CHILDREN
AND
THEIR
LITERATURE

Piping down the valleys wild
  Piping songs of pleasant glee
On a cloud I saw a child.
  And he laughing said to me.

Pipe a song about a Lamb:
  So I piped with merry chear,
Piper pipe that song again—
  So I piped, he wept to hear.

Drop thy pipe thy happy pipe
  Sing thy songs of happy chear.
So I sung the same again
  While he wept with joy to hear.

Piper sit thee down and write
  In a book that all may read—
So he vanish'd from my sight.
  And I pluck'd a hollow read.

And I made a rural pen,
  And I stain'd the water clear,
And I wrote my happy songs,
  Every child may joy to hear.

WILLIAM BLAKE
"Songs of Innocence"

Children AND THEIR *Literature*

CONSTANTINE GEORGIOU
New York University

PRENTICE-HALL, INC. ENGLEWOOD CLIFFS, NEW JERSEY

The color plates, details of which are also reproduced on the cover (along with details of additional color plates), have been reproduced by permission as follows:

The Pied Piper by Kate Greenaway. Copyright 1888. Frederick Warne & Co. Ltd.

Mother Goose, Volland Edition, illustrated by Frederick Richardson. Copyright 1915 P. F. Volland & Co. M. A. Donohue & Company.

The Endless Party by Etienne Delessert and Eleonore Schmid. Copyright 1967 by the author and illustrator. Harlin Quist, Inc.

In A Spring Garden edited by Richard Lewis, illustrated by Ezra Jack Keats. Text copyright 1965 by Richard Lewis. Pictures copyright 1965 by Ezra jack Keats. The Dial Press.

Sleep, Baby, Sleep illustrated by Trudi Oberhänsli. Copyright © 1967 by Artemis Verlag, Zurich, Switzerland. Published in U.S.A. by Atheneum House, Inc.

Moy Moy by Leo Politi. Copyright © 1960 Leo Politi. Charles Scribner's Sons.

The Tailor of Gloucester by Beatrix Potter. Copyright 1903 Frederick Warne & Co. Ltd. (on cover only)

Proserpina, The Duck That Came to School by Constantine Georgiou, illustrated by Bernard Lipscomb. Copyright 1968 by Harvey House, Inc. (on cover only)

Jennie's Hat by Ezra Jack Keats. Copyright 1966 by the author-illustrator. Harper & Row, Publishers, Inc. (on cover only)

Library of Congress Catalog Card No.: 69-10223

Current printing (last digit):

10 9 8 7 6 5 4

PRENTICE-HALL INTERNATIONAL, INC., *London*
PRENTICE-HALL OF AUSTRALIA, PTY. LTD., *Sydney*
PRENTICE-HALL OF CANADA, LTD., *Toronto*
PRENTICE-HALL OF INDIA PRIVATE LTD., *New Delhi*
PRENTICE-HALL OF JAPAN, INC., *Tokyo*

Printed in the United States of America

To
May Hill Arbuthnot
Lillian H. Smith
and
Frederic G. Melcher

*Champions of Children's Literature
who have inspired the production
of this book by their scholarship,
vision, and deep dedication.*

PREFACE

Children and Their Literature is a book designed as a vital reference for those interested in children and what is termed children's literature. It has been prepared in the hope that it will meet the needs of prospective as well as experienced teachers, librarians, school administrators, and others concerned with children and what they read.

This book, although not definitive, does survey the multi-faceted world of children's books with sincerity, thoroughness, and a literary sense. Carefully planned and arranged, this work presents:

- the field of children's books as a portion of universal literature
- various divisions of literature into which children's books may be grouped
- literary genres differentiating between fiction, nonfiction, poetry, and prose
- an historical account of children's books that have become milestones
- approaches in criticism that employ principles basic to all good writing of poetry and prose
- analyses of old and new books considered examples of fine writing and illustrating in each of the divisions classifying children's books
- selections of viewpoints from a variety of other references, book reviews, and the judgment of eminent authorities concerned with what children read
- examples of beautiful and genuinely artistic pictures selected from rare, old, and new illustrated works of excellence

- comprehensive bibliographies carefully annotated and classified according to subject and age appeal for each of the divisions that span the field of children's books
- distinguished art from original sources reproduced without the loss of brilliance in their color or fineness of line

Publishing is a vast and successful enterprise today. It is, therefore, important for one to become acquainted with standards of excellence and to examine books with a sharpened critical sense. I am convinced of the importance of approaching children's books as literature of value and significance and declaring the best in children's literature wherever it is found. To compromise with the substandard, mediocre materials that characterize some aspects of writing for children is to misinterpret the objectives of genuine literature and the book evaluations presented in this text.

I have been assisted in writing this reference by my students, my colleagues, and the many friends whose help and inspiration I acknowledge with deep gratitude.

I am indebted to professors Alvina Treut Burrows, Beatrice D. Hurley, Helen Fleming, George Manolakes, Charles and Mariann Winick for the expert help and direction this text has received. I also wish to express appreciation to Haig and Alice Assatourian, of the Professional Editing and Typing Services, for their suggestions and assistance in the preparation of the manuscript.

For inspiration and comfort I thank my devoted friends Aphrodite and Leon Lianides. Their strong sense of beauty and loveliness lent radiance during dark, tiresome hours of toil.

This book is a tribute to those men and women who have championed the cause of children and their literature: May Hill Arbuthnot, Harvey Darton, Leland Jacobs, Frederick Melcher, Anne Carroll Moore, John Newbery, Frances Clarke Sayers, Lillian H. Smith, Ruth Hill Viguers, to name a few. These distinguished leaders have contributed to a literary legacy and given impetus to the steady growth of literature for children today.

Constantine Georgiou

CONTENTS

CHILDREN
AND
THEIR
LITERATURE

Youth and old age are joined together by the power of a storybook in this finely
detailed drawing by Gustave Doré that prefaces an early edition of Perrault's
Mother Goose Tales.
Bibliothèque Nationale.

Chapter 1 CHILDREN'S LITERATURE

The men and women who have sustained freedom of expression
and genuine creation among these ramparts . . . deserve the gratitude of the
world. The world will have need of what they have here established:
genuine creative literature as interpretation of life; boldness in maintaining an
open, straightforward approach to the minds of children; faith in
the response of the children themselves to honesty, dignity and the demands of
the emotional experience which reading as an art exacts of its
disciples; genuine sharing of all that fires the imagination through beauty in
pictures and design, nor have humor and the need for laughter
been forgotten.

These are the forces from which new life shall come.

— FRANCES CLARKE SAYERS
"Of Memory and Muchness"
The Horn Book Magazine, May 1944

A Portion
of Universal Literature

There exists a portion of universal literature today designated as literature for children. It is the portion of literature that, like an avalanche, has gathered itself, from generation to generation, from adult books or parts of them, and from the literatures of widely separated times and peoples, those materials that meet the developmental needs and interests of children at different stages of their growth.

This portion of universal literature is vast and rich. It is composed of many distinctive works whose themes and treatment express simply and clearly the universal truths, the high purposes characteristic of literature of value and significance, and yet possess childlike appeal.

An Art Form

Historically, only that portion of great literature that possessed appeal for children was included in the realm of children's literature. But, since the eighteenth century, literature has been designed specifically for children and with children in mind. This portion of world literature has grown substantially with its incorporation of considerable content from adult literature as well as materials created especially for children across a wide age range.

Since this literature accommodates children throughout their stages of growth, it is abundant and varied. It constitutes a solid body of material for every occasion and taste. It also reflects some of the best writing with all the true manifestations of a creative art form.

John Dewey's statement "art is experience" relates to children and
the communication between them and their literature. The quality that establishes a book as a piece of literature to a child is that the book is ostensibly an experience. It may be an imaginative experience as in nursery stories and fairy tales, or it may be gained from stories in the other divisions of literature—history, realism, fantasy—that a child explores as he goes through stages in his development. But in each case he acquires bright, new impressions and ideas from his reading that will serve to illuminate subsequent new experiences gained from living and from books. This background equips a child to taste the delights of fine books and in turn stimulates his reading as it widens the base of his experience.

During this expansion of the experiential background a child has grown in stature and awareness as an individual. His perception becomes sharpened and his appreciation of life more zestful. He becomes open and receptive while new ideas nourish his mind and new impressions stir his emotions. He gains something of permanent value that will influence his reading and growth the rest of his life. An experience of this kind is perhaps the most significant part of the learning process, for knowledge and awareness enter subtly through the child's whole being.

A Child's World

Writers of fine children's books exercise a special literary sense in setting out to create a world to suit children—a world scaled down and appropriately distinct from an adult world. Writers who have created this "world of a child" have of necessity actually entered it or have gone back to their own childhood, unconsciously or consciously, before the world of their books came alive.

Best examples of this include the works of Beatrix Potter. This great nursery writer reflects a motherly understanding of childhood's dreams, wishes, and pitfalls in the gently told tales of Peter Rabbit. For older children, there is the literary product of Kenneth Grahame's deep involvement in childhood, *The Wind in the Willows*. Designed with freshness, beauty, and appeal, this book continues to engage the attention of children, awakening them to the wonder and delight of their natural world and calling up in them that deeper humanity which is elemental and universal to childhood. Other distinguished examples include *Rabbit Hill*, *Homer Price*, *The Moffats*, and the sturdy stories of Laura Ingalls Wilder. The writers of these books seem to have found a philosophy or a creed by which a child may order his life. They appreciate the eagerness of youth and the intense curiosity inherent in all children. They understand, too, the narrow confines of most children's environments and their search for a swift passage beyond those boundaries. Sometimes young children find this escape in imaginative play, but often they find it within the pages of a book that allows for the transition to go beyond the limits of their particular world.

The capacity to extend oneself beyond the boundaries of one's own physical existence has been defined as "imaginative power." It is one gift that makes the experience of living rich, meaningful, and vibrant with the color and light of the imagination. Children capable of freeing this power —and most children are—find the passage natural to the enchanted world of children's books.

> For there *is* magic in the writing of these books; a magic that enchants the children who read them as the tune of the Pied Piper lured the children of old Hamelin. It is a magic that eludes definition. The essence from which it is distilled can best be discovered in those books which generations of children have taken to their hearts and have kept alive, books which seem to have an immortality that adult books, so soon superseded by the latest best-seller, seldom attain.[1]

As in all art forms, both the expression and the reception of ideas are involved. A creator of fine children's books has something to say that is vital to the children who read them, and all the while he is writing, he keeps his audience in mind. In this way he employs the appropriate means of expression, carefully blending the content and his style of writing.

Books that reveal the skill and affection that have gone into their writing are books that speak to each individual in the personal, private voice of a friend. And it is with this friendship that a book, whether fact or fiction, establishes a world the child can join, learn from, and grow in; a world where he too can laugh, weep, rebel, and cherish.

The Scope of
Children's Literature

The field of children's books covers a wide area of human accomplishment and knowledge that informs and delights in endless

---

[1]Lillian H. Smith, *The Unreluctant Years* (Chicago: American Library Association, 1953), p. 12.

variety. As one looks around a modern children's library, one becomes aware of the great profusion of books considered suitable literature. The scope of children's literature is aptly described by Beatrice Hurley:

> The scope of literature includes stories of real people of today and yester-day; realistic and fiction tales; stories of animals, machines, and inventions; stories dealing with the world of nature; stories depicting everyday experiences of children at home and abroad; stories of mirth and magic, of fools and silly dolts; tall tales of legendary heroes whose audacious feats afford children a peek into the folklore of a nation; biographies of men and women who have made their indelible imprint upon the history of a nation; books of poetry that sing their way into the lives of boys and girls.[2]

Divisions of Literature

Facing the rich array of books and the steady stream of new books, the student of children's literature needs a basic understanding of the major divisions into which most of these books fall. These divisions will provide the form or structure that will enable a student to approach and utilize the material without being overwhelmed by it.

Children's literature may be divided into three groups: fictional books, factual books, and poetry; or it may be designated as imaginative and informational literature. But whatever terms are used, imagination takes its own shape in books of fiction and poetry. Nonfiction has a decidedly factual slant. For our convenience, the smaller divisions of literature that follow will help in organizing fictional and nonfictional materials.

Description of the Major Divisions

Picture books and picture storybooks. This visual art form provides children with their first experiences in art and literature. It is evolved through the combined efforts of author, illustrator, editor, and printer.

A variety of media is employed in the production of picture books and picture storybooks to convey the message of the text and pictures

---

[2]Beatrice D. Hurley, *Curriculum for Elementary School Children* (New York: The Ronald Press Company, 1957), p. 202.

with the harmonious unity that is common to all forms of graphic art.

Picture books and picture storybooks cover a wide range of topics both factual and fanciful, and reflect an artistic discipline along with the beauty and color of expression that makes them appealing to children.

Poetry. Here ideas are fused with music compressing deepest communication into a few exact, pungent words. Poetry is created through imagery, rhythm, meter, sound, and form.

Poetry is for the ear, for the emotions. There is subtlety in poetry not possible in prose. Its language skillfully stimulates the imagination to arouse deep feelings.

The poet encounters his existence with a depth unknown to the casual observer. He sees with the eye of imagination; he hears with the ear of sensitivity; he touches the intangible; he holds fast the fleeting intensity of experience.

Folk tales, fairy tales, myths, legends, and fables. These tales are considered the "universal literature" of children. With a deep understanding of real life at their base, they mirror in fanciful form the universal truths and passions of humankind. Their portrayal of life is infused with worldly wisdom that knows no boundaries of time or social order. Indestructible, they have transcended time and have come down in literary history as a literary legacy.

Collectively the folk tales, fairy tales, myths, legends, fables, and certain nursery rhymes and tales constitute part of general "folk literature."

Combined groups frequently appear under three separate headings: (1) fairy tales, (2) folk tales, and (3) myths, legends, and fables. On the other hand, nursery rhymes and tales, because of their age appeal, fit logically in the picture book, picture storybook division of children's literature.

Many of these tales are clothed by talented artists in a fresh magic of beauty and richness as new editions of single stories or collections of stories are presented in book form.

Available in several versions, retellings of the same tales may also be found fashioned and illuminated to capture the mood—whether humble or majestic—in picture book or picture storybook format.

Fantasy. Included here are full-length works that bring magic and the irrational into the everyday world. Familiar objects and settings are reshaped in terms of universal themes. Akin to fairy tales, since they possess many traditional elements, stories classified as full-length works of fantasy develop their themes through more complex plots, style of writing, characters, and settings. Although most fairy tales are set in some enchanted country, fantasy stories frequently bring magic and enchantment into the real world. This, at least, is a convenient way of classifying stories that are more properly termed "modern fairy tales."

Historical stories. These stories, a combination of history, chronicle, and imagination, are adventure tales that reconstruct life in the past.

To read historical stories is to live through a period in human history that is telescoped to include the color and the flavor, the thoughts and the emotions, the stirring and momentous events of long ago.

The aim of historical tales is not to teach history but to develop a sense of history and a way of viewing the past.

Realistic stories. This division of literature employs the stuff of everyday living, weaving it into a tale of real adventure that presents to young readers the excitement, the humor, the triumphs and failures, the good and bad in everyday life.

Realistic stories mirror the present world of a child, and capture his interest by flashing back for him the intimate details, manners, and settings of his own life in story form.

Centered around action of characters realistically outlined, books of realism emphasize true-to-life qualities even though the characters and plots are invented.

Informational literature. This material presents factual information with style and visual artistry. It encompasses an enormous area of books designed to inform even the youngest on a wide range of topics. Many areas of the curriculum draw from the vast resources of informational literature.

Aimed to inform, this division of literature meets the standards of fine writing and assists young readers to explore life and living through information and delight.

Many possibilities for children to learn and to be taught are inherent in the division of informational literature. But this must happen naturally, not by imposition, for children may choose books classified as informational literature for their own sake.

Basic Needs of Children
and Characteristics of Their Literature

Literature for children is no substitute for living, but it adds immeasurably to the enrichment of life. The best rewards literature can bring to a young life are those that reach a child by fulfilling his needs and assisting with his growth and development.

At any age, human beings have a basic need to live life to a fuller extent than the limits of their immediate and direct experience make possible. For children particularly, it is in their nature to grow, to stretch minds and horizons, to reach beyond the boundaries of their everyday world, to exercise a power that can extend their actual experience, to be part of a group, to feel the cohesive quality that binds friends who share common interests, to derive a feeling of achievement, to laugh and play, to seek aesthetic satisfaction through enjoyment of beauty, to sit in judgment of the past and envision the future.

Fine literature can contribute to meeting children's needs because its aims include the following:

(1) To afford many opportunities for a child to explore his world in an infinite number of ways—of seeing, of thinking, and of feeling

(2) To nourish the mind and emotions as well as delight the eyes and heart; to invite a child to savor life in a different world, to feel the emotions of someone else, and to view the familiar in a bright, new way

(3) To transmit sound moral values and attitudes communicated through characters in children's books

(4) To provide experiences that sharpen a child's insight into "self" as he searches and encounters that self in stories that allow for identification

(5) To serve as a vital link in preserving and communicating the humanistic tradition from one generation into the next

(6) To broaden aesthetic perception and give an understanding of form and order through language, ideas, and the visual art of picture books

(7) To explore varied contributions, values, ways of life in different cultures—past and present—to give a sense of universal life

(8) To provide for children experiences outside their limited environment—experiences that can be enjoyed vicariously in gaining some of the enchantment of life and a measure of personal fulfillment

(9) To stress themes of natural interest to childhood—dependent, however, upon the extent to which they have been developed through structure and style, with beauty and vitality, and with the essential ingredient: a genius for storytelling

Literature for children exists as a portion of universal literature reflecting excellence in writing, in design, and in the essential features that distinguish an art form.

Children's literature constitutes a substantial collection of fictional, factual, and poetic works designed specifically for children, as well as those drawn from adult literature.

Infinite variety, in agreement with children's interests and tastes, marks this portion of literature that delights and informs children across a wide age range.

Major divisions classify the vast numbers of books that represent the kinds of literary experiences derived by young readers.

Consonant with childhood's stages of growth and development, books satisfy children's needs and interests by supplying the nourishment called for by the children themselves as they go through stages in their reading growth similar to those in their physical and emotional growth.

There is a cumulative value to be gained from succeeding stages of reading and growth. Lasting impressions form the basis for taste in art and literature during the rest of a child's life.

The prose or poetry, fact or fiction, that leaves a notable imprint upon a young life expresses the spirit of children's literature. This spirit, when present in a book—through originality of theme, beauty and dignity of style, masterful characterization that allows for personal identification, and an absorbing plot—arouses in the hearts and minds of children a sense of universal significance that heralds a book as a symbol of civilized life.

References

ADAMS, BESS P., *About Books and Children*. New York: Holt, Rinehart & Winston, Inc., 1953.

ARBUTHNOT, MAY HILL, *Children and Books*, 3rd ed. Chicago: Scott, Foresman & Company, 1964.

————, et al., *Children's Books Too Good to Miss.* Cleveland: Western Reserve University Press, 1953.

BECKER, MAY LAMBERTON, *First Adventures in Reading.* Philadelphia: J. B. Lippincott Co., 1947.

CURRY, CHARLES MADISON and ERLE ELSWORTH CLIPPINGER. *Children's Literature.* Chicago: Rand McNally and Company, 1928.

DARTON, F. J. HARVEY, *Children's Books in England,* 2nd ed. New York: Cambridge University Press, 1958.

D'EVELYN, KATHERINE, *Meeting Children's Emotional Needs.* Englewood Cliffs, N.J.: Prentice-Hall, Inc., 1957.

DUFF, ANNIS, *Bequest of Wings.* New York: The Viking Press, Inc., 1944.

EAKIN, MARY, *Good Books for Children.* Chicago: University of Chicago Press, 1962.

FENNER, PHYLLIS, ed., *Something Shared: Children and Books.* New York: The John Day Company, Inc., 1959.

————, *The Proof of the Pudding.* New York: The John Day Company, Inc., 1957.

HAZARD, PAUL, *Books, Children and Men.* Boston: The Horn Book, Inc., 1960.

HUCK, CHARLOTTE, and DORIS YOUNG, *Children's Literature in the Elementary School.* New York: Holt, Rinehart & Winston, Inc., 1961.

JOHNSON, E., et al., *Anthology of Children's Literature.* Boston: Houghton Mifflin Company, 1959.

MEIGS, CORNELIA, et al., *A Critical History of Children's Literature.* New York: The Macmillan Company, 1953.

MOORE, ANNE CARROLL, *My Roads.* New York: Doubleday & Company, Inc., 1939.

MOORE, ANNIE E., *Literature Old and New for Children.* Boston: Houghton Mifflin Company, 1934.

SAWYER, RUTH, *The Way of the Storyteller.* New York: The Viking Press, Inc., 1942.

SAYERS, FRANCES CLARKE. *Summoned By Books.* New York. The Viking Press, Inc., 1965.

SMITH, DORA V., *Fifty Years of Children's Books.* Champaign, Ill.: National Council of Teachers of English, 1963.

SMITH, IRENE, *A History of the Newbery and Caldecott Medals.* New York: The Viking Press, Inc., 1957.

SMITH, LILLIAN H., *The Unreluctant Years.* Chicago: American Library Association, 1953.

SMITH, PAUL, *Creativity: An Examination of the Creative Process.* New York: Hastings House, Publishers, Inc., 1959.

SPAIN, FRANCES LANDER, *The Contents of the Basket*. New York: The New York Public Library, 1960.

TARG, WILLIAM, *Bibliophile in the Nursery*. Cleveland: World Publishing Company, 1957.

THRALL, WILLIAM FLINT, and ADDISON HIBBARD, *A Handbook to Literature*. New York: The Odyssey Press, Inc., 1961.

TOOZE, RUTH, *Your Children Want to Read: A Guide for Teachers and Parents*. Englewood Cliffs, N.J.: Prentice-Hall, Inc., 1957.

———, and BEATRICE PERHAM KRONE, *Literature and Music*. Englewood Cliffs, N.J.: Prentice-Hall, Inc., 1955.

WALSH, FRANCES, ed., *That Eager Zest: First Discoveries in the Magic World of Books*. Philadelphia: J. B. Lippincott Company, 1961.

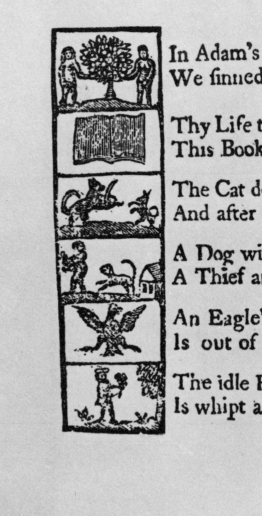

In the *New England Primer,* used in the instruction of Puritan children, crude woodcuts amplify meanings behind rhymed verses keyed to each letter of the alphabet. The alphabet verses are preceded by this solemn rhyme:

He that ne'er learns his A, B, C,
Forever will a Blockhead be:
But he that learns these Letters fair
Shall have a Coach to take the air.

Chapter 2

THE
HISTORY
OF
CHILDREN'S
BOOKS

... children's books keep alive a sense of nationality; but they
also keep alive a sense of humanity. They describe their native land lovingly,
but they also describe faraway lands where unknown brothers live.
They understand the essential quality of their own race; but each of them is a
messenger that goes beyond mountains and rivers, beyond the seas,
to the very ends of the world in search of new friendships. Every country gives
and every country receives—innumerable are the exchanges—and
so it comes about that in our first impressionable years the universal republic of
childhood is born.

— PAUL HAZARD
Books, Children and Men
The Horn Book, Inc., 1960

Beginnings of
a Literary Heritage

Literature written specifically for children, and from a child's point of view, is a new kind of literature. In fact, not until the eighteenth century were books designed especially for children. Prior to this the few books that existed were designed to instruct rather than to entertain. The human interest trends of the eighteenth century included children and so it became distinguished as the first century of children's literature.

But when one examines the vast number of books that constitute the literature for children, one discovers stories and ballads that originated long before the eighteenth century, before the printing press of the fifteenth century, before the hand-illuminated manuscripts of medieval times—even before the art of writing existed! This collection of stories and ballads originated in an ancient, primitive world where little distinction was made between literature for adults and literature for children. Instead, tales were sung or recounted by minstrels and storytellers in great halls or humble homes, for old and young, and have been preserved, collected, and handed down from generation to generation to become part of a time-honored universal literature.

Much of this early literature is now considered part of a great oral tradition, in existence long before men knew how to write; it is due to the abiding memory of children and the work of scholars that these very early stories have been preserved and recorded to become a rich literary heritage.

When young and old listened to these tales, remembered them, and retold the same ones to their children and grandchildren on down through succeeding generations, the tales became a literary legacy whose origins are as dimmed by age as the earliest history of mankind. In a sense, the history of children's stories has become a record of human experience revealing particular features of each era.

Scholars who study this literary inheritance are amazed not only at the incredible age and development of the story themes but also by their universality. For example, the circumstance of magic sleep and the plot of Cinderella are found in many countries and in hundreds of versions.

Various theorists have offered explanations concerning the universality of themes in widely separated countries. One theory holds that these themes are nearly identical because people are essentially the same: they possess the same needs, same emotions, same wonder of life, and apply similar qualities of imagination to reach essentially the same conclusions about human experience.

Upon analysis of early literature for children, one will recognize "above everything else man's effort to explain to himself the forces of which he was so vaguely and reverently aware in the material and spiritual world around him, to explain them without the help of science or the illumination of revealed religion."[1]

This early literature also reveals an imagination and a variety of tastes that "give distinctive character to all the literature that was to come."[2] It possesses a power and a life that have outlasted time, conquests and growth, and vast religious and political changes. But during this time there was "forming among children's minds, as well as among their elders', that basic foundation of taste and imagination and recognition of truth wherever it was encountered which one generation was to pass on to another."[3]

The Early English Period

The literature for children in America had its own early beginnings in England. Aldhelm (640–709), a religious leader of the times,

---

[1]Cornelia Meigs, Anne Eaton, Elizabeth Nesbitt, and Ruth Hill Viguers, *A Critical History of Children's Literature* (New York: The Macmillan Company, 1953), p. 5.
[2]*Ibid.*, p. 4.
[3]*Ibid.*, p. 5.

is recorded as being the first to write books with lessons for children. The lessons were written in Latin and were concerned with mystical significances and virtues of the number seven (septenario) as it is expressed in the Bible, as well as riddles, puzzles (enigmas), and the rules of verse forms (meter). Then followed a treatise on Latin prosody in conversational dialogue between teacher and student. The title of his book is *De Septenario, de Metris, Enigmatibus, ac-Pedum Regulis.*

The Venerable Bede (673–735), a teacher at an English monastery, was another early writer who prepared lesson books for children. Bede's

A page from the Venerable Bede's *De Natura Rerum* that sets down in double-columns Latin lessons for children during the Early English Period. The text deals with natural science, plant life, and the study of stars.
British Museum.

book was entitled *De Natura Rerum* and dealt with natural science, the study of plant life, and the study of stars.

Bede's book was in more understandable Latin and written with greater clarity and more imagination than Aldhelm's. In the tenth century, cut down and translated into Old English, it was widely read and lent "intellectual light" to the Dark Ages in England.

The example of Bede and Aldhelm was followed until 1500. During this period instructional books were written in a question-and-answer form of dialogue or in verse.

Using the question-and-answer dialogue form, Alcuin (735–804), a tutor at Charlemagne's court, wrote lesson books to instruct children studying grammar. Alcuin spent his adult life furthering the cause of education in England. He founded monasteries and schools and wrote a variety of school books for young people. Most of his books followed the established trend of writing in imagined dialogue and were used to instruct children in and out of court circles.

Alfred the Great (849–899), a beloved hero of England, not only drove back the invasions of the Danes but also fostered learning in his country. With the help of a number of scholars, Alfred had Latin works translated into Old English, which was understood by the children studying literature in the monastery schools of the times.

To perpetuate the tradition established by Alfred the Great, Aelfric (955?–1020?), a teacher in a monastic school for boys in Winchester, developed the oldest extant Latin-English dictionary, the *Vocabulary*, which was used in schools for four centuries thereafter.

The *Vocabulary* was accompanied by the *Colloquy*, another school book for children, which consisted of dialogue between student and teacher. The student in the *Colloquy* asked questions on practical, everyday occupations, and the teacher answered. The book was in Latin with Old English translations written between the lines.

Aelfric's *Colloquy* was simple and didactic, but it mirrored the manners and traditions of the times. It also furthered a didactic movement, which produced the first encyclopedia for children. This encyclopedia, compiled and written by Anselm (1034–1109), archbishop of Canterbury, was called the *Elucidarium*. Characteristic of the times, this Latin encyclopedia served to instruct children whose education was entrusted to the clergy. And through the efforts of Christian monks, who lent an altering hand to some of the inherited folklore and added Christian mysticism to some of the stories, children's literature experienced the influence of didacticism that persisted for many centuries to come.

The Middle English Period

In the eleventh century King Alfred's efforts to promote the use of Old English instead of Latin were interrupted when William the Conqueror and his Norman French knights defeated England in 1066. During the Norman conquest French became the language of the ruling English classes and many French words replaced Old English ones. Consequently falling into disrepute, English was considered unworthy of written form until John Cornwall, a schoolteacher, encouraged students to use English. Inspired by John Cornwall's example, other authors began to write in English rather than in Latin or French. Some of their works are *Mandeville's Travels* (1356), *Wycliff's Bible* (1383), and Chaucer's *Astrolabe* (1392). The number of books produced in England totalled 141, with writing and education still in the hands of monastic orders whose influence dominated many features of fourteenth century life in England.

During the fourteenth century education was principally intended for the children of the nobility and was concerned with manners and morals, as can be seen in a well-known work of that period entitled *The Babees' Boke, or A lytle Reporte of how young People should behave.* Containing "the whole duty of children" in 160 lines, the "Boke" opened with an introduction of 56 lines all in a rhymed form.

> *My child, I rede thee be wise and take heed of this rhyme*
> *Old men in proverb said by old time,*
> *A child were better to be unborn*
> *Than be untaught and so be lorn.*

Another didactic rhymed book was divided into three parts. This was *The Boke of Curtasye* which was quite well known just prior to printing. The first two parts deal with acceptable behavior and morals for children, but the third part of the book includes the appropriate conduct and duties of servants in a nobleman's household.

In 1450 Johann Gutenberg, the German printer, invented movable type, making it possible for books, principally the Bible, to be read by many. His invention marked the beginning of modern printing but it was a long time before large numbers of books were published. And in the development of children's books the production was even slower and less imaginative than it was for adult works. When the early printers first began to practice their skill, the books that came off the presses were

A page from *The Boke of Curtasye* in Old English transmitting the morals, manners, and duties of the Middle English Period. Less foreboding than its predecessors, this hand-written text employs some decorations and simpler language without the use of double-columns of an earlier period.
British Museum.

strictly utilitarian and instructional. Education was still in the hands of the clergy, who dispelled any ideas of giving children books they could read for pleasure or entertainment. It was considered of greater value to inform children through their books than to amuse, and to discipline children in the ways of godliness and learning rather than in the ways of amusement and entertainment.

Before the printing press, in the days of hand-written and hand-illuminated books that were costly and rare, it is reasonable to believe that books were limited to learning. It is quite surprising to discover, however, that for a long time printing did little to bring about any appreciable change.

The printing houses, on the other hand, complied with the needs and met the demands that existed. This meant more grammars, more colloquies, more catechisms, and more primers. Of course, there were the perennial books of morals and manners as well as the ancient fables to which tidy morals were attached.

Printing in England was developed by William Caxton (1422–1491). Quality was considered more significant than quantity for, in addition to didactic and moralizing works, William Caxton's printing press produced such best-selling classics of today, as Sir Thomas Malory's *Morte d'Arthur*, Aesop's *Fables*, *The Boke of Histories of Jason*, and *The Historye of Reynart the Fox*. Children able to read would pore over the simpler texts, especially those recounting the Arthurian legends. These legends, which were fast becoming very popular, were first drawn from French and English sources while Malory was a "Knyghte prisoner" in Newgate around 1469 and 1470. Caxton's Malory, however, continued to serve for over a hundred years as the chief source from which numerous adaptations were made. The best among them still echo the haunting prose and the barbaric beauty expressed in the noble legends borne from the mass of medieval tellings.

Although there is no documented evidence to substantiate the exact time and place of the Arthurian legends, it is believed that somewhere between the sixth and eighth centuries fireside tales began to spread of a great leader who championed justice and whose wife divided her love between her husband and a dashing French knight, Lancelot. And only after generations of retelling were these stories written down in the mid-fifteenth century by Sir Thomas Malory, making the names of "Lancelot," "Merlin," "King Arthur," "Guenevere," "Excalibur," and "Camelot" spread to become part of the world's language and a part of universal literature.

Some of these stories, and others that Caxton first printed, have been revised and rewritten for generations of children. Like all true classics, they remain significant and have acquired new significance although the age for which they were written and the conditions under which they were written have passed away.

The Renaissance Period

The fall of Constantinople, the migration of Byzantine scholars into Western Europe, and the revival of classical art forms heralded a rebirth of scholarly and artistic works. In England the art of reading and writing was gaining ground even though there were still very few books being published or even written for children. But children did not confine themselves to materials specifically prepared for them, and

A page from a rare hand-written and hand-illuminated manuscript of unknown authorship. Jeweled colors and leaf gold adorn pages depicting deeds of kings and martyrs set against glorious backgrounds.
British Museum.

many children delighted in the developed art of illuminated manuscripts that contained religious stories and prayers touched with poetry. These manuscripts also included detailed pictures in jeweled colors depicting the lives of saints, scenes from the Bible, and the glorious deeds of kings and martyrs.

The Renaissance monarchies of Henry VIII and of Elizabeth I of England, along with Francis I and Emperor Charles V of France, showed interest in the expansion of knowledge and widening horizons. This was also a time of increased travel, voyages of exploration, and the discovery of the New World bringing remote lands and continents within the scope of England's attention and control. Wealth and learning increased and Western Europe attained an unprecedented height of prosperity not achieved in the Middle Ages.

The Barbers Shop. LXXV.   Tonſtrina.

75

The Barber, 1. ·
in the Barbers-ſhop, 2.
cutteth off the Hair
and the Beard
with a pair of Sizzars, 3.
or ſhaveth with a Razor,
which he taketh out of his
Caſe, 4.
    And he waſheth one
over a Baſon, 5.
with Suds running
out of a Laver, 6.
and alſo with Sppe, 7.
and wipeth him
with a Towel, 8.
combeth him with a Comb, 9.
and curleth him
with a Criſping Iron, 10.
    Sometimes he cutteth a Vein
with a Pen-knife, 11.
where the Blood ſpirteth out, 12.

Tonſor, 1.
in Tonſtrina, 2.
tondet Crines
& Barbam
Forcipe, 3.
vel radit Novaculâ,
quam è Theca, 4. depromit.
    Et lavat
ſuper Pelvim, 5.
Lixivio defluente
è Gutturnio, 6.
ut & Sapone, 7.
& tergit
Linteo, 8.
peſtit Peſtine, 9.
criſpat
Calamiſtro, 10.
    Interdum Venam ſecat
Scalpello, 11.
ubi Sanguis propullulat, 12.
                        The

A page from *Orbis Pictus* by John Amos Comenius and illustrated with woodcuts by Michael Endter. The illustrations and text in Latin appeared first, then English was matched with the Latin text.

The Renaissance awareness of a wider world is symbolized by *Orbis Pictus* (*World in Pictures*) that was produced by John Amos Comenius (1592–1670), a Moravian mystic and bishop who saw the need for educational reforms and the establishment of more vibrant, purposeful practices beginning in early infant schools. Comenius believed that the most meaningful learning for children took place when they were allowed to see things for themselves. It was his contention that: "Boyhood is distracted for years with precepts of grammar, infinitely prolix, perplexed and obscure. Boys are stuffed with vocabularies without associating words with things or indeed with one another."[4]

His philosophy gave rise to what is considered to be the first picture book for children, Comenius' *Orbis Pictus*. Written in Latin in 1637, and translated into English in 1658, it covered a wide and varied range of subjects and attempted to relate pictures with text in order to provide a graphic view of the world in which children lived. Leaving very little unmentioned or unexplained, its 150 chapters, each dealing with a different topic, were illustrated with charming little woodcuts by Michael Endter. This voluminous book not only reflected the spirit of the Renaissance, but the vision of a great teacher who once promised his students, "I will show you everything, I will name all things to you."

The royal courts invited scholars and teachers to "enlighten" the nobility as well as the increasing numbers of students attending the newly founded schools and universities. Reflecting this interest for learning in England, a little rhymed alphabet book for children appeared. Entitled the *Royal Primer* because it "inculcated rudimentary knowledge of religion, morals, and reading" at the prime of childhood, this primer spanned the alphabet from A to Z in the following way:

> A—*In Adams fall*
> *We sinned all*
>
> * * *
>
> Z—*Zaccheus he*
> *Did climb a tree*
> *His Lord to see.*

As a forerunner of the *New England Primer*, published in Boston in 1691, the *Royal Primer* was very popular during the century in England that it served young children as a lesson book.

---

[4]S. S. Laurie, *Comenius* (Syracuse, N.Y.: J. W. Bardeen, 1892), p. 22.

An example of the hornbook made from a paddle of wood on which was fastened a lesson sheet protected by a film of horn.

A less elaborate text than the illuminated or hand-written manuscripts or even the *Royal Primer* was a product of the printing press—a printed sheet tacked onto a paddle of wood. This became known as the hornbook, deriving its name from the transparent film of horn that was fastened to the printed sheet to protect it. Frequently a cord was run through a hole in the handle of the oblong paddle and tied to a child's belt or girdle in much the same fashion as were the keys and crosses of the monastic teachers.

First made in the middle of the sixteenth century, the hornbook became a popular means of handling text for instruction in language, prayers, and some aspects of religious education. The text usually began with a cross, the beginning of a crisscross row, the alphabet in small letters and in capitals followed by groups of syllables: *ab, eb, ib,* and other vowel-consonant combinations. Immediately following these began the Lord's Prayer with, "In the Name of the Father, the Son, and the Holy Ghost." Although the contents of hornbooks differed, their purposes were essentially the same—to teach the child his letters and to continue religious

instruction. Some of these first hornbooks made their way to America
to become one of the earliest devices used to instruct children in the New World.

Around 1746 the hornbook was replaced by a similar kind of lesson book known as the battledore. In the cardboard battledore the lesson was written on one side of Dutch paper decorated with gilt. The larger sheet of three leaves, folded together, made possible the inclusion of alphabet and numerals. Sometimes the reading lesson was illustrated with woodcuts, the process of engraving that became elaborate during the Renaissance. But neither the hornbook nor the battledore presented anything of very good quality that entertained the young; consequently, children still continued to sample and then adopt what they could from adult literature.

Although the passing of the Renaissance saw few strides made in the development of children's books, it was a time of broadening views

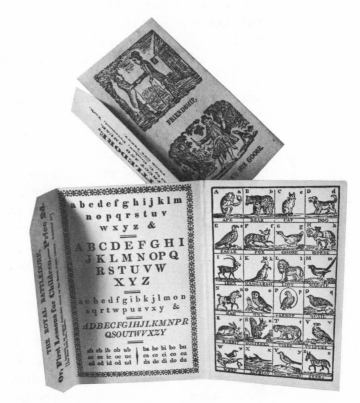

A facsimile of a cardboard battledore folded to include the alphabet, groups of syllables, and pictorial lessons in crude woodcuts.

and horizons. Records of historic events and the reaching out to mythical shores for knowledge and literature had effects on the materials for future generations.

The Puritan Period
in England and America

The seventeenth century, especially between 1620 and 1630, saw the great exodus of Puritans from England to America and the arrival of "good godly books" for children on both sides of the Atlantic. It was a century marked with religious wars, purges, gloom, and terror whose influence was expressed in a crippling form of didacticism that set a trend in the writing for children.

The Puritans, in attempting to cleanse the religious life of England from moral and political corruption, imposed restrictions on the literature for children that delayed any developments sparked by the Renaissance.

Books providing entertainment were looked upon as vain or worldly since time was considered a precious commodity in the light of Puritan theology. The time-honored tales of a much earlier period were frequently collected and burned. The only literary diversion recommended for children was the reading of religious stories and the didactic texts of the times. Even the arithmetics and spellers in Puritan England and America were filled with a morbid pietism that confined the childish imagination to those channels connected with the duty of an early conversion as a prelude to an untimely death.

An examination of some of the typical and most popular children's books of this period will reveal the influences responsible for the gloomy, suppressed, and religion-ruled character of the Puritan New England child. Instruction, not entertainment, prompted the major portion of printed material dictated by church elders who voiced admonition against frivolity. George Foxe, a Quaker, condemned and denounced "the telling of Tales, Stories, Jests, Rhimes and Fables" in his book *Warning to all Teachers*. John Cotton, a newcomer to Massachusetts from England, published the first book for children in America and it clearly revealed the trend of the period. Cotton's book was entitled *Spiritual Milk for Boston Babes in either England, drawn from the Breasts of Both Testaments for their Souls' Nourishment* (1646) and it contained in verse form simple questions and answers that advanced into deep Puritan concepts of religion.

Some of this material later spilled over into the *New England Primer* so widely used on both sides of the Atlantic.

Most "godly" children pursuing the path of virtue were also required to read the Bible, the chief book of New England, from cover to cover with little thought given to the effects some of its passages might have. In every home it was not only the chief source of religious instruction but also the text used for teaching reading and spelling.

After the Bible, the book that was most highly regarded was the *New England Primer*. This tiny text, just big enough to fit snugly into a child's pocket, became the most universally studied school book ever used in America, and more than three million copies of it were printed. Although it was a school book, its contents and general tone were so religious that it has been termed "The Little Bible of New England."

The most distinctive feature of the *New England Primer* was "An Alphabet of Lessons for Youth." This included a set of rhymes designed to aid in learning the alphabet, and each letter with its accompanying rhyme was illustrated with a blurred and grotesque woodcut. Originally the rhymes depicted Biblical characters or incidents, but following the American Revolution they became increasingly more secular in content, reflecting a less religious oriented trend in education.

A book that ranked second only to the *New England Primer* in its wide use by children was Michael Wigglesworth's *The Day of Doom*. As a supplement to the primer, it reflected the same somber aspects of religion and education for children. Consisting of 224 stanzas of eight lines each, the poem is as terrible a description of the final judgment and hell as the human mind can conceive.

The doctrine of necessary preparation for death brought about a group of threateningly awesome writings and publications, the most outstanding example of which is James Janeway's *A Token for Children: being an Exact Account of the Conversion, Holy and Exemplary Lives, and Joyful Deaths of several young Children. To which is now added, Prayers and Graces, fitted for the use of Little Children.*

In this austerely pious book of uncertain date thirteen righteous youngsters die at an early age, having devoted their young lives trying to reform and convert the world about them. They voice their preoccupation with sin and torment and the horror of hell unavoided by sinners who do not repent. In this brooding book, while all the children in it express concern for the careless life of friends and relatives, one exemplary child stresses a broader ideal found in the text that precedes the description of his untimely death:

> [he] was not a little concerned for the whole Nation, and begged that God would pardon the Sins of this Land, and bring it nearer to himself.

It is true that Janeway attempted to provide pleasure for children through the reading of "joyful deaths" and unselfish deeds in conjunction with the acceptance of the "Will of God." It is also true that this was a time when child mortality was high, and awareness of death and the life hereafter seemed important aspects of the educational system, particularly between 1670 and 1720 when Janeway's book was in vogue. Addressing his young audience in the preface of his book, Janeway says:

> You may now hear, my dear Lambs, what other good children have done, and remember how they wept and prayed by themselves, how earnestly they cried out for an interest in the Lord Jesus Christ: you may read how dutiful they were to their parents, how diligent at their book, how ready to learn the Scriptures and their catechisms . . . how holy they lived; how dearly they were loved; how joyfully they died.

A warning in verse form by Abraham Chear appeared about the same time, early in the 1670's, and reveals the contemplations of a young girl who studies herself in the mirror:

> *When by spectators I am told*
> *What beauty doth adorn me,*
> *Or in a glass when I behold*
> *How sweetly God did form me—*
>
> *Hath God such comeliness bestowed*
> *And on me made to dwell.*
> *What pity such a pretty maid*
> *As I should go to Hell!*

Mercifully, the poets of distinction softened their appeal toward children, and brightness glowed in their work sooner than it did in the work of prose writers that followed. Isaac Watts, gentler in his moralizing, wrote *Divine and Moral Songs for Children* in 1715. He prefaced his work accordingly: "to give the minds of children a relish for virtue and religion and . . . raise a young meditation . . . that the rising generation of Great Britain may be a glory among nations, a pattern to the Christian world, and a blessing to the earth."

There is no doubt that morals and manners were quietly stressed by Dr. Watts, who firmly maintained that virtue leads to Heaven and vice to Hell, yet there is poetry in the verses he composed; the metrical version of the ninetieth Psalm clearly stands out as one of his best works. To his credit there also exists a large number of hymns still sung today by young and old: "Joy to the World," "O God, our help in ages past," "When I survey the wondrous cross," and for the youngest, "Hush! my dear, lie still and slumber." From his poem "Against Idleness and Mischief" the following verse still finds its way into poetry books for children in a variety of languages:

> *In works of labor or of skill,*
> *I would be busy too;*
> *For Satan finds some mischief still*
> *For idle hands to do.*

Out of the Puritan period, however, sprang certain great stories that have been adopted by children to become classics in their own right. A leading example is John Bunyan's *Pilgrim's Progress*, first published in 1678. Not intended for children because of passages filled with theological discussion, it was soon adopted by young readers who were drawn by its fairy-tale action and clear, simple language.

John Bunyan (1628–1688) spent much of his life in and out of prison cells. Condemned for preaching against the religious beliefs of his day and for preaching without a license, he was repeatedly arrested and released. When Bunyan did not preach he wrote, and his greatest sermon was a written one. *Pilgrim's Progress*, colorful and imaginative, may have failed in its purpose to bring about soul-searching experiences, but it provided a suspenseful story that has endured to entertain young and old for nearly three centuries.

Following the trend set by *Pilgrim's Progress*, two other books originally written for adults were claimed by children: *Robinson Crusoe*, written in 1719 by the social reformer, Daniel Defoe (1659?–1731), and *Gulliver's Travels*, by Jonathan Swift (1667–1745), published in 1726.

As an allegory, Defoe's story of Robinson Crusoe had many deep meanings that go beyond the understanding of children. Yet as an account of the exciting adventures of a character whose pioneering spirit endeared him to the young, *Robinson Crusoe* continues, even after two centuries, to be the best desert-island story ever written.

Although *Gulliver's Travels* was written as a political satire, its humor and fantasy, especially in the first book dealing with Gulliver's voyage to the land of the Lilliputians, has always appealed to children.

Here, in the tradition of a Punch and Judy show, Mother Hubbard and her dog are depicted on the cover of a chapbook printed by G. Ingram in 1840.

Since the trends in literature during the seventeenth and early eighteenth centuries were religiously and morally oriented, adults frowned upon "feigned fables and wanton stories" produced on crudely-printed little books that became popular soon after they emerged around 1641. Known as chapbooks because they were sold on the streets by peddlers, or chapmen, for a penny or two, "these crudely printed little paper books provided for a penny or more badly retold [stories] which were enjoyed by all ages. Here among the first printed versions of many old tales were such popular stories as *Jack the Giant Killer*, *Tom Thumb*, *Dick Whittington*, and *Robin Hood*. Wide circulation of these chapbooks created a public for later books published for children and preserved many fairy tales and nursery rhymes for a better production."[5]

Many of the stories published in the chapbooks and used by children have disappeared, but the survivors are still popular with children today and find their way into recommended lists of juvenile classics.

Gloom was still widespread in the literature for children in England and America when a "miracle occurred in France with the publication of [Charles Perrault's] *Histoires ou contes du temps passé avec des moralités* (Histories and Tales of Long Ago with Morals), or, more familiarly, *Contes de ma Mère l'Oye* (Tales of Mother Goose)."[6] These tales and nursery rhymes made history by ushering in a brighter movement in juvenile writing and publishing. Charles Perrault (1628–1703), a scholarly member of the French Academy under Louis XIV, developed them from an older folklore collection.

---

[5]Virginia Haviland, "Literature for Children," *American Educator Encyclopedia* (Lake Bluff, Ill.: The United Educators, Inc., 1965), pp. 210–11.

[6]May Hill Arbuthnot, *Children and Books* (Chicago: Scott, Foresman & Company, 1964), p. 36. Copyright © 1964 by Scott, Foresman & Company.

A dramatic Puss-in-Boots and an apprehensive Red Riding Hood are portrayed in a meticulous style by Gustave Doré whose fine drawings grace some of the earliest editions of Perrault's French fairy tales.
Bibliothèque Nationale.

Because it was considered beneath the dignity of an author to write books for children at that time, Perrault's stories did not bear his name but were collected under the name of Mother Goose. His collection began a movement which resulted in an extensive accumulation of stories, rhymes, riddles, and melodies that have become recognized as part of the standard recommended classics for children. Among the best-loved of these are *The Sleeping Beauty*, *Red Riding Hood*, *Puss-in-Boots*, and *Cinderella*.

By 1729, with the translation of his stories into English, Perrault's influence spread to the literature of English-speaking children and began a lighter trend in England and America as these more cheerful tales told by Mother Goose gained popularity.

> No chapbook was ever so thrilling as these eight tales, no "good Godly book" was ever so beloved. At the time, they must have attracted the attention of an English publisher by the name of John Newbery, because not only did his firm later use the title *Mother Goose*, but he may also have discovered through the popularity of the tales the importance of the child as a potential consumer of books.[7]

The Eighteenth Century

The appearance of John Newbery (1713–1767) as a writer, bookseller, and printer of books especially designed for children is a milestone in the history of this literature. In 1744, under the sign of the Bible and the Sun, Newbery established a shop in St. Paul's Churchyard, London, for the publication and sale of children's books that combined instruction with entertainment. The history of books specifically designed for children begins with the publication of John Newbery's first storybook, *A Little Pretty Pocketbook* (1744), subtitled *Intended for the Instruction and Amusement of Little Master Tommy and Pretty Miss Polly*. Like his subsequent books, it was bound in Dutch flowered and gilt paper. After the success of his first storybook, Newbery issued *Mother Goose's Melody or Sonnets for the Cradle*, and *The History of Little Goody Two Shoes* between 1760 and 1765. According to Arbuthnot, this was "a small juvenile novel, the first of its kind to be written expressly for children. Oliver Goldsmith is supposed to have written *Goody Two Shoes*. . . ."[8]

John Newbery and his successors continued to publish other juveniles, demonstrating as they prospered that an extensive market existed among

---

[7] *Ibid.*, p. 37.
[8] *Ibid.*, p. 38.

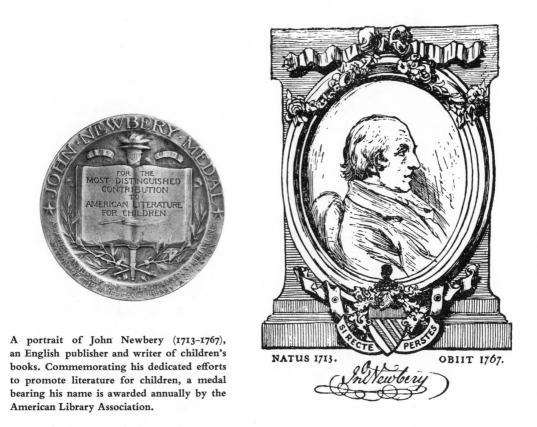

A portrait of John Newbery (1713–1767), an English publisher and writer of children's books. Commemorating his dedicated efforts to promote literature for children, a medal bearing his name is awarded annually by the American Library Association.

NATUS 1713.   OBIIT 1767.

young children for such books. John Newbery is best remembered as a man whose deep and understanding love for children led him to publish books for them that emphasized love rather than the wrath and punishment of God.

The influence of Perrault and Newbery on children's literature, however, was not strong enough to eclipse existing and subsequent movements of didacticism. In 1762 Jean Jacques Rousseau (1712–1778) "proclaimed his theory of a new day for children through his book *Émile*. He believed in the joyous unfolding of a child's powers through a free, happy life."[9] And in its day, *Émile* effected a revolutionary change in people's thinking toward children and the materials used in their education. However, although Rousseau "intended to stand out for the rights of the spontaneous and natural as opposed to those of the mechanical and artificial,"[10] most of his followers misinterpreted his philosophy and began a didactic school of writing in an earnest and solemn attempt to educate children. In so doing they moved in a direction opposite to that of Rousseau.

[9]*Ibid.*, p. 41.
[10]Paul Hazard, *Books, Children and Men* (Boston: The Horn Book, Inc., 1960), p. 14.

35

The moment they took up their pens they disregarded this primitive, spontaneous master whom they had praised so highly. They employed nothing but artifice, and while pretending to liberate the child's soul, they oppressed it still further. Those very pedagogues who boasted that they worked only in the open air, who talked constantly about the benefits of sunshine, rain and even wind, put their plants in hothouses, forced them, pruned them, directed their growth scientifically.

* * *

Perhaps the reason for all this was that each time their master, Rousseau, took three bold steps forward he then took three timid steps back, alternating between revolutionary and reactionary. Regardless of the fact that he had extolled an education without constraint he placed the pupil under a teacher who supervised everything he did, and who, if he found it expedient, faked experiments which were supposed to train him in the knowledge of the absolute truth.[11]

An outstanding example of the didactic school of writing came in Thomas Day's (1748–1789) *Sandford and Merton*. Published in 1773, the highly moralistic novel dealt with a poor, honest boy's attempts to reform a rich, spoiled one.

In the late eighteenth century, poetry expressly written for children began to appear. William Blake's *Songs of Innocence* (1789) and *Songs of Experience* (1794) were about and for children who found their melodic verses appealing. Ann and Jane Taylor wrote *Original Poems for Infant Minds by Several Young Persons* (1804) describing the simple, pleasant life in rural England. In 1807, in the United States, *The Butterfly's Ball and the Grasshopper's Feast* appeared, written by William Roscoe. The poems, fanciful and pretty in rhyme, are considered to be the first original works in American children's literature. In 1822, Clement Moore published "A Visit from Saint Nicholas." This gay story poem was fast-moving and humorous, with rhythm and beat that has sung its way into the hearts of young and old. Edward Lear published a *Book of Nonsense* in 1846, which contained absurd limericks and amusing verses with pictures. Other poets for children include A. A. Milne, Rachel Field, Eleanor Farjeon, Rose Fyleman, and Walter de la Mare.

The Nineteenth Century

Despite the strong influence of Rousseau and his followers, and the temporary lull in children's literature, the nineteenth century saw the beginnings of a succession of books from several authors

---

[11] *Ibid.*, pp. 14–15.

on both sides of the Atlantic who recognized the importance of imagination in literature. As a result, important trends developed that were to
affect later writing done specifically for children. Literature for children
became more imaginative and craftsmanlike. Literary geniuses could now
write openly for children, and in different parts of the world they were
doing so.

In England, Charles and Mary Lamb published *Tales from Shakespeare* for children in 1806. The success of these tales was immediate and
a number of different editions have been produced and are in circulation
today.

Following this success, in 1808 Charles Lamb turned his attention
to the retelling of the *Adventures of Ulysses* for children. "There have been
many children's retellings of Homer since then, but Charles Lamb's
Adventures of Ulysses is a classic in its own right and his is still the most
literary retelling of the story of Ulysses for children."[12] Concerning this
work of Lamb's, an English critic of children's books wrote: "Lamb
achieved the strange feat of getting some of the Odyssey's glorious ease
into what might almost be simple Elizabethan prose ... but the whole
runs with a gracious Homeric speed and smoothness."[13]

In Germany, the scholarly brothers Jacob Ludwig Grimm (1785–
1863) and Wilhelm Karl Grimm (1786–1859) started a trend in folklore.
They traveled about their native land meticulously recording the imaginative household tales recounted by the German folk. Popular stories by
the Brothers Grimm were translated into English in 1824. These stories
were vigorous, humorous, fantastic, terrifying, heroic, and above all,
they reflected the universality of human experience. "The English title
given to Grimm's collection, *Household Tales*, was prophetic, for there is
probably no other children's book which has become so universally a
household word as Grimm's fairy tales."[14]

The immediate popularity of the folklore collected by the Brothers
Grimm showed a way by which the imaginative needs of children could
be nourished. Fresh sustenance of the finest quality was provided by the
Danish genius, Hans Christian Andersen (1805–1875) who is credited with
using a true aesthetic sense in creating some of our greatest original fairy

[12]Lillian H. Smith, *The Unreluctant Years* (Chicago: American Library Association,
1953), p. 26.

[13]F. J. Harvey Darton, *Children's Books in England* (London: Cambridge University
Press, 1958), p. 199.

[14]Smith, *op. cit.*, p. 27.

YALMER'S VOYAGE WITH OLE LUCKOLE

Graceful swans garlanded with roses heighten the fantasy in Andersen's fairy tale of Yalmer's Voyage. Serene, transparent waters shimmer reflections of ships and spires in this beautifully detailed picture.

tales. He enriched children's literature with a volume of tales that "blended successfully for the first time and for all times the strains of fantasy folklore. Andersen's tales contained both elements in a pure state."[15] The *Fairy Tales* of Hans Christian Andersen appeared in England in 1846, translated by Mary Howitt.

Scandinavian folk tales were collected by Norse scholars: Peter Christen Asbjörnsen and Jörgen E. Moe, whose *East o' the Sun and West o' the Moon* was translated into English by Sir George Dasent in 1859. Joseph Jacobs compiled a collection of English, Celtic, and Indian fairy tales, but these were intended more to give pleasure to young children than to preserve folklore. And Andrew Lang began a series of fairy tales in 1889. Meanwhile, in the United States, Joel Chandler Harris wrote the *Uncle Remus* stories in 1880.

---

[15]Darton, *op. cit.*, p. 247.

The success of the movement to collect folklore and to create fantasy folklore encouraged the retelling of ancient legends and epics. In America, Washington Irving wrote imaginary tales about the Hudson River Valley in his *Legend of Sleepy Hollow* and *Rip Van Winkle*. Nathaniel Hawthorne published *The Wonderbook* and *Tanglewood Tales*, and these were followed by Howard Pyle's *The Merry Adventures of Robin Hood* and *The Story of King Arthur and His Knights*. The *Iliad* and the *Odyssey* were translated and retold for children by such literary scholars as Alfred Church, Andrew Lang, and Padraic Colum.

In England, Charles Kingsley reproduced three of the Greek myths in *The Heroes* in 1856. But England's great gifts to children's literature—nonsense and imagination—came from two distinguished writers of the century: one an artist, the other a mathematician. Edward Lear, the artist, brought out the *Book of Nonsense* in 1846 for the sake of being silly and amusing. In 1865, Charles Lutwidge Dodgson (Lewis Carroll), the mathematician, produced a masterpiece that combined fantasy and nonsense in logical, credible terms, and called it *Alice's Adventures in Wonderland*. As a synthesis of fine writing for children, *Alice* can be used as a measuring tool in analyzing children's literature. "Lewis Carroll's *Alice in Wonderland* . . . has the test of time, imagination, genuine emotion, consistent characters, plausible events and plots, distinguished and artistic style that makes a book a symbol of civilized life."[16]

The nineteenth century saw the number of quality books for children rise steadily. The books of this period came from both sides

There was an Old Man who said, "Hush! I perceive a young bird in this bush!"
When they said, "Is it small?" he replied, "Not at all!
It is four times as big as the bush!"

Matching the humor of his verse with pictures, Edward Lear emphasizes the absurdity in his limericks that afford fresh amusement because of their originality of expression.

[16] Joyce Bartell, "The Lewis Carroll Shelf Award," *Elementary English*, XXVI (March 1959), 159.

of the Atlantic and reflected the changes taking place everywhere. Some of these changes were brought about by the Industrial Revolution, which considerably influenced man's values and thinking throughout the world. The westward movement in America, with its emphasis upon individualism and nationalism, led to ideals of freedom and education for everyone; thus education came to be considered as a natural right for children.

During the nineteenth century, the study of human behavior was developing as behavioral scientists such as Wundt, James, and G. Stanley Hall reported their observations and findings, lending new emphasis to life in the present as opposed to a heavy concentration on the life hereafter of an earlier generation.

Living fiction developed in many different directions. *Little Women* by Louisa May Alcott appeared in 1868 to become a prototype of the everyday story for girls. Mark Twain (Samuel Langhorne Clemens) contributed *The Adventures of Tom Sawyer* (1876) and *The Adventures of Huckleberry Finn* (1884) as classics of American boyhood. The adventure-mystery-sea story had a new way opened in 1882 by Robert Louis Stevenson with *Treasure Island* and the jungle story with Rudyard Kipling's *Jungle Book* in 1894.

Increased travel and scientific developments saw the production of books concerned with life in other countries. Through a dramatic family story, *Hans Brinker, or the Silver Skates*, Mary Mapes Dodge gave accurate glimpses of Dutch life in 1865. Life in Switzerland was shared by young readers of Johanna Spyri's *Heidi* in 1884, and the delightful fantasy from Italy, *The Adventures of Pinocchio*, translated into English in 1892, added to the growing list of children's books that have become classics of today.

From the 1860's on, high standards for writing as well as illustrating were established in American magazines for children. *The Youth's Companion* (1827–1929), *Riverside Magazine* (1867–1870), *Harper's Young People* (1879–1899), and *St. Nicholas* (1873–1930) published stories and verse by such distinguished authors as Robert Louis Stevenson, Hans Christian Andersen, Howard Pyle, Sir James Barrie, and Charles Dickens. Artists such as Winslow Homer, Reginald Birch, A. B. Frost, and Randolph Caldecott were also represented.

In the last three decades of the nineteenth century, education began to stress new theories as pragmatists such as Pierce, James, Dewey, and Maria Montessori preached the doctrine of knowledge through experience on the part of childen.

Changes were slowly reflected in the books children of that century read, and although didacticism still continued to be of some importance, books were now written with the child in mind. "Children were considered individuals with unique rights. The attitudes toward religion gave way to secularism and to recognition of play as an acceptable part of child life. Each type of book reflected these social, political, and economic changes. By the end of the century there was a growing body of literature expressly written for children."[17]

From this body of literature came certain books that carry us with distinction from the Victorian period into the twentieth century.

The Golden Age of Children's Books

Outstanding books at the beginning of the twentieth century were *The Wind in the Willows* by Kenneth Grahame, published in 1908, and the miniature stories of Beatrix Potter, beginning with *The Tale of Peter Rabbit* in 1902. Both these masters of children's literature possessed an imaginative power that did not degenerate into trivial fancy as well as a creativeness that did not deteriorate into sweetness and light. Their books possess something that eludes definition but gives them permanent distinction.

> There is, indeed, spiritual kinship between Beatrix Potter and Kenneth Grahame, different as were aspects of their backgrounds and personalities. Both had a liberality of idea . . . which enabled them to treat the seemingly trivial and ordinary in the light of its larger significance. In this respect, they were outstanding, even in a period when writing for children was distinguished by freedom from narrow restrictions of form and content. Both were endowed naturally with a genuine, instinctive understanding of the child's attitude toward life, and of the things a child holds important. Both retained, all their lives, what Kenneth Grahame called the "wonder of the world."[18]

There were other rich contributors to the literary heritage of children. Adding the names of Robert Louis Stevenson and Rudyard Kipling to those of Kenneth Grahame and Beatrix Potter will "make it clear that the passing of the nineteenth century and opening of the twentieth saw the creation of books for children unexcelled in originality,

---

[17]*Ibid.*, p. 2.
[18]Meigs *et al.*, *op. cit.*, pp. 355–56.

The familiar Peter Rabbit is seen amid lush greens and radishes of Mr. McGregor's garden. This sunlit page in delicate pastels reveals the gentle beauty found in these miniature classics. *From The Tale of Peter Rabbit by Beatrix Potter. Reproduced by permission of Frederick Warne & Co., Inc.*

in beauty and breadth of conception and execution, in universality of appeal."[19]

Current Trends in Children's Literature

In the past several hundred years, the field of children's literature has expanded to the extent that it now includes every general field of human knowledge and endeavor. The large number of books published annually has a diversity of content that reflects the social changes and scientific developments of a continuously and rapidly changing world. In this sense, today's books for children have become both an expression of their interests and their times. Many complex subjects—from the stock market to atomic fission, from prehistoric life to modern social problems—are now dealt with in terms that children can understand and appreciate.

In this sweeping panorama of changes and trends, of landmarks among books and writers in the field of children's literature, it is too soon to say which will live and which will not. One can only approach certain of them with respect as one thinks, "These have the stuff of greatness in them; time only will prove whether or not it is the fundamental greatness that belongs to the children of the future as well as the present."[20]

---

[19]*Ibid.*, p. 364.   [20]*Ibid.*, p. 447.

ADAMS, BESS PORTER, *About Books and Children*. New York: Holt, Rinehart & Winston, Inc., 1953.

ARBUTHNOT, MAY HILL, *Children and Books*, 3rd ed. Chicago: Scott, Foresman & Company, 1964.

BECKER, MAY LAMBERTON, *First Adventures in Reading*. Philadelphia: J. B. Lippincott Co., 1947

DARTON, F. J. HARVEY, *Children's Books in England*. 2nd ed., New York: Cambridge University Press, 1958.

DE VRIES, LEONARD, *Little Wide-Awake: An Anthology of Victorian Children's Books and Periodicals*, Selected from the Collection of Anne and Fernand G. Renier. New York: The World Publishing Company, 1967.

ERNEST, EDWARD, ed., *The Kate Greenaway Treasury*. New York: The World Publishing Company, 1967.

HAVILAND, VIRGINIA, "Literature for Children," *American Educator Encyclopedia*. Lake Bluff, Ill.: The United Educators, Inc., 1965.

HAZARD, PAUL, *Books, Children and Men*. Boston: The Horn Book, Inc., 1960.

HUCK, CHARLOTTE and DORIS YOUNG, *Children's Literature in the Elementary School*. New York: Holt, Rinehart & Winston, Inc., 1961.

JAMES, PHILIP, *Children's Books of Yesterday*. London: The Studio, Ltd., 1933.

JORDAN, ALICE M., *From Rollo to Tom Sawyer*. Boston: The Horn Book, Inc., 1948.

MEIGS, CORNELIA, et al., *A Critical History of Children's Literature*. New York: The Macmillan Company, 1953.

MOORE, ANNIE E., *Literature Old and New*. Boston: Houghton Mifflin Company, 1934.

MUIR, PERCY, *English Children's Books 1600–1900*. New York: Frederick A. Praeger, Inc., 1954.

SLOANE, WILLIAM, *Children's Books in England and America in the Seventeenth Century*. New York: Kings Crown Press, 1955.

SMITH, DORA V., *Fifty Years of Children's Books 1910–1960*. Champaign, Ill.: National Council of Teachers of English, 1963.

SMITH, ELVA S., *A History of Children's Literature*. Chicago: American Library Association, 1937.

SMITH, LILLIAN H., *The Unreluctant Years*. Chicago: American Library Association, 1953.

TARG, WILLIAM, *Bibliophile in the Nursery*. Cleveland: World Publishing Co., 1957.

Lining the shelves of children's libraries there are those books whose literary qualities have witnessed the test of time. Designated as classics, these honored works are the touchstones of literary criticism.

Rare book collection, Children's Room, New York Public Library. Photograph by Edwin Gann Snyder.

Chapter 3

LITERARY CRITICISM OF CHILDREN'S BOOKS

Literature is something immeasurably above and beyond the printed
word, of a significance transcending the merely informative, varied as is human
destiny, nonexistent without the twin qualities of beauty of idea
and beauty of expression. It has everlasting meaning, unaffected by changing
literary forms. It deals romantically with the remote, tragic beauty
of "old, unhappy, far-off things," and realistically with the potentialities of the
immediate present.

— ELIZABETH NESBITT
"Hold to That Which Is Good"
The Horn Book Magazine, January-February, 1940

Universal Standards
for Children's Literature

In order to place children's literature in its proper literary perspective one must move into the realm of universal literature. From literary criticism and aesthetics in universal literature come the principles by which we judge children's books.

But "there are those who think of a child's book as just a simpler treatment of an adult theme. This point of view considers children only as diminutive adults and arises from a misunderstanding of childhood itself."[1]

It is true that children's experience differs from that of adults, and therefore the application of standards should be consonant with child life. Nevertheless, one must keep in mind the emotional maturity of the children for whom the book or books are intended. This does not mean that the works must be watered down so as to meet the reading ability levels of young children. On the contrary, some books of lasting value outstrip their vocabulary lists and connect with children on emotional-maturity levels so that they can be understood and enjoyed by the young themselves. However, the standards basic to good writing in adult literature are also basic to good writing for children. Lillian Smith suggests that in literary criticism the judgment of publisher, critic, and librarian, "although arrived at from different points of view, should be based on similar principles; on a knowledge of literature and on a conception of literary standards, for on these the authority of any appraisal rests."[2]

[1]Lillian H. Smith, *The Unreluctant Years* (Chicago: American Library Association, 1953), p. 15.
[2]*Ibid.*, p. 33.

The Problem of Synthesis
of Form and Idea in Literature

In its relationship to the universe of literature, any conception of literary standards for children's books falls heir to a corpus of literary theory and criticism that goes back more than two thousand years. From the time of classical antiquity to the present, it has concerned itself with the problematic blending of—call it genius and craft, or idea and form, or inspiration and rendering—"*making*, the Aristotelian emphasis, and *saying-seeing*, the Platonic and romantic."[3] The synthesis of discovery and creation, or the interrelatedness of the idea and its treatment has been a focus of the literary artist and critic in most eras. An outcome has been classification of genre conceptions or groupings of literary types.

The Organismic Conception
of the Genre of Fiction

The special potentialities of fictitious prose narrative as an art form were first recognized and championed by Henry James at the close of the nineteenth century. He regarded the craftsmanship of certain French writers as doing away with "the perpetual clumsy assumption that subject and style are—aesthetically speaking, or in the living work— different and separable things."[4] How fully organic James' conception was is elaborated in this statement: "... as the work is successful the idea permeates and penetrates it, informs and animates it, so that every word and every punctuation-point contribute directly to the expression."[5] Works of this literary type are conceived as "... all one and continuous, like any other organism."[6]

The Creative Experience

The phenomenon of art—and literature should be approached as art—ought to be seen as one of human life and conduct

---

[3]William K. Wimsatt, Jr., and Cleanth Brooks, *Literary Criticism: A Short History* (New York: Alfred A. Knopf, Inc., 1964), p. 753.

[4]Henry James, *The Art of Fiction and Other Essays*, Morris Roberts, ed. (New York: Oxford University Press, Inc., 1948), p. 120.

[5]*Ibid.*, p. 18.

[6]*Ibid.*, p. 13.

rooted in the warp and woof of all experience: it reflects experience and adds to it. As Wagenknecht observes:

> The best definition of literature that I know—or, for that matter, of art in general, for the creative process is essentially the same in all the arts, is one which, so far as I am aware, I made for myself: Art is the distilled essence of life. Not the actual stuff of human experience, in the narrower, commoner sense, but a selection from experience, somehow recharacterated in the mind of the writer, somehow transformed through the addition to itself of something that is not experience at all.[7]

For Dewey, art *is* experience, experience consciously transformed; it is neither the objective environment alone nor consciousness considered by itself. The artist interacts with his environment in his own particular way: the organization of experience within the artist allows an intensified expression of experience created by his personality, knowledge, memory, and imagination, which are excited into activity by the materials in the environment. "The material out of which a work of art is composed belongs to the common world rather than to the self, and yet there is self-expression in art because the self assimilates that material in a distinctive way to reissue it into the public world in a form that builds a new object."[8] Richards characterized the aesthetic movement, which involves selection from life experience combined with inner organization and results in reorganization of experience, with this idea: "It is in such resolution of a welter of disconnected impulses into a single ordered response that in all the arts imagination is most shown."[9] "The balance is not in the structure of the stimulating object, it is in the response."[10] This response reflects order, unity, balance, and harmony. Thus the organic correctness of a work of art refers to the artist's aesthetically perceptive unity with life in this dual sense: (1) unity with the outer environment of the creator and (2) unity within, which allows him to consciously construct a new whole out of variety.

ART AS COMMUNICATION OF EXPERIENCE

The arts, however, are all a means for the communication of experience. In literature, in fiction particularly, the experience com-

---

[7]Edward Wagenknecht, *Values in Literature* (Seattle: University of Washington Book Store, 1935), p. 4. Copyright © 1928, 1935, 1956 by Edward Wagenknecht.

[8]Joseph Ratner, ed., *Intelligence in the Modern World: John Dewey's Philosophy* (New York: Modern Library, Inc., 1939), pp. 982–83.

[9]I. A. Richards, *Principles of Literary Criticism* (New York: Harcourt, Brace & World, Inc., 1925), p. 245.

[10]*Ibid.*, p. 248.

municated "... depends, in one sense at least, upon the total structure, upon the logic of the whole, the relationships existing among the elements of character and psychology, action, social situation, ideas and attitudes, style, and so on."[11] "If there be no final union of the varied impulses bound by the experience ... if ... the varied details of the poetic experience do not fuse into a final and satisfactory whole ... the experience has not form"[12] for the reader.

As Howard Pyle expressed it, "a man is not an artist by virtue of clever technique or brilliant methods: he is fundamentally an artist in the degree that he is able to sense and appreciate the significance of life that surrounds him, and to express that significance to the minds of others."[13]

SYNTHESIS OF LITERARY ELEMENTS
FOR EXPERIENCE

"The *raison d'être* of literary art is enrichment of life via the communication of life-experience and depends upon the fusion of idea and treatment into an experience. This interfusion of all properties of the medium is necessary if the object in question is to serve the whole creature in his unified vitality."[14] When the artist "succeeds, the value of what he has accomplished is found always in a more perfect organisation which makes more of the possibilities of response and activity available."[15]

Percy Lubbock, in a book that has become a classic formulation, expressed a more abstract aesthetic facet of rendering the experience as a whole: "It is not to be supposed that an artist who carves or paints is so filled with emotion by the meaning of his work—the story in it—that he forgets the abstract beauty of form and color, and though there is more room for such sensibility in an art which is the shaping of thought and feeling, in the art of literature, still the man of letters is a craftsman, and

---

[11]Cleanth Brooks and R. P. Warren, *The Scope of Fiction* (New York: Appleton-Century-Crofts, 1960), p. viii. Copyright © 1960 by Appleton-Century-Crofts, Inc. Reprinted by permission of Appleton-Century-Crofts.

[12]Philo M. Buck, Jr., *Literary Criticism: A Study of Values in Literature* (New York: Harper & Row, Publishers, 1930), pp. 19–20.

[13]Wagenknecht, *op. cit.*, p. 45.

[14]Ratner, *op. cit.*, p. 989.

[15]Richards, *op. cit.*, p. 61.

the critic cannot be less."[16] Like Dewey, Lubbock would have the artist stand above his work to control the production by conscious observation. "Craftsmanship to be artistic in the final sense must be 'loving': it must care deeply for the subject-matter upon which skill is exercised."[17]

Further integration of the work was identified by Wagenknecht: "If a piece of writing would merit consideration as art, it is not enough that it should be true to life: it must also be true to itself."[18] A work lacking fidelity to the nature of the *subject* "is not only bad art, it is bad morals, for it tells a lie about life."[19] "Furthermore, it is not an artistic whole."[20] Artistic faith is seen to be twofold: sincerity and consistency in terms of conviction (1) in the treatment of the subject, and (2) in the communication of life.

THE QUALITY OF EXPERIENCE

For a critical standard of values "the mere presence in a piece of fiction of an idea which is held to be important in itself . . . does not necessarily indicate anything about the importance of the piece of fiction."[21] "The idea is important in a story insofar as it is incorporated into the total structure—insofar as the story lives out the idea and, in the process of living, modifies the idea."[22] In opposition to the blueprint conception of form as a vehicle for the idea, the authors of *The Scope of Fiction* endorse literary style that forces the resolution of conflict in the living story "to take stock of as full a context as possible,"[23] to allow "an appreciation of the more broadly human values implicit in fiction."[24] "The essential greatness of all great literature lies in the fact that it enables us to touch life freely at new points."[25] "This returns us to the notion that the liking for a piece of fiction does not depend upon the satisfaction of threshold interest."[26] As aesthetic and intellectual outcomes, "it is the value of literature, as of all art, that it helps to supply precisely the experiences that enable a mind thus completely to organize itself."[27]

---

[16]Percy Lubbock, *The Craft of Fiction* (New York: Charles Scribner's Sons, 1955), pp. 19–20.

[17]Ratner, *op. cit.*, p. 972.   [18]Wagenknecht, *op. cit.*, p. 33.

[19]*Ibid.*, p. 34.   [20]*Ibid.*, p. 35.

[21]Brooks and Warren, *op. cit.*, p. xii.   [22]*Ibid.*   [23]*Ibid.*, p. xiii.

[24]*Ibid.*, p. ix.   [25]Buck, *op. cit.*, p. 143.

[26]Brooks and Warren, *op. cit.*, p. ix.

[27]Buck, *op. cit.*, p. 143.

Further, "only the artist can make men feel their fundamental human kinship."[28]

RE-CREATION AS EXPERIENCE

The process of discovering and creating is not complete when the artist's work goes to press. "The work of art is complete only as it works in the experience of others than the one who created it."[29] It is a work of art "only when it lives in some individualized experience."[30] "It is re-created every time it is aesthetically experienced."[31] This idea of a living system of creation and re-creation is illuminated by Buck as follows: the "original stimulus . . . is entirely lost. In its place he [the artist] has left us the communicated symbol, which in turn becomes, in its words . . . a new stimulus, provoking our minds into controlled activity which, like his, completes the experience, the work of art."[32]

"The critic creates out of life that is already subject to art."[33] The reader, who is the perceiver, goes through the same process of organization in terms of his interaction between his life, knowledge, and imagination on the one hand, and the artistic object with all that it embodies and suggests on the other. "Books exist for the critic only as they are reflected in his own consciousness."[34] That is one important reason why the critics of children's literature recommend a comprehension of child development as a concomitant to applying universal standards to juvenile literature for, as you are aware, the child's experience is not that of an adult. And also as Richards states, "Criticism, as I understand it, is the endeavor to discriminate between experiences and to evaluate them."[35]

A conception of literary standards based upon the kinds of formal considerations cited above is necessary to the critic and student of children's books.

In literary criticism, however, one also examines certain elements within a work in order to make an accurate appraisal. Some of these are: theme, plot, characterization, setting, and style.

These elements permit one to set up clearly defined standards for judging which in turn serve to interpret works to readers who might otherwise fail to understand or appreciate them.

Although these essentials are considered distinct parts of most literary works they are mutually dependent upon one another and are intrinsi-

---

[28]Wagenknecht, *op. cit.*, p. 49.   [29]Ratner, *op. cit.*, p. 981.
[30]*Ibid.*, p. 983.   [31]*Ibid.*   [32]Buck, *op. cit.*, pp. 23–24.   [33]Lubbock, *op. cit.*, p. 19.
[34]Wagenknecht, *op. cit.*, p. 19.   [35]Richards, *op. cit.*, p. 2.

cally related to give unity to the whole work. For example, this can best be compared to a living organism that is composed of many parts with different functions, all of which contribute to the effective existence of the organism as a whole.

In literature, in full-length works particularly, each literary element performs an important function in making the work come alive. But the degree to which life is experienced in this art form is dependent upon the harmonious unity of the literary elements as they are interwoven into the structure of the book.

Definition and Description of Literary Elements

THEME

By definition, the central and pervading purpose or key idea of a literary work is its "theme." Frequently a single theme dominates a story, and sometimes a central idea with minor themes relating to life is employed in the storytelling. For children, however, the theme has meaning only as it relates to their experiences. If a story has a theme and subthemes that point up concepts not readily comprehended by young readers because of their limited emotional and chronological growth, then the work fails to possess appeal for children, and consequently it fails to be classified as literature for children.

PLOT

Plot is the term applied to a series of progressing, inter-related actions leading to a climax in a story.

The various incidents or episodes in a plot are usually planned, arranged, and designed to unfold in a lifelike way so that the story becomes convincing. Since the story plot is invented and not taken over completely from real life, it depends for this upon its logical sequence and natural outcome.

In fact, a well-knit plot composed of a highly selected series of actions and the characters involved in them serves to simplify life by imposing order upon it and by turning the lens on life in sharp focus.

In fictionalized biographies or true biographies, actual persons are drawn to reveal their true natures and personalities. The creation of imaginary figures—animate or inanimate—is a skill employed in fiction. The test of good characterization is the ability of an author to present characters who are believable even though they may be carved out of his imagination.

If characterization is well done, children can readily identify with the characters and the situations in which they appear. In this sense, characters become the vehicles that carry young readers into the story.

SETTING

The physical and spiritual background against which the story unfolds is called the setting.

The background may constitute the geographical location, the natural scenery, the architecture, and so forth appropriate for the narrative. Background material may also include the customs, manners, and the general way of life during a certain period in history or season of the year in which the story's action is taking place.

On a spiritual level, background includes the emotional climate created by the religious, moral, social, and psychological conditions through which the characters in the story move.

Filled in with a sure hand, the setting in a story can lend authenticity and credibility to an account by the selection of suitable details to sharpen the relief of backgrounds.

STYLE

The arrangement of words and sentences that best express the dominating theme of the literary work is generally described as "style." This implies that an author adapts language to his own ideas so that his expression in words reflects his thinking.

Depending upon the ideas expressed in a piece of literature, the language may include qualities such as imagery, rhythm, emphasis, and sentence structure.

Styles of writing cover a range as wide as their themes and as unique as their authors make them. But regardless of the variety and originality, style should match the ideas expressed by an author so that mood, characters, settings, and themes are developed effectively.

Although these literary elements are found in universal literature—and children's books must be considered as a portion of this literary body—there are specific questions one must ask about those divisions of literature designed for children in order to set up criteria for evaluation. And these questions will grow out of a clear understanding of basic literary elements observable in literature for children. With very few exceptions, the criteria for each literary element are essentially the same as those for literature in general. Leaving aside for the moment factual materials and books of poetry, the essentials of fine prose for children may be determined in the following way.

THEME

- Is the theme made clear?
- Does it reveal the author's purpose and the ideas that emphasize the story?
- Is the theme (or themes) appropriate to the developmental age level for which it is intended?
- Are the ideas in the story worth imparting to children?
- Do these ideas appeal to childhood, regardless of age levels, because they share healthy human emotions and values that reflect universal life?
- Does the theme inspire young readers without moralizing so that "truths worthy of lasting forever"[36] are derived unobtrusively from the books?

PLOT

- Is the action built around the theme of the story?
- Is this "action" expressed through a series of interrelated progressing forces that play upon each other?
- Does the conflict in the book become recognizable as the series of interrelated actions is unraveled?
- Are the incidents or episodes a part of a well-knit plan appropriate to the storytelling?
- Do events follow one another in a logical progression so that following the story is facilitated?
- Is there orderly transition provided from one period to another; from one event or episode to another; and by virtue of characters' actions?
- Is the movement sequential and observable so that the passage of time is understood?

---

[36]Paul Hazard, *Books, Children and Men* (Boston: The Horn Book, Inc., 1960), p. 44.

- Are the events, actions, conflicts, and their interplay in a story plausible?

CHARACTERIZATION

- Is the character portrayal clear and convincing enough to be believed?
- Do the characters lend themselves to reader identification?
- Are the characters drawn with characteristics that give each of them individuality?
- Can the characters, despite their individuality, reflect back to the reader a measure of himself as a human being?
- Do the characters come alive during their development?
- Is their development consistent, real, and true to humankind?
- Are the characters so drawn that they also serve as vehicles for communicating to children sound values of a humanistic tradition?
- Can the memorable characters enter a young reader's life to effect change in his personality?

STYLE

- Does the writing point up the individuality of the author and the ideas he had in mind?
- Is there a measure of originality in the way ideas are expressed, words are used; is craftsmanship demonstrated?
- Does the language, the choice and order of words, express the underlying theme?
- Can the language used in the works be comprehended by the readers for whom it is intended?
- Is clarity, order, and unity developed in the work?
- Is there appropriate use of rhythm, imagery, diction, and is coherence expressed in the literary work?
- Have exact words been utilized to describe settings, define characters, communicate ideas, free healthy emotions when the book makes its impact on a young reader?
- Has the impact been enhanced through the use of fine language?
- If dialogue is used, does the language fit the characters who use it?
- Is the tone quality of a work suitable to the concepts of the division of literature in which the book falls?
- Has the story been written with sincerity, integrity, clarity, and beauty?
- Are the point of view, the ideas, the relief of the setting, the portrayal of characters achieved by a general unity of literary elements?

SETTING

- Is the setting in the story made up of appropriate major and minor details?

- Are these details vital to the story?

- Do the detailed settings give a sense of time, period, place, and emotional climate appropriate to the concepts and story line?

- Do the selections of details in the settings give glimpses of life?

- Is the setting sharp and clear so that the relief of the background is vivid and discernible?

- Are descriptions of the general environment of the characters incorporated into the background?

- Does the background serve to support the action of the story without eclipsing the human interest elements?

Historical Aspects of Criticism

Distinctive criticism of children's books did not appear until the second decade of the twentieth century. By this time an important and significant body of children's literature had formed. "There was still lacking, however, informed and constructive literary criticism of children's books."[37]

In 1918 a fine critical analysis of William Henry Hudson's *A Little Boy Lost* was written by Anne Carroll Moore. This marked the beginning of sound appraisals of juvenile literature. It also established the need for adequate analysis of children's books in America.

"That it [*A Little Boy Lost*] should have been published in England and remain unknown and unread by those who have the education of American children at heart is conclusive evidence of the need of more illuminating reviews of books for children."[38]

This criticism heralded additional criticisms of children's books by Moore and others, and by the early 1920's a variety of periodicals were regularly devoting space to the literary criticism of children's literature. This material, especially Moore's, was subsequently collected in book form to comprise three volumes of *The Three Owls* and a set of *Roads* books which constitute an invaluable record of criticisms for the years 1918 to 1930.

---

[37]Cornelia Meigs, *et al.*, *A Critical History of Children's Literature* (New York: The Macmillan Company, 1953), p. 421.

[38]Anne Carroll Moore, "A Little Boy Lost," *The Bookman*, XLVIII (November 1918), 328.

In 1924 *The Horn Book Magazine*, a periodical devoted exclusively to children's literature, was established, edited by two significant literary critics, Bertha Mahony and Elinor Whitney. This magazine has proved to be a dependable guide through the years and has a fine literary flavor in its own right.

During the years 1927 and 1928 the *Saturday Review of Literature* carried a section called "The Children's Bookshop," which dealt with analyses of children's books. But it was not until 1944 that this periodical established a children's book review department with Mary Gould Davis as editor and critic.

Following the trend set by Moore in *The Bookman*, *The New York Times* and *The New York Herald Tribune* began giving space to children's books in the Book Review supplements of their Sunday editions. In 1930 *The New York Times Book Review* included a biweekly page, "Books for Younger Readers," by Anne Thaxter Eaton. Later this became a weekly feature, with reviews by a variety of literary critics, edited by Ellen Lewis Buell. In 1932 May Lamberton Becker conducted weekly analyses entitled "Books for Young People" in *Books*. Later the analyses appeared in the Book Review section of *The New York Herald Tribune* under the heading, "Books for Boys and Girls" edited by Louise Seaman Bechtel.

By the middle of the twentieth century other newspapers and periodicals included discussions of children's books as well as parts of studies conducted in children's literature.

George W. Norvell,[39] in a significant study of the reading interests of children, heightened the interest in literary criticism by pointing up the necessity for juvenile appeal as well as juvenile appropriateness in books for children.

> Children's books follow children's interests. These interests are broadening today through enlarged school curriculums and through an awareness of a wider world created by [a variety of media]. . . . Emphasis on the one-world theme has resulted in books. . . .
>
> From the multitude of the new and the contemporary, living books will stand on their own merits, recognized by children as the real and the true. The continued reading of such books will determine their survival as modern classics.[40]

---

[39]George W. Norvell, *What Boys and Girls Like to Read* (Morristown, N.J.: Silver Burdett Company, 1958).

[40]Virginia Haviland, "Literature for Children," *American Educator Encyclopedia* (Lake Bluff, Ill.: The United Educators, Inc., 1965), p. 216.

Literary criticism in the field of juvenile literature has mounted in significance and in quality. Contemporary leadership has been assumed by periodicals that have long filled a distinctive role in the criticism of children's books. Many educational journals have set aside space for book analysis, but the most influential reviews continue to appear in *The Horn Book Magazine, Elementary English, Saturday Review, The New York Times, Bulletin of the Center for Children's Books,* and the *School Library Journal.*

Outside of periodicals, established writers have published serious evaluations of selected children's books as literature and have identified their criteria for judgment.

Critics who have continued and accelerated the tradition begun by such pioneers in the literary criticism of children's books as Anne Carroll Moore and Anne Thaxter Eaton include: May Hill Arbuthnot, May Lamberton Becker, Alice Dalgliesh, F. J. Harvey Darton, Paul Hazard, Charlotte S. Huck, Leland B. Jacobs, Alice M. Jordan, Cornelia Meigs, Bertha Mahony Miller, Elizabeth Nesbitt, Dora V. Smith, Lillian H. Smith, Ruth Hill Viguers, George Woods, and Doris A. Young.

The continuity of such work seems assured as a second and third generation of critics have similarly addressed themselves to serious scrutiny of children's literature.

References

BROOKS, CLEANTH, and R. P. WARREN, *The Scope of Fiction*. New York: Appleton-Century-Crofts, 1960.

BUCK, PHILO M., JR., *Literary Criticism: A Study of Values in Literature*. New York: Harper & Row, Publishers, 1930.

HAVILAND, VIRGINIA, "Literature for Children," *American Educator Encyclopedia*. Lake Bluff, Ill.: The United Educators, Inc., 1965.

HAZARD, PAUL, *Books, Children and Men*. Boston: The Horn Book, Inc., 1960.

JAMES, HENRY, *The Art of Fiction and Other Essays*, Morris Roberts, ed. (New York: Oxford University Press, Inc., 1948).

LUBBOCK, PERCY, *The Art of Fiction*. New York: Charles Scribner's Sons, 1955.

MEIGS, CORNELIA, *et al.*, *A Critical History of Children's Literature*. New York: The Macmillan Company, 1953.

NORVELL, GEORGE W., *What Boys and Girls Like to Read.* Morristown, N.J.: Silver Burdett Company, 1958.

RATNER, JOSEPH, ed., *Intelligence in the Modern World: John Dewey's Philosophy.* New York: Modern Library, Inc., 1939.

RICHARDS, I. A., *Principles of Literary Criticism.* New York: Harcourt, Brace & World, Inc., 1925.

SMITH, LILLIAN H., *The Unreluctant Years.* Chicago: American Library Association, 1953.

WAGENKNECHT, EDWARD, *Values in Literature.* Seattle: University of Washington Book Store, 1935.

WIMSATT, WILLIAM K., JR., and CLEANTH BROOKS, *Literary Criticism: A Short History.* New York: Alfred A. Knopf, Inc., 1964.

"John Gilpin's Ride" is struck on the Caldecott Medal, awarded annually by the American Library Association. Honoring the famous English illustrator of children's books, the medal is presented to the artist of the most distinguished picture book published in America for children.

From R. Caldecott's Picture Book No. 1 *illustrated by Randolph Caldecott. Frederick Warne & Co., Inc. Reproduced by permission.*

Chapter **4**

PICTURE
BOOKS
AND
PICTURE
STORYBOOKS

*First impressions of pictures, rhymes and stories are both enduring
and elusive. . . . Here, to my mind, is the normal beginning of any true
appreciation of art and of that folk feeling for other countries which
fires the imagination. No country will ever seem entirely strange whose picture
books have been familiar to us from childhood. Caldecott, Greenaway,
Leslie Brooke, Boutet de Monvel, Walter Crane—best possible fortification
against the vulgarity, the materialistic conceptions and cheap fancy
which characterize many of the popular books for little children.*

*Fine picture books exert a far more subtle influence in the formation
of reading tastes and habits than it is possible to estimate, for their integrity is
unshakeable.*

— ANNE CARROLL MOORE
The Three Owls
The Macmillan Company, 1925

61

Definition of Picture Books and Picture Storybooks

In the field of children's literature, picture books and picture storybooks are regarded as visual art forms, and they are probably the most highly specialized.

The picture book—a simpler unit of text and pictures in relation to the more developed text and fewer pictures of the picture storybook—is ranked among the first media of communication for the very young child. The illuminating power of pictures leads the child to the essentials in his literature: the sounds and meanings of language.

The language of picture books speaks simply and directly to the heart of childhood. Its magic draws the young to look and listen while an adult shares the book with him, and later to return to read the book by himself.

For the very young child, picture books flash back the names and pictures of familiar things in his new-found world where so much is still fresh and wonderful. Then, pages of pictures with little text tell a story with enough dramatic interest to hold him until such time as the picture storybook with more text and fewer pictures absorbs him.

The picture storybook develops the textual story more fully, but, at the same time, it is enlivened by its pictures and inseparable from them. Picture storybooks thus fall into the picture book division of children's literature, the division that emphasizes the union of the textual story and visual art.

The Appeal of Picture Books

A child's initial approach to a picture book is primarily a literary one. He expects the pictures to tell him what he cannot as yet read for himself. And, if the pictures in his first books capture his interest and arouse his curiosity, he will then become absorbed in the art of reading. For at this stage of his development the kind of reading a young child does may be only picture reading with some listening to the slight poetry and prose of these books. But his early involvement in fine picture books will be responsible for the formation of reading tastes and habits that influence his reading during the rest of his life. There is little doubt that the subtle combination of beautiful language and illustrations encourages an aesthetic experience that can develop in a young child the basic elements of good taste in art and literature.

During his earliest and most impressionable years, picture books enter a child's life. They enter through the eyes and ears to stimulate the mind and emotions with heightened impact as the pictures and text develop in accordance with the reader.

Long before a young child can read for himself, he listens to adults read to him. The rhythm and beat of the rhymes and musical jingles often bring pleasurable sensations even before he understands their meaning. This response to rhythmic movement and simple melodies is characteristic of infancy and early childhood. Picture books make their first appeal through a child's ears. He delights in the rhythm and beat of new words, in the pure sound of sentences, in rhyming schemes, and in the melody of language.

At first, bright pictures of familiar things provide a child with the thrill of recognition, but very quickly he will pass from recognizing and naming things to pictures that tell him a story. He will see the names and forms of familiar things but he will also be introduced to new ones in striking design or sudden touching beauty. Picture books offer a child new ways of seeing the world—its wonders, its magic, its fun—and then again, new ways of seeing the same things. A child may see a tree or a cat or a building in his own environment, recognize any one of these arrested in the pages of his picture books, and then see them many more times in the variations of an artist's expression. But from each instance a child gains ways of seeing and sensing the world around him that turn sights into insights heightened by a growing awareness of life and a sense of wonder.

A belief commonly shared is "that children like work that is craftsmanlike, beautiful and real." In the field of picture books an artist proclaims beauty by creating loveliness out of things simple and sublime. He creates a world of interesting shapes and sizes; of form and design; of rhythm and order. Very often a picture book as a whole can be a work of art. Its fine pictures are in harmonious agreement with its fine text. A handsome page is further enlivened with clean, clear type suitable for the eyes of a young child. Paper and binding also contribute to the artistic quality of picture books. And it is when these visual art factors fuse together that a picture book of distinction is born.

Approaches to Picture Books
and Picture Storybooks

The children's picture book field has immense scope, bridged by four centuries of varied picture books, beginning with the first such book by Comenius and continuing in a flood of picture books and picture storybooks that pour off the presses each year.

From this wide variety of books, there are those that stand out as distinguished examples. They mirror excellence and provide standards of criticism germane to this art form of literature for children. Not every picture book or picture storybook merits this designation, nor does an adult's conception of what constitutes a fine picture book always coincide with a child's.

Therefore, one must examine and analyze with a critical mind, a sympathetic heart, and a child's point of view. Final judgment should be based on an understanding of those qualities reflected in distinguished books, the viewpoints of other critics, and, above all, appeal to children. There is no formula that will infallibly reveal what is good in a book and what is not. But the development of a measure gained from familiarity with the best that has been published will help to identify the elements that have lent distinction to picture books and picture storybooks.

We can apply this measure not only to "trade books" for children but also to the bright, new genre of books that supplements the reading diet of schoolchildren today. Frequently these are termed "supplementary books" or "easy-to-read books," and many of them are written by the same trade book writers who can do so much with just a few words.

Although picture books do not as a rule limit their vocabulary for very tender readers, the best of the supplementary and easy-to-read books often use few words and more familiar ones in graceful repetition.

Many books with simple text, disproving the controversial theory that beginning books must stick to a few, repetitive words in a dull, unimaginative style, compete successfully with picture books for children's interest while they help to build reading power as well as delight and inform young readers.

Whether it is intended for school or trade use, writing for children is an art form which employs the mind and emotions. It is not an exact science governed by strict rules and formulas. Each book stands by itself. If the book meets the standards basic in good writing and good illustrating, and is spun with the stuff that is in the tapestry of a child's mind, then the book deserves a place on a bookshelf for children.

This chapter is primarily concerned with distinguished picture books and picture storybooks, but it will also include some of the better easy-to-read and supplementary reading books considered literature for children. These books will be discussed as they pertain to children's interests and reading abilities from the preschool years up through the primary grades. There is really no clear distinction between what entertains and instructs children of preschool years and those who are beginning to read in the primary grades. The trade, easy-to-read, and supplementary reading books used by and recommended for these children often overlap. Much is dependent upon the way the books are used as well as the quality of the books themselves. For even the simplest book, if it is worth using again and again with children, can be used in increasingly sophisticated ways.

In order to select and use trade, easy-to-read, and supplementary reading books more conveniently, we will use the following groupings:

(1) Nursery rhymes and Mother Goose books
(2) Alphabet, counting, and other concept books
(3) Picture stories and easy-to-read books
(4) Picture storybooks

Nursery Rhymes and Mother Goose Books

Transmitted in the oral storytelling tradition, nursery rhymes and Mother Goose tales span a wide stretch of time, from the first such collection, which appeared in Latin during the tenth century, up to today's assortment of anonymous rhymes.

Although tales and rhymes were frequently used together in England and credited to a mysterious Mother Goose, contemporary collections in America restrict themselves to a potpourri of traditional nursery rhymes, melodies, and jingles. This tradition was started in 1791 by John Newbery, who published *Mother Goose's Melody* without the fairy tales that had been translated from French and published in English in 1729. Consequently, Mother Goose now indicates collections of rhymes and verses varying from true nursery rhymes, those specifically composed for children, and a few of the less lusty, politically inspired ones that were once part of a more robust but condemned collection.

Along with some adverse criticism, the Mother Goose rhymes have enjoyed long seasons of applause. Poets have alluded repeatedly to the literary significance of certain Mother Goose rhymes. Walter de la Mare defined them as "tiny masterpieces of word craftsmanship. Her [Mother Goose's] rhymes free the fancy, charm the tongue and ear, delight the inward eye."

G. K. Chesterton, attesting to the poetic value of Mother Goose, singled out the line, "Over the hills and far away," as one of the simplest and yet most beautiful in all English poetry. Andrew Lang speaks of these rhymes as "smooth stones from the brook of time, worn round by constant friction of tongues long silent"—an image that points up the presence of hidden meanings that transcend the nonsense in some of the verses as well as pose problems for the artist who attempts to illustrate them.

Basically, three approaches to Mother Goose have been taken by compilers and illustrators:

(1) A literal and direct interpretation of the text
(2) A more perceptive understanding of meanings and nuances with cleverly designed pictures
(3) An overly sentimentalized collection with cute pictures that distort the verses

We will concern ourselves only with the first two approaches.

In early childhood few, if any, children read by themselves. Most children depend upon adults to read to them, and the well-loved nursery rhymes, rhythmic and musical, delight young listeners whether they understand the words or not—and certainly *not* the nuances and deeper shades of meaning underlying the verses.

Because children possess an inborn musical fancy, the powerful rhythms, the resonance, and the strong lilt of the nursery rhymes appeal to them. The music and beat of the words and sentences catch their fancy and free the responses they make with their bodies, hands, and feet when they listen to the sounds of the more jaunty pieces. *Lavender's Blue*, for example, a collection by Kathleen Lines, offers beautifully colored pages of rhyme and meter that suggest action on the part of children.

> Pat-a-cake, pat-a-cake, baker's man
> Make me a cake as fast as you can:
> Pat it and prick it, and mark it with B
> And toss it in the oven for baby and me.[1]

> Dance to your daddy,
> My little baby,
> Dance to your daddy,
> My little lamb.[2]

Detailed and definite drawings accompany the verses that are probably favorites on both sides of the Atlantic. But the illustrations are free from the baby-cute art that has marked certain contemporary collections. Instead, *Lavender's Blue* is a cheerful collection in muted colors, one of the

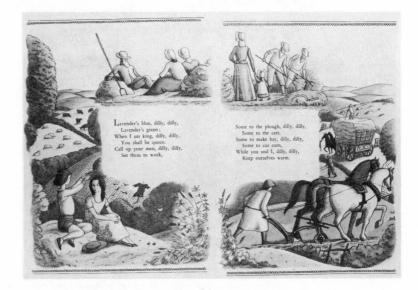

Nostalgic vistas of gently rolling land dotted with patient horses and romantic people provide the background for this lilting English rhyme.
From Lavender's Blue *compiled by Kathleen Lines and pictured by Harold Jones. Copyright* © *1954 by Oxford University Press, London. Reproduced by permission.*

---

[1]Kathleen Lines, *Lavender's Blue* (London: Oxford University Press, 1954).
[2]*Ibid.*

best examples of a literal, direct interpretation of Mother Goose from England.

Another English edition, and this time one in which every shade and nuance is illuminated by fine pictures, is Randolph Caldecott's *Hey Diddle Diddle*. Simplicity in design allows for freedom of interpretation on pages that breathe the life a master artist gave them. "This is the *real* Mother Goose—marvelously imagined improvisations that playfully and rhythmically bounce off and around the verses without ever incongruously straying. If any name deserves to be permanently joined with that of Mother Goose, it is Randolph Caldecott. His picture books, published by Frederick Warne, should be among the first volumes given to every child."[3]

A spirited spoon and dish sprint across a tile floor while cruets and plates dance rhythmically to the tune of a cat's fiddle. Lively movement characterizes the art of this masterful nursery rhyme illustrator.

From Hey Diddle Diddle *illustrated by Randolph Caldecott. Frederick Warne & Co., Inc. Reproduced by permission.*

---

[3]Maurice Sendak, "Mother Goose's Garnishings," *Book Week*, Fall Children's Issue (October 31, 1965).

A literary descendant of Randolph Caldecott is L. Leslie Brooke, whose Johnny Crow books and several Mother Goose collections have caught the magic inherent in the nursery rhymes and verses. Here rhyme and repetition of verse details are enlivened by beautifully balanced drawings in black and white and subtle color. *Ring O' Roses* by Brooke is the best of his Mother Goose collections compiled and illustrated with a humor and delight that taps the flavor of an English setting.

A more recent artist of a more generous collection of rhymes and verses is Marguerite de Angeli. Charmingly illustrated, her *Book of Nursery and Mother Goose Rhymes* includes practically every familiar Mother Goose rhyme, verse, and melody. It is dignified and graceful, and is in possession of precisely the kind of pictures suited to interpret rather literally the mood and meanings of the text. Her pictures, especially the ones of animals and children, are so realistically drawn that no strain falls on the young child's power of inference when he is invited to look at the pictures of this spacious book while the rhymes are read aloud. In this respect Marguerite de Angeli's book succeeds where others fail. The very young child, whose experiential background is slight, should not be expected to make inferences when clear-cut drawings can help him recognize the figures on the page. Only through his first-hand experiences and the visual forms in his first books will a child grasp more clearly the abstract concepts he will meet later on.

Delicate lines trace lovely forms of a cat and a little girl in this softly shaded picture that quietly interprets "I Love Little Pussy."
From Book of Nursery and Mother Goose Rhymes *by Marguerite de Angeli. Copyright 1954 by Marguerite de Angeli. Reprinted by permission of Doubleday & Company, Inc.*

One collection of nursery rhymes selected and illustrated with the youngest child in mind is *Ring-a-Ring o' Roses* by Raymond Briggs. The carefully selected rhymes possess singing rhythm and have the fun and fancy indigenous to early childhood. Warm, beautiful colors heighten the emotional impact, especially since the pictures provide exact, almost microscopic details. From a sensory point of view, full page pictures offer scenes such as the three men in a tub surrounded by salt spray, and sturdy, clear-cut pictures of Simple Simon and the pieman set against the flags and tents of a far-off fair.

Sturdy figures in homespun garments are the focal point of this page depicting the nursery rhyme "Simple Simon." In the distance the fairgrounds are aflutter with tent flags that beckon the little boy and the pieman.
From Ring-a-Ring o' Roses *by Raymond Briggs.* © *1962 by Raymond Briggs. Reprinted by permission of Coward-McCann, Inc.*

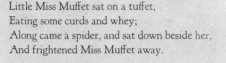

Little Miss Muffet sat on a tuffet,
Eating some curds and whey;
Along came a spider, and sat down beside her,
And frightened Miss Muffet away.

Quaint and comfortable on her backyard tuffet, Little Miss Muffet sits surrounded by ducks and pumpkins while a tiny spider hangs close by.
From Mother Goose *illustrated by Tasha Tudor. Copyright 1944 by Henry Z. Walck, Inc. Reprinted by permission of the publisher.*

A larger collection, though less perceptively interpreted, is the *Mother Goose* book by Tasha Tudor. Her beautiful pictures bring visual brightness to the well-loved verses. The clear, clean pages show portraits of young children who reflect back to the child something of himself, for Tasha Tudor's children possess a fresh-faced vitality that is wholesome and true and reflect the simple honesty that characterizes the nursery. Thus, through these lovely pictures young readers are united with other boys and girls of the Mother Goose age.

Alphabet, Counting, and Other Concept Books

Some examples of the loveliest books that appeal to young children are in the form of alphabets. Classics among them include the *A B C Book* with letter and animal woodcuts by C. B. Falls. Distinct, bright pictures fill each page where figures of the creatures are clearly outlined, recognizable, and ablaze with color.

Though somewhat old-fashioned by modern standards, this book traces forms with grace of line that manages to put on a page something more than just the creatures and the alphabet it depicts. Few alphabet books reveal the beauty and serenity felt in the page designed with "S is for Swan." Done with colorful woodcuts, the work of C. B. Falls exists as a stunning example of order, clarity, and craftsmanship in picture books.

Serene settings and a gracefully curved swan support the shape of the letter *S* to which they are keyed. Distinct letter forms stand out in sharp relief in this vivid picture book.
From A B C Book *by C. B. Falls. Copyright 1923 by Doubleday & Company, Inc. Reprinted by permission of the publisher.*

Another classic example is the charming *A Apple Pie* by the nineteenth century artist Kate Greenaway, who is ranked as one of the first—as well as finest—creators of the modern picture books.

Sturdy lines trace the form of letters while delicate strokes outline children with quaintness and subtlety of color. Boys appear dressed in breeches and tasseled caps, girls in flouncy dresses and bonnets in well-spaced designs on uncluttered pages. The charm of novelty applied to commonplace situations in *A Apple Pie* brings delight to children who read this book, which mirrors natural and frolicsome childhood in beautiful, delicate colors.

In contrast with the delicacy of Kate Greenaway, a modern artist's work, *Brian Wildsmith's ABC*, is exotic in conception and striking in its visual impact. Bold, recognizable pictures of many familiar animals and things, drawn in Wildsmith's vibrant style, provide an excellent beginning for a modern child's first encounter with the alphabet.

Wildsmith reaches children struck by the staccato designs in their neon–lit environment where bold, vivid forms vie for attention. And to focus young eyes on the alphabet, this book offers full, double-page spreads for upper and lower case letters, each beginning the name of an imaginatively drawn object or living thing and set against a backdrop of luminous color.

Complementing a modern collection of distinctive alphabet books is *Bruno Munari's ABC*, which pictures a large variety of familiar animals and objects in brilliant colors and interesting designs.

> *"N is for newspaper,*
> *Nuts on a Nail and*
> *No bird in the Nest."*[4]

Examples such as these link children with elements in their real world. Less imaginative than Wildsmith's, though visually emphatic, Munari's alphabet book ties in with the everyday language and experiences of modern children. No strain is given to inference or recall as familiar objects are flashed on pages with the letters that provide the elements of sound.

Shot through with bright humor is a small cluster of alphabet books with perennial appeal since humor is a quality that lifts and refreshes, and it is frequently needed by children. Just as music and rhythm are almost certain to arouse responses from the young, so are humor and nonsense sure to elicit expressions of delight.

Edward Lear's *A Nonsense Alphabet* presents letters of the alphabet with the names of animals and things they suggest. Each letter in the master humorist's tiny book is accompanied by a nonsense verse. The colorful pictures, animals for the most part, are cleverly drawn with a mischievous sparkle to highlight the humorous text.

> *F was once a little fish,*
> *Fishy,*
> *Wishy,*
> *Squishy,*
> *Fishy,*
> *In a dishy*
> *Little Fish!*[5]

---

[4]*Bruno Munari's ABC* (Cleveland: World Publishing Company, 1960). Copyright © 1960 by Bruno Munari. Reprinted by permission of the World Publishing Company.
[5]Edward Lear, *A Nonsense Alphabet* (New York: Doubleday & Company, Inc., 1962).

Curious George Learns the Alphabet by H. A. Rey helps other young hopefuls to do the same or at least become entertained with a "story-alphabet" book.

Delightful in its presentation of a curious monkey's antics and his attempts at learning the alphabet, this book spins a thin story that chooses alphabet letters to name an article or animal. Wonderful use of color supports the bright text and leads to a surprise ending at "X."

The man with the yellow hat came just in time.
"You don't tear a book apart to find out what's in it," he said. "You READ it, George. Books are full of stories. Stories are made of words, and words are made of letters. If you want to read a story you first have to know the letters of the alphabet. Let me show you."

4

The man took a big pad and began to draw.
George was curious.
"This is an A," the man said. "The A is the first letter of the alphabet."

5

An uncluttered background affords full view of a comical monkey learning the alphabet. Sharply defined letters are traced with clarity in this clever alphabet story. *From* Curious George Learns the Alphabet *by H. A. Rey. Copyright 1963 by Houghton Mifflin Company. Reproduced by permission.*

Counting books provide the elements of the language of mathematics by presenting a few fundamental concepts and their symbols. Their use does not prescribe a particular "method" of teaching that can solve problems of elementary mathematics. Rather, counting books offer material that assists the development of a young child's early concept of "natural number" based on collections of distinct objects. Number names and symbols are attached to each grouping to point up numerical concepts.

A pleasing look-and-listen counting book for the youngest, *3 × 3 Three by Three* by James Krüss, recounts a simple tale in three-line verses. Merriment abounds and pictures glow in this book whose number concept is constant at "three."

There is ease in the way this book uses language to assist in the development of a single number concept, while the book is made bright with color and clear-cut forms on every page where confusion gives way to clarity and order.

A counting book that has additional numerical concepts is *One Step, Two . . .* by Charlotte Zolotow. Large pictures in ripe colors carry off the counting lines in arithmetical progression as preschooler and mother explore the neighborhood.

In *One Was Johnny* by Maurice Sendak, small verses tell a humorous tale of a little boy who counts animals from one to ten as they come to his house. In reverse order the numbers decrease as the animal guests diminish from ten to one. Thus by providing the concepts of increasing and decreasing numbers, a measure of reinforcement can take place, not with dull, repetitive drill, but with ingenuity and humor.

Another counting book, this time in slender verse form with delicate drawings, is Tasha Tudor's *1 is One*. Placid loveliness adorns this small book that matches mathematical language with symbols from one to twenty. Twice emphasizing the tens concept, *1 is One* uses graceful shapes and simple, accurate terms, along with artistically alternating color and black-and-white drawings.

More number concepts are expressed in *Brown Cow Farm* by Dahlov Ipcar. Extending the numerical progression to one hundred, the book itemizes groups of animals in toast-warm colors.

There is one brown horse in a big box stall. . . .

There are two brown hound dogs that sleep in the hay. . . .

There are three brown cats that live in the barn. . . .[6]

---

[6]Dahlov Ipcar, *Brown Cow Farm* (New York: Doubleday & Company, Inc., 1959). Copyright © 1959 by Dahlov Ipcar. Reprinted by permission of Doubleday & Company, Inc.

3 is three swallows

And out in the marshes the ten wild geese build their nests and lay their eggs and hatch their babies. Each wild mother goose hatches ten little goslings.[7]

And so on to multiple groups of ten that add up to one hundred.
Then a final double-page spread graphically sums up the whole farm population.

There are chickens, kittens, a colt, and ducklings. Turkey poults and baby goslings. Puppies, bunnies, piglets, and calves.
And all of their big mothers too. There are lots of animals on Brown Cow Farm. Can you count them all?[8]

Enlivened by distinct pictures, clear-cut text and symbols, this counting book exhances what has been learned from books with single

[7] *Ibid.*
[8] *Ibid.*

up in the sky

Framed with fruits and flowers, each pastel page demonstrates numerical concepts in arithmetic progression. Beautifully spaced and balanced, colored pages alternate with black-and-white in an unusually artistic counting book.

From 1 Is One *by Tasha Tudor.* © *1956 by Henry Z. Walck, Inc. Reproduced by permission.*

or only a very few numerical concepts by its multiple representations of a number system whose base is ten.

Counting books, like alphabet books, point up more specific concepts than books that deal with various dimensions of an abstract idea. The "abstract idea book," or "concept book," a relatively new kind of picture book, explores ideas more deeply, with emphasis given to shape, size, speed, weight, time and so forth. Very often a wise use of color adds immeasurably to concepts expressed by the text and symbols found in this type of picture book, aiming to clarify ideas in an artfully interesting way.

There are chickens, kittens, a colt, and ducklings. Turkey poults and baby goslings. Puppies, bunnies, piglets, and calves.

And all of their big mothers too. There are lots of animals on Brown Cow Farm. Can you count them all?

Groups of multiples are clearly presented in this double-page spread of a counting book that uses farm animals and their young to stress an arithmetic concept. *From* Brown Cow Farm *by Dahlov Ipcar. Copyright © 1959 by Dahlov Ipcar. Reprinted by permission of Doubleday & Company, Inc.*

Roundness. One of the first concept books, which appeared in 1954, explored "roundness" through verse and pictures.

> *A kiss is round,*
> *And so is a hug;*
> *The rim of a glass,*
> *And the lid of a jug;*
> *The top of a hole*
> *When it's carefully dug.*[9]

With the use of comparison, Blossom Budney in *A Kiss Is Round* shows roundness as it exists in the familiar world of a young child.

Weight. The concept of weight—absolute and relative—is symbolized in a faintly humorous, gay little book, *Heavy Is a Hippopotamus* by Miriam Schlein.

Speed. The concept of speed is made personal and relative in another book by the same author-illustrator— *Fast Is Not a Ladybug.*

---

[9]Blossom Budney, *A Kiss Is Round* (New York: Lothrop, Lee & Shepard Co., Inc. 1954). © 1954 by Lothrop, Lee & Shepard Co., Inc.

Size. Size, through comparison, is given a variety of forms in one of the Little Owl books entitled *What Is Big?* by Henry Wing.

Using structured language, flame-colored pages point up concepts with dependable patterns of words and sentences plus amusing drawings of familiar creatures.

> *I am not as big as a goat.*
> *A goat is bigger than I am.*
> *I am not as big as a horse.*
> *A horse is bigger than I am.*
>
> * * *
>
> *I am bigger than a dog.*
> *A dog is bigger than a cat.*
> *I am bigger than a cat.*[10]

In this unusual concept book even the text hints at increasing size by becoming larger in accordance with the biggest thing the little boy in the story uses for comparison.

Shape. Again with comparisons, *Shapes* by Miriam Schlein introduces an observation of shapes familiar to young children. Simple drawings and humming rhymes call attention to the ordinary shapes on the square pages of this sturdy book.

Roundness is stressed by the circular face of a cuckoo clock on this page of a book that employs commonplace objects and happenings to sharpen awareness of shape.
From A Kiss Is Round *by Blossom Budney, illustrated by Vladimir Bobri. Copyright 1954 by Lothrop, Lee & Shepard Company. Reprinted by permission of the publisher.*

---

[10]Henry R. Wing, *What Is Big?* (New York: Holt, Rinehart & Winston, Inc, 1963).

*No, no. A bear is not a square.
Neither is a mare
  or a hare
  or a fox in his lair,
  or a little girl with bows in her hair.*

*A fish in the sea
  or a bird in the air
  can never, no never, no
  never be square!*

     *   *   *

*But the kitty all curled up
is round,
almost round as a ball.*

     *   *   *

*. . . but
no boy, or girl, or lady, or man,
or fish in the water
or beast on the land
or bird in the air
is ever exactly round, or square!*

*Wiggly woggly
here and there—
everything isn't round or square!
Bumpy lumpy
zig and zag—
what other shapes are there?*[11]

Picture Stories
and Easy-to-Read Books

Although a young child's life is marked by rapid changes in growth and development, and his interest in books reflects his own maturity, some books of permanent value never quite lose their appeal. The "Mother Goose Age" may have passed and merely naming or counting may have lost its interest, but the magic of a child's first books will always hold him in its spell, and he may seek them out from time to time and want to look at them and read them in his more mature years.

But no matter how tempting and delicious these earliest experiences may be, a child nurtured on fine first books will eventually want

---

[11]Miriam Schlein, *Shapes* (New York: William R. Scott, Inc., 1952). Copyright © 1952 by William R. Scott, Inc. Reprinted by permission of William R. Scott, Inc.

books whose pictures tell him a continuous story that he can "read" for himself. Or, if the book is a read-aloud book, or an easy-to-read one, it must offer some of the same music and dramatic interest a child has learned to expect from his nursery books as well as tell him a continuous story.

ANIMAL TALES

Beatrix Potter's picture stories are perennial favorites for young children who have always shown a fancy for animal tales. Beatrix Potter's stories, ageless in their appeal, ring true to a world scaled to the understanding and imagination of the young. Her books invite children to live for a moment in another world, to feel someone else's joy or sorrow, to taste the delights of the English spring trapped forever in these tiny books.

The graceful text of this miniature library is true to natural history and lends itself comfortably to a young child's intuitive appreciation regardless of his limited experiences. For example, Peter Rabbit's home life, as well as the home life of many other Beatrix Potter animals, is different from but related to the home life of any child. By touching the conscious experience of a young child such stories allow for the sort of identification that delights and satisfies.

While he gains a deepened self-awareness, a child may be moved by the beauty of language expressed in the animal tales. Beatrix Potter's tuneful patterns of words flow with a gentle ring and convey fundamental truths. No child touched by the power of Beatrix Potter's books remains unchanged.

Although our analysis of this miniature library attempts to separate those elements that are important in children's literature, the pictures and text are, in fact, inseparable. There is a sympathetic agreement between them such that the two exist fused together to give these books their distinctive form and unity.

TALES OF CHILDREN WITH ANIMALS

From close observation of childhood—when little distinction is made between fact and fancy—come some of the works of Marie Hall Ets and Maurice Sendak.

The picture stories and easy-to-read books of these writer-illustrators show unquestioned integrity of conception and design. Their books are consonant with a child's life because they are filled with endearing and quaint human touches, putting them at precisely the right angle to life in early childhood.

Marie Hall Ets' first book in color, *Play with Me*, is judged as her loveliest. Without an excess word or an unnecessary line, her text and drawings blend delicately to tell about a curious child who goes into a meadow to play. Through the pages of this book the little girl helps readers to discover and name the shy creatures of the woods and stream where friends are made through gentleness and patience. Naming the animals, however, is a minor purpose of the book; its main goal is telling a continuous story through full-page pictures and thin text. Fragile pastels and simple drawings spell out the theme naturally and quietly.

In the text, repetition is frequently used, not a deadening repetition in order to drill into a child's head some bite-size words, but a graceful and poetic repetition whose rhythm and beat most young children love to hear. For example, here are a few lines:

> "Grasshopper," I said, "will you play with me?"
> And I tried to catch him, but he leaped away.
>
> *   *   *
>
> "Frog," I said, "will you play with me?"
> And I tried to catch him, but he leaped away too.
>
> *   *   *
>
> None of them, none of them, would play with me.
>
> *   *   *
>
> Oh, now I was happy—as happy could be! For
> All of them—ALL OF THEM—were playing with me.[12]

Another book by this outstanding writer of picture stories is her most imaginative one, *In the Forest*. Its rhythmic, cadenced text is highlighted by rare black-and-white drawings. Here a small boy takes a walk in the forest with a procession of imaginary animal friends just as naturally as a child might imagine doing it.

Once again Ets has constructed a cumulative story with such an economy of words that the simple text is clear and vigorous. Simple as the words may be, however, they never talk down to a young reader. Rather, the concise, lyrical words express the imaginative story with such integrity that this book has become a classic of shared delight for children as well as adults.

A counterpart to *In the Forest* is *Where the Wild Things Are* by Maurice Sendak. With great understanding of young children, it tells about Max, a little boy who is sent to his room for cavorting around in his wolfsuit and acting "like a wild thing." It is the kind of fantasy that adults

---

[12]From *Play With Me* by Marie Hall Ets, copyright 1955 by Marie Hall Ets. Reprinted by permission of the Viking Press, Inc.

When I went for a walk in the forest.

Masterly drawings capture a proud moment of a little boy leading an imaginary parade of animals. Humor vibrates in the detailed portrayal of the forest creatures and the boy with his cap and toy trumpet.

From In the Forest *by Marie Hall Ets. Copyright 1944 by Marie Hall Ets. Reprinted by permission of The Viking Press, Inc.*

will rate highly for its technical, brilliant, and sometimes frightening pictures, but youngsters will claim it as a book written for them.

Through bold, vivid pictures and very few words, Max, while shut in his room, imagines himself traveling off to where the wild things are and ruling over them, but at the same time sharing their rumpus. In agreement with childhood's flight into an imaginary world for a moment of wild excitement, the story returns Max to the warm comforts of reality—his own room where his supper is waiting for him and "it was still hot."[13]

This book offers the momentary escape that most children need. It vicariously provides wild adventure and a refreshed return to a relatively calmer reality. This need for release or escape is common to humankind and to children particularly, on whom so many social limits for conformity are imposed.

---

[13]Maurice Sendak, *Where the Wild Things Are* (New York: Harper & Row, Publishers, 1963).

Excellent craftsmanship is expressed in the finely drawn illustration of little Max and the wild things, who share a rumpus in the swingingest way. Deep, luminous colors add richly to the monstrous beauty of this picture book.
From Where the Wild Things Are *by Maurice Sendak. Harper & Row, 1963. Reproduced by permission.*

BOOKS FOR EASY READING

Once a child has been sparked by the magic of books and their pictures, his attitude toward reading calls for books he can read by himself. These first few books, however, must be chosen carefully if the child is to learn to read with ease and delight and without frustration. Then, caught by the interest and excitement found in good easy-to-read books, a child's desire to read is not only sustained but strengthened.

Since the middle of the twentieth century, books designated as "easy" books have appeared with bright, lively content and color and meanings familiar to the youngest reader. Artistically designed, these easy-to-read books are marked by simplicity and freshness and employ a sensible choice of words and beautiful illustrations. Today's publishing continues the trend for books that rise above the lifeless drone of many textbooks to a sunny, more cheerful variety of books suitable for beginners in reading.

Some delightful examples are published by Harper & Row under the banner of I Can Read Books. Without using condescending language, or the hail-like patter of the first books in many reading series, these simply written stories are made appealing and manageable by the simplicity and originality of their easy-to-read text. Wisely chosen words are used with imaginative pictures that offer clever clues to readers who may be doing their first independent reading.

Many of the books in this series have the added convenience of being set in eighteen-point type, which is large and well-spaced enough to allow for easy reading. Nor has the art work been neglected.

Illustrative of these qualities is *Little Bear's Visit*, one of the four "Little Bear" books, in which Else Holmelund Minarik, a skilled user of bite-size words, gives a tidy account of Little Bear who "came to visit Grandmother and Grandfather Bear in their little house in the woods. This was something Little Bear liked to do." The story moves along to relate the child-like antics of an irresistible little character made even more endearing through the charmingly quaint pictures by Maurice Sendak.

Quaintness lends charm to this page in which an endearing little bear struts off to visit his grandparents.

From Little Bear's Visit *by Else Holmelund Minarik, illustrated by Maurice Sendak. Harper & Row, Publishers, 1961. Reproduced by permission.*

Another group of books in the I Can Read series is the work of Gene Zion and the illustrator, Margaret Bloy Graham. Their stories of Harry, a dog with personality, lend themselves to silent, individual reading because the simple language conveys a meaningful story full of bright humor. Funny, almost cartoon style pictures, splashed across broad, comfortable-to-hold pages, are especially good in *Harry and the Lady Next Door*. But Harry's personality is most pronounced in *No Roses for Harry*, a witty picture storybook with plenty of background details that sharpen the story of a determined dog in search of ways to dispose of a hated rose-covered sweater.

Along these lines, the American Book Company also has published a large selection of supplementary reading books emphasizing variety in themes and in reading difficulty. The primary grade materials in the American Book Company's Reading Round Table series puts no strain on young eyes challenged by a page of text and pictures.

Not taking much for granted, the main books in the series present pages of distilled text and simple drawings expressive of the mood and style suitable for children who are beginning to read. Many of the titles in this collection are by writers of fine trade books for children or young adults. Marked by a color code to identify reading levels, the books in this series utilize language that is skillfully scaled to several grades of difficulty.

Some of the best examples of these titles are Elizabeth Coatsworth's *Seven Sleepers*, Edward Stone's *One Pet Too Many*, and Constantine Georgiou's *The Elephant's Funny Way*, as well as simple retellings of *The Little Red Hen* and *The Gingerbread Boy*. Words are chosen with pungent economy to tell one or more stories that employ elements of surprise, suspense, and a very thin plot free from excessive descriptions.

Another series of lively, imaginative books for beginning readers are the Little Owl Books published by Holt, Rinehart, & Winston. Designed for a wide variety of tastes and abilities, these gaily colored books blend artistry and utility in a convenient package of easy-to-read materials.

The most recent titles with unique formats are those produced by Harvey House Publishers whose Easy-to-Read Picture Books series reveal that poetic prose and distinctive pictures can combine to produce appealing materials for easy reading. Avoiding meaningless words in deadening repetition, the Easy-to-Read Picture Books use lively lines of text matched with pictures that provide context clues simply and directly. To sustain the interest of the youngest readers this series also includes variety in the storytelling art as well as in the art media to encourage beginning readers to sample their first delights in prose and poetry. Bernard Lipscomb's pictures for *The Clock*, one of the Easy-to-Read Picture Books, artistically turn commonplace things into a vital experience for the young. With a minimum of extraneous details and a maximum visual impact his pictures add strength and meaning to the slender lines of text that tell a beautiful story.

And the little mouse lives in me.

11

Clear-cut drawings depict with exactness the details of an old grandfather clock in which a little mouse lives.

From The Clock *by Constantine Georgiou, illustrated by Bernard Lipscomb. Harvey House, Inc., 1967. Reproduced by permission.*

88

*Picture
Books
and
Picture
Storybooks*

Picture Storybooks

Just as a child goes through stages in his physical development, he also passes through developmental stages in his reading tastes and ability. A child will turn from the simple "easy" books to the more complex storybooks with more developed elements of storytelling: themes, sequence, movement, characters, and style of writing. But the growth gained from the bright, imaginative materials is not lost in this transition. Rather, the reading done at the beginning-to-read stage, and the listening skills learned to the music of the nursery rhymes and lilting text of picture books will leave the child with power to unlock meanings and to derive satisfactions from his future reading experiences.

After gaining some reading skill, a child can move in the direction of materials with more developed text with more difficult vocabulary and more complex plots. His earlier reading, mainly a process of identification and visual awareness, was first provided by the picture stories and read-aloud books. Then easy-to-read materials with thin plots and simple characterizations encouraged reading power. At this point, a further transition to picture storybooks is natural and within the ability of children who are eager to read.

The immense scope of picture books and picture storybooks creates a good deal of overlapping of themes that makes the analysis of more developed materials superfluous especially since fine breakdowns have already been covered in the preceding pages. But there is a very important category of themes that emerges in picture storybooks that may be of more significance to children of a later maturity level. This category describes children of different nationalities.

CHILDREN FROM VARIED CULTURES

Although books with far-flung settings may come early in the experience of a young child, the ethnic impact of such books is small compared to the impression these books may make on children of greater maturity. For example Elsa Beskow's *Pelle's New Suit*, the story of a Swedish farm boy, may just as well take place in a preschooler's neighborhood, while later on the same story may serve to broaden a child's understanding of communities outside his own.

Books that explore life in a variety of cultures enlarge a child's horizons. A more developed story line carries a young reader into unknown worlds inhabited by boys and girls with similar needs and interests. A sense of universal life is captured in tales of the joys and sorrows common to childhood.

A heartwarming story of sudden, touching beauty, *Lito and the Clown* by Leo Politi, is aimed at boys and girls with a special fondness for animals. Amid the gaiety of a Mexican town where a carnival is in full swing, one finds a close-up of human feelings and national traits.

Stunning pictures ablaze with color complement the text, whose story line threads its way in and out of narrow cobbled streets in a small city in Mexico. Here Lito loses his little kitten, Paquita. And it is not until a clown on stilts comes to announce the arrival of the carnival that the little kitten is found.

Capturing the mood of fiesta time in Mexico, this beautiful painting reveals beaming faces as a clown on stilts stoops to return Lito's lost kitten. Vibrant colors enhance this story.
From Lito and the Clown *by Leo Politi. Copyright © 1964 by Leo Politi. Reproduced by permission of Charles Scribner's Sons.*

Then Payaco came. He stretched his tall body and reached up very high. Everyone was quiet. Payaco's arms reached up and up. At last he had the kitten in his hands.[14]

Perhaps exposure to this type of picture storybook will not assure the young child of gaining an immediate sense of nationality, but through these books a child unconsciously develops a sense of humanity as well as an artistic approach to the world of the visual arts. These books, in their own subtle way, are capable of connecting cultures by meanings that go beyond the printed page and also of communicating the aesthetic values underlying a genuinely creative work that interprets universal life.

Criteria for Picture Books and Picture Storybooks

THEME

- Is there something original about the themes and the way they are treated?
- Are the themes clearly and vividly presented?
- Are the themes concerned with common experiences of young children?
- Have the themes the potential to extend the experiences of children?
- Can the ideas be readily perceived by young children?
- Are the ideas illumined by pictures?
- Is the content appealing and appropriate?
- Are the various themes capable of arousing a variety of healthy emotions present in early childhood?

PLOT

- Are only the simplest of plots used?
- Are these plots clearly recognizable?
- Can the story line be followed easily?
- Is there "circular motion" to the story line so that it comes full cycle?
- Is the story line interrupted by too much description or by other distracting elements?
- Does the story move along at a rate suitable for its intended age level?
- Does the pace of the story pick up and slow down so as to give a feeling of balance and variation?

---

[14]Leo Politi, *Lito and the Clown* (New York: Charles Scribner's Sons, 1964).

CHARACTERIZATION

91

*Picture
Books
and
Picture
Storybooks*

- Are characters clearly drawn and visible to young children?
- Does the major character stand out as a hero with whom children can identify?
- Are the characters lifelike and real so that they can work out the conflicts in the story without appearing contrived?
- Are the characters genuine enough to give a sense of humanity to young readers?
- Do the characters mirror back to children something of themselves to unite them with the story?
- Do characters in the story say and do the things typical of the age and experience of young children?
- Are the characters capable of serving as vehicles to communicate a measure of the story's message?
- Do even minor characters possess universal characteristics without becoming stereotypes?

STYLE

- Is the style of writing suited to the themes?
- Does the writing impose order upon the ideas?
- Is the writing orderly, clear, and exact?
- Have conciseness and brevity been considered?
- Does the language make the message understood?
- Is there rhythm and music to the text?
- Has the simplicity and beauty of cadenced language been utilized in the prose?
- Is the essence of poetry distilled in the text?
- Has care been given to the choice of words?
- Does the writing, even if just a few words and sentences, come alive on the page?
- Has the appropriate mood or feeling been created?
- Is there ordered sequence in the movement governing the episodes and events?
- Is there discernible logic to this sequenced order?
- Has the sense of wonder, humor, and delight been expressed appropriately?

DESIGN

- Does the artist reflect a strong sense of composition and design?
- Are the pictures clear, interpretive of the text, and well drawn?

- Does the illustrator give careful attention to exactly the right details to catch a child's fancy?
- Is there unity between the text and the pictures?
- Has a suitable medium been used to express the spirit of the text and pictures?
- Have the medium, the design, the various tones in the pictures effectively created an atmosphere or mood?
- Is poetic beauty and grace sympathetically translated by the illustrator's art?
- Is there harmony and order between shapes, forms, colors, and design?

To summarize our discussion of the art of picture books and picture storybooks, here is what Professor Charles Reasoner says about this division of literature:

> Young children live with their literature on visual frontiers created for them by authors and artists of insight and wisdom. Through word-and-picture accounts of arresting segments of life, they help boys and girls find book ways to frontier explorations of literature meanings. Although writers and illustrators can lead young people to the frontier's edge, it is here that they part, for each child must experience for himself. Each must sense and find and formulate his own concepts in the pattern presented him.

> As one prepares to mediate between the young child and his literature, two concerns come immediately to mind. The first urges one to employ all the *sensitivity* at his command to insure high complementation in the selection of the story and the visual medium for extending the child's experience of the story.

> The second concern urges one to take every precaution to retain the *freedom* which the children's artist achieves in his illustrations—a freedom which allows the individual to find his own way through picture and print, to come away from the literature experience with his own interpretation and enjoyment of the story.

> The life the young child sees and lives is not one with a definite purpose for tomorrow but, rather, one which is rich and full of the "stuff of tomorrow"—the sense and nonsense experiences of the moment. So many of these experiences are at his fingertips—between and beyond the covers of his books.[15]

---

[15]Charles Reasoner, "Enjoying Literature Visually," in *Using Literature with Young Children*, Leland B. Jacobs, ed. (New York: Teachers College Press, 1965) p. 47.

References

93

*Picture
Books
and
Picture
Storybooks*

ARBUTHNOT, MAY HILL, "The Artist and the Child's Books," in *Children and Books*, 3rd ed. Chicago: Scott, Foresman & Company, 1964.

AVERILL, ESTHER, "What Is a Picture Book?" in *Caldecott Medal Books: 1938–1957*, Bertha Mahoney Miller and Elinor Whitney Field, eds. Boston: The Horn Book, Inc., 1957.

BROWN, MARCIA, "Distinction in Picture Book," *The Horn Book Magazine*, XXV (September–October 1949), 382–95.

DALGLEISH, ALICE, "Small Children and Books," *The Horn Book Magazine*, IX (February 1933), 158–63.

HUBER, MIRIAM BLANTON, "Illustrated Books for Children," in *Story and Verse for Children*. New York: The Macmillan Company, 1965.

JOHNSON, EDNA, *et al.*, "Picture Books," in *Anthology of Children's Literature*. Boston: Houghton Mifflin Company, 1959.

LANE, MARGARET, *The Tale of Beatrix Potter*. Baltimore: Penguin Books, Inc., 1962.

MITCHELL, MARGUERITE, "Artists and Picture Books," *The Horn Book Magazine*, XIII (May–June 1937), 139–43.

MOORE, ANNE CARROLL, "Leslie Brooke: Pied Piper of English Picture Books," in *My Roads to Childhood*. New York: Doubleday, 1939, pp. 267–71.

NESBITT, ELIZABETH, "The March of Picture Books," in *A Critical History of Children's Literature*, Meigs *et al.* New York: The Macmillan Company, 1953.

SAYERS, FRANCES CLARKE, "Through These Sweet Fields," *The Horn Book Magazine*, XVIII (November 1942), 436–44.

SMITH, LILLIAN H., "Picture Books," in *The Unreluctant Years*. Chicago: American Library Association, 1953.

VIGUERS, RUTH HILL, "The Artist as Storyteller," in *A Critical History of Children's Literature*, Meigs *et al.* New York: The Macmillan Company, 1953.

Picture Books and Picture Storybooks

BOOKS OF MOTHER GOOSE AND NURSERY RHYMES

BOOK OF NURSERY AND MOTHER GOOSE RHYMES
Compiled and illustrated by Marguerite de Angeli. Doubleday & Company, Inc., 1954.

A comprehensive collection of nursery rhymes highlighted by beautiful pictures in color and black-and-white. Each of the 192 large pages is adorned with some drawings while certain pages glow with magical color and the quiet elegance of an English setting. Marguerite de Angeli displays talent in creating delicate pictures that sympathetically interpret the melodic text.

RING-A-RING O' ROSES

*Compiled and illustrated by Raymond
Briggs. Coward-McCann, Inc., 1962.*

A book containing ten nursery rhymes full
of singing rhythm, fun, fancy, and warm,
beautiful colors. The pictures offer an invitation to the senses for one can almost
smell the pies of the pieman going to the
fair and feel the salt spray that surrounds
the three men in a tub. Watercolor illustrations have a lyrical, misty quality.
Artfully designed, each rhyme is delicately
framed by small pen and ink sketches,
adding contrast to the full page color
pictures.

RING O' ROSES

*Compiled and illustrated by L. Leslie
Brooke. Frederick Warne & Co., Inc.,
1923.*

A classic collection of twenty nursery
rhymes enlivened by the simplicity and
freshness that have distinguished the pictures of Leslie Brooke. Each page of both
color and black-and-white drawings is
uncluttered, clear, and designed to facilitate recognition of the animals and characters featured in the rhymes.

CALDECOTT PICTURE BOOKS (4 VOLS.)

*Compiled and illustrated by Randolph
Caldecott. Frederick Warne & Co., Inc.,
1878–1885.*

Devoted to sixteen favorite nursery
rhymes, four in each of the four volumes,
simple line drawings are alive with energetic action whether in color or black-and-
white. The pictures are classics by the great
artist for whom the annual picture book
award is named.

THE HOUSE THAT JACK BUILT

*Compiled and illustrated by Randolph
Caldecott. Frederick Warne & Co.,
Inc., n.d.*

This familiar rhyme is based on repetition
and is conducive to memorization because
of its limited vocabulary. The illustrations
are the highlight of this book. Done in
sepia as well as pastels, they are pert and

clever, appealing to both the eye and the
sense of humor.

LAVENDER'S BLUE

*Compiled by Kathleen Lines.
Illustrated by Harold Jones.
Oxford University Press, 1954.*

Well planned and arranged rhymes with
corresponding pictures fill the pages of
this collection. The detailed, definite drawings invite close observation.

MOTHER GOOSE AND NURSERY RHYMES

*Compiled and illustrated by Philip Reed.
Atheneum Publishers, 1963.*

Charming, colorful wood engravings
adorn clean pages of clear type. Philip
Reed has created whimsical, jaunty, homespun characters and images in keeping with
the spirit of a folk tale.

MOTHER GOOSE

*Compiled and illustrated by Tasha
Tudor. Henry Z. Walck, Inc.,
Publishers, 1944.*

Seventy-seven verses selected and illustrated by a skillful artist of the nursery.
Tasha Tudor's beautiful pictures bring to
the well-loved verses a fresh, bright interpretation. Whether in color or black-and-
white, they reflect order and rhythm in
the simple arrangement of forms, with
pictures of a young child on almost all the
well-designed pages.

ALPHABET BOOKS

SPACE ABC

*Written by Margaret Bruce. Designed
by Ahza Cohen. Bobbs-Merrill Co.,
Inc., 1967.*

This ABC will probably be as interesting
to older members of the family as to
younger ones, for authentic photographs
illustrate each space word. Older children
who wish to read beyond the ABC's and
parents who may need help with their
space vocabulary will appreciate a section
at the back of the book that includes
definitions of terms and descriptions of the
photographs.

A B C Book
Designed and cut on wood by C. B.
Falls. Doubleday & Company, Inc.,
1923.

An alphabet book based upon pictures of animals from the zoo and farmyard. There is no story or rhyme, and some of the words are difficult. Falls uses the wood-cutting technique effectively by printing brightly colored pictures on plain white pages.

The ABC Bunny
Compiled by Wanda Gág.
Hand lettered by Howard Gág.
Coward-McCann, Inc., 1933.

Wanda Gág's ABC book features rabbit drawings with large and clearly defined letters and pictures for the very young. Each illustration in black, soft grey tones, and white reveals a mastery of line drawing.

The Alphabet Tale
Compiled by Jan Garten.
Illustrated by Muriel Batherman.
Random House, Inc., 1946.

Tale or tail—here is an alphabet book that combines both. Jan Garten develops the alphabet with the aid of animal tails. A large double page and a short rhyme is presented for each letter of the alphabet. Illustrations are large and simple. A book with which any youngster can have fun.

A Apple Pie
Compiled and illustrated by Kate
Greenaway. Frederick Warne & Co.,
Inc., 1886.

Letters of the alphabet are presented in a story about a pie. This book is rather old-fashioned in approach but beautiful in composition, and it has much eye appeal. Soft pastel colors effectively complement Kate Greenaway's delicate illustrations of dainty figures in period costumes.

A Nonsense Alphabet
Compiled by Edward Lear.
Illustrated by Richard Scarry.
Doubleday & Company, Inc., 1962.

Each letter in this tiny book is accompanied by a nonsense verse. The colorful pictures, animals for the most part, are clever and mischievous, and capture the general tone and mood of the text. Sample verse: "F was once a little fish,/Fishy,/Wishy,/Squishy,/Fishy,/In a dishy/Little fish!"

All Around the Town
Compiled by Phyllis L. McGinley.
Illustrated by Helen Stone.
J. B. Lippincott Co., 1948.

Capturing sights and sounds from airplanes to the zoo, this alphabet book is rooted in poetry. Clear-cut letter forms correspond with gay pictures made vibrant by their urban dash.

Bruno Munari's ABC
Compiled and illustrated by Bruno
Munari. World Publishing Co., 1960.

A large book for the young child to manage easily. The illustrations are simple and clearly defined and reflect imaginative qualities in color and design. The bold letters are in unusual forms and are interestingly positioned on the pages.

Curious George Learns the Alphabet
Written and Illustrated by H. A. Rey.
Houghton Mifflin Company, 1963.

A delightful book about a very curious monkey named George. Story and text are very entertaining, and there is a valuable concept involved for those just starting to read. The letters are presented as a basis for the wonderful illustrations with each one taking the form of an article or animal. Wonderful use of color supports good, fast reading text. Readers get a surprise when they turn to the letter "X."

A Is for Annabelle
Compiled and illustrated by Tasha
Tudor. Henry Walck, Inc.,
Publishers, 1954.

This is the story of an elegant, old-fashioned doll whose clothes and possessions complete the alphabet. Tasha Tudor uses verse form and delicate drawings in both black-and-white and pastels to make up this charming book. Each picture is oval shaped and wreathed by fruit and flowers.

BRIAN WILDSMITH's ABC
*Compiled and illustrated by Brian
Wildsmith. Franklin Watts, Inc., 1963.*

From his knowledge of what appeals to children, Wildsmith has designed a book ablaze with glorious color and brilliant simplicity of form. Each letter of the alphabet is matched with pictures against jewel-tone backgrounds. A notable book that earned the Kate Greenaway and A.L.A. Awards.

SPACE ALPHABET
*Compiled by Irene Zacks.
Illustrated by Peter P. Plasencia.
Prentice-Hall, Inc., 1964.*

A bright, new idea in alphabet books with a contemporary ring suggestive of the space age. Well-defined letters begin names familiar to space-minded children. "G is for a Galaxy" and "J is for Jets."

BOOKS WITH NUMBER CONCEPTS

JEANNE-MARIE COUNTS HER SHEEP
*Written and illustrated by Françoise.
Charles Scribner's Sons, 1951.*

Childlike pictures and singing text recount the story of a little French girl who hopes for more and more lambkins from her pet sheep, Patapon, while her visions for more and more of her heart's delights increase proportionately. Going as high as "seven," the story returns to "one" as the disappointing sheep gives birth to only one lamb with only enough wool for a pair of socks.

1 2 3 4 5.
*Written by Arthur Gregor.
Photographs by Robert Doisneau.
J. B. Lippincott Co., 1964.*

Photographs replace the usual illustrations in this picture book that counts animals and objects from one to twelve. Very large pages of photographs with corresponding pages of text help to clarify numbers. The photographs are of subjects familiar to children and present numerical groupings in faultless detail.

BROWN COW FARM
*Written and illustrated by Dahlov Ipcar.
Doubleday & Company, Inc. 1959.*

Lovely warm colors illuminate mathematical concepts ranging from one to ten. Multiple groupings add to the progression of numbers showing the animal population on a farm. Pictures of tiny animal babies bring charm to a book whose text is exact to every detail.

3 × 3 THREE BY THREE
*Written by James Krüss. Illustrated by
Eva Johanna Rubin. The Macmillan
Company, 1965.*

A pleasing look-and-listen counting book with winning verses and rustic charm. Emphasis is on a single numerical concept: three. Brilliant color illustrations rest against the clean white pages of a large, beautiful picture book.

OVER IN THE MEADOW
*Adapted by John Langstaff. Illustrated
by Rojankovsky. Harcourt, Brace &
World, Inc., 1957.*

A counting book that develops number concepts through the use of an old counting song. Words, music, and numbers blend for instruction and delight. Charming, clear pictures clarify the concepts of the text.

ONE WAS JOHNNY
*Written and illustrated by Maurice
Sendak. Harper & Row, Publishers,
1962.*

This tiny counting book is part of the miniature Nutshell Library. The small text in verse form tells the story of a little boy and the animals that come to his house one by one beginning with himself, Johnny. When the number of guests has reached ten, the little boy dismisses them one by one until he alone remains. Pale colors and slim line drawings illustrate the increasing and decreasing numbers.

1 IS ONE
Written and illustrated by Tasha Tudor. Henry Z. Walck, Inc., Publishers, 1956.

Pictures wreathed with fruit and flowers adorn pages whose number concepts extend to twenty. Each number, clearly outlined, is illustrated by lovely drawings and slender verses. Pastels alternate with black-and-white pictures throughout the broad, oblong pages of this delicately designed counting book.

ONE STEP, TWO . . .
Written by Charlotte Zolotow. Illustrated by Roger Duvoisin. Lothrop, Lee & Shepard Co., Inc., 1955.

A rather large book that traces steps and numbers from one to twelve during a young child's walk with her mother. Ripe colors and corresponding pages of bold text explore the neighborhood and the mystery of numbers.

BOOKS ABOUT ABSTRACT IDEAS

A FRIEND IS SOMEONE WHO LIKES YOU
Compiled and illustrated by Joan Walsh Anglund. Harcourt, Brace & World, Inc., 1958.

Delicate, diminutive drawings and poetic text gracefully define a friend in childlike terms. Quiet beauty and quaint charm adorn a lovely book for young readers.

DO YOU SEE WHAT I SEE?
Compiled and illustrated by Helen Borten. Abelard-Schuman Limited, 1959.

Handsome designs—sometimes dark and mysterious, sometimes quiet and quickening—present an interesting explanation of the beauty in the world through simple text.

A KISS IS ROUND
Compiled by Blossom Budney. Illustrated by Vladimir Bobri. Lothrop, Lee & Shepard, Co., Inc., 1954.

Many round-shaped items familiar to young children are described in humorous, rhymed verse and illustrations that are distinguished for their clever combination of solids and lines lit by soft, bright colors. In a mood of great fun, this is a book to stimulate and sharpen a child's perception of form.

WHAT DO YOU SAY DEAR?
Compiled by Sesyle Joslin. Illustrated by Maurice Sendak. William R. Scott, Inc., 1958.

Inspired illustrations and text present the fundamentals of manners for young children. Here is an easy book about etiquette that is sparked by the delightfully humorous pictures of a great artist.

LITTLE BLUE AND LITTLE YELLOW
Compiled and illustrated by Leo Lionni. Ivan Obolensky, Inc., 1959.

Told entirely in terms of blobs of color, the gaily amusing account of what happens to Little Blue and Little Yellow because of their close friendship is imaginative and original. As they delight in the adventures of the two friendly blobs of color, young children also gain a deeper understanding of harmony.

SQUARES ARE NOT BAD!
Written by Violet Salazar. Pictures by Harlow Rockwell. Golden Press, Inc., 1967.

A concept book that vividly demonstrates ways of learning about geometric forms as well as tolerance. Squares, circles, triangles, and rectangles, living in separate towns and hating each other, learn that working together produces useful results. By mixing with each other, the geometric forms discover they can make a wagon, a train, or something else depending upon the combination. Especially useful for very young children becoming familiar with colors, shapes, and of course, cooperation.

HEAVY IS A HIPPOPOTAMUS
*Compiled by Miriam Schlein.
Illustrated by Leonard Kessler.
William R. Scott, Inc., 1954*

Factual presentation for the concept of weight is interestingly provided through large, childlike illustrations.

TALES OF ANIMALS

LION
*Written and illustrated by William Pène
Du Bois. The Viking Press, Inc., 1956.*

A brilliant picture book that tells the story of artists who create new animals in a sky factory. Humorous illustrations and lyric read-aloud text describe their experiment with furs, feathers, and rainbow colors that produces a kingly beast.

FOUR FUR FEET
*Written by Margaret W. Brown.
Illustrated by Remy Charlip.
William R. Scott, Inc., 1961.*

Lyrical text wedded to imaginative pictures describe a furry, four-footed animal's walk around the world. Warm, vibrant colors blend naturally to distinguish this sunlit picture book.

WAIT TILL THE MOON IS FULL
*Written by Margaret Wise Brown.
Illustrated by Garth Williams.
Harper & Row, Publishers, 1948.*

The universal theme of a young child's impatience to grow up is tenderly expressed in the story of a little raccoon who wants to see the night but is told by his understanding mother that he must "wait till the moon is full." The author's poetic, lyric text creates a mood of charm and humor, which is matched by the illustrator's gift

for humanizing animals in a moonlit world.

WHERE DOES THE BUTTERFLY GO
WHEN IT RAINS?
*Written by May Garelick. Illustrated
by Leonard Weisgard. William R.
Scott, Inc., 1961.*

Poetic language and soft blue-gray illustrations as fresh and cool as spring rain catch a small child's curiosity about nature's living creatures, particularly when it rains.

THE WILD DUCKS AND DAFFODILS
*Written by May Garelick. Illustrated by
Clare Ross. William R. Scott, Inc.,
1965.*

Warm pictures glow on the pages of this picture book that vividly describes the life of ducklings from springtime to migration time.

LOOK!
*Written and illustrated by Zhenya Gay.
The Viking Press, Inc., 1952.*

Clearly defined pictures present familiar animals for the young child to name and recognize.

ALLIGATOR SMILING IN THE SAWGRASS
*Written by Ira Ironmonger. Illustrated by
Sandra Davidson. William R. Scott,
Inc., 1965.*

A suspenseful story during rainless days in a Florida swamp that has dried under subtropical sun. Thirsty animals follow a trail to the water hole where an alligator luxuriates. An excellent book for reading aloud.

THE STORY OF FERDINAND
*Written by Munro Leaf. Illustrated by
Robert Lawson. The Viking Press, Inc.,
1936.*

In this story of a bull who dares to be different from his fellow bulls, Munro Leaf portrays a beloved yet humorous animal. Ferdinand, the Spanish bull, is gentle and content with life under trees and around flowers. When he is taken to a festive bullfight, his peaceful nature prevents him from participating, and so he returns to his meadow home. Robert Lawson's drawings sharpen a story in which gentleness prevails with clever incongruity.

SWIMMY
Written and illustrated by Leo Lionni. Pantheon Books, Inc., 1963.

An ingenious little fish discovers the beauty of the quiet deep and a way to enjoy it. Delicate watercolors highlight lucid text to make an artistic read-aloud book.

TICO AND THE GOLDEN WINGS
Written and illustrated by Leo Lionni. Pantheon Books, Inc., 1964.

A story with the magic and flavor of the Far East. Magnificent pictures in jewel colors and gold illuminate a legendary tale of a wingless bird whose wish for golden wings is granted. But from his first flight with golden wings he stirs envy among his friends until he uses his gift of gold to help others. Stressing conformity as well as charity, this tale of Tico and his golden wings opens windows on a sunny land.

FREDERICK
Written and illustrated by Leo Lionni. Pantheon Books, Inc., 1967.

While the other field mice are working day and night collecting provisions for the winter, Frederick gathers sun rays and colors and words. In the cold dark days of winter when the supplies are used up, Frederick draws from his summer store and brings touches of warmth and beauty and poetry to the cold, hungry mice. The amusing illustrations are a gay accompaniment to the text.

THE LITTLE ISLAND
Written by Golden MacDonald, pseud. for Margaret Wise Brown. Illustrated by Leonard Weisgard. Doubleday & Company, Inc., 1946.

Luminous pictures depict changing seasons on an island inhabited by kingfishers,

lobsters, spiders, and seals. A young kitten who visits the island in the ocean learns from a fish much about the island and that "all land is one land under the sea." Told in lyric prose, the story is a superb example of wedded text and pictures and merited the Caldecott Medal in 1947.

MAKE WAY FOR DUCKLINGS
Written and illustrated by Robert McCloskey. The Viking Press, Inc., 1941.

When a family of ducklings, raised on the banks of the Charles River, become old enough to travel, their mother proudly leads them through the streets of Boston to establish residence on an island in the Public Gardens. The journey of Mrs. Mallard and her family is told with tongue-in-cheek humor. The strongly drawn illustrations with their wealth of detail show the habits and customs of ducks as well as life in a great bustling city.

THE TALE OF PETER RABBIT
Written and illustrated by Beatrix Potter. Frederick Warne & Co., Inc., 1901.

The first of twenty-two volumes comprising a miniature library of tiny books whose characters are rabbits, ducks, mice, and other woodland creatures. Fragile water colors beautifully complement the graceful text providing a sense of harmony that is distinctive of Beatrix Potter's works.

BRIAN WILDSMITH'S BIRDS
Written and illustrated by Brian Wildsmith. Franklin Watts, Inc., 1967.

In a glorious picture book lit with the radiance of stained-glass colors, Wildsmith has animated varieties of birds and matched them with their appropriate collective-noun names. "A siege of bitterns," "A wedge of swans," and many others. Similar kaleidoscopic delight of color and imagination is expressed in *Brian Wildsmith's Wild Animals* and *Brian Wildsmith's Fishes*. In respective books the distinguished artist has drawn creatures that appear to preen, cavort, chatter, fly, glide, gloat in magnificence.

100

Picture
Books
and
Picture
Storybooks

TALES OF CHILDREN WITH ANIMALS AND IN THE OUT-OF-DOORS

THE DEAD BIRD

Written by Margaret Wise Brown.
Illustrated by Remy Charlip. Scott,
Foresman & Company, 1958.

Children find a dead bird and decide to give him a burial in the woods with flowers, song, and a small marking stone. With consummate skill the author has written a story that deals meaningfully with a situation many young children face when a beloved pet dies. In moving and harmonious simplicity the blues and greens of the illustrations express the gentle serenity implicit in the poetic text.

TIA MARIA'S GARDEN

Written by Ann Nolan Clark. Illustrated
by Ezra Jack Keats. The Viking Press,
Inc., 1963.

The joy and beauty of nature are celebrated in singing words and charming full-color pictures as a small boy and his aunt take the reader along with them on a walk through the New Mexico desert to see the many wondrous things that live and grow there.

GILBERTO AND THE WIND

Written and illustrated by Marie Hall
Ets. The Viking Press, Inc., 1963.

A tiny boy tells of his experiences with Wind in the first person. Soft, muted pictures interpret the gentle movement of a sometimes rustling, sometimes quiet wind, and the lonely boy.

PLAY WITH ME

Written and illustrated by Marie Hall
Ets. The Viking Press, Inc., 1955.

When a little girl goes into the meadow and tries to befriend little wild creatures, they are frightened away by her seemingly aggressive overtures. Discouraged, she sits quietly on a rock and discovers the secret of how to make friends with nature's children. A tender little tale, delicately illustrated in fragile pastels that echo the quiet mood of the story.

A counterpart to this story, *In the Forest,* by the same author, tells of a little boy's meeting with forest animals.

LITTLE BLACK: A PONY

Written by Walter Farley. Illustrated
by James Schucker. Random House,
Inc., 1961.

Fulfilling the need of a young child to feel grown up and important, Walter Farley has written a heartwarming story about a pony who is saddened and discouraged by his inability to compete with a larger horse until he gets his chance to prove his worth by saving a young boy's life. Through sensitively written text and larger double-page illustrations, the young reader is led to experience vicarious satisfaction through Little Black's achievement.

THE BIG YELLOW BALLOON

Written by Edward Fenton. Illustrated by
Ib Ohlsson. Doubleday & Co., Inc.,
1967.

A sunny picture book about Roger's yellow balloon as it attracts a parade of spectators while he walks down the street holding his balloon in the air. Unknown to him there is a policeman puffing after a thief who is sneaking after a lady, who is clacking after a dog catcher, who is stalking a dog, who is chasing the cat that is after Roger's yellow balloon. And just as soon as the cat snatches the balloon there is a big explosion and pile up. Rollicking pictures accompany the jaunty text of this humorous story.

THE BOAT THAT MOOED

Written by Christopher Fry. Illustrated
by Leonard Weisgard. The Macmillan
Company, 1965.

A picture storybook of the quiet beauty and wonder of a small boy's dream-like travel by boat on a river veiled in fog. Gliding past mooing river boats, the boy encounters new experiences: a friend, a new world, and a future as radiant as the sunburst that climaxes this story. The lyrical text is lit by luminous paintings as haunting and fragile as a dream.

THE DAY WE SAW THE SUN COME UP
Written by Alice E. Goudey.
Illustrated by Adrienne Adams.
Charles Scribner's Sons, 1961.

A beautiful picture book that captures the wonder of summer sunrise as two children experience it "before the sun was up until darkness came..."

THE SNOWY DAY
Written and illustrated by Ezra Jack Keats. The Viking Press, Inc., 1962.

A small Negro boy awakens one morning to the miracle of falling snow and joyously faces the prospect of a snowy world to explore. Childlike in its simplicity, the text underscores spacious pictures that combine the subtly muted tones of water color and the textural quality of collage.

THE HAPPY DAY
Written by Ruth Krauss. Illustrated by Marc Simont. Harper & Row, Publishers, 1949.

A satisfying picture story told in broad clear pages of black-and-white drawings superbly matched with text distilled to crystal perfection. The anticipation of woodland animals is caught on each page leading the reader to discover the secret on the last page.

PAVO AND THE PRINCESS
Written and illustrated by Evaline Ness.
Charles Scribner's Sons, 1964.

Despite all the King's efforts, nothing touches the heart of his daughter, the haughty Princess Phoebe, until he decides to give her his favorite pet, Pavo, an exquisite white peacock. How the Princess Phoebe learns to cry makes an endearing and gay tale enhanced by the magical color of the illustrations that depict the elegance and enchantment of a fanciful kingdom in a faraway land.

MANY MOONS
Written by James Thurber. Illustrated by Louis Slobodkin. Harcourt, Brace & World, Inc., 1943.

With his usual charm and gentle wit, James Thurber tells the story of a young princess who longs for the moon and of the amusing efforts of those around her who attempt to grant her this wish. Louis Slobodkin's illustrations capture the magical mood of this fairy tale.

HIDE AND SEEK FOG
Written by Alvin Tresselt. Illustrated by Roger Duvoisin. Lothrop, Lee & Shepard Co., Inc., 1965.

Misty pictures and poetic prose capture young children's response to a mysterious fog that envelops a seaside village on Cape Cod. Fun-packed pages follow a hide-and-seek game among rocks, driftwood, and cottages with a billowy fog that tip-toes in from across the sea.

A TREE IS NICE
Written by Janice May Udry.
Illustrated by Marc Simont. Harper & Row, Publishers, 1956.

Slim text and radiant pictures show the many delights to be had around a tree. The quiet charm of this picture book sharpens one's realization of outdoor beauty.

THE BIGGEST BEAR
Written and illustrated by Lynd Ward.
Houghton Mifflin Company, 1952.

While searching for the biggest bear he can find, Johnny comes upon a lovable little bear cub who immediately finds his way into the young boy's heart and home. With imagination and humor, the author tells how Johnny tries to cope with the problems presented by the bear's rapid growth and enormous appetite. Skillfully drawn illustrations in tones of brown complement the lively text by giving an added dimension of texture to the furry bear's gigantic size and good-natured docility.

102

*Picture
Books
and
Picture
Storybooks*

HARRY THE DIRTY DOG
*Written by Gene Zion. Illustrated by
Margaret Bloy Graham. Harper & Row,
Publishers, 1956.*

Using childhood's common aversion to
baths, Gene Zion tells the story of Harry,
a dirty dog, who desperately needs to be
cleaned before he's even recognizable.
Once this is done, Harry regains his identity though later reverts to being a dirty
dog. A vein of humor runs through the
text and the bold drawings.

IMAGINATIVE TALES

THE STORY OF BABAR: THE LITTLE
ELEPHANT
*Written and illustrated by Jean de
Brunhoff. Random House, Inc., 1933.*

A sophisticated fantasy, in childlike terms,
of a little runaway elephant from the
jungle. Consoled by the vibrant life of a
big city, the little elephant remains a while
before returning to his jungle home to
become king of the elephants. The best in
a series of "Babar" books, this one in
brilliant pictures captures a gay mood with
simple honesty.

THE CAT WHO COULDN'T PURR
*Written and illustrated by Polly
Cameron. Coward-McCann, Inc., 1957.*

Simple pictures interpret the quiet text
about a cat who is too busy to purr until
he travels home to a reunion with his
family. The delight of the successful cat
shines out of the story.

NORMAN THE DOORMAN
*Written and illustrated by Don Freeman.
The Viking Press, Inc., 1959.*

Norman, an ingenious mouse living in the
basement of a museum, wins an art contest
with a creation made from mousetraps.
Allowed to choose his own award, Norman
selects a tour through the museum
unmolested by the guards whose mousetraps actually made the whole thing possible. Whimsical text is accompanied by

colorful illustrations that are highly expressive of the characters, from mean-faced
guards to pompous judges.

WHERE THE WILD THINGS ARE
*Written and illustrated by Maurice
Sendak. Harper & Row, Publishers,
1963.*

This highly imaginative book tells about a
small boy, Max, who has been sent to his
room for "acting like a wild thing." He
imagines himself sailing away to where
the wild things are and being crowned
their king, but at the end he returns to the
warm comforts of his room. Lyric text
and superbly drawn pictures point up the
sound psychological implications.

AND TO THINK THAT I SAW IT ON
MULBERRY STREET
*Written and illustrated by Dr. Seuss.
Vanguard Press, 1937.*

When a small boy gives full rein to his
imagination, even an ordinary horse and
wagon on Mulberry Street can develop
into something stupendous. Brightly
colored illustrations that grow in detail
from page to page faithfully interpret the
gaily rhyming text of this picture storybook that mirrors childhood's imagination.

THE 500 HATS OF BARTHOLOMEW
CUBBINS
*Written and illustrated by Dr. Seuss.
Vanguard Press, 1938.*

Each time Bartholomew Cubbins removes
his hat out of respect to the king, another
hat appears in its place in a seemingly
endless variety of shapes and colors. In
this highly inventive tale, the author taps
a rich vein of rollicking good humor and
pure nonsense in both text and illustrations
to come up with a satisfactory solution to
a perplexing dilemma.

AN ANTEATER NAMED ARTHUR
*Written and illustrated by Bernard
Waber. Houghton Mifflin Company,
1967.*

An imaginative story about an anteater
whose behavior mirrors that of any little

boy growing up. In a series of five episodes related by his understanding mother, Arthur's shortcomings and strengths are charmingly revealed. By reflecting the usual characteristics of most children this bright picture book in three colors should have wide appeal among the youngest.

THE SUGAR MOUSE CAKE
Written by Gene Zion. Illustrated by Margaret Bloy Graham. Charles Scribner's Sons, 1964.

Regal settings provide the background for the jolly tale of a royal cake-making contest in which pastry cooks compete to win the title of Chief Pastry Chef. A tiny mouse figures importantly in the success of the winner of the contest. Well-placed pictures in soft, sugary colors fill almost every page adding icing to the gaily humorous text.

TALES OF INANIMATE THINGS PERSONIFIED

MIKE MULLIGAN AND HIS STEAM SHOVEL
Written and illustrated by Virginia Lee Burton. Houghton Mifflin Company, 1939.

In a thrilling race against time, Mike Mulligan and his steam shovel, Mary Anne, attempt to dig a cellar in a single day to prove that Mary Anne can hold her own with the newer gas and diesel steam shovel. Colorful illustrations join rhythmic text to tell a story with particular appeal to small boys who will find in this exciting adventure realistic details of experiences in their everyday lives.

LITTLE TOOT
Written and illustrated by Hardie Gramatky. G. P. Putnam's Sons, 1939.

Imaginative drawings enliven the bright story of a light-hearted tugboat who assumes his responsibility with appealing good nature. Sturdy text presents challenge in a story in which the little boat wins the respect of other tugboats.

THE LITTLE AUTO
Written and illustrated by Lois Lenski. Henry Z. Walck, Inc., Publishers, 1934.

Bright, clear pictures and simple, straight-forward text provide the information about a little car that a young child wants to know.
Similar books by this author include: *The Little Sailboat, The Little Airplane, The Little Farm, The Little Train, The Little Engine,* and *Cowboy Small.*

THE LITTLE ENGINE THAT COULD
Written by Watty Piper. Illustrated by George and Doris Hauman. The Platt & Munk Co., Inc., 1954.

A heroic little engine successfully pulls a train over the mountain while panting out: "I thought I could." Well-drawn pictures express the train's eagerness to succeed when all other engines refuse to participate.

THE WEDDING PROCESSION OF THE RAG DOLL AND THE BROOM HANDLE AND WHO WAS IN IT
Written by Carl Sandburg. Illustrated by Harriet Pincus. Harcourt, Brace & World, Inc., 1967.

This is an old favorite from Sandburg's *Rootabaga Stories* which Harriet Pincus makes new with whimsical illustrations that charmingly interpret the rhythmic text. When the Rag Doll and the Broom Handle marry, they have one of the grandest wedding processions ever seen. Here march the Spoon Lickers, Tin Pan Bangers, Chocolate Chins, Dirty Bibs, Clean Ears, Easy Ticklers, Chubby Chubs, and Sleepyheads in a procession where the music is provided by the Musical Soup Eaters. Capturing the gaiety of the occasion, the pictures present a wide assortment of creatures and characters in comfortably unguarded moments.

THE LITTLE RED LIGHTHOUSE AND THE GREAT GRAY BRIDGE
Written by Hildegard Swift. Illustrated by Lynd Ward. Harcourt, Brace & World, Inc., 1942.

Once the great gray bridge with its power-

104

*Picture
Books
and
Picture
Storybooks*

ful tower light is completed, the little red lighthouse that nestles under the shadow of the bridge fears that it will no longer be useful. But it makes the happy discovery that land and water traffic need the services of both bridge and lighthouse. The exciting mood of the story set by the lyrical text is matched by Lynd Ward's brightly colored illustrations that capture the spirit of the New York scene against the majestic George Washington Bridge.

TALES OF LIFE IN VARIED CULTURES

THE PAPER FLOWER TREE
Written and illustrated by Jacqueline Ayer. Harcourt, Brace & World, Inc., 1962.

When a traveling peddler in Thailand presents little Miss Moon with a blossom from his paper flower tree, she plants its one seed and patiently waits for it to bloom. The story of a small girl's faith is sensitively told in rhythmically poetic prose and colorful line drawings touched by the magic, beauty, and grace of Thailand.

MADELINE
Written and illustrated by Ludwig Bemelmans. The Viking Press, Inc., 1939.

In rhymed couplets distinguished for their gentle humor and strong sense of rhythm, Ludwig Bemelmans relates the amusing adventures of Madeline, a rugged individualist despite her tender years. Unlike the eleven other little girls who attend the same French boarding school in Paris, Madeline does not take kindly to regimentation. Large, detailed illustrations in bright, glowing colors superbly depict landmarks of Paris.

PELLE'S NEW SUIT
Written and illustrated by Elsa Beskow. Harper & Row, Publishers, 1929.

How a young Swedish farm boy combines ingenuity with hard work to earn a new

suit is told in straightforward text and beautifully drawn pictures in soft, warm colors. Pelle begins by raising his own lamb and then one for each person who helps him with his suit. He also performs various chores in payment for services rendered. Wool processing is presented step by step in preparation for Pelle's new suit.

HENRY-FISHERMAN: A STORY OF THE VIRGIN ISLANDS
Written and illustrated by Marcia Brown. Charles Scribner's Sons, 1949.

More than anything else in the world, Henry wants to be a fisherman. His exciting adventure on his first trip in a fishing boat is told in simple, descriptive text. Glowing pictures in five colors reflect the vivid beauty of the Virgin Islands, the setting for this lively story.

THE STORY ABOUT PING
Written by Marjorie Flack. Illustrated by Kurt Wiese. The Viking Press, Inc., 1933.

Artistic quality marks this picture book of a Chinese duck that lives on a houseboat in the Yangtze. A narrow escape from the jaws of a cooking pot lends suspense and interest to an irresistible story.

WHISTLE FOR WILLIE
Written and illustrated by Ezra Jack Keats. The Viking Press, Inc., 1964.

Vibrant colors and collage combine to illustrate the slight text in a story of a little boy who learns to whistle.

POTATOES, POTATOES
Written and illustrated by Anita Lobel. Harper & Row, Publishers, 1967.

A picture book that depicts a story of two sons attracted by war. Deserting the shelter of their mother's house, the sons join opposing armies: one in the East, and one in the West. Disillusioned, the boys lead their starving regiments to their mother's potato farm, only to find that their wise mother refuses to feed them unless they abandon the war. Sharply drawn and colored pictures depict scenes reminiscent of old military prints while the expressions on the faces of the characters are varied and interesting.

THE PAINTED PIG
Written by Elizabeth Morrow. Illustrated by René D'Harnoncourt. Alfred A. Knopf, Inc., 1930.

Pedro is a young Mexican boy whose greatest wish is to own a china pig like his sister's. The story of his determined efforts to get this pig gives the reader an understanding of the children and customs of Mexico. The illustrator's knowledge of and interest in Mexico is reflected in the brightly colored illustrations that add to the appeal of the story.

LITO AND THE CLOWN
Written and illustrated by Leo Politi. Charles Scribner's Sons, 1964.

Amidst the vibrant festivities of a carnival, a little Mexican boy vainly searches for his lost kitten until a kind clown comes to his rescue. All the gaiety and excitement of a Mexican town at carnival time are captured by the author's bright-colored pictures and singing text.

SONG OF THE SWALLOWS
Written and illustrated by Leo Politi. Charles Scribner's Sons, 1949.

The Mission of San Juan Capistrano, and the swallows' instinctive arrival each year on St. Joseph's Day have been celebrated in song. Now Leo Politi in simple, rhythmic prose tells the story of the Mission and of the customs and festivals of the Mexican-American in California. Softly colored illustrations mirror the serenity of the Mission gardens and the humble devotion of the man and boy who tend them.

ONE MONDAY MORNING
Written and illustrated by Uri Shulevitz. Charles Scribner's Sons, 1967.

A simple little story that skillfully weaves the dream of a little boy with the stark realities of an urban tenement on a rainy day. Matched with detailed pictures of mundane happenings and those of a dream world, this unusual book blends the imaginative with the real, and captures a child's yearning to escape dreariness on Monday.

PLENTY TO WATCH
Written by Mitsu and Taro Yashima. Illustrated by Taro Yashima. The Viking Press, Inc., n.d.

In this record of happy memories, the author and illustrator describe the exciting childhood experience of walking home from their village school in Japan. Simple, concise sentences, wedded to pictures that vibrate with color and life show shops, mills, and factories.

CROW BOY
Written and illustrated by Taro Yashima. The Viking Press, Inc., 1955.

The moving story of Chibi, a shy Japanese boy, whose classmates are helped by their teacher to understand him. This beautiful picture book, lit by colorful illustrations, points up the problems of young children from unusual backgrounds.

SEASHORE STORY
Written and illustrated by Taro Yashima. The Viking Press, Inc., 1967.

This lyrical legend is about a Japanese fisherman who goes away on a turtle's back, swims deep down into the ocean, and inhabits a resplendent palace until, finally, he returns home. Upon his return, he witnesses many changes in his surroundings and in himself as well. As children play in the stillness of a beach like the one where Old Urashima's adventures began, they wonder at the meaning of this provocative story-within-a-story. Lovely pictures enhance the rare beauty in this book.

THE VILLAGE TREE
Written and illustrated by Taro Yashima. The Viking Press, Inc., 1953.

With poetic text and striking illustrations, the author-artist recaptures the feeling of fun and gaiety he and his friends experienced in a village in Japan under the branches of a great tree by a swiftly flowing river.

Kate Greenaway's poetic vision of childhood is expressed in this frontispiece echoing the beauty and grace of her verses. Floral bouquets and quaint attire lend charm to the poetry.

From Marigold Garden *by Kate Greenaway. Frederick Warne & Co., Inc. Reproduced by permission.*

Chapter 5

POETRY
AND
VERSE

*The enjoyment which children receive from poetry is far-reaching
and of many kinds. Martial strains which fire the blood, fairy music ringing in
the ears, half-told tales which set the young heart dreaming, brave
deeds, unhappy fates, sombre ballads, keen joyous lyrics, and small jeweled
verses where every word shines like a polished gem,—all these
good things the children know and love. It is useless to offer them mere rhymes
and jingles; it is ungenerous to stint their young, vigorous imaginations
with obvious prattle, fitted dexterously to their understandings. In the matter of
poetry, a child's imagination outstrips his understanding; his emotions
carry him far beyond the narrow reach of his intelligence. He has but one lesson
to learn—the lesson of enjoyment.*

— A. METHUEN
An Anthology of Modern Verse
David McKay Company, Inc., 1948

Definition and
Types of Poetry

The term "poetry" derives from the Greek verb that means "to give shape," yet it designates a literary art form that eludes definition because of its shape or nature. There is really no single group of words that can claim to provide an exact definition of poetry, nor can the essence of poetry be generalized. However, there is general agreement among literary critics that the word "poetry" indicates creation, and the more energy expended in its creation, the closer the writer comes to pure poetry. This is true because poetry is not the mere arrangement of words, "the best words in their best order"—it is the thought, the feeling, and the emotion behind the ordered language that make a poem an aesthetic experience. And "when a poem says something that could not have been said in any other way, in music, prose, sculpture, movement or paint, then it is poetry."[1]

Just as various artists use various media for expression, a poet uses language in creating poetry. But it is not the same ordering of language found in prose, although some prose may be touched with poetry, especially the prose of picture books. As a literary art form, poetry is basically a richly imaginative way of communicating marked by the poet's ability to compress his deepest thoughts into a few enchanted words. Northrop Frye cogently states that "poetry is the most direct and simple means of expressing oneself in words. . . . Poetry is not irregular lines in a

---

[1]Sybil Marshall, *An Experiment in Education* (Cambridge: Cambridge University Press, 1963), p. 182.

book, but something very close to dance and song, something to walk down the street keeping in time to."[2]

Not unlike music and dance, the language of poetry is characterized by a rhythmic pattern of words arranged in verse form that is achieved in much the same way as a composer arranges musical notes to form rhythmic patterns of music. What is called the "beat" in music and dance is termed the "accent" in poetry; it is the way in which accents are arranged that determines the meter or rhythmic pattern of the poem.

Although it is difficult to provide an exact definition for poetry, there is one clear characteristic that all poetry possesses—rhythm. But essential as it is in all poetry, rhythm varies from poem to poem. For instance, some poets write poetry in very regular metrical or rhythmic patterns:

CLOUDS
Christina G. Rossetti

White sheep, white sheep,
On a blue hill,
When the wind stops,
You all stand still.[3]

RAIN
Robert Louis Stevenson

The rain is raining all around,
It falls on field and tree,
It rains on the umbrellas here,
And on the ships at sea.[4]

On the other hand, some writers prefer not to follow exactly the same rules governing regular, metrical patterns of poetry, and their work reflects a style called "free verse." In much the same way as some writers avoid making use of the same meter all through their poems in order to avoid monotony, writers of free verse digress from a regular pattern to produce lines in which a natural sense of rhythm is felt. Here, in the spirit of Japanese haiku are the expressive lines:

---

[2]Northrop Frye, *The Educated Imagination* (Bloomington: Indiana University Press, 1964), p. 121.

[3]Christina Rossetti, "Clouds," in *Poems for Weather Watching*, compiled by Laurie Israel. (New York: Holt, Rinehart & Winston, Inc., 1963), unpaged.

[4]Robert Louis Stevenson, "Rain," in *A Child's Garden of Verses* (New York: Franklin Watts, Inc., 1966), p. 67.

> *A red morning sky,*
> *For you, snail;*
> *Are you glad about it?*[5]
>
> —Issa

Written simply and directly, this verse has a kind of poetic speech that is fresh with quiet beauty and originality yet not without rhythm as the writer calls attention to great and humble things in a profound way.

In all poetry, however, the language used is that of

a poet speaking out of the depth of himself. He speaks out of his unique experience of life and in a tone of voice and habit of phrasing which are peculiarly his own. That is why a poem is and can be profoundly "true" even when it is making nonsense out of sober reasoning or respected truism;—a good poem is the most genuine expression of the whole personality of the man or woman, of the boy or girl who made it, and for that reason alone it can bring extraordinary insight into a human mind and heart.[6]

Because the language of poetry is more compressed and picturesque than the language of prose or daily speech, it frequently employs similes, metaphors, personification, and other symbols to give color and vitality to the verses. In a sense, the language of poetry implies the use of metaphorical symbols and other intuitive forms for expressing ideas, feelings, and emotions because poetry frequently addresses itself exclusively to the imagination and to the realm of emotive and artistic forms. Therefore, as an art form distinct from prose, poetry must be considered on the bases of beauty of language and conception, structure, and aesthetic impact.

What distinguishes a poet from any one else is his ability to express a great deal with brevity and conciseness, to capture fleeting moments in life and to frame them in a perfected line of words, to bring to clearer vision the unsaid and the unseen, or to give shape and emphasis to a way of seeing and feeling. After all, a poet is one who sees with the eye of imagination; he hears with the ear of sensitivity; he touches the intangible; and he holds fast the fleeting intensity of experience. All those are poets who throw back their heads to catch on their tongues the freshness of rain; or who stretch one finger tenderly to touch a velvet petal; or who gaze entranced at the restless waves licking the sandy shore. The art of the poet is implicit in his firm possession of a sense of wonder, of awareness,

---

[5]Issa, in *In A Spring Garden*, Richard Lewis, ed. (New York: The Dial Press, Inc., 1965), unpaged.

[6]Earle Birney, ed., *Twentieth Century Canadian Poetry* (Toronto: The Ryerson Press, 1954), p. xv.

of being alive—a sense that he skillfully expresses in the distilled language of poetry.

LYRICAL POETRY

The language of poetry is also music and movement. The accented and unaccented syllables and words, the rhythm and the rhyme, the rise and fall of passages, the cadence of lines—all these bring out the melody in a poem that should be heard if full enjoyment is to be gained. Most poems that sing with melody and movement are termed "lyrical" and they comprise much of the poetry that has been composed for children. Lillian Smith says:

> Lyric poetry, by directing sustained attention on a single happening, gives the sensitive reader an intense experience of life. When thought and feeling are joined with music—the music of rhythm and words—we are moved to an awareness of what the poet is trying to express. It may be an intensely remembered event of the past, or perhaps an immediate experience of the beauty and mystery of the world about us. Whatever it is, the degree of awareness that the poem requires of the reader is a measure of its lyric quality.[7]

Touched by the music in the language of poetry, children respond readily to lyrical works just as they do to the music and lilt in their earliest Mother Goose melodies for here, in a sense, music and imagination join to delight ears and hearts.

Among the loveliest of lyrical poems are those of Robert Burns. Because of their lilting cadence, many of them have been set to music.

SWEET AFTON
Robert Burns

*Flow gently, sweet Afton, among thy green braes!
Flow gently, I'll sing thee a song in thy praise!
My Mary's asleep by the murmuring stream—
Flow gently, sweet Afton, disturb not her dream!*

* * *

*How pleasant thy banks and green valleys below,
Where wild in the woodlands the primroses blow;
There oft, as mild Evening weeps over the lea,
The sweet-scented birk shades my Mary and me.*[8]

---

[7]Lillian H. Smith, *The Unreluctant Years* (Chicago: American Library Association, 1953), pp. 106-107.

[8]Robert Burns, "Sweet Afton," in *Poems to Be Read Aloud* (New York: Thomas Nelson & Sons, 1965), p. 17.

Some poets revel in the delightful sounds of language, and they employ music and movement to gain certain desired effects that heighten the tonality in their lyrical poems. Sometimes the sounds they stress subordinate meanings that may not be so important to the poetry as the quality of the sounds the words make. Here is a jaunty example:

MERRY-GO-ROUND

Dorothy W. Baruch

On the merry-go-round
I rode around
On the merry-go-round,
Around
And round
And
Round.[9]

Frequently lyrical poetry evokes intense emotion or a definite mood by focusing closely on familiar things. As a matter of fact, part of the beauty of lyric poetry lies in its concern for the commonplace and the poet's ability to express the wonder and delight behind the familiar things in the everyday world. Animals, sunshine, rain, snow, clouds—anything and everything fall heir to the magical touch a poet can give to turn "pumpkins into coaches . . . and nothing into everything."[10] But behind the words and music so pleasing to the ear shine the keen powers of observation and a love of life that the poet is trying to express through the subtle fusion of music and thought.

Young children particularly, whether they understand all the words or not, respond to poetry almost instinctively because poetry is considered a language that is natural to childhood. But lyrical poetry has specific appeal for the young. It stirs within them an innate sense of rhythm and rhyme, and continues to do so at various stages of their development. A lyrical poem, delicately painted, singing of a joyous experience, can become another adventure for a child who is brought under the influence of genuinely poetic works.

Varied as life itself, lyric poetry covers a wide variety of topics in artfully different ways. But the most appealing ones for children grow out of a world where language and imagination meet. Here "rainbows are for sliding on," "sunbeams are for holding in your hand," and "the earth

[9]Dorothy W. Baruch, "Merry-Go-Round," in *I Like Machinery* (New York: Harper & Row, Publishers, 1933).
[10]Francis Thompson, "Shelley," in *The Dublin Review*, 1908.

and the sun change places, like dancers in dance." Here, every backyard
launches a trip to outer space; while underground a tunnel winds its way
to China. Alongside a rude fence, gnomes and fairies dance right on the
same patch of grass where household pets and earthworms feel equally
at home, and just above the grubby earth an enchanted castle shimmers
atop a nearby tree. This is, indeed, a world of light and color vibrating
with music, yet its language is poetry. Much of the language used in children's lyrical poetry, however, is sparked with a spontaneity and infor-
mality that expresses ideas simply, imaginatively, and in accordance with
children's perceptions at different levels of experiential development.
But regardless of the topic, the lyric poet's gift enables him to crystallize
a single experience so that the entire poem evokes a certain feeling, a mood
appropriate to the verses.

He may use rhyme or blank verse, regular or irregular rhythms,
simple or complex word arrangements to project his impressions and
feelings. He may use everyday language, picturesque language, or even a
style reminiscent of the past to paint his picture and sing his poem. But
whatever technique he uses, a poet strives to communicate his concept of
truth, his intense delight, his own personal way of viewing the world.

Though the full beauty of some poems may escape children "nobody
can possibly tell what will sing its way into a child's spirit, set alight some
flame of his imagination."[11] After all, children are individuals with unique
tastes and interests as well as the capacity for discernment, understanding,
and interpretation. Here, from Ann Nolan Clark's *In My Mother's House*,
is a lyrical poem of quiet beauty whose appeal has no age limit.

> *Mountains are the high places;*
> *They reach up and up*
> *To the blue-blue above.*
>
> *They stand around us,*
> *Looking down at the people*
> *In the pueblo.*
> *In the plaza,*
> *In the fields.*
>
> *I like to know*
> *That mountains are there,*
> *Around me,*
> *So quiet,*
> *So big,*
> *And so high.*

---

[11]Forrest Reid, *Walter de la Mare: A Critical Study* (London: Faber & Faber, Ltd.,
1929), p. 27.

*I have heard
That the Thunder sleeps
In the mountains,
With his great bow
And lightning arrows
By his side.*

*I have heard
That clouds gather
In the mountains,
And that rainbows
Make bridges
Over them.*

*I have heard
That mountains
Are the home
Of the winds
And the night.*

*Perhaps
These things are true;
I have heard them.*[12]

The very sounds of the words with their soft, long vowels and rolling *r*'s and *n*'s seem born of the slumbering thunder. Using personification, the poet sees the mountains as regal giants who shelter the awesome and mysterious phenomena of nature. The very rhythm of the words seems to come from a far-off Indian drum, subdued yet definite. There is also a sense of majesty that pervades the poem giving the music of the language the reverent tone of an anthem.

One type of lyric poetry treats the intangible. Concepts of time, space, and movement are perceptively described with sensory images, personification, and other poetic devices that give shape and form to abstractions. In this way something is made clearer or sharper or more intense than reality can be as the personal feelings of a poet are transmitted by imagination and fine writing. "Swift Things Are Beautiful," a poem by Elizabeth Coatsworth, arrests the beauty of speed and movement:

*Swift things are beautiful:
Swallows and deer,*

---

[12]Ann Nolan Clark, *In My Mother's House* (New York: The Viking Press, Inc., 1941), p. 52.

And lightning that falls
Bright-veined and clear,
Rivers and meteors,
Wind in the wheat,
The strong-withered horse,
The runner's sure feet.

And then, in contrast, there is the second stanza:

And slow things are beautiful:
The closing of day,
The pause of the wave
That curves downward to spray,
The ember that crumbles,
The opening flower,
And the ox that moves on
In the quiet of power.[13]

Some lyric poems sing themselves into the lives of children, often evoking deep human feelings. Poetry capable of doing this possesses the ingredients of permanence and universality. Walter de la Mare is skilled in kindling feelings of the hopelessness or loneliness evoked by the strange or supernatural.

SOME ONE
Walter de la Mare

Some one came knocking
At my wee, small door;
Some one came knocking,
I'm sure—sure—sure;
I listened, I opened,
I looked to left and right,
But nought there was a-stirring
In the still dark night;

Only the busy beetle
Tap-tapping in the wall,
Only from the forest
the screech-owl's call,
Only the cricket whistling
While the dewdrops fall,
So I know not who came knocking,
At all, at all, at all.[14]

[13]Elizabeth Coatsworth, "Swift Things Are Beautiful," in *Away Goes Sally* (New York: The Macmillan Company, 1959), p. 64.

[14]Walter de la Mare, "Some One," in *Peacock Pie* (New York: Alfred A. Knopf, Inc., 1961), p. 12.

The diminutive images, the quiet yet sharp night sounds, the overwhelming contrast between the largeness of the dark and the forest, and the tiny, active creatures awake and at work—all are properly spaced and balanced in humming verses that stir a feeling of tense beauty and haunting suspense.

Although lilting, rhythmic, and rhymed, the slender lines lack the hackneyed beat so obvious in jingles, limericks, rhymes, and lesser verses not to be mistaken for poetry. Poetry need not be childish to appeal to children. Instead, children, constantly discovering, wondering, and creating in their own way respond naturally to a poet whose curiosity and imagination they may share to a large degree. After all, some poets have the ability to remember with a reliving intensity the feeling of being a child, and they express that feeling with the vividness and skill of polished maturity. As Walter de la Mare put it:

> I know too that in later life it is just (if only just) possible now and again to recover fleetingly the intense delight, the untellable joy and happiness and fear and grief and pain of our early years, of an all-but-forgotten childhood. I have, in a flash, in a momentary glimpse, seen again a horse, an oak, a daisy just as I saw them in those early years, as if with that heart, with those senses. It was a revelation.[15]

NARRATIVE POETRY

Along with self-expression, a poet also uses language to express his subjects, varied as they may be, and in doing so he creates an emotional experience that reflects the deep feelings of the poem rather than of the poet himself. A story, for instance, may be told in rhythmic verse by a poet using music, economy of language, and storytelling devices to evoke an emotion that appropriately matches the mood or feeling of the poetry. This type of poetry is called "narrative poetry."

Consistent with a rich storytelling tradition, narrative poetry's first requirement is to tell a story. It is not exempt, however, from meeting some of the requirements basic to verse form: rhythm, symbolism, figurative language, imagery, melody, movement, rhyme schemes, cadence, imaginative power, sound, tone, and skillfully ordered language.

As a matter of fact, many of these qualities are found in a sizable body of poetic literature whose beginnings stretch back to the oral tradition when stirring tales made dramatic recitations along with those sung or chanted in verse form by minstrels, scops, and other bearers of stories.

---

[15]Walter de la Mare, *Bells and Grass* (New York: The Viking Press, Inc., 1942), p. 11.

Eager listeners passed the poem along either by oral recitation or by copy-

ing it down just as the singer sang it. This recording of tales with the
magical beat and swing of language marked the official beginning of
English poetry. Much of this early poetry was narrative in nature. It told
of battles fought and victories won; it rang with the clash of shield and
broadsword of individual combats; it echoed the perils of hunts and
exploits; and it haunted the imagination with tales of demons and spirits.

Epics. Among the earliest of these recorded tales are the heroic
stories of one named Beowulf who tangled with dragons and devils from
the days of his youth. And all through his "life of honesty and nobility"
Beowulf slew monsters and enemies in defense of himself and his fellow
men until he fell victim to the fiery wrath of a dragon. *Beowulf*, first
written down in England around A.D. 700, is thought to be one of the
oldest of Germanic stories. It is written in verse form that depends heavily
upon alliteration and a complicated arrangement of accented and unaccented syllables for its musical effects. And because this long narrative
poem was written in a noble, dignified style to match the heroic feats
performed by its characters, *Beowulf* is termed an "epic"— a term used to
designate narrative poems covering a grand sweep of significant events,
personalities, and drama quite apart from the story itself. Best examples of
the most famous epics are the works of the blind poet Homer who, at
the dawn of Greek history, about 800 B.C., hammered out images of gods
and heroes that have become universal ancestral prototypes.

In his immortal works, Homer glorified gods and heroes alike, but
he gave them credibility by bestowing them with a human naturalness
that has set them apart from other mythical or heroic characters of the
world. Homer's *Iliad* and *Odyssey*, as well as Virgil's *Aeneid*, deal with
battles and heroes linked with the siege of Troy. In each of these epics,
however, the heroes and their exploits are as important as the actual stories
of Troy and its dramatic fall. Based on historical fact, these epics took on
added significance when the archaeologist Heinrich Schliemann went to
Asia Minor in 1871 and excavated remains of a city that matched Homer's
detailed description of ancient Troy.

Just as the Greeks and Romans sang of their gods and heroes,
other countries have produced their own epics to commemorate historical events involving their own national heroes. Other great epics of the
world include the Hindu *Ramayana* and *Mahabharata*, the *Kalevala* transmitted by the Finnish, the epic *El Cid* fashioned in Spain, and the ancient

Babylonian epic of *Gilgamesh*, ranked as one of the greatest literary masterpieces of mankind.

During the Middle Ages, France celebrated the bravery of Roland, one of Charlemagne's peers, in the epic *Song of Roland*. In more recent times, an English poet, Matthew Arnold, described a single episode concerning a Persian hero in *Sohrab and Rustum*, a relatively modern piece of epic poetry with the appropriate dignity and grace. John Milton's *Paradise Lost*, a religious epic, reveals deep spiritual feelings in an exalted style similar to that of the ancients.

Romances. Contrasting with the "true epic," there are romances in English, which, for example, describe the conquests of King Arthur's court. The characters are not as lifelike the and events are of lesser historical importance than in poems more deserving of the designation "epic." However, Tennyson's *Idylls of the King* does have the epic quality marked by a rich, dignified style of writing.

Out of the Middle Ages came Geoffrey Chaucer's masterpiece, *The Canterbury Tales*, a perfection of literary artistry. A collection of narratives, Chaucer's work includes metrical romances, legends about saints, and sundry tales, all told in verse form.

Ballads. Along with epics and romances we find ballads, one of the earliest forms of literature that employs narrative techniques in verses adaptable for singing or recitation. By definition, a ballad may be considered a song that tells a short story, vigorous, impersonal, and direct in its character. Just as most of the English romances during medieval times were composed for the entertainment of the nobility, ballads express feelings and stories common to humbler folk. Frequently connected with communal dances of a distant past, the origins of ballads are now lost. They stretch back to an oral tradition among people who were illiterate and free from literary influences.

Regardless of its origins, the folk ballad was one of the earliest forms of literature in almost every country of the world. There are certain characteristics common to all ballads as they are handed down from one generation to another.

In the early ballads of all literatures certain themes are found frequently: supernatural or great physical feats, mysterious and marvelous phenomena, and the human situations of love, war, loss, tragedy, and death—all the deeds and destinies that touch the lives and experiences of common folk.

Ballads are still being written by poets who express communal thoughts and emotions in verse form. Cowboys of the West strum popular songs that tell a story in much the same style as in the early ballads. Bushmen in Australia and calypso singers of the West Indies produce lilting narratives akin to the ballad with their spontaneous, impromptu chants. Scottish Highlanders still pipe and sing songs of raids north and south of the English-Scottish border. Freedom movements and peace-loving people pour out their hearts in so-called "popular ballads."

Varying enormously in quality, the caliber of many contemporary ballads reveals banal themes, vulgar style, and a simple, pathetic directness that have wider appeal than the ancient ballads of unknown authorship or the works of poets such as Coleridge, Scott, or Wordsworth whose narrative poetry parallels the ballads of old. Yet despite the differences, common qualities in ballads still exist.

Many traditional and popular ballads are composed in simple, four-line verses or stanzas in which the first and the third lines each have four accents and do not rhyme; the second and fourth lines each have three accents and do rhyme. But the ballads that were usually sung tend to shift the accents and alter the rhyme schemes to accommodate the singing, thus making the lines end in imperfect rather than perfect rhymes. An example of a ballad of which the second and fourth lines rhyme perfectly (*a*, *b*, *c*, *b*) is taken from Samuel Taylor Coleridge's "The Rime of the Ancient Mariner":

> *He prayeth best who loveth best*
> *All things both great and small;*
> *For the dear God who loveth us;*
> *He made and loveth all.*

Another ballad, consisting of four-line stanzas in which the second and fourth lines are rhymed imperfectly, is the following from "The Gay Goshawk," a very old love story for which the music is still available:

> *'Woe to you, my sister dear*
> *And ane ill death may you die!*
> *For we left father and mother at hame*
> *Breaking their heart for thee!*

It is true that many of the older ballads are concerned with stories of a remote past and are written in a style that is difficult for some children to appreciate. Nevertheless, certain of the old ballads do serve to transport children to a more primitive past, to wildness, to feudalism, to a time quite different from their own, yet not without flavorsome, musical language. And although the language of the old ballad is archaic, it frequently has soft and pleasing sounds that delight those who listen to them. Most of the ballads sung in Old Scottish or in Renaissance English employ many strange-sounding words that ring with gentle or jubilant tones, evoking a mood that is tranquil and pensive or bright and gay.

A ballad composed in the sixteenth century and adapted to the original music in the twentieth, is entitled "Greensleeves." Hauntingly beautiful, the ballad speaks of unrequited love in the courtly tradition with a stately grace.

> *Greensleeves was all my joy,*
>   *Greensleeves was my delight:*
> *Greensleeves was my hart of gold,*
>   *And who but Ladie Greensleeves.*

Sixteen stanzas follow, enumerating the lover's gifts: "jewels for thy chest," a "smock of silk, both faire and white," "garters fringed with the golde," the "gayest gelding." And then the ballad resolves itself broodingly:

> *Greensleeves now farewel adue,*
>   *God I pray to prosper thee:*
> *For I am still thy lover true,*
>   *Come once againe and love me.*

Ballads whose tales are somewhat more exciting and vigorous include "Robin Hood and Little John," which is long, lusty, and filled with deeds of derring-do. The repetition of the second line is more typical of the sixteenth century ballads than those of earlier times.

> *When Robin Hood was about twenty years old,*
>   *With a hey, down, down, and a down:*
> *He happened to meet Little John,*
>   *A jolly, brisk blade, right fit for the trade;*
> *For he was a lusty young man.*
>
> *Though he was called Little, his limbs they were large,*
>   *And his stature was seven foot high;*
> *Wherever he came, they quaked at his name,*
>   *For soon he would make them fly.*

This jaunty ballad continues for several stanzas, and the language it employs sings along with the bold and vibrant story. It has as much appeal for the present as it did when it was first composed about four hun- dred years ago.

Digressing still further from the four-line stanza and the traditional rhyme scheme is a comparatively simple narrative poem, "The Ballad of the Pilgrim Cat" by Leonard Wibberley. This whimsical story in rhyme tells of a raffish cat who sailed as a stowaway on the *Mayflower*.

When the Pilgrims landed on that strange wild strand
Where they'd make their home in a strange wild land,
There was among them, the least of the crew,
A girl of nine—and a pussycat too.
The little girl's name was Mistress Smith—
Prudent God-With-Us Simplicity Smith.

      *   *   *

As for the cat; 'twas a scandalous tramp,
Missing an ear, a seaport scamp
That roistered in taverns and alleys at night
In Plymouth (England) and had many a fight
With other cats—and mastiffs too.
Among pirate cats he was head of the crew;
A sinful, thievish, graceless knave;
An offense to God; to sin, a slave.

The mellow mood of early America is caught in this affectionate portrait of the little Pilgrim girl and her cat. Authentic details support the lilting ballad.
From The Ballad of the Pilgrim Cat *by Leonard Wibberley, illustrated by Erik Blegvad. The* *Curtis Publishing Company, 1961. Reproduced by permission.*

The cat fell into disfavor because of his curiosity, but later he became a hero among the Pilgrims for ridding them of marauding mice.

There's really not much more to tell;
From that day forward all went well.
The winter passed, the bright spring came,
The Pilgrims sowed their fields with grain.
Then came the harvest, a plenteous hoard
For which the Pilgrims thanked the Lord.
They gave a feast, and to honor the cat
Each Pilgrim Father removed his hat
And bowing politely each one said,
"You worked with us to win this bread.
We thought you worthless, but now we see
We lacked a true humility.
From you we learned to respect the worth
Of the creatures God put on the earth."
The cat hearing this made no demur;
His sole reply was to purr and purr.
And prim Miss Smith, her small head bowed,
Spoke to the Lord (though not aloud).
"Dear Lord, will You kindly grant me that
The next ship from England brings a cat,
So that in this land there will always be
Plenty of kittens for girls like me."
Her prayer was granted. Just look around.
Throughout America cats abound.
And all of them came from the same one that
Saved the Pilgrim Fathers—the Pilgrim Cat.[16]

Story poems. Regardless of their style, narrative poets are master storytellers who stir the pulsebeats and excite the senses with the added melody and movement characteristic of their craft. And children who love to listen to stories, whether they are recited or sung, expect a tale to unfold with a measure of the surprise, anticipation, and excitement aroused by a well-told story.

Stories in verse are composed today, and they continue to be popular with children right up to the present. In the years that have passed since the early English poets wrote their tales of daring deeds, fierce monsters, and great heroes, many distinguished poets have composed narrative verse to tell of love, war, animals, people, places, and things— all the raw materials that inspire a good story. Combining elements found in other narrative works, verse stories, or story poems as they are

[16]Leonard Wibberley, *The Ballad of the Pilgrim Cat* (New York: Curtis Publishing Company, 1962), pp. 13, 42.

sometimes called, cover a wide range of themes and types from soul-stirring accounts of human conflicts to hilariously funny stories universal in their appeal. But, regardless of the theme or style of verse, as poetic works they all express a feeling for the rhythm of language as it underlies and reinforces the message, the humor, the ideas behind the words.

Using her poetic imagination, Elizabeth Coatsworth has adapted the Old Testament story of Noah's Ark to produce the story poem "Journey" for younger children. This picture book uses a simple, direct approach that focuses only on the animals entering the Ark at the time of the impending storm. The lions are the first to open the conversation en route:

> *"It's a long way over the mountains,*
> *it's a long, long, long way to the Ark,"*
> *said the little lion to the great big lion,*
> *"Can we get there by dark?"*[17]

More and more animals, birds, and reptiles join the exodus until the growing numbers of animals, the darkening sky, and the mounting suspense of the story come to a poetic climax:

> *And the animals sighed with contentment*
> *as outside the world grew dark*
> *and they sang, "How far we have journeyed,*
> *but at last we are safe in the Ark!"*[18]

Scope and variety in the drawings allow the energetic action to flow across a double-page spread depicting birds and beasts hurrying to enter the ark before the ominous clouds burst over the land.
From "The Journey" in The Peaceable Kingdom and Other Poems *by Elizabeth Coatsworth, illustrated by Fritz Eichenberg. Copyright 1958 by Pantheon Books, Inc. Reproduced by permission.*

[17]Elizabeth Coatsworth, "Journey," in *The Peaceable Kingdom* (New York: Pantheon Books, Inc., 1958), unpaged.
[18]*Ibid.*

"Listen, rabbit!"
I laughed and cried,
feeling all shiny
and warm inside.
"What a wonderful
secret surprise I've spied,
what a wonderful secret
for you to hide."

I hadn't a pony
or pup
to pet,

I hadn't a rabbit
exactly, yet,

But I
had a nest
like a fur-lined cup

And five baby rabbits
to watch grow up!

Gentle beauty is trapped in this composition lit with shimmering color and touched with tenderness. Invading a rabbit world, pictures and poetry blend to provide a picture book of natural wonder.

From Listen, Rabbit *by Aileen Fisher; illustration copyright* © *1964 by Symeon Shimin. Reproduced by permission of the publishers, Thomas Y. Crowell Company, New York.*

Aileen Fisher's *Listen, Rabbit* is a gently told narrative lit with shimmering colors that correspond with the enchanting verses in brightness. In this story poem for younger children, a little boy finds a rabbit and loves it.

> *"Listen, rabbit!"*
> *I laughed and cried,*
> *feeling all shiny*
> *and warm inside.*
> *"What a wonderful*
> *secret surprise I've spied,*
> *what a wonderful secret*
> *for you to hide."*
>
> *I hadn't a pony*
> *or pup*
> *to pet,*
>
> *I hadn't a rabbit*
> *exactly, yet,*

But I
had a nest
like a fur-lined cup

And five baby rabbits
to watch grow up![19]

A dedicated storyteller, Aileen Fisher invades a child's world with the same magic that charmed the children of old Hamelin. And with her reverence for the natural world, the poet presents her view of the out-of-doors in a fresh, sunny perspective that clearly outlines a rabbit world of wonder and delight.

The Hamelin magic is captured for much older children in Robert Browning's "The Pied Piper of Hamelin," especially in the Warne edition illustrated by Kate Greenaway. There is probably no other edition of this story poem that is so skillfully segmented, illustrated, and then fused together as an artistic whole as this enchanting picture storybook of almost a century ago. Illustrations of quaintly dressed children, piper, and townsfolk enliven the poem whose hero is a mystical figure commissioned to rid a town in Brunswick of its rats by charming them away with his music.

Into the street the Piper stept
  Smiling first a little smile,
As if he knew what magic slept
  In his quiet pipe the while;
Then, like a musical adept,
To blow the pipe his lips he wrinkled,
And green and blue his sharp eyes twinkled,
Like a candle-flame where salt is sprinkled;
And ere three shrill notes the pipe had uttered,
You heard as if an army muttered;
And the muttering grew to a grumbling;
And the grumbling grew to a mighty rumbling;
And out of the houses the rats came tumbling.
Great rats, small rats, lean rats, brawny rats,
Brown rats, black rats, grey rats, tawny rats,
Grave old plodders, gay young friskers,
  Fathers, mothers, uncles, cousins,
Cocking tails and pricking whiskers,
  Families by tens and dozens,
Brothers, sisters, husbands, wives—
Followed the Piper for their lives.

---

[19]From *Listen, Rabbit* by Aileen Fisher, copyright © 1964 by Aileen Fisher. Reprinted by permission of the publishers, Thomas Y. Crowell Company, New York.

But when the Major and the Corporation of Hamelin renege on their promise to pay the Piper, a different procession assembles.

> *Once more he stept into the street,*
> *And to his lips again*
> *Laid his long pipe of smooth, straight cane;*
> *And ere he blew three notes (such sweet,*
> *Soft notes as yet musician's cunning*
> *Never gave the enraptured air)*
> *There was a rustling that seemed like a bustling*
> *Of merry crowds justling at pitching and hustling;*
> *Small feet were pattering, wooden shoes clattering,*
> *Little hands clapping and little tongues chattering,*
> *And, like fowls in a farmyard when barley is scattering,*
> *Out came the children running.*[20]

Following the Piper up the mountainside where a "wondrous portal opened wide," the story concludes with the disappearance of all the children and the man they followed. All except one, a little lame boy, who tells "of all the pleasant sights" the Pied Piper had promised as he led the children to a joyous land

> *"Where waters gushed and fruit trees grew,*
> *And flowers put forth a fairer hue,*
> *And everything was strange and new;*
> *The sparrows were brighter than peacocks here,*
> *And their dogs outran our fallow deer,*
> *And honeybees had lost their stings,*
> *And horses were born with eagles' wings;*
> *And just as I became assured*
> *My lame foot would be speedily cured,*
> *The music stopped and I stood still,*
> *And found myself outside the hill,*
> *Left alone against my will,*
> *To go now limping as before,*
> *And never hear of that country more!"*

To make a connection between past and present, Robert Browning adds to his enchanting story poem that "in Transylvania there's a tribe of alien people . . . risen out of some subterraneous prison, into which they were trepanned long time ago in a mighty band."[21]

---

[20]Robert Browning, *The Pied Piper of Hamelin* (New York: Frederick Warne and Co., Ltd., n.d.), pp. 17–19, 25–34.
[21]*Ibid.*, p. 45–46.

XII.
Once more he stept into the street,
   And to his lips again
Laid his long pipe of smooth straight cane ;

Confident of his magical powers, the Pied Piper steps into the street to lure the children of Hamelin. Against backgrounds of scenic beauty and furnished interiors, the story-poem is splendidly supported.

From The Pied Piper of Hamelin *by Robert Browning, illustrated by Kate Greenaway. Frederick Warne & Co., Inc. Reproduced by permission.*

In his last stanza, the poet adds an admonishing note to his original manuscript:

> *So, Willy, let me and you be wipers*
> *Of scores out with all men—especially pipers!*
> *And, whether they pipe us free from rats or from mice,*
> *If we've promised them aught, let us keep our promise!*[22]

With galloping rhythm to create a mood and movement as important as the story being told, "The Highwayman" by Alfred Noyes rings and moves with the sounds of horses' hoofs. Eerie sounds of language echo a legendary past touched with mystery and terror. But every poet has his

[22]*Ibid.*, p. 47

own particular kind of music that he orchestrates with his own imagination, intuition, and sense of beauty and order. Here Noyes writes movingly with strange, rich imagery as well as musical rhythm that is as constant as a heartbeat throughout his cadenced poem whose theme and language is best appreciated by older children.

THE HIGHWAYMAN
Alfred Noyes

Part One

*The wind was a torrent of darkness among the gusty trees.
The moon was a ghostly galleon tossed upon cloudy seas.
The road was a ribbon of moonlight over the purple moor,
And the highwayman came riding—
    Riding—riding—
The highwayman came riding, up to the old inn-door.*

*He'd a French cocked-hat on his forehead, a bunch of lace at his chin,
A coat of the claret velvet, and breeches of brown doe-skin.
They fitted with never a wrinkle. His boots were up to the thigh.
And he rode with a jeweled twinkle,
    His pistol butts a-twinkle,
His rapier hilt a-twinkle, under the jeweled sky.*

*Over the cobbles he clattered and clashed in the dark inn-yard.
He tapped with his whip on the shutters, but all was locked and barred.
He whistled a tune to the window, and who should be waiting there
But the landlord's black-eyed daughter,
    Bess, the landlord's daughter,
Plaiting a dark red love-knot into her long black hair.*

*And dark in the dark old inn-yard a stable-wicket creaked
Where Tim the ostler listened. His face was white and peaked.
His eyes were hollows of madness, his hair like mouldy hay,
But he loved the landlord's daughter,
    The landlord's red-lipped daughter
Dumb as a dog he listened, and he heard the robber say—*

*"One kiss, my bonny sweetheart, I'm after a prize tonight,
But I shall be back with the yellow gold before the morning light;
Yet, if they press me sharply, and harry me through the day,
Then look for me by moonlight,
    Watch for me by moonlight,
I'll come to thee by moonlight, though hell should bar the way."*

*He rose upright in the stirrups. He scarce could reach her hand,
But she loosened her hair in the casement. His face burnt like a brand
As the black cascade of perfume came tumbling over his breast;
And he kissed its waves in the moonlight,*

(O, *sweet black waves in the moonlight!*)
Then he tugged at his rein in the moonlight, and galloped away to the
   west.

Part Two

He did not come in the dawning. He did not come at noon;
And out of the tawny sunset, before the rise of the moon,
When the road was a gypsy's ribbon, looping the purple moor,
A red-coat troop came marching—
   Marching—marching—
King George's men came marching, up to the old inn-door.

They said no word to the landlord. They drank his ale instead.
But they gagged his daughter, and bound her, to the foot of her narrow
      bed.
Two of them knelt at her casement, with muskets at their side!
There was death at every window;
   And hell at one dark window;
For Bess could see, through her casement, the road that he *would ride.*

They had tied her up to attention, with many a sniggering jest.
They had bound a musket beside her, with the muzzle beneath her breast!
"Now, keep good watch!" and they kissed her. She heard the doomed
      man say—
Look for me by moonlight;
   Watch for me by moonlight;
I'll come to thee by moonlight, though hell should bar the way!

She twisted her hands behind her; but all the knots held good!
She writhed her hands till her fingers were wet with sweat or blood!
They stretched and strained in the darkness, and the hours crawled by
         like years,
Till, now, on the stroke of midnight,
   Cold, on the stroke of midnight,
The tip of one finger touched it! The trigger at least was hers!

The tip of one finger touched it. She strove no more for the rest.
Up, she stood to attention, with the muzzle beneath her breast.
She would not risk their hearing; she would not strive again;
For the road lay bare in the moonlight;
   Blank and bare in the moonlight;
And the blood of her veins, in the moonlight, throbbed to her love's refrain.

Tlot-tlot, tlot-tlot! Had they heard it? The horse hoofs ringing clear;
Tlot-tlot, tlot-tlot, in the distance? Were they deaf that they did not
         hear?
Down the ribbon of moonlight, over the brow of the hill,
The highwayman came riding—
   Riding—riding—
The red-coats looked to their priming! She stood up, straight and still.

Tlot-tlot, *in the frosty silence!* Tlot-tlot, *in the echoing night!*
Nearer he came and nearer. Her face was like a light.
Her eyes grew wide for a moment; she drew one last deep breath,
Then her finger moved in the moonlight,
  Her musket shattered the moonlight,
Shattered her breast in the moonlight and warned him—with her death.

He turned. He spurred to the west; he did not know who stood
Bowed, with her head o'er the musket, drenched with her own blood!
Not till the dawn he heard it, and his face grew grey to hear
How Bess, the landlord's daughter,
  The landlord's black-eyed daughter,
Had watched for her love in the moonlight, and died in the darkness there.

Back, he spurred like a madman, shouting a curse to the sky,
With the white road smoking behind him and his rapier brandished high.
Blood-red were his spurs in the golden noon; wine-red was his velvet
    coat;
When they shot him down on the highway,
  Down like a dog on the highway,
And he lay in his blood on the highway, with a bunch of lace at his
    throat.

And still of a winter's night, they say, when the wind is in the trees,
When the moon is a ghostly galleon tossed upon cloudy seas,
When the road is a ribbon of moonlight over the purple moor,
A highwayman comes riding—
  Riding—riding—
A highwayman comes riding, up to the old inn-door.

Over the cobbles he clatters and clangs in the dark inn-yard.
He taps with his whip on the shutters, but all is locked and barred.
He whistles a tune to the window, and who should be waiting there
But the landlord's black-eyed daughter,
  Bess, the landlord's daughter,
Plaiting a dark red love-knot into her long black hair.[23]

Vividly told, this tragic poem of love haunts the imagination as its imagery and magic create an atmosphere that is suspenseful and ghostly. Linking legend with reality, the poem recounts that certain inhabitants living in the area traveled by the lawless highwayman still hear the sounds of horse's hoofs when the wind howls in the trees and the moon shines like "a ghostly galleon" through the tattered clouds of a wind-swept sky.

---

[23]Alfred Noyes, "The Highwayman," in *Poetry with Pleasure*, eds. Laurence A. Kirkpatrick and William W. Goodfellow (New York: Charles Scribner's Sons, 1965), pp. 91–95.

Attuned to many moods of mankind, poetry reveals the writer's particular mood or emotion in his selection and ordering of words. And the effectiveness of the poet is frequently based on his ability to arouse in his audience the intended emotional response. The emotional element inherent in the writing serves to differentiate the genuine from doggerel or shoddy verses that do not evoke the same intensity of feelings aroused by true poetry.

Because poetry is considered the natural language of children, humorous and nonsensical verses often serve as outlets for laughter and fun. Unlike other forms of poetry, nonsense verse has as its chief purpose to induce laughter. Good nonsensical and humorous verses reveal in the bright, gay use of words a delight in the sounds and rhythm of language. Appealing to young and the young at heart, the finest examples combine sophistication with fun.

Nonsense verses range from the merely humorous to the thoroughly impossible. Characterized mainly by a delight in the absurd, they may deal with familiar things, serious subjects, or just plain nonsense.

The history of nonsense poetry is relatively new even though laughter and quiet chuckles are not. Among the earliest and the finest are the works of Edward Lear. Lear composed limericks, which by definition are written purely for the sake of being inconsequential and amusing. Vibrant with coined words and rhythm, his limericks gain in humor as the stanzas lengthen.

Although limericks possess standard length and form, they are sometimes varied slightly to intensify their emotional appeal. The regular ones are composed mainly of five lines. The first, second, and fifth lines use one rhyme, and the third and the fourth lines another (*a, a, b, b, a*). Here, for example, are two limericks by Edward Lear:

> *There was a Young Lady whose chin*
> *Resembled the point of a pin;*
> *So she had it made sharp,*
> *And purchased a harp,*
> *And played several tunes with her chin.*

> *There was an Old Man who said, "How*
> *Shall I flee from this horrible Cow?*
> *I will sit on this stile,*

> *And continue to smile,*
> *Which may soften the heart of that Cow.*"[24]

This next limerick is by an anonymous writer:

> *I remember a fellow named Louie,*
> *Who ate seventeen bowls of chop-suey;*
> *When the eighteenth was brought,*
> *He became overwrought,*
> *And we watched as poor Louie went blooie!*[25]

An irregular pattern is shown in another anonymous limerick, made even brighter by its unusual form:

> *There was a young man of Spokane*
> *Whose verses never would scan.*
> *When told it was so,*
> *He said, "Yes, I know,*
> *But I always try to get as many words in*
> *the last line as I possibly can."*[26]

With the same sense of humor exemplified in the limericks, sheer nonsense or whimsy is expressed in works where an interplay of words and ideas dominate the writing. In his tongue-twisting poem, "The Quangle Wangle's Hat," Edward Lear gathers together a group of fanciful creatures and sets them up in curious arrangements to evoke humor. Here is a sample:

> *And besides, to the Crumpetty Tree*
> *Came the Stork, the Duck, and the Owl;*
> *The Snail and the Bumble-Bee,*
> *The Frog and the Fimble Fowl*
> *(The Fimble Fowl, with a Corkscrew leg);*
> *And all of them said, "We humbly beg*
> *We may build our homes on your lovely Hat,—*
> *Mr. Quangle Wangle, grant us that!*
> *Mr. Quangle Wangle Quee!*"

---

[24]Edward Lear, *The Complete Nonsense Book* (New York: Dodd, Mead & Company, 1934) pp. 59, 89.
[25]Anonymous, in *Poetry with Pleasure* (New York: Charles Scribner's Sons, 1965), p. 144.
[26]Anonymous, in *Poetry with Pleasure* (New York: Charles Scribner's Sons, 1965), p. 145.

And the Golden Grouse came there,
And the Pobble who has no toes,
And the small Olympian bear,
And the Dong with a luminous nose.
And the Blue Baboon who played the flute,
And the Orient Calf from the Land of Tute,
And the Attery Squash, and the Bisky Bat,—
All came and built on the lovely Hat
Of the Quangle Wangle Quee.[27]

Humorously imagined, this delightful poem—fanciful, jaunty, and gay—resounds with musical words devoid of meanings and nuances.

Matching the humorous imagination of "The Quangle Wangle's Hat" is the more dramatic account of "The Owl and the Pussycat."

The Owl and the Pussy-Cat went to sea
In a beautiful pea-green boat:
They took some honey, and plenty of money
Wrapped up in a five-pound note.
* * * *
They sailed away, for a year and a day,
To the land where the bong-tree grows;
And there in a wood a Piggy-wig stood,
With a ring at the end of his nose.[28]

Another master of nonsense verse is Lewis Carroll who excels in the apposition of sense and nonsense as found in "The Walrus and the Carpenter." For example,

The sun was shining on the sea,
Shining with all his might:
He did his very best to make
The billows smooth and bright—
And this was odd, because it was
The middle of the night.[29]

It is the absurdity of the situation pointed out in such a matter-of-fact manner that arouses a sense of humor in this stanza. More absurdity tinged with logic and common sense appears in the subsequent verses of

---

[27]Lear, *op. cit.*, p. 389.

[28]Lear, *op. cit.* pp. 125–26.

[29]Lewis Carroll, *Through the Looking-Glass* (London: Macmillan and Co., Ltd., 1953), p. 78.

the same poem. And again the mood is changed. This time the audience senses humor tinged with sheepishness from the lines:

> *But four young Oysters hurried up,*
> *All eager for the treat;*
> *Their coats were brushed, their faces washed,*
> *Their shoes were clean and neat—*
> *And this was odd, because, you know,*
> *They hadn't any feet.*
>
> * * *
>
> *"The time has come," the Walrus said,*
> *"To talk of many things:*
> *Of shoes—and ships—and sealing wax—*
> *Of cabbages—and kings—*
> *And why the sea is boiling hot—*
> *And whether pigs have wings."*
>
> * * *
>
> *"O Oysters," said the Carpenter,*
> *"You've had a pleasant run!*
> *Shall we be trotting home again?"*
> *But answer came there none—*
> *And this was scarcely odd, because*
> *They'd eaten every one.*[30]

Wisdom and wit underlie Carroll's poetry as much as coined words and absurdity are the hallmarks of Lear's. Animals and strange creatures represent favorite subjects for both of these writers of humorous and nonsensical verses.

Others who show poetic delight in the humorous use of language include A. A. Milne, whose rhymes by their very nature arouse a sense of humor, and Laura E. Richards, a poet who delights in creating happy nonsense by rhymes and absurdity. Numerous other nonsense poems reveal the interest writers show in producing poetry of fun and fancy lying very close to the heart of childhood.

Childhood is poetic, and poetry is frequently childlike in its simplicity. The experiences of childhood are compounded of exploring, acting, pondering, and creating. The fact that children invent their own poetry in lilting rhythms and rhymes and respond physically as well as emotionally to poetic works is living testimony of their love for the poet's art. And just as the poet views the happenings of his own life freshly, imagina-

---

[30]*Ibid.*, p. 81.

A stout vein of humor runs through this illustration despite the weeping Walrus and the Carpenter. Mock tragedy in verse form about some beguiled oysters is highlighted by superb line drawings.
From Through the Looking Glass *by Lewis Carroll, illustrated by Sir John Tenniel.*

tively, and succinctly, the child also confronts the simple, the ordinary, and the sublime with a faint sense of the miraculous touched with wonder and delight. Very often a child's reactions to the ordinary, simple things in his everyday world vibrate with intense emotion that lifts the mundane into a bright new world—a realm of gold where poets travel.

Criteria for
Books of Poetry and Verse

THEME

· Does the poetry attempt to present a theme or does it stress only the music of language?
· If a particular theme underlies a work, is it clearly presented? Is it implicit in the text?

- Does the poetry avoid presenting its theme or themes in overly abstract terms?
- If the theme is the major basis of the poem, is it within the comprehension level of children?
- Are there concrete references to existing themes within the text of the poetry?
- Are at least some themes universal enough to call up in children intuitive responses?
- Does the poetry, through its expression of theme and ideas, carry children beyond their immediate experiential level to extensions where language and imagination meet?

STYLE

- Is the sound of the language appropriate to the theme and content of the poetry?
- Are the images graphic enough for a child to perceive?
- Does melody flow in the movement of the verse forms?
- Are words and phrases used with economy to amplify meanings present in the poetry?
- Does the poet combine words and phrases in a unique way?
- Are editions of verse made bright by beautiful art work?
- Do the illustrations and word pictures reveal beauty and grace without denying the strength of feeling in the poetry?
- In collections, do the poems cut across a wide range of themes and styles of writing to arouse many moods and emotions?
- Is the style distinguished by technical craftsmanship that illuminates the ideas and projects the poet's feelings?
- Does the style generate a delight for its sounds, its moods, and its rhythm?
- Does the poetry have a distinct lilt in its cadenced lines?

References

ARBUTHNOT, MAY HILL, "Poetry of the Children's World," in *Children and Books*, 3rd ed. Chicago: Scott, Foresman & Company, 1964.

HOLLOWELL, LILLIAN, "Poetry," in *A Book of Children's Literature*. 3rd ed. New York: Holt, Rinehart & Winston, Inc., 1966.

HUCK, CHARLOTTE S. and DORIS A. YOUNG, "Children Respond to Poetry," in

Children's Literature in the Elementary School. New York: Holt, Rinehart & Winston, Inc., 1961.

JOHNSON, EDNA, *et al.*, "Poetry," in *Anthology of Children's Literature.* Boston: Houghton Mifflin Company, 1959.

SMITH, LILLIAN H., "Poetry," in *The Unreluctant Years.* Chicago: American Library Association, 1953.

Books of Poetry and Verse

For younger children

CATS AND BATS AND THINGS WITH WINGS
Written by Conrad Aiken. Illustrated by Milton Glaser. Atheneum Publishers, 1965.

This collection of wise and humorous verse is illustrated with beautiful pictures and is recommended for young children and all others who delight in a glowing book.

TOM, SUE AND THE CLOCK
Written by Conrad Aiken. Illustrated by Julia Maas. The Crowell Collier Publishing Co., 1966.

This charming story poem re-creates the details that make each day a wondrous new experience for children. As the tick-tock of the clock marks the hours of Tom and Sue's day, young readers are linked with the relationship between time and daily activity. The black-and-white illustrations enhance the appeal of the book.

HELLO DAY
Written by Dorothy Aldis. Illustrated by Susan Elson. G. P. Putnam's Sons, 1959.

Here is a collection of very short poems written in the simplest language so that they are easily understood even by pre-school and kindergarten children. Illustrations in black and white appear on almost every page.

ROBIN REDBREAST AND OTHER VERSES
Written by William Allington. Illustrated by Allington, Greenaway, Paterson, and Furness. The Macmillan Company, 1930.

This collection of twenty-nine poems designed for the young child is divided into several categories: playing alone, playmates and pets, fairies and elves, and so forth. Superb illustrations enliven the poetry.

THE SEASONS OF TIME
Edited by Virginia Olsen Baron. Illustrated by Yasuhide Kobashi. The Dial Press, Inc., 1968.

Tanka poetry of ancient Japan is selected here from a Japanese emperor's collections from over a thousand years ago. Written by priests, poets, warriors, and noblemen, this lovely anthology contains some of the most widely used verse form in Japan. Designated as tanka, this frail poetry retains the simplicity of haiku while allowing wider scope for feeling. Brush-and-ink drawings create pictures as fragile as any oriental print.

WINDY MORNING
Written and illustrated by Harry Behn. Harcourt, Brace & World, Inc., 1953.

This group of lyrical verses is appropriate for children five to nine years of age. The content ranges from nonsense verse to fairy poems. Mr. Behn has tastefully decorated his book, giving it added charm.

CALENDAR MOON
*Collected by Natalia Belting.
Illustrated by Bernarda Bryson. Holt,
Rinehart & Winston, Inc., 1966.*

Chosen as an ALA Notable Book, this poetic almanac of moon months has been collected from the folklore of the world. Distinctive, lucent pictures illustrate the mood expressed in the lyrics of this beautifully poetic anthology.

RIDDLE RADDLE, FIDDLE FADDLE
*Composed and compiled by Ann
Bishop. Illustrated by Roy Mathews.
Albert Whitman & Co., 1966.*

An unusual book of riddles with an introduction that traces their origins and consequences back to mythical times. The collection includes many ancient favorites, but it also introduces some fresh, original ones in tune with the present generation of children. Sprightly pictures add verve and dash to this compilation.

SONGS OF INNOCENCE
*Written by William Blake.
Illustrated and with music by Eileen
Raskin. Doubleday & Company, Inc.,
1966.*

William Blake's happy songs are beautifully illustrated here. They express the joy, wonder, and simple emotions of childhood. This is a book for everyone who cherishes the music of words.

RING O' ROSES
*Written and illustrated by Leonard
Leslie Brooke. Frederick Warne
& Co., Inc., 1922.*

This collection of twenty-one ungrouped nursery rhymes designed for the younger child is light and flippant in character. There are illustrations on practically each page.

I MET A MAN
*Written by John Ciardi. Illustrated
by Robert Osborn. Houghton
Mifflin Company, 1961.*

This book of verse is excellent for the beginning reader in that it has a recurring vocabulary of four hundred words. Children may derive pleasure from reading the verses on their own. The range of the poetry is from the simple to the subtle, and there are many light, humorous poems. This delightful collection is illustrated with charming pictures.

THE MONSTER DEN, OR LOOK
WHAT HAPPENED AT MY HOUSE—
AND TO IT
*Written by John Ciardi. J. B.
Lippincott Co., 1966.*

The escape of three children from wearisome restrictions at home may well prove gratifying for younger readers, but this long, well-constructed poem is written chiefly from the parent's point of view, and may not sustain the sympathies and interest of its intended audience.

SUMMER GREEN
*Written by Elizabeth Coatsworth.
Illustrated by Nora S. Unwin. The
Macmillan Company, 1948.*

There is a warm and lighthearted air about the poems in this book. Elizabeth Coatsworth has caught the rapture of summer magic in her tender choice of words.

THE PEACEABLE KINGDOM AND
OTHER POEMS
*Written by Elizabeth Coatsworth.
Illustrated by Fritz Eichenberg.
Pantheon Books, Inc., 1958.*

A quiet picture book of three story poems: "Journey," "Rest in Egypt," "The Peaceable Kingdom." Told in verse, the stories are simply, but beautifully illustrated in accordance with the themes expressed. A wide variety of animals are named and pictured throughout the book making it particularly suitable for younger children.

BEASTLY BOYS AND GHASTLY
GIRLS
*Edited by William Cole. Illustrated
by Tomi Ungerer. World Publishing
Co., 1964.*

A marvelous collection of nonsense verses. Pen-and-ink illustrations are in complete agreement with the poetry.

OH, WHAT NONSENSE!
Written by William Cole. Illustrated by Tomi Ungerer. The Viking Press, Inc., 1966.

This is a book of fifty nonsense poems compiled by Mr. Cole from among the works of Laura Richards, Theodore Roethke, Wallace Irwin, and the prolific Anonymous. From a pot of flea-tea to a spotted cow in a pawpaw tree, the realm of nonsense is given thorough representation. Zany illustrations add stuff to the nonsense.

A POCKETFUL OF POSIES
Compiled and illustrated by Marguerite de Angeli. Doubleday & Company, Inc., 1954.

Pastel illustrations blend delicately with poetry in this collection of nursery rhymes with the flavor of old English life. Young children will be drawn by the warmth and tenderness of de Angeli's artistry.

PEACOCK PIE
Written by Walter de la Mare. Illustrated by Barbara Cooney. Alfred A. Knopf, Inc., 1961.

This group of poems is full of fun and fancy. They are highly imaginative and chock full of witches, fairies, kings, and beasts. The images in the poetry vibrate with the color and light of a poetic imagination. Distinguished drawings intensify the radiance of a masterful touch.

CIRCUS
Written by Beatrice S. de Regniers. Illustrated by Al Giese. The Viking Press, Inc., 1966.

This book of verses reels and sparkles with the colors, sounds, and smells of circus excitement and all the glamor, glitter, and bounce of circus fun.

I OFTEN WISH
Written by Babette Deutsch. Illustrated by Eva Cellini. Funk & Wagnalls Co., 1966.

The poet explores the many things she might be, but is not and, for very good reasons, does not want to be. Black-and-green illustrations add to the amusement.

DRUMMER HOFF
Adapted by Barbara Emberley. Illustrated by Ed Emberley. Prentice-Hall, Inc., 1967.

Ablaze with color, this Caldecott Medal winner recounts the cumulative story of a drummer who fired the cannon that went "Kahbahbloom." The succinct, well-ordered lines of folk verse lend themselves to reading aloud, while vibrating colors make this picture book a bright, visual experience for younger children particularly.

THE CHILDREN'S BELLS
Written by Eleanor Farjeon. Illustrated by Peggy Fortnum. Henry Z. Walck, Inc., Publishers, 1960.

This is a veritable treasure of rich, warm imagery. Some of the poems have a tender touch of humor not exceeding a child's comprehension level. The collection is made enchanting with its gentle poetic ring and delightful pictures.

TAXIS AND TOADSTOOLS
Written and illustrated by Rachel Field. Doubleday & Company, Inc., 1926.

This unique collection is divided into three groups: people, taxis and thoroughfares, stores and storekeepers. The city activities, sounds, and symbols mirror familiar backgrounds for urban children particularly.

LISTEN, RABBIT
Written by Aileen Fisher. Illustrated by Symeon Shimin. Thomas Y. Crowell Company, 1964.

This shining picture book tells in gentle

rhymed narrative the story of a small boy who sees a rabbit and loves it. The verses are so infectious that young readers will be full of its skipping rhythms and lilting phrases. The drawings are enchanting and will be lovingly turned to again and again.

IN THE WOODS, IN THE MEADOW, IN THE SKY
Written by Aileen Fisher. Illustrated by Margot Tomes. Charles Scribner's Sons, 1965.

This is a delightful collection of simple nature poetry expressing feeling for trees, wildlife creatures, stars, and sky. Written on a young child's level, the verses are illumined by lovely ink drawings.

PICTURE RHYMES FROM FOREIGN LANDS
Written by Rose Fyleman. Illustrated by Valery Carrick. J.B. Lippincott Co., 1935.

This anthology of lilting rhymes includes entries from many different lands whose sense of humor and nonsense is captured in pictures and poetry. This unusual collection affords delight from rare sources.

THE PENNY FIDDLE: POEMS FOR CHILDREN
Composed by Robert Graves. Illustrated by Edward Ardizzone. Doubleday & Company, Inc., 1961.

Rich in imagery, this imaginatively treated volume reflects the efforts of outstanding artists who have joined to produce a rare collection of poetry in possession of poetic pictures.

UNDER THE WINDOW
Composed and illustrated by Kate Greenaway. Frederick Warne & Co., Inc., 1879.

Kate Greenaway was known first and foremost as an illustrator. In this book of verse, which is both simple in language and idea, Miss Greenaway has used gentle caricature. Her lines exhibit a true under-

standing of childhood. The poetry is gently old-fashioned but not without grace.

FROGGIE WENT A-COURTIN'
Retold and illustrated by Harriett. Harvey House, Inc., Publishers, 1967.

This centuries-old song appears in picture-book dress adorned with humor and beguiling detail. This enchanting version humorously introduces Mr. Froggie, Miss Mousie, Uncle Rat *et al.* to the youngest. Matching the simplicity of the poetry is the arrangement of the familiar music. An older edition with rollicking illustrations is the Caldecott Medal winner, *Frog Went A-Courtin'*, retold by John Langstaff and illustrated by Feodor Rojankovsky. Harcourt, Brace & World, Inc., 1955.

WHO WILL BE MINE?
Written by Edith Thacher Hurd. Illustrated by Georgia Longini. Golden Gate Junior Books, 1966.

A very personal quest is the matter of this poignant, beautifully photographed book. A little girl looks for a pet of her very own and, by mutual agreement with a puppy, ends her search happily. It is a wistful, satisfying story-poem.

SMALL RAIN
Written and illustrated by Jessie Orton Jones. The Viking Press, Inc., 1943.

This joyously illustrated collection was specifically chosen for its references to childhood. All the verses come from the King James version of the Bible. As a meaningful introduction to the Bible, this richly poetic collection illumines the scriptures for the youngest.

IN A SPRING GARDEN
Edited by Richard Lewis. Illustrated by Ezra Jack Keats. The Dial Press, 1965.

From the dark figure of a snail against the

red morning sky to the bright glow of the firefly against the dark of the evening, haiku poetry and art blend to provide lovely images of a new spring day. Beauty and brevity distinguish the ancient verses of Japan while Ezra Jack Keats' pictures artfully evoke the mood of this ancient art form.

THE MOON AND A STAR AND
OTHER POEMS
Written by Myra Cohn Livingston.
Illustrated by Judith Shahn. Harcourt,
Brace & World, Inc., 1965.

This collection is unique in that it depicts a child describing the world that he sees about him in his own terms. The recognizable language of childhood lends itself to reader identification.

NOAH'S JOURNEY
Composed by George Macbeth.
Illustrated by Margaret Gordon.
The Viking Press, Inc., 1966.

Brilliantly original poems that show the drama played in Noah's Ark when it landed on Mount Ararat. The roles of the animals are augmented by those of thunder, wind, rain, sand, rock, and grass. Strong in concept, text, and pictures, this imaginative book will probably have more appeal for bright, sensitive children.

MAGIC CARPET TO ANIMAL RHYME
LAND
Written and illustrated by Gwyneth
Mamlok. Harvey House, Inc.,
Publishers, 1966.

Young children will delight in meeting both old and new friends. The preschool child will find listening and reciting the rhymes a sheer pleasure. The illustrations are filled with charm and gentle appeal.

ALL DAY LONG
Written by David McCord.
Illustrated by Henry B. Kane. Little,
Brown & Co., 1966.

Fifty beautiful poems present the everyday world in a new dimension. This is the

magic of poetry at its best, and Mr. Mc-Cord performs it admirably. Gaily illustrated, this is a treasure of a book.

FAR AND FEW
Written by David McCord.
Illustrated by Henry B. Kane. Little,
Brown & Co., 1952.

This book of verse has quite a large range, from sheer nonsense to quiet meditation. McCord presents the animal world of the snail, grasshopper, bat, and other "beasties" with a touch of gaiety.

POEMS TO BE READ ALOUD
Edited by Ann McFerran. Illustrated
by Roberta Lewis Clark. Thomas
Nelson & Sons, 1965.

An anthology of well-loved poems recommended by children's librarians for reading aloud. Most of the poetry is standard fare produced by English and American writers, although there is a sprinkling of translated works suitable for English-speaking children. Brief sketches about the poets and their choices of subjects may be interesting to children wanting to know the backgrounds of the verses.

WONDERFUL TIME
Written by Phyllis McGinley.
Illustrated by John Alcorn. J. B.
Lippincott Co., 1966.

Time is personified by the instruments used to measure and capture it in this book of rhythmic, cadenced verses. Full-page, old-fashioned line drawings picture it, and the poet's verses tell about it. Time in all its manufactured and natural aspects is the subject of much poetic speculation.

A WREATH OF CHRISTMAS LEGENDS
Written by Phyllis McGinley.
Illustrated by Leonard Weisgard.
The Macmillan Company, 1967.

Phyllis McGinley's wreath is a garland of fifteen Christmas legends charmingly retold in verse form. A few of these beautifully told tales of the First Christmas will be familiar, but many will be entirely new to the reader. Leonard Weisgard's illustrations are truly a handsome accompaniment to this lyrical collection.

It Doesn't Always Have to Rhyme
Written by Eve Merriam. Illustrated by Malcolm Spooner. Atheneum Publishers, 1964.

The verses in this group offer memorable, fun-filled experiences. As the title implies, not all the poems end in the traditional rhyming manner. There are inner rhymes, repeated beats, and inner chimes that provide imagery and ideas suitable for children.

When We Were Very Young
Written by A. A. Milne. Illustrated by E. H. Shepard. E. P. Dutton & Co., Inc., 1924.

Here is a light-hearted group of verses that skip, dance, and meditate. Milne demonstrates his capacity for understanding both the serious and frivolous moments in childhood. Choice words conjure up indelible images supported by sounds of laughter and delight.

I See the Winds
Composed and illustrated by Kazue Mizumura. Thomas Y. Crowell Company, 1966.

As fragile as an oriental print, this lovely book of free verse is in the spirit of Japanese haiku. Here the variable moods of the wind at seasonal changes are caught with feeling and pungent brevity. The delicate, full-page wash drawings in four colors gracefully interpret the poetry.

Strella's Children
Written by Carol Newman. Illustrated by Fernando Krahm. Atheneum Publishers, 1966.

Strella is the mother of all creatures, both seen and unseen. Bird and beasts, and invisible creatures like the Belled Puglum, the Two-headed Sne-e-e-l, the Burrowing Borksloo, and the Smoke-eating Snarf are all her children.

Collections and Selections
Written by Frances Jenkins Olcott. Illustrated by Milo Winter. Houghton Mifflin Company, 1928.

A varied selection of poetry rich in storytelling elements makes the book suitable for reading aloud or even silently by young readers.

What Is That Sound!
Written by Mary L. O'Neill. Illustrated by Lois Ehlert. Atheneum Publishers, 1966.

Onomatopoeia is the very essence of name-making, and the names for all the sounds of life are imaginatively explored in this excellent collection of sound verses. Charming drawings complement the delightful, well-made poems.

The Lord Is My Shepherd: The Twenty-third Psalm
Illustrated by Tony Palazzo. Henry Z. Walck, Inc., 1965.

An edition superbly illustrating one of the best known and loved poems of the Bible. Each line of the shepherd's song is magnificently interpreted by artfully colored pictures of animals, vegetation, and still waters that blend to provide tranquil harmony in this reverent retelling for the youngest.

Small Child's Book of Verse
Written and illustrated by Doane Pelagie. Oxford University Press, Inc., 1948.

This is an informally grouped collection of poems. The groups are in the following classification: just about me, all through the year, down our street, all out-of-doors, big and little creatures, whither do you wander, and comes the starlighter. This collection is especially appropriate for the young child.

FIRST BOOK OF POETRY
Written by Isabel J. Peterson.
Illustrated by Kathleen Elgin.
Franklin Watts, Inc., 1954.

In this beautifully illustrated book the author has chosen favorites from the scores of poems children read with her each year. There are several lyrical and humorous poems in the collection of one hundred.

RAGGED ROBIN
Composed by James Reeves.
Illustrated by Jane Paton. E. P.
Dutton & Co., Inc., 1961.

A beautiful picture book of poetry consisting of jingles, lyrical verses, and story poems interpreted by line drawings as well as four-color illustrations. Appealing more to the youngest, the poems are ordered in alphabetical sequence—one poem for each letter of the alphabet that begins a title.

TIRRA LIRRA
Written by Laura E. Richards.
Illustrated by Marguerite Davis.
Little, Brown & Co., 1932.

This delightful collection of nonsense verse abounds in the humor and fancy of coined words that afford joyous confusion to the reader. Suitable drawings heighten the humor.

UNDER THE TREE
Written by Elizabeth Madox Roberts.
Illustrated by F. D. Bedford. The
Viking Press, Inc., 1930.

This collection contains many narrative poems to which children will enjoy listening. The simplicity of the poetry has special appeal for the young, and the storytelling elements make the collection entertaining in varying moods.

LAUGHING TIME
Written by William Jay Smith.
Illustrated by Juliet Kepes. Little,
Brown & Co., 1955.

This is a collection of genuinely funny jingles especially good for reading aloud.

A CHILD'S GARDEN OF VERSES
Composed by Robert Louis Stevenson.
Illustrated by Brian Wildsmith.
Franklin Watts, Inc., 1966.

These poems of childhood have been among the best-loved in the English language for many years. They tell of dreams, adventure, and everyday play. The illustrations light up these poems afresh for a new generation.

THE CROCODILE'S MOUTH
Written by Adrien Stoutenburg.
Illustrated by Glen Rounds. The
Viking Press, Inc., 1966.

This is a merry book of folk song stories retold in verse. Among such familiar stories as "Noah's Ark" and "Froggie Went A-Courtin'" are some that may be new to many readers: "The Sow Got the Measles," "Derby Ram," and "The Crocodile's Mouth." Excellent line drawings add a delightful flavor to the verses.

POEMS TO SOLVE
Written by May Swenson. Charles
Scribner's Sons, 1966.

With poems that are riddles, games, and puzzles, the author invites her audience to participate in the challenging business of making verses. The verse games are exciting, although at times a little sophisticated, and they are sure to pique a child's curiosity and his enjoyment of poetry.

FIRST PRAYERS and FIRST GRACES
Compiled and illustrated by Tasha
Tudor. Henry Z. Walck, Inc.,
Publishers, 1952 and 1955.

Reverent beauty is expressed in the simple prayers of thanks and supplication by an artist famed for her delicate pictures. The choices of prayers and graces are especially suitable for small children when they are first introduced to the ancient custom of prayer.

WINGS FROM THE WIND
Written and illustrated by Tasha
Tudor. J.B. Lippincott Co., 1964.

This anthology provides sheer pleasure for the listener as well as the reader. Lovely illustrations serve to enhance the beauty of the poetry.

STARS TONIGHT
Written by Sara Teasdale. Illustrated
by Dorothy P. Lathrop. The
Macmillan Company, 1958.

In this collection Sara Teasdale wanders into the eerie region of outer space. Children will be fascinated by the other side of the moon, shooting stars, and the cause for the changing seasons. In another segment of this group of verse, Miss Teasdale focuses her attention on the world "under the grass." Wonder and delight shine through this galaxy of beautiful poetry.

I LIVE IN THE CITY
Written by James S. Tippett.
Illustrated by Elizabeth Tyler
Wolcott. Harper & Row, Publishers,
1927.

This book is just pocket size. The city comes to life vividly through its verse: elevators, skyscrapers, the subway, and all the confusion that makes up New York. The experiences are seen through the eyes of a poetic child.

SING-SONG: A NURSERY RHYME
BOOK AND OTHER POEMS
Written by Christina Rossetti.
Illustrated by Marguerite Davis.
The Macmillan Company, 1938.

This is a collection of delightful verse especially for the very young child. These verses, slender and lyrical, are full of fun and fancy with sensitive illustrations.

RAINBOW IN THE SKY
Edited by Louis Untermeyer.
Illustrated by Reginald Birch.
Harcourt, Brace & World, Inc.,
1935.

Selected with younger children in mind, this large anthology is distinguished for its range and its illustrations. Old favorites and new ones comprise the five hundred poems included. There is a sizable number of serious works, but humorous poems dominate and are matched with interpretive pictures.

MAGIC CIRCLES
Compiled by Louis Untermeyer.
Illustrated by Barbara Cooney.
Harcourt, Brace & World, Inc., 1952.

This collection of over a hundred poems is certain to delight the young reader. Poetic language matched with superb drawings make this a rare treasury of verse.

THE GOLDEN TREASURY OF POETRY
Selected and with a commentary by
Louis Untermeyer. Illustrated by
Joan Walsh Anglund. Golden
Press, Inc., 1959.

A rich source of poetry selected by a great poet, this is probably the most comprehensive collection for young children. Charming illustrations add color and dash to the poetry.

A ROCKET IN MY POCKET
Edited by Carl Withers. Illustrated
by Susanne Suba. Holt, Rinehart &
Winston, Inc., 1948.

This is an unusual book in that it contains proverbs, spelling rhymes, togue twisters, and autograph album sayings. These are all quite short and thus lend themselves to memorization. The illustrations are simple but meaningful.

For older children

CRICKET SONS
Collected and translated by Harry
Behn. Harcourt, Brace & World,
Inc., 1964.

This well-known poet here turns his attention to translating the nature lyrics of Japanese haiku. Delicate Japanese prints illuminate the fragile unrhymed verses of this small but delightful volume of poetry.

BEOWULF THE WARRIOR
*Retold by Ian Serraillier. Illustrated
by Severin. Henry Z. Walck, Inc.,
Publishers, 1961.*

Probably the best retelling of the Anglo-Saxon epic of the warrior who struggled to rid his land of the monsters Grendel and his mother, and the fiery dragon whose wrath has become legendary in literature. Superb stylized drawings enhance the condensed verses whose drama is heightened by the distillation. Other notable verse narratives by the same poet include: *Ballad of Kon-Tiki* and *Everest Climbed*, published in Britain.

UNDER THE TENT OF THE SKY
*Selected by J. E. Brewton. Illustrated
by Robert Lawson. The Macmillan
Company, 1937.*

A large, delightful collection of poems, all about animals, arranged under amusing and interesting groupings. The collection has beauty, variety, imagination, and humor. The beautiful illustrations add a touch of magic to the book.

POEMS OF ROBERT BROWNING
*Selected by Rosemary Sprague.
Drawings by Robert Galster. Thomas
Y. Crowell Company, 1964.*

This is a well-chosen selection of Browning's poems filled with his enthusiasm for life. His love lyrics express warmth and affection, and his poems of adventure throb with excitement and action. The drawings sensitively speak the romantic language of the poetry.

HAND IN HAND WE'LL GO:
TEN POEMS BY ROBERT BURNS
*Illustrated by Nonny Hogrogian.
Thomas Y. Crowell Company, 1965.*

This collection of favorite poems is designed with grace and enthusiasm to introduce young readers to Robert Burns and to his beloved Highlands. The strong yet sensitive woodcuts capture the very scent of the heather and the majesty of the moors.

SELECTIONS FROM FRENCH POETRY
*Compiled and translated by Kenneth
F. Canfield. Illustrated by Tomi
Ungerer. Harvey House, Inc.,
Publishers, 1965.*

Sixty-three well-selected poems comprise this anthology of some of the best poems from France. As old as the fifteenth century and as modern as the twentieth, the selections consist of many well known poems including the works of Apollinaire, Eluard, and Prévert. English translations on facing pages facilitate the reading of the poems in their original language. Striking illustrations bear out the French flavor in both the English and original versions.

A TASTE OF CHAUCER: SELECTIONS
FROM THE CANTERBURY TALES
*Edited and translated by Anne
Malcolmson. Illustrated by Enrico
Arno. Harcourt, Brace & World,
Inc., 1964.*

A skillful retelling of nine tales from Chaucer and a poetic transcription of his prologue. Strong woodcuts match the spirit and the mood of the ancient epic, and the glossary, notes, and the biographical sketch throw added light on stories from a dim past.

THE SPARROW BUSH
*Rhymes by Elizabeth Coatsworth.
Wood engravings by Stefan Martin.
W. W. Norton & Company, Inc.,
1966.*

The young reader will share pleasure and delight in all the simple rhythms of nature: the flight of the bird, the feel of rain, the change of seasons, and the sounds of a thunderstorm. The wood engravings are brilliantly sensitive.

THE BIRDS AND THE BEASTS WERE
THERE
*Selected by William Cole.
Illustrated by Helen Siegl. World
Publishing Co., 1963.*

Skillfully selected, these three hundred

animal poems cover a wide range of creatures in a variety of moods—playful, nonsensical, lyrical, and reverent. Vividly depicted by splendid woodcuts, this collection presents favorite poetry of well-known writers—Burns, Blake, Wordsworth, Yeats, Frost—as well as new poets. Old or new, together they provide satisfying experiences.

POEMS FOR SEASONS AND
CELEBRATIONS
*Edited by William Cole. Illustrated
by Johannes Troyer. World Publishing
Co., 1961.*

Reflecting many moods, this tastefully selected anthology consists of 140 poems ranging from ancient rhymes to modern light verse by Sara Teasdale, Helen Hunt Jackson, William Blake, Robert Frost, Thomas Carew and many others. Holiday themes underscore this festively decorative collection by a well-known anthologist. Also edited by Cole are: *Poems of Magic and Spells, I Went to the Animal Fair, Story Poems New and Old, Humorous Poetry for Children.*

SELECTIONS FROM ITALIAN POETRY
*Compiled by A. Michael De Luca
and William Giuliano. Illustrated by
Ann Grifalconi. Harvey House,
Inc., Publishers, 1966.*

Another beautiful bilingual selection of poetry consisting of fifty-seven works from Italy and other lands. Spanning eight centuries, this poetic literature has within its scope a prayer of St. Francis; selections from Dante, Petrarch, Ariosto, and Tasso; selections from later poets—Leopardi, Carducci, and D'Annunzio; and works of the Nobel Prize winner Quasimodo. The rich poetry is matched with lyrical drawings in harmony with the poetic tradition of Italy.

REFLECTIONS ON A GIFT OF
WATERMELON PICKLE
*Compiled by Stephen Dunning,
Edward Lueders and Hugh Smith.*

*Illustrated with photographs.
Lothrop, Lee & Shephard, Co., Inc.,
1967.*

Some very frightening as well as wonderfully gentle poems by the best contemporary writers are included in this anthology. These, combined with excellent, artistic photographs, make this book an expecially prized possession for today's very much aware and troubled adolescent.

HE WHO SAW EVERYTHING: THE
EPIC OF GILGAMESH
*Retold by Anita Feagles.
Illustrated by Xavier Gonzales.
William R. Scott Inc., 1966.*

Preserving the spirit of the original cuneiform text, this retelling of the ancient epic is magnificently depicted in paper sculptures and plaster friezes. Appearing for the first time in a picture book format, the epic adventures of Gilgamesh and a friend reveal many moral and ethical problems universal in their appeal and application. Scholarship and simplicity blend to produce a book of rare beauty.

ON A GRASS-GREEN HORN: OLD
SCOTCH AND ENGLISH BALLADS
*Edited and illustrated by Ati Forberg.
Atheneum Publishers, 1965.*

This unique collection of eighteen imaginatively illustrated ballads reveals skill in the selection as well as a sense of pictorial interpretation.

YOU COME TOO
*Composed by Robert Frost. Wood
engravings by Thomas W. Nason.
Holt, Rinehart & Winston, Inc.,
1959.*

Wit and wisdom mark this collection of poems serving as invitations to the outdoors. Sensitively expressed, the pungent verses capture the fragrance and romance of the open world. Wood engravings enhance the woodsy feeling permeating this collection.

THE SILVER SWAN: POEMS OF
ROMANCE AND MYSTERY
*Compiled by Horace Gregory and
Marya Zaturenska. Wood
engravings by Diana Bloomfield.
Holt, Rinehart & Winston, Inc.,
1966.*

A collection of hauntingly beautiful elegies, ballads, and lyric songs that stir a sense of beauty, magic, and mystery as they chant of young lovers, a winter walk, a spell, or death—all touched with delicacy and mystery. The brooding engravings correspond to the mood of the verses, adding richness and dimension. A companion to *The Crystal Cabinet: An Invitation to Poetry*, this outstanding collection is best suited to the upper grades.

AN INTRODUCTION TO HAIKU
*Edited and translated by Harold
G. Henderson. Doubleday &
Company, Inc., 1958.*

Preserving the spirit of the Japanese haiku poetry, this collection of short verses is a fine sampling of an effectively compact literary art. Useful commentaries throw light on each of the nine different chapters of lucidly lyrical and suggestive poetry.

A TREASURY OF IRISH SAINTS: A
BOOK OF POEMS
*Compiled and translated by John
Irvine. Illustrated by Ruth Brandt.
Henry Z. Walck, Inc., Publishers,
1965.*

Put into English words, the gentleness and peace of these lovely lilting lines keeps alive the freshness of the old Gaelic beauty. Sympathetic pictures add reverently to this treasury of poetic literature from Ireland.

THE COMPLETE NONSENSE BOOK
*Written and illustrated by Edward
Lear. Edited by Lady Strachey. Dodd,
Mead & Co., 1945.*

A collection of verse, prose, drawings, alphabets, and absurdities of never-failing delight for young and old alike. To read this charming book is a rare and lasting treat.

POEMS OF EARTH AND SPACE
*Written by Claudia Lewis. Illustrated
by Symon Shimin. E.P. Dutton &
Co., 1967.*

This book of poems reflects the wonder that we all feel in contemplating the atmosphere and knowing that man is exploring this vast unknown. The illustrations echo the feeling of the verses. Suitable for all ages.

THE MOMENT OF WONDER: A
COLLECTION OF CHINESE AND
JAPANESE POETRY
*Collected and edited by Richard
Lewis. The Dial Press, Inc., 1964.*

A very attractive, wide-ranging collection of long and short selections from Chinese and Japanese poetry. Illuminating the gems of rhymed and unrhymed verses are marvelous reproductions of oriental paintings that sympathetically interpret many of the nature poems. Also by Richard Lewis, and very much in the spirit of Japanese haiku, is a lovely book of twenty-two verses matched with striking collages by Ezra Jack Keats, *In a Spring Garden*. The Dial Press, Inc., 1965.

MIRACLES: POEMS BY CHILDREN
OF THE ENGLISH-SPEAKING WORLD
*Collected by Richard Lewis. Simon
and Schuster, Inc., 1966.*

A collection of rare beauty selected by a distinguished teacher of children who demonstrates here his keen appreciation of children's spontaneous and creative expression. Ageless in its appeal, this beautiful collection has samples of poetry that cut across a wide age range.

SELECTIONS FROM CONTEMPORARY
PORTUGUESE POETRY
*Compiled and translated by Jean R.
Longland. Illustrated by Anne Marie
Jauss. Harvey House, Inc.,
Publishers, 1966.*

This bilingual volume serves as a brief introduction to the great outpouring of poetry in modern Portugal, a literature as yet almost unknown in English-speaking countries. The forty-three poems of the twentieth century are faithfully interpreted by black-and-white drawings. The translations here are outstandingly exact to the metrical form of the original works.

A POCKETFUL OF RHYMES
Edited by Katherine Love.
Illustrated by Henrietta Jones.
Thomas Y. Crowell Company,
1946.

A musical collection of verses that point up worlds of light and sound that are full of imagination. Here are lilting poems of stars, the wind, the rain, taxis, and pixies. Nor have nonsense and ancient rhymes been neglected. Suitable for reading even to younger children, the poems by such writers as Eleanor Farjeon, William Blake, Rachel Field, Edna St. Vincent Millay, cover a wide range of appeal, and the older rhymes prove timeless. Also by the same editor, *A Little Laughter*, illustrated by Walter Lorraine.

EDNA ST. VINCENT MILLAY'S POEMS SELECTED FOR YOUNG PEOPLE
Illustrated by Paget Fredericks.
Harper & Row, Publishers, 1951.

Delicacy of style reflects the imagination of a poet perceiving a child's world in diminutive terms. Capturing mischievous moments in childhood, this collection includes poems with gentle humor. Pictures interpret the fragile verses.

TOUCH BLUE
Compiled by Lillian Morrison.
Illustrated by Doris Lee. Thomas Y.
Crowell Company, 1958.

Here are the love charms, rhymed superstitions, and chants that have been repeated through the ages. This collection reveals a sense of the miraculous, mysterious, and deeply poetic. The illustrations are enchantingly delightful in folklore tradition.

A JOURNEY OF POEMS
Edited by Dr. Richard Niebling.
Dell Publishing Company, Inc., 1966.

A beautiful anthology in twelve sections that depicts life as a journey. Through poetic verses, experiences common to humankind are stressed in each of the sections, exploring alternate responses to various stages, places, and periods in the mainstream of universal life. The anthology includes fifty major and minor poets, some of whom are: Shakespeare, Keats, Coleridge, Byron, Browning, Tennyson, Whitman, Frost, Jeffers, Edna St. Vincent Millay, and Vachel Lindsay.

WORDS WORDS WORDS
Written by Mary O'Neill.
Decorated by Judy Piussi-Campell.
Doubleday & Company, Inc., 1966.

Poems that reveal what words can be and say and do. This is a book of the music, the fun, and the beauty that dances within the words of our language. The illustrations are very colorful and most unusual.

LEAN OUT OF THE WINDOW
Written by Sara Hannum and
Gwendolyn E. Reed. Illustrated by
Ragna Tischler. Atheneum
Publishers, 1965.

This anthology of modern poetry is especially appealing to intermediate-grade children. There is depth and variety in the collection, as well as music and rhythm.

SPANISH-AMERICAN POETRY
Compiled and translated by
Seymour Resnick. Illustrated by
Anne Marie Jauss. Harvey House,
Inc., Publishers, 1965.

Forty poems selected from the best of five centuries of Spanish-American poetry, from the sixteenth-century Ercilla to the famous moderns, Neruda and Mistral. Lovely line drawings sharpen the images of each period piece. Also by the same editor, *Selections from Spanish Poetry*, a delightful introduction to classical Spanish poetry for older children.

THE PINE TREE
Written and illustrated by George
Maxim Ross. E.P. Dutton & Co.,
Inc., 1966.

Symbolizing valiant struggle against ravaging elements, the poetry in this book of rare beauty depicts the life of a pine tree from seed to skeleton on a rock-ribbed island off the Maine coast. The text is matched with marvelous sketches.

SELECTIONS FROM RUSSIAN
POETRY AND PROSE
Compiled and translated by
Vladimir Rus. Illustrated by
Elizabeth Korolkoff. Harvey
House, Inc., Publishers, 1965.

This bilingual anthology contains thirty-five charmingly illustrated selections of poetry and prose that span a period of more than three hundred years. Recommended for older children, the fine literary works express universalizing themes without losing their local flavor.

POEMS OF WILLIAM SHAKESPEARE
Selected by Lloyd Frankenberg.
Etchings by Nonny Hogrogian.
Thomas Y. Crowell Company,
1966.

From the richness of Shakespeare's writings, this poet has made an interesting selection. All the lyrical and dramatic uses of poetry are illuminated here. The songs—witty, tender, and gentle—as well as passages that sweep readers through time and space are selected and organized skillfully. The sensitive etchings add much to the beauty of the book.

ST. GEORGE AND THE DRAGON
Written by Edmund Spencer.
Adapted by Sandol Stoddard
Warburg. Illustrated by Pauline
Baynes. Houghton Mifflin Co.,
1963.

The beauty of language and the authentic quality of the gallant era of knights is recaptured in this superb adaptation. In an almost word for word interpretation of the original poem, modern terms replace ancient ones in order to clarify meanings and the ideas of the original poetry, which has not lost its rhythm in the present free verse pattern. Sharp and precise illustrations retain the morbid mood in certain passages without snuffing out the sparks of humor found in other sections of the long poem.

A SNAIL'S A FAILURE SOCIALLY
Written by Kaye Starbird.
Illustrated by Kit Dalton. J.B.
Lippincott Co., 1966.

In polished, perceptive verses the author enters the world of living things, bringing to it a touch of human interest in the social problems of some less renowned animals. These nature poems are often melancholy and nostalgic and always well made. The poet's daughter has beautifully illustrated the book.

THE GREEN ROADS: THE POETRY
OF EDWARD THOMAS
Selected by Eleanor Farjeon.
Illustrated by Diana Bloomfield.
Holt, Rinehart & Winston, Inc.,
1966.

The little-known works of Edward Thomas have been wisely selected for their naturalness and their lack of self-consciousness. Emphasizing a way of seeing, the poetry deepens insights from the natural world whether it sings of cock-crow or melting winters or of the great, wide outdoors. Distinguished drawings lend richness and quality to this most unusual collection.

THE PATHS OF POETRY:
TWENTY-FIVE POETS AND THEIR
POEMS
Compiled by Louis Untermeyer.
Delacorte Press, 1966.

Poetic portraits of twenty-five poets beginning with Chaucer and concluding with Robert Frost. Revealing their struggles, triumphs, and achievements, this delightfully informative book offers a glittering array of writers from whose works Untermeyer has skillfully selected gems that bring out the radiance in the poets' lives.

WALT WHITMAN'S AMERICA
Written by Walt Whitman.
Selected and illustrated by James Daugherty. World Publishing Co., 1964.

The selections here are from Whitman's *Leaves of Grass, Democratic Vistas, Specimen Days,* and writings about Lincoln. Reflecting a strong sense of nationalism, the selections and their sturdy pictures embody the vitality that fired Whitman's writings. This poetic collection may serve as a first taste of Whitman's works.

THE BALLAD OF THE PILGRIM CAT
Composed by Leonard Wibberley.
Illustrated by Erik Blegvad. Curtis Publishing Company, 1961.

A whimsical ballad in rhyme and beguiling pictures that tells of a raffish cat aboard the *Mayflower.* Sailing as a stowaway, the cat falls into disfavor with the Pilgrim Fathers for his curiosity, but he later redeems himself by his instinctive handling of mice that pestered the early colonists.

POETRY AND SONGS

ONE WIDE RIVER TO CROSS
Adapted by Barbara Emberley.
Illustrated by Ed Emberley.
Prentice-Hall, Inc., 1966.

The rollicking song entitled "The Animals Came in Two by Two" is superbly designed in picture-book dress for younger children. Linoleum-block cuts in strong, black outlines are highlighted by vivid colors spread across each page.

THE SEA, SHIPS AND SAILORS:
POEMS, SONGS AND SHANTIES
Selected by William Cole.
Illustrated by Robin Jacques. The Viking Press, Inc., 1967.

Here is a varied collection of poems, songs and shanties celebrating the lure of the sea, the romance of the deep, and the music of the waters. Ballads, nonsensical verses, as well as some touching poetry are selected from Lord Byron to Abe Burrows and provide a tangy variety that is matched with clever line drawings.

FOLK SONGS OF THE WORLD
Compiled by Charles Haywood. The John Day Company, Inc., 1966.

This comprehensive compilation of folk music represents the best in English from Afghanistan to Zambia with informative notes about the dances, the instruments, and the lyrics of each country. Lending an ethnic touch to the book, the text of each song appears in its original language as well as in the English translation.

SOLDIERS' SONGS AND MARCHES
Written by Michael Hurd.
Illustrated by John Miller. Henry Z. Walck, Inc., Publishers, 1966.

With trumpets, drums, and bagpipes the sounds and stories of army music from Pharaoh Tutankhamen's to our own army bands are delightfully explored. The book is both informative and entertaining, providing plentiful interesting detail to keep the budding music historian amused and edified.

SAILORS' SONGS AND SHANTIES
Written by Michael Hurd.
Illustrated by John Miller. Henry Z. Walck, Inc., Publishers, 1965.

The harsh, boisterous, lively, and sometimes somber life and work of the sailor and his ship fills his music and colorful shanties. Each man sings of his work, and a ship can be learned through the songs of her crew. This delightful book presents the sailors' songs in their element.

COCK-A-DOODLE-DOO!
COCK-A-DOODLE-DANDY!
Written by Paul Kapp. Illustrated by
Anita Lobel. Harper & Row,
Publishers, 1965.

Nonsense poems and humorous verses by
Lewis Carroll, Keats, Blake, and others
are set to music in this unusual book.
Sixty-six songs in all, some written by the
author himself, are beautifully illustrated
with pen-and-ink drawings. The music
has a contemporary ring and is easy to
play and sing.

THE STAR SPANGLED BANNER
Composed by Francis Scott Key.
Illustrated by Ingri and Parin
D'Aulaire. Doubleday &
Company, Inc., 1942.

A large, handsome edition of the national
anthem presented with pictures that fit the
stirring text. Done in rich, strong colors as
well as in black and white, the drawings are
skillfully executed, making this book a
valuable one.

BALLADS, BLUES AND THE BIG BEAT
Compiled by Donald Myrus.
Illustrated with photographs. The
Macmillan Company, 1966.

Highlights of American folk singing with
the compelling power and pleasure of
folk singing in all its forms: protest, folk-
rock, hillbilly, old-time ballads, and blues.
The photographs lend interest to a collection born of an old folk tradition.

YANKEE DOODLE
Composed by Dr. Richard
Schackburg. Illustrated by Ed
Emberley. Prentice-Hall, Inc., 1965.

In shouting red, white, blue, and gold,
this vividly illustrated book sets down the
lyrics of a British surgeon who poked fun
at the ill-equipped and poorly dressed
American soldiers who later sang the song
during the British retreat. Capturing a
spirit of patriotism, this dashing book
follows Captain Washington and his men
to their glorious victory. Horses prance,
soldiers stick feathers in their caps, and
townspeople line the streets to cheer the
tattered though courageous Yankee
militia.

LULLABIES AND NIGHT SONGS
Music by Alec Wilder. Illustrated by
Maurice Sendak. Edited by William
Engvick. Harper & Row, Publishers,
1965.

A magnificent collection of traditional
songs, rhymes, and children's poetry from
many backgrounds with old and new
musical arrangements. Highlighting the
melodies are the poetic pictures of Maurice
Sendak that make this brilliant book a rich
source of music and verse.

THE FIRESIDE BOOK OF CHILDREN'S
SONGS
Collected and edited by Marie
Winn. Musical arrangements by
Allan Miller. Illustrated by John
Alcorn. Simon and Schuster, Inc.,
1966.

This is a handsome collection of 105
songs of every type—from light opera to
traditional camp songs; nursery songs and
singing games to American and foreign
folk songs. Letter-names of guitar chords
and easy-to-play piano accompaniments
supplement the melodies. Striking illustrations make this a delightful addition to the
family library.

Suggesting a folk theme, this illustration also stirs a folk feeling as it depicts a humble widow, her two daughters, and their small cottage fenced around with sticks.

From Chanticleer and the Fox *by Geoffrey Chaucer, adapted and illustrated by Barbara Cooney. Copyright © 1958 by the Thomas Y. Crowell Company. Reproduced by permission.*

Chapter 6

FOLK TALES

Folk-literature conserves the accumulating mass of spontaneous,
unscientific thought, feelings, beliefs, fancies, traditions, distortions, superstitions,
and ethical teachings of the common people of all races. It has no
known authors, but, like an avalanche, it gathers into itself, age by age, all that
lies in its path of the natural mental products of the human race.

— Frances Jenkins Olcott
The Children's Reading
Houghton Mifflin Company, 1927

153

Categories
of Folk Tales

Folk literature as a portion of universal literature belongs to everyone, adults and children alike. But it is children who keep alive the dramatically imaginative stories whose sources stretch far back into. the infant years of human history. By returning again and again to these time-honored tales, generations of children have given a permanent place to perennial favorites that adults may have put away as "childish things."

Growing out of the oral storytelling tradition, folk literature reflects and preserves the unscientific thinking, feelings, superstitions, faith, and dreams of simple peoples the world around. Diffused with wisdom and rich in wit and imagination, this folk literature continues to exist today as a body of tales rooted in a humanistic tradition, and it continues to captivate children just as the Pied Piper charmed them with his piping.

What are the characteristics of this portion of universal literature? And what has made these tales so appealing to so many generations of children?

In order to answer these questions the student of literature must approach this art form with a literary sense and impose order and analysis upon some of the best examples "in the folklore of those races whose stories grew out of a genuine art impulse."[1]

Although it is difficult to distinguish clearly between certain stories in the various categories of folklore, especially since many of them contain elements common to several different groups, a convenient classi-

---

[1]Lillian H. Smith, *The Unreluctant Years* (Chicago: American Library Association, 1953), p. 63.

fication can include: (1) folk tales, (2) fairy tales, and (3) myths, fables and

legends. Within these groupings one can find types and motifs that help
to define this great body of literature and the ingredients that give the
tales literary quality and power.

Definition of the Folk Tale

The folk tale is part of the oral storytelling tradition of
a people. Told primarily to present moral values or explanations of the
environment, it is, nonetheless, an art form in its own right. As a tale passes
from storyteller to storyteller, it becomes embroidered and idealized.
The storyteller's desire to use words well, to amuse, or to astound mingles
with the traditional material to create an imaginative work.

The folk tale is usually a short, fast-moving story of an adventurous,
comic, or romantic nature. It is simply constructed, becoming more
involved by the linking of numerous simple motifs, rather than by the
adding of complexity to any one motif. Its characters, animal or human,
are described in just enough detail to further the story's action. The good
and the evil characters, the clever and the foolish ones are clearly opposed.

The plot and characters reflect the culture from which they come,
as do the language and mannerisms of the personalities mirroring a respective culture. Even the settings reflect the cultural environment, whereas
the values and mores of the story emphasize those of the original group.

An ethic is always presented in folk tales. Often, the morality lesson
is tempered or obscured through a humorous treatment of human nature.
But, just as often, the lesson is intensified. Sometimes a world is created
out of the wish of poor folk imprisoned in their mundane environments,
although this world is an idealized one of absolute morality. Here cleverness is not a requisite for justice. The good and the humble are always
rewarded with riches or a marriage to royalty, whereas the irrational,
the proud, the foolish are always punished. Magical forces come into
play to ensure aid and protection to the oppressed, and to secure the over-
throw of the wicked and egotistical.

Magical elements nearly always hold the folk tale together and
move it forward. Yet the climate of the tale is not necessarily fantastical
and lovely as in the pure fairy story. The degree to which the tale appears
ethereal and unreal depends on the degree of realism or the sense of reality
possessed by the supernatural character. The other characters' speech as
well as the setting and the tone of the author may further serve to coun-
terbalance or emphasize the magical event.

Origins of Folk Tales

There has been a great deal of exchange of folk tales and folk motifs among cultures. The common situations of primitive, peasant, and noble in different cultures are not an adequate explanation for the countless similarities among the tales of different peoples.

Theorists in the nineteenth century implied that all folk tales had come from a single group. The Grimm brothers suggested the Aryan race. Deslongchamps in France suggested India. Today it has become reasonably well established that no single group is responsible for the origin of all tales (and that all groups have some tales that are completely their own). It is generally agreed, however, that Egypt and India have provided a substantial base of motifs for Indo-European folklore.

Tales were transmitted largely through four groups: the missionaries of Buddhism and Hinduism, the Hebrews, the Romans, and, later, the Crusaders. The animal tales of Buddhism were translated into Persian and Arabic and spread throughout the Islamite lands of North Africa, and then, through trade relations into Western Europe. Jewish migrations contributed Hebrew translations, and the Romans spread Greek myths and legends in their conquests. Significantly, all of them were apt to translate these stories in their terms, and then claim them as their own.

Not only did migrant or conquering people bring home tales from other lands, but they also carried tales to the places they visited. English folk tales, for example, are a mixture of Celtic, Scandinavian, and French motifs, for these are the groups who, through the centuries, settled in England. On the other hand, the Southern Negro folk tale uses African motifs as variations on basic themes.

Types of Folk Tales
and Motifs in Folk Tales

There are five main types of folk tales common to many cultures. They are

(1) the reversal-of-fortune story
(2) the superhero story
(3) the droll story
(4) the animal story
(5) the explanatory story.

These categories are not clear-cut, and many stories fit into several of
them.

THE REVERSAL-OF-FORTUNE STORY

The reversal-of-fortune story is the Cinderella story.
It is the "fairy" story. In it, the oppressed, unrecognized innocent or
beautiful character (who is usually close to nature) is seen for what he is.
Through his nature, or through magic, his situation is overcome, and he
gains in wealth or status through marriage to royalty or monetary reward.
The situation of the character differs from tale to tale, as do the complications and solutions. But the plight of the character and the final outcome
of the tale are invariably the same.

Initial situations. There are several major variants on the initial
situation of the sympathy-evoking character in the reversal story. As in
Perrault's well-known version of "Cinderella," there is the plight of the
innocent and beautiful stepdaughter who is oppressed by her stepmother
and sisters. In "Vasilisa the Beautiful," a Russian tale, a young girl is sent
by her stepmother to the house of a witch since she is too popular with
the young men of the community. The Indian "Punchkin," in which a
wicked stepmother demands the death of seven stepdaughters so that her
own daughters may claim their wealth, is still another example. Similar,
too, are the plights of small children innocent and beautiful in their youth
(Hansel and Gretel), or lovely maidens, either hidden away (Snow White,
Rapunzel) or mismatched (the princess in "Ivan, the Firebird and the
Gray Wolf").

A more dire variant of this motif is the situation in which a person,
child or adult, has been transformed by a malign force and is a prisoner in
his altered shape. The German "The Seven Ravens" and "The Twelve
Brothers" from the Grimm brothers' collections of *märchen*, the Scottish
"The Laidly Worm" and the Irish "The Children of Lir" are examples
of this situation. Each is poignant and pathetic. Indeed, the situation of
the children of Lir is nearly tragic. In some of these tales, the transformed
characters are restored to their original shape through the faith or for-
bearance of a sibling, and all of them eventually live happily ever after.
The children of Lir, however, are doomed to be swans for nine hundred
years, until a marriage between North and South is secured. They sing
sadly of their longing for their passing youth. "Save us, father!" Fionuala
cries, as they pass over their father. "I want to run again and to feel the

soft grass beneath my feet,"[2] sighs the youngest. But they are transformed too late, and have time only to view each other, gray and hoary, and to die.

A less obvious variation on this theme may concern a seemingly foolish (often poor and usually youngest) brother and, less often, sister. For his innocence and goodness of heart, he seems in the eyes of the world to be a ne'er-do-well. Jack of the English tale "Jack and the Beanstalk," "so often full of wonder at all the things he saw that sometimes he forgot to work!"[3] is one.

Similar examples include satisfying tales of rewards, such as "Lazy Jack," whose foolishness makes a princess smile and subsequently wins for him her hand. Another is the young man in the Russian tale "Martin, the Peasant's Son" who takes a bag of sand rather than a bag of silver and gold and sets out to seek his fortune. And, in the lyrical Russian tale "The Language of the Birds," the younger of two sons spends a week in the woods learning the language of birds instead of using an allotment of money in an approved, enterprising way.

The complication. Complications arise in many ways, often out of the initial situation. The innocent one seeks to overcome the evil that he encounters or that has him in its grasp.

Evil presents itself in both human and supernatural form. Sometimes, as in "Cinderella," "Hansel and Gretel," or "Vasilisa the Beautiful," it assumes the form of a wicked and jealous stepmother. The evil person may be wicked and beautiful ("Punchkin") or wicked and ugly ("The Two Sisters" or "Cinderella"). It may be a folk-person who is very old and has magical powers (the Baba Yaga in "Vasilisa the Beautiful") or a magician ("Punchkin" or "Aladdin's Lamp").

Evil can present itself in the form of a supernatural monster ("Jack the Giant Killer") or as a natural animal (the wolf in "Ivan, the Firebird and the Gray Wolf"). It can present itself in the more subtle form of power which is not evil in itself but as an irresistible force. The Irish fairies of the legend "Connla and the Fairy Maiden" and of "Oisin in the Land of Youth" are beautiful, but they make men lose their will. The sea god in the Russian "Sadko" is frightening in the same way. Most subtle of all,

[2]Eileen Colwell, "The Children of Lir," in *A Storyteller's Choice* (New York: Henry Z. Walck, Inc., Publishers, 1964), p. 94. © 1963 by The Bodley Head Ltd. Reprinted by permission of Henry Z. Walck, Inc.
[3]Flora Annie Steel, "Jack and the Beanstalk," in *English Fairy Tales* (New York: The Macmillan Company, 1962), p. 97.

evil appears as a threatening situation such as the one that the hero of the
Russian "Martin, the Peasant's Son" and Grimm's "Six Who Traveled the
World" faced—of having impossible tasks to complete successfully in a
limited amount of time.

Often the innocent himself is responsible for the threat or occurrence.
He exhibits a character flaw of anger or pride or a kind of *hubris* and is
punished for it. The father of seven sons and a daughter in "The Seven
Ravens" angrily wishes them transformed into birds, and is unable to undo
the charm. Ivan of "Ivan, the Firebird and the Gray Wolf," like the boy
in the Pawnee story "The Dun Horse" and like "Cinderella," takes magical aid for granted, and ignores the warning of his magical friend, the
worl, not to dally with the princess he must bring back to the Czar if
he is to save his neck. A kind of pride and overconfidence goads him to
forget his humble position as less than supernatural, and he forfeits his
prize. Usually, the magical creature pities or forgives the hero's "sin" of
pride, but, until he is safe again, the hero is in danger, and the reader feels
he has brought his trouble on himself.

The solution. The complication is resolved as a result of the
central character's initial traits. Either he resolves it through his own
cleverness or shrewdness, or his kindness, prudence, and goodness are
rewarded by magical intervention.

In "The Master Cat" ("Puss-in-Boots"), the clever cat, magical only
in that he speaks, succeeds in winning the hand of the king's daughter for
his master. He plays people and circumstance against each other, and
convinces the king that his master is a rich marquis. He is perceptive
enough to recognize the vulnerable points of those he must manipulate—
the fear that motivates the peasant, the impression that the trappings of
wealth make on wealthy people, and the superficiality of their judgment.

Similarly, in the Irish tale "Hudden and Dudden and Donald
O'Neary," Donald uses cleverness and perception to outwit two brothers
who live near him and are trying to cheat him. He recognizes, first of
all, their dullness—this is also true in the cases of the German "gallant
tailor" and the English Jack the Giant Killer—and plays on it. The
brothers kill his cow, but to compensate for the loss he cuts slits in its
skin, puts coins in the slits, and makes a good profit by selling it as magical.
He convinces the brothers to try to sell the skins of their cattle, and gets
even with them when no one will buy the skins of the greedy brothers'
freshly killed cattle.

One does not necessarily have to work one's own way out of a confrontation with danger or evil, however. A character who is kind or generous or courageous is usually helped by magic. In "Cinderella" the girl is aided by a fairy godmother solely because of her nature and her plight.

More often than not, though, the person helped has done some act of kindness for an elderly person who turns out to be a magical being, or for an animal, or even for an inanimate object. In "Toads and Diamonds," a Perrault tale, the youngest daughter helps an old woman draw some water from a well, and is rewarded by being enabled to speak real jewels. In "How the Raja's Son Won the Princess Labam," an Indian tale, the Raja's son removes a thorn from the foot of a tiger who later helps him when he has impossible tasks to perform. Martin, the peasant's son, is helped for a similar reason. To the scorn of the townsfolk, he saves a dog and cat, and later the grateful animals help him.

"The Language of the Birds" is an interesting variant of the motif of assistance by grateful animals. The boy is taught the language of birds as a gift from birds he has helped. He then has a tool with which to help himself when he is faced with impossible tasks.

A character wins magical aid, too, through just or courageous action. "The Little Hump-Backed Horse" is won for the youngest son because he does not shirk his duty and honestly tries to find out who is stealing his father's grain. Similarly, Ivan, in "Ivan, the Firebird and the Gray Wolf" wins the wolf's respect by courageously confronting him.

THE SUPERHERO STORY

In the superhero tale, the morality and plot complications of the reversal story reappear in a different form. Goodness, courage, and cleverness are presented as virtuous characteristics that win out over evil, selfishness, and stupidity, but instead of bringing a reward to a previously unacclaimed hero through the plot action, they are embodied in an exaggerated hero of enormous physical size and superhuman, even magical capabilities. He can do no wrong and has his magical assistance—the reward of the reversal hero—built in. Although he is fantastic in his exaggerated characteristics, he is described in a realistic way, and embodies the cultural characteristics of his native background as well as the abstract qualities of goodness, courage, and cleverness. Thus, in the eyes of the folk from whose culture he comes, he is doubly a representative of these abstractions, as he is the epitome of their own favorite characteristics.

Here the strapping figure of Paul Bunyan stands squarely beside his ox. Looming larger than in real life, the exaggerated proportions subordinate details of the environment and symbolize the super-hero qualities found in the American tall tales. *From* Legends of Paul Bunyan. *Copyright Alfred A. Knopf, 1947, 1955. Reproduced by permission.*

A fine example of this kind of superhero is Paul Bunyan, the legendary character of Northern lumber camps. Wallace Wadsworth, his chronicler, describes him as follows in "Paul Bunyan's Great Flapjack Griddle":

> Paul Bunyan was of tremendous size and strength, the strongest man that ever swung an ax. . . . the estimate [of his height] which seems most nearly correct is that Paul was so big that ninety-seven ax-handles would just barely measure him from hip to hip.[4]

He is a manly symbol of American ingenuity and freshness. He has curly black hair that he combs with a great crosscut saw and parts with an ax,

---

[4]Wallace Wadsworth, "The Hero of the Lumber Woods," in *Paul Bunyan and His Great Blue Ox* (New York: Doubleday and Co., Inc., 1926, 1944), p. 13.

and a fine black beard. He is invariably proud and sure of himself, yet unaffected and good-natured.

Fin M'Coul and his wife Oonagh are the comparable superheroes of Irish peasant culture. Fin is good-natured and joking and willing to let his wife do the hard work to get rid of the giant Cuhullin; Oonagh is a loving wife, a little on the bossy side, but very shrewd and clever. They have a superlove to match their size, as the following quotation proves:

> "Fin, an' you're welcome home, you darlin' bully," said Oonagh. There followed a smack that is said to have made the waters of the lake at the bottom of the hill curl, as it were, with kindness and sympathy.[5]

Their superkiss generates the sympathy and kindness implicit in Oonagh's warm, colloquial welcome.

Plots in superhero tales. For the most part, the plot of the superhero tale unfolds with humor. Often, as in the reversal story, the

In this dramatic picture a giant's hand stretches to grasp the ship rowed by Finn Mac Cool's men. Aiming at the sensitive mole in the huge palm, the marksman of Finn's crew shoots an arrow that kills the giant.

From The High Deeds of Finn Mac Cool *retold by Rosemary Sutcliff* © *1967, illustrated by Michael Charlton, E. P. Dutton & Co., Inc., New York and The Bodley Head Ltd., London. Illustration* © *1967 by The Bodley Head Ltd.*

---

[5]Joseph Jacobs, "A Legend of Knockmany," in *Celtic Fairy Tales* (New York: G. P. Putnam's Sons, n.d.), p. 173.

hero is involved in combating evil or foolishness. The exaggerated
capabilities of the hero and his use of common sense and cleverness to
outwit his adversary make the humor of the story real. In many instances, however, exaggeration and the possibilities it provides to amuse
are excuse enough for the spinning of a tale.

"Fin M'Coul and the Giant" is a good example of the first kind of
story. Oonagh and Fin find themselves threatened by Cuhullin, a huge
giant who keeps a flattened thunderbolt in his pocket to show his enemies
what he can do. He has heard of Fin, and wants to meet him and fight
with him. Oonagh puts Fin into an enormous baby cradle, and through
her own ingenuity, impresses Cuhullin with the strength of her "absent"
husband, until Cuhullin flees, glad to have missed an encounter with
such a brute as Fin. Her bravado is brilliant! She fills bread with iron
griddles and tells the giant that Fin will not eat it because it is too soft.
Then she exchanges it for a dough bread and gives it to the "baby."
The giant's dullness gives the reader great delight, but it is Oonagh's coup
in the tradition of the Irish wife and Fin's good-natured sitting pretty—
again, in Irish tradition—while admiring his wife, that charms and entertains most conclusively.

"The Boomer Fireman's Fast Sooner Hound" is an interesting variation of the first kind of story. It is not the fireman who is the superhero
here; it is his hound. The fireman, who applies for a railroad job, is told
that his dog cannot accompany him in the car. The Boomer answers that
the dog is used to running alongside the car:

> "Why, he ain't no trouble," said the Boomer. "He just runs alongside, and
> when I'm on a freight run he chases around a little in the fields to pass the
> time away. . . . It's a little bit tiresome on him having to travel at such
> a slow gait, but that Sooner would do anything to stay close by me. . . ."[6]

The fireman's implied exaggeration is that the Sooner runs faster
than a train, and it is the slow drawl that takes this so completely for granted, that amuses. The hound must prove his speed to the railroad against
the enormous odds that the company puts up. It is the hound's easy victory
contrasted with the fast and frantic efforts of the railroad to prevent his
victory that amuse. The victory is not exactly over a foolish or an evil
enemy except in the context of the story. A disbeliever in the exaggerated
abilities of a superhero is certainly foolish, and those who stand between a
man and his dog are almost always evil.

---

[6]Jack Conroy, "The Boomer Fireman's Fast Sooner Hound," in *A Treasury of American Folklore*, ed. B. A. Botkin (New York: Crown Publishers, 1944), p. 534.

"The Boomer Fireman's Fast Sooner Hound" is a story that fits into the second group of superhero stories, too. But "Paul Bunyan's Great Flapjack Griddle" is the classic example of the story written strictly to amuse through exaggeration. Paul, who is worried about getting enough flapjacks for his men to eat, has a great griddle built. "So big was this griddle," Wadsworth says, "that the cookees greased it with telephone poles, on the ends of which were tied great bunches of gunny sacks for swabs."[7] The story revolves around the unwieldiness of the griddle and Paul's difficulties in transporting it to the camp and in flipping the flapjacks. He settles on using dynamite (when block-and-tackle fails) to provide his loggers with the best and the most food around. The story ends with a picture of thousands of thousands of men seated at miles and miles of table, all of them eating flapjacks. Paul's ingenuity and the preposterousness of his plights and solutions have endeared Paul to Americans as a folk hero.

THE DROLL STORY

The "droll" story presents a more realistic world than that of the reversal or superhero tales. Its ethic is implicit as it presents the world with its fallible population. As the play of vanity, hypocrisy, cleverness, deceit, and foolishness is presented, the reader is not told what values must prevail before people will stop misbehaving. It is usually obvious, but the teller of the droll tale does not wish to moralize. He seems to enjoy people as they are, and to get a good laugh out of their little deceptions.

The humor of the story generally derives from either the misfortunes of a foolish person who deserves to be laughed at or from the reader's recognition of himself in characters who represent or characterize the folk.

"Hudden and Dudden and Donald O'Neary," an Irish tale, is of the first type. Donald's outwitting of the two brothers who seek to ruin him and their misfortunes at his hand are funny because of Donald's ingenuity, the brothers' unthinking cooperation in their own downfall, and because the brothers so roundly deserve what they get.

The English tale "The Three Sillies" is an example of the second type as well as the first. A young girl's betrothed enters her home and finds her and her parents crying. The girl, sent to the cellar to draw some cider, had spotted a wooden mallet suspended from the beam of the ceiling. She

---

[7]Wadsworth, "Paul Bunyan," *op. cit.*, pp. 102–103.

had begun to speculate on what might happen if the mallet were to drop.

> "For," thought she, "supposing him and me was married, and supposing
> we was to have a son, and supposing he were to grow up to be a man,
> and supposing he were to come down to draw cider like as I'm doing,
> and supposing the mallet were to fall on his head and kill him, how dread-
> ful it would be!"[8]

Her romantic picture of the tragedy becomes so real to her that she
begins to weep. Her parents have become so involved that they start
weeping, too. The youth rejects the girl and says he will return to her
only if he can find three people more silly than they. The rest of the tale
relates his episodic encounters with three greater sillies. He returns to the
girl, and, having acquired greater insight into human nature, he feels
that though she is romantic and silly, she is not as silly as many other folk.
The humor of the story is in the silliness that the youth finds during his
adventures, and in his and our final understanding of the young girl's
romantic silliness.

Occasionally a story occurs in which the characters are more than
sketched in, and in which the humor lies in the folk-manner and language
of the character. "King O'Toole and His Goose" is such a story. The
King, except for his title, is very much of the land. He is shrewd and a
little distrustful, tactless, and direct. His speech and manner are unpolished
and full of brogue. The story is about the King's encounter with St.
Kavin when the saint, disguised as a man, offers to give renewed life to the
King's sole diversion, a goose. The humor of the tale is in the King's
manner and speech and in their incongruity with his station as King. The
King meets St. Kavin as he is walking around a nearby lake.

> "God save you," says the king to the young man.
> "God save you kindly, King O'Toole," says the young man.
> "True for you," says the king. "I am King O'Toole," says he, "prince and
> plennypennytinchery of these parts," says he; "but how came ye to know
> that?" says he.
> "Oh, never mind," says St. Kavin.[9]

The casual ways of both the King and St. Kavin work into their extraordinary meeting. The King's uppity snappiness and his undisguised sur-

---

[8]Flora Annie Steel, "The Three Sillies," in *English Fairy Tales* (New York: The
Macmillan Company, 1962), p. 73.
[9]Jacobs, *op. cit.*, pp. 103–104.

prise are humorous to the reader, who knows of St. Kavin's presence. St. Kavin's retort, never condescending, always in the same tone as the King's, amuses the reader further.

Most amusing, though, is the fact that the King's manner—and St. Kavin's, too—does not change at all, once the King has found out St. Kavin's identity. His tone is the same gruff, terse, straightforward one he used before. It is more humble, but the King still seems to be talking to a fellow country person:

> "Oh, queen of heaven!" says the king, "... is it the great Saint Kavin," says he, "that I've been discoursing all this time without knowing it," says he, "all as one as if he was a lump of a *gossoon*?—and so you're a saint?" says the king.
>
> "I am," says Saint Kavin.
>
> "By Jabers, I thought I was only talking to a dacent boy," says the king.
>
> "Well, you know the difference now," says the saint.[10]

Seldom does the narrator of a tale enter into the effect his characters have on the reader in the way he does here. It is his interjection of "he says," and his colloquialisms, which are so charming and which were so familiar to the original listener.

THE ANIMAL STORY

The animal story resembles the droll in its presentation of insights into human nature and the ways of the world. It too points to the realities of the world rather than presenting an idealization.

The animal story had its beginnings as an instructive religious parable (the Buddhist *Jatakas*, the Hebrew *Midrash*, the Hindu *Panchatantra*) or moral tale (Aesop's fables). It developed as a kind of humorous folk literature with animal characters who resemble humans in their actions. The degree of development in the animal characters and the degree of direct moralizing or humor in the tale depends upon its original purpose.

"The Lion and the Crane," a parable from the Buddhist *Jatakas*, and Aesop's "The Ant and the Grasshopper" are similar in character depiction and in presentation of a moral. In the first story, a crane saves a lion who has a bone caught in his throat by flying into the lion's mouth and fetching the bone, but only after the lion promises that he will not harm him. Having done the deed, the crane expects gratitude, but the proud lion says that the bird should be glad to be alive. The crane, who is

---

[10]*Ibid.*, p. 107.

Buddha, sings a song berating the lion's pride. In the latter, a grasshopper, who fiddled through the summer while his ant friend industriously stored food, comes shivering to his friend in the winter, and pleads for food. The ant says that he should not have fiddled and shows him no mercy.

In both of these stories, the characters are stylized embodiments of human traits and vehicles of the moral. The lion represents pride; the crane symbolizes mildness and pitying kindness. The ant stands for industry; the grasshopper seems to embody a carefree, imprudent attitude. The characters have no individuality, though they do speak. It is the narrator, of whom we are conscious, rather than the character.

That the story is a moral lesson is clear. In both cases the tale is too brief for the reader to mistake either its intention or the moral itself. In the first we see that pride is not desirable; the second shows that prudence and industry are desirable. However, there is a difference in the way the moral is implemented in each. In the first, the crane (Buddha) *tells* us that the lion's pride is not commendable. In the second, we see through the outcome of the story that imprudence is foolish. Showing rather than telling occurs more and more completely as the animal story moves away from its religious beginnings.

"Why Mr. Possum Loves Peace," an Uncle Remus story chronicled by Joel Chandler Harris, is an animal story developed as humorous folk literature. Though far removed from the religious parable, it has many similarities to it.

The characters in the tale are far more developed than those of any parable or fable. Brer Coon is a tough fighter, ready to defend himself: "'Ef he [a dog] run up onter me, I lay I give 'im one twis',' sezee."[11] Brer Possum is cowardly and not above lying to protect his honor. He may not even confess his cowardliness to himself. Mr. Dog attacks the two, and Brer Possum simply lies down and leaves the fight to Brer Coon. Brer Coon meets him later and refuses to "soshate" with Brer Possum. "I ain't runnin' wid cowerds deze days,"[12] he says. Brer Possum indignantly maintains that he is not a coward but ticklish. He claims that the dog's attack hit him in such a way as to incapacitate him completely: "I laughed twel I ain't had no use er my lim's."[13] Righteously, he maintains, "Git me in a row whar dey ain't no ticklin' 'lowed, en I'm your man."[14]

---

[11] Joel Chandler Harris, "Why Mr. Possum Loves Peace," in *Uncle Remus* (New York: Appleton-Century-Crofts, 1929), p. 12.

[12] *Ibid.*, p. 14.

[13] *Ibid.*, p. 15.

[14] *Ibid.*, p. 15.

Here is demonstrated the strategy of Brer Rabbit in outwitting Brer Wolf. Preserving the spirit of the folktale, the pictures reflect the verve and vitality found in much of American folklore.

From Uncle Remus, His Songs and His Sayings *by Joel Chandler Harris, illustrated by A. B. Frost. D. Appleton-Century, Co., Inc.*

Neither character speaks very much, but the lines each has and the narrator's description of their interaction reveal a real personality. Their speeches identify them as Southern folk of a certain type, and the way they react to each other establishes them further as real characters, but they are still symbolic in the manner of the fable. Each represents one or more characteristics, and we see these as well as the characters.

The story is told by Uncle Remus much more for the pleasure of telling the little boy about those funny personages, Brer Coon and Brer Possum, than for making any moral point, as "one should not lie." His whole story expresses Brer Possum's hypocrisy and its obviousness to everyone but the righteous possum. Nevertheless, this tale is a development of the parable and fable.

THE EXPLANATORY TALE

The explanatory tale provides a reason for natural phenomena. This kind of tale is generally narrated in a straightforward, matter-of-fact tone, but its object may not always be a sincere explanation. Sometimes the description of an occurrence is a way of moralizing; sometimes it is a flight of charming fantasy.

Originating in primitive religion, the tale represents one way of coming to terms with an environment. However, it becomes difficult, even in primitive culture, to distinguish how much of the tale's explanation is believed and how much is a moral lesson or perpetuation of a tradition or just a tale.

The Pawnee story "Why the Coyote Is the Color of the Ground" is an example of a relatively primitive culture's moral lesson. According to the tale, the coyote passed an oasis and saw his reflection in the water. He wished to be blue and was turned to that color but when he returned to the desert, he had lost his natural protective coloring and could be seen running like a blue streak. He regretted the change in color, and so he became the color of the sand, instead of his original beautiful gray color. This is a warning against envy and an encouragement to accept oneself. It is presented in a straightforward, believing tone, but the moral is so pronounced and the character is so plainly a vehicle that the tale is obviously a lesson.

The German *märchen* "The Straw, the Coal and the Bean" is a *pourquoi* tale that at the same time is both a moral lesson and a good story. It tells how the bean got its black seam by laughing at the plight of a straw and a coal who could not successfully cross a bridge. The moral is lightly put: the bean splits his side for laughing at others' misfortunes, but he is repaired by a compassionate tailor. He bears the scar of his "sin," but he recovers. In this story, too, the characters are developed only to further the plot. As in the animal story, they stand for characteristics.

The folk atmosphere of these tales that makes them such an accurate reflection of a culture is found in their settings and in the creatures and situations depicted. The Western Indian chooses from his environment the coyote and builds his story around a lesson vital to him—survival in the desert. From the hearth-cottage situation comes the German peasant's tale about beans, straw, and coal and their planned escape from an old woman's hearth.

Component Elements

The component elements of these five kinds of tales form the framework for most modern children's fiction. Story plots follow one or more of these patterns. A hero confronts a complication and through his or someone else's ingenuity, or by magic, overcomes his adversary. Or a central character deals with a situation imposed by magical intervention. Some plots use the patterns of the animal tale and the explanatory tale. Talking animal and human characters in realistic situations point to the ways of people and of the world. Realism rather than fantasy is emphasized.

Simple folk characters are ideal for children, partly because they need clearly defined characters with set positions, and partly because of their preoccupation with the plot action of a story rather than with descriptive elements.

The morality or ethic, which is invariably present in the folk tale, also appears in children's fiction. It is subtly covered over with humor or with engaging characters and plot, or it is made plain by the narrator that the child is to "see what happens if—." It is the nature of the adult's relation to the child that he should want to tell the child what is good and what is not, or that he should provide him with moral lessons to point out that goodness and cleverness are commendable and that duplicity and wickedness are not. The exaggerated justice and the often humorous results of cleverness versus duplicity, in any case, appeal to a child's desire for action.

The whimsy and delicacy of the fairy story, the devices of broad comedy and exaggeration that the folk tale employs, appear again and again as essential tools of the modern children's writer.

The Narrator in the Folk Tale and in the Modern Story

In the folk tale, one is almost incapable of locating "the narrator." There is a voice speaking, and it reveals a good deal about itself in its emphasis on certain parts of the story, but it is the voice of many people. The story has gone from person to person, from oral to written form and back again, almost obscuring a single voice. This is responsible for the straightforward, matter-of-fact tone that works to lend all but the most fantastic tales credibility. It is responsible for the undecorated, terse style of the folk tale.

The "literary" folk/fairy tale, the tale that has a single author and is generally fairly recent, often is written in a more poetic style. Its single romantic author, nostalgic about the innocence of animals and children, and sentimental about the whimsy of fairies and magic, creates a work in which each sentence is a complicated flight of imagination. Or the sophisticated author uses the vehicle of the folk or fairy tale for adults, subordinating the action of the story to a satiric development of characters.

The narrator in the children's story bridges the gap between the folk tale narrator and the "literary" tale narrator, but his effect is closer to the former's.

For example, in *Charlotte's Web*, a modern fantasy, E. B. White is unobtrusive as narrator, and his presentation is simple and straightforward. His characters serve his plot rather than himself. One is aware of his delightful sense of humor and overwhelming human sympathy—he is as fond of his characters as we are—but he gives his characters an identity of their own.

A. A. Milne is not quite so unobtrusive. His characters are delightful and do have identity, but one can always hear him behind them on a sophisticated level telling us what people are like. He does try to maintain the simplicity of the folk story in his narration, however.

The narrator's role in the works of these two authors is reminiscent of the Perrault tales written by single authors in the court of Louis XIV, but the language adheres more closely to the simplicity of the common folk tale. The teller's position, however, changes depending on the tale, and a story for children may fail because of the satiric or descriptive focus of the prose, which interferes with the action of the story and with a child's interest and understanding.

In summary, the folk tale, a simple moral story, makes an invaluable contribution to modern children's literature. The reader's familiarity with the patterns of folk stories presented in this chapter will confirm this.

In a plot of action, comedy, and romance, in the introduction of simple characters, in the use of magic and of subtle or exaggerated moralizing, the folk tale provides the basis for modern children's literature.

References

ARBUTHNOT, MAY HILL, "Old Magic," in *Children and Books*, 3rd ed., Chicago: Scott, Foresman & Company, 1964.

COLWELL, EILEEN, *A Storyteller's Choice*. New York: Henry Z. Walck, Inc., Publishers, 1964.

FITZGERALD, BURDETTE S. *World Tales for Creative Dramatics and Storytelling*. Englewood Cliffs, N.J.: Prentice-Hall, Inc., 1962.

GARRY, RALPH, F. B. RAINSBERRY, and CHARLES WINICK, eds., "The World of the Young Viewer," in *For the Young Viewer*. New York: McGraw-Hill Book Company, 1962.

HUBER, MIRIAM BLANTON, "Folk Tales: Value, Origin and Use," in *Story and Verse for Children*. New York: The Macmillan Company, 1965.

HUGHES, LANGSTON, and ARNA BONTEMPS, *Book of Negro Folklore*. New York: Dodd, Mead & Co., 1958.

JOHNSON, EDNA, *et al.*, "Folk Tales," in *Anthology of Children's Literature*. Boston: Houghton Mifflin Company, 1935, 1948.

SAWYER, RUTH, *The Way of the Storyteller*, New York: The Viking Press, Inc., 1942, 1962.

THOMPSON, STITH, *The Folktale*. New York: The Dryden Press, Inc., 1946.

Multiethnic Folk Tales in English

COLLECTIONS WITH MULTIETHNIC BACKGROUNDS

TOLD UNDER THE MAGIC UMBRELLA
Compiled by the Association for Childhood Education Literature Committee. The Macmillan Company, 1939.
Well-loved folk tales and other stories compiled for their imaginative and realistic qualities. Tales cover a wide range of appeal.

THE TALKING TREE AND OTHER STORIES
Selected and told by Augusta Baker. Illustrated by Johannes Troyer. J. B. Lippincott Co., 1955.
Twenty-eight tried and true favorites from fifteen out-of-print folk tale collections, selected by testing children's reactions during story hours. Beautiful pictures add dash to the tellings.

THE EARTH IS ON A FISH'S BACK
Told by Natalia Belting. Illustrated by Esta Nesbitt. Holt, Rinehart & Winston, Inc., 1965.
Tales of beginnings taken from the folklore of the world and retold with regard for their sources.

THE SUN IS A GOLDEN EARRING
By Natalia Belting. Illustrated by Bernarda Bryson. Holt, Rinehart & Winston, Inc., 1962.
Poetic images of men's wondering about the heavens, beautifully illustrated and collected from all over the world.

THE ELEPHANT'S BATHTUB
Told by Frances Carpenter. Illustrated by Hans Guggenheim. Doubleday & Company, Inc., 1962.
Twenty-four tales representing sixteen countries of the Far East are told in simple, graphic style with unique and humorous black-and-white drawings.

RIDE WITH THE SUN
Edited by Harold Courlander for UN
Women's Guild. Illustrated by
Roger Duvoisin. McGraw-Hill
Book Company, 1955.

Sixty stories, each from a different country in the United Nations as of 1955, divided by continent into categories. Rich illustrations add charm and authenticity to backgrounds.

TALES TOLD AGAIN
Told by Walter de la Mare.
Illustrated by Alan Howard. Alfred
A. Knopf, Inc., 1961.

Nineteen familiar stories with lively conversation and characters of universal appeal. Vigorous illustrations bring the time-honored tales to life.

HOW THE PEOPLE SANG the
MOUNTAINS UP: HOW AND WHY
STORIES
Selected and retold by Maria Leach.
Illustrated by Glen Rounds. The
Viking Press, Inc., 1967.

People everywhere have their explanations of how and why things are the way they are. A distinguished folklorist has included in this dignified collection for older children the serious and mythical, the entertaining and legendary, in a world-wide assortment of how and why tales. Included here are stories about earth, sea, sky, man, animals, birds, fish, plants, constellations and many others in sometimes amusing, sometimes reverent retellings.

AFRICAN INFLUENCE

AFRICAN WONDER TALES
Told by Frances Carpenter.
Illustrated by Joseph Escourido.
Doubleday & Company, Inc., 1963.

Twenty-four African tales told with skill and matched with handsome illustrations.

THE COW-TAIL SWITCH
Told by Harold Courlander and
George Herzog. Illustrated by Madye

Lee Chastain. Holt, Rinehart &
Winston, Inc., 1962.

Twenty tales revealing customs and ways of thought of West African peoples through a philosophical as well as fanciful turn of the stories. Strong, silhouette illustrations capture the jungle-village mood.

THE COCONUT THIEVES
Told by Catharine Fournier.
Illustrated by Janina Domanska.
Charles Scribner's Sons, 1964.

A marvelous African folk tale in picture book format about a dog and a turtle who outwit a selfish leopard. Pictures in near-primitive style add charm and humor to this book.

WAKAIMA AND THE CLAY MAN
Told by E. B. Kalibala and M. G.
Davis. Longmans, Green & Co.,
Inc., 1946.

A handsome collection of Baganda tales from East Africa that reveals the origins of the "Uncle Remus" collections.

MIDDLE EASTERN AND PERSIAN INFLUENCES

TALES OF THE HODJA
Retold by Charles Downing.
Illustrated by William Papas. Henry
Z. Walck, Inc., Publishers, 1965.

Vignettes of folklore from the Middle East personifying the historical and celebrated Nasreddin Hodja in his shifting role of preacher, magistrate, dupe. Brilliant, full-color illustrations.

TEN THOUSAND DESERT SWORDS
Retold by Russell Davis and Brent
Ashabranner. Illustrated by Leonard
Everett Fisher. Little, Brown & Co.,
1965.

The epic story of a Bedouin tribe drawn from the legends of the Bani Hilal with the essence and sweep of an Arabian romance.

THE SULTAN'S FOOL AND OTHER
NORTH AFRICAN TALES
Compiled and told by Robert

*Gilstrap and Irene Estabrook.
Illustrated by Robert Greco. Holt,
Rinehart & Winston, Inc., 1958.*

Wit and wisdom mark these tales whose illustrations breathe life and light into lesser-known stories from the once Dark Continent.

ARABIAN NIGHTS
*Told by Andrew Lang. Illustrated
by Vera Bock. Longmans, Green &
Co., Inc., 1951.*

The expertly told tales are enhanced by beautiful pictures. Capturing an aura of mystery and elegance, the stories unfold with artistic grace.

THE FIRE ON THE MOUNTAIN AND
OTHER ETHIOPIAN STORIES
*Told by Harold Courlander and Wolf
Leslau. Illustrated by Robert Kane.
Holt, Rinehart & Winston, Inc.,
1950.*

Well-told tales of many kinds that represent cultures from Africa, the Middle East, the West, and some very primitive groups. Spicy with local flavor, the tales are given an added dash of interest by the stylized drawings.

THE FEARSOME INN
*Told by Isaac Bashevis Singer.
Translated by the author and
Elizabeth Shub. Illustrated by
Nonny Hogrogian. Charles Scribner's
Sons, 1967.*

The eternal struggle between good and evil is treated in this tale of enchantment radiating the spirit and imagination of Eastern Jewry. The story is told about three girls who are held captive as servants by an evil witch and her half-devil husband. When three young men arrive at the inn where the girls are held captive, the evil couple attempts to apply their usual witchcraft. But one ingenious young man imprisons the couple in a magic circle and forces the husband and wife to return to the underworld where they belong. Their departure brings about a marriage between the young men and the captive

maidens, and the once fearsome inn becomes a haven for all travelers.

PERSIAN FOLK AND FAIRY TALES
*Retold by Anne Sinclair Mehdevi.
Illustrated by Paul E. Kennedy.
Alfred A. Knopf, Inc., 1965.*

A beautiful blend of fun and fantasy spun from the repertory of Nana Roosie, a Persian nurse. Paisley-decked pictures effectively translate much of the mood.

NORTH AMERICAN INDIAN INFLUENCE

DOWN FROM THE LONELY
MOUNTAIN
*Retold by Jane Louise Curry.
Illustrated by Enrico Arno.
Harcourt, Brace & World, Inc.,
1965.*

Twelve animal tales retold with simplicity and directness. Collected from California Indian lore, the tales show care in selection, retelling, and accurate illustrating.

ONCE UPON A TOTEM
*Told by Christie Harris.
Illustrated by John Frazer Mills.
Atheneum Publishers, 1963.*

Five stories of the West Coast Indians—the people of the totem poles—with interesting illustrations.

THE WORLD OF MANABOZHO
*Told by Thomas B. Leekley.
Illustrated by Yeffe Kimball.
Vanguard Press, 1965.*

Fifteen tales of the Chippewa Indians and the wonder worker Manabozho. Drawn from Algonquin mythology, the tales are true to an ancient civilization.

AMERICAN INFLUENCE (UNITED STATES)

PECOS BILL, THE GREATEST
COWBOY OF ALL TIME
Told by James Cloyd Bowman.

Illustrated by Laura Bannon. Albert Whitman & Co., 1937.

A hilariously funny tall tale of a cowboy hero whose achievements ride out of the picture book and into the imagination of young readers.

HIGH WIND FOR KANSAS
Told by Mary Calhoun.
Illustrated by W. T. Mars.
William Morrow & Co., Inc., 1965.

A tall tale of Windwagon Jones's invention that captures the flavor and humor of the Midwest.

THE JACK TALES
Edited by Richard Chase.
Illustrated by Berkeley Williams, Jr.
Houghton Mifflin Company, 1943.

A wonderful collection of Appalachian folklore featuring Jack as conqueror of giants, dragons, and kings. Authentic illustrations stress the integrity of the stories. Very good for reading aloud or for storytelling hours.

PECOS BILL AND THE MUSTANG
Told by Harold W. Felton.
Illustrated by Leonard Shortall.
Prentice-Hall, Inc., 1965.

One of the wildest tall tales to come out of the great plains of the West. Told in straightforward, exaggerated style, the story is enhanced by gay pictures in pink and gold. Rip-roaring adventure is packed in this book about the great pacing mustang and wild longhorn cattle that roamed the plains.

AMERICAN NEGRO INFLUENCE

THE COMPLETE TALES OF UNCLE REMUS
Compiled by Richard Chase from the Joel Chandler Harris collection.
Illustrated by Arthur Frost and

others. Houghton Mifflin Company, 1955.

A marvelous collection of authentic folklore of the American Negro. Whimsy and folklore humor is spun with dialect that lends itself to reading aloud or storytelling. Homespun pictures complete the collection.

UNCLE REMUS
Retold by Miriam B. Huber.
Illustrated by Arthur Frost.
Appleton-Century-Crofts, 1935.

Charming animal stories with endearing pictures of lovable Brer Rabbit who is "sassy as a jay bird" and so much a trickster that young children love to identify with him.

BIG ROAD WALKER
Compiled and told by Eula Duncan.
Illustrated by Fritz Eichenberg.
Frederick A. Stokes Company, 1940.

Negro tall tales told with superb ease. Dialect enlivens the humor of the story tracing the giant steps of Big Road Walker as he goes "steppin' a mile a step."

JOHN HENRY AND HIS HAMMER
Told by Harold W. Felton.
Illustrated by Aldren A. Watson.
Alfred A. Knopf, Inc., 1950.

Based on the authentic accounts of John Henry's strength and powerful undertakings, this well-illustrated book makes the stories convincing.

CENTRAL AND SOUTH AMERICAN INDIAN AND LATIN AMERICAN INFLUENCE

THE TIGER AND THE RABBIT AND OTHER TALES
Told by Pura Belpré. Illustrated by Tomie de Paola. J. B. Lippincott Co., 1965.

Folksy tales resembling fables are matched with equally charming pictures. A vein of humor runs through many of these Latin American tales.

PEREZ AND MARTINA
Told by Pura Belpré. Illustrated by Carlos Sánchez. Frederick Warne & Co., Inc., 1961.

Transmitted by an oral tradition, this charming folk tale of Puerto Rico recounts in straightforward language interesting anecdotes about Perez and Martina. Authentic drawings add to the story.

THE BOY WHO COULD DO ANYTHING
Told by Anita Brenner. Illustrated by Jean Charlot. Scott, Foresman & Company, 1942.

Twenty-four Mexican tales, many of them of ancient Indian origins, told with legendary grace and ease. Strong Mexican designs are in keeping with the stories.

TALES FROM SILVER LANDS
Gathered and told by Charles Finger. Illustrated by Paul Honoré. Doubleday & Company, Inc., 1924.

Outstanding folk tales of South American Indians told with superb simplicity and colored woodcuts. A winner of the Newbery Medal.

STORIES FROM THE AMERICAS
Edited by Frank Henius. Illustrated by Leo Politi. Charles Scribner's Sons, 1944.

Twenty folk tales, some with legendary quality, drawn from folklore popular among peoples in Mexico and Central and South America.

THE KING OF THE MOUNTAINS: A TREASURY OF LATIN AMERICAN FOLK STORIES
Told by M. A. Jagendorf and R. S. Boggs. Illustrated by Carybé. Vanguard Press, 1960.

Over fifty tales from a wide variety of Latin American countries told with charm and illustrated with a flair.

THE BURRO BENEDICTO AND OTHER FOLK TALES AND LEGENDS OF MEXICO
Told and illustrated by Philip D. Jordan. Coward-McCann, Inc., 1960.

Lovely legends and folk tales, with handsome color illustrations, based on Aztec and Christian beliefs.

ANGLO-EUROPEAN INFLUENCE

English

DICK WHITTINGTON AND HIS CAT
Told and illustrated by Marcia Brown. Charles Scribner's Sons, 1950.

A classic tale of a young orphaned boy's rise to wealth and high office in London. Strikingly bold linoleum cuts are vividly imposed upon clear white backgrounds to depict and tell a medieval story.

CHANTICLEER AND THE FOX
Retold and illustrated by Barbara Cooney. Thomas Y. Crowell Company, 1958.

Magnificent illustrations illumine the clear, simple retelling of Chaucer's tale.

COCK ROBIN
Collected and illustrated by Barbara Cooney. Charles Scribner's Sons, 1965.

A delightful recitation of the well-known Cock Robin tale and the not-so-well-known story of the Cock Robin and Jenny Wren wedding. Outstanding illustrations bring rare beauty to this narrative poetry.

DON'T COUNT YOUR CHICKS
Told and illustrated by Ingri and Edgar Parin d'Aulaire. Doubleday & Company, Inc., 1943.

Bright, clear pictures support the sturdy text of this homespun tale, which is found in other cultures as often as in English editions.

A Penny a Day
Told by Walter de la Mare.
Illustrated by Paul Kennedy. Alfred
A. Knopf, Inc., 1960.

Six English stories told by a master story-teller. Fine illustrations are as high in quality as the distinctive selection of tales from English folk literature.

The Three Wishes
Retold and illustrated by Paul.
Galdone. McGraw-Hill Book
Company, 1961.

A classic folk tale with wonderfully comic illustrations.

King Arthur and His Noble Knights
Written by Mary MacLeod.
Illustrated by Henry Pitz. J. B.
Lippincott Co., 1949.

A direct and simple version of the Arthurian legends that follows Malory closely. Small but spirited colored illustrations.

Tom Tit Tot
An old English folk tale illustrated by
Evaline Ness. Charles Scribner's
Sons, 1965.

Vigorous woodcuts lend vitality to the old tale of a girl who ate five pies. Language and pictures of a high order distinguish this picture storybook.

Mr. Miacca: An English Folk Tale
Retold and illustrated by Evaline
Ness. Holt, Rinehart & Winston,
Inc., 1967.

A vigorous retelling of what happens to disobedient children who go around the corner when they have been warned against doing so. Here the imminent results are told in a humorously scary story with its pictorial equivalent. The book relates how Mr. Miacca boils and eats bad little boys who get in his way. Twice he catches Tommy Grimes, pops him in his bag, and carries him home for dinner. Tommy's

resourcefulness in escaping, plus a richly glowing cast in a Victorian mold, makes this Old English nursery tale sheer delight.

Hector Protector and As I Went over the Water
Told and illustrated by Maurice
Sendak. Harper & Row, Publishers,
1965.

Superbly imaginative illustrations interpret the humorous story behind the simple Mother Goose verses. A beautiful blend of colors distinguish and enliven the old tale of rebellious Hector and the aggressive captain Victor.

Beowulf the Warrior
Retold by Ian Serraillier. Illustrated
by Severin. Henry Z. Walck, Inc.,
Publishers, 1961.

In this treatment of the oldest English verse epic, the author closely follows the pattern of the original poem with eight hundred lines of striking, well-wrought verse. Excellent stylized illustrations.

The Hound of Ulster
Retold by Rosemary Sutcliff.
Illustrated by Victor Ambrus. E. P.
Dutton & Co., Inc., 1963.

A lyric and imaginative rendering of the Cuchullin saga and its Champion of Ulster.

Scottish

Gaelic Ghosts
Told by Sorche Nic Leodhas.
Illustrated by Nonny Hogrogian.
Holt, Rinehart & Winston, Inc.,
1963.

The author has collected ten Scottish Highland stories from her family and native storytellers. Superb woodcuts.

Ghosts Go Haunting
Told by Sorche Nic Leodhas.
Illustrated by Nonny Hogrogian.
Holt, Rinehart & Winston, Inc.,
1965.

Ten Scottish tales of wit and charm in the latest collection by an award-winning storyteller.

HEATHER AND BROOM: TALES OF
THE SCOTTISH HIGHLANDS
Told by Sorche Nic Leodhas.
Illustrated by Consuelo Joerns. Holt,
Rinehart & Winston, Inc., 1960.
Eight Scottish Highland tales by a story-teller of grace, inspiration, and Celtic background. Lovely pictures.

THISTLE AND THYME. TALES AND
LEGENDS FROM SCOTLAND
Told by Sorche Nic Leodhas.
Illustrated by Evaline Ness. Holt,
Rinehart & Winston, Inc., 1962.
Ten tales of the Scottish Highlands, well illustrated, and lyrically written.

ALL IN THE MORNING EARLY
Told by Sorche Nic Leodhas.
Illustrated by Evaline Ness. Holt,
Rinehart & Winston, Inc., 1963.
A lovely Scottish folk tale about a little boy who goes to the mill one morning and picks up an unusual collection of companions on the way. An outstanding book in picture book format.

Irish

LITTLE DERMOT AND THE THIRSTY
STONES
Compiled and illustrated by
Richard Bennett. Coward-McCann,
Inc., 1953.
Eight wonderful Irish folk tales superbly told with special appeal for younger children. Attractively illustrated.

THE KING OF IRELAND'S SON
Told by Padraic Colum. Illustrated
by Willy Pogány. The Macmillan
Company, 1962.
Beautiful retellings of the doings of a

brave young lad in seven Irish folk tales that breathe the genius of storytelling.

CHILDREN OF THE SALMON AND
OTHER IRISH FOLK TALES
Selected and translated by Eileen
O'Faolain. Illustrated by Trina
Hyman. Little, Brown & Co., 1965.
An attractive collection of Irish tales sparked by the gaiety of the illustrations. Particularly suited for storytelling.

THE WONDER SMITH AND HIS
SON
Retold by Ella Young. Illustrated
by Boris Artzybasheff. Longmans,
Green & Co., Inc., 1955.
A series of adventures of the ancient Irish folk hero, Gubbaum Saor, retold by a master with great spirit and inspiration. Stylized drawings provide appropriate backdrop.

Welsh

WELSH LEGENDARY TALES
Told by Elisabeth Sheppard-Jones.
Illustrated by Paul Hogarth. Thomas
Nelson (Edinburgh), 1959.
A collection of lovely Welsh folk tales with beautiful illustrations in color.

CENTRAL EUROPEAN INFLUENCE

Dutch

LEGENDS AND FOLKTALES OF
HOLLAND
Told by Adele Deleeuw. Illustrated
by Paul Kennedy. Thomas Nelson
(Edinburgh), 1963.
Twenty-eight neatly turned tales by an author who has done scholarly work in

studying the origins of the tales. Beautifully written and sympathetically illustrated.

French

STONE SOUP
*Told and illustrated by Marcia
Brown. Charles Scribner's Sons,
1947.*
All the flavor of French soup and a roadside town caught in a wonderful tale about three soldiers who outwit the townsfolk by making soup of stones. In picture book dress, the book links the reader with a lovely land.

THIS IS THE HOUSE THAT JACK
BUILT
*Told and illustrated by Antonio
Frasconi. Harcourt, Brace &
World, Inc., 1958.*
Tidy woodblock pictures in green, yellow, and pink light up the pages of a book full of humor and imagination. The use of French adds interest and local color.

A TREASURY OF FRENCH TALES
*Told and translated by Mary Mian.
Illustrated by Pauline Baynes.
Houghton Mifflin Company, 1954.*
Forty tales are told with vigor and humor and enlivened by clever pictures.

German

NIBBLE, NIBBLE MOUSEKIN
*Told and illustrated by Joan Walsh
Anglund. Harcourt, Brace & World,
Inc., 1962.*
A gentle retelling of the Hansel and Gretel folk tale with lovely pictures that match the text in simplicity and grace.

MILLIONS OF CATS
Written and illustrated by Wanda

Gág. Coward-McCann, Inc., 1928.
The flavor of an old German folk tale is expressed in the rhythmic text and illustrations of a picture book designed in black and white. Tracing the wants and fulfillment of an old man and an old woman, the book has become a classic in children's literature.

THE TRAVELING MUSICIANS
*Collected by the Brothers Grimm.
Illustrated by Hans Fischer. Harcourt,
Brace & World, Inc., 1955.*
A handsome picture book with lilting text that captures the mood of Central Europe.

THE SEVEN RAVENS
*Collected by the Brothers Grimm.
Illustrated by Felix Hoffmann.
Harcourt, Brace & World, Inc.,
1963.*
A moving folk tale of a young girl's courage as she travels to the ends of the earth to free her seven brothers turned into ravens. A marvelous translation and retelling.

THREE GAY TALES FROM GRIMM
*Collected by the Brothers Grimm.
Retold and illustrated by Wanda
Gág. Coward-McCann, Inc., 1943.*
Lively narratives enhanced by simple, natural pictures that preserve the German flavor.

GONE IS GONE
*Collected by the Brothers Grimm.
Retold and illustrated by Wanda
Gág. Coward-McCann, Inc., 1935.*
An old homespun story narrated with simplicity and freshness. Visual artistry highlights the text about a man who exchanged household duties with his wife for a day.

EASTERN EUROPEAN AND ASIATIC INFLUENCE

Armenian

ARMENIAN FOLKTALES
*Told by I. Khatchatrianz in
Russian. Translated by N. Orloff.
Illustrated by M. Saryan. Colonial
House Publications, 1946.*

Sixteen folk tales with a Russo-Armenian flavor. Told with dazzling details, the narratives provide rich material that the artist has used in his illustrations.

Polish, Russian, and Ukrainian

SEVEN SIMEONS
*Retold and illustrated by Boris
Artzybasheff. The Viking Press,
Inc., 1937.*

This Russian picture book is imbued with native qualities—amusing, imaginative, and ironic. Precision and delicacy of design add to the richly colored illustrations. Suited to reading aloud for kindergarten through third grade children.

UKRAINIAN FOLK TALES
*Translated by Marie Halun Bloch,
from the original collections of Ivan
Rudchenko and Maria Lukiyanenko.
Illustrated by J. Hnizdovsky.
Coward-McCann, Inc., 1964.*

Twelve endearing stories translated not only to read well but to sound good when read aloud. Pleasant illustrations.

THE GOLDEN SEED
*Told by Maria Konopnicka.
Adapted by Catharine Fournier.
Illustrated by Janina Damanska.
Charles Scribner's Sons, 1962.*

A folk tale of European medieval life in charming four-color illustrations that complement the dignity of this Polish tale.

OLD PETER'S RUSSIAN TALES
Told by Arthur Ransome.

*Illustrated by Dmitrii Mitrokhin.
Thomas Nelson (Edinburgh), 1963.*

A new edition of a favorite book.

BORIS AND HIS BALALAIKA
*Told by Esphyr Slobodkina.
Illustrated by Vladimir Bobri.
Abelard-Schuman Limited, 1964.*

A musical telling of Boris and his one talent—playing the balalaika. Pictures add gaiety to this charming story.

THE MITTEN
*Told by Alvin Tresselt. Illustrated
by Yaroslava. Lothrop, Lee &
Shepard Co., Inc., 1964.*

A notable book of exceptionally fine detail retells the story of a small boy's lost mitten in which animals struggle to find shelter from the snow. A lovely book brightened by peasant designs.

RUSSIAN WONDER TALES
*Told by Post Wheeler. Illustrated
by Bilibin. Thomas Yoseloff Inc.,
Publisher, 1957.*

Sixteen Russian skazki (wonder folk tales) with illustrations that revive the enchanted lands of a distant Slavic past.

SALT
*Adapted by Harve Zemach from a
literal translation by Benjamin
Zemach. Illustrated by Margot
Zemach. Follett Publishing
Company, 1965.*

Humorous pictures retell a famous Russian story about Ivan the Fool. Decked out in fine picture-book dress, this skillfully decorated book is also pleasingly written.

NORTHERN EUROPEAN INFLUENCE

Danish

THIRTEEN DANISH TALES
Retold by Mary Hatch. Illustrated

by Edgun. Harcourt, Brace &
World, Inc., 1947.

Retold from Sven Grundtvig's Folkaever-tyr, the stories incorporate lively word pictures and conversation enlivened by comic sketches.

MORE DANISH TALES
*Retold by Mary Hatch. Illustrated by
Edgun. Harcourt, Brace & World,
Inc., 1949.*
Fifteen traditional and humorous stories from Sven Grundtvig's Folkaevertyr in Miss Hatch's second collection of Danish folk tales.

Finnish and Czechoslovakian

THE SHEPHERD'S NOSEGAY
*Retold by Parker Fillmore. Edited by
Katherine Love. Illustrated by
Enrico Arno. Harcourt, Brace &
World, Inc., 1958.*
A new edition of eighteen favorites from Parker Fillmore's collections of Czechoslovakian and Finnish tales.

TALES FROM A FINNISH TUPA
*Written by James C. Bowman &
Margery Bianco from a translation by
Aili Kolehmainen. Illustrated by Laura
Bannon. Albert Whitman & Co.,
1936.*
Stories of humble, everyday routines told with distinction and illustrated handsomely.

Scandinavian

EAST OF THE SUN AND WEST OF THE
MOON
*Collected by Peter Asbjörnsen and
Jörgen E. Moe. Illustrated by
Hedvig Collin. The Macmillan
Company, 1953.*
Wonderful Norweigan folk tales told with

strength and illustrated with a Scandinavian sense of beauty.

THE THREE BILLY GOATS GRUFF
*Collected by Peter C. Asbjörnsen and
Jörgen E. Moe. Illustrated by
Marcia Brown. Harcourt, Brace &
World, Inc., 1957.*

The popular tale of the three goats saved from a troll by Big Billy Goat Gruff is dramatically told and illustrated with stunning pictures.

SOUTHERN EUROPEAN INFLUENCE

Greek

ANDY AND THE LION
*Adapted and illustrated by James
Daugherty. The Viking Press Inc.,
1938.*
The age-old Greek story of Androcles told with humor, originality, and skilled drawings.

TALES OF CHRISTOPHILOS
*Told by Joice M. Nankivell.
Illustrated by Panos Ghikas.
Houghton Mifflin Company, 1954.*
Strains of folklore and legend are blended with modern-day life to weave stories about a Greek peasant boy who lives in a sunlit corner of a lovely land.

Spanish

THREE GOLDEN ORANGES AND
OTHER SPANISH FOLK TALES
*Told by Ralph Steele Boggs and
Mary Gould Davis. Illustrated
by Emma Brock. David McKay
Co., Inc., 1936.*
Ten Spanish stories told and illustrated with flair and radiance.

Italian

PICTURE TALES FROM THE ITALIAN
*Told by Florence H. Botsford.
Illustrated by Grace Gilkison.
Frederick A. Stokes Company, 1929.*

Well-told stories come alive with humor
and exaggeration. Beautifully illustrated,
the book is a delightful picture of a sunny
part of the world.

FAR EASTERN INFLUENCE

Indian and Pakistani

WHY SO MUCH NOISE?
*Retold and illustrated by Janina
Domanska. Harper & Row,
Publishers, 1965.*

Striking illustrations enliven an old Indian
tale about a mouse deer and his ingenuity
in tricking a tiger into saving an elephant.
Wonderful storytelling qualities.

THE VALIANT CHATTEE-MAKER
*Retold and illustrated by Christine
Price. Frederick Warne & Co.,
Inc., 1965.*

Pleasing pictures spark a humorous Indian
folk tale about an unwilling hero.

THE BLIND MEN AND THE ELEPHANT
*Told by Lillian Quigley. Illustrated
by Janice Holland. Charles Scribner's
Sons, 1959.*

A popular tale about the blind men of
Hindustan who describe what they "see"
when they feel the elephant.

TOONTOONY PIE AND OTHER
TALES FROM PAKISTAN
*By Ashraf Siddiqui and Marilyn
Lerch. Illustrated by Jan Fairservis.
World Publishing Co., 1961.*

Since both author and illustrator resided in
Pakistan, the research is sound and the
collection well chosen with its twenty-two
humorous Pakistani folk tales full of
indigenous birds and beasts.

Chinese

FIVE CHINESE BROTHERS
*Written by Claire Huchet Bishop.
Illustrated by Kurt Wiese.
Coward-McCann, Inc., 1938.*

A popular Chinese tale retold in picture
book dress. The cleverness of the brothers
in outsmarting the law holds the attention
of young readers.

YOU NEVER CAN TELL
*Adapted and illustrated by Janice
Holland. Charles Scribner's Sons,
1963.*

An old Chinese tale with a moral that
points up the acceptance of joy and sorrow
as a way of life. Cleverly told and illustrated.

THE TREASURE OF LI-PO
*Told by Alice Ritchie. Illustrated by
T. Ritchie. Harcourt, Brace &
World, Inc., 1949.*

Six fairy tales told with dignity in the
manner of traditional Chinese folk tales.

Japanese

ISSUN BOSHI, THE INCHLING
*Told by Momoki Ishii. Translated
by Yone Mizuta. Illustrated by
Fuku Akino. Walker & Company,
1967.*

A bright, shining picture book retelling the
story of Tom Thumb in a Japanese idiom.
Without losing much of its ancient oriental quality, this translation captures the
flavor of authentic settings against which
little Tom struts around in a charming
story.

THREE STRONG WOMEN: A TALL
TALE FROM JAPAN
*Told by Claus Stamm. Illustrated by
Kazue Mizumura. The Viking Press,
Inc., 1962.*

A funny but believable story about a
conceited wrestler who meets his match
with three women. Clever pictures translate some of the humor and strength of
the story.

THE SEA OF GOLD AND OTHER
TALES FROM JAPAN
*Adapted by Yoshiko Uchida.
Illustrated by Marianne Yamaguchi.
Charles Scribner's Sons, 1965.*

A collection of wise old tales full of
Japanese humor and highlighted by handsome charcoal drawings.

THE DANCING KETTLE: AND
OTHER JAPANESE FOLK TALES
*Told by Yoshiko Uchida. Illustrated
by Richard C. Jones. Harcourt,
Brace & World, Inc., 1949.*

Beautiful tales reflecting the peasant life
of Japan with glimpses into humble
households and into rural Japan. Charming pictures.

THE GOLDEN CRANE: A JAPANESE
FOLKTALE
*Told by Tohr Yamaguchi.
Illustrated by Marianne Yamaguchi.
Holt, Rinehart & Winston, Inc.,
1962.*

A heartwarming tale of a mute orphan
and an old man who befriend a wounded
sacred crane. Illustrations fragile as a
Japanese print adorn the lovely tale.

In this delicate drawing a sturdy tree dominates the scene as it serves to shelter a wide variety of fairy-tale characters and props. This artist's compositions have dignity and grace in keeping with her subjects.
From Tasha Tudor's Book of Fairy Tales *edited by Dana Bruce, illustrated by Tasha Tudor. The Platt and Munk Co., Inc., 1961. Reproduced by permission.*

Chapter 7

FAIRY
TALES

Know you what it is to be a child? It is something very different
from the man of today. It is to have a spirit yet streaming from the waters of
baptism; it is to believe in love, to believe in loveliness, to believe
in belief; it is to be so little that the elves can reach to whisper in your ear; it is
to turn pumpkins into coaches, and mice into horses, lowness into loftiness,
and nothing into everything, for each child has its fairy godmother in its soul.

— Francis Thompson
"Shelley"
The Dublin Review, 1908

Definition of
Fairy Tales

Fairy tale is the term that best describes that strain of folk literature which embodies a universal truth in highly imaginative fanciful form. In its simplicity and lyricism, a fairy tale is not unlike other forms of folk literature—a short narrative with an uncomplicated plot. It is its use of extraordinary and supernatural happenings that differentiates it from other tales of folklore. Lit with magical cadence that is neither too pretty, too vague, nor inconceivable, the fairy tale flows with storytelling ease from its beginning, past its fantastic events, to a satisfying climax with a realistic approach.

Although the aesthetic pattern of the story mirrors some aspects of reality, the form creates a special aura of the marvelous and the magical peopled with the supernatural—a fertile field for the imagination. Through wonder and challenge a child may be drawn subconsciously into the stories and held spellbound. And because the tales fulfill their first requirement, which is to entertain, they sustain a young reader's interest and delight.

Origins of Fairy Tales

Fairy tales of unknown authorship go back to the origins of the human race. Like all traditional folk literature, fairy tales were common to peoples in widely separated as well as neighboring lands. Born out of the oral storytelling tradition, many magnificent tales of supernatural adventures have survived to be collected by scholars such as Grimm, Asb-

jörnsen, and Moe who have preserved them in books that now hold an important place in children's literature. 187
Fairy
Tales

Modern fairy tales, however, are the products of imaginative minds and known authorship. Whether old or modern, fairy tales, considered the beginnings of man's expression of fantasy, have acquired new significance with time, including twentieth-century psychological and anthropological interpretations. The tales are said to have evolved as an imaginative expression of man's aesthetic need. Fairy tales use images of magic and marvels to amuse, to entertain, and to provide for refreshing escape. They are unlike most other folk literature in that they neither explain natural phenomena, as do the myths, nor present exaggerations of what human beings would like to be, as do many hero and superhero tales; nor do they show social behavior through story characters, as do many "earthy" folk tales.

Regardless of certain differences, folk literature is essentially the same with no sharp distinctions between the kinds of tales. From a literary point of view, much of folklore possesses elements basic to good writing and storytelling. As Annie E. Moore states:

> Literary critics [use folk tales] as striking examples of story construction, dramatic quality, pervading tone, character delineating, clarity of theme, intensity of action, effective dialogue, and other significant traits ... because the best of these tales exhibit striking qualities free from the complexities of a more sophisticated literature. The student of children's literature should be no less aware of the factors which contribute to the excellence of stories which long since became the especial property of the young.[1]

Folk Tales
and Fairy Tales

One finds some overlapping in types and expression between folk and fairy stories, which makes it difficult to generalize about differences or types and structure. For example, in "Beauty and the Beast" ordinary people live in life-like conditions and behave in much the same way as ordinary people do until an awesome "beast" appears. And it is his transformation into a handsome young man that switches a traditional story with a traditional folk setting into a fairy tale with supernatural events and the fairy tale ending, "they lived happily ever after."

---

[1] Annie E. Moore, *Literature Old and New for Children* (Boston: Houghton Mifflin Company, 1934), pp. 95–96.

From the moral and social perspective common to folklore, "Beauty and the Beast" inspires a young reader with goodness and charity since Beauty proves to have high moral character in the midst of corrupting vicissitudes of fortune. She is moved by compassion to look beyond the Beast's surface for spiritual beauty.

As a fairy tale, however, it augments the moralizing by telling an aesthetically pleasing story. Through its fairy-tale action, a world of wonder and enchantment is opened. Here, a supernatural change takes place just as it might in the world of a child's imagination. Consequently, fairy tales offer food for the imagination that lifts readers above the mundane into a world of magic and marvels. The story satisfyingly entertains with the drama, romance, fun, and fancy that are characteristic of the finest fairy tales. This is the heart of the fairy story, and it may be described as its essential distinction—aesthetic value.

The Aesthetic Qualities
in Fairy Tales

Inherent in fairy tales are the qualities of great literature—aesthetic transformation of reality with emotional impact in a style appropriate to and evocative of its ideas.

First of all, they are exciting stories that begin dramatically, and are full of action, conflict, and suspense, which is maintained by provoking the reader into asking how this can be or what will happen next. With hair-raising rapidity, Jack in "Jack and the Beanstalk" proceeds to outmaneuver the giant in order to get money, the hen that lays golden eggs, and the harp. Suspense is maintained to the last moment when Jack stops the giant by cutting down the beanstalk.

Themes in fairy tales unfold in the plots—what characters do and what happens to them—for the idea of the story is not told but enacted. Human qualities—courage, industry, love, kindness, goodness, wickedness, vanity, morality—are dramatized for the reader because the stories have a single point, and a unity of interest is maintained. Snow White's stepmother, for example, reveals her vanity through a dialogue, "Mirror, Mirror on the wall, who is the fairest of us all?"[2] and through the disguises she affects in order to harm Snow White. Each action gets progressively worse until the queen chokes with passion and dies of vanity.

---

[2]May Hill Arbuthnot, "Snow White and the Seven Dwarfs," in *Time for Fairy Tales* (Chicago: Scott, Foresman & Company, 1961), p. 53.

The immortal fairy tale of Snow White and the seven dwarfs is depicted here by Walter Crane whose highly skilled drawings flow deftly to evoke the shifting moods of this story.

From "Snow White" in Household Stories *by the Brothers Grimm, illustrated by Walter Crane. First published by The Macmillan Company in 1886.*

189

The point of view from which the fairy story is told is impersonal, and therefore one's experience of the story is direct and uninterrupted by a narrator. The story tells itself, and judgment is reserved for the reader. The unobtrusive opening of "Little Red Riding Hood" gives no preconceptions about the central character. The adjectives used to describe her are not subjective in nature. "Once upon a time there was a little girl who was called little Red Riding Hood, because she was quite small and because she always wore a red cloak with a big red hood to it, which her grandmother had made for her."[3]

Action that reveals character may take the form of tasks and trials or problems to be overcome. Hansel and Gretel, in a brother-sister relationship held together by the bond of faith and love, through endurance and courage persist in solving their problem of poverty so they can return to their father. Contrast in actions shows the antithesis of good and evil; coincidence and fortune favor the well-prepared man.

Sometimes the story focuses on a single central action: winning a maiden, freeing oneself from sorcery, improving one's state, or overcoming odds. At other times a series of actions must be accomplished. For example, in "Cinderella," the central action of the story is winning the Prince to prove one's worth; but in "Six Servants" there are several goals to attain: getting a ring at the bottom of the Red Sea, eating three hundred plump oxen, keeping the princess in sight while enchanted. The action is further complicated by a mother-witch queen, a servant with X-ray vision, a croucher who can hear everything—characters whose peculiar idiosyncrasies make the deeds they perform seem plausible and real. The story interprets and makes concrete the more abstract themes of searching for love, striving for self-realization, winning the respect of others. The sequence of actions is the logical development of a problem situation within a moral framework. Through fortuitousness and contrivance, things finally fall happily into place.

The simplicity of form that truth takes in these tales deepens its significance. Structure and point of view elaborate the concentration on action. Structure puts events and parts of the story in relationship to each other and to the whole in accord with the main idea or theme.

The title of a fairy tale often embodies a contrast and gives one a hint as to what the story will do as in "How Jack Went Out To Sell His

---

[3]Flora Annie Steel, "Little Red Riding Hood," in *English Fairy Tales* (New York: The Macmillan Company, 1962), p. 191.

Fortune," "Cinderella, or the Little Glass Slipper," "King O'Toole and His Goose," "Beauty and the Beast," "Clever Manka."

The introduction throws us into the world of the story situation, showing us who's who, pointing to a problem, and creating a mood. Brevity is part of its charm. "Once upon a time there was an old sow who had three little pigs, and as she had not enough for them to eat, she said they had better go out into the world and seek their fortunes."[4] In another introduction, "There was a man, he had a daughter who always tried to use her brains as much as possible and so she was called Clever Elsie."[5]

Descriptions in introductions are sketched in their universal aspects, leaving the rest to be filled in. In time and place the story's setting is anywhere common to man's experience—a poor man's hut, a forest, a bridge, just a place where something is going to happen. In "Spindle, Shuttle and Needle," we are told: "At the edge of a village lived an orphan girl and her godmother. They were poor and lived in a tiny cottage."[6] The introduction affords a vantage point for looking at a still life.

With no time to react, the reader finds that everything has started moving. Events occur so quickly that he becomes a part of the action and is drawn on into the story for more entertainment and excitement.

In the body of the story things really start moving: tasks and searches begin, flights get underway, obstacles appear, protagonists are reduced to despair. Action after action, event after event, disaster after disaster. How will Cinderella and her prince ever get together between the magic and transformation? How far can the fisherman's wife's avarice lead her? The wife lives in a vinegar jug, she wants a hut. She gets a hut, she wants a mansion. She gets a mansion, she wants a castle. She gets a castle, she wants to be king. She becomes king, she wants to be emperor. She becomes emperor, she wants to be pope. She is pope and wants to be God. So back she goes to her vinegar jug. Steadily mounting action leads the reader to a climax which brings it all to a head and leads quickly to a resolution of the situation.

After the helter-skelter jumble that has just occurred, one is again gazing at a still life. There is no lingering over retribution. Good is victorious, virtue is rewarded, villains are defeated. The end gives a sense of finality and is satisfying as only wishes can be. At the end of "Snow White,"

[4]Steel, "The Three Little Pigs," *ibid.*, p. 122.

[5]Wanda Gág, "Clever Elsie," in *Tales from Grimm* (New York: Coward-McCann, Inc., 1936), p. 123. Copyright © 1936 by Wanda Gág. Reprinted by permission of Coward-McCann, Inc.

[6]Gág, "Spindle, Shuttle and Needle," *ibid.*, p. 65.

for example, the queen dies of vanity, and the prince and princess live happily ever after. At the end of "Hansel and Gretel," the stepmother and the witch are disposed of, and the children live happily ever after with their father. When Aladdin gets rid of the wicked magician, evil is gone from the world and peace and happiness reign forever. In the "Six Servants," with tasks successfully completed and the witch queen destroyed, the fruits go to the victor. Good triumphing over evil in the happy resolution of conflict provides for a catharsis of feeling, a sublimated joy that satisfies the need for justice and successful achievement, and fulfills the aesthetic need for beauty and delight.

Repetition in structure and images ties one incident to another to form a total pattern, giving emphasis and continuity to the main idea and leaving the reader with a unified impression. Examples of repeated verbal patterns are:

> "No! No! No! by the hair of my chinny chin chin! . . . Then I'll huff and I'll puff and I'll blow your house in."[7]

> "Manye, Manye, Timpie Tee,
> Fishye, Fishye in the sea,
> Ilsebill my wilful wife
> Does not want my way of life."[8]

> "Oh, Grandmamma, Grandmamma,
> what big ears you've got!"
> "Oh, Grandmamma, Grandmamma,
> what big teeth you've got!"[9]

Children find security in the familiar. Repetition of verbal patterns throughout the story makes the unknown gradually familiar to the child drawing him into the story through identification with the known. He feels he is a part of the world of the tale as well as comfortable in it.

Unity of interest is maintained in a fairy tale because the story tells itself with no exhaustive literary descriptions to interfere with the story.

The beauty, simplicity, and dignity of words in fairy tales account for their pure and direct force:

> Rapunzel was a winsome child, with long luxuriant tresses, fine as spun gold. When she was twelve years old, the witch took her off to the woods and shut her up in a high tower. It had neither door nor staircase but at its very top was one tiny window.[10]

---

[7]Steel, "The Three Little Pigs," *op. cit.*, p. 123.
[8]Gág, "The Fisherman and His Wife," *op. cit.*, p. 151.
[9]Steel, "Little Red Riding Hood," *op. cit.*, p. 193.
[10]Gág, "Rapunzel," *op. cit.*, p. 139.

The royal prince took Rapunzel with him into his kingdom and made her his queen, and they lived long and happily ever after.

Consonant with the language in fairy tales, this illustration emphasizes beauty, simplicity, and dignity of design. Here is a panoramic view of a far-reaching sea sailed by stately ships. Beyond the harbor lies a walled kingdom of turrets and towers to which the royal prince takes Rapunzel to make her his queen.

From Rapunzel *by the Brothers Grimm, illustrated by Felix Hoffmann. Copyright © 1949 for illustrations by Amerbach-Verlag, Basle (Switzerland), © 1960 by Oxford University Press. Reproduced by permission of Harcourt, Brace & World, Inc.*

Then she feel asleep instantly, and only woke up to hear the clock saying, "Beauty, Beauty," twelve times in its musical voice, which told her she was really in the palace once more. Everything was just as before, and her birds were so glad to see her, but Beauty thought she had never known such a long day. She was so anxious to see the Beast again that she felt as if suppertime would never come.[11]

The imagistic quality of the language appeals to the senses as well as to the emotions and the mind:

The moon did come out, full and round and bright, and it shone on the white pebbles which Hansel had strewn along the way. With the glistening pebbles to guide them, they found their way back easily enough.[12]

---

[11] Arbuthnot, "Beauty and the Beast," *op. cit.*, p. 114.
[12] Gág, "Hansel and Gretel," *op. cit.*, p. 7.

They were dressed in satin and silk. Their bustles were puffed, their bodices stuffed, their skirts were ruffled and tufted with bows; their sleeves were muffled with furbelows. They wore bells that tinkled, and glittering rings; and rubies and pearls and little birds' wings![13]

The rhythmical patterns of sound and sense, cadenced to suit the tale's tempo and mood, give a pervasive lyrical power to the story, as evidenced in the refrains mentioned earlier. All these aspects of language combine to create a variety of moods in the tales. The total effect of language, however, is twofold:

(1) A concrete story is narrated in words that induce pictorial visualization and interpretation.
(2) Various abstract moods, feelings, and states are evoked through sensory effects.

Combining and relating the two levels of language into the oneness of the tale creates the magical quality in a story so that in it, anything can happen! At Sleeping Beauty's christening, for example, "There was placed before every one of them a magnificent cover with a case of massive gold, wherein were a spoon, knife and fork, all of pure gold set with diamonds and rubies."[14] Aladdin's mother, in preparing a gift for the sultan, "fetched a napkin and laid in it the magic fruits from the enchanted garden, which sparkled and shone like the most beautiful jewels."[15]

The storytelling language, however, is conversational, direct, and flowing. In "The Three Little Pigs," the dialogue between the wolf and pig proceeds as follows:

"Little pig, I know where there is a nice field of turnips."

"Where?" said the little pig.

"Oh, in Mr. Smith's home-field, and if you will be ready to-morrow morning I will call for you, and we will go together, and get some for dinner."

"Very well," said the little pig, "I will be ready. What time do you mean to go?"

"Oh, at six o'clock."[16]

But the words that describe people—few as they are in fairy tales—take us right to their souls. Snow White's stepmother was "so proud that she could not bear to think that any one could surpass her."[17] When

---

[13]Gág, "Cinderella," *op. cit.*, p. 104.
[14]Arbuthnot, "The Sleeping Beauty in the Wood," *op. cit.*, p. 99.
[15]Arbuthnot, "Aladdin and the Wonderful Lamp," *op. cit.*, p. 169.
[16]Arbuthnot, "The Three Little Pigs," *op. cit.*, p. 11.
[17]Arbuthnot, "Snow White and the Seven Dwarfs," *op. cit.*, p. 53.

characters speak they reveal their values, attitudes, and natures. Words that picture the action are almost inseparable from the action itself.

The moods and states evoked by language are sheer poetry. Images to describe feelings are appropriate and delicate. We cannot picture these effects, we feel them. Images in many instances become symbols for human feelings, desires, and fantasies.

Through aesthetic images of the marvelous and fantastic, a world of beauty is created in fairy tales. The language of the stories evokes pictures of mental, emotional, and sensory experiences, and adorns the ordinary with art.

Characters are both concrete and abstract. They serve the interests of themes, and provide dramatic contrasts of good and bad, strong and weak. Characters generally sustain the simplistic form of the tales, which calls forth an intuitive response, in that they represent single human qualities. They are not drawn as flesh and blood characters but as essential types. The characters in "Cinderella" form a world of good and bad. The cinder girl represents goodness, kindness, and industry. In contrast, her two stepsisters illustrate false vanity, petty self-indulgence, and laziness. Her father's weakness outweighs his other qualities, for he is dominated by a selfish stepmother. Prince Charming is all that can be wished for in romance. The characters are believable, for they stimulate genuine and spontaneous emotion in a reader. Snow White, though passive, evokes our sympathy for her innocence and the wickedness contrived against her. The dwarfs are lovable for their helpfulness and for the way they try to take care of the princess.

Adult characters as well as child figures have a childlike simplicity and purity in their depiction. They are active, daring heroes and heroines attempting impossible tasks and succeeding by their persistence and courage. Actions and dialogue are consistent with character, translating abstract qualities into the concrete action. Dialogue conversationally establishes the attitudes of the speakers. We note in "Beauty and the Beast":

"Good evening, old man. Good evening, Beauty."

The merchant was too terrified to reply, but Beauty answered sweetly, "Good evening, Beast."

"Have you come willingly?" asked the Beast. "Will you be content to stay here when your father goes away?"[18]

Beauty answers bravely that she is quite prepared to stay. Each sentence, each action serves to reveal character, and thus maintains the unified impression of the story.

---

[18]Arbuthnot, "Beauty and the Beast," *op. cit.*, p. 110.

Animals are characters and personify human behavior. The Three Bears are almost little people. When they discover someone has been in their house, they say: "Somebody has been at my porridge!... Somebody has been sitting in my chair!"[19]

It is possible to clarify our view of things by watching animals in the tales. They are accomplices and friends. They are placated and exploited in serving the characters. Identification with animals provides a release for children, for they see the creatures doing things they might like to do.

In fairy tales, supernatural characters appear who are not found in usual folk stories. These elves, sorcerers, witches, giants, ogres, and fairies facilitate the action and effect a magical bond between reality and fantasy —by their power they are true to themselves, by nature they are fanciful. Ultimately, they help fortune or chance work the right way. They often cause problems for the protagonist to overcome. The bad supernatural characters, motivated by their own wicked reasons, allow the good of the hero to be demonstrated. Enchantments and wicked spells can be broken by the self-sacrificing hero, driven by love. But, in the end, it is often the good supernatural characters who point the way to happiness or make a wish come true.

Fairy tales have emotional value that satisfies children's needs. Moral ideas, human qualities, and universal forces are abstracted from reality so that they become larger than life without confusing and distracting aspects. In these tales we find things as we would like them to be.

Issues and characters are clear-cut. Since good triumphs over evil, virtue is rewarded, and cruelty and evil punished, a child's faith in a moral and just universe is reinforced without being belabored and confused by the ambiguity of retribution. Strength and support is given to righteous inner forces. The world of fairy tales is the world as it is sometimes imagined to be. The real world exists only in terms of social organization—people, incidents, work, and places where things happen.

We read for knowledge and understanding, excitement and suspense, laughter, mystery, comfort, security. Different tales awaken pity and terror or kindle wonder and imagination, all of which contributes to a child's understanding and insight in a direct and intuitive way.

Although the content of the tales mirrors human nature and beliefs, the world of fairy tales is one to wonder at and marvel in. The relationship

[19]Steel, "The Story of the Three Bears," *op. cit.*, pp.15–16.

Distinguished ink drawings contrast the magnificence of courtly splendor to the humble manner in which Cinderella fits the coveted shoe. French opulence adds majesty to this tale.

From "Cindrillon" in Les Contes de Perrault *illustrated by Gustave Doré. Bibliothèque Nationale.*

between reality and imagination is necessarily complex to children whose dreams are real. What is real and what is imaginary are distinctly recognized in the stories, but the fusion of the two creates the new reality of the fairy tale. The tales are aesthetic and emotional experiences that transform reality to convey experience. The change occurs through magic, enchantment, and wonder in such a way that the real becomes unbelievable and the incredible true, depending on the point of view at a certain point in the story. This is the art of the fairy tale: aesthetic transformation.

Precise realistic details early in the story suggest the world as we know it. Then complications, problems, obstacles appear until resolution seems impossible. How can the Prince find Cinderella? And then, poof, magic or supernatural intervention, and the dust of the fantastic is sprinkled over our world and change is effected. A pumpkin is changed into a coach, a rat into a coachman, lizards into footmen. Cinderella's rags are turned into gold and silver, covered with jewels.

The ordinary is transformed by art to the wonderful and marvel-ous. When the complications are resolved, the clouds disappear and one is back where one started, having had a dream-like experience. Often within one story we have been led back and forth from real to fantastic. The story ends, but images of another world remain in the mind's eye.

The magic has worked subconsciously, for consciously one has been comfortably and securely aligned with reality. A child's readiness and willingness to have faith, to believe in fantasy, romance, and wishes make his journey in and out of reality possible.

What elements can we find in the tales which mix real and imagined to create fairyland reality?

46 They spent the whole night in weaving a net out of the pliant willow bark and stout reeds, and it was large and strong. On it Elisa lay down, and when the sun came up and the brothers changed into wild swans, they gripped the net in their beaks and flew high up towards the clouds, with their dear sister, who was still asleep. The sunbeams fell hotly on her face, so one of the swans flew above her head, that his broad wings might shade her.

47 They were far from land when Elisa awoke. She thought she was still dreaming, so strange it seemed to her to be borne over the sea, high through the air. At her side lay a branch with beautiful ripe berries on it, and a bundle of sweet-tasting roots. Her youngest brother had gathered them and laid them by her; and she smiled gratefully at him, for she knew it was he who was flying straight over her head and shading her with his wings.

In a brooding fairy tale of untiring devotion, the artist uses cool shades of gray and black warmed with touches of coral to haunt the imagination. In this picture the bewitched swan brothers transport their sister, Elisa, over a sparkling sea. Language and pictures join to convey a sense of majesty and movement as well as the serene loveliness of a sister's loyalty.

From The Wild Swans *by Hans Christian Andersen, illustrated by Marcia Brown. Illustrations copyright © 1963 by Marcia Brown. Reproduced by permission of Charles Scribner's Sons.*

In this dreamlike picture of detailed splendor, the Sleeping Beauty is contrasted with a vigorous young prince. Shafts of light stream into a chamber overrun with vines, as if to dispel the gloom of witchcraft found in this dramatic fairy tale. From "*La Belle Au Bois Dormant*" *in* Les Contes de Perrault *illustrated by Gustave Doré.* Bibliothèque Nationale.

Magical settings have the verisimilitude of reality because they are created from objects of our world. The castle in "Sleeping Beauty" contains familiar objects and typifies domestic life. Realistic settings and descriptions are sketched in their universal aspects—a hut, a cottage—leaving us to fill in our own details. "Hansel and Gretel" begins "In a little hut near the edge of a deep, deep forest..."[20]

Time in the tales is not clock time but emotional time. It combines past, present, and future into a direct immediacy as if they were all part of the now. The time in "Beauty and the Beast" when Beauty leaves home to return to the Beast is dream time, ticking according to a feeling instead of a clock. In "The Fisherman and His Wife," things happen according to

[20]Gág, "Hansel and Gretel," *op. cit.*, p. 3.

the time of will. As wishes are granted, cottage, castle, and mansion appear and life is transformed in an instant.

In repetitious verbal and action patterns, we find a changing emphasis on the real and unreal. Movement within the structure is flexible from real to imagined for the framework is conventionalized and familiar to us. The refrain, "Mirror, Mirror on the wall," in "Snow White" is a device that moves the reader between two worlds, the queen's reality and Snow White's retreat in the woods.

The impersonal presentation of the tales does not distinguish between real and unreal, as both are presented in the same matter-of-fact way. Although many things that occur are of a highly fantastic nature, the events are related in a logical plausible manner. The fabulous is conceived with imaginative truth and is often humanized. In "Jack and the Beanstalk," as soon as we accept the giant as imaginatively real, Jack's actions and the situation are believable. The chase down the beanstalk ending with Jack's chopping it down and thus eliminating the giant is a logical conclusion. In "Sleeping Beauty," when the prince breaks the spell after so many others have failed to enter the castle in the woods, his triumph fulfills the sequential working out of the prophecy. Again, if we accept the supernatural framework of the story, the action is believable, ordered, and logical.

Although characters are essential types, in their depiction there are flashes of flesh. All princesses are not the same. Snow White has black hair, white skin, red lips. Others have blond hair, dark skin. The princess in "The Frog Prince," by her actions and words tries actively to defy her fate.

> "Oh, dear father, as I was playing under the linden tree by the well, my golden ball fell into the water. And because I cried so hard, the frog brought it back to me; and because he insisted so much, I promised him that he could be my playmate. But I never, never thought that he would ever leave his well. Now he is out there and wants to come in and eat from my plate and drink from my cup and sleep in my little bed. But I couldn't bear that, papa, he's so wet and ugly and his eyes bulge out!"[21]

But Sleeping Beauty is less articulate and more passive than this princess, and is resigned to her fate.

Themes in the stories exist on two levels. Abstractly, they reflect ethical, moral principles and concepts such as justice, goodness triumphing over evil, industry and kindness rewarded. Concretely, the protagonist's

---

[21]Gág, "The Frog Prince," *op. cit.*, p. 183.

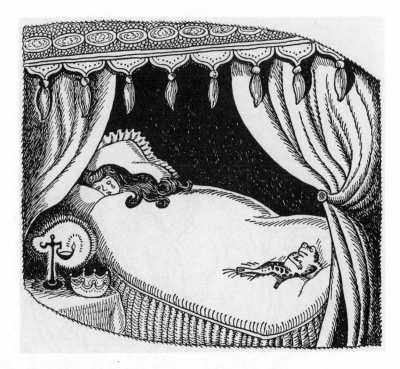

Here a softly weeping princess cries herself to sleep while a goggle-eyed frog dozes off at the foot of her bed. Kindness and humility are rewarded in this fairy tale when the frog turns prince in the morning. Sturdy peasant pictures support the magic in Wanda Gág's edition of this märchen, "The Frog Prince."

From "The Frog Prince" in Tales From Grimm *by Wanda Gág. Copyright © 1936 by Wanda Gág. Coward-McCann, Inc. Reproduced by permission.*

efforts to win security, find a place in the world, accomplish a task, escape from an enemy, outwit a wicked scheme, or the like are part of a pattern that culminates in justice and accomplishment. Through the juxtaposition of real and unreal, the abstract is made concrete, and the concrete is generalized into the abstract. On one level in "Cinderella" industry and goodness rewarded is contrasted with vanity and meanness unrewarded. On the story level, we see the drama of a vain stepmother and her vainer daughters thwarted in their efforts to obtain the prince in marriage alongside the happily-ever-after story of the cinder girl.

The language of the tales conveys the convergence of real and imagined. Art adorns the ordinary. In "Hansel and Gretel," we find a dark night evoked imagistically: "The moon was shining brightly, and the white pebbles which lay in front of the house glistened like silver coins."[22]

---

[22]Gág, "Hansel and Gretel," *op. cit.*, p. 5.

201

Supernatural characters speak words that symbolize human feelings and emotions. In "Rumpelstiltskin," when the queen discovers the name of the little dwarf, he screams out:

> "The devil told you that! the devil told you that!" . . . and in his anger he stamped with his right foot so hard that it went into the ground above his knee; then he seized his left foot with both his hands in such a fury that he split in two, and there was an end of him.[23]

Enraged that the queen discovered his name, the little dwarf stamps in anger as he screams out. True to the symbolism in the language of the fairy tale, the violent behavior of the gnarled dwarf symbolizes impassioned human emotions.
From "Rumpelstiltskin" in Household Stories *by the Brothers Grimm, illustrated by Walter Crane. First published by The Macmillan Company in 1886.*

The lushness of fairyland appeals to the senses. For example, the palace in "Aladdin and the Wonderful Lamp" is quite spectacular:

> . . . he said to the genie: "Build me a palace of the finest marble, set with jasper, agate, and other precious stones. In the middle you shall build me a large hall with a dome, its four walls of massy gold and silver, each side having six windows, whose lattices, all except one, which is to be left unfinished, must be set with diamonds and rubies."[24]

Marvelous happenings are related in a journalistic way. In "Six Servants," extraordinary feats, like the fetching of a ring at the bottom of the sea or

---

[23]Arbuthnot, "Rumpelstiltskin," *op. cit.*, p. 62.
[24]Arbuthnot, "Aladdin and the Wonderful Lamp," *op. cit.*, 171.

the eating of three hundred oxen, are reported as having been accomplished with ease. Thus, the simplicity of the language gives the imagined a sense of directness and honesty.

Stories often swing from the real to the unreal and back so one can hardly tell what is happening. Fantasy brings the irrational, wished for, and imagined into our world of the rational, observable, and real. Because the improbable takes off from the probable, it is believable. The tales constantly stimulate our emotions in a variety of ways. Within one story, one can feel, think, and see pity, anger, fear, tenderness, wonder, joy, sadness, suspense, admiration, humor, sympathy, beauty, enjoyment—an emotional impact conveyed by an aesthetic that makes the tale a real as well as a vicarious experience. One can identify, one's fears are allayed, and one cannot help but be enriched, for the stories penetrate to those realms beyond consciousness.

References

"American Folklore," *Compton's Pictured Encyclopedia*. Chicago: F. E. Compton and Co., 1956.

ARBUTHNOT, MAY HILL, *Time for Fairy Tales Old and New*, rev. ed. Chicago: Scott, Foresman & Company, 1961.

FISHER, MARGERY, *Intent Upon Reading: A Critical Appraisal of Modern Fiction for Children*. Market Place, England: Brockhampton Press Ltd., 1961.

FITZGERALD, BURDETTE S., "The Fairy of the Dell," in *World Tales for Creative Dramatics and Storytelling*. Englewood Cliffs, N.J.: Prentice-Hall, Inc., 1962.

"Folk Tales Around the World," *Compton's Pictured Encyclopedia*. Chicago: F. E. Compton and Co., 1957.

JORDAN, ALICE, *Children's Classics*. Boston: The Horn Book Inc., 1960.

LANE, MARGARET, *The Tale of Beatrix Potter*. Baltimore: Penguin Books, Inc., 1962.

MABIE, HAMILTON W., *Fairy Tales Every Child Should Know*. New York: Doubleday and Company, Inc. 1914.

MEIGS, CORNELIA, *et al.*, "The Deepest Roots: The Quality of Saxon Fancy, Celtic Fairyland, The Piskey Folk of Cornwall, Genius Concerns Itself with Fairies in Ireland, The Fairy World and the Welsh, The Cinderella Story," in *A Critical History of Children's Literature*. New York: The Macmillan Company, 1953.

SAYERS, FRANCES CLARKE, and DORA V. SMITH, "Lose Not the Nightingale," *American Library Association Bulletin*, XXXI (October 1, 1937), and XXXII (January 1938).

SMITH, DORA V., "More Literature for Children," in *Fifty Years of Children's Books*. Champaign, Illinois: The National Council of Teachers of English, 1963.

SMITH, LILLIAN H., "The Art of the Fairy Tale," in *The Unreluctant Years*. Chicago: American Library Association, 1953.

TOLKIEN, J. R. R., *Tree and Leaf*. Boston: Houghton Mifflin Company, 1965.

WEBBER, F. E., "Children Glory in the Gory," *Progressive Education*, XXXII (March 1955), 48.

Multiethnic Fairy Tales in English

GENERAL COLLECTIONS WITH MULTIETHNIC BACKGROUNDS

FAIRY TALES OF THE ORIENT
Selected and edited by Pearl S. Buck. Illustrated by Jeanyee Wong. Simon and Schuster, Inc., 1965.

A magnificent collection of fairy tales from, among others, China, Japan, India, Persia, and Arabia, made sumptuously beautiful by color and line drawings.

CASTLES AND DRAGONS
Compiled by the Child Study Association of America. Illustrated by William Pène du Bois. The Crowell-Collier Publishing Co., 1958.

A carefully selected group of fairy tales concerned with splendid castles, fierce dragons, supernatural happenings and magical images. Artistic illustrations illumine the narratives.

FAIRY TALES
Written by E. E. Cummings. Illustrated by John Eaton. Harcourt, Brace & World, Inc., 1965.

These four exquisite fairy tales of known authorship have no regional boundaries but seem to spring from the conscious experiences of a young child. Luminous images emerge from the tales lit with the color, light, and sound of a delicate fantasy. Soft washes of color perfectly complement the stories.

THE ENCHANTED BOOK
Told by Alice Dalgliesh. Illustrated by Concetta Cacciola. Charles Scribner's Sons, 1947.

Superb tales of enchantment drawn from a number of different sources. Fine pictures trace out portions of the stories with deftness and add a magical touch.

CHIMNEY CORNER FAIRY TALES
Told by Veronica Hutchinson.
Illustrated by Lois Lenski. Minton,
Balch & Company, 1926.

A rather old-fashioned edition by modern standards, but comprised of charming stories and sturdy drawings by an outstanding author-illustrator for younger children.

THE BLUE FAIRY BOOK
Edited by Andrew Lang. Illustrated by
Reisie Lonette. Random House, Inc.,
1959.

An outstanding collection of fairy tales from a master storyteller. Pictures with a sense of fairy elements add luster to a colorful collection.

A FATHER READS TO HIS
CHILDREN
Selected by Orville Prescott. E. P.
Dutton & Co., Inc., 1965.

This anthology offers a wide variety of literary works. In addition to choices from Hans Christian Andersen's original fairy tales and the Brothers Grimm, it also includes Padraic Colum, T. H. White, and Nathaniel Hawthorne, to name a few. The selection reflects beauty and grace.

THE ARTHUR RACKHAM FAIRY
BOOK
Selected and illustrated by Arthur
Rackham. J. B. Lippincott Co., 1950.

Twenty-three beloved fairy tales with eight full color and over fifty black-and-white illustrations in fascinating Rackham style.

FAR EASTERN INFLUENCE

Chinese

OLD WIND AND LIU LI-SAN
Written by Aline Glasgow.
Illustrated by Bernard Glasgow.
Harvey House, Inc., Publishers,
1962.

Tenderness and beauty distinguish this story drawn from an ancient Chinese fairy tale about a mysterious Old Wind that brings good fortune to a little boy and his family. In picture book format, this tale is an exceptionally fine first book for young children.

THE BLACK HEART OF INDRI
Told by Dorothy Hoge. Illustrated
by Janina Domanska. Charles
Scribner's Sons, 1965.

This Chinese fairy tale, with a distinct Far Eastern flavor, lends itself well to the delicate pictorial interpretation the artist has given it. Although closely resembling tales of ill-favored toads transformed to something finer, it is lifted from the routine by its dramatic yet tender quality.

THE TREASURE OF LI-PO
Told by Alice Ritchie. Illustrated by
T. Ritchie. Harcourt, Brace &
World, Inc., 1949.

Six original fairy tales with the flavor of folk tales in their structure, sincerity, and dignity. These less delicate fairy stories are appropriately illustrated by an artist who has worked closely with the author.

THE NIGHTINGALE
By Hans Christian Andersen.
Translated by Eva Le Gallienne.
Illustrated by Nancy Ekholm Burkert.
Harper & Row, Publishers, 1965.

Majestic pictures mark this exquisite fairy tale as a picture book of distinction. Told with the fluidity and ease of a master, the story of the valiant Nightingale has a poignant poetic cadence.

Fairy Tales

Japanese

JAPANESE FAIRY TALES
Told by Lafcadio Hearn and others.
Illustrated by "Kay." Liveright
Publishing Corp., 1953.

A rich and varied collection of fairy tales told with a simplicity and beauty reflective of the quiet grace of the Japanese. Delicacy in the pictures preserves the ancient quality found in Oriental prints.

LITTLE ONE-INCH
Told by Florence Sakade. Illustrated by
Yoshisuke Kurosaki. Charles E.
Tuttle Co., 1958.

A collection of favorite Japanese fairy tales told with simplicity and subtle humor. Reflecting variants of fairy tales from other lands, especially the Danish "Thumbelina," the tales preserve much of the flavor of their ethnic origin.

THE MAGIC LISTENING CAP
Told and illustrated by Yoshiko
Uchida. Harcourt, Brace &
World, Inc., 1955.

The power of magic is featured in a collection of spellbinding tales whose rhythm and simplicity make them ideal for storytellers.

Korean

WHICH WAS WITCH?
Told by Eleanore M. Jewett.
Illustrated by Taro Yashima. The
Viking Press, Inc., 1953.

Fourteen tales of ghosts and magic from Korea that convey Far Eastern qualities: delicacy of expression, beauty, and wisdom. Most of the tales use familiar themes, but some employ fresh, beautiful ideas unknown in Western tradition. All have qualities relevant to a storyteller's art.

Indian and Pakistani

INDIAN FAIRY TALES
Edited by Joseph Jacobs. Illustrated by
J. D. Batten. G. P. Putnam's Sons, 1892.

Ancient fairy tales gathered from the Hindus that stress magical and metaphysical elements. The Sanskrit tales and those concerned with the birth of Buddha, especially beautiful, are enhanced with brooding pictures.

TALES OF THE PUNJAB
Collected by Flora Annie Steel.
Illustrated by J. Lockwood Kipling
with notes by R. C. Temple. The
Macmillan Company, 1894.

Magnificent tales for older children. Spun with the magic of a storyteller's art, the language is graceful and adorned. Gentle illustrations highlight the collection of tales told by the people from the "land of five rivers."

MIDDLE EASTERN AND PERSIAN INFLUENCE

Arabian

THE FLYING CARPET
Told and illustrated by Marcia
Brown. Charles Scribner's Sons,
1956.

This story from the Arabian Nights collection comes decked out in lavish picture book dress touched by the magic of an Oriental fairyland.

PALACE IN BAGDAD
Told by Jean Russell Larson.
Illustrated by Marianne Yamaguchi.
Charles Scribner's Sons, 1966.

Seven tales from Arabia told with mystery and humor and full of colorful characters. The quiet beauty and romance of a distant land is conveyed well.

ARABIAN NIGHTS: TALES OF
WONDER AND MAGNIFICENCE
Collected and told by Padraic Colum.
Illustrated by Lynd Ward. The
Macmillan Company, 1953.

An outstanding retelling of magnificent tales based on Edward Lane's translation of *The Thousand and One Nights*. Drama and imagery blend to provide a feast of fairy tales drawn from the ancient Saracen civilization.

THE ARABIAN NIGHTS: THEIR
BEST KNOWN TALES
Edited by Kate Douglas Wiggin and
Nora A. Smith. Illustrated by
Maxfield Parrish. Charles Scribner's
Sons, 1909.

Rich colors and beautiful language join in telling these popular tales from the Arabian Nights.

Persian

PERSIAN FAIRY TALES
A Persian collection decorated by
Valenti Angelo. Peter Pauper Press,
1939.

Beautiful fairy tales with magical settings and happenings from ancient Persia. Handsome decorations adorn these tales for older children.

ANGLO-SAXON-CELTIC INFLUENCE

English

THE HOUSE IN THE WOOD AND
OTHER OLD FAIRY STORIES
Told and illustrated by L. Leslie
Brooke. Frederick Warne & Co.,
Inc., 1962.

Ten marvelously told tales with illustrations indicative of the artistic integrity that has distinguished this author-artist.

FAVORITE FAIRY TALES TOLD IN
ENGLAND
Retold by Virginia Haviland.
Illustrated by Bettina. Little, Brown
& Co., 1959.

Six simply told familiar fairy tales with illustrations suitable for the youngest. A lovely retelling of some of England's fairy treasures.

ENGLISH FAIRY TALES
Told by Joseph Jacobs. Illustrated
by John D. Batten. G. P. Putnam's
Sons, n. d.

Forty-four short, delightful legends from English folklore with selected dialect and lively pictures in black and white.

Irish

FAVORITE FAIRY TALES TOLD IN
IRELAND

Retold by Virginia Haviland.
Illustrated by Artur Marokvia.
Little, Brown & Co., 1961.

Lively fairy stories resplendent with the magical qualities that abound in the Emerald Isle. Handsome colored illustrations further enhance this collection.

CELTIC FAIRY TALES
Selected and edited by Joseph
Jacobs. Illustrated by John D.
Batten. G. P. Putnam's Sons, n. d.

Twenty-six tales chosen for fairy elements that reflect beliefs and superstitions found among the Irish. A superbly told collection with much Irish wit, wisdom, and imagination.

Scottish

THE MAGIC BAGPIPE
Told and illustrated by Gerry and

George Armstrong. Albert Whitman & Co., 1964.

The short narrative of a rescued fairy who gives MacCrimmon a magic bagpipe that only he can play told with a Highland flair that makes the tale endearing.

NORTHERN EUROPEAN INFLUENCE

Danish

THE WILD SWANS
Translated from Hans Christian Andersen. Illustrated by Marcia Brown. Charles Scribner's Sons, 1963.

Quiet beauty and grace mark one of the loveliest of fairy tales. Pictures on every page accompanied by gentle lines of text tell the tale of the bewitched swan brothers. Touches of coral give warmth to pages of pen-and-wash drawings in black and gray tones.

FAIRY TALES
Translated from Hans Christian Andersen. Illustrated by children of eighteen nations. Orion Press, 1958.

Some of Andersen's gentler tales tenderly told and sympathetically illustrated with childhood's touch. The pictures frequently reveal interpretations native to the children rather than to the stories' region.

THUMBELINA
Translated from Hans Christian Andersen. Illustrated by Adrienne Adams. Charles Scribner's Sons, 1961.

An exquisite picture book graced with beautiful water colors that enhance the charm of this lovely fairy tale. Superbly told and well illustrated, this single edition of an Andersen story is a book of rare beauty.

THE UGLY DUCKLING
Written by Hans Christian Andersen. Translated by R. P. Keigwin. Illustrated by Adrienne Adams. Charles Scribner's Sons, 1965.

A fresh interpretation of a classic fairy tale sympathetically interpreted by lovely pictures. Brooding qualities are contrasted with splendid fulfillment across the broad, well-designed pages.

SEVEN TALES
Written by Hans Christian Andersen. Translated by Eva Le Gallienne. Illustrated by Maurice Sendak. Harper & Row, Publishers, 1959.

Seven of Andersen's beautifully told tales superbly illustrated by Sendak make this a special literature treasure.

Norwegian

EAST OF THE SUN AND WEST OF THE MOON
Collected by Peter Asbjörnsen and Jörgen E. Moe. Illustrated by Hedvig Collin. The Macmillan Company, 1953.

Twelve stories by the classic collector of Scandinavian fairy tales. Suitable for reading aloud to very young children, the imaginative tales include favorites such as "The Princess on the Glass Hill" and "The Giant Who Had No Heart in His Body." The stories are dramatically enlivened with strong Norse drawings.

TRUE AND UNTRUE AND OTHER NORSE TALES
Edited by Sigrid Undset. Illustrated by Fred Chapman. Alfred A. Knopf, Inc., 1962.

Based on Norse stories collected by Moe and Asbjörnsen, these twenty-seven tales deal dramatically with classical fairy tale situations. The powerful drawings use costumes of the Middle Ages.

Swedish

THE WONDERFUL ADVENTURES OF
NILS
*Told by Selma Lagerlöf. Illustrated
by Hans Baumhauer. Pantheon
Books, Inc., 1947.*

Moving stories interwoven with folkways
of Sweden tell about a goose-boy who is
changed into an elf and must travel with
the wild geese. Beauty and pathos convey
the moral in this fairy tale of a boy who is
punished for his misdeeds.

Finnish

TALES FROM A FINNISH TUPA
*Told by James Cloyd Bowman and
Margery Bianco. Illustrated by Laura
Bannon. Albert Whitman & Co.,
1964.*

Based on Aili Kolehmainen's translation,
these Finnish fairy tales retain the values
present in the original stories. Magic,
humor, and fable-like elements are woven
into this outstanding collection.

CENTRAL EUROPEAN INFLUENCE

French

RAMINAGROBIS AND THE MICE
*Told and illustrated by Harold
Berson. Seabury Press, Inc., 1965.*

Charming drawings in black and white
join slender text in telling a fairy tale based
on an eighteenth century La Fontaine
character. Raminagrobis and his villainous
designs on four mice living in an abandoned tower bring humor to a highly
imaginative tale.

CINDERELLA: OR THE LITTLE
GLASS SLIPPER
*Translated and illustrated by
Marcia Brown. Charles Scribner's
Sons, 1954.*

Adapted from the original French collection by Charles Perrault, this storybook
is graced with artistry in text and pictures.

PUSS IN BOOTS
*Told and illustrated by Marcia
Brown. Charles Scribner's Sons,
1952.*

Again from Charles Perrault's collection, a
superbly told story about a faithful cat,
matched by the author-illustrator's
pictures, which enliven a favorite among
children.

FAVORITE FAIRY TALES TOLD IN
FRANCE
*Retold by Virginia Haviland.
Illustrated by Roger Duvoisin.
Little, Brown & Co., 1959.*

More delightfully produced fairy tales in
the series. Duvoisin makes a child's
enjoyment of these five stories memorable
with his illustrations.

PERRAULT'S COMPLETE FAIRY
TALES
*Translated by A. E. Johnson.
Illustrated by W. Heath Robinson.
Dodd, Mead & Co., 1961.*

A superb collection of fourteen favorite
fairy tales, elegantly produced, and illustrated with beautiful fantasy.

CINDERELLA
*Adapted and illustrated by Beni
Montresor from the opera version by
Gioacchino Rossini. Alfred A.
Knopf, Inc., 1965.*

Perrault's graceful tale decked in stage
settings to match those of the Metropolitan
Opera Company. Contrasting with quieter
editions, this one lights up in gaudy colors
suggestive of toy theatres.

THE WHITE RAT'S TALE
*Written by Barbara Schiller.
Illustrated by Adrienne Adams.
Holt, Rinehart & Winston, Inc.,
1967.*

A fragile medieval French fairy tale wound around a white lady rat who is so wonderful that the king and queen, with no daughter of their own, have her changed into a real royal princess. The wedding day, however, brings problems because the princess is hard to please, especially since she wants the most powerful man in the world for a husband. When the espoused turns out to be a splendid gray gentlemen rat, the princess is once again changed to her former state and presumably lives happily ever after as a lady rat. Adrienne Adams' delicate drawings are a perfect complement to this lyrical fairy tale.

German

JORINDA AND JORINGEL
*Translated from the Brothers
Grimm by Elizabeth Shub. Illustrated
by Adrienne Adams. Charles
Scribner's Sons, 1968.*

This lovely fairy tale, translated from the German, tells in lyrical prose the love story of two sweethearts lost in the woods. Straying close to a witch's castle Jorinda falls under the evil spell that has already turned thousands of girls like herself into imprisoned nightingales. Vowing to free his sweetheart, Joringel searches for the magic flower that will break the witch's spell. He succeeds and they are united to live happily ever after. Graceful illustrations trace beautiful forms abounding in this fairy tale.

THE SLEEPING BEAUTY
*Translated from the German
collection of the Brothers Grimm.
Illustrated by Felix Hoffmann.
Harcourt, Brace & World, Inc.,
1960.*

A beautiful picture book that reveals sympathetic agreement between its radiant pictures and fairy tale text. A favorite of old and young, Sleeping Beauty comes vividly to life in the illustrations.

SNOW WHITE AND ROSE RED
*Translated by Wayne Andrews from
the German collection of the
Brothers Grimm. Illustrated by
Adrienne Adams. Charles
Scribner's Sons, 1964.*

A fairy tale of enchantment and romance and of good and evil. Magical pictures in beautiful colors filtered with light create an illusion appropriate to the fantasy.

THE SHOEMAKER AND THE ELVES
*The tale from the Brothers Grimm
translated by Wayne Andrews.
Illustrated by Adrienne Adams. Charles
Charles Scribner's Sons, 1960.*

A sensitive retelling wedded to delightfully expressive pictures mark this as a notable book that richly interprets the fairy tale world.

GRIMM'S FAIRY TALES
*By the Brothers Grimm. Illustrated
by Arnold Roth. The Macmillan
Company, 1963.*

One hundred tales including less familiar ones as well as the universally beloved.

THE WOLF AND THE SEVEN LITTLE KIDS
*By the Brothers Grimm. Illustrated
by Felix Hoffmann. Harcourt, Brace
& World, Inc., 1957.*

A fairy tale delightful for small children with endearing and artistic illustrations.

THREE GAY TALES FROM GRIMM
*Told and illustrated by Wanda Gág.
Coward-McCann, Inc., 1943.*

Three delightfully absurd stories with apt illustrations.

ONCE UPON A TIME
Retold by Rose Dobbs. Illustrated by

Flavia Gág. Random House, Inc., 1950.

Twenty endearing, familiar tales are divided into sections on timelessness, why and how, and fun. Comical drawings in black and white.

THE WISH WORKERS
By Aliki. Illustrated by the author.
The Dial Press, Inc., 1962.

Modern fairy tale of the vain Twiddle, who foolishly uses up his three wishes.

MEDITERRANEAN INFLUENCE

THE ROSE FAIRY BOOK
Edited by Andrew Lang. Foreword
by Mary Gould Davis. Longmans,
Green & Co., Inc., 1948.

Romantic tales from Mediterranean backgrounds. The magical loveliness of these tales reflects the art of the storyteller who brought them to English-speaking children.

Italian

ITALIAN PEEPSHOW
Told by Eleanor Farjeon. Illustrated
by Edward Ardizzone. Henry Z.
Walck, Inc., Publishers, 1960.

An unusual Florentine fairy tale of fun and fancy interlaced with Italian tales full of poetic inventions. Enchanting pictures by an outstanding artist.

FAVORITE FAIRY TALES TOLD IN
ITALY
Retold by Virginia Haviland.
Illustrated by Evaline Ness. Little,
Brown & Co., 1965.

Six sunlit tales adapted for younger children whose interest in other lands will be heightened by the glorious pictures that interpret the magical stories with a Mediterranean flavor.

OLD NEAPOLITAN FAIRY TALES
Selected from Il Pentamerone and
told by Rose Laura Mincieli.
Illustrated by Beni Montresor.
Alfred A. Knopf, Inc., 1963.

Twelve tales from a collection first set down in Naples during the seventeenth century. Large type and vivid pictures enhance the usefulness of these ancient fantasies.

Spanish

TALES OF ENCHANTMENT FROM
SPAIN
Told by Elsie Spicer Eells.
Illustrated by Maud and Miska
Petersham. Dodd, Mead & Co.,
1950.

Resplendent with magic, these tales from Spain convey much of the enchantment of that sunny land. The romance in these stories makes them outstanding since they retain values found among Mediterranean peoples.

FAVORITE FAIRY TALES TOLD IN
SPAIN
Retold by Virginia Haviland.
Illustrated by Barbara Cooney.
Little, Brown & Co., 1963.

Imaginative and beautiful water colors glowing with the warmth and sunshine of Spain illuminate six stories well chosen for their splendid read-aloud texts.

EURASIAN INFLUENCE

THE GOLDEN LYNX
Selected and told by Augusta Baker.
Illustrated by Johannes Troyer. J. B.
Lippincott Co., 1960.

A collection of traditional tales from Europe and Asia by a storytelling specialist who has tried them all out with children. Selected for their beauty and enchanting elements, these tales possess the added brilliance provided by the illustrator.

Russian

BABA YAGA'S SECRET
*Told by Nancy K. Ford. Illustrated
by Kurt Werth. J. B. Lippincott Co.,
1959.*

A witch and a harassed cat serve as the principals in an animal fairy tale that features talking beasts. Russian-oriented pictures echo the vigor and imagination expressed by the stories themselves.

FAVORITE FAIRY TALES TOLD IN
RUSSIA
*Retold by Virginia Haviland.
Illustrated by Herbert Danska.
Little, Brown & Co., 1961.*

Five lively stories with large print and excellent illustrations aimed at younger children. Concerned with magic and superhuman feats, the collection points up characteristics indigenous to the culture that influenced them.

THE STORY OF PRINCE IVAN, THE
FIREBIRD, AND THE GRAY WOLF
*Translated from the Russian by
Thomas P. Whitney. Illustrated by
Nonny Hogrogian. Charles Scribner's
Sons, 1968.*

This classic Russian fairy tale is well told in English and glowingly illustrated for young readers. Relating the fabulous adventures of Prince Ivan during his search for the Firebird, the story abounds in splendid creatures, a beautiful Princess Elena, and a magnificent Firebird. Rare beauty marks this most unusual fairy tale.

NORTH AND LATIN AMERICAN INFLUENCES OF AFRO-ASIAN ORIGIN

THE MAGIC CALABASH
Edited by Jean Cothran. Illustrated

*by Clifford N. Geary. David
McKay Co., Inc., 1956.*

Sixteen glorious tales of Eskimo, Polynesian, Negro, and similar origins. Superbly told, these tales bring a wealth of wisdom, wit, and fantasy from America's islands and Alaska. Many of the beautiful stories could be classified as myths, fables, and folk tales as well as stories of magic.

NORTH AND LATIN AMERICAN INFLUENCES OF EUROPEAN ORIGIN

THE GOLDEN PHOENIX AND
OTHER FRENCH-CANADIAN
FAIRY TALES
*Compiled by Marius Barbeau.
Retold by Michael Hornyansky.
Illustrated by Arthur Price.
Henry Z. Walck, Inc., Publishers,
1958.*

Eight French-Canadian tales well written and beautifully illustrated with the flavor transmitted by French colonists some three hundred years ago. Included are some magnificent tales of magic.

PEACOCK PIE
*Told by Walter de la Mare.
Illustrated by Barbara Cooney.
Alfred A. Knopf, Inc., 1961.*

Dancing rhymes tell about witches, fairies, and farmers. Luminous pictures by an outstanding illustrator highlight this collection.

THE WONDER CLOCK
*Told and illustrated by Howard
Pyle. Harper & Row, Publishers,
1915.*

This handsome collection is made up of old fairy tales rooted in European backgrounds and retold by a great storyteller. The collection consists of "four and twenty marvelous tales, being one for each hour of the day."

THE MAGIC FEATHER DUSTER
*Told and illustrated by Will and
Nicolas. Harcourt, Brace & World,
Inc., 1958.*

In this tale of magic, reminiscent of an old
European fairy tale, kindness and unself-
ishness triumph over avarice. Intended for
younger children, this picture book is
marked by simplicity and good taste.

NORTH AND LATIN AMERICAN INFLUENCES OF NATIVE ORIGIN

THE WITCHES' RIDE AND OTHER
TALES FROM COSTA RICA
*Translated, retold and illustrated by
Lupe de Osma. William Morrow
& Co., Inc., 1957.*

Twelve fairy tales illustrated with charming pictures that stress peasant humor and
local color with delicacy and authenticity.

IN MEXICO THEY SAY
*Told by Patricia Ross. Illustrated by
Henry C. Pitz. Alfred A. Knopf, Inc.,
1942.*

A beautiful collection of fairy tales steeped
in strong elements of fantasy and superstition. Authentically flavored pictures
adorn a rich collection of tales.

FAIRY TALES FROM BRAZIL
*Told by Elsie S. Eells. Dodd,
Mead & Co., 1917.*

Stories that resemble fables but with many
more supernatural and magical elements.
The Brazilian settings retain a Latin
American flavor.

THE GOLDEN WEDGE
*Told by Maud H. Lovelace and
Delos Wheeler Lovelace. Thomas
Y. Crowell Company, 1942.*

South American Indian tales that preserve
some of the ancient magic of dwindling
tribes. Poetic prose recounts supernatural
feats that give the collection a mythical
slant.

Fiery horses and mythical deities wing their way out of pillared palaces across a sea of clouds in this illustration that jackets a book of myths.

From A Treasury of Greek Mythology *by Alisoun Witting, illustrated by James Barry. Harvey House, Inc., 1965. Reproduced by permission.*

Chapter **8**

MYTHS,
FABLES,
AND
LEGENDS

*Religion, philosophies, arts, the social forms of primitive and historic
man, prime discoveries in science and technology, the very dreams that blister
sleep, boil up from the basic ring of myth.*

—Joseph Campbell
The Hero with a Thousand Faces
Pantheon Books, 1949

215

Definition
of Myths

The word "myth" comes from the Greek "mythos," meaning tale or story. Today the word myth refers to the kind of story that ancient man composed to explain nature, or to perpetuate the heroic deeds of gods and men.

Like the rest of the world's folklore, myths have come down from an obscure and distant past. Their origins are lost, yet they reveal a freshness and a significance that transcends time itself. Although the world in which the myths were first hammered out has faded away, they have endured and continue to undergo interpretations in keeping with the times. But whatever the interpretations, the myths undeniably address themselves to all men in all ages that feel their impact in the indelible impressions they have made on every aspect of civilization.

Civilizations derive their life force from man's endless pursuit of knowledge about himself, the world in which he lives, and his relationship to this world. Primitive man, for example, living in an aura of mysticism and fear, had three ways of obtaining such knowledge: his careful observations of nature, his firsthand experiences of life, and his vivid imagination. With these tools, he attempted to organize his existence by creating explanations for the mysteries that surrounded him.

As he observed such natural phenomena as the rising and setting of the sun, the phases of the moon, changes of seasons, and the succession of day and night, primitive man was filled with wonder, curiosity, and awe. He sought order and meaning beneath the surface of these things, and he used his imagination to explain that which puzzled him. He interpreted these events subjectively and intuitively, for he had no knowledge of a scientific method of hypothesizing, experimenting, and verifying. In a sense, primitive man's thought processes closely parallel those of the young child who also relies upon his intuition for explanations, and whose egocentricity colors his every belief and action. Similarly, thousands of years elapsed between the evolution of myths and the scientific discovery that man was not at the center of the universe.

Every group of people has composed similar stories to explain the natural phenomena of the universe. This chapter will focus on the myths of the Greeks, Romans, and Norsemen.

The Greeks

The ancient Greeks, a lively, imaginative people of rare literary talent, excelled in mythology. They are credited with creating some of the most fascinating tales in literature. The Greeks were

> by nature artistic; they instinctively expressed their ideals, the truth as they saw it, in poetry, story and sculpture, and because imagination, insight, and love of beauty were united in them, their stories and their art have an appeal that is universal.[1]

When the Greeks began to record myths, they also included legends that were based on historical fact; Homer's epics, the *Iliad* and the *Odyssey*, fall into this category of lyrical history.

The Romans

The early Roman myths were concerned more with social functions and interpretations of conduct than with spiritual matters. Later, when the Romans adopted many of the Greek gods, they continued their tradition of treating the gods as exemplary citizens rather than as spiritual models. For reference, a catalogue of corresponding Greek and Roman gods follows:

---

[1] Jessie M. Tatlock, *Greek and Roman Mythology* (Appleton-Century-Crofts, 1917).

GREEK	ROMAN	TITLE
Zeus	Jove or Jupiter	*King of the gods*
Hera	Juno	*Wife of Zeus, goddess of women and marriage*
Kronos	Saturn	*God of time and agriculture*
Poseidon	Neptune	*God of the sea*
Ares	Mars	*God of war*
Apollo	Apollo	*God of the sun and youth*
Hades or Pluto	Dis	*God of the underworld*
Eros	Cupid	*God of love*
Dionysus	Bacchus	*God of the vine*
Athena	Minerva	*Goddess of wisdom*
Aphrodite	Venus	*Goddess of love and beauty*
Artemis	Diana	*Goddess of the moon and the hunt*
Demeter	Ceres	*Goddess of agriculture*
Hermes	Mercury	*Messenger of the gods*
Hephaestus	Vulcan	*God of fire*
Hestia	Vesta	*Goddess of home and hearth*

The gods peculiar to the Romans probably originated in the Stone Age, for they had dominion over plants and animals, and festivals in their honor closely resemble early fertility rites. Roman mythology was far less sophisticated than Greek. The Romans' apparent insecurity and practicality are revealed in the many *numina* or spirits whom they believed controlled their destiny and whom they placated with many offerings and prayers.

The Norsemen

The Germanic tribes had an analogous tradition of mythology, but because they had no architecture or written literature and were essentially hostile toward each other, the myths were not retained when the tribes scattered and came in contact with other cultures. By the time these myths were recorded, in the early fourteenth century A.D., only the Norsemen who had settled in northern Germany (Scandinavia) had preserved any of the ancient tales. The Norseman's view of life, as

portrayed in these myths, was tragic, for the climate was harsh and un-
compromising. Even their gods were mortal and it was believed that
they would perish with man in a terrible battle at the end of the world—
the twilight of the gods. This is a sharp contrast to the immortal Greek
and Roman gods, who lived in a sympathetic climate, and were free
to make sport under the Mediterranean sun.

Using his intuitive knowledge, man endowed natural elements with
spiritual life, thus creating a hierarchy of gods that corresponded to natural
forces. So it was that primitive man came to understand the many marvels
of his world. Gathering these strands of knowledge, he wove them into a
fabric of life that sustained him by dispelling the paralyzing fear of the
unknown.

Types of Myths

Myths can be divided into two broad categories: 1) explanatory myths, which interpret the creation and the causes of natural
phenomena; and 2) exemplary myths, which deal with gods, heroes, and
other persons whose actions are to be emulated.

Of primary importance to all early peoples was the need to explain
their origins as races, and to account for the mysteries of everyday life.
Primitive man realized that some superhuman force had created order out
of the apparent chaos in the universe by giving each aspect of life a specific
place and function. Thus the creation myth usually lays the groundwork
for other explanatory myths.

The Greek and Roman myth of Pluto (Dis) and Persephone (Proserpina) is an explanation of the change of seasons. Persephone, the maiden
of spring and daughter of Demeter (Ceres), the goddess of agriculture,
is abducted by Pluto and taken to his kingdom in the underworld, where
she must stay for part of every year. During Persephone's absence, Demeter grieves and the earth becomes cold and desolate, but when she returns,
the earth blooms again. Similarly, the death of Balder, the best loved of
the Norse gods, leaves the earth dark and barren, for he represents the
sun.

While delighting their audiences, tales of the gods and heroes also
provided an excellent medium for transmitting codes of behavior. Such
myths resemble fables, brief stories that illustrate moral lessons. Fables
take "abstract ideas of good or bad, wise or foolish behavior and attempt to
make them concrete and striking enough to be understood and remem-

bered."[2] The characters in fables are usually coldly impersonal animals or inanimate objects that stand for personality traits such as pride, ignorance, or impatience, for example. The moral is presented at the end of the story in the form of an axiom or proverb, as illustrated by Louis Untermeyer's version of "The Fox and the Grapes":

> The Fox had gone without breakfast as well as without dinner, so when he found himself in a vineyard his mouth began to water. There was one particularly juicy-looking bunch of grapes hanging on a trellis. The Fox leaped to pull it down, but it was just beyond his reach. He went back a few steps, took a running start, and jumped again. Again he missed. Once more he tried, and once more he failed to get the tempting prize. Finally, weary and worn out, he left the vineyard. "I really wasn't very hungry," he said, to console himself. "Besides, I'm sure those grapes are sour."

There is comfort in pretending that what we can't get isn't worth having.[3]

Spying the grapes growing on this gnarled vine, a fox reaches for them but without success. Sturdy woodcuts imprint the fruit and the beast with rustic simplicity.
From an original German woodcut from Aesop's Life and Fables, *Ulm, about 1476–77.*

[2]May Hill Arbuthnot, *Children and Books* (Chicago: Scott, Foresman & Company, 1964), p. 298.
[3]Louis Untermeyer, "The Fox and the Grapes," in *Aesop's Fables* (New York: Golden Press, Inc., 1965), p. 23.

Just as the fables used animals with human characteristics to project their morals and spin their stories, the ancient myths employed gods and heroes to stage the drama of life. The Greeks and Romans were especially able to identify with their gods who were endowed with many human characteristics. Thus the Greeks were amused by Zeus' numerous affairs and instructed by Penelope's faithfulness; the Romans attempted to follow Aeneas' example of reverence for the gods and his father, and commiserated with Orpheus' lack of faith; the Norsemen reveled in Loki's mischievous pranks and strove to pattern their lives after Sigurd's so that they too would be accepted into Valhalla as heroes after death.

Examples of Creation Myths

The creation myth is a fundamental document in a culture's mythology, for it is the story of the origins of a race. The Romans have no extant myth of creation; it is typical that their "creation" story relates the founding of Rome by Romulus and Remus, the mythical twins who were raised by a she-wolf. The founding of their city and civilization was more significant to the Romans than discovering the origins of their people. They adopted the Greek's version of the origins of life in addition to borrowing many of the Hellenic gods.

The Greek and Norse stories of creation depict matter formed either from Chaos or from opposing forces of heat and cold giving the reader deep insight into basic differences between the temperaments and lifestyles of these two civilizations.

The climates in which they flourished were as polar as the differences reflected in their myths. Greek man was made out of the warm Mediterranean clay by Prometheus, the fire-giver. The man of the North was created from a tree by Odin, Vili, and Ve, descendants of the frost giant Ymir. Clay is pliable, trees are resilient; there is a finality in wood that pottery does not suggest: once cut, a tree cannot be reconstructed, but a broken earthenware jug can be fired down and reshaped. The doom of the Norseman was clearly written in the nature of the fiber of his creation, while the dust of the Greek mingled with clay for the continuation of life.

GREEK CREATION MYTH

Before the creation of heaven and earth and the ocean, there existed a shapeless and formless mass which held the seeds for all things. Out of this vast emptiness, which was called Chaos, came Nox, the goddess of night, and Erebus, the darkness of the deep. Because these two were very lonely, they bore Eros, the great power of love. The earth goddess, Gaia, who brought forth the deep seas and the world in which we live, and the starry sky called Uranus also appeared.

From the union of Gaia, the earth, and Uranus, the heavens, came an immortal race called the Titans. They were enormous in size, handsome to behold, and mighty in their strength. But Uranus proved a cruel and savage father who hated certain of his children who were monstrous and ill-formed. When Gaia called together the twelve Titans to help her against the cruelties of Uranus, only Cronus, the youngest of them, dared do the deed demanded by his mother. With a jagged sickle of the strongest metal formed by Gaia, Cronus dealt his father a terrible blow.

Cronus thus became ruler of the universe and took as his wife his sister Rhea. Cronus ruled for many years and the period of his reign was the start of the Golden Age. It was during this time, some say, that Prometheus, the son of the Titan Iapetus, formed man from the clay of the earth and made him in the image of the gods. Unlike the animals whose form makes them look down at the earth, man was made to stand upright so his eyes might easily turn toward the starry heavens.

This early time was a period of joy and innocent happiness. Earth brought forth food, flowers sprang up from the ground, springs ran with milk and nectar. There was no need for plows or swords or spears. Animals lived in harmony with men and men lived in harmony with one another.

NORSE CREATION MYTH

In the beginning of time there was nothing—no sand nor sea nor salty waves. There was no earth below nor heaven above, only a deep and yawning chasm. The sun, the moon, the stars were not yet in the sky.

To the north was Niflheim, a land of mist and icy frost. And to the south was Muspelheim, the home of fire. When burning sparks from Muspelheim rose to touch the northern frost, there formed a huge cloud whose icy drops became Ymir, the first giant. There also grew a giant cow named Audhumla, who nourished Ymir with her milk.

For food Audhumla licked the hoary frost, which held the salt of life. One day as she licked these salty blocks of rime, the head and then the form of man appeared. Fair and strong and brave, he was Buri, the first of the gods. From his son, who was called Borr, came Odin, the all-father, and his brothers, Vili and Ve.

Depicting the creation of the first gods and giants in Norse mythology, this spread pictures the frost giant, Ymir, and the hornless ice cow. Offspring sprout from Ymir while the cow brings about life by licking the brim of the salt pit.
From Norse Gods and Giants *by Ingri and Edgar Parin d'Aulaire. Copyright © 1967 by the d'Aulaires. Doubleday and Company, Inc. Reproduced by permission.*

From the beginning there was enmity between the giants and the gods. When at last a great battle was fought, Ymir, the mighty frost giant, was slain. So huge was he that from his flesh the gods could form the earth, and from his skull they shaped the sky. His bones became the barren hills. From his hair grew the trees. And from his blood flowed the rivers of the earth and the waters of the sea. Then the gods used his eyebrows to build a wall around Midgard, which was to be the home of man.

But still the world was not complete. So the gods took an ash tree from the shore and formed a man. And from an elm they made woman. To these two, who had nothing, Odin gave life and spirit, Vili gave wisdom and understanding, and Ve gave sight and speech and hearing, along with form and shape for their bodies.

The man they called Ask and the woman they named Embla. From these two came all mankind.

Examples of Exemplary Myths

The exemplary myth covers and rounds out the skeleton of the creation myth by giving substance and depth to the fundamental story of a race. By adding the human element, and allowing all men the opportunity to aspire to a mortal godhead—heroism—the exemplary myth propounds the national creed. A god receives reverent worship and almost blind obedience, but a hero must earn his place in the hearts of his people.

Perseus of Greece and Sigurd of Scandinavia are such mortals who achieved the greatness of the gods by their valorous actions on earth. Once again, the essential differences in the life styles of the Greeks and Norsemen can be seen in their myths. Perseus performed glorious deeds to protect his mother and to please the gods. His concern lay with this world. Sigurd, on the other hand, upheld the tradition of the Volsungs. Of foremost importance to him, as a Norseman, was to die heroically in battle while fighting for his king and his people.

These two heroes, equal in valor, faced monsters and slew them. One, Perseus, fought with aid from the gods; he was fortified with a divine shield and sword and armed with moral strength from Athene. Without this help, his quest would never have succeeded. The other, Sigurd, stood alone with the sword of his ancestors and faced a monster and a treacherous man before winning fame and a place in Valhalla, the hall of the heroes.

GREEK EXEMPLARY MYTH

Perseus was the son of Danae and Zeus, who had come to the beautiful daughter of the King of Argos as a shower of gold. Because an oracle had once told King Acrisius that the son his daughter bore would kill him, the king imprisoned the two in a chest and cast them out to sea.

Through the protection of Zeus, the box with the beautiful Danae and the boy Perseus washed ashore on an island. There Danae taught Perseus to revere the gods and saw him grow into a handsome, strong young man with grace and courage befitting the grandson of a king and the son of a god.

Polydectes, the cruel king of the island, desired Danae as his bride but knew he had no chance of winning her as long as the brave Perseus was near to protect her. So as a challenge to the youth and to remove him forever from the island, King Polydectes sent Perseus to seek the head of Medusa. This creature was one of the Gorgons, horrible, scaly monsters whose heads were covered with ugly, writhing snakes instead of hair. So fierce and so ugly were the Gorgons that anyone looking at them was turned instantly to stone.

As he started on his quest, the young hero found allies among the gods and goddesses. Hermes told Perseus to polish the shield Athene had given him until it was mirror-bright and so shiny that what it reflected was as clear to Perseus as if he had gazed on the object directly. Hermes presented Perseus with his sword, the only one strong enough to slice through the scales of Medusa's neck.

PERSEVS RESCVES ANDROMEDA

Atoning for her mother's sins, Andromeda prepares to sacrifice herself to the sea monster. Shooting down like a star, Perseus challenges the scaly creature by flashing before him the Gorgon's head that freezes the monster into a stretch of black rock.
From The Heroes *by Charles Kingsley, illustrated by H. M. Brock. First published in 1855. Copyright © 1962 by Macmillan and Co., Ltd. Reproduced by permission.*

Still further help came from the nymphs who provided Perseus with a helmet to make him invisible and with winged slippers to make him fleet of foot and able to travel swiftly through the air. Their third gift was a small, magic pouch that expanded to fit the size and form of whatever was thrust into it.

With Athene and Hermes at his side, Perseus reached the home of the Gorgons. There, surrounding these horrible creatures, were fields filled with stone statues, figures of those whose eyes had dared a flickering glance at the monsters. Even in sleep the Gorgons were frightening, for the snakes that formed their hair restlessly hissed and tossed about.

His companions pointed out Medusa and urged Perseus to be swift, to strike and be away before the Gorgons awoke and made his task impossible. Perseus drew closer, always keeping Medusa's image reflected in his shield, for he did not wish to be turned to stone as others had. Quickly he slashed at Medusa's head, snatched it from her body, and thrusting it into his magic pouch, leaped high into the air to escape the fury of her awakened companions.

On the long journey home, Perseus stopped to rescue Andromeda, the beautiful daughter of the Ethiopian king, just as she was about to be devoured by a sea monster. He claimed her hand in marriage and together they flew back to his island home.

Perseus knew now that the cruel King Polydectes was a wicked tyrant who had intended that the task of beheading Medusa would cause the death, not of Medusa, but of Perseus himself. When the king and his friends refused to believe that Perseus had really accomplished his task of slaying the Gorgon, the young hero snatched the head from his bag for all to see—and they were instantly turned to stone.

NORSE EXEMPLARY MYTH

Sigurd, son of Sigmund, was the greatest of the Volsungs. All knew him as the noblest of men, fearless and swift, far above all others in strength, stature, and deeds of daring. He was of the race of the sons of Odin.

Regin, the skilled craftsman, was his boyhood tutor, teaching him all a mighty warrior must know. When Sigurd grew to manhood, Regin told a tale of ancient wrong, how Regin's brother Fafnir killed their father for his gold and turned himself into a dragon to guard his priceless hoard on Guitna Heath.

And Regin told how fierce this serpent Fafnir was, how strong his venom, and how his breath so seared the earth that no man dared go near.

To destroy this dragon, this enemy of men and gods, Regin said, was a worthy task for the son of the brave race of the Volsungs. And Sigurd knew the time had come for him to venture forth and prove himself.

For this deed and for his other battles with men and kingdoms far and near, Sigurd sought a mighty horse. From the herd of the king he selected Grani, the swiftest of stallions, said to be descended from Sleip-ner, Odin's eight-footed steed.

To have a blade of keenest steel for his own, Sigurd took the frag-ments of his father's sword, once the gift of Odin, and had Regin reforge for him the sword called Gram. So strong was this sword that with one stroke it split apart Regin's anvil and so sharp was the blade that it cut in two a lock of wool that floated down the river.

For the first task of his manhood, Sigurd decided to avenge his fa-ther's death. Only when this deed was done did he set forth to find the dragon Fafnir. Together Regin and Sigurd devised a plan to kill the beast, but Regin, in truth, was plotting Sigurd's death. At last Sigurd saw through the wicked plan and saved himself as he delivered a death wound to the dragon. With just two swift strokes Sigurd slew the serpent and rid the world of this vile beast forever.

The Significance of Myths
to Their Creators

THE GREEKS

In early Greek civilization, during the Mycenean period (roughly 1600 to 1100 B.C.), two forces produced the tales of gods and heroes: the need to explain natural phenomena, and the need to create a history and tradition of the great wars and the heroes who had fought in them. These myths were set in the cities, palaces, and countryside of that time, making them very real to the people. Centuries later, in the Golden Age of Greece, the Age of Pericles (800 to 600 B.C.), the validity of these histories could be attested to by the continued existence of these sites. Three thousand years later, late in the last century, the place names served as valuable information to archeologists who sought to validate these records and to find clues to these early civilizations.

As the history of this era was transmitted to each succeeding genera-tion, deeds of individual heroes were expanded, thus creating a heroic tradition. Concurrently, interest in the world about them motivated the Mycenaeans to seek explanations for the outside forces that controlled

The imposing figure of the Trojan Horse stands garlanded in the assembly place as Greek warriors of Agamemnon's army overtake Troy. Classic simplicity hallmarks the art in this book.
From The Iliad of Homer *retold by Barbara Leonie Picard, illustrated by Joan Kiddell-Monroe. Copyright 1960 by Oxford University Press. Reproduced by permission of Henry Z. Walck, Inc.*

their lives. Indeed, the early stories of gods are focused upon the crops and weather. The establishment of gods to personify natural forces led to sacrificial worship, for a farmer could easily connect adversity with a god's wrath. Even after all of the gods had been propitiated, misfortunes still occurred; man then explained such catastrophes as the way of the inscrutable gods. Both heroes and gods were very real to the Greeks; humans and deities were assembled into a body of myths, founded on historical truths and curiosity about nature. Myths were both religious and secular for the Greek, and thus were a functional part of Greek life.

THE ROMANS

Prior to Hellenization in the sixth century B.C., the Romans had already established their own body of gods and heroes. Besides protecting households, the early gods dictated the social order and provided standards of behavior. Each Roman home had an altar dedicated to the gods (Lares) who protected the household and its human and animal inhabitants. Worship of the gods took a very personal form then. Between the sixth and third centuries B.C., Greek influences began to filter into

Roman life. The assimilation was so smooth that Greek gods stood beside
those of ancient Rome and were incorporated into the existing rituals. With the rise of the Roman Empire, the religion that had grown up around mythology was gradually admitted into administrative functions. The gods of Rome were thus secularized and made a part of common state ritual. They served more as practical guides to behavior than as sources of inspiration.

The myths had perhaps greatest significance for the Norsemen who had no codified system of laws or great cities to stabilize their culture. Thus the myths served as a central point of reference for the people of the tribes. Myths were multifaceted documents for the Norsemen, functioning as religion, ethical code, history, and entertainment. The *Eddas* influenced the Norseman just as the Homeric tales molded the Greek.

The Significance of Myths Today

MYTHOLOGY AND CHILDREN'S LITERATURE

The world of mythology is a natural source of literature for children, for the child has, within his imagination, the seeds of all experience from the beginning of time. Each child discovers fire again and sees the sun rise for the first time. He invents the wheel, and makes his home in trees, in caves, in huts, in boats, in tunnels. He lives beneath the waves, and he even launches flights to outer space.

There is no path that men have traveled that has not been rediscovered by children who will continue to chart the realm of imagination as long as there is childhood and its strong sense of wonder and curiosity, as well as the urge to live and grow.

The child's mind operates on many levels. The little boy who walks down the street taking great care not to step on any cracks lest he "break his mother's back," is not in the least surprised to come home after stepping on cracks to find that she is none the worse for his oversight. He can believe and yet not believe simultaneously. He can know that rain is condensed vapor, and yet know, just as certainly, that it is the tears of a god; he is capable of believing firmly in a number of explanations for one natural phenomenon. Therefore, the more alternatives he accepts, the richer he is. These contradictory explanations do not confuse him, for every child has an innate tendency toward "that willing suspension of disbelief" of which Coleridge speaks as a necessary element in comprehending poetry.

The great myths are poetry in the fullest sense; they are the poetry of whole cultures—great metaphors that can enlighten, delight, and render more human the child who reads them. Basically, myths are attempts to explain natural phenomena, or to glorify noble deeds, but they are also living documents of human experience, and as such can never diminish in importance to the child.

Myths, as they represent the various levels of man's emergence from the shadowy, fantasy-filled existence of primitive life into the relative clarity and sophistication of the civilized world, parallel the development of childhood itself in terms that can be understood at each successive stage of growth and development.

For the younger child, whose mind is geared toward endowing natural objects with life and bestowing human attributes on animals and plants, there are the tales created at the earliest stages of man's development to explain in simple and meaningful terms the causes of natural phenomena. When thunder rolled and lightning flashed, it was only Thor driving his chariot and throwing his hammer.

As the child grows older and becomes more concerned with his own emerging image, the marvelous adventures and exciting contests of the gods and their superhuman achievements offer many significant opportunities for identification. Perseus accomplished the almost impossible feat of slaying the Gorgon, serving as an example to those children who in their own lives are faced with similar seemingly impossible tasks that are a part of the difficult process of growing up.

And for those children who stand at the threshold of adulthood, ready to assume its attendant responsibilities, there are the more complex and symbolic myths representing the highest and most perfect expression of man's view of himself and the larger world in which he lives. For them, the story of Pandora has a profound significance in its implication of how the actions of one affect the lives and welfare of many.

Stemming from the consciousness of man, myths are, in a way, a mirror of life, reflecting the prototype of every human experience at many levels of interpretation, and offering an infinite variety of possibilities for meaningful learning experiences for children of all ages.

MYTHOLOGY AND LANGUAGE

The significance of mythology for boys and girls extends even further than its role as a source of literature. Myths have become a part of Western culture and thinking. Words in English, for example, are derived from the names of characters that appear in these tales. One speaks of herculean tasks requiring the superhuman strength of a Hercules, vulcanized tires are toughened with the same kind of intense heat produced by Vulcan, the Roman god of fire; a mercurial person is quick like Mercury, Roman messenger of the gods.

In another realm the names of planets are taken from the Greek and Roman gods:

PLANET	TITLE
Mercury	*Messenger of the gods (R)*
Venus	*Goddess of love and beauty (R)*
Mars	*God of war (R)*
Jupiter	*King of the gods (R)*
Saturn	*God of time (R)*
Uranus	*Personification of heaven (G)*
Neptune	*God of the sea (R)*
Pluto	*God of the underworld (G)*

Days of the week as we know them in English are identified with Roman and Norse gods, and come to us through the Anglo-Saxons:

DAY	GOD
Monday	*Moon's (N)*
Tuesday	*Tiw's day (N)*
Wednesday	*Woden's day (N)*
Thursday	*Thor's day (N)*
Friday	*Frigga's day (N)*
Saturday	*Saturn's day (R)*
Sunday	*Sun's day (N)*

Stories of mythology can, therefore, serve as a focal point in an enrichment program designed to help children learn more about their language in an interesting and meaningful manner. Eventually, upon this foundation an appreciation for and understanding of literature, music, drama, art, and dance will be built, for all of these reflect the influence of mythology.

Mythology exists as a rich source of stories that have withstood time and that are as pertinent today as in the days when they were first created.

Whether the myths explain natural phenomena or stress human ideals, they owe their immortality to a single ingredient—the art of storytelling. Evoking a sense of beauty, the lyrical language of the myths intones the wisdom of the ages, for in a way, the mythology of a people is an insightful commentary of human drama and experience.

The myths of deathless deeds and destinies are ageless in their appeal and their frequent retellings speak simply and directly to children. Caught in the spell of the ancient storytellers, children who have been nurtured on simpler tales find enchantment in traveling to mythical lands of winged horses, magic swords, one-eyed giants, sea serpents, dragons, talking beasts, Elysian fields, gods, and heroes—all the elements of a poetic imagination, which, in a sense, are akin to the kinds of pictures children paint in their dreams and daydreams.

General Criteria
for Folklore of the World

THEME

- Is the theme (or themes) in the tale objective and understandable?
- Is the theme suitable for the age group using the tale?
- Do some of the talking beast tales point up appropriate morals such as the folly of credulity, or the rewards of courage, ingenuity, and independence?
- Are the themes in the stories diverting and suitable for good entertainment?
- Do the fairy tales and myths in particular capture children's interest and fanciful imagination?
- Do the highly imaginative tales provide for a measure of wish fulfillment?
- Is the "romance" found in some folk tales remote and impersonal?
- Are the themes vital enough to be concerned with: winning security, earning a living or a place in the world, accomplishing impossible tasks at personal risk, escaping from powerful enemies, outwitting wicked schemes and schemers, and succeeding with nonchalance?
- Do some of the stories put their stamp of approval upon certain values held in high esteem by certain groups?
- Do some of the stories accommodate the values and morality common to childhood?
- Do some of the tales stress human ideals: modesty, kindness, honesty, courage, and so forth?

- Do the stories make virtue seem worthwhile because it is rewarded and evil unprofitable because it is punished?
- Do the tales portray a moral code that has ethical significance for and gives emotional satisfaction to young readers?
- Is the tale or tales in some way a reflection of the people?
- Are the themes in the stories set in symbolic forms that appeal and satisfy man's basic emotional needs?

STYLE

- Does the story possess the charm and characteristic language patterns suitable for storytelling?
- Is the language of the story characteristic of the particular type of tale, and is it readily understood by the listeners or readers?
- Is the language in most of the tales cadenced, or witty, or romantic in accordance with the theme and mood of the tales?
- Does the conclusion demonstrate skill in breaking off and sending the listener or reader back to his real world?
- Is the dialogue in the story so natural that real people seem to be talking?
- Do the words in swift interchange suffice to establish the attitude of the speakers?
- Do the folk and fairy tales in particular have a minimum of plot and maximum rhythm suitable for young children?
- Do most of the tales stress a melodious oral pattern in which rhymes frequently appear?
- Is the vocabulary and style of writing used in the story expressive of the people and area influencing the account?
- Are some colloquialisms, idioms, distinctive phrasing, rural obsolete words used, adding flavor and uniqueness to the tales?
- Do the more imaginative fairy tales, myths, and legends create beautiful images of lovely paraphernalia?

PLOT

- Is the plot dramatic, exciting, full of suspense, action, and smashing climaxes that make children eager to hear more?
- Do the episodes in the accumulative tales follow each other neatly and logically in a pattern of cadenced repetition?
- Is the conflict of the plot launched with no distracting details?
- Does the development or plot carry forward the note sounded in the introduction?
- Does the action mount steadily until it reaches a climax when the conflict is resolved?

- Does the plot preserve unity of interest, that is, the centering of attention on the theme?
- Does the conclusion follow swiftly on the heels of the climax and end everything started in the story?
- Do the heroes and heroines achieve a happy solution for their efforts? And are the villains accounted for and punished accordingly?
- Do the droll and silly characters in some stories effectively carry out appropriate episodes, which though improbable, are possible?

CHARACTERIZATION

- Does the portrayal of the characters in the story reveal understanding of humans?
- Does the story interpret the ways of human beings with one another?
- Do the animals embody certain human traits such as loyalty, slyness, cleverness, and so forth?
- Do some of the story characters accurately portray local people and their customs?
- Do the characters give expression to deep universal emotions: joy, grief, fear, jealousy, wonder, triumph?
- Do the characters reap the results of greed, selfish ambition, or quiet courage and humane treatment?
- Are the characters typed as good or bad, but individualized sufficiently to arouse sympathy or antagonism by brief characterizations?
- Do characters in the tales mirror the lives, tendencies, beliefs, and emotions of people the world over?
- Do the myths, in particular, cut across a wide range of human emotions and human situations, but at the same time loom larger than life as ancestral prototypes?
- Are the characters in myths and legends drawn so that they appear vivid and alive despite their antiquity and fantastic forms?
- Are gods and heroes "believable," with certain qualities of human naturalness?
- Are the stories of legendary heroes based on some historical fact?

SETTING AND DESIGN

- Do the books of collections or single editions blend beautiful retellings with fine illustrations, format, paper, print, binding and design in general?
- Do the illustrations faithfully interpret the story they accompany?
- Do the pictures create a suitable atmosphere by clearly depicting scenes and settings from the story?
- Do the illustrations transport readers to the scene of the story?

- Are the pictures suggestive of the geographical location pointed out by the tale?
- Have the characters in the illustrations been clothed in costumes that authentically depict the period in which the story is told?
- Is there a sense of mystery and magic in the pictures for such stories?
- In pictures for younger children especially, has the artist exercised the rare ability to trace recognizable and unusual details that are most appealing in books of folklore?
- Do the illustrations and design of the books generate interest by skillful use of drawings, color, shading, shapes, beauty, and balance?

References

ARBUTHNOT, MAY HILL, "Fables, Myths, and Epics," in *Children and Books*, 3rd ed. Chicago: Scott, Foresman & Company, 1964.

HUBER, MIRIAM BLANTON, "Legends and Hero Tales," in *Story and Verse for Children*. New York: The Macmillan Company, 1965.

HUCK, CHARLOTTE S., AND DORIS A. YOUNG, "Myths and Legends," in *Children's Literature in the Elementary School*. New York: Holt, Rinehart & Winston, Inc., 1961.

JOHNSON, EDNA, *et al.*, "Myths and Legends," in *Anthology of Children's Literature*. Boston: Houghton Mifflin Company, 1959.

SMITH, LILLIAN H., "Gods and Men," in *The Unreluctant Years*. Chicago: American Library Association, 1953.

Multiethnic Myths in English

COLLECTIONS WITH MULTIETHNIC BACKGROUNDS

A BOOK OF FAMOUS MYTHS AND LEGENDS
Told and edited by Thomas B. Aldrich. Illustrated. Hall & Locke Co., 1901.

An excellent, well-written collection of twelve stories from many countries by several authors. Stories include: "The Golden Touch," "The Argonauts," "The Odyssey," "Beowulf," and "Rip Van Winkle." There are twelve color illustrations.

MYTHS OF THE WORLD
Collected by Padraic Colum. Illustrated by Boris Artzybasheff. The Macmillan Co., 1930.

This book includes a very interesting section on the significance of mythology in which the mythology of the seventeen races included in the book is discussed. The book has fifty-seven stories, and is universal in its geographical scope. The twenty ink drawings with shading are appropriate. The book does possess an uncommon item in the literature of this area—an excellent index.

A BOOK OF MYTHS
Selected and retold by Roger L.
Green. Illustrated by Joan
Kiddell-Monroe. E. P. Dutton &
Co., Inc., 1965.
This makes an excellent first book covering world mythology with the exception of the Orient. The nineteen stories in this collection are from a cross section of the ancient world including Phoenician, Hittite, Cretan, and Phrygian lore. The language is appropriate for children in the intermediate grades. There are twenty-eight stylized line drawings, with a single color added.

MYTHS AND LEGENDS OF ALL
NATIONS
Told by Herbert Spencer Robinson
and Knox Wilson. Garden City
Books, 1960.
A fascinating collection of myths and folk tales from many parts of the world. The stories are well written but the book suffers greatly from a textbook-like format that is devoid of the illustrations that might enhance it.

THE GOLDEN TREASURY OF MYTHS
AND LEGENDS
Adapted by Anne Terry White.
Illustrated by Alice and Martin
Provensen. Golden Press, Inc., 1947,
1965.
This book is truly a golden treasure with beautiful color illustrations covering perhaps one out of two pages. Its pages are large, with stylized figures, classical in

design. The eighteen stories are predominantly European and a majority of them Greek, with one story each from Morocco and Iran. The stories are easy to read. An extremely well done book.

CLASSICAL GREEK INFLUENCE

FAMOUS MYTHS OF THE GOLDEN
AGE
Retold by Beatrice Alexander.
Illustrated by Florian. Random
House, Inc., 1947.
The eleven myths of varying length in this book are from the Golden Age of Greece. Most of the more renowned stories are included in the smooth-flowing prose. The illustrations, in color and black and white, possess a soft, mythical quality.

STORIES OF THE GODS AND
HEROES
Collected by Sally Benson.
Illustrated by Steele Savage. The
Dial Press, Inc., 1940.
This collection of twenty-eight Greek myths contains the well-known stories. The book reads easily but is by no means simple. It has twenty-eight pen-and-ink drawings, with eight in color. This modest book has the tried and true illustrations, with very little originality.

A BOOK OF MYTHS
Selections from Bulfinch's Age of
Fable. Illustrated by Helen
Sewell. The Macmillan Company,
1956.
Though one is not certain, one must assume the illustrator chose the thirty myths in this collection. The clarity of the original text has been left intact. The illustrator used many full-page line drawings, many with a Grecian blue background and figures in black and white.

The cameo effect is modern but retains classic lines somewhat along the lines of contemporary Greek vases.

THE GOLDEN FLEECE AND THE HEROES WHO LIVED BEFORE ACHILLES

Told by Padraic Colum. Illustrated by Willy Pogány. The Macmillan Company, 1921.

This is a smoothly written story of Jason and his adventures with other heroes of Greek mythology. The book is enhanced by beautiful line drawings in black and white.

GREEK MYTHS

Told by Olivia E. Coolidge. Illustrated by Edouard Sandoz. Houghton Mifflin Company, 1949.

This prolific author has written a clear, interesting book, but the language is suitable for older children. The twenty-seven stories are divided into seven sections. The twelve full-page pen-and-ink illustrations are interesting and show individuality, but are uneven in quality.

TALES THE MUSES TOLD

Related by Roger L. Green. Illustrated by Don Bolognese. Henry Z. Walck, Inc., Publishers, 1965.

A sparsley illustrated but beautifully written collection of some of the best of the Greek legends including the stories of Damon and Pythias, the two bears, Cygnus the Swan, Daphne and Apollo, and Clytie and the Sunflower.

THE RISE OF THE THUNDERER

Told by Tom Galt. Illustrated by John Mackey. Thomas Y. Crowell Company, 1954.

A delightfully written story of the history of the earth as told by the Greek gods, with special emphasis on the period relating to Zeus. The scanty black-and-white illustrations and the author's style seem suited to middle-grade readers.

THE GOLDEN TOUCH

Told by Nathaniel Hawthorne. Illustrated by Paul Galdone. McGraw-Hill Book Company, 1959.

A superbly written and illustrated edition of the famous story from Greek mythology. The clear, relatively simple text and many color drawings are well suited for the lower and middle grades.

THE HEROES

Told by Charles Kingsley. Illustrated by Vera Bock. The Macmillan Company, 1954, 1964

This well-known children's author has concentrated on three heroes of Grecian mythology: Perseus, Theseus, and the Argonauts. The language is modern, and the author succeeds in conveying readers to another era and land. The illustrator creates an interesting effect in twelve full-page black-and-white illustrations and line drawings with solid beige overlays.

ADVENTURES OF THE GREEK HEROES

Told by Mollie McLean and Anne Wiseman. Illustrated by W. T. Mars. Houghton Mifflin Company, 1961.

Simplified adaptations of Greek mythology written in a smooth, lucid style. Included are the stories of Hercules, Perseus, Theseus, Orpheus, Meleager, and the Argonauts. Three color line drawings add much to the text. For middle grades.

THE WAY OF DANGER

Told by Ian Serraillier. Illustrated by William Stobbs. Henry Z. Walck, Inc., Publishers, 1963.

This well-written narrative of Theseus, son of the king of Athens, is told through legends from Greek mythology. It includes battles with monsters, Theseus' rise to ruler of Athens, and his sad death.

Illustrated with well-drawn black-and-white pictures.

THE GODS OF MOUNT OLYMPUS
Retold by Robert Penn Warren.
Illustrated by William Moyers.
Random House, Inc., 1959.

This is an excellent small volume to introduce young readers to the stories or myths relating to the principal gods and goddesses of ancient Greek mythology. Told simply and clearly, the retellings have the lustre, ease, and grace of the original works. The author's distinctive prose is matched with pictorial equivalents.

A TREASURY OF GREEK MYTHOLOGY
Selected by Alisoun Witting.
Illustrated by James Barry. Harvey
House, Inc., 1965.

This collection of thirteen stories, including one dealing with fifteen gods, reads easily, has appeal, but is not very imaginative. Some of the myths are not encountered in the usual anthologies. The type is extremely readable, and the illustrations are classic, nicely stylized in a wash using brown, gold, and black very effectively. The figures are large and clear, with sharp, uncluttered lines.

NORDIC INFLUENCE

LEGENDS OF THE NORTH
Told by Olivia Coolidge. Illustrated
by Edouard Sandoz. Houghton
Mifflin Company, 1951.

With sparsely spread pen-and-ink sketches, the four sections contain thirty-four stories, but the mystical and wonderful flavor of reading the Norse sagas is lost. The stories are interesting to readers of many ages. One good feature is a two-page table of the chief Northern gods and a one-page pronunciation guide for proper names.

NORSE GODS AND GIANTS
Told and illustrated by Ingri and
Edgar Parin d'Aulaire. Doubleday &
Co., Inc., 1967.

A vibrant introduction to Nordic mythology in glowing picture book format. Valhalla sized, this collection with well over 100 pages of illustrations offers stories that range from the humorous to the mysterious. Here stride the one-eyed Odin with his band of Valkyries; huge Thor, who once dressed as a blushing bride to retrieve a magic hammer; the mischievous Loki; Freya, the goddess of love and beauty; as well as the mysterious three Norns who spin a fine thread for every life on earth. In informal style the rough-and-tumble world of ancient Nordic myth comes alive in visual brilliance.

THE FIRST BOOK OF NORSE LEGENDS
Told and Illustrated by Kathleen
Elgin. Franklin Watts, Inc., 1956.

A collection of charming Norse tales centering on Thor, Odin, and Loki and their problems with the frost giants. Written in a slightly clumsy style with a series of two and three color drawings. For middle grades.

THUNDER OF THE GODS
Collected by Dorothy Hosford.
Illustrated by Claire and George
Louden. Holt, Rinehart &
Winston, Inc., 1952.

This inexpensive book of Norse myths contains sixteen stories. The language is simple and ideally suited for the retelling of these tales of the North. The pen-and-ink drawings are appropriate, though meager in number. A pronunciation guide of proper names is included.

FAR EASTERN INFLUENCE

JAPANESE TALES & LEGENDS, RETOLD

Retold by Helen and William
McAlpine. Illustrated by Joan
Kiddell-Monroe. Henry Z. Walck,
Inc., Publishers, 1959.

This book conveys an oriental flavor
throughout its thirty stories. They are
interesting, though their level would
recommend them for children in the intermediate grades. The six full-page illustrations use tints of royal blue and shades of
gray admirably, adding an oriental fragil-
ity. Numerous small line drawings are
interspersed as fillers.

CHINESE MYTHS AND FANTASIES
Retold by Cyril Birch. Illustrated by
Joan Kiddell-Monroe. Henry Z.
Walck, Inc., Publishers, 1961.

The six full-page color illustrations,
complemented by many line drawings,
possess a flavor of authenticity and the
deliberate delicateness of painted silk.
The eighteen stories are divided into three
sections. The earlier stories dealing with
the myths of creation may be difficult
for the occidental mind to follow.

THE LEGEND OF THE WILLOW
PLATE
Told by Alvin Tresselt and Nancy
Cleaver. Illustrated by Joseph Low.
Parents' Magazine Press, 1968.

In this lovely picture book the familiar
pattern of blue and white willow on
dinnerware is illumined in a legend that
stems from ancient China. The story is
based on the tragic love life of a wealthy,
high-born girl forbidden to marry a poor
peasant poet. Escaping the anger of her
father, Koong-se elopes with the poet
for only a brief spell before both lovers
become immortalized. This legendary
story is now gracefully preserved in a
picture book for children as it has been
popularized the world over on rare and
inexpensive china.

THE FIVE SONS OF KING PANDU:
THE STORY OF THE MAHABHÁRATA
Adapted by Elizabeth Seeger from
the English translation of Kisari
Mohan Ganguli. Illustrated by
Gordon Laite. William R. Scott,
Inc., 1967.

In a lucid style the ancient Indian epic is
retold. Although the original work included 110,000 couplets of 32 syllables
each and comprised 18 books, the present
edition comprises a core extracted from the
collection of myths, fables, legends, religious incidents around a central idea.
Deftly handled, the present story presents
the struggle between families of early
rulers and the eventual victory of one of
them, the Pandavas, who establish rule
over northern India. Through the story
emerges a fund of ethical teachings, pious
meditations, acts of chivalry, and many
other aspects of social behavior. Graceful
illustrations reflect the lyrical beauty of
this adaptation of the longest work in
literary history.

THE WHITE ARCHER
Told and illustrated by James
Houston. Harcourt, Brace & World,
Inc., 1967.

This Eskimo legend is distinguished by its
pungent economy of words and sharp
illustrations. Kungo, an Eskimo boy, vows
vengeance on the Indians who slaughter
his parents and carry off his sister. He
travels to the distant island home of Ittok
who, though old and nearly blind, is
still a great hunter and the only man able
to draw the mighty bow Kigavik.
Kungo learns many things from old Ittok
and his wife, but he cannot forget his
mission of revenge. But as his age increases
so does the wisdom that enables him to
return home at peace with himself and the
world. Despite the story's brevity, its
epic quality matches the dignity of the
poetic Eskimo civilization.

Floating away over the roofs of the houses

Soaring over rooftops, Mary Poppins hangs from her parrot-handled umbrella that keeps her aloft. Realistically detailed drawings lend credence to this buoyant fantasy.

From Mary Poppins *by P. L. Travers, illustrated by Mary Shepard. Copyright 1934 and 1962 by P. L. Travers. Reproduced by permission of Harcourt, Brace & World, Inc.*

Chapter 9

FANTASY
IN
CHILDREN'S
LITERATURE

*. . . fantasy is a medium that reflects reality through unreality,
that interprets life through illusion and plays with shimmering implications and
urgencies over human experience and human character. . . . It deals
in prophecy; through satire, burlesque, and make-believe it assays human
qualities; through poetic mirage it penetrates to the realities of the
human heart. . . . Its values are the values of imagination: as a means of
conveying emotional or intellectual perception of truths not openly
presented; as a detonator of the high explosive of ideas; as a weapon of
mockery for attack or defense; as a stimulus to the sense of beauty
and the sense of humor; and as release of the spirit of wonder and frolic that
belongs to the eternal child within us.*

— HELEN E. HAINES
What's in a Novel
Columbia University Press, 1942

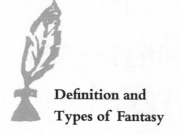

Definition and
Types of Fantasy

Fantasy is that portion of literature which brings the magical and the irrational into the world of actuality. Sometimes the term fantasy describes a literary fairy tale—a fanciful story possessing certain traditional elements found in the folklore of the world. Fantasy is the product of the imagination that comes meaningfully alive to the reader even though it may deal with intangibles and abstractions. Its roots, however, run deep into the reality of the everyday world. Familiar settings and things are reshaped and rearranged to suit the occasion and to put into a clearer light that which may be hidden from vision but visible to the mind's eye.

Like poets, writers of fantasy struggle for expression—expression of truth clothed in allegory or metaphors. Many books classified as fantasy tell their stories through a skillful blend of familiar elements of reality and figments of a creatively expressive imagination—the power of the mind to formulate ideas and images beyond those drawn from the tangibles experienced through the senses. But the blends of familiar and fanciful elements in fantasy are so reshaped and rearranged that even the most commonplace objects and scenes vibrate with color and light up the concepts clothed in symbols and allegory.

Fantasy, for children in particular, deals with a wide assortment of events, things, and people against a background that has its own order. A make-believe world with a logic all its own is supported by the realignment of experienced realities from an everyday world. In an imaginative situation kettles and kittens, clocks and kings, plates and spoons, toys and

242

tiny creatures all move about in curious arrangements and on a principle
that rings true to a child. For example, a young child has only to dress a
puppy in doll's clothes and tuck it into a doll's bed to regard it, literally,
as a baby. To this child, the everyday world has not really changed. Nor
has something totally out-of-the-way happened. The roles of animals
and things have merely been rearranged to create a world that the child
can control and order and where nothing is impossible. This is why the
world of Peter Rabbit or Jemima Puddle-Duck seems real and lifelike to
young children who accept the ways and workings of humanized animals
and objects as being very near to fact even though these may be ostensibly fantastic rearrangements of realities.

But even in the most imaginative works of fantasy, the story is
anchored by the most precise details born of real life. Founded on the facts
of everyday, characters and episodes take on fantastic turns that make the
unreal seem real, and the incredible seem credible. That is to say, beyond
its first requirement of telling a good story, well-drawn fantasy affords
new insights into reality and contributes a sense of life to many worlds.

As a serious work of literary art, fantasy follows a logical course of
development that leads through rich depth and perspective beyond the
symbols and allegories to the fundamental truths underlying the story.
Of *Alice's Adventures in Wonderland*, Paul Hazard says: "It is nonsense. But
it is not pure invention. . . . We laugh for some profound reason of which
we are hardly conscious, but which takes shape in our mind. The idea is
caricatural, but it is not completely false. On the contrary, it touches us
by the element of truth that it contains."[1]

In its broadest meaning fantasy includes the fairy tales as well as the
myths and legends of unknown authorship, but it also designates that
portion of literature consisting of slender and full-length works of modern
fantasy by known authors who have used traditional elements in their
storytelling.

Earliest examples of fantasy can be traced back to the rich inherited
folklore of tales dealing with magical and supernatural elements existing
long before writing was invented. Down through the centuries these tales
of marvels and magic have been told and retold until they are polished and
shining and form the bedrock of imaginative works for children. Built
upon this solid inheritance are the more modern stories by well-known
creative authors who have brought enchantment that is at once human and
supernatural into books intended for the young.

---

[1]Paul Hazard, *Books, Children and Men* (Boston: The Horn Book, Inc., 1960), p. 140.

In contrast with the early fairy tales of unknown authorship, the more modern stories classified as fantasy bear the names of distinguished authors of original works. The giants among them are the producers of renowned classics out of the Victorian Era: Lewis Carroll, the mathematician, who originated *Alice's Adventures in Wonderland* with as much logic as there is in an equation; Kenneth Grahame, a lover of wildlife, who packed rustic wisdom into his *Wind in the Willows;* and James Barrie, who provided exciting adventures in Never-Never Land with Peter Pan, the little boy who never grew up.

In recent times, more men and women of literary stature have endowed children's literature with stories rich in character improvisations, settings, plots, and artistry in writing. In varying degrees these authors have made the realm of fantasy enchanting with magic and wonders offering new insights into reality while expressing universal truths. Rumer Godden, a graceful storyteller, managed to scale domestic drama to the miniature world of a dolls' house and other doll stories. E. B. White, Robert Lawson, and Hugh Lofting wrote with great dignity and faith about animals, and Pamela Travers, Mary Norton, and J. R. R. Tolkien transmitted by imagination and fine writing a sense of expansion from magical happenings.

Significance of Fantasy

Books of fantasy possess perennial appeal and freshness due to their dramatic ingredients, imaginative power, and deeply satisfying conclusions. Just as children's first picture books appeal to their senses and provide enriching experiences, so fantasy captivates children with a magical power that can draw upon their experiential background and make greater demands on their imaginative process.

But without this background of experiences gained from their first books and from life itself, children may fail to become interested in the more developed stories that employ the subtle blending of the natural with the supernatural. There is little doubt, however, that children savoring the delights of their first fairy tales and other stories with simple incidents will reach for the more complex works of fantasy later on in their development.

Because good fantasy, no matter how fantastic, is firmly founded on truth, a child capable of perceiving it will discover for himself the elements that ring true and will tie them in with what he learns from his everyday experiences. And should a child not yet have had these experiences, it is possible that he will recognize similarities in situations and connect them when they are encountered. This connection not only drives a meaning home to a child, it also strengthens his awareness of real life by the recreation of a fresh experience worthy of lasting forever. For if a child, especially a young child, ponders over a piece of fantasy repeatedly and for a long period of time, much of the story will become a part of the child's "reality system" since the boundary between reality and fantasy is less distinct for a young child than for an adult. A daydream, for example, is something just as "real" as playing with his toys or walking down the street. And very often what is meant to be reality in a story may be perceived by the young child as fantasy, and the other way around. However, distinct pleasure is derived from the encounter with real and make-believe worlds, and the travel between them proves refreshing and satisfying.

Then, too, young children show characteristic interest in behavior that is somewhat savage and cannibalistic. Although regarded as questionable, this kind of behavior may not be acted out by children though it may be experienced vicariously in the stories of fantasy employing "uncivilized acts." In *Little Red Riding Hood* a wolf eats the grandmother, or, in *The Tale of Peter Rabbit*, a little bunny is warned by his mother not to enter a farmer's garden lest he suffer the same fate as his father who "had an accident there; he was put in a pie by Mrs. McGregor." Of course, a young child is not fully aware of society's mores, restrictions, and points of view about threats of killing, gobbling up, or being cut up and put in a pie for someone's dinner. The child responds to such fantasies, but not in the way expected by the culture whose restrictions at this time are just beginning to have effect upon him. Winick, in supporting this theory, indicates: "Content of this kind is enjoyed by a child, as he realizes that he is not alone in experiencing feelings that are alien to the adult world."[2]

This earlier interest of children in fairy tales leads in a developmental progression to the preadolescent's enthusiasm for the richer forms of fantasy found in folklore and full-length stories that are similar to fairy tales, though more sophisticated. Some examples of these include *The Borrowers, The Hobbit*, and *The Castaways in Lilliput*—tiny people who have a distinctly separate society; stories like *Stuart Little, The Great Geppy*, and *Pinocchio* cut across similar lines of interest.

---

[2]Charles Winick, "How the Child Views the World," *For the Young Viewer* (New York: McGraw-Hill Book Company, 1962), p. 147.

Adolescents and young adults, on the other hand, call for stories more developed than the simple fantasies, even though they may revert occasionally to early childhood interests. But more mature readers show characteristic enthusiasm for intricate plot schemes involving the fabulous, strange, and wonder worlds of science fiction for symbolisms of growing up. They look beyond the magical happenings for the feeling of human relations and for stories probing into depths of mystery and meaning.

Significantly enough, a book of fantasy reaches out beyond its characters and inventions into the fundamental questions of universal life: questions of good and evil, of morals and ethics, of customs and traditions, of lasting values as opposed to temporal ones, and of the inconsistencies in real life matched with certain illogical consistencies. For example, there is fantastic logic in what the White Queen says in Lewis Carroll's *Through the Looking-Glass:* "The rule is, jam to-morrow and jam yesterday—but never jam *today*." Or the wealth of meaning embedded in the statement of the Red Queen: "Now, *here*, you see, it takes all the running *you* can do, to keep in the same place."

Treated in this metaphorical way, deep meanings may be brought into sharper focus and proper perspective while a child's world is being enlarged and his experiences confirmed through fantasy.

Along with glimpses of life and loveliness, children also derive a deep sense of satisfaction from the medium of fantasy through the magic and marvels that they experience in what Jung calls the "collective unconscious." Here in fantasy, they find their love for adventure, nonsense, and humor fulfilled; their everyday world is illumined; their aesthetic needs are satisfied, because much of fantasy is rich allegory touched with poetry; and their imaginations are stretched to help them identify and realign the natural with the supernatural.

Approach to Fantasy

Fantasy adheres to the storytelling requirements and basic principles that underlie each division of literature, but it also has certain special qualities. The strength of most fantasies lies in the writer's ability to project reality into an original dimension. However, the effectiveness is judged on the basis of mastery of style, depth of emotion, originality of

idea, strength and development of story pattern, credible characters, no
matter how fantastic they may be, and a faint sense of the miraculous,
which allows the story to move more freely than in any other division of
literature.

One approach toward better understanding of fantasy is to evaluate
and analyze the literary elements—theme, plot, characterization, style,
settings—so that qualities germane to this division can be examined more
closely.

THEME

Because fantasy projects meanings and original ideas into
unique dimensions, originality of expression and projection dominate the
other literary elements. The originality of idea, however, is frequently
projected in a piece of fantasy that may reflect the author's concern with
the fundamental issues of universal life.

For children these issues may be those which deal with imagination
and wonder, right and wrong, good and evil, and, for young children in
particular, rebellious pleasures matched with imminent results. An example
of this latter theme is expressed in Sendak's *Where the Wild Things Are.*
Self-revealing and therapeutic, this vivid dream-fantasy allows children
to confront the rebellious in themselves as well as their monstrous identities and to cope with them. Consequently, many highly imaginative books
for primary-grade children utilize strange blends of the monstrous and
other supernatural creatures in a make-believe land. And often these
bizarre characters in a young child's book may very well reflect behavior
characteristic of the stage of human growth and development for which
the book has greatest appeal.

Themes in fantasy also express a wide range of human emotions
and human situations reshaped and rearranged so as to reveal new depths
of meaning understandable at many levels. The story of *Alice's Adventures
in Wonderland* makes an exciting adventure beyond reality into the land
of the unreal. Full of fantastic characters in varied situations, parts of the
story may be used even with the very young, but it also serves as a complex work revealing rich depth and perspective to be penetrated by much
older children and adults.

The deceptively simple stories of Beatrix Potter exemplify the
presentation of fundamental truths conveyed by pretty kittens, ducks,
and rabbits who reveal the reality of struggle for survival in the animal

world. From the Potter books one is made aware of the fact that humans trap small animals who in turn prey on each other, although fair play always enters in to balance the toughness of reality without exaggerated sentimentality.

Some themes concern themselves with children's psychological problems. *Peter Pan* portrays a little boy who does not want to grow up. Children identifying themselves with Peter Pan and other story characters may derive therapeutic value from the confirmation that there are others who share the same anxieties and problems of growing up.

PLOT

The strength of well-written fantasy lies in the uninterrupted storytelling even though the story line weaves in and out of magic and marvels, introduces new and exotic characters, swings freely from reality to the imaginative, and involves a fantastic turn of events in the climax. Through this action, fantasy avoids clashes with reality so as to impart a sense of actuality.

In spite of all its play with marvels, well-drawn fantasy remains anchored by the most precise details of real life with limits of its own preventing the story from swinging out beyond the comprehension of children. This is where certain writers of fantasy excel whereas others give in to elaborate descriptions that eclipse the story line and diminish credibility.

The successful fantasy owes its strength and vitality to a single, unquestioned ingredient: a well-knit story balanced and proportioned by an economy of truth and invention. Also, its success depends upon the degree of human naturalness that it incorporates to make the unreal seem real and the incredible seem credible. Consistently and strongly developed, the story line must move swiftly, carrying young readers with it to a satisfying, "fairy tale" conclusion that children expect from a story made iridescent with magic and marvels.

CHARACTERIZATION

A fantasy carves out characters that are human, humanized, or animated, depending on the story. Often they mingle together in a tale touched with magic. But no matter how fantastic or magical the adventures, characters in fantasy remain true to their natures through-out the book. They also remain faithful to themselves.

In books that utilize humanized animals, it is natural to find crea-tures of woods and stream wearing human clothes and revealing human attributes. But it is bad art that falsifies the nature of the animals them-selves in characterizations that inaccurately portray natural fact.

Distinguished writers of fantasy, Kenneth Grahame, Beatrix Potter, and Rumer Godden, paint humanized animals but preserve something of their naturalistic, animal selves. Some of their stories bring in animals that behave just as they would in their natural habitats. But for the purposes of the tale and in order to heighten the appeal more directly for children, these animals appear dressed as humans. In other words, Peter Rabbit behaves in the way rabbits do; Jemima Puddle-Duck has all the instincts of a real duck; Mole, Rat, and Badger, who reveal recognizable human traits, still remain true to their animal natures. Vast understanding of nature and the habits of animals goes into successful characterizations of creatures with unique personalities and personal idioms of their own.

Inanimate objects in fantasy come alive as personified characters, depending upon the author's ability to bestow life and appropriate per-sonality upon even the humblest of objects in the story. Touched with the magic of imaginative storytelling, the simplest things become enchanted, lifelike, and then, in a twinkle, common things once again in accordance with the concepts of the tale.

Hans Christian Andersen is credited as being the supreme example of a storyteller with deep insight into the "private lives" of simple, com-mon things—a teapot, a candle, old china, a bell. He imagined them as living characters in the poignant drama of his most searching fairy tales, and he gave them unique personalities. When one reads Andersen, how-ever, the characters, no matter how humble, never fail to make an impact on the reader because they are drawn with more than enough talent and conviction to convey the message of their maker. Whether it's a teapot or a darning needle in an Andersen fantasy, they rarely fail to tug at the heart strings while communicating axioms rooted in real life.

Characterization in fantasy, more than in any other division of literature, stresses individuality and inventiveness. And much of the ef-fectiveness of characters in a piece of fantasy lies in their consistent devel-opment, reasoning, and behavior so that they display no inconsistencies or uneasiness while moving from one world to another.

Stories of fantasy owe their beauty and vitality to artistic storytelling. Taken simply as stories, they are the most imaginative in literature. When matched by poetic imagery, they become the beautifully balanced prose that charms a child's senses and moves his imagination.

Rich, graceful writing is enlivened by the imagination of fantasy writers. Concrete images are drawn to reflect much the same beauty and form that children create in dreams. With an artist's eye for detail, words are chosen to depict exactly the shapes, patterns, or colors that give authority to a work. Sometimes delicate details underline the blends of truth and art, and sometimes deep, encrusted designs are used. But whichever style is chosen, it must conform to the theme and background of the story so as to lend a sense of reality to even the most imaginative stories pushed to the farthest edge of fantasy.

Because writers of fantasy find an expression for ideas and feelings by rearranging realities and matching them with inventions, they struggle to devise an original dimension to project the ideas. Lewis Carroll, for example, injects satire into his strange amalgam of realities and inventions by projecting the story into another dimension: "wonderland" or "through the looking glass." Here the fantasy is free from stereotyped moorings. A magic land beyond the ordinary is created by detailed descriptions, marvelous images, consistent characters, and "logical" dialogue. As a child's story, *Alice's Adventures in Wonderland* is magnificent with symbols and metaphors. It is philosophical, yet entertaining. And its most fantastic incidents seem probable and are presented with beautiful clarity.

In fantasy, more than in the other divisions of literature, a fusion of the materials of poetry is imperative to give a moving, flexible style rather than one composed of rigid, detached incidents.

SETTINGS

Whether backgrounds in fantasy are real or imagined, similar standards of quality, restraint, and pungent economy must be imposed. Even in the most beautifully imagined story, superbly told, a writer can accommodate only the essentials of detail. Fantasy is vulnerable to excessive use of nonfunctional material and sometimes suffers from details that cannot be justified on realistic grounds because they eclipse the story line and destroy the atmosphere. The essentials in settings acquire value when they present human interest details that conjure up scenes, costumes, and images with impressive accuracy even though some of these may be figments of a creative imagination.

Landscapes in fantasy reveal much that is unique to the story, and against this background move unique characters in unique situations. Each story stresses its own devices and its own original settings, incorporating naturalistic and invented details to the degree appropriate for the story's development.

But no story is worthy of the designation fantasy if it is merely a series of long descriptions of landscape, costumed characters, and events that reflect no logical order and no restraint. Convincing fantasy is a fusion of elements interrelated with artistic integrity and a sense of proportion that add depth and dimension shaded by essential details.

The literature of fantasy encompasses a vivid spectrum of subjects that stem from the deep, personal involvement of writers who have dealt with their most cherished moments, memorable scenes and characters, and the driving desire to go "through the looking glass" for an exploration of life and adventure. Some have shared their devotion for the outdoors, for the tiny creatures of woods and stream. Others, like Beatrix Potter, have shared their love for animals and their natures set against beautiful backgrounds of authentic habitats, and the simple beauty of homelike things such as rag rugs, sprigged calico, pretty pie plates, saucepans, and flat-irons. Still others have endowed inanimate things with life and compassion in order to deepen insights as the reader encounters his identity in the personalities of the inanimate coming alive in the stories.

Deeply felt and beautifully imagined, fantasy comes through on a high level of literature touched with poetry and suspended by magic so that when young readers move in and out of its wonderlands they derive a sense of beauty and expansion. Drawn by the power of the imagination, children often return to the books they had once read when they were very young. These books of fantasy undeniably address themselves to large audiences since many fine stories are written on more than one plane so that they can be reread long after added experiences of life have been gained at different levels of growth and development.

Analysis of Fantasy

The literature of fantasy tends to separate into certain groups, each reflecting one similar pattern even though it may be expressed with originality and with varying degrees of imaginative power. Some stories, on the other hand, defy classification because their writers have used—and may have used successfully—more than one pattern in designing the fantasy.

Because the literature of fantasy is such an enormous division, a comprehensive analysis of all the patterns expressed in the stories is beyond our scope. Distinguished examples, however, are used, and an annotated list of selected books follows this chapter. For practical purposes, these categories following certain recurring patterns in fantasy will be considered, classified by age and grade levels:

> *Nature, Animals, and Humans*
> Books for younger children
> Books for intermediate-grade children
> Books for upper-grade children
>
> *Tiny People, Toys, and Things*
> Books for younger children
> Books for intermediate-grade children
> Books for upper-grade children
>
> *Magic, Dreams, and Wonderlands*
> Books for younger children
> Books for intermediate-grade children
> Books for upper-grade children

Nature, Animals, and Humans

Nature and animals, one of the most significant patterns in fantasy, are frequently intermingled with humans and natural phenomena. Sometimes animals alone are used to symbolize the natural, human-inhabited world. But whatever the combination, well-drawn works, especially the more developed ones, that utilize nature and animals mirror universal human experiences.

BOOKS FOR YOUNGER CHILDREN

A small picture story book of great beauty is Beatrix Potter's *The Tailor of Gloucester*, a miniature classic for younger children. As an example of total integration of visual and verbal elements, this tiny fantasy is woven from an old tailor's fevered dream, a legend of Christmas Eve, and an ancient city silenced in snow and moonlight.

Choice words skillfully tell the story of a humble tailor commissioned to sew the Lord Mayor's waistcoat before Christmas. Alone with his cat, Simpkin, the tailor struggles to perform the impossible task of finishing the garment. But intricate embroideries consume his time, thread, and money. Soliciting the assistance of Simpkin, the tired tailor gives his cat some money to buy the necessary thread and some milk. While the cat is away the kind-hearted tailor takes pity on the mice in his small home by freeing them from the cups under which they had been trapped by Simpkin. In return for this kindness, the mice come to the tailor's rescue by scampering off to the tailor shop with the thread Simpkin had bought and nimbly finishing the work on the Lord Mayor's waistcoat.

Constructed with great skill and precision, *The Tailor of Gloucester* is as subtle a fantasy as any that has rolled off the printing press. The whole book rustles with light, gentle sounds of mouse feet in the night and the fevered breath of a deliriously ill tailor haunted by the thoughts of an unfinished garment and no more thread to work on it.

Based on very close observation of the habits of small animals as well as of details of architecture, landscape, china, and original embroideries, the story takes on an air of actuality that makes the fantasy come convincingly alive in cadenced prose style. Though grounded by precise details, the story moves swiftly from the real world of a frugal tailor's shop, past ancient streets of cobbles and gables, to the homelike setting of the tailor's room where the story shifts from reality to art. Here, animal characters take over while the human tailor falls into a dream. True to their own natures, each creature—mouse or cat—reveals its own particular temperament. The independently selfish cat fends for himself by preying on the mice, who madden him after their release by tempting scamperings. On the other hand, the mice flit as lightly as mice can, yet not without the haste that is in keeping with their nervous natures. And, in accordance with the legend of animals talking at midnight, the household animals not only act but talk in character so as to lend credence to a spellbinding story.

The pictures, exquisitely detailed, are an integral part of this miniature classic. Suffused in soft pastels of pink, sepia, and rose matched with greens, grays, and browns, the full beauty of the embroideries, particularly, comes into clearest focus only under a magnifying glass. This artistry in the water colors produces an exact pictorial equivalent for the well-turned text that makes *The Tailor of Gloucester* a fine example of literature and art scaled to the world of children.

BOOKS FOR INTERMEDIATE-GRADE CHILDREN

At the heart of Robert Lawson's engaging animal fantasy, *Rabbit Hill*, is love for the animals themselves and the Connecticut countryside that they inhabit. The philosophy of "live and let live" emerges from this kindly tale of a rabbit family and other wildlife creatures surrounding the "Big House" on a hill.

Vacant a long time so that the garden had grown wild and the grass and weeds had run rampant, the "Big House" was the subject of much speculation when it was rumored that "new folks" were coming and they might be "planting folks." The first to sing the tidings was Little Georgie, a high-leaping rabbit who belonged to the rabbit family of Father, a bluegrass gentleman, Mother, a worrier, and agitating, illiterate Uncle Analdas. Delightfully individualized, the rabbit family and a host of minor animal characters interact, fuss, and play throughout a story in which the new "planting folks" provide generously for their small needs and improve the hard times that had once plagued the little creatures on Rabbit Hill.

Told with sympathy for even the humblest of small animals, the fantasy is founded on a wide understanding of nature and wildlife creatures. Each creature is given a distinct personality not unlike his own natural one. But the characters are drawn with an artist's eye and a poet's heart so that the animals on Rabbit Hill stand out as perhaps the most humanizing community of wild animals ever to appear in a child's book.

The gentle story, *Rabbit Hill*, is frequently matched with *The Wind in the Willows*, a similar tale for older children. Both of these nature fantasies rely heavily on the characterization of the animals and on the spirit of the open world accurately portrayed in beautiful descriptive writing to tell their stories. Moreover, *Rabbit Hill* pleads for a world where animals and men can live together in harmonious freedom—freedom from the traps, guns, and fences that endanger the lives of the small animals. In return for human kindness, Lawson expresses wildlife gratitude in the following passage from *Rabbit Hill*:

> Slowly, solemnly, the procession circled the garden until they had all returned to the little lawn where the Good Saint stood. The Red Buck snorted again and all gave attention as he spoke.

**Textured pictures of wildlife enliven beautifully balanced prose endowing person-
ality to each animal. Mother Rabbit, a worrier, is contrasted with the serene father
and the slumbering Little Georgie.**
From Rabbit Hill *by Robert Lawson. Copyright 1944 by Robert Lawson. Reproduced by permission
of The Viking Press, Inc.*

"We have eaten their food," his voice rang out impressively. "We have
tasted their salt, we have drunk their water, and all are good." He tossed
his proud head in the direction of the garden. "From now on this is forbidden ground." His chisel-sharp hoof rapped the earth. "Does anyone
dispute me?"

None did and there was a silence, broken at last by the voice of Uncle
Analdas. "Haow 'bout them dingblasted Cutworms?" he called. "They
don't know no laws or decent regulations."

The Mole, who had been a little slower than the rest, leaned his elbows on
the earth as he reared up from his just completed tunnel and turned his
blind face toward the sound.

"We'll patrol," he said smiling, "me and my brothers, night and day,
turn and turn about."[3]

---

[3]From *Rabbit Hill* by Robert Lawson, copyright 1944 by Robert Lawson, pp. 125-26.
Reprinted by permission of the Viking Press, Inc.

And finally as in *The Wind in the Willows*, a satisfying ending sings out contagious rapture—a reminder of Little Georgie's song that was chorused by all the animals in *Rabbit Hill*:

> All over the Hill voices of the Little Animals were rising in a chorus, and they were singing *his* song—the Song of Little Georgie!... Way up near the house he could hear Porkey's unmusical bellow,
> New Folks comin', Oh my!
> New Folks comin', Oh my!
> New Folks comin', Oh my!
> Oh my, Oh my![4]

And the reader, with everyone else, wants to sing—and believes.

In nature fantasies such as *The Wind in the Willows* and *Rabbit Hill*, animals are humanized to the extent that they not only talk but wear clothes and live among furnishings even though they inhabit holes and burrows deep in the ground. In contrast, certain fantasies utilizing the pattern of animals and nature employ talking beasts that do not wear human trappings but live in exactly the way animals of their kind usually do. Yet they reveal human attributes through personification.

E. B. White in his *Charlotte's Web*, for instance, develops a story of talking animals and their involvement in human affairs by using a piglet about to be butchered because of his abnormal size and two heroines: the first is a little girl called Fern and, later on in the story, a spider called Charlotte appears who works "miracles" to save the pig's life and also to bring him fame and glory. As a result of their efforts, Wilbur, the pig, attains a feeling of self-worth and becomes a pig loved and admired by many. Successfully drawn, the story pushes farm life close to the edge of fantasy, though never beyond, by means of a miracle-working spider.

Restrained in its use of "magic" or "miracles," the story makes the reader conscious of the irrational that underlies events of everyday farm life, and it does this while still keeping the animal and human characters real, lifelike, and in possession of personal identities and idioms. Fern, the little girl who saves the runt from slaughter, remains consistently the same without shifting her point of view, which is straightforward and humane. Charlotte, the barnyard spider, demonstrates friendship and tenderness along with the rare talent to spin life-saving words in her web. And through her the author projects his own philosophy of life that speaks sensibly to any age:

> "You have been my friend," replied Charlotte. "That in itself is a tremendous thing. I wove my webs for you because I like you. After all, what's

---

[4]*Ibid.*, pp. 57–58.

life, anyway? We're born, we live a little while, we die. A spider's life can't help being something of a mess, with all this trapping and eating flies. By helping you, perhaps I was trying to lift up my life a trifle. Heaven knows anyone's life can stand a little of that."[5]

E. B. White's particular contribution to a fantastic, rural adventure is the way he describes certain of his characters—man and beast—with such succinctness and variety that he brings the whole account in direct line with actuality. And mirrored in the personalities of the barnyard population are human characteristics that always override whatever bizarre intimations there may be. A description of the rat, for example:

> The rat had no morals, no conscience, no scruples, no consideration, no decency, no milk of rodent kindness, no compunctions, no higher feeling, no friendliness, no anything. He would kill a gosling if he could get away with it—the goose knew that. Everybody knew it.[6]

Artistic integrity makes this barnyard fantasy believable. Unaffected drawings reveal facial expressions in varying moods. Here the geese show contempt for the rat, who rolls a rotten egg.
From Charlotte's Web *by E. B. White, illustrated by Garth Williams. Copyright 1952 by E. B. White. Harper & Row, Publishers. Reproduced by permission.*

---

[5]E. B. White, *Charlotte's Web* (New York: Harper & Row, Publishers, 1952), p. 164.
[6]*Ibid.*, p. 46.

Similarly, descriptions of the barn are nailed down with sharp details that freely allow the intrusion of a miracle-working spider so that she becomes quite credible within the framework of her everyday world.

> The barn was very large. It was very old. It smelled of hay and it smelled of manure. It smelled of the perspiration of tired horses and the wonderful sweet breath of patient cows. It often had a sort of peaceful smell—as though nothing bad could happen ever again in the world. It smelled of grain and of harness dressing and of axle grease and of rubber boots and of new rope. And whenever the cat was given a fish-head to eat, the barn would smell of fish. But mostly it smelled of hay, for there was always hay in the great loft up overhead.[7]

Defying the fantasy are the statements made by Dr. Dorian in defense of the most fantastic feature in the story—that of a spider spinning words in her web.

> "But for that matter I don't understand how a spider learned to spin a web in the first place. When the words appeared, everyone said they were a miracle. But nobody pointed out that the web itself is a miracle."[8]

Anchored by truth and sturdy realism, the superb story *Charlotte's Web* stands out as the sort of fantasy that even the most sensible reader will find irresistibly logical with its sound arguments, clear-cut descriptions, contrasting characters, and the eternal theme of friendship that runs stoutly through a satisfying book.

BOOKS FOR UPPER-GRADE CHILDREN

Kenneth Grahame's *The Wind in the Willows* also uses the pattern of the natural world but in a more complex way than either of the aforementioned writers. Grahame has blended satire, allegory, humor, and natural history in something that might well be termed a sociological commentary. Grahame himself, in a letter to President Theodore Roosevelt, pronounced his book as "an expression of the very simplest joys of life as lived by the simplest beings." Symbolizing human strengths and frailties, and at the same time presenting the glories of nature, *The Wind in the Willows* exemplifies writing rich in imagery and cadenced with style that heightens the striking designs woven by the language and the ideas infused with other materials of poetry.

The Wind in the Willows tells primarily of the adventures of four wildlife friends: Mole, Water Rat, Badger, and Toad. Together they picnic and dine, stray and run around, and each in his own characteristic

---

[7]*Ibid.*, p. 13.
[8]*Ibid.*, p. 109.

way shares in a series of experiences varying in intensity of emotion. Sometimes the experiences are leisurely, sometimes impetuous. Now and then they become ominous and frightening, as in Toad's rescue from his life of folly and his encounter with "The Piper at the Gates of Dawn." But always there is "the spirit of divine discontent and longing"—a theme played throughout the book in a number of different keys.

The story is also humorous and philosophical with profound regard for the simple joys of the natural world. Here human, universalizing values lying close to the heart are set in a world of wildlife dominated by instinct and urges. Human frailties and follies are mirrored by gentle humor and a strong sense of friendship.

Told with dignity and grace, *The Wind in the Willows* is a carefully constructed nature fantasy possessing purity of style, clearness of vision, and detailed accuracy in its observation of the natural world. Bound by economy and gravity, the book has carved archetypal portraits symbolizing the real world although its roots are deep in meadow and riverbank. Familiar things and situations are presented in such a sensitive way that young readers are forced to see the world with new wonder and delight. Here for instance, is a graphic description composed with utmost simplicity and beauty of a familiar landscape from a poetic angle:

> The line of the horizon was clear and hard against the sky, and in one particular quarter it showed black against a silvery climbing phosphorescence that grew and grew. At last, over the rim of the waiting earth the moon lifted with slow majesty till it swung clear of the horizon and rode off, free of moorings; and once more they began to see surfaces—meadows widespread, and quiet gardens, and the river itself from bank to bank, all softly disclosed, all washed clean of mystery and terror, all radiant again as by day, but with a difference that was tremendous.[9]

Grahame has done admirably in bringing the out-of-doors into such sharp focus for children whose irresistible urges seem more closely akin to those felt in the natural world. And at the same time, he has made his nature story sing with exuberance for life itself. The essential themes are hopes, and fears, and desires, and friendship—the emotions readily aroused by readers on the threshold of maturity, and the underlying message is that, despite man's weaknesses, life remains meaningful, vibrant, and kind. The illustrations, too, in earth tones and perceptive designs, remain an integral part of the heart-warming story they parallel.

---

[9]Kenneth Grahame, *The Wind in the Willows* (New York: Charles Scribner's Sons, 1940), p. 95

TODAY, HOWEVER, THOUGH THEY WERE CIVIL ENOUGH,
THEY SEEMED PREOCCUPIED

In a fantasy that sings the joys of the outdoors, the humblest of creatures offer glimpses of life along riverbanks, woodlands, and roadsides. Here field mice and harvest mice busy themselves.

From The Wind in the Willows *by Kenneth Grahame, illustrated by Arthur Rackham. Copyright © 1908 by Charles Scribner's Sons. Reproduced by permission.*

Young children in particular take pleasure in playing with small things. Somehow toys and tiny people go together in a world more appropriately scaled than the world of reality. Adults, like giants, tower over the very young who, with their three-foot-high vision of the world, can readily identify with people, toys, and things in miniature.

Close to the surface of the earth, children experience many of their early delights. With intense curiosity they study eyes of flies, knee bones of grasshoppers, the glassy stares of cats and beetles. Here they experience sharp enjoyment—a kind of kinship with a down-to-earth world of insects, tiny animals, toys, and things.

Writers of children's fantasies have also discovered this tiny world with its life lying close to the ground and only a few feet away from chairs and tabletops. With a poet's eye for precious details, many of these writers have sharply focused on its mysteries and wonders. As a result, fantasies for children have been produced with the indefinable charm of being scaled perfectly for their themes as well as for their young audiences.

Some stories, like Rumer Godden's toy fantasies, afford miniature domestic drama as in *The Dolls' House*, a book sharpened by vividly accurate details of minutely scaled life. Yet beyond the myriad details of dolls and settings, the author has projected her own views of life—broad, clear, and universal.

Other writers, with an equally sharp vision of microscopic things, have detailed to perfection some "lilliputian" fantasies —J. R. R. Tolkien's *The Hobbit*, and Henry Winterfeld's *Castaways in Lilliput*. Mary Norton, on the other hand, has brought into existence a whole race of tiny imaginary people called the Borrowers. Of course their utterly human personalities, together with their clever use of common things, dispel doubts of their existence, especially when small, necessary objects get lost.

Utilizing the familiar dilemma of humans subject to misplacing things, Mary Norton explains this human predicament by creating tiny people who do not actually steal but merely "borrow" the misplaced objects—matchboxes, safety pins, watches, and chessmen—that are required for their own purposes. Perfectly accurate in their personification, *The Borrowers* in miniature portray humans in actuality. And it is through these tiny people—sometimes visible and sometimes not—that children acquire insightful information about humans and what they are really like.

BOOKS FOR YOUNGER CHILDREN

An enchanting story composed by an imaginative team of writer and illustrator is *The Velveteen Rabbit*. Touched by the poetic talents of Margery Bianco and William Nicholson, this toy fantasy recounts the friendship and devotion between a little "Boy" and his "Rabbit." Exposed to the usual handling a toy gets from a playful owner, the Rabbit shows wear and tear that earns him criticism from adults but affection from the little Boy who "loved him so hard that he loved all his whiskers off, and the pink lining to his ears turned grey, and his brown spots faded. He even began to lose his shape, and he scarcely looked like a rabbit any more, except to the Boy."[10]

A bout with scarlet fever forces the little owner to bed and brings about the contamination of the Rabbit who lies tucked "under the bedclothes, with just his head peeping out." Condemned to burning by the doctor, the Rabbit is taken away from the Boy and left behind a fowl house so that the gardener can light a bonfire and dispose of the germ-infested books and toys. At this point the fantasy swings away from the ordinary settings of sickroom and backyard to a transformed, magical world. Because the sack to be burned has been left untied, the Rabbit, coming alive, wriggles out and wanders down familiar paths where he had played with his little owner. And as he reminisces, "a great sadness" comes over him while a miniature panorama quietly unfolds to echo the past. "And a tear, a real tear, trickled down his little shabby velvet nose and fell to the ground. . . . For where the tear had fallen a flower grew out of the ground, a mysterious flower, not at all like any that grew in the garden."[11]

A fairy steps out of the beautifully described blossom and addresses herself to the little Rabbit. She explains that she cares for all the toys that children have loved, and because the little Boy had so dearly loved the velveteen Rabbit he is to be transformed into a real little rabbit now.

Suddenly the common and the ordinary are sparked with magic and vibrate with the color and brilliance of the imagination, but the sensitive balance between the unreal and the real is never tipped in favor of one or

---

[10]Margery Williams Bianco, *The Velveteen Rabbit* (New York: Doubleday Company, Inc., 1926), p. 25.

[11]*Ibid.*, p. 29.

the other. Fine writing sharpens the luminous world into which the fantasy shifts:

> It was light now, for the moon had risen. All the forest was beautiful, and the fronds of the bracken shone like frosted silver. In the open glade between the tree-trunks the wild rabbits danced with their shadows on the velvet grass, but when they saw the Fairy they all stopped dancing and stood round in a ring to stare at her.[12]

Here she presents the once-toy rabbit to the living rabbits and with a kiss puts him on his own. From the Fairy's kiss life and strength are bestowed upon the Rabbit. He can run and play. He becomes soft, brown, and shiny. Kick and vitality propel him to jump and whirl with all the exuberance of a happy woodland creature.

Then swinging back to reality, the fantasy concludes with a satisfying scene in which the little Boy and the Rabbit meet again. The two of them stare at each other in surprise, for there is little doubt in the Boy's mind that here at last is his velveteen Rabbit come to life.

Appealing to children in the primary grades, this shining toy fantasy beautifully develops a nursery theme involving affection between toys and children who frequently believe that, "loved long enough, toys and things will come to life."

Children's perception of toys and imaginative play are again expressed by the same author in a set of toy fantasies that reveal vivid memories of toys and children's feelings toward them. *The Adventures of Andy, Poor Cecco, The Little Wooden Doll,* and *The Skin Horse* afford children a wonderful chance to confront themselves and to live vicariously through delightful adventures shared by children and playthings everywhere. Sensitively written, these unusual stories highlighted by exquisite illustrations demonstrate the skill that goes into making inanimate things reflect life and personality to the delight of children.

Similar well-loved works are the products of A. A. Milne's creative imagination. Because of their craftsmanship, wit, and rhythmical qualities they defy criticism and remain gems of verse and prose. Matched with apt drawings by E. H. Shepard, the works of Milne seem to call up something elemental in children that gives these books their deserved immortality. The prose fantasies especially seem to stem from a genuine creative impulse. Christopher Robin makes his appearances in *Winnie-the-Pooh* and its sequel *The House at Pooh Corner*—two original toy fantasies involving a little boy and his toy animals. Pooh, a teddy bear, undeniably

---

[12]*Ibid.,* p. 31.

expresses best the author's ability to bestow life and personality on a plaything as well as warmth of genuine affection that a child gives it.

BOOKS FOR INTERMEDIATE-GRADE CHILDREN

A more mature vision of the world may be found in the stories of Rumer Godden who has chosen doll characters to serve as models in domestic dramas that will be favored mainly by girls. When the front of *The Dolls' House* is lifted a world in miniature is disclosed. Candy Floss, a coconut-shy mascot; Impunity Jane, a pocket-size Victorian doll; and Holly of the toyshop—all key figures in these doll stories —also serve as vehicle to communicate issues fundamental to human experience.

The miniature world of dolls and teddy bears is akin to the miniature world of tiny people. *The Borrowers*, however, prefer to live only in quiet country homes ordered by tradition and well-formed patterns of living. The movement of modern life is disturbing to them and to their schemes. Adopting the names of the places they inhabit are Borrowers such as the Clock family, the Overmantels family, and the Harpsichord family. Safe if not "seen," these tiny people, Pod, Homily, and Arrietty, living under the kitchen floor of an old English house, are comfortable until the daughter, Arrietty, wishes to go exploring and see a wider world. Once seen, the Borrowers are forced to escape disaster by emigrating. So, their fortunes are followed in sequels entitled *The Borrowers Afield*, *The Borrowers Afloat*, and *The Borrowers Aloft*, the end of the series.

In all her books about the Borrowers, Mary Norton blends truth and tenderness into poetry that pulsates with a stout vein of humor. Because she has given such close attention to details, the comic points in her stories stand out brightly even though the first of her four books about the Borrowers strikes a rather sad note when it tolls the end of quiet elegance for "human beans."

Completely free of magic's power, Mary Norton's stories exemplify fantasy drawn from dilemma in real life and scaled to life in miniature. After all, the Borrowers appear as real little people with characters so precisely delineated that they are readily accepted by the reader even though no "fairy magic" makes them work. But once doubts of their existence are dispelled, the happenings of these little people seem to work out convincingly in the stories. Handled in realistic terms, the details, development of character, clear, strong prose, and, above all, the originality of the idea distinguish these books as landmarks in children's literature.

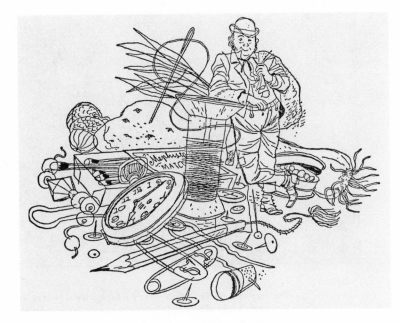

Scaled down to the size of his borrowings, Pod's tiny form stands waist high to a spool of thread he uses as an armrest. Precisely drawn, the figures in the pictures add to the credibility of the fantasy.

From The Borrowers *by Mary Norton, illustrated by Beth and Joe Krush. Copyright 1952 and 1953 by Mary Norton. Reproduced by permission of Harcourt, Brace & World, Inc.*

BOOKS FOR UPPER-GRADE CHILDREN

Gulliver's Travels, especially the first part, "A Voyage to Lilliput," is another fantasy concerned with a society of small people. Not originally intended for children because of its satirical overtones, the fascinating adventures of an "imaginary hero" in a land whose inhabitants are no taller than six inches, has nevertheless become a classic in children's literature.

Inventiveness of detail and clear portraits of the characters who people the Lilliputian world sharpen this picture of a nonexistent land. Here is a graphic presentation of a world in miniature with all the artifacts that appeal to childhood. And to carry the story along, unadorned language free of grandiloquence has been employed so that the story, written more than two centuries ago, still remains as a model of simple, straightforward English.

The precise delineation of settings and characters is as exact as an architect's scaled drawings and gives Jonathan Swift's imaginary adven-

Gulliver lies resting while myriad Lilliputians swarm around him industriously.
Scaled to a world whose inhabitants are no more than six inches high, Gulliver is
gigantic in proportion.
From Gulliver's Travels *by Jonathan Swift, retold by Padraic Colum, illustrated by Willy Pogany.*

ture an inescapable conviction. Consequently, children can readily identify
with either the tiny Lilliputians if they recognize themselves as "little
people," or with the heroic Gulliver if they prefer to perceive themselves
as giants. But whatever choice the reader makes, the story can meet many
a child's longing for size and power, and, above all, satisfy a yearning for
adventure beyond the limits of actuality.

The movement from one world to another in this subtle fantasy
is handled without self-consciousness, and the reader, traveling from reality to unreality and back again, can do so without uneasiness. For mature readers, there is an opportunity to probe into the meaning of real
life and society.

Another delightful fantasy, though less satirical and profound than
Gulliver's Travels, brings three children to an island visible only in a
mirage. Like their predecessor, Gulliver, the children discover that they
are giants to the tiny inhabitants of Lilliput. *Castaways in Lilliput*, written
by Henry Winterfeld and illustrated by William M. Hutchinson, updates
the voyage to the land of Lilliputians originated by Jonathan Swift in
the eighteenth century. In more modern times, Lilliput is detailed with
television, helicopters, superhighways, and tractors all worked into an
imaginative story supported by wit and freshness.

From their earliest years children reveal fascination for the world in which they live. Their intense curiosity leads them to discover new and strange worlds of wonders at each new stage of their growth and development. At first, the bright new scenes and objects in their immediate environment arouse interest. But widening horizons soon include worlds peopled with fabulous beings selected from the fairy tales that may have been read aloud by adults, the various media children view and listen to, and their own imaginations. Elves, goblins, fairies, and dragons all move about in curious arrangements acting and talking in accordance with child morality and in the childlike terms exemplified in fairy tales. Here is a world peopled by daring extroverts with unorthodox ethics who rob giants, as in "Jack and the Beanstalk," or who invade the home of "The Three Bears"—all at considerable personal risk! This is also a world where sharp wits pull one out of trouble either by white lies, magic, or some unrecommended ingenuity.

For the adult, however, the traditional fairy tale or modern fantasy for children that expresses such peculiar morality seems distinctly apart from the world of the pervading social order. But, after all, fantasy is a wonderland in which children can wander at will and command the images of heart and mind in any way they wish. And not all disapproved behavior is condoned in fantasy; much of it is not. Forgetfulness, failure to obey orders, breach of promise, and ingratitude frequently carry harsh penalties in fairy tales as well as in full-length fantasy. However, this is all part of child society, and the behavior reflected in the stories that children cherish is, ostensibly, their own behavior because fantasy is for them a source of vicarious experiences stemming from a wonderland where wishes come true.

Children growing up discover for themselves more and more new worlds projected in totally original dimensions in which their imaginations may have free play. Fantasy, whether traditional or modern, conjures up imagery of the familiar and the nonfamiliar that vibrates with the color and light of the imagination and lifts the reader into strange and marvelous new wonderlands. Even the aesthetic of the grotesque— witches and wizards; giants and ogres inhabiting weird domains—has a peculiar power to transport a reader, as if by magic carpet, to extensions of reality.

Sometimes children find this travel to and from a wonderland possible through their dreams or daydreams. Sometimes the voyage is facilitated by writers of fantasy who have created dream worlds where the strange and the marvelous dominate. Made luminous with beautiful pictures that children usually create in a dream, much of fantasy is spun with the stuff of which dreams are made, yet touched with poetry that gives depth and distinction to the particular category of Fantasy: Magic, Dreams, and Wonderlands.

BOOKS FOR YOUNGER CHILDREN

Fantasy and reality are beautifully blended and balanced in an extraordinarily artistic picture book, *The Troll Music*, by Anita Lobel. Visual and verbal elements join forces to express the power of the troll magic that besets a group of traveling musicians who are reminiscent of medieval minstrels.

Beginning realistically, the story presents the "group of musicians who played beautiful music" against a detailed background of closely clustered houses, walled towns, and richly glowing costumes.

The musicians halt in their travels to rest with their instruments by their sides, and it is at this point that the story swings into a magical world where troll power presides. The juxtaposition of the mundane and the fabulous is in a style akin to folk and fairy tales. Here the fantastic action is made believable with incidents that are lifelike in their alignment with reality and with human situations that are probable.

The story progresses as an angry troll appears. He is irritated by the music, so, while the players are sleeping, he causes all the instruments to "moo," "honk," and "cluck" like barnyard animals. When the musicians awake and go about their work they discover the troll's intervention and go about trying to remedy the situation.

Although a certain number of fantastic elements creep into the story, a measure of wit and wisdom is also expressed. For example, when the musicians attempt to appease the troll, they begin by tempting the troll's wife who is quick to accept the delicious gifts they offer. Her children also picnic on the delights provided for appeasement. But nothing so far tempts Mr. Troll. Unwilling to sacrifice his pride to the cunning musicians and his persistent wife, he relentlessly refuses to remove the spell. But he is no match for Mrs. Troll who threatens him with a punch in the nose and cajoles him with a promise of cake. At last the grouchy sprite submits, and the musicians, whose instruments are in tune again,

continue their travels from town to town making music "everyone agreed
... was the best in the land."

There is a human situation in this magical story, and the personalities
of the fairy-like creatures resemble human counterparts. But viewed from
an angle of fantasy, the meanings behind the situations, the conflicts
between the characters, and the domestic drama in the story itself seem
humorously clever and entertaining. At the same time, they offer an
opportunity to confront a human dilemma found in reality and to learn
to cope with it.

The author/illustrator has devoted care and attention to fine details
bordering the pictures. Edges toned in pink, orange, yellow, green, and
russet are balanced with pen-and-ink lines that frame the softly colored
full-page illustrations. Reminiscent of medieval tapestries, the figures in

In this double-page spread a moonlit world of make-believe pulsates with the
vitality of dancing trolls, prancing animals, and the accompanying musicians.
Beguiling details dot this vibrant painting.

From The Troll Music *by Anita Lobel. Copyright © 1966 by Anita Lobel. Harper & Row,
Publishers. Reproduced by permission.*

this lovely picture book call up the art of another era which the artist has so skillfully recreated with the same craftsmanship exercised by the artists of the Middle Ages.

BOOKS FOR INTERMEDIATE-GRADE CHILDREN

Tom's Midnight Garden, a magnificent fantasy, spans time when a boy, escaping the boredom of an aunt and uncle's home in England, involves himself in the lives of former inhabitants of an old restored house. Beautifully told by Philippa Pearce, the book was awarded the Carnegie Medal in 1958.

In this story time moves beyond the limits of actuality for two of its principal characters, Tom and Mrs. Bartholomew, who share a mysterious sympathy as the past melts into the present with convincing naturalness. Unlike traditional fairy tales, this beautifully written fantasy does not depend on supernatural performance to turn the trick. Rather, it is the magic of the characters' personalities and of the mysterious movement in time that lifts this story beyond the usual time and dream fantasies in children's literature.

The book opens with Tom, cross and resentful, standing alone on the doorstep of his home where his brother lies ill with the measles. He waves good-bye to his brother and mother as well as to the garden whose pleasures of tree-climbing and outdoor excitement must be left behind as Tom broodingly drives off to live with his uncle and aunt until the quarantine is over.

In this haunting picture the present melts into the past soon after midnight when Tom steals out of bed to enter the world of yesteryear. Shadowy forms intensify the eeriness in the scene.

From Tom's Midnight Garden *by Phlippa Pearce, illustrated by Susan Einzig. Copyright © 1958 by Oxford University Press. Published in the United States by J. P. Lippincott Company. Reproduced by permission.*

While living with his relatives in a large apartment of their restored house, Tom begins to miss his brother and the garden at home where they used to play together. Lack of exercise and overly rich food keep him awake at night listening to the "striking of the grandfather clock . . . in the silence of those nights when everyone else was asleep."

Then, from these realistic beginnings the story shifts into fantastic adventure. One night the old clock strikes thirteen. Tom goes downstairs despite his promise not to get out of bed before breakfast and opens the back door. He is in a mysterious garden where he meets a little girl, Hatty, who becomes his friend in a Victorian world of the past. Although Tom must return to the present, he is convinced that he can share in everything affecting his playmate in the strange garden. But this is not so. Hatty grows out of childhood even while she plays with Tom, and the garden, in accordance with the strange passage of time, fades away with Hatty's childhood.

Tom's growth, on the other hand, does not keep up with Hatty's because time in his world stands still while he plays in yesteryear. Then, suddenly, Tom witnesses a fantastic phenomenon—Hatty, his child-playmate, becomes a young woman with all the mannerisms and characteristics typical of the Victorian era.

Soon the "dream" is over, and so is Tom's stay with his relatives. At this point the story swings back to reality once more as Tom, ready to return home, actually meets Hatty—she is now old Mrs. Bartholomew who occupies an upstairs apartment of the house.

Philippa Pearce's particular contribution to this fantastic adventure in time is in the way she makes her characters come alive with natural dialogue, colloquial at times, but breezy and clear-cut. Tinged with poetry, the beautiful narrative is firmly rooted in reality and presented in probable terms. Although the brilliant projection into the past may not be fully understood by some children at the intermediate level, it will become clear when these same children reread the story in their later years.

BOOKS FOR UPPER-GRADE CHILDREN

In the last half of the nineteenth century, Lewis Carroll, employing nonsense and powerful imagination, created *Alice's Adventures in Wonderland*—"the spiritual volcano of children's books." With its sequel, *Through the Looking-Glass*, it has become the most successful story ever written expressly for children. Both books belong to the category of dream or wonderland fantasy, and they both recount the imaginative adventures of Alice, who tumbles down a rabbit hole in

Alice's Adventures in Wonderland, and who passes through a sitting-room mirror in *Through the Looking-Glass*.

Long an innocent staple for children, the collection of Alice's adventures has, since Freud, been subjected to the scrutiny and analyses of psychologists and psychiatrists who, finding the stories rich sources of symbolism and meaning, have labeled them with less innocent impulses of adults.

Despite the psycho-oriented interpretations, perhaps no other fantasy for children has survived so many attacks to be so generally termed a classic as *Alice's Adventures in Wonderland* with its ageless and timeless appeal. Or, as Alice M. Jordan states: "It delights us when we are young, it is cherished, reread and quoted for its philosophy and humor when we are old. There are so many apt conversations in it, so many occurrences called to mind in our everyday life, so many characters reminding us at times of ourselves or our friends. Always there is the sweet wholesome laughter that follows the inconsequential turn of events in that book and in *Through the Looking-Glass*."[13]

A good edition combining both books, so that they appear as one, is published by Macmillan under the banner New Children's Classics. Although designated as a book for intermediate-grade children, its humor and profundity are better appreciated by older children who may revel in the jokes, mathematical puzzles, parodies, allusions and other curiosities *in* the stories rather than just books of riddles, puzzles, and humor for their own sake. Parts of *Alice* may appeal to the youngest, its humor and symbolism to older children, and its poetry of oddity may give delight to all. *Alice* may be used wisely at many levels of children's growth just as other fine works of art and literature have many levels of appeal.

As a brilliant dream fantasy, *Alice* springs very quickly from actual settings to strange lands. In the first book, *Alice's Adventures in Wonderland*, the little girl is "tired of sitting by her sister on the bank and of having nothing to do . . . So she was considering in her own mind (as well as she could, for the hot day made her feel very sleepy and stupid), whether the pleasure of making a daisy-chain would be worth the trouble of getting up and picking the daisies, when suddenly a White Rabbit with pink eyes ran close by her."[14]

---

[13] Alice M. Jordan, *Children's Classics* (Boston: The Horn Book, Inc., 1960), p. 3.
[14] Lewis Carroll, *Alice's Adventures in Wonderland and Through the Looking Glass* (Chicago: The John C. Winston Company, 1923), p. 1.

Seated at a table under a tree, the March Hare, the Hatter, the Dormouse, and Alice are humorously portrayed in "A Mad Tea-Party." Tenniel's pictures remain insepa-rable from this fantasy.
From Alice's Adventures in Wonderland *by Lewis Carroll, illustrated by Sir John Tenniel.*

Following the rabbit down an underground passage, Alice has a fantastic series of adventures and meets some of the most unusual charac-ters ever to appear in literature.

She grows larger and smaller, swims in a pool of tears, matches wits with a hookah-smoking Caterpillar, attends to a baby that turns into a pig, joins a mad tea-party, withstands the impulsive arguments of the King and Queen of Hearts, listens to the Mock Turtle's story, watches a Lobster-Quadrille dance, and witnesses a wildly bizarre trial to determine who stole the tarts. In the final scene, Alice and the story return to reality after a whirlwind adventure.

Through all this the author weaves a splendid design of word pic-tures whose richness, depth of perspective, and shades of meaning become more intense as one reads, rereads, and grows. As Lillian Smith adds, it "builds up striking patterns of language and idea, each part held in subtle relation to the others. The unity of the book is not in the design alone, but also in the consistent point of view. The story is Alice's dream as Alice dreamed it; the point of view is invariably that of the rational child in an irrational dream. The language is the language of nonsense, but at the same time we are sensible of the essence of truth it contains."[15]

The topsy-turvy world of Wonderland is replaced by a more ordered, though equally irrational, world just on the other side of Alice's drawing-room mirror in Carroll's *Through the Looking-Glass*. Bored playing with her cat and kittens in a stuffy Victorian room, Alice allows free reign to her imagination as she climbs the mantle, faces the large mirror over it, and pretends "the glass has got all soft like gauze, so that we can get through." Melting away "like a bright silvery mist" the glass allows Alice to enter an extension of reality where, freed from the mundane moorings of an ordinary drawing-room, the story is projected into another dimension. Here the pictures on the wall are alive, clocks grin, chessmen walk about two and two, castles walk arm in arm, and the Red King and Queen, the White King and Queen, Pawns, and Knights all move about in curious arrangements. Subsequently, events in this ornately imagined story take place in rapid succession and cover a broad sweep of fantastic creatures and happenings, calling up deeper meanings in human experience. For example, this dialogue between Alice and the Red Queen when they start running:

> The most curious part of the thing was, that the trees and the other things round them never changed their places at all: however fast they went, they never seemed to pass anything. "I wonder if all the things move along with us?" thought poor puzzled Alice. And the Queen seemed to guess her thoughts, for she cried, "Faster! Don't try to talk!"
>
> * * *
>
> Alice looked round her in great surprise. "Why, I do believe we've been under this tree the whole time! Everything's just as it was!"
> "Of course it is," said the Queen. "What would you have it?"
> "Well, in *our* country," said Alice, still panting a little, "you'd generally get to somewhere else—if you ran very fast for a long time as we've been doing."
> "A slow sort of country!" said the Queen. "Now, *here*, you see, it takes all the running *you* can do, to keep in the same place. If you want to get somewhere else, you must run at least twice as fast as that!"[16]

In practical terms the dialogue seems pure nonsense, but it holds the distilled essence of a much higher truth not discernible by the mere logical deductions of the everyday world. Though echoing the frantic hustle and bustle of most humans, this incident in *Alice* is clothed in humorous,

---

[15]Lillian H. Smith, *The Unreluctant Years* (Chicago: American Library Association, 1953), p. 154.
[16]Carroll, *op. cit.*, pp. 184–85.

allegorical garb that allows a reader to view his life and laugh at it. There are very few incidents in Lewis Carroll's work that do not inject meanings that touch us by the element of truth they possess, and children capable of grasping the ideas behind the symbols and allegories will find themselves viewing life from another angle and so becoming more and more conscious of their own world while still enjoying the vibrant storyland of Alice.

Despite the high-flying action in this picture, the Queen's statement to Alice is rooted in reality: "Now, *here*, you see, it takes all the running *you* can do, to keep in the same place."
From Through the Looking Glass *by Lewis Carroll, illustrated by Sir John Tenniel.*

This is possible because there is rollicking entertainment in this story. Alice enters the room on the other side of the looking glass, tours Looking-glass House; wanders up and down in a garden of live flowers; encounters an angry Red Queen confidently; rides in "a very queer carriage-full of passengers"; listens to reams of poetry—nonsense and otherwise; listens also to profound beliefs ". . . I've believed as many as six impossible things before breakfast"; meets Humpty Dumpty, the Lion and the Unicorn, a strange Knight; and even presides as Queen Alice before waking up to actuality. After all, *Alice* stands as a supreme example of literary art. Its dream world offers a new view of reality and gives young readers a sense of expansion from the imaginative experience, which, in the end, is the test of any good fantasy.

Criteria for Fantasy

THEME

- Is the idea (or ideas) original in its expression and is it projected into an original dimension?
- Are the ideas projected in the fantasy firmly founded on truth?
- Does the theme lend itself to promoting a sense of expansion?
- Does the central idea dominate the fantasy so that the concepts, no matter how abstract, can be made concrete through development in other literary elements?
- Are the concepts in the story believable even though they may be clothed in symbols and allegories?
- Does the fantasy concern itself with fundamental questions of universal life?
- Does the theme reveal a general symbolic significance that children may grasp at, either at once or in future readings of the story?
- Does the fantasy concern itself with the fundamental question of universal life regardless of its allegorical or metaphorical approaches?
- Are the themes based on imagination and wonder so that they can arouse in children curiosity and concern for the natural and the supernatural?

PLOT

- Is there a strong story line affording the delights of imaginative entertainment yet still exercising the imagination of children?
- Is the story line strong enough to weave through magic and marvels without being eclipsed by these elements of fantasy?
- Is the plot, for all its play with magic and marvels, still anchored in the real world?
- Is the plot constructed so that the fantasy swings freely from reality to the imaginative without weakening the story?
- Does the plot legitimately break free from the experienced realities inherent in the story yet still spin a convincing fantasy?
- If the fantasy is placed in direct contact with real life, are real-life means then used to solve serious problems so that the balance of the story is not weakened?
- Has the fantasy been developed so that it has its own limits that prevent it from swinging out beyond comprehension?
- Do the fantastic events and inventions avoid serious clashes with their counterparts in real life?
- No matter how inventive the fantasy, does the plot reveal a consistency of action?

- Are the events unobtrusively interrelated so that the fantasy does not seem contrived or made up of loosely linked episodes?
- Has the fantasy managed to translate characters into action?
- During the process of the action has the story utilized a neat proportion of suspended disbelief, fantastic turns of events, magical and irrational elements, all climaxed in a convincing, satisfying conclusion?

CHARACTERIZATION

- Are the characters believable in spite of their fantastic adventures?
- Does the touch of magic in the fantasy kindle vigor and fresh life in characters?
- In spite of the fantasy, are the characters delineated precisely enough to become convincing and lifelike?
- Whether the characters are human, supernatural, or animations, do they remain true to their natures throughout the story?
- Do these characters, human or imagined, develop so that they become convincingly real with unique personalities and personal idioms of their own?
- Do the human, humanized, or animated characters lend themselves to human identification?
- Is the story distinguished by colorful characterization?
- Is there a lifelike air to the characters even though some of them may be pure inventions?

STYLE

- Is the style distinguished by exquisite writing in accordance with the kind of fantasy expressed?
- Does the fantasy have a rich, graceful style of writing with overtones of meanings?
- Does the writing reveal a measure of the writer's poetic imagination?
- Are images conjured up by skillfully used words, phrases, symbols, and allegories?
- Does the writing afford some of the whimsey that is distinctive of fantasy?
- Is the language capable of bringing before a young reader a series of images that seem credible and satisfying?
- Despite the profundity in the story, is the language used to communicate with the recognizable tongue of childhood?
- Does the language reflect a measure of respect for the supernatural so that the magical inventions do not lose authority?

- Is the language powerful enough to make the incredible seem credible and the unreal seem real within a fantastically logical framework?

- Is the author's style vibrant enough with color, light, and imagery to lift the fantasy beyond the boundaries of the mundane so as to afford a sense of expansion?

- Does the writing reveal a balance between real and unreal, between fact and fancy?

- Has the writer demonstrated skill in deepening insights into the imaginative and private worlds of the animate and inanimate?

- Has the fantasy as a whole been so expressed that it succeeds as a genuine work of the creative imagination stemming from a genuine creative impulse?

SETTING

- Are the settings detailed enough so as to catch the radiance of the marvelous and magical in a fantasy?

- Is there a sense of proportion about the inventive details that add dimension and deepen faith in the fantasy?

- Do the details of the settings give an air of reality to the most fantastic scenes, characters, costumes and inventions?

- Are the settings concretely drawn with the details taken from actuality; do the inventive ones express originality and imagination?

- Do the details remain true to their backgrounds without distorting or falsifying the locale in the fantasy?

- Are the settings sharpened by some intricate details?

- No matter how elegant or splendid the background for the story, has the writer exercised a degree of restraint to avoid elaborate descriptions?

- Have the settings been designed with the artistry, whimsey, and charm that frequently highlight fantasy?

- Are the settings fashioned so as to provide beauty and atmosphere tinged with the strangeness that allows for an illusion?

- Do the settings in general reflect a balance of delicacy, preciseness, sureness of touch combined with originality of idea and beauty of design?

References

ARBUTHNOT, MAY HILL, "New Magic," "Once Upon a Time," in *Children and Books*, 3rd ed. Chicago: Scott, Foresman & Company, 1964.

DAVIS, MARY GOULD, "George Macdonald," "Hans Christian Andersen," "Aristocrats and Griffins: Fanciful Tales of Frank R. Stockton," in *The Three Owls*, Anne Carroll Moore. New York: The Macmillan Company, 1925.

EATON, ANNE THAXTER, "Betwixt and Between," in *Reading with Children*. New York: The Viking Press, Inc., 1940.

FISHER, MARGERY, "Mrs. Bunny and the Rabbits," "The Land of Faerie," "Magic Carpets," in . . . *Intent upon Reading*. Leicester, England: Brockhampton Press, Ltd., 1961–62.

HOLLOWELL, LILLIAN, "Traditional Fairy Tales," in *A Book of Children's Literature*. New York: Holt, Rinehart, & Winston, Inc., 1961.

HUBER, MIRIAM BLANTON, "Make-Believe Stories," in *Story and Verse for Children*. New York: The Macmillan Company 1965.

HUCK, CHARLOTTE S., and DORIS A. YOUNG, "Modern Fantasy," in *Children's Literature in the Elementary School*. New York: Holt, Rinehart & Winston, Inc., 1961.

JOHNSON, EDNA, *et al.*, "Fantasy," in *Anthology of Children's Literature*. Boston: Houghton Mifflin Company, 1959.

MEIGS, CORNELIA, *et al.*, "A Landmark in Fantasy," in *A Critical History of Children's Literature*. New York: The Macmillan Company, 1953.

SMITH, LILLIAN H., "Fantasy," in *The Unreluctant Years*. Chicago: American Library Association, 1953.

TOLKIEN, J. R. R., "On Fairy-Stories," in *Tree and Leaf*. Boston: Houghton Mifflin Company, 1964.

VIGUERS, RUTH HILL, "The River's Source," in *Margin for Surprise*. Boston: Little, Brown & Co., 1964.

Fantasy in Children's Literature

NATURE, ANIMALS, AND HUMANS

For younger children

JAGLON AND THE TIGER-FAIRIES
Written and illustrated by L. Frank Baum. Reilly & Lee Co., 1953.

An animal fantasy about an orphaned Royal Tiger, Jaglon, who is raised by tiger-fairies, and, who through courage and nobility, eventually becomes king of the inner circle of the wilderness. Set against a realistic background, the story travels through exciting adventures warmed by their emotional impact. Many of the situations in this jungle fantasy parallel those in human experience, which makes closer identification with the characters possible.

SHAWNEEN AND THE GANDER
*Written and illustrated by Richard
Bennett. Doubleday & Company,
Inc., 1937.*

An enchanting fantasy about a little boy,
Shawneen, who sees a golden bugle in a
store and makes plans to obtain it. A
leprechaun lends beguiling advice, but
it is a lowly gander who is principally
instrumental in the achievement of the
boy's goal. Distinguished text and pictures mark a story that is reminiscent of an
Irish fairy tale sparked with magical
elements.

THE MOUSE AND THE
MOTORCYCLE
*Written by Beverly Cleary.
Illustrated by Louis Darling.
William Morrow & Co., Inc.,
1965.*

A down-to-earth fantasy that refreshingly
presents a mouse named Ralph who borrows a boy's toy motorcycle. Subsequent
friendship develops between Ralph and
the little boy, Keith.

PETUNIA, I LOVE YOU
*Written and illustrated by Roger
Duvoisin. Alfred A. Knopf, Inc.,
1965.*

An adventure in pictures about an innocent goose Petunia, this very short tale
follows her on her short walk through the
woods with Raccoon as she unknowingly
foils all his attempts to eat her.

MY FATHER'S DRAGON
*Written by Ruth Stiles Gannett.
Illustrated by Ruth Christman
Gannett. Random House, Inc., 1948.*

A humorous, fanciful tale of a small boy
who travels to Wild Island to rescue a
mistreated, striped baby dragon. The story
is filled with continuous action as "my
father" outwits an assortment of animals
with ridiculous problems. His imaginative
use of mundane objects delights the reader.
Illustrations depict the animals in a sympathetic, loving manner.

MOUSE HOUSE
*Written by Rumer Godden.
Illustrated by Adrienne Adams. The
Viking Press, Inc., 1957.*

A little story about little creatures, Mouse
House is an enchanting nursery masterpiece presented in the Beatrix Potter
manner. Scaled to an audience between
five and eight, the suspenseful tale follows
the adventures of Bonnie, a mouse who is
crowded out of her nest and who moves
upstairs to a comfortable miniature house
that is just right for mice-tenants. Her new
home belongs to a kind little girl who
carefully places it in a safe and fitting
locale, and whose role it becomes to house
the homeless. Charming illustrations are
as lovely and perceptive as the prose they
accompany.

NUBBER BEAR
*Written by William Lipkind.
Illustrated by Roger Duvoisin.
Harcourt, Brace & World, Inc.,
1966.*

A strikingly beautiful picture book
interprets a story reflective of a human
condition. Nubber Bear, representing any
little boy or girl who wants to be obedient
but also independent, strays to "the Middle Wood" for forbidden honey. The
consequences are a bee sting and a spank-
ing, but not without a consoling bear hug.
Remarkably clever drawings strengthen
the storytelling in this enchanting animal
fantasy.

MARTHA THE MOVIE MOUSE
*Written and illustrated by Arnold
Lobel. Harper & Row, Publishers,
1966.*

Arnold Lobel brings humor and his own
understanding of home and happiness
into this touching story of a homeless
mouse who eventually finds both in a
movie house. Told with rhyme and delightful three-color pictures, the book
captures the special flavor of life in a movie
theatre.

MRS. PIGGLE-WIGGLE
Written by Betty Heskett
Macdonald. Illustrated by Richard
Bennett. J.B. Lippincott Co., 1947.

Mrs. Piggle-Wiggle is lovable, eccentric, and ingenious in her amusing ideas for curing harassing children. In this book of stories-with-a-moral, some odd and naughty habits and attitudes of four-to nine-year-olds are humorously presented and cleverly dealt with. The most familiar situations described and satirized are of the Won't-pick-up-the-toys, Answer-back, and Never-want-to-go-to-bed variety. In between laughs both children and adults can learn from Mrs. Piggle-Wiggle's surprising skill and originality in coping with each funny or nonsensical problem. Illustrations by Richard Bennett are well drawn but the 1940's style and settings are dated.

A BIRTHDAY FOR BIRD
Written and illustrated by Diane
Redfield Massie. Parents' Magazine
Press, 1966.

This fresh, colorful picture book tells of a bird and his birthday. Verses and pictures join to convey the doubts and delights of the approaching event and then the event itself. All the gaiety of a birthday party complete with gifts is expressed in this bright book whose furred and feathered characters reflect the feelings of young children.

BLUE'S BROKEN HEART
Written by Jean F. Merrill.
Illustrated by R. Solbert.
McGraw-Hill Book Company,
1961.

This tender and purposeful little fantasy about an animal doctor who mends a dog's broken heart is carried along with lilting prose and unusually attractive illustrations. Kindness is stressed with great simplicity and a sense of humanity.

THE TAILOR OF GLOUCESTER
Written and illustrated by Beatrix

Potter. *Frederick Warne & Co., Inc.,*
1903.

A miniature classic by an outstanding author/illustrator of the nursery who has produced a veritable library of tiny books for children. *The Tailor of Gloucester* is ranked as one of her best fantasies. It is concerned with an ailing tailor and his completion of the Lord Mayor's waistcoat. Tiny mice come to his rescue and complete the garment with a precision possible only from creatures as nimble and small as they. Beautiful language echoes the stir and quiet sounds of an ancient city hushed by snow, of hurrying, scurrying mouse feet, and of tolling bells at midnight. Soft pastels blend with fuchsias and greens in pages of rare beauty, dignity, and grace.

PARTOUCHE PLANTS A SEED
Written and illustrated by Ben
Shecter. Harper & Row, Publishers,
1966.

This humorous beast-fable, lying near the borders of fantasy, has as its hero a vegetable-loving pig. Partouche, who loves to munch the corn in Madame Gounard's backyard, decides to put an end to Madame's fussing by planting corn of his own. He finds a corn seed, plants it, nurtures it, and, with the help of his fieldmouse assistant, saves it from tragedy to provide enough corn for a summer picnic for Partouche and his friends.

BELLING THE TIGER
Written by Mary Stolz. Illustrated
by Beni Montresor. Harper &
Row, Publishers, 1961.

There is wisdom to be perceived in this witty and imaginative story that disproves the fable by Aesop that says a mouse cannot bell a cat. Two humble little cellar mice are ordered by their chief to accomplish this act, but at one point during their terrifying mission they find themselves on a tropical island where there is much bigger game—like tigers. When they return home, no one will believe their great feat. But now the task of belling the old cat, Portman, is as nothing to the mice who belled a tiger. Illustrations by Beni Montresor add to the beauty of this well-designed book.

Miss Suzy
Written by Miriam Young.
Illustrated by Arnold Lobel.
Parents' Magazine Press, 1964.

A fantasy that solicits the aid of toy soldiers to achieve its climactic fulfillment is told with brevity and charmingly imaginative pictures. A little gray squirrel, Miss Suzy, is rudely chased away from her cozy oaktree home by a band of quarrelsome red squirrels. In her search for a new home, Miss Suzy finds a beautiful dollhouse and a box of toy soldiers asleep for years. By mothering the toys that come alive, Suzy wins their affection and aid in driving the rude squirrels from her original home.

Mr. Rabbit and the Lovely Present
Written by Charlotte Zolotow.
Illustrated by Maurice Sendak.
Harper & Row, Publishers, 1962.

A fantasy made iridescent by luminous watercolors filtering soft light from sun, stars, moon, and wildflowers about a rabbit who helps a little girl find a birthday present for her mother. The magical pictures create an illusion that is difficult to break because they are drawn with details of reality that make the fantasy, in text and pictures, seem so credible.

For intermediate-grade children

The Cat and Mrs. Cary
Written by Doris Gates. Illustrated by Peggy Bacon. The Viking Press, Inc., 1962.

Mrs. Cary understands everything The Cat says to her in this witty account of her exciting summer with smugglers, The Cat, a little boy, and new neighbors. All the characterizations are excellently executed with humor in both words and pictures.

Alonzo and the Army of Ants
Written by Murray Goodwin.
Illustrated by Kiyo Komoda.
Harper & Row, Publishers 1966.

One inhabitant of a South American village of jungle animals is Alonzo, the anteater, who is a great character to have around in an emergency such as an invasion of marauding ants. He leaves his village because of a quarrel with a peccary but returns in time to unite and organize the animals to fight off their threatening invaders. This perceptive fantasy tale is made effective by sharp dialogue that gives each animal a distinctive personality.

Rabbit Hill
Written and illustrated by Robert Lawson. The Viking Press, Inc., 1944.

Through words and pictures, Robert Lawson creates a memorable community with sensitive portrayals of the animals who inhabit Rabbit Hill. Familiar with the ways of the wild, Lawson adds humanizing touches to make this a superb combination of fact and fantasy. The exquisite illustrations add new dimensions to the personalities of the wildlife creatures.

The Tough Winter
Written and illustrated by Robert Lawson. The Viking Press, Inc., 1954.

Robert Lawson again depicts a wildlife community with skill and sensitivity as he creatively exposes the helplessness of little animals. The picturesque language conveys the beauty of the countryside, action, humor, and respect for all living creatures. A keen understanding of the animals and their environment is revealed through subtle details in the illustrations.

The Voyages of Doctor Dolittle
Written and illustrated by Hugh Lofting. J. B. Lippincott Co., 1922.

One of the classic series of stories about

John Dolittle, M. D.—the adorable doctor, animalinguist, explorer and naturalist of Puddleby—this beloved and whimsical tale takes children to a faraway land called Spidermonkey Island. Through the kindhearted doctor's conversations and dealings with his animal friends, children come to love and respect each living creature. All characters come to life through the author's simple and delightful language and his gay and amusing illustrations. A Newbery Medal winner.

Other Doctor Dolittle stories by the same author/illustrator: *The Story of Doctor Dolittle, Doctor Dolittle's Post Office, Doctor Dolittle's Circus, Doctor Dolittle's Zoo, Doctor Dolittle's Caravan, Doctor Dolittle's Garden, Doctor Dolittle in the Moon, Doctor Dolittle's Return, Doctor Dolittle and the Secret Lake, Doctor Dolittle and the Green Canary,* and *Doctor Dolittle's Puddleby Adventures.*

THE CRICKET IN TIMES SQUARE
Written by George Selden.
Illustrated by Garth Williams.
Farrar, Straus & Giroux, Inc.,
1960.

A whimsical mixture of fantasy and logic runs throughout this capricious and creative plot about the cricket, Chester, who is carried in a picnic basket from Connecticut to the Times Square subway station in New York. City images, sounds, and characters are authentic backgrounds to the delightful and fantastic situation that makes up the ensuing story. Chester settles in the Bellini family's newsstand, and befriends their son Mario. Then, to repay Mario's kindness, the cricket brings success to the Bellinis through his unusual musical talent and saves their almost bankrupt newsstand business. This captivating and cheering tale is full of wise and humorous dialogue and wonderful images and personalities that will appeal to children between the ages of eight and twelve. Garth Williams' illustrations are beautiful and help to make this an outstanding work.

HIGGLETY PIGGLETY POP! OR
THERE MUST BE MORE TO LIFE
Written and illustrated by Maurice Sendak. Harper and Row, Publishers, 1967.

Although Jennie is a restless Sealyham terrier who has everything, she comes to believe there is more to life than all that she has so far. She sets out to star in the World Mother Goose Theatre, but first she must have the required experience. This she has—even to the point of discovering that there is more to life than having nothing. Jennie eventually reaches the Castle Yonder and becomes the finest leading lady the World Mother Goose Theatre ever had. Maurice Sendak's distinctive and hauntingly magnificent pictures illumine his imaginative fantasy.

THE RESCUERS
Written by Margery Sharp.
Illustrated by Garth Williams.
Little, Brown & Co., 1959.

An amusing fantasy of three brave mice who rescue a Norwegian poet from imprisonment. Told convincingly, the story has appeal for the more mature, skeptical reader who demands factual descriptions as well as a sturdy story line. Garth Williams' drawings amplify the account with conviction.

CHARLOTTE'S WEB
Written by Elwyn Brooks White.
Illustrated by Garth Williams.
Harper & Row, Publishers, 1952.

A rare, tender, and imaginative story of a beautiful friendship between farmyard characters, *Charlotte's Web* offers magic, humor, and delight for older children and for adults with a corner of childhood in their hearts. There is wisdom, wit, and pathos in this irresistible fantasy about the little girl Fern, the runty pig Wilbur, and the philosophical spider Charlotte who weaves miraculous webs to save the pig's life and morale. All the human and animal creatures are realistically and believably portrayed to represent various characteristics of humankind: they are good and bad, warm and cold, kind and selfish, intelligent and ignorant. Garth Williams' fine pen drawings depict settings, characters, and situations faithfully, and they also trace the fragile intricacies of spider webs in delicate lines.

For upper-grade children

THE CAT WHO WENT TO HEAVEN
*Written by Elizabeth Coatsworth.
Illustrated by Lynd Ward. The
Macmillan Company, 1930.*
Imbued with the delicacy and depth of an ancient oriental print, this beautiful, poetic story is based on Japanese legends and the spiritual teachings of Buddhism. It tells of how a humble artist is commissioned by the temple priests to paint the dying Buddha surrounded by adoring animals and of the compassion he shows his patient little cat by including him in the picture. This is a brave act, which infuriates the priests, for legend has it that of all animals only the cat did not accept Buddha's teachings. But the miraculous outcome of this tender story helps the young reader to understand a religion that recognizes and blesses all living creatures on earth. Illustrations reflect the beauty and sensitivity of the tale and seem to become individual parts of the Japanese artist's temple picture.

THE TWENTY-ONE BALLOONS
*Written and illustrated by
William Pène du Bois. The
Viking Press, Inc., 1947.*
Fact and fantasy mingle in a book that unravels fabulous adventures like a constantly unrolling map. Here a wearied Professor William Sherman explains how he came to land in the Atlantic Ocean with twenty-one balloons when he had started his trip over the Pacific with just one. The explorer's adventures include landing on a volcanic island whose destruction is historical fact. Other fabulous accounts heighten the fascination of this book which won the Newbery Medal.

THE WIND IN THE WILLOWS
*Written by Kenneth Grahame.
Illustrated by E. H. Shepard.
Charles Scribner's Sons, 1933.*
A favorite treasure and a beautiful, deeply moving experience for all. Episodes of life on the river bank with Rat, Mole, Badger, and Toad run the gamut of emotions in this classic that appeals to many levels of understanding with warmth, humor, wisdom, and beauty. Throughout their adventures, the four animal friends mirror the weaknesses and strengths of man and reflect the joys and pains of living. "The Piper at the Gates of Dawn" is unforgettable, and reaches rare heights of beauty and great depths of feeling. Mr. Grahame's vivid characters, images, and descriptions have been sympathetically interpreted in the lovely pen drawings of Ernest Shepard.

THE ANIMAL FAMILY
*Written by Randall Jarrell.
Illustrated by Maurice Sendak.
Pantheon Books, Inc., 1965.*
This beautiful book defies placement in any one age grouping. Blending real and unreal with poetic beauty, this simple story tells about a lonely hunter who finds a mermaid and takes her to live with him. He goes on to adopt a bear cub, a lynx kitten, and a small boy adrift in a lifeboat. Superior storytelling sharpens the focus on domestic details. Graceful style points up overtones of meaning, and exquisite illustrations deepen the inner delight aroused by the storyteller. Pamela Travers has stated "the story is a medley of lyrical factuality" and is "a paean to family life and its long unending thread."

TINY PEOPLE, TOYS, AND THINGS

For younger children

PENNY
Written by Beatrice Schenk De

Regniers. Illustrated by Marvin Bileck. The Viking Press, Inc., 1966.

Scaled to suit its diminutive character, Penny, this small book, minutely detailed, tells the story of a tiny girl found by an old couple who had wanted a child of their own. Charming the couple as well as the animal members of the family, the little girl grows older but no bigger. When sixteen, Penny flies away on the back of a bird to find a husband her size. Resembling Andersen's *Thumbelina*, *Penny* moves with fairy-tale action to a satisfying conclusion.

ZEEE
Written by Elizabeth Enright.
Illustrated by Irene Haas.
Harcourt, Brace & World, Inc., 1965.

The miniature world of the tiny fairy Zeee is a lovely, fragile one described here in elegant detail. She is a pretty eight-and-a-half-year-old, just bumblebee-size, who almost becomes an ill-tempered, antisocial human-hater because big people who can't see her are always accidentally wrecking her homes or inadvertently frustrating and threatening her. Each of her domestic arrangements—a sandpail cottage on the beach, a pagoda tent of leaves, and a home in an empty wasp's nest—is upset. But Zeee's luck and outlook change when one good person comes into her life and offers her comfort and everlasting friendship. A spell of enchantment is woven throughout this story with threads of invention and reality, sentiment and good sense, happiness and light wit. Irene Haas' many intricate and humorous drawings allow the reader to travel through fairyland with Zeee in full color and in black and white.

SHERWOOD WALKS HOME
Written and illustrated by James Flora. Harcourt, Brace & World, Inc., 1966.

The adventures and difficulties of a toy wind-up bear are humorously told.

Forgotten in the park in the rain, he arrives home just as his motor runs down. Marvelously funny pictures detailed in bold, gay colors alternate with black-and-white double-page spreads that give contemporary enhancement to a fantasy of love and loyalty.

THE GINGERBREAD RABBIT
Written by Randall Jarrell.
Illustrated by Garth Williams. The Macmillan Company, 1964.

In this slight, pleasant fantasy for the very young a gingerbread rabbit who was to have been a mother's surprise gift for her little girl comes to life and escapes being baked in the oven. When he runs away to the forest, he meets squirrels, a fox who wants to eat him, and a real rabbit who rescues and adopts him. Garth Williams' fine line illustrations enhance this happy-ending tale.

THE JOURNEY OF BANGWELL PUTT
Written and illustrated by Mariana.
Lothrop, Lee & Shepard Co., Inc., 1965.

Once distributed as a limited edition of hand-lettered and hand-colored books, this publication preserves the rare and antique quality of the original. It is the story of an old museum doll named Bangwell Putt who is sent to a big New York museum in a box marked "Christmas Loan of Old and Rare Objects." On her journey she meets other tiny antique characters and toys from museums around the world. When they are all assembled in New York, it is a dashing Hessian soldier riding a Horseandsnail who carries her off to the Museum ball on Christmas Eve.

WINNIE-THE-POOH
Written by A. A. Milne. Illustrated by Ernest H. Shepard. E. P. Dutton & Co., Inc., 1926.

Winnie-the-Pooh is a compilation of short, humorous fantasies anchored by the exact detail used to describe the characters and the forest that they inhabit. Through their association with human characters, these stuffed animals become very real. There is Winnie-the-Pooh, the simple-minded, lovable "bear of very little brain"; Eeyore, the old gray unhappy donkey; Rabbit, with his many friends and relations; Kanga, with a very motherly concern for baby Roo; Piglet, the friend of all; and Owl, the sage. The illustrations portray these animals as they are: charming, warm, and friendly.

THE HOUSE AT POOH CORNER
Written by A. A. Milne.
Illustrated by Ernest H. Shepard.
E. P. Dutton & Co., Inc., 1928.

In this sequel to *Winnie-the-Pooh*, Mr. Milne has re-created the charming and delightful world of Christopher Robin and his stuffed-animal friends. Melodic language is used to relate the whimsical, humorous adventures of the personified animals. Mr. Shepard's delicate pen-and-ink drawings are well suited to the mood of the stories and beautifully interpret the feelings and the personalities of the characters.

THE ELF WHO DIDN'T BELIEVE IN HIMSELF
Written by Geraldine Ross.
Illustrated by Kurt Werth.
Steck-Vaughn Co., 1966.

This beautifully illustrated book for the very young is a small tale of a small elf who doesn't believe that he exists. He meets two little boys who believe in him so strongly that they almost bring him into being through sheer will power.

THE MUFFLETUMPS
Written by Jan Wahl. Illustrated by
Edward Ardizzone. Holt,
Rinehart & Winston, Inc., 1966.

Author and illustrator both contribute to the charming, humorous storytelling in this book about four Victorian dolls who climb out of their attic trunk every summer when the Bediggian family leaves for

their holiday. They take over all the chores and duties of running the big house. The absurd antics of these dolls-come-to-life will give delight to very young children who project personalities into inanimate toys.

LITTLE OLD BEAR
Written and illustrated by Hilda Van
Stockum. The Viking Press, Inc.,
1966.

Based on a familiar, old-fashioned, and quaint theme, this is a simple story of an old, discarded teddy bear who finds a little boy to love and hold him. It will be loved by young children who are never too modern to find meaning in this sort of tale.

BENEATH THE OAK TREE
Written by Nathan Zimelman.
Illustrated by Carol Rogers.
Steck-Vaughn Co., 1966.

As if viewed through a magnifying glass, the miniature world of busy life beneath an oak tree comes to life in this vividly detailed and sensitive story. The enchantment of this fantasy is heightened by beautiful and colorful illustrations that help the reader to see into the tiny realm.

For intermediate-grade children

MISS HICKORY
Written by Carolyn S. Bailey.
Illustrated by Ruth Gannett. The
Viking Press, Inc., 1946.

A staunch little New England doll made of an Applewood twig body and a hickory nut head faces abandonment by her family at the end of summer vacation with bravery and ingenuity. Fortune is with her in the person of Crow who helps her make a home for the coming winter in a robin's nest. An unexpected development is her discovery by Squirrel. The four seasons in New England are painted with great delicacy and charm in lovely lithographs and enchanting prose. Miss Hickory herself is a thoroughly engaging personality in this delightful book where fantasy becomes reality.

FIVE DOLLS AND THEIR FRIENDS
Written by Helen Clare. Illustrated by Aliki. Prentice-Hall, Inc., 1968.

This doll fantasy, full of unpredictable escapades, is about five dolls and their friends: Elizabeth Small, a little girl who is magically able to reduce herself to doll-size; Vanessa, a bossy doll; Jacqueline, a saucy French doll; tiny Lupin; funny Armanda; and pretty, poetic Jane. Joining in the adventures of the dolls are a mischievous monkey, a lovely black kitten, a mimicking parrot, and a baby robin. The delightfully drawn fantasy compares with the other doll stories this same author has produced: *Five Dolls in a House, Five Dolls and the Monkey, and Five Dolls in the Snow.*

THE ADVENTURES OF PINOCCHIO
Written by C. Collodi. Translated by M. A. Murray. Illustrated by Fritz Kredel. Grosset & Dunlap, Inc., 1946.

This is the classic story of a little puppet's metamorphosis into a living puppet whose mischievous ways get him into horrendous situations. Finally, through the acquisition of a conscience, Pinocchio undergoes a second metamorphosis into a real, flesh-and-blood little boy. His lovable papa, Gepetto, creator of the original puppet, welcomes him back as a real boy in one of the most heartwarming happy endings in literature. Pinocchio is a fascinating, beautifully drawn character whose history has universal appeal.

HITTY: HER FIRST HUNDRED YEARS
Written by Rachel Field. Illustrated by Dorothy P. Lathrop. The Macmillan Company, 1929.

Here are the memoirs of a very personable, spirited doll, written against the rich historical background of nineteenth-century America. Her adventures are full of excitement and action as she travels aboard a whaling vessel from New England to the South Seas and India and back again to the land of her birth where she encounters more adventures. "What is a mere hundred years," she asks at the close of the book, "to well-seasoned mountain-ash?" Even now, as she sits in the window of a New York antique shop, she is as eager as she was that day, long ago, in Maine when the Old Peddler carved her. The charm of her pure, simple, slightly antique English makes this a most readable story.

THE DOLLS' HOUSE
Written by Rumer Godden. Illustrated by Tasha Tudor. The Viking Press, Inc., 1948.

A bewitchingly beautiful story about a small wooden doll whose wisdom shines through a toy fantasy made even more enchanting by delicate drawings scaled down to a world of playthings. Realistically portrayed, the characters in this, the best of all Rumer Godden's doll stories, come alive to point up a theme about "good things and bad things.... They can only wish hard for the right thing to happen."

IMPUNITY JANE
Written by Rumer Godden. Illustrated by Adrienne Adams. The Viking Press, Inc., 1954.

What could a "fivepence halfpenny doll" hope for? Patient Impunity Jane hopes, through four generations of little girls who insist on keeping her caged in an uncomfortable doll's house, for nothing more than to travel in someone's pocket looking out at soldiers, bugles and bells, yachts and trees, and the open sea. Only a little boy could fulfill such a hope, and that is exactly what little Gideon does. But Impunity Jane and Gideon both have a moral decision to make before life is finally exactly what they want. The illustrations leave much to be desired, but the story is thoroughly satisfying and delightful.

THE FAIRY DOLL

*Written by Rumer Godden.
Illustrated by Adrienne Adams. The
Viking Press, Inc., 1956.*

The fairy doll, brought out once a year to adorn the top of the Christmas tree, is the instrument by means of which little Elizabeth learns to gain self-confidence. This is a touching story of a youngest child who suffers badly in comparisons with her elder brothers and sisters. Elizabeth can't do anything right until Great Grandmother and the fairy doll begin to work their magic. The magic is Elizabeth's own, but she does not realize this until she loses the doll and with it, temporarily, the confidence she had gained. The story is written with delicacy and perception of a very real little girl's heroic triumph over her own timidity.

THE STORY OF HOLLY AND IVY

*Written by Rumer Godden.
Illustrated by Andrienne Adams. The
Viking Press, Inc., 1958.*

Three wishes come true at Christmas time —for a lovely doll named Holly, a little orphan named Ivy, and childless Mrs. Jones. Ivy, the only orphan at St. Agnes orphanage who has nowhere to go on Christmas, wishes for a grandmother. Holly, in a toy shop on Christmas eve, wishes to be owned by a little girl. Mrs. Jones wishes for a child of her own, and all three come together in this wistfully charming story, perfectly visualized in delicate illustrations. It is a story of faith and love and of happy endings that are really happy beginnings.

THE LITTLE MAN

*Written by Erich Kästner.
Illustrated by Rick Schreiter.
Alfred A. Knopf, Inc., 1966.*

Little Maxie, whose bed is a matchbox, is a funny, brave, inspired, and ingenious two-inch high boy who tours the capitals of Europe as a circus performer. He attracts audiences with his artistry and then is kidnapped by a band of gangsters whom he manages to outwit. Maxie's problems, emotions, and secret longings make the otherwise humorous surface story a beautiful and moving experience. This simple translation from the German is illustrated with whimsical line drawings.

THE GAMMAGE CUP

*Written by Carol Kendall.
Illustrated by Erik Blegvad.
Harcourt, Brace & World, Inc.,
1959.*

A group of rugged individualists live among the Minnipins who inhabit "Slipper-on-the-water," a tiny town surrounded by unclimbable mountains. In a clash with the authorities, the reactionary "Periods," the nonconformists are banished from the town, only to become heroes in a daring rescue of the village from its ancient enemy, the Mushrooms. The story is rich in satire and high imagination, with illustrations that perfectly match the original text. It is an exciting and amusing experience—a fine and witty tribute to individualism.

THE BORROWERS

*Written by Mary Norton. Illustrated
by Beth and Joe Krush. Harcourt,
Brace & World, Inc., 1953.*

When things disappear and are miraculously rediscovered where they never should have been, the Borrowers have been afoot. The Borrowers are a family of little people who depend for their livelihood on the things they borrow from people's houses. This unique, completely captivating story is so convincing in its detail that it is nearly impossible to doubt the existence of these little culprits. Conceived and written with great imagination, full of humor and suspense, beautifully illustrated, this book is a delightful experience.

THE BORROWERS AFIELD

*Written by Mary Norton. Illustrated
by Beth and Joe Krush. Harcourt,
Brace & World, Inc., 1955.*

Their home under the kitchen floor is disrupted, and the tiny Clock family of Borrowers sets up temporary quarters in an old shoe. In this tentative existence many exciting adventures and close escapes from danger unfold before the little people can return to the big house that is home. The writing is highly imaginative, and the characterizations in this sequel to *The Borrowers* are as vivid and true to life as the fantasy they people. Charming line drawings capture this delightful little world.

THE BORROWERS AFLOAT
Written by Mary Norton. Illustrated by Beth and Joe Krush. Harcourt, Brace & World, Inc., 1959.

The six-inch-high Clock family of Borrowers, in constant trouble with the human world, venture via a drain pipe to a new home in a tea kettle beside a river. Their old enemy, Mild Eye the gypsy, is in pursuit, but each member of the plucky family meets danger after danger with characteristic fortitude. This delightful microcosm is depicted with vibrant realism, and all the members of the Clock family are fascinating studies of human nature in miniature. The writing is of the highest quality.

FLOATING ISLAND
Written and illustrated by Anne Parrish. Harper & Row, Publishers, 1930.

A house of ten dolls is shipwrecked in transit to the tropical home of their prospective owner, Elizabeth. It is on Floating Island that the amusing misadventures of the doll family unfold. The story is told with spontaneity and wit. With its delightfully made illustrations, its footnotes that speak in realistic asides directly to its audience of children, and its beautifully, yet lightly written text, this book creates a unique world of fantasy, full of fun and captivating adventure.

For upper-grade children

THE LITTLE PRINCE
Written and illustrated by Antoine de Saint-Exupéry. Harcourt, Brace & World, Inc., 1943.

A philosophical and deeply touching tale of wonder and love, this is about a little prince from a tiny and peaceful planet who owned three volcanoes and a flower of unmatchable beauty and pride that became the ruin of his serenity. He learns the secret of what is important in life when he journeys to Earth and shares his new spiritual and aesthetic insights with an aviator who is forced down in the Sahara desert. Soft wash drawings are as simple and lovely as the author's verbal images.

GULLIVER'S TRAVELS
Written by Jonathan Swift. Illustrated by Arthur Rackham. E. P. Dutton & Co., Inc., 1952.

First published in 1726 as an English political satire for adults, this classic has been adopted into the realm of children's literature. Gulliver's famous voyage to the miniature land of Lilliput, where the people are less than six inches tall, makes for fascinating and imaginative reading. Gulliver and the Lilliputians dwarfed by him become oddly believable, and their relationship and interaction is thoroughly entertaining. Though more than two centuries old, the book has needed no revising because of its skillful and simple style.

THE HOBBIT: OR, THERE AND BACK AGAIN
Written and illustrated by J. R. R. Tolkien. Houghton Mifflin Company, 1938.

A richly imaginative tale set in a fantastic land of dwarfs, elves, wizards, goblins, and dragons. Bilbo Baggins, a small creature called a Hobbit, sets out on a complicated mission to recover stolen treasure from Smaug, the dragon who guards it deep inside a mountain. Bilbo regrets having to go after dragon-guarded gold when he encounters an extraordinary, malicious creature near an underground river. His marvelous adventures show veins of magic and mythology and create a suspenseful fantasy written with precision, imagination, and profound thought. Quiet humor seasons the tale to perfection.

CASTAWAYS IN LILLIPUT
*Written by Henry Winterfeld.
Translated by Kyrill Schabert.
Illustrated by William M.
Hutchinson. Harcourt, Brace &
World, Inc., 1960.*

The castaways are three little children whose raft brings them through a curtain of air surrounding this famous island. It is the same Lilliput first discovered 250 years ago by Lemuel Gulliver in his famous travels, but it is now equipped with all the modern conveniences. The story of the three children and their adventures on the island is a thoroughly engaging and satisfying one, written with great imagination and deep insight into a child's craving for size and power.

MAGIC, DREAMS, AND WONDERLANDS

For younger children

BROWNIES—HUSH!
*Written by Gladys L. Adshead.
Illustrated by Elizabeth Orton Jones.
Oxford University Press, 1938.*

Illustrated in soft browns and reds, this is a new version of the old tale of the kindly brownies who helped the little old man and the little old woman until a reward was left for them, after which they vanished forever. A remarkable story beautifully illustrated by an outstanding artist.

THE TWELVE DANCING PRINCESSES
*Illustrated by Adrienne Adams.
Holt, Rinehart & Winston, Inc.,
1966.*

Elegantly illustrated by Adrienne Adams, this familiar French fairy tale is presented here in full, rich color. The hero is a young cowherd who is an incorrigible

daydreamer. He sets out to prove that, backed up with effort and action, seemingly impossible dreams can come true. His one dream, to marry a princess, impels him to try his luck. But first he must solve a puzzle, break a strange spell cast on twelve princesses who live in a nearby castle, and pass a difficult test. The mystery of the twelve princesses who wear out their slippers by dancing all night every night is of an enchantment equaled only in make-believe.

THE WITCH OF HISSING HILL
*Written by Mary Calhoun.
Illustrated by Janet McCaffery.
William Morrow & Co., Inc.,
1964.*

An entertaining fantasy about an old witch called Sizzle who raises wicked witch cats. Brilliantly bold pictures lend snap and dazzle to a highly imaginative book by a writer of smooth descriptive prose. Other picture-book fantasies by the same author include: *Wobble, The Witch Cat,* and *The Hungry Leprechaun.*

DINDLE
*Written by Paul Fenimore Cooper.
Illustrated by Marion Erskine
Cooper. G. P. Putnam's Sons, 1963.*

Lovely ink sketches illuminate this book about a boy who lives in a kingdom threatened by a dragon. The people are quaintly depicted, and illustrations of the kingdom show it as being just the way children believe kingdoms are.

THE MAGIC FISHBONE
*Written by Charles Dickens.
Illustrated by Walter Crane.
Frederick Warne & Co., Inc., n.d.*

This little-known funny fairy tale appeared in a Dickens collection for children published in 1874. Its comic plot concentrates on good little Princess Alicia and her father, King Watkins the First, who has nineteen children and not enough money. Alicia's cranky old Fairy Grandmarina comes to their rescue by giving the princess a magic fishbone that will grant her just one wish in life. Bravely coping with the accidents, illness, and strife that befall the household, Alicia uses her own ingenuity and fortitude, wisely reserving her fishbone for a final emergency. She realizes, when the occasion arises, that one must resort to magical powers only after one has done his very, very best, and it is still not enough. Beautiful watercolor illustrations by Walter Crane portray this royal family in their proper Victorian setting.

THE GREAT GEPPY
Written and illustrated by William Pène DuBois. The Viking Press, Inc., 1940.

In this grave nonsense tale, The Great Geppy is a red and white striped horse who succeeds in solving the mysterious safe robberies in a circus. This highly original and inventive picture book offers a great deal of excitement spiked with dashes of wild humor. The unexpected turns in the story demonstrate the author/illustrator's skill.

TATSINDA
Written by Elizabeth Enright. Illustrated by Irene Haas. Harcourt, Brace & World, Inc., 1963.

High above the mists is a magic place of fabulous animals, giants, a good witch, a prince, and an entire population of white-haired and blue-eyed people. This is the setting for the lovely fairy tale of Tatsinda, a little blonde girl with brown eyes, who has many problems and overcomes them. Delicate line drawings depict her adventures and her delightful make-believe world in color.

SPACE WITCH
Written and illustrated by Don Freeman. The Viking Press, Inc., 1959.

Tilly Ipswitch is a modern witch who zooms through the skies in her homemade space ship. With her reluctant black cat as a fellow passenger, she blasts off on a Halloween trip to frighten inhabitants on other planets. Drawings in blue and black record her action-filled adventures, in an appropriately funny and eerie way.

THE WISHING SHOE
Written and illustrated by Frank Jupo. Abelard-Schuman Limited, 1955.

A message of social significance may be read between the lines of this humorous fantasy based on life's lessons. A magical shoe grants Mr. Pin and his children Jeff and June their wishes to live as the rich do, recapture the "good old times," and to "take things easy" on a South Sea island. But they come to realize that an effortless life leaves much to be desired.

AMANDA REMEMBERS
Written and illustrated by Robert Kraus. Harper & Row, Publishers, 1965.

Reliving the adventures a little girl once shared with her toys, this brooding picture book captures the various moods of a child whose mother has tossed out a beloved doll and a toy dog. Something of a dream fantasy, the quiet story begins realistically with the girl's mother throwing away the old toys, and then it shifts into a low key of recollections tracing the joys and sorrows connected with the discarded toys. The story is satisfactorily resolved when it returns to the realities of the child's own room. Her dreams come true when her father rescues the toys and brings them safely home to her. Faint, mysterious, pastel pictures interpret a haunting story.

THE TROLL MUSIC
Written and illustrated by Anita Lobel. Harper & Row, Publishers, 1966.

The power of troll magic is expressed imaginatively in an account describing the efforts of a group of musicians who played beautiful music until a nasty troll bewitched their instruments into producing animal sounds. But by appeasing the troll and his family, the musicians are able to regain their reputation. Soft hues light up full-page illustrations that lend enchantment to a fresh and lively fantasy.

A BOOK OF WITCHES
Written by Ruth Manning-Sanders.
Illustrated by Robin Jacques. E. P.
Dutton & Co., Inc., 1966.

Twelve traditional tales about witches have been collected here from diverse sources and illustrated with drawings that are consistent with the mood and shivery subject. The stories are humorous or eerie, and the witches involved vary in personality—good, bad, beautiful, ugly, shrewd, stupid, or frightening. Some familiar witches are met again in fluent retellings of favorites such as "Rapunzel" and "Hansel and Gretel."

THE LITTLEST WITCH
Written by Jeanne Massey.
Illustrated by Adrienne Adams.
Alfred A. Knopf, Inc., 1959.

Illustrations in subdued colors capture the mood of Halloween and the sensations and sounds of the wind and of witches on their broomsticks. Littlest Witch is left far behind when she joins other witches in a race to the moon because she stops on the way to help a kitten, a pumpkin, and a small boy. But though she does not win the racing prize and cannot emulate the other witches, she discovers that she has a special kind of magic that is all her own.

THE INCOMPETENT WIZARD
Written by Robert M. Oksner.
Illustrated by Janet McCaffery.
William Morrow & Co., Inc.,
1965.

Humor and wizardry blend in a story about Bumble, an eager and diligent spell-caster who never quite masters his art. His unpredictable results touch off hilarious incidents of the kind that delight

children. His most unique act of incompetence occurs when a little girl asks him to fix her broken doll. His attempts to do so turn the doll into a basset puppy. Attempting the spell once more, Bumble turns the dog into a dragon. This happy mistake and an unexpected crisis earn Bumble the right to be called a competent wizard. Pictures, too, cast a magic spell in this engaging book.

THE LITTLE WITCH
Written by Otfried Preussler.
Translated by Anthea Bell.
Illustrated by Winnie Gayler.
Abelard-Schuman Limited, 1961.

A delightful little book about a small witch who is given a year to prove herself worthy of her title, because she is considered unorthodox, and not at all spooky. Black and white illustrations make everything very eerie, except for the little witch.

MANY MOONS
Written by James Thurber.
Illustrated by Louis Slobodkin.
Harcourt, Brace & World, Inc.,
1943.

This modern fairy tale about a little princess who wanted the moon captures the tenderness, instinctive wisdom, and fantasy-wishes characteristic of childhood. Sensitive, gently humorous drawings reflect the mood of the story.

TAL AND THE MAGIC BARRUGET
Written by Eva-Lis Wuorio.
Illustrated by Bettina. World
Publishing Co., 1965.

Barruget is a bottle imp who resembles a leprechaun, and Tal is an eight-year-old Welsh lad. Working together they help to beautify Santa Eulalia and make it the prettiest of all the villages of Ibiz, one of the Balearic Islands. A strong, realistic note enters the story when Tal's father brings home a "new mother." How the boy learns to accept his step-mother with the assistance of the bottle imp is touchingly narrated. Enticing images of island life and landscapes highlight the story.

THE WITCH WHO WASN'T
Written by Jane Yolen. Illustrated by Arnold Roth. The Macmillan Company, 1964.

This slight Halloween tale promises to bewitch and amuse young readers between five and eight. It is about little Isabel, an endearing "non-witch" whose family and ancestors are famed for the black arts of witchery. But Isabel's powers are limited to white magic. Her spells turn a snake into a chocolate cake and a bug into a cuddly creature because she does not really want to be bad or scary. The remorse she feels at being different and a disgrace to her kind is resolved at a witches' meeting one Halloween Eve where she becomes a delightful success by trying "her worst." Arnold Roth's very funny drawings of witches and their mad paraphernalia are highly inventive, and rendered in appropriate tones of orange, yellow, and night-time blues.

For intermediate-grade children

THE WIZARD OF OZ
Written by L. Frank Baum. Illustrated by W. W. Denslow. The Macmillan Company, 1962.

A wonderful fantasy tracing the adventures of a little Kansas girl named Dorothy who is carried by a tornado to the magical land of Oz. She meets her memorable friends the lion, the Scarecrow, and the Tin Woodman. On the way to the Emerald City, the home of a magnificent Wizard, the story follows a hazardous yet humorous course resplendent with paraphernalia from the natural and supernatural worlds. Consistent with movement in fairy tales, this story easily swings from one world to another and back to the reality of Kansas.

THE MUMMY MARKET
Written by Nancy Brelis. Illustrated by Ben Shecter. Harper & Row, Publishers, 1966.

The three Martin children live with a housekeeper they call "Gloomy" who advises them to go out and shop for a mother. At the Mummy Market children can pick and choose a type of mother that best suits them, try her out at home, and return her if not satisfied. The Martin children experiment with three—a homemaker who wants to be called "Mimsey," a rugged, outdoor "Mom," and a psychology-oriented beatnik guitar player. They finally select a mummy who hasn't yet been chosen by children, and together they invent past memories to share and unite them as a family. Rich in detail, and filled with meaning, this imaginative story has sophisticated overtones and an enchantment that must be pondered.

HILDY AND THE CUCKOO CLOCK
Written by Ruth Christoffer Carlsen. Illustrated by Wallace Tripp. Houghton Mifflin Company, 1966.

The Fortin family has two mottoes: "Treat each day as an adventure and it will be one," and "Never believe that the unbelievable is impossible." They become very appropriate when a mischievous little ghost joins their household and strange things begin to happen. It all starts when the old cuckoo clock mysteriously appears in their fireplace. Then bottles move by themselves, the house fills with bubbles, and it snows in July. Hildy and Rob Fortin find the three-year-old ghost Willy irresistible and fun-loving, and they share some lively adventures with him in this book of chuckles and hilarious antics.

CHARLIE AND THE CHOCOLATE FACTORY
Written by Roald Dahl. Illustrated by Joseph Schindelman. Alfred A. Knopf, Inc., 1964.

There is humor on two levels in this unusual and inventive story that subtly includes some familiar moral lesson within each chapter. The surface plot tells how Charlie and four nasty children win a chance to tour Mr. Willy Wonka's mysterious chocolate factory and of the uproarious situations and extraordinary happenings that befall them there. A fast pace carries young readers right into the adventures of the five children with whom they can easily identify. The underlying theme of this book is that goodness reaps its rewards whereas nastiness or obnoxious behavior is punished. Each of the four bad characters here meets a befitting disaster, but good, obedient, earnest Charlie triumphs by winning the day and the entire factory. Accompanying pictures are as lively as the action and nonsense throughout.

JAMES AND THE GIANT PEACH
Written by Roald Dahl. Illustrated
by Nancy Ekholm Burkert. Alfred A.
Knopf, Inc., 1961.

A gem of an adventure story especially attractive for young boys. The story is a delightful fantasy of a magical peach with a strange cargo of huge friendly insects and a little boy named James Henry Trotter. They travel in various ways across the Atlantic from England to New York City—landing on top of the Empire State Building. Many exciting happenings occur on the voyage including an attack by sharks in the sea and moon-men in the sky. The illustrations are beautifully drawn with great detail and clear color.

THE MAGIC FINGER
Written by Roald Dahl. Illustrated
by William Pène Du Bois. Harper
& Row, Publishers, 1966.

An unusual book dealing with a family of duck hunters and the sense of justice that overtakes them when a little girl casts her spell on them by means of "the magic finger." Quite believable, this poetic account possesses a delightful vein of humor that runs through the heart of the story.

CHITTY CHITTY BANG BANG:
THE MAGICAL CAR
Written by Ian Fleming. Illustrated
by John Burningham. Random House,
Inc., 1964.

A magical racing car is salvaged from a junkyard by Commander Caractacus Pott and is appropriately dubbed "Chitty Chitty Bang Bang" for the two sneezes and two explosions with which it starts. Here begins a funny, fast-moving and thrilling plot about the Pott family's motoring escapades in England and France with their new miracle car that can fly or float, outwit a group of gangsters, and get its owners out of some troublesome situations. The car is a brilliant invention of the author's and is described in such fascinating and accurate detail that its magical powers become wholly convincing to the reader. Quaint sketches in black and white of Chitty, the Potts, the villains, and French towns illuminate this imaginative adventure story and add to the fun.

THE MAGIC PIN
Written by Ina B. Forbus.
Illustrated by Corydon Bell. The
Viking Press., Inc., 1956.

Especially appealing to little girls, this gentle fantasy is about Neelie, the seventh granddaughter of a seventh granddaughter. Already "different" because of her place in her family's lineage, Neelie becomes even more extraordinary after being given her grandmother's pin. Possession of this piece of magic jewelry endows her with the ability to understand the language of animals. The account of the amazing things that happen to her is a happy one, with some tense moments.

THE HEART OF STONE
Written by Wilhelm Hauff. Retold
by Doris Orgel. Illustrated by David

Levine. *The Macmillan Company, Inc., 1964.*

This recent translation of a beloved nineteenth-century fairy tale from Germany, also known as "The Little Glassman," is simple and forthright. Qualities such as good and evil, charity and greed, and ignorance and enlightment are all dealt with in this story of poor, foolish Peter Munk who wishes for money and success overnight. A kindly spirit of the forest named Glassman offers Peter good advice for happiness. But, instead, Peter bargains with a giant, trading his heart for one of stone in exchange for being made a millionaire. After many experiences and misadventures, the boy finally comes to realize that being content with little is better than having riches and no heart. The black and green ink drawings that border each page resemble old German woodcarvings and beautifully complement the text.

YOU BETTER COME HOME WITH ME
Written by John Lawson. Illustrated by Arnold Spilka. Thomas Y. Crowell Company, 1966.

A quest fantasy told with dignity and grace and full of wit and wisdom. Set deep in the world of long blue mountains, this story springs from a colloquial parting invitation: "You better come home with me." Accepting the invitation from Scarecrow, a wandering boy finds himself in Appalachian country. Here he works the farmland and exercises great skill as "water diviner." His roots sink deeper and deeper in the country's soil, and his own identity grows clearer. With the grace of a poem and the dramatic range of a novel, this convincing fantasy comes alive as something of a legend anchored by the most accurate rural realities.

THE BLACK GULL OF CORRIE LOCHAN
Written by Margaret MacAlpine

Illustrated by James Armstrong. Prentice-Hall Inc., 1965.

A haunting fantasy in which Morag Ban often finds a strange black gull circling in the night air above Roway Tarn or resting near a pool or flying off to the crags of Ben Storr. But the whereabouts of this beautifully mysterious bird lends intrigue and suspense to a story that involves two children searching for their father through the wind-lashed moors of Scotland. Strong pictures support this sturdy story pushed to the edge of fantasy but not beyond.

TOM'S MIDNIGHT GARDEN
Written by Philippa A. Pearce.

Illustrated by Susan Einzig. J. B. Lippincott Co., 1958.

Drawn to the edge of fantasy, this hauntingly beautiful story recounts a boy's life by day at his aunt's home in England and his life of fantasy at night. Projecting himself through fantasy experiences, Tom participates in the world of the past. An example of a well-developed time fantasy, this story reflects impeccably fine writing highlighted by occasionally poetic and rhythmical prose.

THE ENCHANTED SCHOOLHOUSE
Written by Ruth Sawyer. Illustrated by Hugh Troy. The Viking Press, Inc., 1956.

Irish fairy folklore comes to Maine in this delightful and humorous tale in the romantic tradition of leprechauns and miracles. The story of how Brian Gallagher brought a fairyman to America and how they plotted and schemed to get a schoolhouse for the children of Lobster Cove is involved, convincing, and very well told. Fine black-and-white illustrations by Hugh Troy are charming and add to the entirely inviting presentation.

THE MAGIC FLUTE
Retold by Stephen Spender.

Illustrated by Beni Montresor.
G. P. Putnam's Sons, 1966.

With the rich grace of Mozart's opera, vivid colors and poetic text blend to re-create a fantasy for children. Spun with magic and marvels, the story follows a youthful prince in his search for a beautiful princess whom he must rescue. Fabled beasts and majestic creatures in wonder-land settings lead to a fairy-tale conclusion as resplendent as the finale in a dramatic opera. Here all the elements of a highly imaginative fantasy support a brilliant story line.

THE GRIFFIN AND THE MINOR CANON
Written by Frank R. Stockton.
Illustrated by Maurice Sendak.
Holt, Rinehart & Winston, Inc., 1963.

Rooted in a Gothic tradition, this whim-sical fantasy is about a Griffin who is the last of his species and is unable to see what he really looks like. He visits a distant town where his image is sculptured in stone over the great door of a church. The Griffin's visit frightens the citizens even though it brings prestige to a minor canon with whom the Griffin strikes up an omi-nous relationship. Superbly drawn pic-tures add an exciting dimension to an old, revived fairy tale.

MARY POPPINS
Written by Pamela L. Travers.
Illustrated by Mary Shepard.
Harcourt, Brace & World, Inc., 1934.

The arrival of Mary Poppins, a most un-usual and unpredictable nursemaid, changes everyday activities in the Banks household when she blows in on a high wind one day with her magical umbrella. Funny and fantastic things happen when she takes charge of little Michael, Jane, and the twins and flies with them through space in all directions of the compass. She also has a magic bag of tricks and goodies, and ability to understand dogs, and the power to make medicine taste like strawberry ice. Although she is priggish, conceited, and elusive, she comes to be adored by the children she disciplines and entertains. They, and all her young readers, can never tell exactly where the real world merges into make-believe during the fanciful adventures they share with her. When Mary is carried away from their lives by a wild west wind, the youngsters find com-fort in the hope that she may as suddenly return some time in the future. Illustra-tions are amusing and appropriately placed and match the whimsical, highly imaginative style of writing.

MARY POPPINS COMES BACK
Written by Pamela L. Travers.
Illustrated by Mary Shepard.
Harcourt, Brace & World, Inc., 1935.

Since Mary Poppins left, sailing over the rooftops in the wake of her umbrella, the Banks household has been in an uproar—nothing *ever* goes right! And just when all are at wits' end, who should appear out of the blue but that stern and haughty nurse-maid herself. In a twinkle, she has things in order, and those strange, delightful adventures begin again. Circumstances are essentially unchanged: characters and incidents are as unique and refreshing as in the first book.

MARY POPPINS FROM A TO Z
Written by Pamela L. Travers.
Illustrated by Mary Shepard.
Harcourt, Brace & World, Inc., 1962.

This sequel to Mary Poppins is a shortened series of skits about that wonderful and eccentric nursemaid. Told simply in alphabetical order, this version is well illustrated with plentiful and detailed drawings.

FOR UPPER-GRADE CHILDREN

THE BLACK CAULDRON
Written by Lloyd Alexander. Holt.
Rinehart & Winston, Inc., 1966.

Continuing the chronicle of the imaginary
land of Prydain, this second book in the
series is somber and moving. The story of
how Prince Gwydion leads the attempt to
destroy the Black Cauldron, a weapon of
evil powers owned by the Lord of the Land
of Death, is filled with adventure, sacrifice,
love, and even some light humor. Some of
the unforgettable characters of the first
book, *The Book of Three*, are met again
in this wonderful fantasy.

THE CASTLE OF LLYR
Written by Lloyd Alexander. Holt,
Rinehart & Winston, Inc., 1966.

Inspired by ancient legend and mythology, this third volume in the Prydain series
continues the endless war between good
and evil forces. This one tells of how
Princess Eilonwy is rescued from a bad
enchantress and how she inherits the
dangerous power of magic. Personalities
and dialogue are presented with skill and
humor in a story of struggle, triumph,
and high adventure.

PETER PAN
Written by James M. Barrie.
Illustrated by Nora S. Unwin.
Charles Scribner's Sons, 1950.

In one of the most appealing journeys in
literature, the three Darling children fly
with Peter Pan to Never-Never Land
where no one ever grows up. Here they
live through many exciting and amusing
adventures before flying back to their
nursery and the real world. The story is
peopled with fairies like Tinker-Bell
and evildoers like Captain Hook and his
gruesome crew of pirates, and it is filled
with the richest provender that fantasy
offers. Beautifully illustrated, the book in
its entire conception and execution is a
true classic, founded as it is on the universal wish to remain a child.

PETER PAN IN KENSINGTON
GARDENS
Written by James M. Barrie. Retold
by May Byron. Illustrated by Arthur
Rackham. Charles Scribner's
Sons, 1930.

This simplified retelling of the Peter Pan
story, made with permission from the
author, is about the adventures of Peter
and the birds, fairies, and children who
stay in Kensington Gardens after lockout
time. The fine childlike illustrations sustain a delightful, imaginative reality.
Some of the atmosphere and high quality
of the original work is lost in this adaptation for younger readers, but it does serve
as an adequate introduction to the classic
story of the little boy who never grows
up.

THE CHILDREN OF GREEN KNOWE
Written by Lucy M. Boston.
Illustrated by Peter Boston.
Harcourt, Brace & World, Inc.,
1955.

Tolly is a nine-year-old English boy who
visits his great-grandmother's marvelous
old house and comes to learn about his
ancestors who, as children, grew up in this
house many years ago. Through Granny's
stories and his own vivid imagination, he
journeys into the past and alternately lives
in the world of fantasy and of reality.
Mysterious and beautiful events take place
then at Green Knowe and make this tale
wholly enchanting.

THE TREASURE OF GREEN KNOWE
Written by Lucy M. Boston.
Illustrated by Peter Boston.
Harcourt, Brace & World, Inc.,
1958.

Sensitively and spiritually written, this
sequel to the first story of Tolly is primarily a mystery in which the boy again
takes an excursion into the past. He revisits
Green Knowe and becomes acquainted
with his nineteenth-century ancestor
Susan, a blind girl, who lived in the old

house when part of it was destroyed by fire and the family jewels disappeared. Tolly's search for the long-lost treasure and the story-within-a-story of the brave Susan combine in creating a strong plot and a perfect blending of past and present in this memorable book.

THE CASTLE OF YEW
Written by Lucy M. Boston.
Illustrated by Margery Gill.
Harcourt, Brace & World, Inc.,
1965.

Delicate and precise botanical drawings reproduce the magical mood of a mystical garden in which two small boys become finger-size as they enter the door of a yew-bush clipped in the shape of a castle. Stepping into the realm of fantasy-play, the boys invent their own ceremonial language and engage in quests and tests in this brilliant adventure story where real and unreal can be juxtaposed at will. They are free to leave their green garden world as easily as they entered it, which makes believable the garden owner's words: "You can go anywhere you want if you really want to."

PILGRIM'S PROGRESS
Written by John Bunyan. Retold by
Mary Godolphin. Illustrated by
Robert Lawson. J. B. Lippincott Co.,
1939.

Now one of the immortal classics of children's books, this Puritan adventure tale first appeared in 1678 for adult reading and was shortened and simplified for younger readers by Mary Godolphin in 1884. An essentially religious story, it also has all the fabulous elements of a complex fairy tale. In a fantastic world, giants, monsters, characters that represent virtue and sin, and heroes act out a happy-ending drama based on a universally appealing theme: Man's strength and endurance in his search for a Promised Land is un-

defeatable. Though he meets danger, ill fortune, ridicule, defeat, and despair, he faces and overcomes all opposing forces in order to reach his goal. Robert Lawson's modern black-and-white drawings are alternately delicate, beautiful, humorous, satirical, or darkly ominous depending upon the text.

ALICE'S ADVENTURES IN WONDERLAND AND THROUGH THE LOOKING GLASS
Written by Lewis Carroll. Illustrated
by John Tenniel. The Macmillan
Company, 1963.

One of the most quoted books in English literature, this classic fantasy is unrivaled in its logical nonsense. Little Alice is an unforgettable heroine expressing wonder, curiosity, courtesy, wisdom, and surprising sophistication as she journeys through Wonderland and reacts to its strange characters and events. Most outstanding are the funny and brilliant dialogues among all the personalities, which come to impress the reader as being perfectly plausible in the mad and incredible setting of Carroll's world where the impossible and unreal bear a remarkable resemblance to our own everyday world. Tenniel's illustrations are now as familiar and famous as Carroll's text.

THE SUMMER BIRDS
Written by Penelope Farmer.
Illustrated by James J. Spanfeller.
Harcourt, Brace & World, Inc.,
1962.

A group of children spend an enchanted summer flying like birds over the beautiful English countryside and seashore in this strange, rather sad story about the deep pain of growing up. The ecstasy of flight is introduced to them by an anonymous, mysteriously compelling boy who is invisible to everyone but them. Charlotte is the twelve-year-old heroine who best understands and communicates with the boy, whose true identity is disclosed to her. It is also she who must make the profound and mature decision at the end of the summer not to follow the boy to his enticing world in the sky. The nostalgia she feels for the passing away of the golden summer and the severing of a soaring love relationship is indicative of the slipping away of childhood and all its attendant flights of fancy.

A LITTLE BOY LOST
Written by W. H. Hudson.
Illustrated by A. D. McCormick.
Alfred A. Knopf, Inc., 1958.

Six-year-old Martin follows a mysterious mirage that lures him into a fantasy world of nature. Henceforth, he resolves to wander in this world until, at the end, he is taken into the arms of the sea. It is a world seemingly veiled in symbolism, a little overpowering in its strangeness, and, except for a brief time when he is cared for by the Lady of the Hills, Martin is alone in his confrontation of it. For these reasons, the book will probably be appreciated only by exceptional children.

THE PHANTOM TOLLBOOTH
Written by Norton Juster.
Illustrated by Jules Feiffer.
Random House, Inc., 1961.

Wisdom and whimsey fill this allegorical fantasy about a boy's amazing journey through the Mountains of Ignorance to rescue the princesses Sweet Rhyme and Pure Reason. The book has something wonderful to offer the mature youngster of intellect who relishes more rigorous reading.

THE DIAMOND IN THE WINDOW
Written by Jane Langton. Illustrated by Erik Blegvad. Harper & Row, Publishers, 1962.

In this suspenseful mystery, two children discover a secret attic playroom from which two of their young ancestors vanished one night long ago. In a New England setting, and in the atmosphere of an old turreted and gabled house, the children explore and play detective in order to find the lost youngsters. Terror is balanced with humor throughout, and satire and symbolism are included in a tale that ends happily.

A WRINKLE IN TIME
Written by Madeleine L'Engle.
Farrar, Straus & Giroux, Inc., 1962.

An exciting, mysterious fantasy in which three children—Meg and Charles Wallace Murry and Calvin O'Keefe—travel in search of Mr. Murry. They travel by "tesseracting" (using a fifth dimension) to the planet of Camazotz where all persons are regimented and controlled by IT, an oversized brain. Mr. Murry, a prisoner in Camazotz, is rescued by the three children with the aid of three witches —Mrs. Whatsit, Mrs. Who and Mrs. Which—one of whom never completely materializes. There are overtones of science fiction. Characterizations are marvelously drawn, especially that of Meg, the twelve-year-old daughter, who demonstrates typical adolescent insecurities and concerns. A Newbery winner.

THE LION, THE WITCH AND THE WARDROBE, *Book 1*
Written by C. S. Lewis. Illustrated by Pauline Baynes. The Macmillan Company, 1950.

This is the first book in the Narnia series, which is based on religious allegory. The forces of Light struggle with the powers of Darkness in an outstanding fantasy that is beautiful, magical, frightening, and wise. The setting is the mysterious land of Narnia, a strange and other-worldly place under the spell of a wicked White Witch, where it is always "winter and never Christmas." The story follows the thrilling experiences of four English children who meet giants, satyrs, fauns, and talking animals in Narnia, and of the noble lion Aslan who frees the enchanted country from its curse. Fine line drawings depict the light and darkness of Narnia's landscapes and its inhabitants.

PRINCE CASPIAN, BOOK 2
Written by C. S. Lewis. Illustrated
by Pauline Baynes. The Macmillan
Company, 1951.
C. S. Lewis has succeeded in creating an irresistible fantasy in which a "good" prince with an army of Talking Beasts conquers the Telmarines. Vivid, poetic prose creates a mood of spellbinding delight, which is heightened by the illustrations. Subsequent chronicles of Narnia by the same author and illustrator include: *The Voyage of the "Dawn Treader,"* Book 3; *The Silver Chair,* Book 4; *The Horse and His Boy,* Book 5; *The Magician's Nephew,* Book 6; *The Last Battle,* Book 7.

AT THE BACK OF THE NORTH WIND
Written by George MacDonald.
Illustrated by Ernest H. Shepard.
J. M. Dent & Sons, Ltd. (London),
1956.
Here is an outstanding dream fantasy studded throughout with mysticism and images of inspiring and dazzling beauty. The language is so poetic and deeply moving that its wonder is impossible to describe. The romantic and haunting story of a sensitive little boy, Diamond, and his strange love relationship with the North Wind carries the reader up out of this world into one of magic and fantasy. One travels with the boy, riding at the back of the wind, and shares his profound sensations and awe of the wonderful sights he sees. This marvelous book

promises to enlarge the reader's vision, senses, and heart. Lovely watercolor illustrations by E. H. Shepard are in keeping with the delicacy and dreamlike quality of the story.

THE PRINCESS AND THE GOBLIN
Written by George MacDonald.
Illustrated by Nora S. Unwin. The
Macmillan Company, 1951.
Another MacDonald story of loveliness and rarity imbued with spiritual values for the pure of heart, this fantasy adventure creates a magic mountain kingdom in which a good miner's son and the little princess Irene triumph over wicked goblins who threaten their world. Also by the same author and illustrator: *The Princess and Curdie.*

A GRASS ROPE
Written by William Mayne.
Illustrated by Lynton Lamb. E. P.
Dutton & Co., Inc., 1962.
The haunting beauty of the Yorkshire Downs is the background for the story of two children who become fascinated by a puzzling legend about their ancestors from Crusader days. The intriguing ancient riddle they finally solve features a unicorn, a pack of silver-collared hounds, and a love affair. There are notes of tenderness, pathos, reproach, and humor in this touching tale, which is illustrated with pen sketches and flavored with dialogue in the Yorkshire idiom.

THE ENCHANTED CASTLE
Written by Edith Nesbit. Illustrated
by Betty Fraser. The Platt & Munk Co.,
Inc., 1966.
A magnificent fantasy that leads three children from a garden to a world of magic. Their imaginative adventures include an enchanted castle, a talisman ring whose power makes wishes come true,

a "sleeping-beauty" princess aroused after a hundred years, ancient statues that descend from their pedestals to swim in a moonlit lake, and garden scarecrows that come alive. Intrigue and excitement fill this story of rare beauty.

THE KING OF THE GOLDEN RIVER
Written by John Ruskin. Illustrated.
World Publishing Co., 1946.

Reading like a medieval legend, this dramatic story of good little Gluck and his two cruel and selfish older brothers is built upon a series of exciting incidents and trying tests that each of them must meet and attempt to conquer. Its contrasting values, colorful descriptions, and vivid portrayals merit the book its outstanding place in children's literature. The powerful plot that tells how Gluck wins back the inheritance lost by his evil brothers is resolved in a way that will satisfy young readers.

Across history's broad tapestry a strange succession of people and events weaves rich and rare designs as in this picture inspired by legend and chronicle. Recreating scenes from medieval Spain, the fabric ties in symbols of Moslems, Christians, and Jews.

From Casilda of the Rising Moon *by Elizabeth Borton de Trevino. Farrar, Straus & Giroux, 1967. Reproduced by permission.*

Chapter **10**

HISTORY
IN
CHILDREN'S
LITERATURE

It is true that in its nature the historical novel is fiction, not history:
a work of imagination, not a record of fact. It seeks to recreate, not to transcribe;
and the novelist is free to choose any subject that interests him
and to write about it from any point of view that he wishes to take. But it is
also true that his concern is with history in fiction and that he is
under certain obligations to historic fact. He may . . . transpose time or reshape
minor events to fit into his plot scheme; but he may not falsify
history's fundamental record.

— HELEN E. HAINES
What's in a Novel
Columbia University Press, 1942

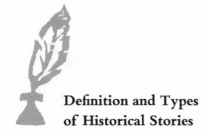

Definition and Types
of Historical Stories

Fine historical stories invite readers to live an adventure in the past vicariously. Young readers can thus witness historical events, meet historical characters, recapture the flavor of an era, and enter a new world whose experiences can deepen and broaden.

Historical stories constitute a sizable body of literature that may be divided into two types: works that are "truly historical" and those that are "historical realism."

THE TRULY HISTORICAL

These stories telescope and explore times when momentous events took place and certain memorable characters existed, or they may record a way of life that has disappeared or is fast disappearing. These books are modern, and yet they present an accurate picture of life in the past. Certain facts of history are skillfully interwoven with imaginative creations to produce a spectacle that serves to entertain rather than to teach.

> Spectacle is the word that expresses the essence of traditional historical romance: spectacle as distinguished from drama. In the best of historical romance the spectacle has meaning: in its totality it achieves grasp of an age, illustration of a general truth of human nature.[1]

Examples of this type of historical story include *Adam of the Road*, a tale that grew out of the medieval period in England; *Men of Iron*,

[1]John T. Frederick, "Costain and Company: The Historical Novel Today," *English Journal*, XLIII (April 1954), 173.

another medieval story; and *The Door in the Wall*, a story that makes life in England during the Middle Ages come alive. Augmenting this list of books with a European background are the books with a truly American flavor: *Johnny Tremain*, a story that carries the reader through two dramatic years of America's history; *Caddie Woodlawn*, another spirited story that explores a historical movement during American expansion; and *The Matchlock Gun*, which tells a tale based on an actual incident made memorable in the annals of New York's history.

Such books as these, whose total conception is historical, are considered "truly historical."

HISTORICAL REALISM

This kind of story presents a picture of the times during which it was written. Stories such as *The Adventures of Tom Sawyer, The Adventures of Huckleberry Finn, Little Women*—classics written more than seventy-five years ago—were considered realistic stories of their period. These works do not point out large movements and trends or momentous events in history, nor do they necessarily portray great historic characters. And when a child reads these works, he derives from them a feeling of immediacy rather than a feeling of having relived a great moment of history.

But the passage of time has given historical value to these period stories since they tell us about life during the times in which they were written. Consequently, these time-honored tales, now clothed in an aura of history, have earned the designation "historical realism." Though they are fewer in number as compared with recently written tales utilizing historical backgrounds, they do have a special place in children's literature for preserving life in the past in a moving and dramatic way.

The Significance of Historical Stories

There is inherent fascination and perennial appeal in literature that provides young readers with a glimpse into the past and at the long road man has traveled. Children are captivated by the differences in life as it was long ago. These differences, sharpened by scrupulously accurate detail and the picturesque language of a particular period, have the romantic appeal of a time that cannot be lived again. Yet despite the differences in detail, young readers observe a similarity about life then and now, because the truth of human experience is unchanging. This is what makes a good piece of historical literature timeless rather than topical.

Historical stories, through fusion of chronicle and imagination, can bring to children a sense of the significance and flavor of other times and what it must have been like to live in the past. In other words, by identifying with great personages and by entering a world of historical settings, children can view the events and the way of life during another period of human history. Thus involved, children may perceive life from another angle whose perspective arouses the emotions and deepens impressions of characters as well as images never to be forgotten—heralding the historical story as a rich source of vicarious experiences.

The past can be seen in a more orderly and less complicated way than the swiftly moving events of today thus making it possible to view the great sweep of human history and to sense a relationship with all humankind. As Professor Leland Jacobs points out:

> Life, in its continuous flow, period into period, generation to generation, is illuminated, and though one may be alone in the flesh, he is inextricably related to others who walked their lone ways, in the past. For a child, through fiction, to feel his place in the great sweep of human destiny and to link it with others now gone is a big, big experience, one that both enlightens and matures the beholder.[2]

Approaches to Historical Stories

This division of literature is no different from any other in that its first requirement is to tell a good story. But there are some qualities germane to this division just as there are to each of the other divisions. To understand and identify these qualities that are characteristic of historical stories, a sensible approach is to analyze the literary elements— theme, plot, characterization, style, settings—as they are expressed in this genre of writing.

THEME

Probably the most important element for differentiating historical stories, theme carries the broad central ideas basic to human nature. For example, the theme in a book may stress the dignity and

---

[2]Leland B. Jacobs, "Historical Fiction for Children," *The Reading Teacher* (January 1961), 192.

worth of man while it tells a story of struggle for independence. *Johnny Tremain* exemplifies this technique in a story of America's fight for freedom. Honorable causes in support of civil rights, abolition of serfdom, triumph over handicap, tyranny, or injustice rank high among the broad themes stressed in historical stories. Of course these themes may be skillfully expressed or developed amid myriad details, and the themes may be quite unobtrusive at first, but nevertheless the central idea will run all through the story and may not be fully realized until long after a book has been completed.

After all, in a historical story what matters most is the impression the idea makes on the reader. The reasons and facts governing "why" a battle was fought mean far more than "who" fought it and with "what" weapons even though these facts are appealing. Novelist John Hersey has commented very aptly with regard to historical stories:

> Palpable facts are mortal. Like certain moths and flying ants, they lay their eggs and die overnight. The important flashes and bulletins are already forgotten by the time yesterday morning's newspaper is used to line the trash can to receive today's coffee grounds. The things we remember for longer periods are emotions and impressions and illusions and images and characters: the elements of fiction.[3]

PLOT

In well-written historical stories, major facts of the times in which the story is set are adhered to with scrupulous accuracy so that the story will ring true to its period and seem indivisible from its settings. Minor details, however, may be imaginative creations that support the story as it weaves through the facts of history. Because most of the stories are fictional in nature, a measure of imagination is necessary to supply all the facts used to tell the tale. And even though a book echoes the spirit of its period, it does not attempt to set down the literal truth. Rather, the historical facts and the imaginative inventions fuse so naturally that the facts do not appear as cold facts of a well-documented commentary, but come alive as the warm essentials that leave an impression of history.

Some historical stories use a plot that consists of events and episodes in chronological sequence. For younger readers especially, this type of

---

[3] John Hersey, "The Novel of Contemporary History," *Atlantic Monthly*, CLXXXIV (November 1949), 80. Copyright © by The Atlantic Monthly Company. Reprinted by permission of The Atlantic Monthly Company.

plot structure is less difficult than one that uses many flashbacks, or that shows the problem in the beginning and then regresses in time to tell how it all came about before moving forward to unravel the plot completely. Or the other type of historical story which begins at the end, moves back to the beginning and travels on to find what triggered the whole thing.

But no matter how the plot is constructed or for whatever age group it is intended, a logical sequence and a basis for the cause and effect in the occurrences is important in the historical literature children will read.

CHARACTERIZATION

Many historical stories carve out a character whose whole personality and image appear in heroic proportions. Johnny Tremain, for instance, looms over other figures as a hero in a noble period of American history, and Mafatu, a young Polynesian, personifies courage in the legendary style of a story of primitive life, *Call It Courage*. Tom Sawyer and Huckleberry Finn stand out as archetypes of American boyhood in stories that are now considered historical realism.

Characterization in well-written historical stories brings into sharp relief memorable personages who serve as vehicles to communicate the underlying themes and also to call up universal human feelings. Such convincing characters, not mere cardboard ones dressed in historical costumes, can deepen insights regarding universal human needs, and provide for the identification that strengthens involvement in the story which taps the essence of life in some other era.

STYLE

In historical literature a very significant style characteristic is the picturesque language used. Interesting words, colorful dialogue, suitable names, choice human interest details, all well blended, lend credence to the story and help to create a sense of living in another age.

There is appealing romance in archaic language as well as in idioms and expressions that have now become obsolete. Books that make a wise use of the fine differences of language can preserve the dignity of the past if overindulging in grandiloquence or out-of-date usage is avoided. These devices help to catch the flavor and drama appropriate to the theme. In this way many fine books recounting historical events provide the flavor of the period in the telling of a story that still preserves a way of viewing the past and go beyond mere historical details. Best examples of this are: *Adam of the Road*, which telescopes life in medieval England with teeming humanity, events, and conditions rearranged without distortion;

Ivanhoe, which sharpens our perception of medieval tourneys and the siege of Torquilstone; *Island of the Blue Dolphins*, which preserves in unadorned language some choice historic facts that link a decimated people with men of succeeding generations; and *The Door in the Wall*, which serenely captures the flavor of the Middle Ages while recounting a historical event.

SETTING

No historical story for young readers avoids graphic details for colorful backdrops. Clipper ships, covered wagons, castles, cottages, and the like are the artifacts that set the stage for the story. Here authentic details of time, place, and the social order play a part in providing a truthful picture of history.

Scrupulously accurate details, even the smallest ones, essential to the story are filled in with a sure hand so as to avoid anachronisms. Quaintness and antiquity grace the sets depicting life in the past while the issues of the period are clarified and a sense of history is gained. But if the settings and the details of characters do no more than stage a parade of costumes and regalia without enlarging the past so that it is a memorable experience for young readers, the book is not worthy of the designation historical fiction. A good example of adventure in the past uses significant details only as a backdrop for a genuine historical story.

Assisted by language, the novelty of difference in the details sharpens the focus of attention because children are captivated with quaintness and oddities, colorful costumes and customs, log cabins and wagon wheels—the authentic details in the recreation of life long ago. Not drawn to excess, these accurate details paint the canvas of the times and deepen the dramatic impact of the story.

Historical stories, be they "truly historical" or historically oriented, must be approached with certain specific considerations in mind. They are not exempt from the standards basic to all literature, particularly fiction. As Dr. Jacobs cogently states:

> Historical fiction is, in certain respects, no different from any other kind of fiction. The story must move through genuine conflict to reasonable climax to plausible resolution. The writing must be original and effectual. But, in addition, the genre has some unique characteristics, which make it distinctive as prose fiction. . . . The heightened moment of sensitivity for the reader of fine historical fiction is that in which he feels himself in and of the past and is bigger today for having been with yesterday.[4]

---

[4] Jacobs, *loc. cit.*, 193–94.

Analysis of Historical Stories

Any comprehensive analysis of historical works of either the truly historical or the "historical realism" types would be impossible since the titles are numerous and the themes varied. But distinguished examples of historical stories will be discussed here and an annotated list of carefully selected books follows this chapter.

In order to make this sizable body of books a little more manageable, categories have been designed to classify them. However, no arbitrary classification can possibly include all the books ever written as historical stories, and no single classification is adequate enough for the wide reading tastes of children. But a sense of order is gained from the establishment of categories for a genre of writing that is so rich in content and style and suitable for different age and grade levels.

Consequently, books with American backgrounds can be grouped together as distinct from the group of books about ancient civilizations. Similarly, other groups are separated according to the backgrounds and times in which the stories are set. Such groups include some books designed for younger children whose reading tastes, abilities, and sense of time correspond with the themes and styles of writing in picture storybooks and other less complicated stories.

On the other hand, since most of the books in this division of literature are really full-length works, the reading and developmental levels fall comfortably within the range of intermediate- and upper-grade children. Therefore, each of the groups is subdivided into age and grade levels:

Stories of American Heritage
Books for younger children
Books for intermediate-grade children
Books for upper-grade children

Stories of Primitive Life
Books for younger children
Books for intermediate-grade children
Books for upper-grade children

Stories of Ancient Civilizations
Books for younger children
Books for intermediate-grade children
Books for upper-grade children

Stories of Life in the Middle Ages and Modern Times
Books for younger children
Books for intermediate-grade children
Books for upper-grade children

Stories of American Heritage

The strength of this category lies in the noble themes and well-drawn characters it presents. Adventure, courage, heroism, and loyalty overshadow lesser attributes in stories from America's past, but the best of the kind provide moving close-ups of momentous times from the point of view of children. They are written with an awareness and understanding of the period and the issues as they affected the lives of people that fills out the framework of American history.

BOOKS FOR YOUNGER CHILDREN

Outstanding examples of picture storybooks suitable for even very young children are the works of Alice Dalgliesh whose skillfully told historical narratives depict life in early America in beautiful detail.

In this reverent retelling of Pilgrim adventure, hardship, and bounty, stylized drawings emphasize the stark simplicity of dress and possessions characteristic of this Pilgrim family.
From The Thanksgiving Story *by Alice Dalgliesh, illustrated by Helen Sewell. Copyright 1954 by the author and illustrator. Reproduced by permission of Charles Scibner's Sons.*

Her *The Thanksgiving Story* is a very simply written account in words and pictures. Beginning with somber tones, the pictures and the story develop into a climax of delicious autumn colors portraying Pilgrims and Indians at a Thanksgiving feast.

Although the story is centered on the adventures of a single family traveling to America, it affords glimpses of life as it must have been soon after the Pilgrims landed. Skirting stereotyped incidents and characters, the story covers the period from the sailing of the three ships off the English coast to the bountiful feast a year or so later in America.

Children, honestly portrayed, figure largely in this story of Pilgrim adventure, hardship, and bounty. Puritan names and values seep in with quiet tones that then shift to warm, glowing ones in pictures of American primitives. This beautiful tale of the early Pilgrims catches a feeling of Americana in its reverent telling in words and illustrations.

BOOKS FOR INTERMEDIATE-GRADE CHILDREN

Among the historical stories affording a genuine portrait of American pioneer life is the series of books by Laura Ingalls Wilder. Frequently known as the "Little House Books," the series is unexcelled in the use it makes of authentic background details, lifelike characterization, and themes appropriate to the sturdy pioneers.

The first in the series is *Little House in the Big Woods*, an outstanding little story of a log-cabin family that lived on the edge of the "big woods" in Wisconsin. Based on the author's childhood experiences, the whole series unravels family-oriented incidents of pioneering and settling in the Midwest. Concepts are within the understanding of children from eight to ten who will be gripped by the power of the engaging relationships between pioneer children and adults in the story.

Great simplicity and beauty are expressed in the descriptions of humble things:

> The attic was a lovely place to play. The large, round, colored pumpkins made beautiful chairs and tables. The red peppers and the onions dangled overhead. The hams and the venison hung in their paper wrappings, and all the bunches of dried herbs, the spicy herbs for cooking and the bitter herbs for medicine, gave the place a dusty-spicy smell.[5]

There are rag dolls and warm mittens as Christmas gifts; calico, nails, and feed from a general store; horse-drawn wagons, campfires, and a wide

---

[5]Laura Ingalls Wilder, *Little House in the Big Woods* (New York: Harper & Row, Publishers, 1953), p. 20. Copyright 1932 by Laura Ingalls Wilder. Reprinted by permission of Harper & Row, Publishers.

This cozy scene confirms the warmth and joy of life in a little log house of pioneer times. Here Laura and her sister sit on comfortable pumpkins while onions and peppers dangle overhead.
From Little House in the Big Woods *by Laura Ingalls Wilder, illustrated by Garth Williams. Harper & Row, Publishers, 1953. Reproduced by permission.*

starlit sky—all the honest, vivid realities that were woven into the broad tapestry of American expansion. Along with frontier history are included the sturdy values characteristic of a truly American way of life. In the "Little House Books" family life is honored and the emphasis is on family unity and joint human efforts in keeping soul and body together. And through it all, a warm sense of comfort and security is projected as young readers are touched by the integrity and the sincerity expressed in these stories.

BOOKS FOR UPPER-GRADE CHILDREN

An outstanding historical novel for adolescents and young adults stands alone in its literary quality and conception—*Johnny Tremain* by the award-winning Esther Forbes.

The stirring quality of *Johnny Tremain* echoes the heartbeats and drumrolls of a noble period in American history. The authentic background of Revolutionary days in Boston throws into sharp relief details of domestic life and memorable characters who championed the cause of American independence. But all this is done with such uncanny skill that characters, scenes, and events come alive. Young readers feel as if they were living spectators to the momentous events surrounding Lexington, Boston, and North Creek. Here, indeed, is history treated with scru-

Johnny Tremain's erect posture in this illustration dramatizes the noble theme of this historical story that rings true to the period when Otis said, "We give all . . . that a man can stand up."

From Johnny Tremain *by Esther Forbes, illustrated by Lynd Ward. Houghton Mifflin Company, 1943. Reproduced by permission.*

314

pulously accurate details of events and characters, all supporting the theme that runs through the lively plot: man's struggle for freedom.

The story also portrays through its characters a variety of universal human traits. Johnny Tremain displays arrogance, impudence, and an immature disregard for others and for authority. Only his own feelings seem at all important. But his involvement in patriotic activities, after an injury to his hand ends his apprenticeship as a silversmith, challenges his strengths and weaknesses.

Although Johnny's personal problems and his activities in the revolutionary movement comprise the bulk of the work, readers may also identify with a wide variety of historic characters while living through stirring moments of American history with them. Assisted by the vivid text they can scent the fragrance of "salt-water tea"; help Paul Revere set out on his ride—"one if by land and two if by sea"; witness Billy Dawes, disguised as a drunken farmer, go merrily on his way; envision Yankee Doodle riding to town with blood in his eye and rage in his heart; and hear the impassioned speech of James Otis who said: "We give all we have, lives, property, safety, skills . . . we fight, we die for a simple thing. Only that a man can stand up."

And with clear, lucid language appropriate to the enduring theme of freedom, the story achieves its climactic fulfillment with an emotional ring that establishes *Johnny Tremain* as a great American junior novel. Though set in the past it possesses power to illumine the present when America still struggles for "a simple thing . . . that a man can stand up."

So Johnny became an unselfish man and an honest American. "He could smell turned earth and gummy buds. . . . His nostrils trembled. . . . So fair a day now drawing to its close. Green with spring, dreaming of the future yet wet with blood. This was his land and these his people."[6]

Stories of Primitive Life

BOOKS FOR YOUNGER CHILDREN

Because children's concept of time is hazy at best, stories of man's earliest history become difficult for them to comprehend. As a result, few books in this category are written with the youngest in mind, although children in the intermediate and upper grades can sample a

---

[6]Esther Forbes, *Johnny Tremain* (Boston: Houghton Mifflin Company, 1943), p. 255.

richer variety of stories with backgrounds of primitive and ancient peoples. But there is perennial appeal in stories of Indians, Eskimos, and of lesser known tribes whose way of life has anthropological and historical significance. Details of ancient and primitive life, however, are sometimes woven into fast-moving stories where primitive tribes are treated as heroic savages or as bloodthirsty beasts, and the impressions gained from stories such as these become colored by injustice and sentimentality making them unsuitable for younger children in particular.

Capturing the spirit of a Hawaiian tribe, William Lipkind's book, *Boy of the Islands*, deals with life before the advent of the white man with integrity and frankness. Never does he descend to maudlin sentiment or brutality. Because he writes for younger children, Lipkind's well-told story focuses on the human interest aspects of Lua, through whose eyes are witnessed sports, voyages, and the training of a chieftain. *Boy of the Islands* is written with simplicity and strength and rings true as a story out of the distant past. Dominated by the theme of growth through participation and interaction, the book also reveals storytelling skills that set it apart as an authentic account of a disappearing way of life.

Other notable books of this kind for younger children tell tales of adventures among various tribes and groups of people whose primitive way of life can still reveal to children the universality of human experience. The poetic works of Ann Nolan Clark describing the life of Indian children are significant contributions. Based on a complete understanding of Indian life and art, her dignity of language communicates the order, beauty, and peace of Indians in the West with tenderness and truth. A most distinguished example is her *In My Mother's House*.

BOOKS FOR INTERMEDIATE-GRADE CHILDREN

A descendant of Sir Walter Scott, Scott O'Dell, has fashioned from historical fact and his own imagination a book entiled *Island of the Blue Dolphins*. Years of research must have gone into this book to arrange facts in such a palatable way yet remain true to human experience.

O'Dell has used choice bits of history about the Ghalas-at Indians to tell a story of a girl who finds herself marooned on an island. Told in the first person, her strange and beautiful story reveals the strongest of human attributes: courage, endurance, and greatness of spirit. Nor are loyalty, beauty, serenity, and peace overlooked. Perfectly blended together, these qualities portray a character who arouses in the reader the fullest sense of character identification so that the whole story becomes a living and lasting experience.

The setting of this haunting tale is a remote California island where an Indian girl, known to history as the Lost Woman of San Nicholas, lived alone. Bereft of her people when tragedy destroys the tribe, Karana manages to exist by bringing simple comforts and aesthetic delights into her solitude. She tames creatures of the brush and patiently observes those of the sea. She studies the ways of nature and takes joy in the grass and flowers that blanket the island. She makes friends with the gentle and wild animals surrounding her primitive dwelling. But most of all, she seeks the companionship of her devoted dog, Rontu. For eighteen years she lives alone on the Island of the Blue Dolphins until a missionary group sails to her village after learning that she had returned to the island in an attempt to save her brother's life.

Adorned with clear storytelling images of characters and episodes, this beautiful book of outstanding quality runs parallel with another great desert-island adventure story, *Robinson Crusoe* by Daniel Defoe. Both of these books portray the spell of isolation and the urgency for survival amid chaos and apparent despair. Caught in this predicament, both characters demonstrate courage and ingenuity while they carry young readers through adventures where life is primitive and savage, yet manageable and kind. These moving stories have the essential ingredients of good literature: they offer children the experience of living through hazardous moments in a world distinctly apart from their own— one on which they can vicariously impose order and control.

BOOKS FOR UPPER-GRADE CHILDREN

Conquest of fear is at the heart of *Call It Courage*, a powerful story said to have become a legend among Polynesians. Originating in a dim past, the book unfolds the story of life on an island in the South Seas where a young boy, Mafatu, struggles to overcome his fear of the sea and earn an honored place in a society of stout-hearted islanders.

Armstrong Sperry tells a gripping story of the South Sea Islands and carves out a character who is at once human and superhuman, and he does both with integrity and great sympathy. The gradual development of the brave boy is highlighted by the vivid images in the story. There is a strange island, a perilous voyage, a savage boar, and the hostility of even more savage man-eaters.

With these convincing details of early Polynesian life, Sperry spins a yarn with native storytelling ability. From the knowledge he gained of South Sea Islanders through personal travel among them and from having listened to the seafaring tales of his great-grandfather, the author has created an exciting, action-packed adventure story that is suspenseful enough to hold wide appeal.

Here is great adventure dominated by the sea and drawn with ancient details of a little-known group of primitive islanders whose legendary story is as timely today as it was when Mafatu, "The Stout Heart,"

In this compelling tale of high adventure the author-artist has carved out a brave boy, Mafatu, who is here guided back to his island home by an albatross.
From Call It Courage *by Armstrong Sperry. Copyright* © *by The Macmillan Company. Reproduced by permission.*

won his ultimate victory over his fears and returned to his island triumphant.

Stories of Ancient Civilizations

For younger children particularly, stories of the ancient world may lose much of their historic importance, whereas older children can develop a feeling for antiquity through a well-told tale that recreates the magnificence of an ancient culture.

The ancient world, more than any other period in human history, lends itself to historical storytelling by the nature of the refined, classical backgrounds through which colorful characters have walked.

Transcending time, brilliant scholars, philosophers, priests, and kings of ancient civilizations have left blueprints of their achievements from which future generations, esteeming the stature of these men, have founded institutions that echo the spirit of a noble past. The ancient world is the source for many ideas expressed today in art and architecture, as well as in mathematical and related scientific developments. Children reading the inspired stories derived from a glorious past can readily link the remote with the present since much of what they witness and experience in the present stretches back to classical times.

However, the ancient world not only provides rich sources for storytelling themes, characters, and settings but is a principal source as well of great literature. Today, in schools and institutions of higher learning, the literature of Greece, Rome, and other civilizations that made rich contributions is recommended. Corner drugstores peddle paperbacks of Homer and Plato. Dramatists draw from the rich resources of Sophocles, Aristophanes, Euripides, and Aeschylus whose works have stood as prototypes of fine dramatic art. There are great examples of noble poetry from ancient Egypt, the great Sumero-Babylonian epic of Gilgamesh, and famed Hebrew writings in the earlier books of the Old Testament.

But if one examines the stories from a purely human viewpoint, one can see that it was the ancient Greeks who first conceived of looking at things from a perspective that dealt with fundamental problems facing human beings daily and directly. And this, in a measure, explains why many of the best historical stories for children have survived to become classics in literature. They tend to focus on a wide range of issues from a certain period enriched by the glow of history yet without crowding out the human interest elements that make a good story.

Few books for this age group concern themselves with the ancient world as well as the artistic *Master of the Royal Cats* by Jerzy Laskowski with outstanding illustrations by Janina Domanska.

This lovely picture book is drawn from ancient Egyptian art and has the right storytelling elements to convince a young reader that this imaginative account might have taken place. For young adventurers who show an interest in ancient peoples, and especially in the storied land of pyramids and Pharaohs, this book is a fine first.

Using illustrations of life in ancient Egypt that resemble archeological discoveries, the author and illustrator show the flavor of wealth, the impact of Pharaonic power, the role of animals, and, above all, the ingenuity of a small boy named Anpu. In both word and picture, ancient Egypt is beautifully portrayed. Especially fine, however, are the carefully drawn pictures whose simplicity and beauty make *Master of the Royal Cats* a picture book of rare charm.

Up the Nile swam the big crocodile, with Anpu on his back holding tight to the sack full of cats. He swam so fast that in no time at all they caught up with the boys and the dogs in the boat.

"Jump on my back," said the crocodile to the dogs. And he upset the boat with a mighty flip of his tail. "The boys can swim home," said the crocodile.

So it was that Anpu and the dogs and the cats arrived at the royal palace to find Pharaoh in a terrible state of nerves.

Replicating the art found in tombs and palaces of ancient Egypt, this book uses historical details to tell of Anpu's imaginative excursion up the Nile with a sack of cats.

From Master of the Royal Cats *by Jerzy Laskowski, illustrated by Janina Domanska. Copyright © 1965 by the author and artist. The Seabury Press. Reproduced by permission.*

Surrounded by accurate details of the Old Kingdom, the exciting story line carries young readers on an imaginative excursion through the art of ancient Eygpt. The hero of the story is a little boy who sets out on a search with two disloyal friends to find Pharaoh's lost dogs who were used to keep rats away from his grain. Anpu, through his kindness and the blessings of good fortune, makes friends with a crocodile who helps him find not only the lost dogs but rat-hunting cats.

Authentic details of time, place, and the social order lend credibility to an ancient account of the importance of cats during the days of the Pharaohs. Having taken on legendary proportions, this ancient story is still told in Egypt to explain the role of the cat in Egyptian history and to account for the subsequent influence the cat exerted on the various art forms and beliefs of that ancient civilization.

BOOKS FOR INTERMEDIATE-GRADE CHILDREN

Inspired by an incident in history, *The Hand of Apollo* by Elizabeth Coatsworth recreates the splender and shadow of ancient Greece.

In this fine historical story, the poet's impressive talents are focused on Corinth during the invasion by the Romans. Dion, the son of Hermonax, is granted a safe conduct to leave his doomed city. By chance the boy is sheltered by a sea trader who risks his life to harbor Dion aboard his ship. From this point to the end of the story Dion finds himself hiding on a sacred islet off Apollo's own island of Delos and tormented with "nightmare memories that cried for vengeance of his lost family and city and his own dream of serving a god, [while] he waited for a sign. And when the time came for Dion to leave the sanctuary with Agios the Athenian," it seemed as if the hand of Apollo himself guided him.

Serenely told, the book shares an ancient vision that becomes splendidly credible. Elizabeth Coatsworth's mastery of the classic period enables her to choose details of dress, speech, terrain, and religion that make the background for the book very vivid. Along with this there is the richness of language, so skillfully used that the rush of events is never impeded. A young reader can become enthralled with a story that shows the power of a boy's conviction which "meant learning to give himself to creation rather than to destruction" even though it involved going against his father's wishes. Dedicated to poetry, the sensitive and fine portrait of an ancient youth stands as a testimony of deep, personal convictions.

In this sensitive picture a young man dedicates himself to peace and poetry even while murders and destruction haunt his memory. Dignity and grace mark the pillared architecture and high hills of Greece.

From The Hand of Apollo *by Elizabeth Coatsworth, illustrated by Robin Jacques. Copyright © 1965 by Elizabeth Coatsworth. Reproduced by permission of The Viking Press, Inc.*

Robin Jacques has captured the solemn beauty of the text in pictures that are true to the design and order of a classical period in history.

BOOKS FOR UPPER-GRADE CHILDREN

Hatred turned to love is the theme underlying *The Bronze Bow* by Elizabeth George Speare, the 1962 Newbery Medal winner. Inspired by the Biblical quotation from II Samuel 22:35—"He trains my hands for war, so that my arms can bend a bow of bronze"— the author tells an action-filled adventure story set at the time when Christ lived on the earth.

Anticipating the coming of Messiah as the deliverer of the Israelites during Roman occupation of the Holy Lands, Daniel forsakes his family to join a band led by Rosh whom he believes to be the savior. But this small band of believers does not command the same respect as another group led by Jesus of Nazareth. Hate and revenge burn within Daniel until he comes in contact with the gentler persuasion of Christ. Touched by the healing doctrine of love and peace, Daniel realizes that "love, not hate, is strong enough to bend the bow of bronze."

True to historical fact, this stunning story of a bitter Israelite pitted against the Romans is powerful and breathtakingly real. Anger and revenge dominate a story where the gentle theme of love over hate develops slowly but surely, though with great subtlety. The issues of the period are made clear as well-drawn characters give expression to the impact that historical events had upon those who lived through such times as those of Roman conquerors.

The portrait of Jesus, particularly, is superbly developed. Great skill is shown in bestowing the gentle teacher with characteristics that are neither sentimental nor weak. Instead, Jesus of Nazareth's character reflects strength, conviction, and persuasive leadership in accordance with the existing evidence about him rather than with the conceptions expressed by some artists.

Stories of Life in the Middle Ages and Modern Times

The Middle Ages marks the period in European history when Christianity's influence was manifested in many forms of human endeavor. None was more colorful, however, than the serene medieval magic permeating forms of religious life.

All over Europe graceful cathedrals raised their stately spires, monasteries dotted the countryside, universities were founded and matched ideas of freedom and learning with much older traditions.

This was an era when Byzantium flourished and spread from its ancient capital, Constantinople, to widely separated continents. And the most beautiful expressions of Byzantine spirit were found in the ecclesiastical arts adorning places of worship and learning. Here the arts of mosaic, fresco, and miniature painting developed. For more than ten centuries iconography, reliquaries, crosses, and sacred vestments continued to preserve the mystical spirit and character of the Middle Ages passing along, as into an epic, the creative ideals of a glittering civilization.

Another complete expression of Byzantine spirit was found in the music and literature of the times. Illuminated manuscripts blended art and writing to make resplendent images for the eye and mind. Haunting chants and ballads entered into many different kinds of medieval life: churches, castles, universities, great halls, inns, markets, and fairs. In this way it touched even the simpler folk—the farmer, the miller, the silversmith, the baker, and all the rest of teeming humanity—so that some of their wisdom and myths mingled with the lyrics and mysticism prevalent at the time.

Because of the richness and variety found in this period of history, many exciting books for children have been inspired by its ideas, beliefs, and pageantry as well as by the minstrels, monks, and kings who make up the tapestry of the Middle Ages and still influence life today.

Of course, the momentous events of the contemporary world will become the history of tomorrow. The twentieth century has already seen historic movements, episodes, characters, and trends that overshadow many other periods in history. So there are already books in print that reflect the historically significant details of this century and do so with enough authentic, realistic background and spirit to make them stand out as distinguished historical stories for children.

BOOKS FOR YOUNGER CHILDREN

Beautiful details of monastic life are teamed with convincing character portrayals in a gentle story entitled *Saint Jerome and the Lion* by Rumer Godden and illustrated by Jean Primrose.

Combining medieval beauty with poetic grace, cadenced verses reveal a story of devotion, humility, and obedience. Legendary facts are used reverently to tell in a devout style of writing the inspiring tale of friendship between a human being and a lion.

A form of illumination is used for the initial letters in key passages of the story, which is made continuous by charming anecdotes disclosing Saint Jerome's friendship with the lion: the beast's admission to a cloister, the animal's services as guard over the monks' donkey, which caused him to be unjustly accused of eating the she-ass, and the satisfying solution that proves the lion innocent.

Told and illustrated with a fine strength and simplicity, even though an archaic style is used, this medieval story may be termed the best of its kind for children. The picturesque life of the religious order provides for younger children a rare glimpse into a monastery during the Middle Ages.

Faithfully interpreting this glorious tale are the well-drawn pictures whose tone is much in harmony with the incantation of the language. And in unison, text and pictures provide fresh delights for the ears, eyes, and hearts.

Marguerite de Angeli's *The Door in the Wall*, another Newbery Medal book, is a heart-warming story set in thirteenth-century England about a boy's victory over a physical handicap.

Robin is a dependent, rather petulant ten-year-old of noble birth whose father has gone off to fight in the Scottish wars while his mother is serving the ailing Queen. Left all alone, the crippled boy is also deserted by the household servants who flee London when some of them die of the plague that is spreading like wildfire.

But Brother Luke, a friar from St. Mark's, takes the little crippled boy to stay at the hospice, described with authentic details that give us glimpses of life in London and in the hospice, which served as an inn for wayfarers as well as a hospital.

One learns about the almonry where food and clothing are given to the poor, about the scriptorium where poems and psalteries were copied, and the ordered way of life of the monks who teach Robin to make use of his hands as well as his head when they recite: "For reading is another door in the wall. . . ."

Under expert tutelage, Robin gradually learns to carve, to read and write, to study music, astronomy, and history, as well as to make crutches with which he learns to swim. Consequently his arms develop strength and his bad temper softens. His patience increases too when he identifies with the boys with whom he plays the games popular with children in medieval England.

After Robin is taken to the castle of Sir Peter de Lindsay to be trained as a page, the story threads its way through more instruction, more patience, more stress on courage until the castle is besieged and Robin performs heroically to rout the enemy.

At last the troops from the Scottish wars return led by the King and Queen and Robin's parents. During a great celebration made vibrant with the rich, festive details of a medieval Christmas, Robin is knighted.

Warmth and love flow from the poignant tale of a boy crippled and haunted by fear. His triumphant victory over handicap stands out clearly in language that is appropriately tender, and matched with beautiful illustrations.

Deep spiritual values also rise to the surface of this inspiring tale of triumph over misfortune and handicap. On several occasions during the telling of the tale the friar and others speak of finding a door in the wall, which is symbolic of a solution to a problem, a way to success. And according to the religious teachers, success is earned by: "What we do with what we have."

Reminiscent of an illuminated manuscript, this title-page picture heralds a magnificent story set in the Middle Ages. Crippled Robin courageously triumphs over handicap in a beautifully illustrated book with feeling for pageantry.

From The Door in the Wall *by Marguerite de Angeli. Copyright 1949 by the author-illustrator. Reprinted by permission of Doubleday & Company, Inc.*

Considered an epic of courage and a book of high principle in today's world to inspire teenagers, *Ring the Judas Bell* by James Forman is a deeply serious story reflecting the fury, destruction, and pathos of modern-day unrest.

Charged with electricity and tenderness, this book is compelling for its tension, power, and solid grasp of character. Unbearable conflicts and tragic episodes are handled with the stark realism that goes to the heart of the issues behind the times.

Nicholos, a shepherd boy of fifteen, and son of the local priest, Father Lanaras, emerges as the hero of a story that grew out of World War II and the civil war in Greece after the Nazi occupation had ended. The immediate scene of the story is the sunlit island of Serifos graced by a little chapel whose bell Father Lanaras regards as "the voice of God calling to people." This Judas bell, as it is commonly known, hangs from a white-washed belfry to symbolize the islanders' faith and Father Lanaras' ideal: to keep the people of the village spiritually united.

However, a harrowing day comes to the island when "Andartes" (communist partisans) turn the "peace" of World War II into the worst civil war in the history of Greece. The idealist, Father Lanaras, for all his dedicated efforts, is unable to prevent the pillaging, burning, and savage brutality to which the village is exposed.

And during this feverish unrest, the Judas bell of Serifos falls taking with it the ideals and hopes of the destitute inhabitants.

Compounding the horrors of Serifos, communists kidnap all the children of the island. Among them are Nicholos, the priest's son, and his sister Angela who are later imprisoned in a camp beyond the high hills of Greece, somewhere in Albania.

In developing its dominant theme, "the power of the spirit to triumph even when it seems to fail most bitterly," the story traces the plans for escape that courageous Nicholos makes with the embittered children and his antagonistic sister. Sustained only by the memories of his idealistic father and the ideals for which the bell stood, the sturdy youth manfully leads the children past every imaginable hardship to their village home.

Tragically true to history, the boy now faces even more crippling conditions on his own island: antagonism, rejection, starvation, and deep, personal despair. But the most painful condition of all is the awareness that his once dedicated father is no longer a priest but a soldier turned cold and cynical.

Impressively, the stalwart youth decides to pick up the pieces and try to rebuild a decent way of life in his island home. Here he must once again raise the Judas bell or forever deny its power.

Although cruel and pitiful, the story is graced with truth and tenderness because it is written with integrity and from conviction. Stark, vivid realities fill in the framework of a historical structure that is sound and compelling. And without falsifying "history's fundamental record" of events during the dark years of Greek civil war, the book gives a poignant, dramatic account of ruthlessness and despair, yet not without pointing up the optimistic theme of man's power to triumph even in the midst of chaos and failure.

As an Honor Book, *Ring the Judas Bell* tolls still another message: it reminds young readers and the world of war's grim and savage futility.

Books with historical stories serve to recreate the past and to illumine the present and future. And because the truth of human experience is unchanging, good historical stories are timeless and link generations of readers with their universalizing power.

Each period of history, each generation, each momentous event, each historical character—the props in the moving drama of time—are reordered by the storytelling art that confirms for young readers "the solidarity of man and the universality of the human soul."

Criteria for Historical Stories

THEME

- Is the theme (or themes) historically basic to human experience?
- Does the theme concern itself with human worth and dignity and other ideas deserving of children's attention?
- Is the choice of theme in the story comprehensible to the age group for which the book is intended?
- Is the theme strong enough to communicate without condescension at the appropriate emotional level of children?
- Is the underlying theme in a story original enough so as to afford a fresh perspective for viewing life in the past?
- Are the basic ideas dominating the story capable of lending themselves to the re-creation of life long ago so that the people, places, and issues of the times appear as alive as those of today?
- Does the theme remain constant with the truth in human experience, especially in developmental levels of childhood?

- Is the theme of a caliber high enough to satisfy young readers so that they become inspired by life in the past?
- Do the themes in the stories of long ago confirm for children a fundamental truth of human experience so as to link them with the ebb and flow of human life?

PLOT

- Is the story a genuine adventure in the past?
- Is the adventure concerned with action and resolution of conflict characteristic of the times the book tries to re-create?
- Is the action paced closely enough to make the story move swiftly through historical details?
- Does the movement of action intensify the interest in the story so that it grows more absorbing?
- Are the events, actions, conflicts, characters, settings, tightly interrelated in developing the basic idea?
- Have details of time, place, and the social order been used naturally with imaginative inventiveness?
- Is there adequate chronological sequence to the events in a book so as to afford a sense of time's passage?
- Does the story line weave itself strongly through the facts of history so as to form an indivisible whole?
- Is the story paced in keeping with the rate of living during the period of history retraced in the book?
- Are the details in the story used to point up the human interest elements?

CHARACTERIZATION

- Do characters come alive within the historical framework of the story?
- Are the characters drawn with close, human details that sharpen their relief against a period background?
- Do the characters serve as vehicles to communicate underlying themes or message in a story of the past?
- Have the significant characters in the story been drawn so as to represent memorable personages in history?
- Do these characters possess many attributes worthy of emulation?
- Can present-day youngsters readily identify with characters drawn from the past because of the universality they reveal in the story?
- Have these long-departed characters been depicted with convincing characteristics?
- Are the characteristics, mannerisms, speech, dress, and attitudes of the characters a genuine reflection of the period in which they lived?

STYLE

- Is the style of writing in keeping with the theme and period stressed in the story?
- Have colorful words, phrases, names, dialogue been utilized skillfully so as to paint an accurate picture of the times?
- Are some elements of language archaic enough to afford a feeling of long ago?
- Have accurate idioms and obsolete expressions been effectively used to capture the flavor of a period in history?
- Does the style of language preserve the dignity of the past without excessive use of idioms, archaic terms, and the like?
- Is a sense of history gained from the language used in the story?
- Is the writing free of sentimentality as life is approached from a historical perspective?
- Are the perspective, the point of view, the theme, historical backgrounds, and character portrayals achieved through clarity, order, and unity in the writing of a period story?
- Has authenticity been preserved in affording glimpses of life long ago or life that is fast disappearing?
- Can the style of writing give young readers an opportunity to "live" rather than just "witness" history?
- Is the writing true to the times, settings, peoples, and issues so that there is obvious integrity about the book?
- Is the book designed so that in no way does it "falsify history's fundamental record" even though the style of writing has utilized invention?

SETTING

- Has the story employed historical details to stimulate a sense of awareness of life long ago?
- Are the historical details graphic enough to form a colorful background against which characters and episodes can move convincingly?
- Do these graphic details of time, place, and the social order give an authentic, truthful picture of history?
- Are major and minor details scrupulously accurate so as not to be in the least unfaithful to the period in which the story takes place?
- Have accurate details of a period been presented to demonstrate captivating quaintness and the charm of antiquity?
- Does the unity of elements in the settings—those of time, places, people, beliefs, costumes—remain faithful to the spirit of a period in history?

ARBUTHNOT, MAY HILL, "Other Times and Places," in *Children and Books*, 3rd ed. Chicago: Scott, Foresman & Company, 1964.

BUTTERFIELD, HERBERT, *The Historical Novel: An Essay*. London: Cambridge University Press, 1924.

HAINES, HELEN E., *What's in a Novel*. New York: Columbia University Press, 1942.

HUBER, MIRIAM BLANTON, "History of Children's Books," in *Story and Verse for Children*. New York: The Macmillan Company, 1965.

SHEPPARD, ALFRED TRESIDDER, *The Art and Practice of Historical Fiction*. London: H. Toulmin, 1930.

HUCK, CHARLOTTE, and DORIS YOUNG, "Children Identify with their Historical Heritage," in *Children's Literature in the Elementary School*. New York: Holt, Rinehart & Winston, Inc., 1961.

MEIGS, CORNELIA, et al., "Adventures in the Past," in *A Critical History of Children's Literature*. New York: The Macmillan Company, 1953.

REPPLIER, AGNES, *Old Wine and New*. Boston: Houghton Mifflin Company, 1897.

SMITH, LILLIAN H., "Historical Fiction," in *The Unreluctant Years*. Chicago: American Library Association, 1953.

TOOZE, RUTH, and BEATRICE PERHAM KRONE, *Literature and Music as Resources for Social Studies*. Englewood Cliffs, N. J.: Prentice-Hall, Inc., 1955.

History in Children's Literature

STORIES OF AMERICAN HERITAGE

For younger children

THE SOD HOUSE
Written by Elizabeth Coatsworth.
Illustrated by Manning De V. Lee.
The Macmillan Company, 1954.
Little Ilse is the heroine in this story of a German family migrating from Boston to Kansas in the days before the Civil War. They fight not only the physical hardships of pioneer life, but also the immorality of slavery. Struggling to maintain their own freedom, this brave family helps to make Kansas a state free from slavery. Far more inspiring than the story of the geographical frontier that the Traubels forge is the clearly and simply told tale of courage that establishes moral frontiers. Large, well-done black and white illustrations admirably suit the text.

POCAHONTAS
Written and illustrated by Ingri and Edgar Parin D'Aulaire. Doubleday & Company, Inc., 1946.

Although the language is a trifle strained, the pictures are poetically conceived and correct in detail. Pocahontas is presented as a very real little Indian girl, energetic and alive, whose marriage to an Englishman and reception by the Queen of England has become an American fairy tale. The authors' respect for the English language is apparent. Illustrations blend authentic Indian feeling with an individual style.

THE THANKSGIVING STORY
Written by Alice Dalgliesh.
Illustrated by Helen Sewell.
Charles Scribner's Sons, 1954.

Revolving around the Hopkins family whose child, Oceanus, is born on the Mayflower, this familiar story of the first Thanksgiving is told with simplicity and directness without loss of significance and dignity. The strong and dramatic illustrations in the style of American primitives admirably reflect the somber life of the early Plymouth pilgrims and build to a colorful autumnal climax with the celebration of the feast. It is an excellent read-aloud book with clear text and apt illustrations bringing scenes and characters to vivid life.

BEARS ON HEMLOCK MOUNTAIN
Written by Alice Dalgliesh.
Illustrated by Helen Sewell. Charles Scribner's Sons, 1952.

A trip over Hemlock Mountain to borrow an iron kettle from an aunt becomes an adventure for eight-year-old Jonathan who feels uneasy about the rumored presence of bears on that mountain. The story is told with lively humor and enticing suspense. An abundance of sensory detail and brilliance of characterization bring to life the robust country family of which Jonathan is a member. The illustrations, in deep blue and black, provide a delightful

complement to the text, and together with it, make an excellent read-aloud book especially designed for those who love to get the shivers.

THE 4TH OF JULY STORY
Written by Alice Dalgliesh.
Illustrated by Marie Nonnast.
Charles Scribner's Sons, 1956.

This effectively illustrated picture book tells the story of the fight for independence from England, the making and signing of the Declaration of Independence, and the spreading of the news throughout the land. It is a most distinguished book with many full-page illustrations that succeed in presenting this subject vividly to children. It is historically accurate, but not so overburdened with facts as to dim the excitement and drama of the events.

AMERICA BEGINS
Written by Alice Dalgliesh.
Illustrated by Lois Maloy. Charles Scribner's Sons, 1958.

The settlement of the New World is narrated and illustrated with coherence and great accuracy. Stories of Leif the Lucky, Columbus, Marco Polo, Vasco Da Gama, Ponce de Leon, Balboa, Magellan, Cartier, Coronado, Drake, and Champlain are presented against a background of America before the white man. Color and black-and-white illustrations and concise narrative combine to give a living, connected history of the settlement of America and of the men who forged its frontiers.

THE COLUMBUS STORY
Written by Alice Dalgliesh.
Illustrated by Leo Politi. Charles Scribner's Sons, 1955.

Precisely the right details of Columbus' life, from boyhood dreams of the sea, through his studies and first voyage, to the start of the second are presented in simple, meaningful prose and in illustrations that recapture the flavor of the Old World and the drama of voyaging to the

New. It is an excellent read-aloud picture book, visually delightful and written with historical accuracy and insight into a child's imagination.

COLUMBUS SAILS
Written and illustrated by C. Walter Hodges. Coward-McCann, Inc., 1939.

The narrative is skillfully presented as though by eye-witness of a monk, a sailor, and an Indian who returned with Columbus to Spain. Historical accuracy and artistic perception in the choice of appropriate incidents make it a story of truth and drama in which Columbus is realized as a man of great vision. The pictures by the author are convincingly drawn, and, together with imaginative writing, they build an inspiring story.

LEIF ERIKSSON
Written by Katherine B. Shippen. Harper & Row, Publishers, 1951.

Leif Eriksson is acknowledged as the true discoverer of America in this beautifully written book. Despite the paucity of information on the subject, the author has not overfictionalized his story but has remained faithful to the facts known. She has gleaned enough to make of Eriksson a living historical figure in an exciting, forcefully written tale. The language is simple and dignified in this remarkable book of pre-Columbian adventure into the New World.

OLD ABE: THE EAGLE HERO
Written by Patrick Young. Illustrated by John Kaufmann. Prentice-Hall, Inc., 1965.

The hero is a bald eagle taken as mascot by the Eighth Wisconsin Infantry Volunteers during the Civil War and named after President Lincoln. Inspiring his regiment by his tireless vigil, standing on his perch, screaming at the enemy, and hated by the Confederate soldiers, Old Abe becomes a Northern legend. His story is told from his prewar days, through his adventures in battle and on to his later renown.

Narrative and illustrations combine to make a stirring story of this historical bird.

For intermediate-grade children

JOHNNY REB
Written by Merritt P. Allen. Illustrated by Ralph Ray, Jr. David McKay Co., Inc., 1952.

In a vigorous style, which brings the Civil War alive, the story is told of a young orphan, of Northern parentage, but living in South Carolina, and of his coming to maturity in the Cavalry legion led by Wade Hampton. Historical accuracy, lively dialogue, and skillful characterization make this one of the better historical novels. It is a story grim in its realism, yet genuine in its touches of humor, a story told with fairness to the courage of both the Northern and Confederate soldiers, but fully conveying the horror of war.

A HEAD ON HER SHOULDERS
Written by Gladys Baker Bond. Illustrated by Richard Kennedy. Abelard-Schuman Limited, 1964.

This is an exciting tale concerning the trek of a Midwestern pioneer family to the Idaho Territory in 1885. It is the story of Brita Ward, thirteen years old, who, although separated from her parents, responsibly manages family, livestock, and possessions. The novel points out the life of the pioneers in natural enough circumstances and offers the reader vicarious satisfaction in Brita Ward's accomplishment.

DRUMS
Written by James Boyd. Illustrated by N. C. Wyeth. Charles Scribner's Sons, 1936.

James Fraser is sent by his Tory father to England in the hope that he will thereby escape the revolutionary influence, but the boy's encounter with John Paul Jones brings him into active participation in the battle between the *Bonhomme Richard* and the *Serapis*. This is social history in the best sense of the word. It is a meticulously accurate reconstruction of the country with authenticity subtly revealed through the characters, their speech, and the pervading atmosphere. It is a vital story written with deep feeling and sound information.

CADDIE WOODLAWN
*Written by Carol Ryrie Brink.
Illustrated by Kate Seredy. The
Macmillan Company, 1935.*

This story, based on the reminiscences of the author's grandmother, embraces one year in the life of a pioneer family in Wisconsin—a family that decides unanimously, despite the inheritance of an estate in England, to remain in Wisconsin. The year is 1864 and Caddie Woodlawn is eleven years old. Because of her basic frailty, Caddie is encouraged to live an outdoor life in which she flourishes as an adventure-loving tomboy. Clear characterization, confidently drawn background, an abundance of lively incidents, and fine black and white illustrations, which revel in the spaciousness and freedom of the frontier, all make this book a rewarding adventure into pioneer days. A Newbery Medal winner.

JOHN BILLINGTON, FRIEND OF
SQUANTO
*Written by Clyde Robert Bulla.
Illustrated by Peter Burchard.
Thomas Y. Crowell Company,
1956.*

Because of little John Billington's friendship with the Indian Squanto, peaceful relations are developed between the Pilgrims and the Cape Cod Indians. The hardships as well as the more attractive elements of Pilgrim life are realistically represented. The black-and-white illustrations in a clean, simple format, and a clear narrative style make this a splendid book—a delightful introduction to the story of the Pilgrims' first difficult year in Plymouth Harbor.

SWORD OF THE WILDERNESS
*Written by Elizabeth Coatsworth.
Illustrated by Harve Stein. The
Macmillan Company, 1936.*

The scene is laid in Maine and Canada in the winter of 1689—the time of the French and Indian War. Seth Hubbard spends this bitter winter as a captive of the Abenakis. The author's style has beauty that is genuine and moving as it unfolds the logical alliance of the French with the Indians against England. It is a vividly told story, constantly contrasting the Indians and the New England settlers, and dramatizing the inevitable outcome of the unhappy war.

THE FAIR AMERICAN
*Written by Elizabeth Coatsworth.
Illustrated by Helen Sewell. The
Macmillan Company, 1951.*

Escaping from the horrors of the French Revolution, Pierre, sole survivor of his family, is taken as cabin boy by Captain Peterson of the *Fair American*, a ship bound for the New World. Pierre meets the captain's wife, their son, Andrew, and their niece, Sally, who teaches him new manners that will prepare him for his life in his new country. It is an appealing story of a little boy's adaptability to challenging circumstances.

BOSTON BELLS
*Written by Elizabeth Coatsworth.
Illustrated by Manning De V. Lee.
The Macmillan Company, 1952.*

Skillfully, the author brings to life Boston during the Knowles riots when British press gangs were invading the city. The short narrative revolves around a few significant days in the life of John Singleton Copley, a nine-year-old boy who lives with his widowed mother in a shop on Boston's Long Wharf. John's lucky escape from the British Navy, despite his proximity to the sea, makes an exciting, action-packed story, efficiently told, and well supplemented by excellent, detailed pictures.

ADAM AND THE GOLDEN COCK
Written by Alice Dalgliesh.
Illustrated by Leonard Weisgard.
Charles Scribner's Sons, 1959.

Adam is a boy who lives in Connecticut during the Revolutionary War. His friend, Paul, whose father is a Tory, does not share Adam's enthusiasm over the arrival of General Rochambeau and his French soldiers. The story is one of the confusion and the problems encountered by a young boy in the Revolutionary War. Historically accurate, it gives a vivid insight into this period in American history. The black and yellow illustrations lend a New England flavor to this story of fighting and freedom.

THE COURAGE OF SARAH NOBLE
Written by Alice Dalgliesh.
Illustrated by Leonard Weisgard.
Charles Scribner's Sons, 1954.

Sarah Noble is a little girl whose courage shines through a timidity that has no place in the hard life of the pioneers. Along with her father she participates in the founding of New Milford in the Connecticut wilderness. The story is based on an actual incident and is told with a simple dignity that makes this remarkable child of the pioneers a truly sympathetic little heroine. The illustrations give the book a fine sense of authenticity.

THEE, HANNAH!
Written and illustrated by
Marguerite de Angeli. Doubleday &
Company, Inc., 1940.

This is the story of a little Quaker girl whose love of very un-Quakerish frills is a source of constant exasperation to her family. Her plain Quaker bonnet, however, proves instrumental in helping her to save an escaping Negro slave, and thereafter she has a deeper understanding of the simple Quaker uniform. Quaker family life in Philadelphia is affectionately portrayed, and Hannah is a thoroughly engaging and distinct personality. Historical truth enlivens the whole story, and the lovely illustrations lend a visual insight into the Philadelphia of the 1850's.

THE MATCHLOCK GUN
Written by Walter Edmonds.
Illustrated by Paul Lantz. Dodd,
Mead & Co., 1941.

The bloody facts of early American life are re-created with a rare sense of reality. Ten-year-old Edward Van Alstyne and his mother stand guard in their house with a great Spanish matchlock gun while Mr. Van Alstyne is away from home in search of Indians. The inevitable Indian attack comes, and Edward plays the part of a hero in a story of suspense and mounting terror. The illustrations, rich lithographic drawings in black and white and vivid colors, do not shy away from the lurid aspects of the story. Dutch phrases spice the simple and dramatic narrative with an authentic ring. A well-made story.

HITTY: HER FIRST HUNDRED
YEARS
Written by Rachel Field. Illustrated
by Dorothy Lathrop. The Macmillan
Company, 1929.

Hitty is a wooden doll carved from ash and the author's imagination into a very live and fascinating personality whose memoirs of adventure throughout the world are delightfully told in language spiced with an antique flavor. The book is most unusual in its conception, and in its masterful development of the character of this one-hundred-year-old, ageless doll. She has the irresistibility of a living character, and her life in a realistically drawn America of the 1800's is never dull, yet never sentimentalized. The drawings are a perfect visual supplement to this very literary, perfectly appealing book. A Newbery Medal winner.

BRADY
Written by Jean Fritz. Illustrated by
Lynd Ward. Coward-McConn,
Inc., 1960.

Brady is a sensitive but irresponsible boy

whose unexpected entry into the activity of the underground railroad provides him with an opportunity to prove his maturity. The boy's character and that of his preacher father are developed with credibility. Although the story begins somewhat slowly, it evolves with mounting interest to present a picture of Pennsylvania's Washington County in 1836, a community torn by the question of slavery. It is a perceptive, satisfying story of a boy's development and thoughtful, attractive illustrations support the orderly text.

The Cabin Faced West
Written by Jean Fritz. Illustrated
by Feodor Rojankovsky.
Coward-McCann, Inc., 1958.

Ann Hamilton faces the loneliness of pioneer life away from her Gettysburg friends with equanimity after entertaining General Washington with her mother in their Pennsylvania frontier home. The story is based on the reminiscences of the author's great-great-grandmother, and is told with genuine charm and a feeling for the hardships of pioneer life. The illustrations—black-and-white pencil sketches—have a homespun charm that adds immeasurably to the warmth and humor of the book.

Puritan Adventure
Written and illustrated by Lois
Lenski. J. B. Lippincott Co., 1944.

Young Aunt Charity of the Partridge family comes from England to New England, and in the process of spreading her Old World charm among solemn New Englanders she inspires both warm friendships and bitter enmities. Her attempts to desolemnize the Puritans, and the consequences of those attempts, provide sharp contrasts between the English and their Puritan cousins. It is a work in which research is evident, though unobtrusive, giving the action and characters freedom in which to be sincere and honest.

Indian Captive
Written and illustrated by Lois
Lenski. J. B. Lippincott Co., 1941.

The actual story of Mary Jemison, "white woman of the Genesee," captured by Indians in 1758 at the tender age of twelve, is fictionalized without any loss of authenticity. Mary is realized as an appealing personality whose absorption into the Indian culture, in which she is forced at first to live, gradually becomes complete in a sensitively told story. This is also an excellent study of Seneca Indian life, customs, and ideas.

By Secret Railway
Written by Enid Meadowcroft.
Illustrated by Henry C. Pitz.
Thomas Y. Crowell Company,
1948.

David, a white boy, and Jim, a young freed Negro, exchange assistance in times of peril. Jim helps to rescue David's younger brother from drowning, and when Jim is spirited out of Illinois into a slave state by slave traders, it is David who seeks him out. Together they make a dangerous trip back to Chicago by underground railroad. It is an exciting, well-written story, accurately documented, and told with a feeling for pre-Civil War days. Excellent illustrations complement the text.

On Indian Trails with Daniel Boone
Written by Enid Meadowcroft.
Illustrated by Lloyd Coe. Thomas
Y. Crowell Company, 1947.

Daniel Boone's children are central to this story of the means and reasons used by Daniel Boone to guide his friends and family over the Wilderness Road to Kentucky. It is a vitally told, factual story, developed with simplicity and a sense of life. The lively dialogue lends depth to the characterizations of the Boone children, and the dramatic sketches with which the book is illustrated sharpen the visual awareness.

MASTER SIMON'S GARDEN
Written by Cornelia Meigs.
Illustrated by John Rae. The
Macmillan Company, 1929.

With pungent economy the theme of thrift and brisk practicality runs through a superbly told story rooted in Puritan New England. Supporting the theme and adding to its significance is a clearly carved character, Master Simon, who tends and develops a glorious garden run riot with herbs and flowers. As an expression of his love and sympathy, the garden grows in direct contrast with the morbid suspicions abundant in the neighborhood. Continuing through generations and into the Revolutionary War, this colorful tradition stands for tolerance and understanding even when Master Simon's great-grandson Stephen fights for freedom.

Other historical stories by this same author include: *Clearing Weather*, illustrated by Frank Dobias, Little Brown & Co., 1928; *The Covered Bridge*, illustrated by Marguerite de Angeli, The Macmillan Company, 1936; *Swift Rivers*, illustrated by Peter Hurd, Little, Brown & Co., 1937; *The Willow Whistle*, illustrated by E. B. Smith, The Macmillan Company, 1931; *Wind in the Chimney*, illustrated by Louise Mansfield, The Macmillan Company, 1934.

THE PERILOUS ROAD
Written by William O. Steele.
Illustrated by Paul Galdone.
Harcourt, Brace & World, Inc.,
1958.

A ten-year-old boy's loyalties are torn between his brother in the Northern army and the memory of the Yankee invasion of his father's farm. The story of danger and suspense, courage, and the horrors of the "Brothers' War" unfolds with intense realism and excitement. Vividly portrayed are the hatred and meanness engendered by war, and the importance of exercising tolerance in dealings with others. The narrative is based on authentic

backgrounds and is well integrated with the suitable illustrations.

THE STAR-SPANGLED BANNER
Written by Neil and Anne Swanson.
Illustrated by Norman G. Rudolph.
Holt, Rinehart & Winston, Inc.,
1958.

Fourteen-year-old Lex is present at the thrilling moment when the words of the national anthem are living realities. He has come from captivity on a British ship to the *Surprise* where he encounters Francis Scott Key and from which he witnesses the bombardment of Fort McHenry. Momentous and rarely told incidents, such as the British burning of Washington in 1814, are brought into historical perspective in a dramatic and fast-moving story that thrills with suspense and excitement.

A YANKEE MUSKET
Written by Hildreth T. Wriston.
Illustrated by Jo Polseno. Abingdon
Press 1960.

Fort Ticonderoga and control of the Champlain-Hudson Valley are the prizes in this struggle of the American forces with the British, and the hero is young Stephen Tuttle. Stephen, the head of his family, is responsible for leading his mother and the two younger children to safety. War is a sadly maturing influence on the boy, and the story is written with great insight into the experience, making of Stephen a thoroughly sympathetic character.

LITTLE HOUSE IN THE BIG WOODS
Written by Laura Ingalls Wilder.
Illustrated by Garth Williams.
Harper & Row, Publishers, 1953.

This story, a first-hand telling of the experiences of the author and her family on the edge of the Big Woods in Wisconsin is a refreshing, genuinely enjoyable account of life in a log cabin. Incidents are chosen from experience with an accurate account the things in the daily doings of a family that are important and interesting to children. The muscular, earthy drawings reflect the vigor and strength characterizing this very real family of pioneers. Other titles in this series of Little House books are: *Little House on the Prairie*, *On the Banks of Plum Creek*, *By the Shores of Silver Lake*, *The Long Winter*, *Little Town on the Prairie*, *These Happy Golden Years*, and *Farmer Boy*.

For upper-grade children

LITTLE WOMEN
Written by Louisa M. Alcott.
Illustrated by Jessie Willcox Smith.
Little, Brown & Co., 1943.

A moving story in which four teen-age girls are featured. Reflecting the life and manners of their times, the four March sisters come alive as nineteenth century New England girls leading uneventful lives but with roots that run deep into American soil. The lifelike character studies of the March sisters mirror the dilemmas, fun, and pathos of family experience. Sentimentality runs high in this classic story of American girlhood but it is in keeping with the emotional period when girls first come in contact with this book. As a family chronicle, this plotless story honestly reveals everyday happenings with accurate details that mark the account as a social history of the nineteenth century. Like *The Adventures of Tom Sawyer* and *The Adventures of Huckleberry Finn*, *Little Women* has acquired historical significance through time as "historical realism."

DANIEL BOONE
Written by Esther Averill.
Illustrated by Feodor Rojankovsky.
Harper & Row, Publishers, 1945.

Copiously illustrated in color and black and white, this simply written book is infused with the adventure of the first settlers: their hardships and dangerous dealings with hostile Indians. The story covers Daniel Boone's life, his settlement and exploration of Kentucky, and his aid to and in defense of the settlers and their families. It is a book that does not shy away from the bloodier aspects of pioneer life but presents a sharply revealing picture of its realities.

VALIANT CAPTIVE
Written by Erick Berry. Chilton Books, 1962.

This is the story of Margaret Eames and her younger sister who are captured in 1676 by the Indians of the New Settlement, which was to become Framingham, Massachusetts, and of their trek to Canada where they are traded to the French. Although somewhat self-conscious in its re-creation of the period, the book gives a vivid intensity to the two sisters' struggle for existence and accurately describes life among the Indians. It is a fictionalized account of actual incidents that took place during King Philip's War.

CAPTIVES OF THE SENECAS
Written by John Brick. Duell, Sloan & Pearce, 1964.

In this exciting story, set in the early frontier days of America, the Seneca Indians capture several settlers. The narrative concerns the captives' struggles, endurance in captivity, and final escape. The illustrations add to the excitement of the story.

TREE OF FREEDOM
Written by Rebecca Caudill.
Illustrated by Dorothy B. Morse.
The Viking Press, Inc., 1949.

The Venables are a pioneer family of 1780 who move from California to Kentucky to find that the peace they had hoped to win is difficult to attain. The heroine is thirteen-year-old Stephanie Venable whose far-seeing vision about the issues of the Revolutionary War give her a surprising maturity. This story of family loyalty is told with rich humor and convincing drama. It is a story of hardship in the

wilderness, of action and near tragedy—
an altogether rewarding reading experience.

THE RED BADGE OF COURAGE
Written by Stephen Crane.
Appleton-Century-Crofts, 1895.

This is the great novel of the Civil War. It
is not a book of historically accurate
information—in fact, the hero is as confused as the reader will be by the vaguely
presented particulars of battles and issues—
but Crane's intention to present a "psychological portrayal of fear" is perfectly
consummated. Henry Flemming's experience of the war is a subtle metaphor of
redemption as he discovers the disparity
between the vainglorious dreams that
were his initial impulse in going to war
and the real ugliness and pettiness of
private fear, and as he learns to know the
humble nature of true heroism. It is a
true classic of the American literary
tradition.

DANIEL BOONE: PIONEER
Written and illustrated by James
Daugherty. The Viking Press, Inc.,
1939.

This fictionalized biography of the great
pioneer is a tribute to the heroism that
built America. An authentic pioneer
flavor permeates this book in which the
prose sings with virility and strength,
and the illustrations echo the vitality and
endurance that tamed the wilderness. It is
a genuinely beautiful book throughout,
and winner of the Newbery Award of
1940.

A SPY IN OLD NEW ORLEANS
Written by Anne Emery. Illustrated
by Emil Weiss. Rand McNally &
Co., 1960.

A fourteen-year-old boy, Ned, plays an
exciting role in the War of 1812 by helping to secure munitions for the army of
Jean Lafitte, one of the most controverisal
and truly colorful personalities in the
history of America. The story is based on

accurate historical knowledge of the period
and issues. Characters are well rounded,
and the tale unfolds with great dramatic
impact. Admirable illustrations add
further immediacy to the exciting events.

A SPY IN OLD PHILADELPHIA
Written by Anne Emery. Illustrated
by H. B. Vestal. Rand McNally &
Co., 1959.

Skillful plotting and suspenseful writing
characterize this book which centers on
young Johnny Monroe, a fervently patriotic boy, and his exploits in the crucial
first two years of the Revolutionary War.
Johnny suspects his father of being a Tory,
and he is envious of his brother's part in
the rebel fighting. It is an adventure story
rich in historical facts and absorbing in its
dramatic daring.

JOHNNY TREMAIN
Written by Esther Forbes. Illustrated
by Lynd Ward. Houghton Mifflin
Company, 1943.

This proud, gifted young man is one of
those characters in literature who have the
intensity of living people and whose very
vitality lifts them from fiction into real
life. An orphan, apprenticed to a Boston
silversmith at the age of fourteen, Johnny
lords it over his less talented fellow workers
until an accident incapacitates him as a
silversmith. His subsequent role in the
Revolutionary War, in which he develops
as a heroic, thoughtful youth, and his
eventual return to his silversmithing with
a cured hand makes an inspiring, unforgettable story. The book is written with
wit and humor and an uncanny insight
into the characters' personalities. It is
truly a literary masterpiece.

EARLY THUNDER
Written by Jean Fritz. Illustrated by
Lynd Ward. Coward-McCann, Inc.,
1967.

Salem just before the Revolution is a town
torn by the differences between Whig and
Tory. Young Daniel West, a member of a

family with Tory sympathies, tries to hold to his belief that freedom involves the right to differ. Events slowly push him toward the choice he must make. Daniel's struggle represents the problem many people in the American colonies faced in choosing between their desire to remain loyal to the King and their right to govern themselves. The illustrations of Lynd Ward add dimension to this excellent portrayal of a colonial town just prior to the start of the Revolutionary War.

THE SYCAMORE TREE

Written by Marion B. Havighurst.
World Publishing Co., 1960.

Teen-age Anne Rogers finds herself torn between loyalty to two brothers, one of whom is fighting in the Union Army, the other in that of the Confederacy. The story of the conflict that threatened the unity of the country and burdened the hearts of its citizens is told gracefully and with genuine feeling. The book brings to life the important issues as well as the personalities involved in the "Brothers' War." It is a book with dramatic impact and a source of vividly presented historical information.

ACROSS FIVE APRILS

Written by Irene Hunt. Follett
Publishing Company, 1964.

The story of Jethro Creighton, nine years old at the time of the attack on Fort Sumter, covers five years of the Civil War. Fragile Jethro takes on the responsibility of his family's Illinois farm when his brothers leave for the war and his father has a heart attack. The characterization is brilliant, making the development of the individuals far more interesting than the accounts of the war. It is written with insight and compassion for the torn loyalties suffered by families in the Civil War. It is a well-written historical novel, intriguing and beautiful—the deserved winner of the 1964 Charles W. Follett award.

DAWN AT LEXINGTON

Written by Nora Wood James.
Illustrated by Nedda Walker.
Longmans, Green & Co., Inc.,
1957.

The hero is young Jeremiah Cutler, a bookseller's apprentice, whose participation in the great battles of the American Revolution makes an exciting venture into this period in American history. It is an absorbing story that credibly and skillfully portrays momentous events in Boston, Cambridge, and New York. It is a fast-moving, action-packed adventure with a touch of romance and an abundance of historical incident.

RIFLES FOR WATIE

Written by Harold Keith. Illustrated
by Peter Burchard. Thomas Y.
Crowell Company, 1957.

General Stand Watie leads the Cherokee Indians in raids on the Union Army, and young Jefferson Davis Bussey, a Kansas farm boy, tries to learn where Watie is procuring his rifles. Much of the detail is gathered from actual journal accounts and veterans' reminiscences so that the view presented is one of authenticity and breadth. The political problems of the Indians themselves, as well as the issues of slavery and states' rights, are given dramatic representation in a book truly worthy of the Newbery Medal.

REBEL SIEGE

Written by Jim Kjelgaard.
Illustrated by Charles B. Wilson.
Holiday House, 1953.

At the Battle of King's Mountain, fourteen-year-old Kinross McKenzie and his father, a noted rifle maker, join the Carolina backwoodsmen in a valiant struggle with the British and Tory troops. The story of this brave father and son of the American Revolution is told with an accurate sense of the times and with great insight into the sympathies and impulses of the revolutionary Americans.

SPY IN WILLIAMSBURG
Written by Isabelle Lawrence.
Illustrated by Manning De V. Lee.
Rand McNally & Co., 1956.

A masterful job is done of marrying fact to fiction in this mystery story of pre-revolutionary Virginia. The blacksmith hero is a fully realized character, and the feelings rampant in Virginia in the days just previous to the Revolutionary War are portrayed in an accurate and colorful narrative. The black-and-white illustrations admirably combine with the imaginative writing to bring this thrilling period in American history to life.

YANKEE DOODLE BOY
Written by Joseph Plumb Martin.
Illustrated by Victor Mays.
William R. Scott, Inc., 1965.

This is a poignant, vividly told story of a young soldier's reminiscences of the American Revolutionary War. His story is presented against an authentic background and is told movingly. Robust illustrations round out this clear picture of Revolutionary times and personalities.

TITUBA OF SALEM VILLAGE
Written by Ann Petry. Thomas Y.
Crowell Company, 1964.

This brilliant novel, set in the demented witch-hunting Salem Village of 1692, tells of the bigotry that pursued an innocent Negro, Tituba, until she suspected herself guilty of the incredible charge of witchcraft. The timely implications cannot be mistaken. Tituba is drawn with great simplicity, and she emerges as a person of profound spiritual beauty. This fictionalized biography of the Negro woman and her husband, John Indian, from the day they were sold in Barbados, through their years in the Puritan home of Reverend Samuel Parris, to the final Salem witchcraft trials gives important insights into the workings of the bigoted mind and the tragedy of molested innocence.

THE LIGHT IN THE FOREST
Written by Conrad Richter. Alfred
A. Knopf, Inc., 1953.

In a book of refreshing charm and simplicity the story is told of the conflicting loyalties experienced by a fifteen-year-old white boy, John Butler. It is the story of John's rescue from the Delaware Indians who captured him as a child and with whom he has lived for eleven years. He attempts to return to the Indian family he has inevitably learned to love. The contrast between the civilized life of white society and the natural life of the Indians is vividly portrayed. It is an accurate presentation of Indian life told with a genuine passion for nature and with deep sympathy for the hero's plight.

THE WITCH OF BLACKBIRD POND
Written by Elizabeth G. Speare.
Houghton Mifflin Company, 1958.

The story centers on a little girl's brave rebellion against her puritanical environment and the bigotry of her people in colonial Connecticut. The heavy atmosphere of Puritan witch-hunting is dramatically presented in a narrative characterized by strong plot and fully developed characters. The historical background of colonial New England is vividly drawn in this excellent historical novel which won the Newbery Medal.

RAILROAD TO FREEDOM
Written by Hildegard Swift.
Illustrated by James Daugherty.
Harcourt, Brace & World, Inc.,
1932.

This is a fine, spirited account of the life of Harriet Tubman, a Negro girl and escaped slave who became a conductor in the underground railroad and led over three hundred Negroes up from slavery. Her story up to the time of the Civil War is told in a style characterized by simplicity and a touch of poetry that catches the nobility of the life portrayed. Illustrations capture the tension between bound and free and heighten the over-all magnetism of this exciting book.

THE ADVENTURES OF TOM SAWYER and THE ADVENTURES OF HUCKLEBERRY FINN
Written by Mark Twain, pseud. for Samuel Clemens. Illustrated by Norman Rockwell. Heritage Press, 1952.

Portraying American boyhood of a century ago, these glorious tales are exciting adventures along the Mississippi. Vigorous, original writing marks these books of a great American writer who has created the young immortals Tom Sawyer and Huck Finn. Spanning American life among respectable and less respectable groups, Twain covers a broad spectrum of society yet avoids lurid details. Here humor and excitement blend as decent codes of life emerge throughout the stories. Passage of time has given an aura of history to these realistically drawn adventures.

MASSACRE AT SAND CREEK
Written by Irving Werstein.
Charles Scribner's Sons, 1963.

The white man's betrayal of the Indians is caught in the account of an actual United States Cavalry troop that brutally attacked a Cheyenne camp during the Civil War after having signed a peace treaty. It is a timely story, centered on the character of the ambitious man who led the attack. His politics come from a wellspring of hate and intolerance. This historically accurate book conveys an invaluable message for modern children.

STORIES OF PRIMITIVE LIFE

For younger children

IN MY MOTHER'S HOUSE
Written by Ann Nolan Clark.
Illustrated by Velino Herrera. The Viking Press, Inc., 1941.
Describing accurately the life of Indian

children near Santa Fe, this book is distinguished by poetic text and masterfully done illustrations. Dignity of language communicates the ordered life of the pueblo people. Based on a complete understanding of Indian life and art, the rhythmic text and pictures preserve the color, beauty, and peace of Indian life in the West.

RIEMA: LITTLE BROWN GIRL OF JAVA
Written by Kathleen Morrow Elliot, Illustrated by Roger Duvoisin.
Alfred A. Knopf, Inc., 1937.
Presenting Javanese life in distinctive text and pictures, this beautiful book gives accurate, authentic details of primitive peoples against tropical backgrounds of lush vegetation, sun, and sea. A companion book to *Soomoon*, this one is told from a girl's point of view. *Jo-Yo's Idea*, another book by this author, tells about a festival in the South Sea Islands.

SOOMOON: BOY OF BALI
Written by Kathleen Morrow Elliot.
Illustrated by Roger Duvoisin.
Alfred A. Knopf, Inc., 1938.
A Balinese tale depicting Hindu temples, deities, mud huts, fighting cocks, and fiery volcanoes. Running through the authentic details is the story of an orphan boy through whom one sees the primitive customs and way of life that have existed for centuries in the South Seas. The boy's adventures may not point up momentous events or important historical characters, yet Soomoon, his white cock, and the brilliant end of this journey provide glimpses of primitive peoples and events that make up their own Balinese history.

KINTU: A CONGO ADVENTURE
Written and illustrated by Elizabeth Enright. Holt, Rinehart & Winston, Inc., 1935.
This sensitive story about Kintu, the son of an African Congo chief, deals with the aspirations of an eldest son who will be chief one day. He must become skilled in

many things: shooting with a bow and arrow, dancing the devil dances for rain and good hunting, playing the drums to send messages across the villages, and throwing the lethal spears with faultless marksmanship. Authentic details of primitive life are presented with clarity, liveliness, and historical value.

GREAT DAY IN GHANA: KWASI
GOES TO TOWN
Written by Geraldine Kaye.
Illustrated by Valerie Herbst.
Abelard–Schuman Limited, 1962.

The theme of freedom and justice underlies this gaily illustrated story of a boy in Ghana who must visit his grandmother on Independence Day. All the gala festivities of music, dancing, sailing, and a night full of fireworks heighten the excitement of the little boy's day. Story and pictures provide a vivid, authentic glimpse of life in Ghana today and a reflection of the movement that freed a primitive society.

BOY OF THE ISLANDS
Written by William Lipkind.
Illustrated by Nicolas Mordvinoff.
Harcourt, Brace & World, Inc.,
1954.

A well-told story of a Hawaiian boy, Lua, with a background that stretches back to before the white man. Anthropological details flesh in the skeleton of the story as the author provides glimpses of primitive life through a boy's participation in sports, tribal voyages, and the training of a chieftain. Recreating the spirit of the people in terms of their social and religious traditions and with well-chosen episodes, including a suspenseful escape, this book stands out as an authentic account of a disappearing way of life.

BOY WITH A HARPOON
Written by William Lipkind.
Illustrated by Nicolas Mordvinoff.
Harcourt, Brace & World, Inc.,
1952.

This story in text and pictures about an Eskimo boy and a little seal in the northern part of Alaska serves as the structure for accurate, convincing information about the Eskimo people whose primitive mode of living is rapidly·being eliminated by technological developments. While preserving the picture of a fading way of life in the North, the book also spins a charming story of how a little boy wins the right to go on a whale hunt with the mature males in the village.

THE CORN GROWS RIPE
Written by Dorothy Rhoads.
Illustrated by Jean Charlot. The
Viking Press, Inc., 1956.

This marvelous blend of story and pictures tells of a momentous year in a boy's life. Stunned by his father's death, he grows up suddenly to become man of his family. Woven through the story are the ancient customs, ceremonial festivals, and religious traditions of the historic Mayan Indians of Yucatan. Full of the drama of seasons and superstitions, this book shows the grace and strength, the magic and faith, the human interest details of the Mayas and their surroundings.

THE GOLDEN FROG
Written by Anico Surany.
Illustrated by Leonard E. Fisher. G. P.
Putnam's Sons, 1963.

This is the story of Aurelio, a small Indian boy whose home is the island of Mulatuppu, off the Panamanian coast. Aurelio's wish, to help raise money for a village trading vessel and to give an original gift, is told with verve and blazing color. Based on a historic move to establish trade relationships between San Blas Islanders, this picture storybook dips into a legendary past for its supply of ceremonial artifacts and primitive traditions.

For intermediate-grade children

WATERLESS MOUNTAIN
Written by Laura Adams Armer.

Illustrated by Sidney Armer and Laura Adams Armer. Longmans, Green & Co., Inc., 1931.

An unusual story of Navajo Indian life. A boy makes new songs for himself by listening to and learning from the songs of the medicine men. The tribal customs and beliefs are wonderfully woven into the fabric of the narrative. The story reveals the innate desire of the Indian for mysticism and his love of beauty. This story of a Navajo poet and his search for beauty is superbly written and filled with comparable pictures.

VALIANT CAPTIVE
Written by Erick Berry. Chilton Books, 1962.

This story is based on the true account of Margaret Eames and her little sister who were captured by the Indians from the New Settlement during King Philip's War in 1676. After a long trek to Canada, they are traded to the French. For the most part, the story moves swiftly and with excitement. Life among the Indians is vividly described, yet the book lacks a certain emotional intensity because the conclusion is rather weak.

HAH-NEE OF THE CLIFF DWELLERS
Written and illustrated by Mary and Conrad Buff. Houghton Mifflin Company, 1957.

The life of thirteenth-century Ute Indians in the Southwest is depicted through the story of Hah-Nee, a youth who is rescued and reared by a neighboring tribe. Authentically documented, the book presents a down-to-earth picture of the drought that compels the cliff dwellers to abandon their ancestral homes and seek sanctuary further south. The authors' finely drawn lithographs and smooth, effective writing help spice this refreshing account of pre-Columbian times in the United States.

VIKING ADVENTURE
Written by Clyde Robert Bulla.

Illustrated by Douglas Gorsline. Thomas Y. Crowell Company, 1963.

Sigurd is a young Viking boy who is being trained for his adventurous voyage aboard a Viking ship. The story describes the rigorous training he receives and the long voyage to Wineland (America) during which Sigurd's endurance is put to the test many times. The story is easy reading and dramatic, with illustrations that heighten the excitement of a unique voyage.

SECRET OF THE ANDES
Written by Ann Nolan Clark. Illustrated by Jean Charlot. The Viking Press, Inc., 1952.

An Inca Indian boy named Cudi helps an old Indian herder guard the precious and irreplaceable flock of llamas while learning the traditions and folklore of his people. The site is a high valley in the Peruvian mountains, which is hidden from the rest of the world. The mystic Incan songs appeal to young readers touched by the beauty and power of the book. The descriptions of the unvisited grandeur of the high Andes are made vibrant by the art work. Awarded the Newbery Medal.

ISLAND OF THE BLUE DOLPHINS
Written by Scott O'Dell. Houghton Mifflin Company, 1960.

Based on historical fact, the story is told of a Ghalas-at Indian girl marooned on an island for eighteen years. Resourcefully she learns to protect herself and to perform the tasks necessary for survival. She tames some of the wildlife and even brings a measure of beauty into her otherwise desolate existence. Graced with truth and tenderness, this book depicts a unique remnant of a lost tribe. Her greatness of spirit transforms drudgery and loneliness into a moving experience in a well-written book that earned the Newbery Medal.

THE FIRST LAKE DWELLERS
Written by Chester G. Osborne.
Illustrated by Richard A. Osborne.
Ambassador Books, Ltd., 1956.

The precious breath of life is the essence of this powerfully characterized story. A crude Neolithic village is destroyed by Warth and his fierce warriors. The young hero, Arvi, loses contact with his father and conceives a daring plan for his family's survival. His father escapes from Warth and recognizes the unique value of the plan, developing from it a new concept for community living. They become lake dwellers, work for the common good, and defeat the enemy. An exciting tale, it mingles historic fact with fiction in a delightful way.

CALL IT COURAGE
Written and illustrated by Armstrong Sperry. The Macmillan Company, 1940.

Mafatu is a Polynesian boy who has feared the sea since childhood in direct contrast to his society's worship of courage. Mafatu is driven from his native home by indifference, which at times can be worse than violence. This legendary tale goes on to show how Mafatu, traveling alone, overcomes his fear and grows into Mafatu, "Stout Heart." Even today the people of Hikueru sit around their evening campfires and retell this story of how a former tribal member was able to conquer his deepest fear. A Newbery Medal winner.

For upper-grade children

WHITE FALCON
Written by Elliot Arnold. Illustrated by Frederick T. Chapman. Alfred A. Knopf, Inc., 1955.

John Tanner is kidnapped from his Kentucky home by the Chippewa Indians in the late 1770's and taken to Canada where he becomes the adopted son of the chieftess of the tribe. Later he becomes White Falcon, leader of the tribe, and helps The Northwest Company defeat the Hudson Bay Company is a struggle for the for trade. The story is based on true incidents and has the vigor of narrative, depth of understanding, and knowledge of Indian life that make a stirring tale of historical adventure.

THE LAST OF THE MOHICANS
Written by James Fenimore Cooper. Illustrated by N. C. Wyeth. Charles Scribner's Sons, 1826; 1919.

This wonderful American classic was first published in 1826. It is the story of Indian and frontier life during the French and Indian Wars in central and western New York State. This is the second in the series of The Leatherstocking Tales. Two daughters of General Munro have escaped a massacre at Fort Henry but have been captured by the Indian Magua. Hawkeye (the Leatherstocking of the series), with his Indian friends Uncas and Chingachgook, attempts to rescue the captives. This is an exciting tale of rescue, escape, and pursuit set among American Indians of colonial days.

HAKON OF ROGEN'S SAGA
Written by Erik Christian Haugaard. Illustrated by Leo and Diane Dillon. Houghton Mifflin Company, 1963.

Hakon of Rogen is a thirteen-year-old prince of the island of Rogen in Norway. After his father's death, he is put under the watchful eye of his uncle whose aim is to kill Hakon and gain permanent possession of the island. Learning of this, the young prince flees to the hills and, together with many loyal followers, regains his birthright. The character of Hakon grows and matures as he struggles for his life and identity. The story has the suspense of a Norse saga during the Viking period and is beautifully illustrated by the Dillons.

ARROW IN THE SUN

*Written and illustrated by Carl
Kidwell. The Viking Press, Inc.,
1962.*

Netzah is a fourteen-year-old prince of the
Acolhuans of ancient Mexico. With the
help of his uncle, he is taught patience in
waiting for the opportune time to avenge
the death of his father. To die for his
people, although noble, would be of no
lasting value to them. They need him alive,
not dead. The illustrations give the reader
a strong sense of this historic past.

FIRE-HUNTER

*Written by Jim Kjelgaard. Illustrated
by Ralph Ray. Holiday House, 1951.*

Hawk is a member of a wandering prehistoric tribe. As a young spearman he
displeases the rest of the tribe by not
following their customs and is cast out
into the wilderness. Comforted by a
young girl who is also abandoned because
of an injury, the boy manages to survive
by bringing ingenuity and adventure
into his experience. Careful illustrations
give the young reader a deep understanding of what primitive life must have been
like.

WOLF BROTHER

*Written by Jim Kjelgaard. Holiday
House, 1957.*

The story is centered on a sixteen-year-
old Apache Indian of the late nineteenth
century who has spent six years at a
Jesuit school. When he returns to his home
on an Arizona Indian reservation, he experiences brutality and injustice. Aligning
himself with an Indian outlaw, Cross
Face, the young Apache is pitted against
a well-equipped army. The story stresses
the Indians' point of view and calls up
sympathetic understanding for the brave
Apaches.

THE STONE DAGGERS

*Written by Paul Lauring. Illustrated
by Ib Spang Olsen. The Macmillan
Company, 1965.*

This prize-winning book is set in the
Bronze Age and tells of the struggle of
a thirteen-year-old brother and sister
with slave traders. The story goes on to
describe how the two children fend for
themselves in this primitive era.

LAST HORIZON

*Written by Reginald Maddok.
Illustrated by Douglas Relf.
Thomas Nelson & Sons, 1961.*

In this engrossing tale of a lost and forgotten people in a bygone era, the
characters and setting are uniquely developed. The story is centered on the heroic
leadership of Jonny Strong Arm. He
leads his people, the Bushmen, in defense
of the Boers for the last time. After their
defeat, they withdraw to the Kalahari
desert. The vigorous narrative is charged
with a real feeling for the beauty of antiquity and for the vastness of the desert.

BLACK FIRE

*Written by Covelle Newcomb.
Illustrated by Avery Johnson.
Longmans, Green & Co., Inc., 1940.*

This is an informative, brisk account of
the life of Henri Christophe who became
the first king of Haiti. Adventure is
splashed throughout a biography that is
completely absorbing. The problems Henri
encounters as a slave, the struggles to
free his people, his eminent successes,
and, finally, his demise are all skillfully
handled. Excellent illustrations add flavor
to this well-done narrative.

WARRIOR SCARLET

*Written by Rosemary Sutcliff.
Illustrated by Charles Keeping.
Henry Z. Walck, Inc., Publishers,
1958.*

Drem's crippled arm keeps him from at-
taining the symbol of manhood in his
tribe, the "Warrior Scarlet," won by
killing a wolf. Drem is forced to leave the
tribe and live with The Little Dark People
of the hills as an outcast until in unexpected
circumstances he is able to prove himself
a man and a warrior. This story, set in the
Bronze Age of southern England around

the year 900 B.C., is an exciting and well-written story with excellent descriptions of life in that era. The characters are real and the story is moving. The illustrations interpret the mood of the times and harmonize beautifully with the text.

STORIES OF ANCIENT CIVILIZATIONS

For younger children

MASTER OF THE ROYAL CATS
Told by Jerzy Laskowski.
Illustrated by Janina Domanska.
Seabury Press, Inc., 1965.

A lovely picture storybook drawn from ancient Egyptian art and with storytelling elements to convince a young reader that this imaginative account set in the Egypt of the Pharaohs might have taken place. Archaeologically flavored illustrations convey the aura of wealth, the impact of Pharaonic power, the role of animals, and, above all, the ingenuity of a small boy named Anpu in telling of how the Egyptians first domesticated the cat for use as a rat chaser. Although the text is somewhat awkward, the pictures are drawn with simplicity and beauty to distinguish *Master of the Royal Cats* as a picture storybook of rare charm.

For intermediate-grade children

SONS OF THE STEPPE
Written by Hans Baumann.
Illustrated by Heiner Rothfuchs.
Henry Z. Walck, Inc.,
Publishers, 1958.

This is the story of two grandsons of Genghis Kahn who are being carefully trained in the art of war and to be relentless, unfeeling, unquestioning conquerors of their enemies. Arik-Buka embraces the cruel life of the warrior, but Kublai slowly comes to abhor the constant pursuit of enemies and desires to learn and practice the art of peace. This brings him into conflict with his brother and with all the old established traditions of the Mongols. This is an engrossing and thought-provoking book. It is the compelling story of the conflict a boy faces when he tries to discover for himself the important values in life. There is a subtle character study of the two princes in a book distinguished by historical accuracy and a swiftly flowing plot.

OMEN OF THE BIRDS
Written and illustrated by Harry Behn. World Publishing Co., 1964.

Set in the Etruscan Golden Age, this story of the young lovers Caele (later the first Etruscan king of Rome) and Tanaquil, his queen-to-be, promises to enchant children of the intermediate grades. Combining legend and prophesy with archaeology, Mr. Behn's simple and subtle tale, complemented by his own beautiful and suitable drawings, is provocative and intriguing.

STORIES FROM HERODOTUS
Written by Glanville Downey.
Illustrated by Enrico Arno. E. P. Dutton & Co., Inc., 1965.

Giving a historic panorama of ancient Greece during the Persian invasion—an important period in determining the fate of Western civilization, and including the battles of Marathon, Thermopylae, and the sea encounter at Salamis—these three lively and popular tales of Croesus, Darius, and Xerxes have been selected and almost literally translated from the works of the ancient historian Herodotus. Mr. Downey retells them simply, in modern language—but without paraphrasing or losing the flavor of the detailed, animated, and personal anecdotes of the original. Presented in handsome format, visualized by Enrico Arno in stylized drawings that resemble Greek vase-paintings, and with a glossary and fine reference map, this book is geared to interest young people.

NIKO: SCULPTOR'S APPRENTICE
Written by Isabelle Lawrence.
Illustrated by Arthur Marokovia. The
Viking Press, Inc., 1956.

Niko, a young apprentice to the sculptor Phidias in ancient Greece, comes to have a small part in creating the figures of the Parthenon in this brisk narrative that is informative, intimate, and a good picture of one aspect of the Golden Age.

FORGOTTEN DAUGHTER
Written by Caroline Snedeker.
Illustrated by Dorothy Lathrop.
Doubleday & Company, Inc.,
1933.

An interest in Greek and Roman history might be awakened by this stirring, imaginative book about a young girl, Chloe, who spends her childhood in slavery and exile and then meets and comes to love Aulus Gracchus. The plot, set in Rome, ends with Chloe returning to her father's home, leaving her grim way of life behind her. Dorothy Lathrop's pictures suggest Greek vase-paintings, most appropriate to the text.

A TRIUMPH FOR FLAVIUS
Written by Caroline Snedeker.
Illustrated by Cedric Rogers. Lothrop,
Lee & Shepard Co., Inc., 1955.

A well-written, easy-to-read short story about a Roman boy, Flavius, and his Greek teacher-slave Ariphron. Barriers that normally exist between master and personal slave give way when the two come to understand and love one another. This dramatic tale is set in ancient Rome, which is portrayed colorfully and in well-documented detail. Cedric Rogers' wash-drawings are stunning and full of action, and the type is large and especially fine.

THE WINDSWEPT CITY: A NOVEL
OF THE TROJAN WAR
Written by Henry Treece.
Illustrated by Faith Jaques.
Meredith Press, 1968.

This is a dramatic retelling of an ancient conflict between the Greeks and the Trojans. In this case the events are seen through the eyes of Asterius, a slave to the now sick and aging Helen of Troy. And through the lyrical narrative stride the immortal heroes Odysseus, Hector, Achilles, Agamemnon displaying that measure of humanity that makes their fate all the more tragic.

HITTITE WARRIOR
Written by Joanne Williamson.
Alfred A. Knopf, Inc., 1960.

A good book for introducing children to the earliest history of the Bible lands. Based on the story of Uriah of the Old Testament, historical fact and archaeological detail convincingly re-create an ancient period and culture in a complicated story of the Hittite Uriah's adventures with the Canaanite army and his acceptance of the Israelite nation and their God.

For upper-grade children

THE TREASURE OF TENAKERTOM
Written by Robert E. Alter.
Illustrated by Frank Aloise. G. P.
Putnam's Sons, 1964.

In ancient Egypt, Kemheb is rescued from bandits. He and his rescuer, a young soldier of Tutankhamon, then join in the exciting search for the lost city of Tenakertom.

I MARCHED WITH HANNIBAL
Written by Hans Baumann.
Illustrated by Ulrik Schramm.
Henry Z. Walck, Inc., Publishers,
1962.

A historical novel, a portrait of the ruthless warrior-leader Hannibal, an attack on war and conquest, a thirteen-year-old boy's fighting adventures and sufferings, and an informative account of the use and psychology of elephants come together in one complex book. The story, however, is mainly about a mystical sort of love relationship between a boy and his elephant (who is the real hero of this legend) and their dangerous journey over the Alps with the daring Hannibal who alternately merits suspicion, admiration, and hatred from the boy. It was Hannibal's armies that killed his family and destroyed his home in Spain, and to those ruins he finally returns as an old man.

THE PRINCESS AND THE LION
Written by Elizabeth Coatsworth.
Illustrated by Evaline Ness.
Pantheon Books, Inc., 1963.

A young princess named Miriam plots her brother's escape from prison in Abyssinia. By a strange twist of events, she finds out that her brother is heir to the throne and will soon be the next king. Now her task is to reach her brother and prevent him from escaping and possibly losing his life. The story is based on historical fact. The double-page illustrations are very powerful.

THE EXPLOITS OF XENOPHON
Written by Geoffrey Household.
Illustrated by Leonard Everett
Fisher. Random House, Inc., 1955.

A distillation of Xenophon's classic "Anabasis," retold and condensed to one-quarter of its length, this version for younger readers is effectively illustrated and includes maps for reference. It is a recount of a heroic and disciplined Greek army that, although unable to reach Persia, returned through a thousand miles of enemy territory in order to get back to the homeland. This volume is a magnificent study in ancient history.

AUGUSTUS CAESAR'S WORLD
Written and illustrated by Genevieve
Foster. Charles Scribner's Sons, 1947.

The life and times of Augustus, first emperor of Rome, and the world he lived in—its political philosophies and movement, its social forces and events, its varied religious sects—is told here with dramatic flair. The period of that civilization (44 B.C. to A.D. 14) is clearly and effectively presented in Mrs. Foster's verbal and visual images, and in her drawings and designs.

THE LION IN THE GATEWAY
Written by Mary Renault.
Illustrated by C. Walter Hodges.
Harper & Row, Publishers, 1964.

An outstandingly dramatic and well-written historical account of three famous battles in the Greek and Persian Wars: Marathon, Salamis, and Thermopylae. The author depicts the richness and splendor of Persia, the beauty and pride of Greece, the heroic stature of men from both armies, and the stirring action and strategy of the battles. But the deepest message of the book is found in its conclusion: had the Greeks lost their country to Persia, democratic forms of government and justice and freedom would never have been developed— and so, our Western civilization today might never have happened.

THE BRONZE BOW
Written by Elizabeth G. Speare.
Houghton Mifflin Company, 1961.

Daniel of Galilee joins a brave underground movement that is concentrated on "bending" the bronze bow of Rome. After his parents' crucifixion and its effects on his sister Leah, the embittered Daniel promises vengeance against the hated and feared Romans. But the boy's blind anger is gradually turned to love with his introduction and exposure to the teacher-prophet Jesus. For young readers whose prejudices are not yet formed, this powerful story of David's growth and change, and the influences on his life, presents its message without any overtones of preaching. This memorable tale from the Bible is presented in the reality of its era and is a most significant piece today.

EAGLE OF THE NINTH
Written by Rosemary Sutcliff.
Illustrated by C. Walter Hodges.

Henry Z. Walck, Inc., Publishers,
1954.

A young Roman soldier searches for his father's lost Ninth Legion, which carries the eagle standard as a symbol of honor. They have mysteriously disappeared in the wilderness of Britain (in that area which is Scotland today). The story of the determined boy's sleuthing and tracking down of his father is a distinctive one, and the author, in her scholarly way, vividly re-creates that period of history.

PIANKHY THE GREAT
Written and illustrated by E.
Harper Johnson. Thomas Nelson
& Sons, 1962.

E. Harper Johnson takes the reader back to the mysterious country of Egypt during the years 744–712 B.C. The story is an authentic one of the king who ruled in the Nubian Valley of the Nile during those years. The author's own illustrations lend a historical authenticity to the vivid text.

THE HONORABLE SWORD
Written by M. D. Lewis. Houghton
Mifflin Company, 1960.

Two young boys are the lone survivors of castle defenders in feudal Japan. There are many narrow escapes in their attempt to sneak through enemy lines to reach their leader, the Shogun. During the fighting the ancient and revered sword of Nippon was given over to the besiegers rather than let it be destroyed by fire. The adventure deepens when the two young men of thirteen resolve to reclaim the sword. The story is well written and based on historical fact.

THE GOLDEN GOBLET
Written by Eloise Jarvis McGraw.
Coward-McCann, Inc., 1961.

The theft of a golden goblet from a pharaoh's tomb and the ensuing story of a stone-cutter's apprentice who finally finds his life's dream presents life in ancient Egypt. The goldsmith's craft of making rare and treasured objects for tombs and the religious beliefs and customs are described. Portrayal of everyday affairs of the era, as well as of people and settings, is detailed and realistic.

MARA, DAUGHTER OF THE NILE
Written by Eloise Jarvis McGraw.
Coward-McCann, Inc., 1953.

This swiftly paced and engrossing book about a young slave girl of Thebes who is involved in dangerous espionage reads like an ancient Egyptian mystery-thriller. The heroine Mara acts as spy and interpreter for a nobleman who helps restore Thutmose III, half-brother and rival of Queen Hatshepsut, to his rightful place on the throne. Mara's own love story is unusual, for she marries into nobility. Egypt of that age becomes almost three-dimensional through the author's colorful descriptions of settings, costumes, details of daily life, and dialogues full of rich images. Recommended especially for older girls.

STORIES OF LIFE IN THE MIDDLE AGES AND MODERN TIMES

For younger children

THE FRIENDLY BEASTS
Adapted by Laura Nelson Baker.
Illustrated by Nicolas Sidjakov.
Parnassus Press, 1959.

A fine adaptation of a medieval story based on the Christ Child's birth in a stable. Humbly the animals—"sheep with curly horn," "cow all red and white," and "the doves from the rafters high"—decide to present the Baby with a gift. Their practical ideas afford warm comfort for the tiny Christ Child. "Thus every beast, proudly and well . . . sang a song to tell of the gift he was giving Emanuel." Illuminating the text are jewel-colored illustrations that resemble stained-glass windows.

THE LITTLE JUGGLER
Written and illustrated by Barbara
Cooney. Hastings House Publishers,
Inc., 1961.

As an adaptation of an old French legend of the Middle Ages, this story is touched with poetry and medieval richness. Sharp, detailed drawings in color and black and white support the singing text of a young juggler's devotion and reward. Without pointing up momentous events or historical characters, the story stands as a lovely example that depicts a way of life in the Middle Ages.

THE LOST DRAGON OF WESSEX
Written by Gwendolyn Bowers.
Illustrated by Charles Geer. Oxford
University Press, 1957.

Calling up visions of King Arthur and tales of the Round Table, the author entices the reader with a legendary prophecy. It concerns an armband worn by an orphan boy, Wulf, at court in the times of Alfred the Great. This enthralling story clearly depicts court life, customs, and ceremonies of the period. Children can readily gain a deeper understanding of life in the days of King Arthur.

ST. JEROME AND THE LION
Told by Rumer Godden. Illustrated
by Jean Primrose. The Viking Press,
Inc., 1961.

Beautiful details of monastic life are teamed with convincing characters in a gentle story of St. Jerome and a lion. Combining medieval beauty with poetic grace, cadenced verses reveal devotion, humility, and obedience in rare combination. Select facts about the saint reverently tell a tale of the man whose devotion to a lion has become a legend. The writing effectively captures the flavor of life in a monastery.

For intermediate-grade children

THE APPLE AND THE ARROW
Written by Mary and Conrad Buff.
Illustrated by the authors. Houghton
Mifflin Conpany, 1961.

In a beautifully illustrated book with many color and pencil sketches, the Buffs recount the William Tell story from the point of view of eleven-year-old Walter, who had faith enough to stand perfectly still while his father shot at the apple on his head. Though set in 1291, this timely, moving story of the Swiss struggle for freedom is told with freshness and integrity.

JON, THE UNLUCKY
Written by Elizabeth Coatsworth.
Illustrated by Esta Nesbitt. Holt,
Rinehart & Winston, Inc., 1964.

Jon, a young Dane orphaned at the age of nine, after hardships and wanderings, discovers a hidden valley where the descendants of Leif the Lucky dwell. Literate Jon takes the place of the last scholar in the valley and eventually solves the problem of his survival. Told with verve, tension, and power, the book also demonstrates a solid grasp of character. Watercolor illustrations complement the lucid text.

THE DOOR IN THE WALL
Written by Marguerite de Angeli.
Illustrated by the author. Doubleday
& Company, Inc., 1949.

Set in the Middle Ages, the sufferings and successes of a crippled castle page make for an entertaining story ideally suited for intermediate-age children. One can easily identify with the youth as he courageously saves the castle from the besieging Welsh. Moreover, the interesting and colorful illustrations complement the story because they are done in fine, graphic style. Feeling for pageantry and historic events permits the reader to gain a sense of this period in history.

BLACK FOX OF LORNE
Written by Marguerite de Angeli.
Illustrated by the author. Doubleday
& Company, Inc., 1957.

Internecine strife between tenth century Scot and invading Saxon is the background of this absorbing tale. Into this setting, identical twin sons of a lord are involved in a struggle for survival. Separated by a sea disaster, one of the boys is taken prisoner. The reader is captivated by the manner in which the twins take each other's place, effect escape, and defeat Gewin, the sinister Black Fox of Lorne. Good story, beautiful illustrations, and fast-moving text make the novel easy and entertaining reading.

NACAR, THE WHITE DEER
Written by Elizabeth Borton de Trevino. Illustrated by Enrico Arno. Farrar, Straus & Giroux, Inc., 1966.

Based on historical facts from the seventeenth century, this tender tale tells of a white deer from the Orient who arrives in Mexico too ill to travel any more. A little mute herder ministers to the deer to restore him to health. A keen understanding of animals is revealed in this well-written story. By the author of the award-winning *I, Juan de Pareja*.

ESCAPE FROM MOSCOW
Written by Constantine Georgiou. Illustrated by Enrico Arno. American Book Company, 1963.

Czarist splendor mingled with Bolshevik uprisings form the background for this story of escape, intrigue, and courage. Full of local color and details of life in an exciting period of Russian history, the book traces the flight of a noble family from the Palace of Facets in the Kremlin past many historic landmarks, momentous events, gypsies, the billowy wheatfields of the Ukraine, and into safety. Glowing touches of Byzantine influence are interspersed with views of serfdom and the unrest of the period.

THE ARK
Written by Margot Benary-Isbert. Translated by Clara and Richard Winston. Harcourt, Brace & World, Inc., 1953.

Based on the author's own experiences during the forties, a heart-felt and sympathetic story unfolds concerning the tribulations an uprooted East German family encounters in fashioning a new life in West Germany. Personalities are in sharp focus and the four youngsters assume identities almost like children next door. The book presents a clear picture of war-torn Europe and displaced persons.

RASMUS AND THE VAGABOND
Written by Astrid Lindgren. Illustrated by Eric Palmquist. The Viking Press, Inc., 1960.

Set against the Swedish countryside of long ago, this adventure story follows an orphan, Rasmus, in search of someone who wants a boy with straight hair. Filled with excitement and a gallery of interesting characters, this appealing book is graced with truth.

A MIRACLE FOR MEXICO
Written by Josefina Niggli. Illustrated by Alejandro Rangel Hidalgo. New York Graphic Society, 1964.

This historical novel, involving a complex, violent plot set in the Mexcio of 1531, interweaves the politics of Cortez with the story of a humble Mexican boy affected by the Miracle of the Virgin of Guadalupe. Historical and emotional contact are quickly made. Nevertheless, the plot is demanding and interest is not easily sustained. The illustrations paint the times excellently and express a feeling of authenticity.

THE TREASURE TROVE OF THE SUN
Adapted by M. Prishvin. Illustrated by Feodor Rojankovsky. The Viking Press, Inc., 1952.

A home-spun story about two children in Russia who discover the swampland and its vegetation and the wildlife of field and pond. The superstition and beliefs, foods and clothing of a fading way of life are captured in this unusual book decorated with lovely art.

MEN OF IRON
Written and illustrated by Howard
Pyle. Harper & Row, Publishers,
1930.

The story portrays a knight's life in four-teenth-century Britain. The reader finds himself a part of the life in the great castles of that era. The authenticity in which the author reveals the training of young nobles for knighthood during the days of Henry IV of England is exemplary. Prince Hal, who later becomes King Henry V, and other historical characters give the story an authentic historical background.

BLACK TOWERS
Written by E. K. Smith. Illustrated
by Nancy Sager. Vanguard Press,
1957.

Two little brothers are knee-deep in fifteenth-century English palace intrigue. Embroiled in events beyond their control, these children of the Queen seek a sanc-tuary. Their reactions to danger are child-like and believable. The happenings are seen through the boys' eyes, and this adds dimension and reality to the story. Vivid impressions remain from the book's text and illustrations.

THE MAN WITH TWO COUNTRIES
Written by James Playsted Wood.
The Seabury Press, 1967.

This is a well-written historical novel of the dark conflict between England and Ireland. Neatly turned phrases, precise character delineations, and sound historical details flesh out the skeleton of a story "as old as the world" where one man or na-tion desires and pursues what some other man or nation would keep at considerable sacrifice. Without falsifying history's fundamental record, the story is told with drama and suspense and with all the other elements of a classic.

For upper-grade children

THE SWORD IN THE TREE
Written by Clyde Robert Bulla.

Illustrated by Paul Galdone.
Thomas Y. Crowell Company,
1956.

An eleven-year-old boy named Shan finds that his wicked Uncle Lionel has taken possession of his father's castle, leaving him disinherited. With his father missing, Shan and his mother seek help at King Arthur's court in Camelot. The story is centered around the hardships and dan-gers that are encountered by Shan. The story is mainly for middle-grade readers who find it difficult to read more detailed stories about knighthood and for older children who have reading difficulties. The book includes many illustrations in black and white.

I, JUAN DE PAREJA
Written by Elizabeth Borton de
Trevino. Farrar, Straus & Giroux,
Inc., 1965.

"When Velazquez was painting his mas-terpieces at the Spanish court in the seven-teenth century, his colors were expertly mixed and his canvases prepared by his Negro slave, Juan de Pareja. The great painter soon recognized the intelligence and gentle breeding which were to make Juan his indispensable assistant and com-panion—and lifelong friend. In this novel, which depicts both the beauty and the cruelty of the time and place, Elizabeth Borton de Trevino tells the story of Juan, who was born a slave and died an accom-plished and respected artist." Taken from pamphlet prepared by Farrar, Straus & Giroux, Inc. for this Newbery Medal book.

THE WHITE ROSE OF STUART
Written by Lillian de la Torre.
Thomas Nelson & Sons, 1954.

The story concerns Flora MacDonald and Charles Stuart who live in eighteenth-century Scotland. The childhood account of Flora makes her a very real person: she is responsible for helping the prince escape through enemy lines to safety.

Scottish poems and songs are part of the text.

BELISARIUS: YOUNG GENERAL OF BYZANTIUM
Written by Glanville Downey. E. P. Dutton & Co., Inc., 1960.

The story is centered around a famous campaign of the sixth century A.D. Belisarius is made general at the age of twenty-two. His triumph over the Vandals is highlighted by his return to Constantinople with the famous Vandal treasure. This is an interesting literary biography.

RING THE JUDAS BELL
Written by James Forman. Farrar, Straus, & Giroux, Inc., 1965.

Nicholas, a shepherd of fifteen and son of the local priest, has already known suffering. His mother, taken as hostage in the "Hitler War," had been executed. Even after the Nazis left the Greek villages, he knew no peace, for Communist partisans hiding in the hills continued to bedevil the country. Nicholas and his sister, Angela, are kidnapped by the partisans and sent to a camp in Albania. Surviving every imaginable ill, Nicholas finally returns home to discover that his father is no longer a priest but a soldier. The realism of these brutalities, combined with a plot rich in incidents, makes the spiritual testing of Nicholas the kind of heroic tale that appeals to boys of high school age. An epic of courage, this superbly written story carves out a way of life during a grim period on Greece's history. Another book by the same author, *The Skies of Crete*, is about World War II.

ADAM OF THE ROAD
Written by Elizabeth Janet Gray. Illustrated by Robert Lawson. The Viking Press, Inc., 1942.

Set in thirteenth-century England, this is a realistically told story of a boy, Adam, and his travels on the open road and of the people he meets: pilgrims, minstrels, merchants, and farmers. Never dull or lagging in action, this story moves swiftly along the trail of a boy who sets out to find his stolen spaniel. The story is full of historical details that are sound, making the book come alive with charm and a sense of humanity. Superb illustrations capture scenes of countryside, castles, towers, inns, and wayfarers.

THE NAMESAKE
Written and illustrated by C. Walter Hodges. Coward-McCann, Inc., 1964.

In the early years of King Alfred's reign, Danish warriors invade Saxon England. Alfred-the-One-Legged, the King's namesake and scribe, tells of violent times and of the noble warriors under King Alfred's leadership who hold back the Danes. Here is a stirring tale that assumes epic proportions with its poetic prose, vivid settings, and superb characterization.

THE HIDDEN TREASURE OF GLASTON
Written by Eleanore M. Jewett. Illustrated by Frederick T. Chapman. The Viking Press, Inc., 1946.

On a stormy night in the Middle Ages a crippled boy named Hugh is left by his father at the abbey of Glastonbury. He and his friend Dickon discover a secret underground vault that leads to the unearthing of treasures related to the life and death of King Arthur. This delightfully told story throws the warmth of human light on monasticism in the twelfth century.

THE TRUMPETER OF KRAKOW
Written by Eric P. Kelly. Illustrated by Angela Pruszynska. The Macmillan Company, 1928.

A tale of exciting adventure is woven

around the possession of the Great Tarnov Crystal with its indefinable fascination and its occult powers. Drawn with authentic, historical details, the story involves a fifteen-year-old trumpeter from Krakow. Viewed through the eyes of the lad, the panorama of Poland throbs with invaders, pillaging Tatars, and refugees of the fifteenth century. Historic traditions, picturesque language, beauty and grandeur of landscape add to the dramatic tale. The illustrations are excellent; they were made in Krakow.

THE SWEDISH NIGHTINGALE:
JENNY LIND
Written by Elizabeth Kyle. Holt Rinehart & Winston, Inc., 1965.
This biographical novel is a moving account of Jenny Lind's rise to greatness as a singer. Readers will be inspired by her successful struggle to overcome voice failure during her early twenties when she fled Sweden to study in Paris. The novel is straightforward and skillfully written. Its realistic language and sympathetic treatment of the plight of Jenny Lind make the book appealing to junior high school students.

JIM DAVIS
Written by John Masefield. Illustrated by Bob Dean. The Macmillan Company, 1951.
Mr. Gorsuch comes to the conclusion that Jim is learning too much about his band of smugglers and their operation off the coast of England. He is taken captive and goes on two exciting trips with them. The young prisoner finally escapes, and Mr. Gorsuch repents for his evil ways after being wounded. The story is a robust, vigorous, sea-going adventure that takes place around the time of the French wars.

THE GOLDEN SPUR
Written by Eugenia Miller. Illustrated by Leonard Everett

Fisher. Harcourt Brace & World, Inc., 1964.
In this story that takes place at the start of the French Revolution, a horse, named Isabeau, in the stable of Louis XVI is threatened. Twelve-year-old Jacques Renauld, often one of the King's stable-boys, tries to save the animal and in the process saves the King as well. Movingly told, the theme shines through to strengthen the story.

LOST JOHN
Written by Barbara L. Picard. Illustrated by Charles Keeping. Criterion Books, Inc., 1963.
Fifteen-year-old John Fitz William sets off to avenge his father's death. Captured by outlaws, John is made a member of Ralf the Red's notorious band and squire to this leader. He admires Ralf even though both he and his father had been victims of outlaws. When Ralf's son joins the band, John's jealousy and conscience are stirred. This tale of the Middle Ages is remarkably realistic and suspenseful with strong characterization and a good plot.

BEORN THE PROUD
Written by Madeleine Polland. Illustrated by William Stobbs. Holt, Rinehart & Winston, Inc., 1962.
Ness, a fourteen-year-old Irish girl, is the only survivor of a village plundered by a Viking raid. She is taken captive by Beorn, a Viking prince, who takes her back to his home in Denmark. Ness begins to like the Viking prince and gives him support and aid in time of trouble, showing him the meaning of Christian kindness. Ness even dreams of going back to Ireland someday with Beorn. The opposition between paganism and Christianity is clear, and the plot has all the excitement of a ninth-century Viking drama. The illustrations are powerful and complement a strong story.

ICE FALCON
Written by Rita Ritchie. W.W. Norton & Company, Inc., 1963.

This is a tale of tenth-century Norsemen. Kurt, his brother, and their father are on a falcon hunt when the latter two are captured by a Viking band. The only ransom that will free his father and brother is a wild, white Ice Falcon. Kurt's hunt leads him through adventures and war. When he finally catches the falcon, his problem is to keep it from enemies. The story gives the reader a glimpse into Icelandic customs, medieval life, Viking ships, and falconry.

THE EMPEROR AND THE DRUMMER
Written by Ruth Robbins.
Illustrated by Nicolas Sidjakov.
Parnassus Press, 1962.

Jean and Armand, two drummer boys, are given exciting duties when Napoleon reviews his fleet at Boulogne. On the day of the review, the Admiral refuses to order the ships to quit their moorings because of a brewing storm. Napoleon gives the orders himself and during the storm is witness to the flotilla's destruction from the shore. Jean fears Armand is lost. But he sees something red and blue bounding on the waves in the distance. It is Armand floating on his drum. Out of this incident, based on history, the author and artist have made an extraordinary book, harmonious in every respect.

DOBRY
Written by Monica Shannon.
Illustrated by Atanas Katchamakoff.
The Viking Press, Inc., 1934.

Dobry is a Bulgarian peasant boy who wishes to become a sculptor. His mother does not approve at first. However, his understanding grandfather fosters his ambitions and finally Dobry goes away to art school in Sofia. When he leaves, he finds that his mother's blessings are upon his endeavor. Many of the traditions, customs, and folklore of the Bulgarian people are woven into the story so as to provide a rich treasury of Balkan life with historic significance. Atanas Katchamakoff uses

his childhood memories of his grandfather's farm in Bulgaria to give a rich and rewarding background to the story. The book design is distinctive and original.

QUEEN'S CHAMPION
Written by Shaun Sutton. St.
Martin's Press, Inc., 1962.

This is a story of treachery against Queen Elizabeth. Fourteen-year-old Roger Penlynden has just received the inherited symbol of loyalty—a small gold statue known as the Queen's Champion. Suspense is built rapidly until England is saved by the destruction of the Spanish Armada. Although this story is not to be compared with some of the historical adventure Britain has to offer, it does have a good period background and enough wild flights, pursuits, duels, and noble sacrifices to stimulate an adventurous boy's appetite to go on to even better stories of this genre.

SEVEN KINGS OF ENGLAND
Written by Geoffrey Trease.
Vanguard Press, 1955.

The text gives brief character sketches of seven Kings of England chosen by the author for their interesting personalities and some unique aspects of their lives. Included are: Alfred the Great, William the Conqueror, Richard the Lion-Hearted, Charles I and II, William III, and George VI. This informative text should prompt an interest in more involved texts on this subject.

SILENCE OVER DUNKERQUE
Written by John R. Tunis.
William Morrow & Co., Inc.,
1962.

During the retreat at Dunkirk, Sergeant Williams, together with one of his men, is left behind. Their help comes from a fourteen-year-old French girl named Gisele. It is because of her and other French people that the two English soldiers are finally able to escape to England. The story gives glimpses into the realities of war and the confusion of retreat and evacuation. The details are extremely realistic.

PEPYS' BOY
Written by Rachel M. Varble.
Illustrated by Kurt Werth.
Doubleday & Company, Inc., 1955.
Life in Restoration England is illuminatingly described in this book, which fashions a character, Toby, out of the diary of Samuel Pepys. Employed as a page, Toby thrives on misadventure. Although many of the escapades seem exaggerated, the tale is exciting and well written. It should whet the reader's appetite for more works of this kind.

LARK
Written by Sally Watson. Holt,
Rinehart & Winston, Inc., 1964.
When irrepressible Lark runs away from her stern Puritan uncle's household she is befriended by a handsome young Royalist spy who takes her to be a mere child, easily returnable to her family. Lark's assistance in saving her friend's life heightens the interest and excitement of this seventeenth-century story set in England. Not without humor, this escape story travels across a broad landscape studded with the gypsies, tavern keepers, Roundheads, and Cavaliers of Cromwell's time.

The satisfactions that come from sharing and possessing are expressed in the beaming faces of two small brothers who live in an overcrowded apartment. Urban realities are handled honestly in the unpretentious pictures amplifying the simple text.
From Evan's Corner *by Elizabeth Starr Hill, illustrated by Nancy Grossman. Copyright © 1967 by the author and illustrator. Reproduced by permission of Holt, Rinehart & Winston, Inc.*

Chapter 11

REALISM
IN
CHILDREN'S
LITERATURE

*... it remained for realism to assert that fidelity to experience and
probability of motive are essential conditions of a great imaginative literature.
... When realism becomes false to itself, when it heaps up facts
merely, and maps life instead of picturing it, realism will perish too. Every true
realist instinctively knows this, and it is perhaps the reason why
he is careful of every fact, and feels himself bound to express or to indicate its
meaning at the risk of over-moralizing. In life he finds nothing
insignificant; all tells for destiny and character; nothing that God has made is
contemptible. He cannot look upon human life and declare this
thing or that thing unworthy of notice, any more than the scientist can declare
a fact of the material world beneath the dignity of his inquiry. He
feels in every nerve the equality of things and the unity of men; his soul is
exalted, not by vain shows and shadows and ideals, but by realities,
in which alone the truth lives.*

— WILLIAM DEAN HOWELLS
Criticism and Fiction
Harper & Bros., 1892

Definition and Types
of Realistic Stories

Realism in children's literature is a broad division that encompasses every aspect of life. Animal, family, sports, and sea stories are just a few of the many categories that present an accurate picture of life to the reader. In these stories the reader will sometimes find that he can identify with characters who have similar backgrounds or experiences. But realistic stories also describe people who are different from the reader, and, by seeing how others differ, he can grow to understand himself better.

In the nineteenth century people believed that books influenced a child's character, and to make sure the effect was a good one a moral might be added at the end. The purpose of realism in children's literature is no longer to preach sermons but instead to expose the child to true-to-life drama and everyday living. Today, stories of realism are not presented in a one-sided manner. They may portray people who are victims of social injustice. Good does not always triumph and evil is not always punished. These books do not shelter children from the realities of life but make them aware of existing conditions. In *The Hundred Dresses* by Eleanor Estes a group of school children realize too late that their cruelty has destroyed the happiness of a poor Polish girl and her family. The ostracism that the Petronskis experience compels them to leave the community. This thought-provoking book helps a child to understand what values are truly important and also shows him that mistakes cannot always be rectified.

The Significance of Realistic Stories

Realistic stories have a perennial appeal because most children are confronted with similar delights and pains. "The pain of feeling unique and isolated is somewhat assuaged by the knowledge not only that there are others in the same boat, but that adults are also aware of the predicament and care enough to write about it."[1] If a troubled child is subtly introduced to a book that deals with his problems, some of his anxiety may be relieved. The child without a friend finds comfort in *Play with Me* by Marie Hal Ets. The middle child in the family might profit by reading Eleanor Estes' *The Middle Moffat*, and the handicapped child may gain new courage and strength from *The Door in the Wall* by Marguerite de Angeli.

Not only do these realistic stories, past or present, concern themselves with problems that are critical to the child, but very often they fulfill a need that cannot otherwise be met. An unwanted child may be drawn to a book that depicts a home where there is warmth and understanding. He is removed from his own unhappy setting even if it is only for a short while. Another need that may be partially assuaged is that of the child who has not been successful as an athlete. He may compensate for his lack of skill by reading books on sports and emulating his favorite heroes. Such a child would find it inspiring to read of the effort and hard work often involved in winning a coveted championship.

In reading realistic books, a child can best relate to what his background and development have made possible for him to understand. In other words, for a child to identify fully with a character or an event, he must have had prior experiences with similar characters in his own life. For example, a child who is self-conscious because of his unusual height will empathize with a fictional character who is tall and will feel the same frustrations and insecurities because he is different. Most children feel secure in knowing that they are not dissimilar from their peers. They strive for acceptance by imitating the actions and attitudes of those around them. Often when they perceive themselves to be unlike the others, it affects them deeply and makes a lasting impression on their personalities, which are easily influenced by first-hand experiences as well as by the books children read.

---

[1] Josette Frank, *Your Child's Reading Today* (Garden City, N.Y.: Doubleday & Company, 1960), p. 155.

Approaches to Realistic Stories

The purpose of a good piece of literature usually is to tell a good story. However, as Oliver Wendell Holmes once noted, "The best of a book is not the thought which it contains, but the thought which it suggests; just as the charm of music dwells not in the tones but in the echoes of our hearts." The division of realism has basically the same goals as the other divisions of literature and uses the traditional approaches to produce a story that is true to life. In order to understand better some realistic stories, one must examine separately the traditional literary elements of theme, plot, characterization, style, and setting.

THEME

The theme differentiates realism from the other divisions in literature. In realistic stories the theme reflects human ideals of the time. For example, a book might stress bravery and courage as in *The Boy Jacko* or *The Call of the Wild*. The former depicts man courageously fighting man in order to reach America and claim what is rightfully his. The latter story tells of animals in the wild North struggling against both nature and man to survive. In realistic stories it is the theme that makes the most powerful impression on the reader.

PLOT

In realistic stories the plot echoes the spirit of the times by an accurate portrayal of the events and feelings of contemporary people. The reader, however, is not presented with a literal truth but with the fusion of fact and fiction. The result is a vivid, interesting picture of life in the present. Most realistic stories describe the events in a chronological sequence, although there are some authors who utilize the techniques of flashback or of isolated episodes. In *The Moffats* by Eleanor Estes a new adventure unfolds in each chapter. Though the chapters are in no logical sequence, they form a unified whole as they describe the continuous adventures of one family.

CHARACTERIZATION

In many realistic stories, the character's personality is of paramount importance. The hero may have a powerful personality that affects the other characters and the mood of the story. Burgess Leonard creates such a character in *Stretch Bolton, Mister Shortstop*. Stretch, a former baseball manager, is concerned with winning the World Series fairly. Distressed by the actions of fellow major league players, he endeavors to bring to public view the unethical practices that he witnesses. Though his teammates resent his actions, he continues his crusade. Eventually, Stretch proves that his convictions are sound, and he gains the respect of players and baseball fans alike.

In realistic stories, because the characters are so fully developed and convincing, the spirit of the times is captured. Through effective characterization, the author appeals to the reader's emotions and involves him in the themes of the book.

STYLE

Since the purpose of realism is to give an accurate picture of life, the language must parallel the language of the times. Therefore it must be colorful and varied in order to include the regional and social differences of the people whom it describes. *It's Like This, Cat* by Emily Neville is written in the vernacular of a fourteen-year-old living in New York City. Its dialogue reflects the attitudes of an adolescent boy and his peers and gives the reader deeper insights into his character.

Colorful language, however, does not necessarily mean flowery prose. Because the author's intent is to be realistic, he often presents the story in a straightforward manner, eliminating the more eloquent style characteristic of some other divisions of literature. A fantasy depends upon imaginative passages to enrapture the reader, but realistic stories concern themselves with reporting thoughts that reflect everyday life.

SETTING

There is no limit to the number of settings that may be employed by the author of realistic stories. The settings may range from the uninhabited regions of the North to the familiar surroundings of one's own backyard.

Very often the setting determines much of what is to happen in the story. For instance, E. Nesbit's *The Railway Children* describes small children living by a railway line through which they get much of their contact with the outside world. This setting has an influential role in the unraveling of the plot.

Yet, the setting of a book involves more than the physical location of the story. Accurate detail and vivid description are also important.

Forerunners of Realistic Stories

Before discussing the categories of present-day realism, it is necessary to examine realistic stories from other times, the forerunners of modern realistic fiction for children. In the nineteenth century such stories as *Little Women*, *The Adventures of Tom Sawyer*, and *The Adventures of Huckleberry Finn* were beloved for their authentic portrayal of life and today are considered classics in children's literature.

Little Women by Louisa May Alcott has been a favorite book of older children for over eighty years. It deals with four teen-age girls, Meg, Jo, Beth, and Amy, and their disappointments and triumphs in growing up. The Marches struggle with poverty, but they are held together and sustained by love for one another. The treatment is not overly sentimental so that the joys and tragedies of the March family remain realistic.

Another author, Mark Twain, contributed much to American literature when he wrote of life during the nineteenth century. As a great humorist, he recorded robust characters that have become an important part of children's literature. Tom Sawyer and Huck Finn appeal to youngsters who want adventure and action.

In *The Adventures of Tom Sawyer* Mark Twain has created a red-blooded American boy who has a great capacity for mischief and imaginative adventures. This tale, packed with the typically Western humor for which Mark Twain was noted, is told in excellent prose with precise character portrayal. Though the book was written in the nineteenth century, Tom could easily be placed in a twentieth-century environment because he is a universal character with whom boys of any age can readily identify.

Another favorite character from the annals of children's literature is Huck Finn, who is a more solitary character than Tom. He has never really been cared for by anyone, and he knows that no one in the world is concerned with his welfare. *The Adventures of Huckleberry Finn* is also set against the mighty Mississippi, and, in a sense, it is about the great river itself.

Although these books are often thought of as historical realism, their discussion at this time is pertinent, for they laid the foundation for the realistic stories of today.

Analysis of Realistic Stories

Since there are overwhelming numbers of books in this division, it is necessary to arrange them into smaller categories. By judicious selection of the stories for each category, one gains a sense of order and a better understanding of the subjects included. Although the division of realism encompasses many categories, the following are so arranged that most stories fall comfortably into one grouping or another.

Stories of Animal Life
Books for younger children
Books for intermediate-grade children
Books for upper-grade children

Stories of Family Life
Books for younger children
Books for intermediate-grade children
Books for upper-grade children

Stories of the Sea
Books for younger children
Books for intermediate-grade children
Books for upper-grade children

Sports Stories
Books for younger children
Books for intermediate-grade children
Books for upper-grade children

Stories of Animal Life

Animal stories comprise a large section in the division of realism in children's literature. These stories are not confined to one basic theme but touch upon many different subjects. They range from adventures in the North to domestic tales of a household pet and may be narrated by the author, an animal in the story, or another character. In this way, the reader is able to see animals from many different points of view.

Animal stories have always been popular subjects for children's books. Utilizing a variety of topics, these books can draw upon a rich abundance of material for each age group.

BOOKS FOR YOUNGER CHILDREN

One Kitten Too Many by Bianca Bradbury is a delightful book for young children, who will enjoy following the antics of two kittens. The pictures are so realistic that they have a photographic quality. Catching the kittens in a variety of positions, the vivid illustrations enhance the brief plot.

The warm kitchen where Tabitha, a Siamese cat, lives is suddenly invaded by a strange kitten who takes over with no reservations. Tabitha is overwhelmed by the rude cat who decides to take her pillow and warm milk. But when the new cat wins the attention of the lady of the house, Tabitha forces her to learn how to be polite, and the two live happily together in the kitchen, sharing the comfortable pillow and the good food.

Barn Cat by Belle Coates describes a new addition to a South Dakota farm, a cat. Everybody likes him, but no one can think of a suitable name. During the month of May, an unexpected blizzard strikes during the night. The children hear strange sounds and discover the barn cat outside. He leads them to the barn where they discover that the latch has broken and the snow has blown in on the floor, the cows, and a new calf. The children struggle back to the farmhouse to get help. Finally the cows are safe, and the children have found just the right name for their pet— Barney, for barn cat, of course.

Not only is this story bright and amusing, but it gives the reader an idea of what farm life is like. The true-to-life illustrations add much to the development of story line, plot sequence, and characters.

The Puppy in the Pet Shop by Joseph Schrank is the story of a little black puppy who lives in a pet shop with many other animals. He is a shy little dog who always stays at the back of the window when people come to view the animals. People buy the other dogs but never pay any attention to him. One day a little girl pauses at the window. She returns each day hoping that she will be able to buy him, but the dog costs more than her family can afford. One day, she gets an inspiration while watching television. She enters a children's contest, but on the day of the program she is heartbroken to learn that the puppy has been sold to someone else. She does not win the contest, but she is happily surprised when she learns that her consolation prize is the little black puppy from the pet shop window. Bright, lovely pictures accompany the text.

Wonderful Things, written and illustrated by Zhenya Gay, is predominantly a picture book for the younger child. This story begins with the first day in the life of a newborn colt and follows his development, impressions, and first activities. The black-and-white illustrations are excellently done and may help the nonreader to understand the life of a young colt.

BOOKS FOR INTERMEDIATE-GRADE CHILDREN

The Last Little Cat by Meindert DeJong is the touching story of a tiny black cat, the last and smallest of the litter, born in a barn that is now a dog kennel. The little cat is always the last to get milk and warmth from its mother. One day the mother and her kittens leave the nest to explore the world, but the tiny cat, too small to take on the adventure, is left behind. Quite by accident, he falls into the cage of the old blind dog who belongs to the owner of the kennel. The two become good friends, and the kitten finds security at last. On a warm day the owner moves the cage outside into the sun so the old dog can enjoy its warmth. The little kitten, overwhelmed by the world, leaves the cage and ventures out into the unknown. When he returns at night, he discovers that the familiar cage is gone and his friend is nowhere in sight. He experiences a lonely, unhappy night as he learns that the cold world does not always provide a warm place to sleep and milk to drink. Finally, when morning comes, the cat is reunited with the old dog and is happy again.

A Pony for Winter by Helen Kay is a poignant account of a little girl who desperately wants a horse of her own. The owner of an amusement park is looking for someone to care for his ponies over the winter, so Deborah gets her parents to consent to her taking care of one of them. She takes such good care of the horse that the man asks her if she would like to have it again next winter. This story shows that caring for a pet is a great responsibility.

Another beautiful story expressing care and love for animals is Marguerite Henry's *King of the Wind*. This Newbery Medal winner is the exciting story of a thoroughbred horse, an ancestor of Man O'War. Beginning in Morocco, the story sweeps across France and into England with rich details of background that sharpen a sense of place and period for young readers.

King of the Wind is a flashback story about an Arabian horse named Sham who lived two hundred years ago. Shipped out of Morocco to France, the horse is rejected by the French king who does not understand his value and puts him out to unpleasant work. A long line of subsequent owners intensifies the pain and deepens the scars of rejection for Sham until the Earl of Godolphin recognizes the true worth of this small horse and gives him a more noble role and surroundings.

> The Godolphin Arabian stood very still, his regal head lifted. An east wind was rising. He stretched out his nostrils to gather in the scent. It was laden with the fragrance of windflowers. Of what was he thinking? Was he re-running the race of Lath? Was he rejoicing in the royal purple? Was he drawing a wood cart in the streets of Paris? Or just winging across the grassy downs in the shafts of the sun?[2]

---

[2]Marguerite Henry, *King of the Wind* (Chicago: Rand McNally & Company, 1948), p. 169.

Eyes flash in amazement while anticipation mounts in this picture of a deaf-mute stable boy, a handsome horse, and a barn cat. Care in the use of real-life details gives the pictures the vitality they reflect.
From King of the Wind *by Marguerite Henry, illustrated by Wesley Dennis. Copyright* © *1948 by Rand McNally & Company. Reproduced by permission.*

King of the Wind is a magnificent example of a story that is drawn from a strong sense of realism and a love for a horse. The detailed, authentic settings and well delineated characters reflect the artistry of Marguerite Henry and her sympathetic illustrator Wesley Dennis. Together they produce outstanding animal stories that remain unsurpassed for their excellence in word and picture.

Other titles by this same team include *Misty of Chincoteague*, a marvelous story about two children who capture and tame two wild ponies; *Sea Star*, a poignant account of the wild ponies of Chincoteague; *Stormy, Misty's Foal*, a true-to-life and thrilling story of Misty's baby born right after a devastating storm that swept Chincoteague Island; and many other books that display deep love and understanding of animals, especially horses.

Tough Enough, written and illustrated by Ruth and Latrobe Carroll, tells of a mischievous little dog, "Tough Enough." His playful actions

368

have annoyed his family because they always result in destruction, but Beanie has faith in his dog and loves him in spite of all the trouble he creates. His faith in his dog is justified when the dog saves the children from a flood.

The text here is descriptive and straightforward in style. The illustrations, in blue and gray hues, are most appropriate for the Smoky Mountains setting and they effectively convey the humor of the story.

Another Kind of Puppy by James Sterling Ayars is about the Olivers' futile search for their lost kitten. He is nowhere to be found and so Molly decides to buy a dog. Although her parents are willing to give her any breed, she chooses to keep a scrawny puppy who has followed her home. This story of a compassionate child is well illustrated in black, white, and rust hues.

Muley-Ears: Nobody's Dog by Marguerite Henry is about a dog who lives on the island of Jamaica in a house that is rented to families each month throughout the year. They have all loved and taken care of Muley-Ears, but one month a man arrives who pays no attention to him. At the end, the man realizes how hostile he has been and the two become friends. The watercolor illustrations capture many picturesque scenes of Jamaica and Jamaican life, including piers with banana boats and fishing wharfs.

BOOKS FOR UPPER-GRADE CHILDREN

The Call of the Wild by Jack London is an exciting adventure story for the upper-grade child. This book tells of Buck, a Saint Bernard who gradually reverts to the untamed life of the wild. At the end of the book we see that Buck "... is not always alone. When the long winter nights come on and the wolves follow their meat into the lower valleys, he may be seen running at the head of the pack. . . . "

White Fang is another thrilling story by Jack London of the wild North. In this book, the theme is reversed and a wild wolf is domesticated.

Faithful readers have enjoyed several series of animal tales, one of which is Walter Farley's Black Stallion series. *The Black Stallion's Courage* seems to be one of the most widely read of this particular group. The book is a complex animal saga dealing with real problems and emotions. This action story has an element of mystery woven into the fiber of the plot. Here is real drama and excitement at its best for the older reader.

Alec Ramsey has great faith and determination as he and Henry Daily, his horse trainer, ignore the advice of everyone, and prepare the Black Stallion for the Kentucky Derby. A thrilling tale of racing unfolds, authentic to the last detail. With colorful words and phrases, Walter Farley conveys an atmosphere of excitement that involves the reader completely.

During the latter half of the nineteenth century when sentiment toward animals ran high, there appeared a book for children whose timely theme gave it tremendous popularity. This book was Anna Sewell's *Black Beauty*, which was first published in 1877.

Suitable for more mature readers, this realistically told animal story remains a paradox in that the horse whose tale is told stays true to its own species but possesses human attributes of speech and thought. Written in a convincing style that combines elements of truth and poetry, *Black Beauty* tells of an animal whose life reveals unbearable hardships, fears, tragedies, and some of the joys of living.

Stemming from a genuine creative impulse that was aroused by compassion for animals, the story stirs a sense of humanity and more humane consideration for animals. In this respect especially, *Black Beauty* has benefited many helpless creatures because it was written to protest serious cruelties to which horses and other animals were subjected.

Revealing the anguish of the tired horse, the drawings here are in sympathy with the story protesting the hardship of tightly-reined animals.
From Black Beauty *by Anna Sewell, illustrated by John Groth. Illustrations* © *1962 by The Macmillan Company. Reproduced by permission.*

Family stories have strong appeal because they describe situations that directly relate to a child's own life. Displaying many different backgrounds and settings, these stories offer a multitude of experiences, both humorous and sad. Caught in various predicaments, characters never fail to demonstrate courage and strength, which impart hope and reassurance in facing the problems of life.

BOOKS FOR YOUNGER CHILDREN

Country Mailman by Jerrold Beim is a family story for the beginning reader. Ben waits at the mailbox every day and hopes in vain for a letter. The mailman gives Ben letters for everyone in his family, but nothing ever comes for Ben. During a storm, a tree falls and blocks the road: the mailman is not able to get through until Ben helps him. A few days later, to everyone's surprise, letters arrive for Ben. The neighbors are writing to thank him for his help in removing the tree from the road. *Country Mailman* is a delightful book, and every child who longs to receive a letter will empathize with Ben.

Pelle's New Suit is an example of realism for the youngest. Marion Letcher translated this picture book, which was written and illustrated by Elsa Beskow. Pelle raises a lamb and has various people help him in making a suit from the lamb's wool. For each person who helps him he performs a service. For instance Pelle goes to his grandmother and says,

Warmth radiates from this picture of a homespun boy tipping his cap to the lamb whose wool provided him a new suit. Broad, comfortable pages are swept clean of extraneous details for maximum visual impact.

From Pelle's New Suit *told and illustrated by Elsa Beskow. Harper & Row, Publishers, 1929. Reproduced by permission.*

"Grandmother dear, please spin this wool into yarn for me!" "That I will gladly do, my dear," says his grandmother, "if while I am spinning it you will tend my cows for me!" This book is cherished by many young children for its fine text and beautiful illustrations.

The Swimming Hole, written for the younger child by Jerrold Beim, depicts a warm, generous Negro child, Larry. Larry plays with his white friends in the swimming hole. One day a new boy, Steve, ties Larry's clothes in knots and refuses to play with him because he is colored. The boys tell Steve to leave, and as he does so they notice that he is red from being out in the sun all day. Larry says, "Why don't we tell him we won't play with anyone that color?" It is then that Steve realizes that it does not matter what color a person is.

The Snowy Day, written and illustrated by Ezra Jack Keats, is another minority group story for the youngest child. It describes the delightful experience of a little boy named Peter with his first snow.

One winter morning Peter woke up and looked out the window. Snow had fallen during the night. It covered everything as far as he could see.

Upon viewing this picture one enters Peter's room and looks with him out the open window onto a snow-covered neighborhood. Strong colors in collage vibrate in the telling of a small boy's adventures in the snow.

From The Snowy Day *by Ezra Jack Keats. Copyright © 1962 by the author–illustrator. All rights reserved. Reproduced by permission of The Viking Press, Inc.*

Paralleling Peter's adventures in a snowy neighborhood, Moy Moy's daily life with family and neighbors threads through Chinatown and Los Angeles. The quaint customs, warm-hearted folk, and gaily decorated streets and shops described by Leo Politi in *Moy Moy* provide a strong sense of real life as it flows in a throbbing city. Transcending the reality, tiny Moy Moy's wide-eyed wonder and visions of imaginative toys give this gentle story its humanizing power.

Marcia Brown, the author and illustrator of many fine children's books, has written a sparkling and fresh account of a day in the lives of Pepineddu and the rest of his merry band of "soldiers" in *Tamarindo*. This story for the youngest age group is about the mysterious disappearance of a donkey and the boys who decide to find him. As Pepineddu and his friends wander through Sicilian olive and lemon groves, the reader gets a brief glimpse of life in another country. The illustrations are as lively and bright as the rollicking text. This story teaches children that, though cultures may be different, people are essentially the same everywhere.

Because most young children are familiar with home and school surroundings they will always want stories that make use of recognizable settings as well as themes common to childhood. *Evan's Corner* is just such a picture storybook. Here Elizabeth Starr Hill tells her story against the backdrop of a crowded two-room city flat, congested neighborhood streets, and a typical urban school.

The story is slim but the idea behind it is broad in its appeal. More than anything else in the world, Evan, a small boy in a large family, wants a place of his own. Sympathetic to his needs, Evan's mother manages to provide her son with a corner right by the only window in the flat. Ingeniously Evan tidies his little spot by hanging a picture he painted, by placing a flower pot on the sill, and by adding a goldfish bowl with a turtle in it near his plant. But this is still not enough to satisfy Evan who is quietly aware that something else is missing. Only when he helps his little brother brighten his own corner does Evan feel his wish has been realized.

Rising above the grim details of overcrowdedness is the warm realistic atmosphere of the humble home in which Evan lives and grows. Despite the congestion, one gains from the story a strong sense of urban reality as cluttered details of recognizable home-like and other familiar things come into sharp relief. The story also brings into clear focus two basic needs of childhood—to possess and to share. Although it is very difficult to interplay these two themes, the author and the artist Nancy Grossman have collaborated in this picture book to convey their message honestly and with beautiful simplicity.

Many modern stories point up in realistic terms certain psychological problems of children and how they cope with them. Evaline Ness'

Sam, Bangs and Moonshine, a Caldecott winner, is just such a book. Universal in its understanding portrayal of a lonely child's predilection for daydreams, this striking picture book sharpens the difference between uncontrolled flights of fantasy and the real world for a motherless little girl called "Sam,"—short for Samantha.

The story, simple and touching, is about a fisherman's orphaned daughter who resorts to inventing fantasies in order to escape her own dreary world of the fishing village. She imagines her mother as a mermaid; she glides along on the back of a resplendent dragon; she pretends to possess a real live kangaroo for a pet. Of course, no one believes Sam—no one except Thomas, who is anything but a doubter in this true-to-life tale. But each time Thomas asks to see the mermaid mother or the golden

Grief strikes Samantha when she learns from her father that her playmate and cat nearly met disaster because of her farfetched tales. True-to-life details do not spare the feelings of the readers of this book.

From Sam, Bangs and Moonshine *by Evaline Ness. Copyright © 1966 by the author-illustrator. Reproduced by permission of Holt, Rinehart and Winston, Inc.*

dragon or even the kangaroo, Sam devises still another story, or "moonshine" as her father calls her exaggerations, and Thomas must wait until another time.

Suspicious of Sam's inventions, the fisherman warns his daughter against the perils of "moonshine" and he firmly recommends, ". . . for a change, talk REAL not MOONSHINE." But not until her farfetched talk pushes her only friend Thomas and her beloved cat Bangs to the edge of destruction is Sam made aware of the difference between "real" and "moonshine."

Despite the well-drawn exaggerations and without frills, the clear-cut language paints a genuine world that young children inhabit; a world peopled with imaginary characters and real ones too; a world where grown-ups can be discouraging as well as sympathetic; a world where compassion may find a response in the most unusual place. In Sam's case, a gerbil from a banana boat serves to link her make-believe world with blunt reality in the satisfying climax of the story.

Supporting the straightforward text, the author-illustrator's handsome pictures, beautifully spaced and balanced for maximum visual impact, provide a sense of place and immediacy with a minimum of extraneous details.

BOOKS FOR INTERMEDIATE-GRADE CHILDREN

Beverly Cleary's *Henry Huggins*, like many nine-year-olds, cannot stay out of trouble. His life seems to consist of one humorous situation after another. He decides a thin, hungry dog needs a home, but the only way he can get the dog to his house is to smuggle it onto a bus. He manages to do this successfully but the dog suddenly jumps out of the bag and into the laps of several passengers. The reader cannot help but laugh as the dog pounces on a stranger and scatters broken eggs all over the bus.

Beverly Cleary's books are enjoyed for their humorous, true-to-life episodes. After reading *Henry Huggins*, many children go on to read *Henry and Beezus*, *Henry and the Paper Route*, and *Henry and Ribsy*.

In *Mitch and Amy* this sensitive author brings to her writing the usual bright humor that has characterized the Beverly Cleary books. With convincingly real illustrations by George Porter, *Mitch and Amy* focuses on some of the sights and sounds of school life. The story involves nine-year-old twins who, despite their loyalty to each other, indulge in periodic spats and quarrels that reveal some of the everyday aspects of family life.

In addition the school scenes, peppered with the problems and paraphernalia of the average American school, present the twins in further vigorous action. Here the reader of the same or similar age has plenty of opportunity to identify with children in conflict with the neighborhood bully or to empathize with Mitch's book-report difficulties and Amy's struggles with arithmetic. Yet, in this true-to-life book the reader is not robbed of a chance to laugh at certain exaggerations that heighten the humor in a superbly written realistic story.

Beverly Cleary's ability to understand children and to portray humorous situations is matched by Eleanor Estes, who wrote *The Moffats*, *The Middle Moffat*, and *Rufus M.*

In *The Moffats* each chapter depicts a different predicament for the Moffat children. In one chapter Jane Moffat hides from a policeman in a box where he eventually discovers her. The reader laughs with the policeman as Jane explains that she had strutted up the street behind the superintendent of schools imitating him, and now she is afraid she will be arrested. The Moffat family is an endearing one that will not be quickly forgotten by the intermediate-grade reader.

Many third and fouth grade children delight in the realistic characters Carolyn Haywood has created in *B is for Betsy*, *Little Eddy*, and *Annie Pat and Eddie*. In the last, a lovable little boy, Eddie, goes to the seashore with Annie Pat. They spend a wonderful summer together and share many experiences.

It is not unusual for the fifth and sixth grade child to be enchanted with E. Nesbit's books. *The Railway Children* is about an ordinary family in which there are three children, Roberta, Peter, and Phyllis. One day their father goes away and does not return. As a result, the family moves to a small cottage in the country by a railroad line. In their new surroundings they are faced with many problems, one of which they solve by writing the following letter:

Dear Mr. We do not know your name.

Mother is ill and the doctor says to give her the things at the end of the letter, but she says she can't afford it and to get mutton for us and she will have the broth. We do not know anyone here but you . . . Father will pay you, or if he has lost all his money, or anything, Peter will pay you when he is a man. We promise it on our honer. I.O.U. for all the things Mother wants. . .[3]

---

[3]E. Nesbit, *The Railway Children* (New York: Coward-McCann, Inc., 1958), p. 58.

In the end, father returns and everyone is happy. *The Railway Children* is highly recommended for the intermediate-grade child.

It's Like This, Cat by Emily Neville, a Newbery Medal winner, is a contemporary story for an intermediate-grade or upper-grade child. The illustrations are lively and realistic, capturing the mood of the story. Emily Neville depicts the experiences of an adolescent boy, Dave Mitchell, growing in up New York City. The opening paragraph reflects the humorous tone of the book. "My father is always talking about how a dog can be very educational for a boy. This is one reason I got a cat."[4]

Dave is a sensitive fourteen-year-old boy who makes friends with a stray tomcat, a troubled nineteen-year-old boy, and an eccentric old lady who has a house full of cats. *It's Like This, Cat* is written in the vernacular of a New York City boy, yet the book's message gives it broader appeal. This is probably one book urban children will not want to miss.

Exploring New York City from its East Side, Ruth Sawyer's *Roller Skates* throws light on rarely visited shops and corners accessible only to a bouncy little girl called Lucinda. Through the eyes of this youngster a reader views life in a city bustling with activity and teeming with humanity. Here a rich gallery of characters is meticulously portrayed. The different personalities come alive in a story that the author admits to being a part of her personal diary of childhood experiences during the 1890's in New York City. Here one meets the salty cab driver, the kind yet firm policeman, a most colorful fruit seller, a musician, a newspaper reporter, varied shopkeepers, and many others who make up the assorted inhabitants of the Big City.

Lucinda's experiences on roller skates comprise the bulk of this shining story with crisp humor and fine writing. Ruth Sawyer, a distinguished storyteller, has bestowed life upon each of her characters, who manage to express their individuality no matter how crowded the scenes into which they gravitate. By reading her Newbery Medal book one gains not just the delights of the storytelling but also a sense of life and a feeling for the actuality of life in New York City.

Running counterpoint to the Big City stories are those books that have distinctly rural backgrounds, such as *Rebecca of Sunnybrook Farm*. Written at the turn of the century, this forerunner of present-day stories ranks high as a work of realistic fiction for children. The most distinctive feature of Kate Douglas Wiggin's book is the portrayal of the child

---

[4]Emily Neville, *It's Like This, Cat* (New York: Harper & Row, Publishers, 1963), p. 1.

character, Rebecca. Completely dominating the story, this memorable child emerges exuberant with enthusiasm for a life of joys and sorrows. The account of her experience vibrates with warmth and affection against a sharp relief of New England settings and characters.

Paralleling Rebecca's story is that of Garnet Linden on a modern Wisconsin farm. *Thimble Summer* by Elizabeth Enright reveals the author's insights into the concerns of childhood and the characters who share these concerns in a beautiful real-life drama that sings with the joy and contentment of a little girl whose roots sink deep into a well-loved farm home.

As a Newbery Medal book *Thimble Summer* underscores the dignity of family life on a Midwestern farm which happens to be oppressed by a scorching drought. Finally, rain brings relief and Garnet finds a thimble made of silver. Accepting this as a good omen, the small girl believes the thimble will bring her a lucky summer. The events that follow somewhat fulfill her prophecy, but more than that, they entertain the reader greatly with their humor, excitement, and delightful characterization.

Rachel and Herman by Mina Lewiton is a sequel to *Rachel* and a wonderfully warm family story for the intermediate-grade child. Rachel moves uptown with her family and finds the adjustment quite difficult. Gradually she makes friends and then cousin Boris, a man of the world, arrives. Cousin Boris is lively, full of wonderful schemes, and brightens everyone's life. The story of Rachel and her brother Herman is among the best family stories written for young children.

Mary Nash's *While Mrs. Coverlet Was Away* is the story of the Persever children and how they manage on their own. Their father is in New Zealand on business when their housekeeper Mrs. Coverlet is called away. The Persever children are left to care for themselves and at times find it quite a struggle to make ends meet. At one point they even have to sell their cat. This is a fast-reading book that will be enjoyed by the intermediate-grade child.

Bright April, written and illustrated for the intermediate-grade child by Marguerite de Angeli, is the story of a nine-year-old Negro girl and her family. Many of the episodes in the book touch on racial issues that are very real to April. For example, at a Brownie dinner a new girl does not want to sit next to April, but eventually they become good friends. Some critics of the book feel that there are too many problems in *Bright April*. The author, however, presents her character realistically and the story rings true to life.

BOOKS FOR
UPPER-GRADE CHILDREN

379
*Realism
in
Children's
Literature*

Spurs for Suzanna by Betty Cavanna is a fast-moving family story written for the adolescent. It is about Suzanna Scott, a spoiled fifteen-year-old who has much growing up to do. With the help of the Ballantine family and their three horses, Suzanna matures and develops as a person. Most teen-agers will love reading about Suzanna, the horses, and her exciting summer.

A book that escapes the stereotyped superficiality of many teen-age novels is the 1967 Newbery Award winner, *Up a Road Slowly*, by Irene Hunt. Miss Hunt relates with warmth and sympathetic insight the story of a young girl's growth to maturity, from the age of seven when her mother dies to the day of her graduation from high school at seventeen.

Julie Trilling goes to live in the country with her aunt about five miles from the little town where her father is a college professor. The aunt is a no-nonsense sort of person whom Julie often resents but whom she eventually learns to love and respect. Although Aunt Cordelia is strict, she has compassion and understanding.

The adult characters are portrayed as real people and are not simply shadowy backdrops for the activities of the young. There is the story of Aunt Cordelia's lost romance, when as a young woman she did not marry the man she loved because of family responsibilities. Uncle Haskell, Aunt Cordelia's brother, is shown as a charming, irresponsible drunkard and a pathological liar. He does not wish to be a "good, gray uncle, full of wisdom," but there are a few times when he plays the part in spite of himself. He encourages Julie's desire to write and demands her best, he rescues her from herself and an amorous beau, and reaching beyond the family, he is exceedingly kind to the mentally ill wife of the man Aunt Cordelia once loved.

There are no really dramatic adventures in Julie Trilling's life, but the story of her problems with her family and friends, her loves, her quarrels, her small triumphs and disasters form a book that is, on the whole, a delight. The story is real, it has dimension, its characters are alive, it moves with a fine pace, and it is beautifully written. Young girls experiencing much of the pain and heartbreak, as well as many of the joys, of growing up will read *Up a Road Slowly* with sympathetic understanding and enjoyment.

Stories of the Sea

BOOKS FOR YOUNGER CHILDREN

Little Tim and the Brave Sea Captain, written and illustrated by the distinguished Edward Ardizzone, is a rare and impressive example of a sea story for the youngest.

The book launches a series of spirited adventures which feature a little boy in a thrilling way—especially since it all began with Little Tim playing innocently among the boats and seashells on the beach. Here a young child is brought into contact with salty excursions that lead to strange port towns, while a shipwreck and rescue with the Brave Sea Captain heighten the excitement that follows. The high adventure packed

Just as they were about to sink beneath the waves Tim gave a great cry. 'We're saved. We're saved.'

Realism flows in the story line as well as in the pictures that record a tense moment at sea. Firm line drawings distinguish the work of an artist who adds washes of color to highlight this sea story.

From Little Tim and the Brave Sea Captain *by Edward Ardizzone. Copyright* © *1955 by Henry Z. Walck, Inc. Reproduced by permission.*

into this superb picture book reveals the artistry of Ardizzone, who has
endeared himself to boys in particular with seafaring yarns matched with
powerful pictures of seascapes and seafaring men.

The Life-Savers, written and illustrated by Anne Cleveland, is a
wonderful sea story for younger children. Sandy, Jeff, and Jane are invited
to visit their Aunt Martha at the lake. Noah, Aunt Martha's big dog, is
told to guard Sandy so he will not drown, but in the end it is Sandy who
saves Noah.

Children create a private world of their own, one completely set
apart from adult supervision or criticism. They form their own clubs and
secret societies with codes of rules and ethics. Mildred Myrick in *The
Secret Three* perceptively describes three boys who have begun such an
association. Mark and Tom, both seeking a new adventure, discover a
message in a sealed bottle washed up on the shore. Through it they form
a secret club with the son of a lighthouse keeper. When the boys finally
meet, they become fast friends and design their own secret words, codes
signals, and handshakes.

BOOKS FOR INTERMEDIATE-GRADE CHILDREN

In *Cabin Boy Ballast* by Barbara Reynolds, Mr. Andrews
sails with his family from the United States to Japan, a voyage that has
always been a family dream. Their trip, however, turns out to be far
from pleasant; it is filled with fear and danger. This story has lots of
excitement and will be a challenge for the intermediate-grade child.

But for sheer excitement few books can rival Robert Louis Stevenson's *Treasure Island*, one of the most remarkable adventure stories ever
written. It was first published as a serial in the *Young Folks* magazine in
1881 under the pseudonym of Captain George North, and a year after
its serialization it appeared as a full-length book with Stevenson's by-line.
Written to entertain Lloyd Osbourne, the author's bored stepson living
in Scotland, the book is ranked among the best realistically-drawn sea and
treasure island stories written specifically for children.

This excellent example of an adventure story unfolds a tightly-knit
plot concerning a few guileless gentlefolk in the hands of villainous pirates
led by the colorful Long John Silver. Sailing on the pirate ship *Hispaniola*
there is a boy named Jim Hawkins. Through Jim much of the story is
told in a way that a boy would see it and with the morality of a young
adventurer. Departing from the stereotyped story where virtue triumphs
over villainy, *Treasure Island* lures young readers down pirate trails, to

buried treasure, on high adventure with seafaring men and salty thrills. Here is a robust account in the idiom of boyhood. Here, a "smooth and formidable" villain transports young hopefuls along an adventure-packed route with blood, rum, and the haunting song of "Fifteen men on the dead man's chest." (Actually this quote was the result of a typographical error that made the passage even more lusty than it should have been. Dead Man's Chest was intended to be the name of the island in the pirate zone rather than part of a corpse.) But whether by accident or intent, the story remains exciting with high adventure, extraordinary thrills, and unforgettable characters.

Inherent in *Treasure Island* are not only the qualities of Stevenson's creative imagination exercised in the storytelling art but also his masterly prose style, which gives life and integrity to his characters and at the same time sharpens the relief of the route they travel. So strongly vivid are his descriptions and so exact are his picturesque words that the whole story readily becomes imprinted upon the young reader's imagination as if he had actually undergone a strange, exciting, and real experience.

BOOKS FOR UPPER-GRADE CHILDREN

A thrilling adventure story for the upper-grade child is *Lost Off the Grand Banks* by Arthur Catherall. Geoff and Kinney, lost at sea, board the *Lucky Mactear*, only to find that the boat is deserted except for an injured captain. To make matters worse, the ship is about to collide with an iceberg. The boys also discover that an American submarine is caught in the ice with seventy men aboard, but Geoff is finally able to radio ashore for help.

For more mature readers the great sea story of *Moby Dick* by Herman Melville remains unrivaled. This is a story of magnitude that along with others of its kind marked the beginning of realism in the books American children read.

"To write a mighty book," Herman Melville once remarked, "you must have a mighty theme." To that prescription he wrote *Moby Dick*. And focusing on the mightiest of human themes he used a mighty symbol, a creature from the watery depths.

Packed with high adventure, drama, and suspense, the story follows the impetuous voyages of an obsessed captain determined to take revenge against the white whale that once injured him. Scouring the seas in maniacal pursuit, Captain Ahab finally brings an end to his own life and to members of his ill-fated whaler crew in this, one of the best sea stories ever written.

Moby Dick, however, does not exist on a single level of meaning, and some of its levels may escape even the most precocious children. But as a narrative of masterful prose, ingenuity, and deep inner meanings, this novel succeeds where so many others fail.

Melville is a master of the literary art. In *Moby Dick* he combines a wonderful array of metaphors and symbols with a special talent for character development and a rare understanding of mankind and the kind of men who venture to "go down to the sea in ships, that do business in great waters."

With remarkable precision and expertise, Melville creates a gallery of striking personalities. His treatment of characters is sufficiently detailed to disclose a variety of human attributes and yet not so precise as to limit their possibilities for action. Melville relates the story through Ishmael, the only survivor of the ill-fated crew, and this point of view distinguishes the novel as a classic written in the first person. But whether speaking through Queequeg, Father Mapple, the obsessed Captain Ahab, or any other character in the story, the author arouses a sense of humanity and elicits a variety of emotions from the reader. Anger, compassion, love, hate, revenge, prejudice, serene piety—all are experienced or witnessed as the problems and mysteries of the plot are revealed and ultimately resolved.

Moby Dick has been termed an epic, a novel, a poem, a drama, a tragedy, and a history of whaling. For children it is all of these; but first it is an adventure story possessing the ingredients common to childhood: there are sailors, animals, strange men, strange names, a tatooed harpooner, an Indian Tashtego, a savage, a sea captain with scarred face and ivory leg, and a boy named Pip.

Sports Stories

Sports stories have been traditional favorites of boys of all ages and the selection has expanded in the twentieth century to include many tales of great interest to girls as well.

Along with the story may come some information about the techniques used in a specific activity. These realistic stories provide an opportunity for the young reader to see that hard work and determination are important ingredients in winning a game or accomplishing a feat.

Young children are concerned with their own abilities. When they try to imitate the activities of older brothers and sisters, they are sometimes discouraged because they are not physically mature enough to succeed.

By reading about other children who are faced with the same problem, they find comfort and relief from their anxieties.

On the other hand, the older child seeks information about a specific sport or a particular hero, and he finds satisfaction in acquiring more knowledge in his chosen field.

BOOKS FOR YOUNGER CHILDREN

Ben on the Ski Trail, written and illustrated by Leonard Shortall, is an exciting story for the younger reader. Ben borrows skiing equipment and sets out to learn the sport. At first he feels very awkward and discouraged, but his perseverance helps him to succeed. He becomes so proficient that he is asked to help the ski patrol in a rescue. The text and illustrations are lively and accurate as they take the reader through the beginning phases of skiing. Though the style is not complex, the story is interesting and will hold the attention of many young readers.

In *Who Will Be My Friends?* written and illustrated by Syd Hoff, a little boy who has just moved into a new neighborhood searches for someone with whom he can play. He tries to join a group of boys playing baseball, and finally they agree to let him play because he can catch and throw. He feels very accomplished and enjoys the company of his new friends.

Children all over the world enjoy sports. Through books of other cultures, children learn about the interests of other peoples and about the

Lines flow lucidly in this double-page spread full of exotic color from Thailand. Oriental forms of kites and costumes enhance the panorama drawn for this favorite sport of a distant land.
From Nu Dang and His Kite *by Jacqueline Ayer. Copyright © 1959 by the author–illustrator. Reproduced by permission of Harcourt, Brace & World, Inc.*

Nu Dang's kite was
It ran swiftly with th
and chased the birds
Nu Dang was the ha
He was the happiest
He was the happiest
Nu Dang was *just* tha

countries in which they live. *Nu Dang and His Kite*, written and illustrated by Jacqueline Ayer, is set in Siam. With simple lines the illustrations capture the spirit of that exotic country as well as Nu Dang's neighbors.

Another book set in a foreign land is *Chie and the Sports Day* by Masaka Matsuno. Chie has no one to play with since her brother Ichiro began school. She admires him and everything he does, and so looks forward to the school "Sports Day." But Ichiro dreads it, for he is the slowest boy in his class. Just as he feared, Ichiro loses his race, but he is entered in another race which he must run with a little girl. He chooses Chie, and together they win the three-legged race. The book is truly charming, as are the illustrations that accompany the delightful text. The author proves that she has a clear understanding of young children as she fills a realistic tale with warmth and humor.

Kiki Skates, written and illustrated by Charlotte Steiner, is the story of a little girl who visits her grandmother in the country where she learns about winter sports. This book for the youngest age group has delightful illustrations of young children enjoying snow sports and the text is very simple and easy to follow.

BOOKS FOR INTERMEDIATE-GRADE CHILDREN

In *Little Leaguer's First Uniform* by Paul Jackson, Johnny Cook fears that his brother, a star Little Leaguer, will catch the mumps from

him before the team leaves for the Little League World Series. Hank does come down with the mumps and Johnny, wearing his uniform, is sent as his replacement. During the Series he hears the laughter of the crowd as they ridicule him for his size and his large uniform, but he proves to everyone that he is a valuable member of the team as he catches the ball that saves the game. Johnny's determination and his deep sense of pride and responsibility make him a sympathetic character. Realistically presented, this book moves at a fast pace. The illustrations mirror the joys and anxieties of the players.

The Big Basketball Prize by Marion Renick deals with a boy's dreams and aspirations and his perseverance in achieving them. Timmy wants to enter the basketball contest, but he is so awkward that he thinks he should not even try. His neighbor tells him that he needs "perfect muscular control," and his grandmother gives him some secret advice. Timmy wins the contest and attributes his success to his grandmother's secret. The collaboration of illustrator and author has resulted in an exciting story that will delight many a young basketball fan.

Tommy Carries the Ball by James and Marion Renick is the story of a little boy who is not good enough to make the football team. One day while watching the university team at practice he meets the star of the collegiate team, who offers to help him learn how to play the sport well. Tommy finally does get to play as his skill improves, and he becomes the star of an exciting football game. This is an excellent book for young boys who are interested in learning about football. The reader traces the development of this little boy as he faithfully practices the new techniques that his hero teaches him. It illustrates that stick-to-itiveness is an important factor in determining whether a goal can be achieved or not.

BOOKS FOR UPPER-GRADE CHILDREN

In *Touchdown Maker* by Dick Friendlick, Russ Harkness decides to forget football now that he is in a new town and a new high school. He does not want to become part of after-school activities and resents the small-town attitudes of the people. But he reevaluates some of his own ideas and attitudes when his father has a serious accident and is helped by everyone in the community. The reader comes to know Russ and sympathize with him as he makes difficult decisions and grows up.

Highpockets by John R. Tunis is the story of Cecil McDade, "Highpockets," a rookie for the Brooklyn Dodgers who is interested only in his own score and batting average. But when he accidentally hits a boy while driving his new car, he comes to realize that there are other things more important than baseball. He learns how to give of himself and ultimately receives a great deal in return. Excellent character study makes this an important book. Authentic, blow-by-blow descriptions keep the reader enthralled as he traces the development of a man and a ballplayer.

Another exciting story about baseball is *Stretch Bolton, Mister Shortstop* by Burgess Leonard. Stretch Bolton is the manager of a major league baseball team, but when he loses the pennant and the World Series he is traded to another team as a shortstop. This new adjustment is a hard one for him to make. His goal is to win, but fairly, and his team resents this. When he is asked to fill in as manager temporarily, their antagonism grows, but he pulls the team together in time to win the World Series. This book goes beyond baseball to deal with personality conflicts, doubts, and anxieties. The characters are down-to-earth people who must cope with difficult problems.

Children move quickly from one stage of development to another, and there are thousands of books from which they can choose according to their individual interests and personalities. The division of realism, with its many categories, supplies the child with an abundance of material to suit any mood or need.

Criteria
for Realistic Stories

THEME

- Are the themes in the stories aligned with the realities of the here-and-now in child life?
- Are the themes expressive of the real problems, concerns, and delights characteristic of the emotional level for which the book is intended?
- Are the stories built around themes of reassurance, security, and ideals of humankind?

PLOT

- Does the plot sufficiently convey the theme?
- Is there lively and vigorous action appropriate to a realistic story?
- Does the plot incorporate a realistic element of suspense?
- Is the action of the plot consistent and sequential?
- Is there a clear-cut and satisfying conclusion?
- Does the plot emphasize achievement of goals rather than defeat?

- Is the child readily able to identify himself with the plot because it is drawn from real life?
- Does the plot help fulfill the child's basic needs—security, acceptance, competence, knowledge, and diversity—the needs of his actuality?
- In an animal or natural science story, does the plot stay true to the nature and ways of each species?
- Is the plot convincingly real?
- Does the plot incorporate a child's responses to and view of the world rather than an adult's?
- Does the plot lead the child to a greater understanding of himself and other people?

CHARACTERIZATION

- Are the characters real people, and do they talk and act as real people in their situation?
- Do the characters relate to their particular educational and cultural background?
- Are the characters alive and memorable?
- Are the characters more than mere stereotypes?
- Are some of the characters lovable, exasperating, heroic, absurd, delightful, humorous, sentimental, or romantic?
- Do the characters give the child greater confidence in approaching the next level of life?
- Are the characters built upon a theme of reassurance?
- Can a child acquire self-knowledge and an understanding of life from the characters?
- Can the child gain added experiences through the characters who figure in a story with realism?

STYLE

- Does the book have lasting value because of the excellence of its artistic expression?
- Is the author's style of writing distinctive despite its less imaginative story?
- Does the author's choice of words reveal a measure of imagination?
- Do the words convey sound and create vivid imagery in a realistic way?
- Is the style appealing and forthright with those dramatic elements appropriate to the realistically told story?
- Does the writer see the world with integrity and express the truth without clothing it in symbols and allegory?

- Does the story give the young reader or listener a sense of reality without distortion?

SETTING

- Are the special elements of realism in the story accurately drawn?
- Are concepts of time, life and place presented with simplicity, avoiding telescoping action and flashbacks?
- Are the settings convincingly real and true to life?
- Is the setting skillfully used in the development of the story to give a sense of immediacy?
- Do descriptions and pictures realistically depict the time and place?
- Are pictures, drawings, and descriptions of places familiar and recognizable in stories of contemporary life?
- Are the costumes, scenery, and landmarks realistic and memorable in stories of other peoples and lands?
- Are descriptions and pictures of places, people, and things presented realistically?
- Do the pictures of the settings create an atmosphere of reality by use of color, shapes, figures, humorous composition, detail, and beauty?
- Do the pictures transport the reader to the scene so that a sense of actuality is stirred?
- Do the pictures and images capture the spirit of the story in a realistic sense?
- Does the setting, no matter how realistic, appeal to the child's basic love of beauty and adventure?
- Are the pictures and descriptions appropriate to the experiential level, maturity, and background of the child?

References

ARBUTHNOT, MAY HILL, "Here and Now," in *Children and Books*, 3rd ed. Chicago: Scott, Foresman & Company, 1964.

HOLLOWELL, LILLIAN, "Fiction," in *A Book of Children's Literature*, 3rd ed. New York: Holt, Rinehart & Winston, Inc., 1966.

HUCK, CHARLOTTE S., and DORIS A. YOUNG, "Children Have Special Interests," in *Children's Literature in the Elementary School*. New York: Holt, Rinehart & Winston, Inc., 1961.

SMITH, LILLIAN H., "Stories," in *The Unreluctant Years*. Chicago: American Library Association, 1953.

Realism in Children's Literature

ANIMALS, CHILDREN, AND THEIR ENVIRONMENTS

For younger children

SARAH AND SIMON AND NO RED PAINT
Written and illustrated by Edward Ardizzone. Delacorte Press, 1966.

Sarah and Simon live with their father, a painter, their mother and baby brother, in a big room called a studio. Father is too poor to finish his masterpiece—until his two resourceful children take charge of the family's finances. The illustrations are charming and delightful to look at.

THIN ICE
Written by Jerrold Beim. Illustrated by Louis Darling. William Morrow & Co., Inc., 1956.

An inspired little story that deals with a small boy's ambivalent feelings toward his many sisters, this is a satisfying literary experience for young readers. The bold gray wash drawings beautifully depict the everyday life of a child.

BALLET FOR MARY
Written and illustrated by Emma Lillian Brock. Alfred A. Knopf, Inc., 1954.

Amusing story of "Sudden" Mary, an eight-year-old who is all angles and awkwardness, who decides that she would like to join her best friend in taking ballet lessons. Her family fears that this will simply mean more upset and broken furniture, but they agree to let her try. Although she does not become exactly graceful, she does, as her mother says, learn to "bump into things more skillfully," and when the class gives its first recital, Mary inadvertently becomes the star performer. The author has written with warmth and humor of real and exceedingly likable people.

BENJY'S BLANKET
Written by Myra B. Brown. Illustrated by Dorothy Marino. Franklin Watts, Inc., 1962.

Benjy's baby blanket gives him security, but everyone teases him about it. Not until Benjy becomes more mature emotionally does he give it up. Gently sympathetic to early childhood's needs, this simple little story is tenderly supported by pictures in black, gray, and gold.

DID YOU CARRY THE FLAG TODAY, CHARLEY?
Written by Rebecca Caudill. Illustrated by Nancy Grossman. Holt Rinehart & Winston, Inc., 1966.

Carrying the flag is the reward for the most helpful child each day in The Little School. Charley Cornett seems least likely to merit it because of his exuberant curiosity, his uncontrollable desire to explore, and his attention-getting shenanigans. How Charley eventually gets to carry the flag is told in this true-to-life story, which is written with honesty and matter-of-factness.

HENRY HUGGINS
Written by Beverly Cleary. Illustrated by Louis Darling. William Morrow & Co., Inc., 1950.

A genuinely funny and captivating story

of a boy named Henry who adopts a stray dog, and with him, lots of trouble. The charm of this story lies in its depiction of everyday life and a believable boy that together add up to something uncommonly funny.

THE LAST LITTLE CAT
Written by Meindert DeJong.
Illustrated by Jim McMullan.
Harper & Row, Publishers, 1961.

This is the touching story of a cat, the last of a litter born in a kennel. Neglected by his mother, the cat forms a bond of mutual love with the kennel owner's old blind dog. The black-and-white illustrations are expressive and appealing in this realistic story of a little cat who is looking for warmth, food, and comfort.

OASIS OF THE STARS
Written by Olga Economakis.
Illustrated by Blair Lent.
Coward-McCann, Inc., 1965.

Lyrical prose and lovely pictures tell of Abu, a little nomadic boy, who wishes for a permanent home in an oasis. His yearning for a real home is captured in a setting of desert beauty.

ANGELO: THE NAUGHTY ONE
Written by Helen Garret.
Illustrated by Leo Politi. The
Viking Press, Inc., 1944.

Angelo is a Mexican boy who loves to wallow in the mud and hates to take baths. The book portrays the common childhood inclination to get dirty and the great difficulty of staying clean.

PROSERPINA: THE DUCK THAT CAME TO SCHOOL
Written by Constantine Georgiou.
Illustrated by Bernard Lipscomb.
Harvey House, Inc., Publishers,
1968.

Paul's duck Proserpina, named after the mythical goddess of ancient Greece, lives and grows in a classroom until she is taken to live in Rock Creek Park.

One day she is missing from the park and Paul decides that she is not lost but that she has been transformed to shine as a star along with the goddess for whom she was named. The lovely illustrations haunt the imagination as they interpret the quiet text with sympathy and tenderness.

WHOSE LITTLE RED JACKET?
Written by Mary McBurney Green.
Illustrated by Tony de Luna.
Franklin Watts, Inc., 1965.

Jimmy loves his little red jacket, but he outgrows it and passes it along to Andy and then to Molly and Sally. It gains as many alterations as wearers. Unexpectedly, Jimmy receives the jacket again—altered to fit him now that he is older. The return of the cherished possession to its original owner is quaintly depicted in this picture book.

THE WORLD IN A CITY BLOCK
Written and illustrated by Natalie
Hall. The Viking Press, Inc., 1960.

Nine-year-old Nick misses his older brother who has left home to join the Merchant Marine, so he too decides to see the world by getting to know the people of many nationalities who are his neighbors on his own city block. The pictures fortify the qualities of precision and inspiration found in the text, and the result is a book children will truly enjoy.

PROJECT: SCOOP
Written and illustrated by William
D. Hayes. Atheneum Publishers,
1966.

The school paper keeps an editor in hilarious difficulties. This is a book to delight any young reader's adventuresome heart.

MULEY-EARS: NOBODY'S DOG
Written by Marguerite Henry.
Illustrated by Wesley Dennis. Rand
McNally & Co., 1959.

Set in exotic Jamaica, this story tells about a dog who belonged to no one and yet to everyone. The heart-warming account is illumined with outstanding illustrations in color and black and white.

EVAN'S CORNER
Written by Elizabeth Starr Hill.
Illustrated by Nancy Grossman.
Holt, Rinehart & Winston, Inc.,
1967.

In a warm realistic atmosphere of a crowded home the themes of sharing as well as possessing are honestly conveyed. More than anything else in the world, Evan, a small boy in a large family, wants a place he can call his own. Difficult as this may be, Evan's mother manages to provide a corner for each one in the family and there is one for him as well. Here Evan struggles for privacy and strives to beautify his corner with a picture he painted in school, a plant he potted himself, a goldfish bowl with a turtle, and so on. The completion of the corner brings about Evan's satisfaction only when he shares his skill to fix up his little brother's corner across the crowded room. Pleasing pictures in line drawings and color washes blend to produce a fine book for younger children.

ONE MORNING IN MAINE
Written and illustrated by Robert
McCloskey. The Viking Press, Inc.,
1952.

The loss of a first tooth is always a momentous occasion in a young child's life. All the anxiety, excitement, and anticipation that are part of this important event are movingly captured in this warmly written story of that special morning in Maine when Sal loses her first tooth. The large double-page lithographs in dark blue filled with the feeling of the woods, beach, and sea along the coast of Maine add to the magical quality of the day.

TIME OF WONDER
Written and illustrated by Robert
McCloskey. The Viking Press Inc.,
1957.

The breathtaking beauty and mystical elements of nature are vividly described in this story of children vacationing on an island in Maine. From a foggy spring morning through to the approach of fall, a sense of seasonal sequence is given by the poetic text and superb watercolors.

BLUEBERRIES FOR SAL
Written and illustrated by Robert
McCloskey. The Viking Press, Inc.,
1948.

Sal and her mother enjoy picking blueberries in the pasture, as do Little Bear and his mother. As Sal and Little Bear wander along, more interested in eating the sweet blueberries than in watching where they are going, they each inadvertently follow the wrong mother. How this situation is solved is told in humorous text and appropriate blueberry-colored drawings.

SAM, BANGS AND MOONSHINE
Written and illustrated by Evaline
Ness. Holt, Rinehart & Winston,
Inc., 1966.

An understanding portrayal of a lonely child's predilection for daydreams, this striking picture book spells out the difference between uncontrolled flights of fantasy and the real world. Not until her farfetched talk pushes her only friend, Thomas, and her beloved cat, Bangs, to the edge of destruction does Sam become aware of the difference between "real" and "moonshine."

CITY BOY, COUNTRY BOY
Written by Miriam Schlein.
Illustrated by Katherine Evans.
Children's Press, Inc., 1955.

Bright pictures and simple, lilting text contrast the lives of two boys from different backgrounds: city and country. Bringing in much of the wonder of both boys' backgrounds, this beautiful book holds rare appeal for young children.

SAM
Written by Ann Herbert Scott.
Illustrated by Symeon Shimin.
McGraw-Hill Book Company, 1967.

In a sensitive and touching urban story, a little Negro boy, Sam, dramatizes experiences common to childhood. Sam, who lives in a throbbing city, wants to play amidst the busy surroundings of his home. But when he wants to play, his mother is busy in the kitchen, his brother is busy with homework, his sister defends her dolls from her playful brother, and his father is too busy at the typewriter to take time out to play with him. Then after a tearful outburst Sam gets the attention he is seeking, and warm human relations shine through in this skillfully written and realistically drawn book.

ANDY WOULDN'T TALK
Written by Jane Thayer. Illustrated by Meg Wohlberg. William Morrow & Co., Inc., 1957.

Because he is so shy, Andy talks only with his mother and his dog, Gertrude. One day when Andy and Gertrude are lost, and Andy has to speak up to save his dog, he learns the joy of conversation. Cheerful pictures and large print make this book both appealing and easy to read for the young child.

LET'S BE ENEMIES
Written by Janice M. Udry. Illustrated by Maurice Sendak. Harper & Row, Publishers, 1961.

This is a story of the ups and downs of a friendship between two young boys. The brief text and clear, buoyant pictures that tell the tale in themselves appeal to very young children who will identify and respond to the situations.

ANNIE'S SPENDING SPREE
Written by Nancy Dingman Watson. Illustrated by Aldren Watson. The Viking Press, Inc., 1957.

Annie is faced with tantalizing decisions when she is given a dollar to spend on the day before her birthday. The story, which offers painless practice in arithmetic, has a happy surprise-party ending. Even young

children may be able to read the simple text and follow the gay, detailed pictures.

THE TWO REDS
Written and illustrated by Will and Nicolas. Harcourt, Brace & World, Inc., 1950.

One Red is a boy, the other a cat. One day when Red is being chased by a neighborhood gang and the cat by a fisherman, they escape together and become good friends. The story reveals only a small measure of originality, but the pictures are excellent.

BIG SISTER AND LITTLE SISTER
Written by Charlotte Zolotow. Illustrated by Martha Alexander. Harper & Row, Publishers, 1966.

A charming little girls' story describing a small child's need to give as well as to receive. Young readers will love the story about two sisters and what they learn from each other. The minutely detailed illustrations are done in pink and green pastels.

For intermediate-grade children

MY BROTHER BIRD
Written by Evelyn Perkins Ames. Illustrated by William Pène du Bois. Dodd, Mead & Co., 1954.

Smoky, an ordinary New York pigeon hatched on a Park Avenue window sill, loses his mother, so the Bennets adopt him and take him to Long Island with them. The author's observation of birds is precise and poetic, and the illustrator has caught the personalities of the children and the free spirit of the pigeon in his sensitive drawings.

NINO
Written and illustrated by Valenti Angelo. The Viking Press, Inc., 1938.

Based on the author's boyhood in Tuscany, this is the story of Nino, who lives in an Italian village with his mother and grandfather until the family moves to America to join Nino's father. The dominant impression left by this book is one of beauty—beauty of format, illustrations, and text.

THE BELLS OF BLEECKER STREET
Written and illustrated by Valenti Angelo. The Viking Press, Inc., 1949.

The story takes place on Bleecker Street, near the end of the Second World War. Joey Enrico and his friend, Pete the Squeak, go through many small but exciting adventures in this satisfying and realistic picture of New York's "Little Italy." The author exhibits his understanding of the Italian temperament with warmth and vitality.

THE TALE OF A DONKEY
Written and illustrated by Valenti Angelo. The Viking Press, Inc., 1966.

Cherubino, a little gray donkey, is sold to three men who treat him cruelly until he runs away. Carlo nurses the donkey back to health and treats him with a kindness he has not known before. Valenti Angelo's artistry, his love of the Italian countryside, and his compassion for all creatures shine through in both text and illustrations.

BIG LITTLE ISLAND
Written and illustrated by Valenti Angelo. The Viking Press, Inc., 1949.

The pattern of family life in New York today, colored and shaped by Italian warmth and vivacity, is the background for this moving story of a war orphan's struggle to find himself amid the confusion and alien beauty of Manhattan. Valenti Angelo writes of the boy's spiritual loneliness with understanding and gives it true perspective with exuberant descriptions of family celebrations and tempestuous island excursions.

THE MARBLE FOUNTAIN
Written and illustrated by Valenti Angelo. The Viking Press, Inc., 1951.

Two young Italian boys, orphaned during the war, help rebuild the village where they come to live. This touching and arresting story is filled with humor, action, and a significant message about the results of war that a young reader will be able to comprehend. Simplicity, gentle humor, and compassion for people add beauty and balance.

THE HONEY BOAT
Written and illustrated by Valenti Angelo. The Viking Press, Inc., 1959.

The simple tale of Italian customs is filled with happy personalities, interesting anecdotes, curious facts, and good descriptions. The setting is the author's native Tuscany. Andrea and his family, who belong to the beekeeping colony along the River Po, go cruising in the blossom-filled springtime. This is a story of happy adventure and family strength to which the author brings a very special understanding.

TROUBLEMAKER
Written by Alberta Armer. Illustrated by J. C. Kocsis. World Publishing Co., 1966.

Twelve-year-old Joe Fuller has been placed in a detention home because he is guilty of petty thievery; his father is in jail and his mother in a state hospital. When the welfare board sends him to stay with foster parents, the Murrays, Joe is prepared to dislike them. Conscious of the inadequacies of his real parents, Joe tells spun-sugar fantasies about his hospitalized mother. Not until she recovers and comes for a visit is Joe able to face reality and admit that his life with the Murray family has a warmth and satisfaction that he hopes to find when his own home is re-established. The story has a message, but no moralizing, and the characterizations are perceptive and sympathetic.

THE SMALLEST BOY IN THE CLASS
Written by Jerrold Beim. Illustrated by Meg Wohlberg. William Morrow & Co., Inc., 1949.

Jimmy, the smallest boy in the class, is nicknamed Tiny. One day at a picnic, Tiny has a chance to show that being big is not always a matter of size. Children will find it easy to identify with this character and to see that important values overshadow lesser ones. The illustrations are realistic and convincing.

A DASH OF PEPPER
Written by Thelma Harrington Bell.
Illustrated by Corydon Bell. The
Viking Press, Inc., 1965.

Clyde Downing's dream horses, Pepper and Salt, are for sale but his parents refuse to let him have a horse of his own. The Downing's family doctor tells Clyde why his parents refuse even to talk about horses—a reason deeply rooted in grief. Corydon Bell's distinguished drawings add vividness and reality.

SEA PUP
Written by Archie Binns. Illustrated
by Robert Candy. Little, Brown &
Co., 1954.

An unusually lively and amusing animal story about Clint Barlow and the baby seal he rescues and raises. Buster makes friends with Clint and his pet, and paves the way for Clint to begin his life work as an oceanographer. An excellent mixture of humor, adventure, and excellent characterization.

A PRESENT FROM PETRO
Written by Claire Huchet Bishop.
Illustrated by Dimitris Davis. The
Viking Press, Inc., 1961.

On the Island of Rhodes, Petros and his donkey, Kyrios, are hired for the summer to guide and amuse ten-year-old Susan Spenser. The little American girl is so good to Petros that he plans a way to give her a present—his donkey. Drawings by the talented Greek artist convey the loveliness of Petro's island and of his gift. The child's keen awareness of reality is entirely credible, and the humor is sufficient to save the story from sentimentality.

THE HOUSE AT 12 ROSE STREET
Written by Mimi Brodsky.
Illustrated by David Hodges.
Abelard-Schuman Limited, 1966.

The problems of a twelve-year-old Negro boy whose family has moved into a white neighborhood are not easily solved, but they are deeply probed in this skillfully written and timely story. The characterizations are well rounded and the conflicts perceptively presented.

SKINNY
Written by Robert Burch. Illustrated
by Don Sibley. The Viking Press,
Inc., 1965.

Skinny is an illiterate twelve-year-old orphan who is the heart and soul of a small-town hotel in Georgia. The regional dialogue and genuine humor heighten the pleasure of knowing this memorable boy. A warm and vivid picture of rural life in the South that avoids both sentimentality and sensationalism.

REGGIE'S NO-GOOD BIRD
Written by Nellie Burchardt.
Illustrated by Harold Benson.
Franklin Watts, Inc., 1967.

Whenever there is mischief in the city housing project where he lives, Reggie Thompson seems to be right in the middle of it. When he throws a crushed tin can and hits a baby blue jay, he suddenly finds himself in possession of a bird whose presence in the crowded apartment must be kept secret from his parents. The problems of feeding and hiding a noisy little bird are amusingly and sympathetically told. Harold Benson's pictures show distinct agreement with the straightforward text.

THE INCREDIBLE JOURNEY
Written by Sheila Burnford.
Illustrated by Carl Burger. Little,
Brown & Co., 1961.

A young Labrador retriever sets out with two companions, a Siamese cat and an old bull terrier, on a journey through the

Canadian wilderness. Together they battle starvation, exposure, and wild animals, resisting the human beings who try to detain them. Courage and devotion keynote this story, which is a mixture of fact and fiction without sentimentality. Each animal has a unique personality, which strengthens the realism. The author manages to invest her tale with suspense, drama, and a close feeling for the kinship between man and beast.

Borghill of Brooklyn
Written by Harriet H. Carr.
Illustrated by Dorothy B. Morse.
Farrar, Straus & Giroux, Inc.,
1955.

A young Norwegian girl moves to midtown Manhattan to live with her Americanized aunt and family but finds more compatible friends and family in the Norweigan colony in Brooklyn. This realistic and convincing story with a significant theme is notable also for its description of the Norwegians who settled in Brooklyn.

Little Navajo Bluebird
Written by Ann Nolan Clark.
Illustrated by Paul Lantz. The
Viking Press, Inc., 1943.

The story of Doli, a charming little Navajo songstress, whose heart carries the burden of her people and who does her best to further the old customs and ways. Through the sympathy and wisdom of her brother's wife, she comes to see that the Red Man's Trail and the White Man's Trail may meet. Illustrations are done excellently in soft pencil. There is a quiet rhythm in the writing making it a deeply sympathetic book.

In My Mother's House
Written by Ann Nolan Clark. Illustrated
by Velino Herrera. The Viking
Press, Inc., 1941.

This story of everyday life in a Pueblo village is written as if a Tewa child were speaking simply and beautifully of the small world he knows and holds dear. The cadenced prose of this text is matched by the beauty of the black-and-white illustrations. This book gives a real sense of knowing Indian boys and girls and the feeling of experience shared.

The Trail of the Hunter's Horn
Written by Billy C. Clark.
Illustrated by Veronica Reed. G. P.
Putnam's Sons, 1957.

A sensitive, beautifully written story of a young boy in the Kentucky mountains who is given a pup that is blind in one eye. Bitterly ashamed of the dog at first, the boy gradually comes to an awareness of his responsibility for helping it to overcome its handicap, and in the process he takes a long step toward maturity. The story shows great understanding of a young boy's reaction to a difficult situation.

Dorp Dead
Written by Julia Cunningham.
Illustrated by James Spanfeller.
Pantheon Books, Inc., 1965.

Gilly Ground learns that Kobalt, the laddermaker, "is cruel, not just hardhearted" in this grimly enthralling tale of an orphan boy's emergence into a smiling world. (Emotionally mature readers.)

Adopted Jane
Written by Helen Form Daringer.
Illustrated by Kate Seredy.
Harcourt, Brace & World, Inc.,
1947.

This is the touching story of Jane Douglas, a ten-year-old girl who has been brought up in an orphanage. The author creates in Jane a realistic central character, small, quiet, sensitive, wishing to be loved and to love. This is a moving, well-written story with high emotional appeal.

The House of Sixty Fathers
Written by Meindert DeJong.
Illustrated by Maurice Sendak.
Harper & Row, Publishers, 1956.

During China's war with Japan, Tien Pao is separated from his parents. This is the story of a small boy's courage, his desperate search for his parents, and his adventures with an American soldier until he and his family are reunited. This is a moving account of a child caught in the horror of a war-torn world.

BRIGHT APRIL
Written and illustrated by
Marguerite de Angeli. Doubleday
& Company, Inc., 1946.

April, a little Negro girl, has a happy middle-class home, school, and social life. She is unaware of racial prejudice and encounters it for the first time at a Brownie party when a girl refuses to sit next to her. April accepts this girl's intolerance and wins her over as a friend. With the aid of her family and scout leader, April is able to cope with and understand racial discrimination.

THE HUNDRED DRESSES
Written by Eleanor Estes. Illustrated
by Louis Slobodkin. Harcourt,
Brace & World, Inc., 1944.

Wanda Petronski, a girl of Polish descent, comes from a poor family. When she is teased by her classmates about her name and lack of clothes, she tells them that she has one hundred dresses and proves it by winning a class contest with her entry of one hundred sketches of beautifully designed clothes. The author describes the lack of tolerance and the cruelty that can be demonstrated against someone of different background. The story is simple, hard-hitting, and to the point.

THE MOFFATS
Written by Eleanor Estes. Illustrated
by Louis Slobodkin. Harcourt,
Brace & World, Inc., 1941.

Here is the warm, humorous story of a poor Connecticut family consisting of four young Moffats and Mama Moffat, seen through the eyes of nine-year-old Janey. The illustrations by Louis Slobod-

kin are realistic and lend much to the warmth of this book.

BLUE WILLOW
Written by Doris Gates. Illustrated
by Paul Lantz. The Viking Press,
Inc., 1940.

Janey Larkin is the ten-year-old daughter of a migrant worker who faces hardships with courage and inner strength. She cherishes her Blue Willow plate, the last remembrance of a time when her family was prosperous. The author brings to light the social implications of the migratory worker's family through the main character, Janey, and the constant struggle for financial, physical, and emotional security. To cushion the harshness of life for migratory families, the author presents a close-knit, happy family relationship in which a child is able to make the best of her circumstances.

THE KARTERS
Written by William Gault. E. P.
Dutton & Co., Inc., 1965.

In a story about Tom and Elwood Roberts, William Gault shows young boys how exciting, safe, and healthy an interest in the sport of kart racing can be.

FROM THE MIXED-UP FILES OF
MRS. BASIL E. FRANKWEILER
Written and illustrated by E. L.
Konigsburg. Atheneum Publishers,
1967.

This Newbery Medal book tells superbly about the elegant running-away planned by a girl named Claudia and her little brother, Jamie. Choosing the Metropolitan Museum in New York City as their hiding place, these two children manage to live for a week before they are gently jolted to return home. The author-illustrator is also the producer of *Jennifer, Hecate, Macbeth, William McKinley and Me,* and *Elizabeth,* another amusing book written with care.

BETSY-TACY
*Written by Maud Hart Lovelace.
Illustrated by Lois Lenski. Thomas
Y. Crowell Company, 1940.*

This is a perfect story for young girls between the ages of eight and ten. The everyday lives of Betsy and Tacy become adventures, and the story of their friendship and its growth is the story of every child and a best friend. The illustrations by Lois Lenski ideally supplement the text.

HOMER PRICE
*Written and illustrated by Robert
McCloskey. The Viking Press, Inc.,
1943.*

This is a group of stories about Homer and his attempts at helping his uncle Ulysses in a restaurant. He helps by not making a few doughnuts as instructed but a few hundred. The cartoon drawings help to make this fantastic tale located in a small midwestern town seem real. It is a good book to read aloud to all ages.

LENTIL
*Written and illustrated by Robert
McCloskey. The Viking Press, Inc., 1940.*

This is a story of a young boy, Lentil, and his outstanding talent in playing the harmonica. Lively black-and-white drawings and sturdy text capture the energy and humor of a boy and his need to achieve.

THE MOST WONDERFUL DOLL IN
THE WORLD
*Written by Phyllis McGinley.
Illustrated by Helen Stone. J.B.
Lippincott Co., 1950.*

This is the story of a little girl, Dulcy, and the working of her imagination when she loses her favorite doll. This charming book will appeal to any little girl who enjoys playing with dolls.

SEA BEACH EXPRESS
*Written by George Panetta.
Illustrated by Emily McCully.
Harper & Row, Publishers, 1966.*

This realistic story bubbles with many of the good things in life. There is nine-year-old Tony's fat mama who sighs from the sweltering heat, Tony's father, Salvatore, an elevator operator who just wants to stay home on his day off. And around the table loaded with chicken cacciatore and wine, there is love, laughter and song. The Sea Beach Express goes to Coney Island, and even though the windows are dirty, "how wonderful it is to be alive on this day in Coney Island." Jews and Italians ride the subway, fat people wear bathing suits, and one little Puerto Rican boy doesn't wear anything at all. The line drawings let you know where you are every step of the way.

BIRKIN
*Written by Joan Phipson. Illustrated
by Margaret Horder. Harcourt, Brace
& World, Inc., 1966.*

The plight of a motherless calf, Birkin, draws together three oddly matched children: Frances, awkwardly growing out of childhood, Tony, who limps, and Angus, whose foreign accent subjects him to ridicule by the children of a small, rural Australian town. The three provide food for Birkin and defend him against the threats of angry townspeople whose yards he has trampled. During the year of care and concern, the children convincingly overcome or face up to their own problems.

HAMLET AND BROWNSWIGGLE
*Written by Barbara Reynolds.
Illustrated by Robert Henneberger.
Charles Scribner's Sons, 1954.*

Hamlet and Brownswiggle are hamsters, and the pets of fifth-grade Ricky Stern. Ricky had difficulty remembering the things he was supposed to do until he was told that if he could learn to accept responsibility, he would have a chance to have a hamster. This story is rich in humor concerning the characters and their situations.

A BRAND-NEW UNCLE
*Written and illustrated by Kate
Seredy. The Viking Press, Inc.,
1961.*

Two elderly people try to recapture youth by escaping from their children only to find that to have youth they must be with children. The problems conveyed are adult ones and young readers may not be mature enough to appreciate the warm human values implied. The superb illustrations help to convey the deep affection that an older child will feel in this warm and tender story.

ROOSEVELT GRADY
Written by Louisa R. Shotwell.
Illustrated by Peter Burchard.
World Publishing Co., 1963.

This is a story of migrant family life. Despite their lack of food and money, the family is happy because they have affection, humor, and love. This moving, tender book is enhanced by sensitive drawings.

BEST FRIEND
Written by Shirley Simon.
Illustrated by Reisie Lonette.
Lothrop, Lee & Shephard Co., Inc., 1964.

This is a story of the friendship of Jenny and Dot. The question that arises from this book is whether an adolescent should have a best friend or not. The realistic black-and-white illustrations help to make this story an enjoyable reading and learning experience.

ALL-OF-A-KIND FAMILY
Written by Sydney Taylor.
Illustrated by Helen John. Follett Publishing Company, 1951.

A story of five sisters in a Jewish family living in the New York of 1912. It describes the importance the Jewish holidays and the library have on these girls. Through its text and charming illustrations, a view of a loving, warm, and happy family is presented.

IN-BETWEEN MIYA
Written by Yoshiko Uchida.
Illustrated by Susan Bennett.
Charles Scribner's Sons, 1967.

As the daughter of the village priest, twelve-year old Miya wonders what it would be like to live in a beautiful house and have no worries about money. An invitation to Tokyo to help in the household of a wealthy uncle and aunt, a serious financial loss affecting a friend, and other events of the summer show Miya the true value of the integrity and simple dignity of her own family's life.

THE JAZZ MAN
Written by Mary Hays Weik.
Illustrated by Ann Grifalconi.
Atheneum Publishers, 1965.

This realistic depiction of modern existence throbs with the honest rhythms of city life. From a Harlem tenement nine-year-old Zeke, lame and a truant, watches his little world—the windows across the court. The woodcuts are carved out of a real Harlem world.

JUNKET
Written by Anne H. White.
Illustrated by Robert McCloskey.
The Viking Press, Inc., 1955.

This is a story of a dog named Junket who likes everything "just so" and tries to get his family to see his point of view. Here is a very lighthearted humorous book both in text and its black-and-white illustrations.

For upper-grade children

THE FAMILY UNDER THE BRIDGE
Written by Natalie Savage Carlson.
Illustrated by Garth Williams.
Harper & Row, Publishers, 1958.

Armand is a jaunty Parisian hobo who lives under the bridges of Paris. He is a saucy old man whose aversion to children has no effect on the three little redheads he finds one day, camping with their mother in his spot. Made Grandfather in spite of himself, Armand takes command of his plucky little family throughout the hard Paris winter. It is a heartwarming story of family unity, told with wit and pathos, and with illustrations exuding the charm of old Paris.

THE SINGING HILL
Written by Meindert DeJong.
Illustrated by Maurice Sendak.
Harper & Row, Publishers, 1962.

Ray is a timid, lonely country boy who finds and befriends an old horse. This gentle and touching story is beautifully written in quiet, sensitive prose. The illustrations capture the reality and the tender mood of the tale.

WHEEL ON THE SCHOOL
Written by Meindert DeJong.
Illustrated by Maurice Sendak.
Harper & Row, Publishers, 1954.

This story takes place in Shora, a small Dutch fishing village. One day, the school children wonder why there are no storks in their town. The children, their teacher, and, eventually, the rest of the towns-people become involved in correcting the storkless situation, and go about searching for wheels (to act as nest bases for the birds) to put on their roofs. This story is told with much humor in the everyday language of children, and the illustrations by Maurice Sendak fit the story. A New-bery Medal winner.

HANS BRINKER
Written by Mary Mapes Dodge.
Illustrated by G. W. Edwards.
Charles Scribner's Sons, 1915.

Holland, with its canals, windmills, water-roads, dikes, customs, and traditions, comes to life in the homey tale of Hans and Gretel and the silver skates.

BIG BLUE ISLAND
Written by Wilson Gage. Illustrated by Glen Rounds. World Publishing Co., 1965.

A young orphaned boy goes to live on a lonely island with his great-uncle, but he is bored with the slow life and plans to run away. His plans change as the result of an accident, and he eventually grows to understand and sympathize with his uncle's way of life. Nature is brought into sharp, vivid focus through clear writing and warm, tender character portrayal.

THE TROUBLED SUMMER
Written by Ben Haas. Bobbs-Merrill Company, Inc., 1966.

A very real and complex situation of modern life is presented vividly and fac-tually. Clay Williams, a Negro high school student, is caught up in a violent hatred of white men engendered by the fact of segregation and reinforced by a beating from two Klansmen. Clay is attracted to FREE, a civil liberties organiza-tion conducting a drive in his community, and the story revolves around the impact of the organization on Clay and on his small Southern community. At the con-clusion loose ends are tied up a little too neatly, but the author does not over-simplify the human problems involved.

KING OF THE WIND
Written by Marguerite Henry.
Illustrated by Wesley Dennis.
Rand McNally & Co., 1948.

This is the partly true, partly fictional story about Godolphin Arabian and a little mute stable boy who travels with him to France and England. The efforts of the loyal and devoted boy help the horse become famous. The story is written movingly and is matched by the well-drawn illustrations of an outstanding artist. A Newbery Medal winner.

MISTY OF CHINCOTEAGUE
Written by Marguerite Henry.
Illustrated by Wesley Dennis.
Rand McNally & Co., 1948.

One of the best horse stories ever written, it is about a wild pony who loves his free-dom and two children on two islands just off the shores of Virginia. Deft characteri-zation is combined with the magnificent setting of the Atlantic in this absorbing story. Strengthening the book are the superb illustrations alive with feeling and movement.

MUSTANG
Written by Marguerite Henry.
Illustrated by Robert Lougheed.
Rand McNally & Co., 1966.

The fictionalized story of a real woman—Mrs. Annie Johnston—whose dedication to saving the wild mustangs of the West from slaughter and extinction won for her the name of "Wild Horse Annie." As a result of her efforts, legislation was passed in 1959 outlawing the use of planes and trucks in roundups. It is an inspiring biography, told with spirit and imagination.

TRUST A CITY KID
Written by Anne Huston and Jane Yolen. Illustrated by J. C. Kocsis. Lothrop, Lee & Shepard Co., Inc., 1966.

Reg Johnson, a young Harlemite, is fearful that his ignorance of country ways will shame him when he leaves for the summer to live with a Quaker family, but he looks forward to learning to ride the Bradshaw's horse. Resentment of his hosts builds when the horse dies and he is left without resources with which to build his pride and alleviate his homesickness. In the rescue of an old workhorse from the slaughterhouse, the boy's pride is rescued, too, in a credible and effective characterization. Unfortunately, the roundness of Reg's character stands out among the flatly drawn Bradshaws.

ONION JOHN
Written by Joseph Krumgold.
Illustrated by Symeon Shimin.
Thomas Y. Crowell Company,
1959.

A warm story about the friendship between a young boy, Andy, and Onion John who emigrated from Europe and is now selling vegetables and doing odd jobs in Andy's town. It deals with our understanding of people with a foreign culture and different ways of life. The story has everything that children love: conflict, humor, drama, and very good portrayal of character.

AND NOW MIGUEL . . .
Written by Joseph Krumgold.
Illustrated by Jean Charlot. Thomas Y. Crowell Company, 1953.

Miguel Chavez, a twelve-year-old boy, tells his own story simply and with touching earnestness. Miguel's searching spirit and the wisdom and dignity of the theme give this book a biblical quality. Its factual details concerning the raising of sheep anchor it firmly to the reality of New Mexican life.

HIGH-RISE SECRET
Written and illustrated by Lois Lenski. J.B. Lippincott Co., 1966.

A realistically told story of the difficulties of urban living. The five Murphys find bickering, noise, and hoodlum trouble when they move into a high-rise urban renewal project. Troubles with neighbors, landlord, and local boys are presented with no softening of their grimness, but progress is made toward more civilized living through the efforts of the tenants themselves. It is a truthful portrayal of mixed community living where individual differences are faced realistically.

THE SHY ONE
Written by Dorothy Nathan.
Illustrated by Carolyn Cather.
Random House, Inc., 1966.

Problems that are not unique to the place and time (Oregon, 1921) beset a painfully shy little girl who learns that her grandmother and young uncle are coming from Russia to live with her family. Dorothy suffers all the agony of the first generation American child who fears that the foreignness of her family will make her an outcast from her classmates. The story is handled with humor, warmth, and verisimilitude, and is accompanied by illustrations that evoke the historical setting.

IT'S LIKE THIS, CAT
Written by Emily Neville.
Illustrated by Emil Weiss. Harper & Row, Publishers, 1963.

Here is a straightforward story of a young boy's experiences while growing up. His dates, friendship with another boy, affection for a pet, and learning to understand his father are universal steps in the growth to manhood. Written and illustrated in a humorous yet reflective style, it is also a good picture of city life. A Newbery Medal winner.

HEIDI
Written by Johanna Spyri. Illustrated by Agnes Tait. J. B. Lippincott Co., 1948.

A story of the beauty of Switzerland—its scenery and gentle life. Reading about the kindness, generosity and loyalty that the little girl of the mountains, Heidi, gives to others can be a moving experience for an older child. The illustrations in color and beautiful, soft black and white help to convey the joy of life and the beauty in the world that this book presents.

SEA STORIES

For younger children

THE CRUISE OF THE SANTA MARIA
Written by Eilis Dillon. Illustrated by Richard Kennedy. Funk & Wagnalls, 1967.

John's grandfather has antagonized everyone by bragging that his boat will be the finest hooker ever made. The men of the small Connemara fishing village say the *Santa Maria* is made for misfortune because of her foreign name and because a red-haired woman, old Tom's daughter, had a hand in building her. When John and a friend take the *Santa Maria* on her first voyage, they are caught in a storm and beached on a strange island. Its only inhabitant helps mend their boat and persuades them to sail to Spain to bring back his daughter, who has married a Spaniard. How the boys prove the seaworthiness of the *Santa Maria* makes an exciting story

which is given dimension by well-drawn characters and colorful settings.

OTTO AT SEA
Written and illustrated by William Pène du Bois. The Viking Press, Inc., 1958.

Otto is a heroic giant dog whose bravery and heroic action aboard the SS *Caesar*, during Hurricane Nancy win him a special medal from the mayor of New York.

OLEY: THE SEA MONSTER
Written and illustrated by Marie Hall Ets. The Viking Press, Inc., 1947.

Oley, a sad little seal lonesome for his mother, frightens the people of Chicago who think he is a sea monster. How he gets into the waters of Lake Michigan and how he finally gets back to the Atlantic Ocean is told in short sentences with numerous, detailed drawings in rose and black. The drawings not only advance the action but show real humor and fun.

FISHING WITH DAD
Written and illustrated by James Flora. Harcourt, Brace & World, Inc., 1967.

Although not an outstanding piece of literature this book deals honestly with father-son relationships in an exciting sea story. It is a big day for Daniel when his father decides to take him out with the crew of the *Kitty Q*, a commercial fishing boat. Daniel cleans the deck, steers the boat, works in the galley, and helps sort the fish caught in the big net. Here he also learns about the dangers of the sea when an ocean liner almost runs down the fishing boat during the dark hours of a foggy night. The catch of a torpedo along with fish heightens the excitement of the tale.

SWIMMY
Written and illustrated by Leo Lionni. Pantheon Books, Inc., 1963.

Alone after all his brothers and sisters have been swallowed by a tuna, Swimmy, the only black fish of the school, finds happiness as he explores the wonders of the ocean. He comes upon a school of little fish like himself and devises a way for them to live safely and happily. The mood of the story is conveyed by the beautiful illustrations.

BURT DOW: DEEP-WATER MAN
Written and illustrated by Robert McCloskey. The Viking Press, Inc., 1963.

This is a delightful, tongue-in-cheek story about an old fisherman, his pet gull, and their Jonah-like adventure with an understanding whale. Everything turns out well in the end thanks to a can of peppermint-striped bandages. Vividly colored pictures capture the spirit of the narrative. Although the story itself is flamboyantly incredible, the character of the old seaman is warm and realistically drawn.

WINGFIN AND TOPPLE
Written by Evans G. Valens, Jr. Illustrated by Clement Hurd. World Publishing Co., 1962.

Young Topple wonders why he has such long fins until Wingfin teaches him to fly. After he escapes from a net because of his ability to fly, he appreciates the freedom of the air. Lovely pictures add to the enjoyment of the story.

For intermediate-grade children

THE GREAT WHITE
Written by Jane and Paul Annixter. Holiday House, 1966.

This moving story gives the feeling of life close to nature. Iskwao and Nunker, Eskimo boys, are matched in power and courage to make a story that is at once compelling, suspenseful, and interesting.

THE SECRET SEA
Written by Richard Armstrong. David McKay, Co., Inc., 1967.

A story of modern whaling with all the mystery and excitement surrounding that little known aspect of life at sea. This book combines a detailed description of whaling with the thrill and suspense of an adventure story. No illustrations, but a great deal of blood and gore in the text.

THE SEA EGG
Written by L. M. Boston. Illustrated by Peter Boston. Harcourt, Brace & World, Inc., 1967.

An imaginative blending of reality and fantasy is accomplished in this story of two youngsters spending their summer on the Cornish coast. A strange and beautiful egg-shaped stone, which they hide in a sheltered pool reached only at low tide, hatches a wonderful summer companion for Toby and Joe. The boys learn to swim like sea creatures with their new friend, a boy triton. The characterization, dialogue, and sparkling description of sea and shore help make this a believable tale.

I HAVE JUST BEGUN TO FIGHT
Written by Edward Ellsberg. Illustrated by Gerald Foster. Dodd, Mead & Co., 1960.

A fictional account of the story of John Paul Jones, naval hero, through the eyes of young Tom Folger. The language is quite suitable for the intermediate levels.

THE "BEAR": SHIP OF MANY LIVES
Written and illustrated by Stella F. Rapaport. Dodd, Mead, & Co., 1962.

This story has only one hero—the ship whose name is the title. Built in 1874 in Dundee, Scotland, the *Bear* rescued survivors of Admiral Greely's antarctic expedition, sailed as Admiral Byrd's flagship, and served with distinction in World War II. U. S. Coast Guard photographs and drawings by the author enliven the text. This non-fictional book won the Dodd, Mead Writing Award.

THE LIGHT AT TERN ROCK
*Written by Julia L. Sauer. Illustrated
by George Schreiber. The Viking
Press, Inc., 1951.*

Tern Rock is a lonely, sea-swept light-house. The lighthouse keeper tricks Ronnie and his aunt into spending two weeks alone at the lighthouse and then stays away much longer. The boy's aware-ness of the sea and its workings is sen-sitively revealed. The illustrations are profusely spread throughout the book.

TREASURE ISLAND
*Written by Robert Louis Stevenson.
Illustrated by N. C. Wyeth. Charles
Scribner's Sons, 1924.*

An outstanding example of sea and treas-ure island adventure by a renowned writer for children. Here unfolds an absorbing story of pirates and hidden treasure and a few guileless gentlefolk in the hands of villainous pirates. Suspense, mystery, and high adventure come vividly to life in a thrilling tale.

THE FREEDOM OF THE SEAS
*Written by Catherine Storr.
Illustrated by Peggy Fortnum.
Duell, Sloane & Pearce, 1965.*

A little boy, overshadowed by his older brother and sister, desperately tries to find a way to excel. His wish is granted when he finds a seashell that gives him magical powers, thus helping him to avoid a tragedy at sea. Delicate black-and-white drawings provide just the right frame for this portrait of a sensitive young hero.

THE SINGING SCHOONER
Written by Diana Walker. Abelard-Schuman Limited, 1966.

In this absorbing Nova Scotia tale, the romance of the sea finally prevails over crass commercialism. The *Nancy Kelly*, a neglected and abandoned schooner, is on the verge of being turned into a hot dog stand. But the would-be entrepreneur has not counted on the determination of fifteen-year-old Gabrielle Leblanc who

loves ships and the sea. With the help of a friend, Jean-Pierre, she overcomes all obstacles and, needless to say, is aboard ship when the venerable *Nancy Kelly* comes in first in an exciting schooner race. A fast-moving story with excellent charac-terization.

For upper-grade children

THE BLOOD OF THE BRAVE
*Written by Betty Baker. Harper &
Row, Publishers, 1966.*

This book is based on a true sixteenth-century adventure. Juan signs with Her-nando Cortez for a voyage from Cuba to Aztec Mexico. Their long sea journey is arduous, but they find treasure, conquest, and much more.

FAMOUS SMALL BOAT VOYAGES
*Written by Walter Buehr. G. P.
Putnam's Sons, 1967.*

Stories of nine different voyages of adven-ture. The courage shown by these crews against unbearable odds is almost unbeliev-able. Yet the accounts are realistically convincing while they blend facts with fiction.

PETER THE WHALER IN SOUTHERN SEAS
*Written by Max Colwell. Illustrated
by Geoffrey Ingleton. St. Martin's
Press, Inc., 1965.*

This story of whaling in the Southern Seas has no conventional hero. It describes the slaughter that almost caused the extinction of the gentle balaena, the right or bay whale, and the great sperm whale.

THE ROPE'S END
*Written by Reginal B. Hegarty.
Illustrated by Wallace Tripp.
Houghton Mifflin Company, 1965.*

Hegarty tells the story of his year on his father's whaler as the youngest member of the crew. He gives an interesting account of his experiences in learning about ships, the sea, and the whaling business. Told with freshness and integrity, this strong sea adventure is as compelling as the sea itself.

The Dark Frigate
Written by Charles B. Hawes with frontispiece in color by Anton Otto Fischer. Atlantic-Little, Brown, 1959.

Especially written for boys, this story of a frigate, the *Rose of Devon*, tells of the rescue of twelve men in midocean. The rescued men seize the ship and sail toward the Caribbean, where they hope to plunder Spanish towns and galleons. Superbly written, this salty tale won the John Newbery Medal.

Captains Courageous
Written by Rudyard Kipling. Doubleday & Company, Inc., 1897.

This classic in the field of children's literature relates the story of a spoiled American youth who is washed overboard and picked up by a fishing vessel. Forced to work for a living instead of depending solely upon his millionaire father, the boy gains in stature and character. His greatness of spirit, his acceptance of reality, and his growth as a man make this sea story a source of inspiration for young readers.

Mutiny in the Bay
Written by Richard S. Lambert. Illustrated by Joe Rosenthal. St. Martin's Press, Inc., 1963.

A dramatic account of Henry Hudson's last voyage during his search for the Northwest passage to China. The crew, led by the treacherous Harry Greene, mutinied and set Hudson adrift in an open boat with seven of his loyal followers.

The Bird of Dawning; or, The Fortune of the Sea
Written by John Masefield. The Macmillan Co., 1943.

Probably one of the most exciting sea stories ever written by an author who is

a sailor and poet of distinction. Here he writes vividly of a sailing-ship race from the Pagoda Anchorage to the Thames. The briny account combines lucid and engaging plots with very fine character delineation as well as extraordinary descriptions of the sea, ships, and sailors.

Phantom of the Blockade
Written by Stephen W. Meader. Illustrated by Victor Mays. Harcourt, Brace & World, Inc., 1962.

A story based on actual experience aboard a Confederate blockade runner from Bermuda to the South describes hairbreadth escapes as the *Gray Witch* makes dangerous voyages to bring arms and other supplies for Lee's hard-pressed men. Packed with action and suspense, the thrilling text is matched with haunting pictures of sea danger.

The Black Pearl
Written by Scott O'Dell. Illustrated by Milton Johnson. Houghton Mifflin Company, 1967.

A graceful, haunting story that blends reason with superstition as it tells about a youthful pearl diver, the great pearl he finds, and the giant manta he angers. When he is sixteen, Ramon Salazer learns to dive and he finds the great Pearl of Heaven. An old Indian warns him that it belongs to the Manta Diablo, the monster of the sea, who will not rest until he has the pearl back—and Ramon's life with it. The struggle for possession of the rare pearl makes an exciting tale of rare beauty.

Sea Fever
Written by A. H. Rasmussen. Illustrated by Ray Bethers. Hastings House Publishers, Inc., 1960.

A fine sea story for the older child. The author's descriptions of a sailor's boarding house, life on an East Coast brig, a shipwreck, a voyage to Pernambuco, and another to Central American in the logwood trade are very convincing.

THE ENEMY SEAS
*Written by Gordon D. Shirreffs.
Westminster Press, 1965.*

During World War II two young sailors are rescued by a submarine crew as it proceeds through enemy waters on a secret mission. Excitement mounts as the boys are assigned to duty and learn every phase of submarine service.

SPORTS STORIES

For younger children

NU DANG AND HIS KITE
Written and illustrated by Jacqueline Ayer. Harcourt, Brace & World, Inc., 1959.

Here in wide panoramic spreads, the author-illustrator has lucidly traced in lines and language a lilting story about a boy and his friends flying kites in Thailand. Nu Dang's kite, "the boldest and bravest," wins over all the other kites that race in the stiff breeze and makes the little boy ecstatic with joy. Throughout the story are also woven Far Eastern designs of life and location that provide for the reader a sense of adventure as well as sport in a distant land.

WHO WILL BE MY FRIENDS?
Written and illustrated by Syd Hoff. Harper & Row, Publishers, 1960.

A straightforward story about a little boy who has moved into a new neighborhood and searches for someone with whom he can play. Proving himself capable of catching and throwing a ball he is allowed to join a group of boys playing baseball in a nearby field. Enjoyment of the game as well as in making new friends give satisfaction to young readers.

CHIE AND THE SPORTS DAY
Written and illustrated by Masako Matsuno. World Publishing Co. 1965.

A tender little story about Chie who has no one to play with since her brother, Ichiro, started going to school. With great admiration for her brother the little girl looks forward to the school "Sports Day." Ichiro, however, dreads the big event because he is considered the slowest runner in the class, and just as he feared, he loses the race. But running in a three-legged race with his little sister gains him a victory. Told in warm, lyrical text this lovely book is also highlighted with beautiful pictures reflecting the Orient.

BEN ON THE SKI TRAIL
Written and illustrated by Leonard Shortall. William Morrow & Co., Inc., 1965.

An exciting sports story for the youngest, *Ben on the Ski Trail* tells how Ben borrows skiing equipment and sets out to learn to ski. Awkward and discouraged at first, he perseveres and succeeds to ski well enough so that he joins the ski patrol in a rescue. The lively text and illustrations entertain and inform as they join to tell a true-to-life tale about a winter sport.

For intermediate-grade children

LONG SHOT FOR PAUL
Written by Matt Christopher. Illustrated by Foster Caddell. Little, Brown & Company, 1966.

Glenn and Judy Marlette decide to teach their brother Paul how to play basketball so he can play with the Sabers and get to know other boys. This takes a great deal of patience, because Paul is mentally retarded and does not learn easily. Coach Munson lets Paul join the team, but the other boys often get impatient with Paul's errors and ignore him. Paul's hard practice pays off and in a crucial moment helps the team win.

THE TEAM THAT COULDN'T LOSE
Written by Matt Christopher. Illustrated by Foster Caddell. Little, Brown & Company, 1967.

With a team of rookies and a coach who

knows nothing about football, the Cougars look like sure losers at the beginning of the season. But using a brand-new play that someone anonymously mails to their coach each week, they become league leaders. How the boys solve the identity of their mysterious helper and learn to have faith in themselves as players makes an exciting and breezily told story.

ROUGH ICE
Written by Beman Lord. Illustrated by Arnold Spilka. Henry Z. Walck, Inc., 1963.

Eddie MacDougal is afraid he won't live up to his father's reputation as a former star hockey forward. He tries out for goalie in the Pee Wee league when he realizes his weak ankle will prevent his winning a berth as forward. Though he proves to be a good goalie, he can't bring himself to tell his father he is not following in his footsteps. Eddie's problems are finally resolved during an exciting game in the arena. Easy reading with lively pictures about an exciting sport.

FOOTBALL BOYS
Written by Marion Renick. Illustrated by Donald C. Lynch. Charles Scribner's Sons, 1967.

When Kevin and his friends in the high-rise apartment house show they are serious enough about football to stop rough-housing in the halls and elevators, tenants become more sympathetic to their campaign to use part of the yard for sports. Nearly every apartment in Skytop has someone involved in what becomes a community project. Through all the effort and practice, Kevin also learns there is no such thing as an "instant football player."

THE CONTENDER
Written by Robert Lipsyte. Harper & Row, Publishers, 1967.

The problems of a high school drop-out trying to find himself are revealingly depicted in this novel that realistically points up the grim and the hopeful aspects of life in Harlem. When Alfred Brooks is beaten by hoodlums he has refused to join, he takes up boxing at Donatelli's gym. Although he never becomes a champion, he does learn the importance of being a contender. The strict discipline and training in boxing help him attain strength and courage in his own life. Relationships with understanding adults of both races are warmly portrayed.

BACKFIELD BUCKAROO
Written by Jackson Scholz. William Morrow & Co., Inc., 1967.

Rodeo and football are the two big sports at Buckskin University and Hank Tabor is a natural for both teams. When Hank is thrown by a tricky bronco at the beginning of the season and doesn't seem to reach his full potential on the football field, there is talk that "Tabor can't mix rodeo with football." How Hank finally conquers the wily bronco and redeems himself on the football field makes an exciting sports story.

HIS ENEMY, HIS FRIEND
Written by John R. Tunis. William Morrow & Company, 1967.

John Tunis is a crack writer of sports stories who frequently employs realistic details of wartime. Here in a powerfully compelling junior novel he weaves a tale that links the war years of World War II with aftereffects twenty years later. Hans, who is stationed in Normandy, earns the reputation of "butcher" because of reprisal killings connected with an underground incident aimed at the Germans. Confronting his past on a soccer field when the French and German teams meet in a championship game, Hans finally plays out his tragedy. Crispness and simplicity mark this well-written story that underscores the brutality of war.

MYSTERY AND DETECTIVE STORIES

For younger children

THE STRANGE DISAPPEARANCE OF
ARTHUR CLUCK
*Written by Nathaniel Benchley.
Illustrated by Arthur Lobel. Harper
& Row, Publishers, 1967.*

Designated as an "I Can Read Mystery" for the youngest readers, this handsome little book wittily recounts the mysterious disappearance of a distracted hen's chick and his eventual recovery. Mrs. Cluck, the hen, is understandably upset when her son, Arthur, disappears. None of the other barnyard animals can tell her where he might be, but Ralph, the wise owl, promises to stand guard at night to see what he can find out about the mysterious disappearance. As Ralph waits and watches, he has his own adventures before he solves the mystery.

THE CASE OF THE CAT'S MEOW
*Written and illustrated by Crosby
Bonsall. Harper & Row, Publishers,
1965.*

When Snitch's cat disappears, the four private eyes, Wizard, Tubby, Skinny, and Snitch, go into action. After some amusing misadventures with other cats and dogs, a homemade alarm, and a plate of food in a tin of flour, the boys come up with a plan that leads to Mildred's discovery. Mildred provides her own surprise for the boys in a delightful ending to this puzzling mystery for younger children.

THE HORSE IN THE CAMEL SUIT
*Written and illustrated by William
Pène du Bois. Harper & Row,
Publishers, 1967.*

Why does the camel suit used in Swami Tarragon's Curiosity Parade smell like a stable full of hot horses? With the help of a broken-down horse bettor, a country editor, and Officer Dillingham, the town

policeman, the young detective hero attempts to find the answer and capture the criminals in the carnival act. A stunning detective story with bright pictures that add to the mystery and merriment. Suitable for the ablest readers among young children.

SHERLOCK ON THE TRAIL
*Written by James Holding. Illustrated
by Aliki. William Morrow & Co.,
1964.*

Sherlock, Marjory's bloodhound, helps her when she finds that her piggy bank is missing. He sniffs a handkerchief left at the scene of the crime and, never lifting his nose from the ground, leads Marjory and the policeman directly to the culprit in the Law Office Building. Discovery of the culprit makes everybody laugh and is sure to bring amusement to young readers particularly as they discover his true identity.

For intermediate-grade children

THE MYSTERIOUS SCHOOLMASTER
*Written by Karin Anckarsvard.
Illustrated by Paul Galdone.
Harcourt, Brace & World, Inc.,
1959.*

Translated from the Swedish, this fast-moving story portrays a teacher in the local school and the spy plot in which he figured during World War II. Fine writing and a tightly knit plot distinguish this excellent mystery.

THE HORSE WITHOUT A HEAD
*Written by Paul Berna. Illustrated
by Richard Kennedy. Pantheon Books
Inc., 1958.*

Set in Paris, this book was first published in France and was awarded the Grand Prix Littéraire du Salon de l'Enfance. The story concerns ten poverty-stricken Parisian street urchins whose prize possession is mysteriously stolen. To retrieve their loss, the ingenious children devise clever schemes that heighten the suspense of this beautifully written mystery.

THE MYSTERY OF MOUND KEY
Written by Robert F. Burgess.
Illustrated by Vic Donahue. World
Publishing Co., 1966.

With vivid details about boating, fishing, and scuba diving, this lively adventure story along the Florida coastal waters follows Jib and Shandy in their search for buried treasure, which is also being sought by someone else. A mysterious map etched on a telescope launches this unusual story.

HARRIET THE SPY
Written and illustrated by Louise
Fitzhugh. Harper & Row,
Publishers, 1964.

A wryly told mystery for younger children about an intensely curious little child, Harriet, who keeps a secret notebook filled with honest jottings about her parents, classmates, and very close friends. When her notebook is discovered and read by those Harriet writes about, a tense situation follows. Unpretentious drawings accompany this interesting story of a nosey, brash 11-year-old spy.

DIAMOND CAVE MYSTERY
Written by Franklin Folsom. Harvey
House, Inc., Publishers, 1962.

In this mystery story a long-lost cache of diamonds is sought from a set of clues entered in an old Bible. Two curious boys, Chuck and Hal, follow the clues, and one leads them to explore New Mexico's Carlsbad Caverns. Fascinating information about speleology and caves enriches the work of this mystery writer for children. Other books by the same author are: *Sand Dune Pony Mystery, Indian Mummy Mystery, Mystery at Rustlers' Fort, Mystery at Payrock Canyon,* and *Forest Fire Mystery.*

THE TWO HELENS
Written and illustrated by Eleanor
Frances Lattimore. William Morrow
& Co., 1967.

When the three Dunbar children discover an apparently deserted house with a tower near their summer home, an unfriendly man chases them away. Later eight-year-old Helen returns to the old house, learns the identity of the mysterious "dragon" her parents talk about, and finds that the dragon, her great-aunt Helen, is really a lovely person after all. The warmth of happy family life is quietly woven into the story.

MYSTERY AT THE RED HOUSE
Written by Cornelia Meigs.
Illustrated by Robert MacLean. The
Macmillan Company, 1961.

An exciting mystery story that involves a whole family. Valuable jewels in an old well and a deserted room serve as the props to carry the suspense of this well-written tale by an outstanding author for children.

THE DOG SHOW MYSTERY
Written by Eileen Thompson.
Illustrated by James Russell.
Abelard-Schuman Limited, 1966.

The disappearance of a fox terrier leads Brian and his friend, Cindy, to investigate. At a dog show, their investigations become exciting when the villain attempts to keep the champion out of the ring. Also by the same author: *The Blue Stone Mystery, The Spanish Deed Mystery,* and *The Apache Gold Mystery.*

COLONEL SHEPERTON'S CLOCK
Written by Philip Turner. Illustrated
by Philip Gough. World Publishing
Co., 1966.

This well-balanced book is by a British Carnegie Medal winner who is distinguished for his deft characterization, dialogue, and stout story lines. Here, the author presents a detective-type story of young boys whose curiosity leads them to an old newspaper article with clues regarding an act of espionage during the First World War.

LIBBY LOOKS FOR A SPY
Written by Catherine Woolley.
Illustrated by Liz Dauber. William
Morrow & Co., Inc., 1965.

Cape Cod serves as the setting for this suspenseful story in which a little girl named Libby plays a crucial role detecting the spy she first suspected from overhearing a conversation. Sleuthing takes Libby in and out of the woods and enlivens her winter in a lonely resort town. The clever story line is full of woodsy detail and eventful episodes.

For upper-grade children

THE STRANGE INTRUDER
Written by Arthur Catherall.
Lothrop, Lee & Shepard Co., Inc.,
1965.

Only sixteen-year-old Sven and the aged men of the community are left to protect the women and children in Mykines, the most remote of the Faroe Islands. A marauding bear and the exciting rescue of a shipwrecked crew provide a memorable tale of suspense and high adventure.

YUGOSLAV MYSTERY
Written by Arthur Catherall.
Lothrop, Lee & Shepard, Co., Inc.,
1964.

Josef's father, a fearless Yugoslav partisan, returns to his poor island village after fifteen years of unjust imprisonment. He is pursued by the Ustashis, looters of churches, whom he had once fought. Impersonating the secret police, they hope to force him to reveal the secret of stolen church treasures. Josef and his grandfather care for the wounded man and hide him from his pursuers until the real police arrive. Tension and suspense heighten the excitement of this adventure story.

THE CAVE
Written by Elizabeth Coatsworth.
The Viking Press, Inc., 1958.

This is the story of a young Navajo Indian boy who is hired as a sheepherder to accompany the flock on a long journey. The boy's warm, courageous character is revealed through his bravery and through his friendship and understanding for Fernando, the mysterious and changeable sheepherder. The narrative is impressive and has a generous amount of intrigue and suspense.

THE MISSING MASTERPIECE
Written by Helen Girvan.
Westminster Press, 1965.

Seventeen-year-old Nan, who is always sent to visit relatives in the summer, spends her vacation with an aunt she has never met. Nan finds herself involved in a mystery that combines cryptic offshore signals with a stolen Degas. Nan forms a friendship with Ross that corresponds with her aunt's growing involvement with Warren Blake, Nan's guardian.

CRUISING TO DANGER
Written by Priscilla Hagon.
Illustrated by William Plummer.
World Publishing Co., 1966.

Joanna Forest is hardly the "ordinary" girl she pretends to be in order to win her vacation job as companion to two children on a Mediterranean cruise. She becomes entangled in a mystery far more sinister than the stories she hopes one day to write. As the ship travels from port to port, Joanna finds herself increasingly involved with danger and excitement, atomic spies, and international intrigue. Good-looking Charles adds to the romance of the cruise and is the one person Joanna dares trust with her secret.

MYSTERY AT LAND'S END
Written by Marg Nelson. Ariel
Books, 1961.

When 15-year-old Marcie comes to Land's End to spend her sophomore year with relatives, she looks forward to an ordinary, pleasant year of making new friends and participating in school activities. She finds unexpected excitement in helping to solve a mystery that involves a prowler and a strange old house with interesting inhabitants. The touch of romance added to the mystery makes an enjoyable and exciting book for older girls.

MYSTERY OF THE CARROWELL NECKLACE
Written by Eugenie C. Reid.
Illustrated by Barbara Werner.
Lothrop, Lee & Shepard Co., Inc.,
1965.

Twelve-year-old Lou isn't at all sure she wants to visit her Great-aunt Isobel until she learns about the missing diamond necklace hidden by her great-grandfather fifty years before. She wonders if her cousins, Joe and Caroline, also visiting their aunt, will be looking for the necklace too. When the three children pool their information, the pieces begin to fall into place as they seek out the missing clue that may hold the answer to an exciting mystery.

THE MYSTERY OF 22 EAST
Written by Leon Ware.
Westminster Press, 1965.

Fifteen-year-old Tom is traveling alone on a freighter to England, via the Panama Canal. The trip brings Tom face to face with an exciting rescue at sea, a violent storm, a stowaway, and a disappearing monkey. But most sinister are the two characters who enter Tom's cabin to look for a hidden roll of microfilm.

SECRET OF THE SPOTTED SHELL
Written by Phyllis A. Whitney.
Illustrated by John McCray. The
Westminster Press, 1967.

Wendy Williams looks forward to living with her cousins on the Virgin Islands but finds a household disrupted by Cousin Marion's illness over the disappearance of her husband in Vietnam. Wendy tries to adjust to the problems of the adults, but only Uncle Paul seems concerned about her. A special shell in Cousin Gordon's collection holds the clue to his disappearance. Wendy's involvement in the mystery and her relationship with her relatives make an excitingly believable story.

Consonant with the diversity of information found in factual books for children, this picture presents a vivid display suggesting many areas of interest encompassed by this division.

From Science and the Secret of Man's Past *by Franklin Folsom, illustrated by Ursula Koering. Illustration copyright © 1966 by Harvey House, Inc. Reproduced by permission.*

Chapter 12 INFORMATION
IN
CHILDREN'S
LITERATURE

I like books of knowledge; not those that want to encroach upon
recreation, upon leisure, pretending to be able to teach anything without
drudgery. There is no truth in that. There are things which cannot
be learned without great pains; we must be resigned to it. I like books of
knowledge when they are not just grammar or geometry poorly
disguised; when they have tact and moderation; when, instead of pouring out
so much material on a child's soul that it is crushed, they plant
in it a seed that will develop from the inside. I like them when they do not
deceive themselves about the quality of knowledge, and do not claim
that knowledge can take the place of everything else. I like them especially
when they distill from all the different kinds of knowledge the most
difficult and the most necessary—that of the human heart.

— PAUL HAZARD
Books, Children and Men
The Horn Book, Inc., 1960

413

Definition of
Informational Literature

Curiosity is one of the most significant characteristics of a child's mind, and it is extended by his growing ability to observe and understand the various experiences he encounters. With his constantly growing and developing powers of observation, he sees the world around him as a vast area for exploration and discovery.

In his attempt to find out about the many-faceted world of which he is a part, a child seeks answers to the multitude of questions that arise naturally out of the wide-eyed curiosity with which he greets the experiences of each new day. Because there is so much to learn, it is not surprising that, as soon as he can read, a child is attracted to books that will clarify those things which are mysterious and unknown to him. But clarification in itself is not enough.

The fundamental role of informational books is to provide the child with a body of information that as it answers old questions will stimulate him to ask new ones. It is in this perpetual cycle of questions and answers, in which vague imaginings become knowledge and truth, that a child's precious gift of wonder and desire to know becomes the foundation upon which significant learning experiences are built.

Since informational books explain to children the world around them and within them, it is not surprising that the list is so extensive. With the latest technological advances in the fields of communication and transportation, a child's world is no longer limited to his immediate environment. As soon as he is able to watch television or listen to the radio, the child of today becomes a spectator at such provocative and stimulating events as the launching of a satellite or the inauguration of a president. He learns, too, about other countries and other cultures much earlier in his development than did his counterpart of a generation ago. Consequently, not only must there be books available to explain many areas of interest to a child, but these books must provide the kind of explanation that the young mind will find satisfying.

The books that cover the broad range and scope of informational literature for children discussed in this chapter fall into most school curriculum interests and groupings:

(1) Science and mathematics
(2) Social studies
(3) Biography
(4) Fine arts
(5) Games and hobbies
(6) Holidays
(7) Language skills
(8) Reference books

Under each major heading are subtopics that deal with more specific areas of interest within the particular subject. In these subdivisions, books are arranged according to their suitability for different age groups as well as for their application to the school curriculum and use in the classroom. Some examples will be discussed to serve as guidelines in understanding this large division of literature.

SCIENCE AND MATHEMATICS

Science books written for children today are much more specialized than those of many years ago, and the demands made even by first and second graders for information about the sun and moon, light, sound, electricity, space travel, dinosaurs, and inclined planes are endless. Children can ask staggering and still unanswerable fundamental questions: "Where do the stars come from?" "Why is the world round?" and "How big is everything?" But they also ask questions that have answers, and these may be explained to them in science books of interesting and illuminating facts. Even the youngest readers can choose from many available picture books that effectively introduce the universe and the wonders of nature in a vivid, visual way—through beautiful photographs and drawings accompanied by simple and accurate captions.

Science books published for youngsters can be divided into three main categories: the physical sciences, the natural sciences, and mathematics.

Those in the first group deal with the subject matter of physics, chemistry, and astronomy—how the universe works, what things are made of, and the laws governing cause and effect. The second group includes studies in biology—plants, animals, insects, and the human body—and in world geography, natural resources, and the conservation of soil, trees, water, and wildlife. Both of these categories allow the young reader to travel through space, beneath the earth's surface, or back in time to confront ancient living creatures. They broaden his capacity for wonder and widen his vision, too, as he sees through the telescopic or microscopic lenses provided by illustrations. Books in the third major grouping, mathematics, range from brain teasers and logical puzzles for fun through simple arithmetical problems to discussions of the application of mathematical principles to the universe.

SOCIAL STUDIES

Social studies covers the vast areas of history, geography, economics, government, and important aspects of living in all cultures. History books about the shaping of America and other nations of the world are countless. It is through the pages of these books that a child views the vast panorama of events and men that contributed to his human

Here the artist affords us a panoramic view of life in a busy seaport. East meets West over a variety of transactions and exchanges. Blending facts from geography and history, the picture opens windows onto a social highroad.

From America Begins *by Alice Dalgliesh, illustrated by Lois Maloy. Copyright © 1938 by Charles Scribner's Sons, renewal copyright © 1966 by Lois Maloy. Reproduced by permission.*

heritage. The child is also given some understanding of current problems and a perspective on revered laws and traditions. When he reads about present life in other lands and the cultures of other peoples, his concept of himself and his place in the world enlarges; he can see himself as a member of the large, global community of Man. The child arrives at these things not only by projecting himself through historical and geographical reading adventures, but also through other books that deal with anthropological concepts. This last category introduces him to all the different customs, laws, and values as well as the governments and economies of other societies and his own.

BIOGRAPHY

Biographies provide children with an ability to witness history in the making through the eyes of an actual participant whose personality and talents contributed toward influencing and changing the world and time in which he lived. By reading biographies, the child experiences a more personal link with the rich heritage of the past and comes to know the kind of people who shaped his nation and the world. Moreover, the stories of the lives of great people serve as inspiring examples of reality that ambitious young readers might aspire to emulate.

Images of heroes, of noble characters with sound values, are often the vehicles to transport humanistic ideals. Children also come to recognize in biographical accounts that heroes are as human as they—with weaknesses and strengths—and that they struggled, made mistakes, and even experienced failure. Those who grew and profited from a lesson in defeat developed a deeper understanding of themselves and still another kind of strength. It is this kind of heroic personality with whom a child can identify and emphathize. He is given a pattern of reality from which he can draw elements to inspire and comfort him when he experiences disappointment or some temporary failure.

FINE ARTS

Books about the fine arts cover the areas of visual arts, music, drama, and the dance. They are becoming an integral part of children's informational literature on all age levels. Their popularity and

The rich heritage of fine arts is symbolized in this beautiful painting that assembles rare books of literature, musical scores, and instruments in an artistic composition. *"Music and Literature" by William Harnett.*

appeal seem to be growing in direct proportion to today's emphasis on creating an atmosphere of welcome to the young listener and viewer in concert halls, theatres, and museums. The sounds and sights of the arts may be so beautifully and effectively introduced to a child through pictures and the written word that he may become a lifelong art lover, equipped with a standard of aesthetic values. Also, children endowed with a special talent in any one of the arts may be recruited into the art world through an inspiring book. There is a great need, then, for more good books that will inform, clarify and stimulate further investigation into a rich and deeply satisfying area that can, with proper nourishment, grow and flower as a youngster proceeds from childhood to the world of the adult.

GAMES AND HOBBIES

Games and hobbies make up another broad area of informational books that includes the "how-to," make-it-yourself, and rules-of-the-game series. This area of literature is the answer to those periods of play and leisure time that a child may use creatively by actively experimenting, constructing, exploring, and developing in some realm that is most vital to him in terms of its interest and appeal. For boys and girls with athletic ability, there are books concentrating on world sports and games and physical feats; for those with an artistic bent there are numberless volumes that introduce methods, techniques, tools, and instruments used in music, painting, sculpture, the crafts, puppet plays, and dramatics; and young scientists can find a wealth of books on nature-study, home experiments, and three-dimensional and abstract puzzles to probe and solve. Little architects, ballplayers, collectors, cooks, designers, divers, gardeners, mechanics, and zoologists can all improve their unique abilities by following a blueprint, diagram, recipe, or list of instructions that are usual aids in these books.

HOLIDAYS

The observance and celebration of holidays has always held an important place in the school curriculum and in the life of a child. Children are naturally fascinated and pleased by the color, pageantry, excitement, and display of familiar paraphernalia, symbols, and rituals that accompany the festivities of the year's red-letter days. It is the primary function of books dealing with holidays to extend and elaborate upon the child's enjoyment by providing him with a meaningful background and

5
Valentine Symbols
and the Story of Cupid

Holiday books not only give information about a particular holiday but also depict with beauty the symbols associated with each. Here Cupid hurls an arrow at hearts, while ribbons and fans add decorative touches to expressions of love and friendship.
From Valentine's Day *by Elizabeth Guilfoile, illustrated by Gordon Laite. Copyright © 1965 · by the author. Garrard Publishing Company. Reproduced by permission.*

flavorful history of those days we have designated as important enough to celebrate. Whether they commemorate an outstanding man, event, or idea in history, their origins and significance may be variously presented to young readers in the forms of stories, legends, historical accounts, biographies, compilations of verse and songs, or as short surveys of customs practiced in different countries throughout the ages. Children love a festival, party, or parade along with the music, costumes, and decorations associated with special days. By being aware of the "who," "what," and "why" that underlie celebrations, children's interests are heightened and the base of their experience may be broadened.

LANGUAGE SKILLS

As a social instrument language is interrelated with experiences in everyday life. Instrumental chiefly in communication, language involves listening and expressing in a variety of ways. Children's books, however, express ideas that may be listened to or read by the young themselves, and frequently these ideas become the answers to questions

420

children ask as they seek out books of information. Once a child has gained ideas, he organizes them and assimilates them through the magic of his own individuality, making what he has read, or heard, or felt, or expressed a part of himself—a new experience.

The chief function of books about language skills is to extend children's experiences in gaining, organizing, and expressing ideas through pages that afford opportunities in listening, speaking, reading, writing, and dramatizing. Sometimes the information in books about these subjects may be simply historical—telling a child how writing came to be developed or how printing was perfected. Other books about language may only offer a few language concepts in palatable style as in Tom Funk's *I Read Signs* in which a little boy and his dog find a multitude of signs and discover the meanings of each. But, in each instance, understanding about language, foreign or one's own, is acquired.

REFERENCE BOOKS

Reference books are invaluable aids to the child who wants to look something up quickly and easily or study an area of interest in depth. These are almanacs, dictionaries, and encyclopedias. Almanacs are packed with brief factual data, figures, dates, and comparative listings

Locating information is difficult without the aid of reference books ranging from pocket-sized to oversized volumes of dictionaries, atlases, and other works.
From Libraries and You *by Pekay Shor, illustrated by Stephen P. Peck. Copyright © 1964 by Prentice-Hall, Inc. Reproduced by permission.*

and are reissued annually to include the most recent news and statistics available. Special picture dictionaries and school dictionaries are published for children. In content they range from the simplest words accompanied by a descriptive picture and short sentence to more extensive volumes for older children who want to know more words and more about them as their vocabulary steadily increases. Dictionaries in the latter category divide the words into syllables, give a pronunciation key, and tell what part of speech it belongs to. Better volumes have a thumb index, include proper names, and contain plentiful illustrations and definitive maps. Encyclopedias are more elaborate and detailed reference books or sets of books whose last volume is dedicated to an extensive index, arranged alphabetically, of topics and names that are conveniently cross referenced. These books are made up of factual articles that give descriptions and backgrounds of an amazing number of subjects and offer every age level something of value—from pictures, maps, and simple text to more advanced and technical areas. Some editions include nonfactual material as well: stories, poems, and selections from fiction. Reference books should be available to every child because the gesture of looking something up easily becomes a good habit and may very well lead to more intensive research into other sources.

General Criteria
for Informational Books

An informational book must be accurate, clear, and, above all, up to date. Regardless of the age level for which the book is written, it must get at the essence of its subject. The child must have confidence in the authority of the writer who, in turn, must achieve a balance of detail and comprehensiveness that alters with audiences of different ages.

The book's style must not be so irregular as to be unclear, yet, in maintaining a clarity it must not rob the area discussed of the emotion of discovery. Indeed, the exceptional informational book must capture the wonder of discovery in its style.

Illustrations and format are a crucial part of an informational book, too. Illustrations must explain the text and, in many cases, must open up possibilities to the imagination of young people.

Interestingly enough, the very nature of informational books is responsible for their transitory success. A book must be up to date to be valuable. It must be clear and accurate. Often, the book that is written in an undistinguished style is more satisfactory for answering questions than the one written in a "literary" style. Biographies, histories, and certain standard scientific books, however, are not as likely to become outdated as some other kinds of informational books more subject to swiftly moving events and developments.

Perhaps it is in the format and illustrations that the key to "literature" in informational books lies. A book of luxurious size or especially beautiful illustrations or photographs put together in a simple way is of lasting value to children regardless of whether the book is the most recent on the subject or not. Though text and information are equally essential, illustrations, photographs, and diagrams are invaluable sources for communicating information.

Criteria for
Specific Subject Areas

The criteria stated above are fundamental in selecting the exceptional informational book from the many, many books that are published each year. There are certain questions, however, that one must ask in selecting the exceptional book within a specific subject area. Here, for example, are a few criteria applicable to specific informational books:

SCIENCE AND MATHEMATICS BOOKS

- Is the information scrupulously accurate?
- Is the text clear and understandable but not insulting to a child's intelligence?
- Is the scientific information up to date?
- Are the examples and illustrations illuminating to the text?
- Are there some kinds of examples provided and experiments conducted in a way that a child can carry out himself?
- Does the book stimulate a child's curiosity so that he pursues the study still further?
- Does the book contribute to a child's conceptual development either in science or mathematics?
- Does the book give due consideration to any questions a child might have?

Tracing the growth patterns of life in an egg, the clear-cut pictures sharpen an awareness of the life cycle. The accuracy in the photographs stresses the scientific method used in the experiment of incubating chicks in a classroom. *From* Wait and See *by Constantine Georgiou, illustrated by Janet and Alex D'Amato. Copyright © 1962 by Harvey House, Inc. Reproduced by permission.*

SOCIAL STUDIES BOOKS

The same criteria apply to social studies with these added considerations appropriate to books in this area:

- Are some of the illustrations provided more than just diagrams or simple sketches but fine examples depicting scenes and characters with vividness and integrity?
- Does the book provide readable maps and charts that satisfy a child's reference requirements?
- Does the book utilize the kind of language that gives a sense of time and place to the young reader?

BIOGRAPHIES

Depicting the history of an individual's life, a biography offers its readers authentic details that are informative as well as interesting in either a fictionalized or a purely factual account. As informational literature, however, the nonfictional biographies are grounded by scrupulously accurate facts about a person's life presented in good literary style.

Not exempt from meeting standards basic to good writing as an art form, biographies subtly interweave literary elements inherent in well-developed stories so that the characters and their personalities loom large as life and stay true to their original selves, times, and convictions. The characters in biographies serve as models for identification and emulation, and the books themselves serve as significant sources of historical facts carefully selected and artistically presented.

Many historical stories provide biographical episodes or glimpses into the lives of men and women who became famous in their times, and some fictional biographies develop their themes around characters whose lives were colorful and engaging enough to become stories for young readers. But whatever the treatment, biographies paint portraits in vivid details that breathe life and vigor into their subjects and show the human interest touches that intensify their appeal for children.

Some helpful criteria pertinent to biographies include the following:

· Does the book represent sound research of informative details set in an interesting style of writing?

Biographies, unlike books of fiction, reveal the lives and personalities of real people. Great leaders such as Lincoln, Gandhi, and King become key figures in books about them.
From Martin Luther King: The Peaceful Warrior *by Ed Clayton, illustrated by David Hodges.* © *Copyright 1964 by Prentice-Hall, Inc. Reproduced by permission.*

- Does the book retell episodes and events in the life of a person with honesty and conviction?
- Are the personalities drawn deftly enough so as to make the biographical portraits seem alive and natural?
- Are the speech and dialogue anchored by the tenor and idioms of the times in which the characters lived?
- Do the biographies introduce children to characters worthy of emulation?
- Can some sense of history be gained from the biography?
- Are the period, place, and social order accurately handled?
- Is there unity and balance of literary elements?
- Has the character been re-created with power so as to make a deep imprint on the lives of young readers?

FINE ARTS BOOKS

The best in this category are aesthetic entities in themselves—beautifully designed, handsomely and artistically produced. Frequently they are filled with color plates that faithfully reproduce the artistry of original works. The following criteria may be applied to specific books in the area of the fine arts:

- Are the pictures reproduced appropriate for a child interested in finding out about a topic in the fine arts?
- Are the pictures selected from among the best examples of artistic works—paintings, sculpture, crafts, dance forms, instruments, and so forth?
- Do the color plates register clearly and without blur? Do they do justice to the artist's palette?
- Can the choice of paintings and illustrations elicit aesthetic responses at the appropriate age level for which the book is intended?

ABOUT HOBBIES AND GAMES

To help children develop their hobbies and find out more about them are the twofold purposes of books concerned with such specialized activities as collecting, building, photography, and various crafts. In addition, books on games frequently provide instructions for playing or information about the rules of particular games, which children may find interesting. Explanations and directions are set down in easy-to-follow steps that lend encouragement instead of stifling hobby and sports interests. Also, some additional criteria may be helpful to consider:

- Are there sufficient varieties of books to meet all the interests of children?

Detailed directions become helpful guides for those desirous of learning to make puppets or toys. The well-worded text is often accompanied by clear-cut diagrams. *From* The First Book of Puppets *by Moritz Jagendorf, illustrated by Jean Michener. Copyright* © *1952 by Franklin Watts, Inc. Reproduced by permission.*

- Are the books designed with distinct diagrams, labels, and directions that are easy for children to follow?
- If photographs are included, are they clear-cut and informative rather than decorative?
- Do the sport stories and other activity books arouse enthusiasm for actual participation and/or imaginative play?
- Does the text recommend a variety of ways for performing an activity along with the one demonstrated in the book?
- Do the books provide instructions for the care of materials used with hobbies?
- Do the books inspire children to try different activities rather than to center on just one all the time?

BOOKS ABOUT HOLIDAYS

Aimed to inform as well as delight, books about holidays come in either single picture-book editions or in collections that offer stories and facts about various holidays. Ranging from the hauntingly mysterious tales of Halloween to the gentler stories of Christmas, the

427

books also offer biographical accounts and rich historical details in accordance with holidays celebrated in memory of national figures.

Here the criteria for picture books and picture storybooks apply as well as the general criteria basic to informational books, but some of the unique characteristics include the following:

- Is the story about the holiday historically correct insofar as the events and portrayal of life during the times is concerned?
- Does the author capture the spirit of the holiday giving children the appropriate flavor of the event?
- Is there sufficient background in the book about a particular holiday to assist children to understand the significance of the event?
- If the book tells a story about a holiday, is it presented with a theme and an interesting plot?
- Is the story told so that the people involved in it seem real and alive?
- Is the story presented simply enough so that children can readily understand and appreciate it?
- Are there fine illustrations illuminating the meanings of the holidays and customs?
- Does the book deepen insights and lend inspiration for the celebration of holidays?

BOOKS ABOUT LANGUAGE SKILLS

Books dealing with different aspects of language and the language skills reflect interests ranging from the simplest elements in the content areas to the highly technical development of the communication skills. The center of focus in elementary school curriculum books is on four facets of communication: listening, speaking, reading, and writing. Augmenting these are books of poetry, plays, histories of printing and writing, and other broader, yet interrelated, aspects of the language arts. Some helpful criteria pertinent to this far-reaching field of study include:

- Is the book distinguished for its clarity and unusually fine use of language?
- Is the book free of inaccuracies in syntax, structure, and content?
- Does the book reveal through its lucid text some methods of study by which content is authenticated?
- Does the content of certain of the books in a language arts collection have sufficient breadth and depth to afford children a sense of change and development in language?
- Are there books that give children a sense of connection between them, the culture, and the communication skills?

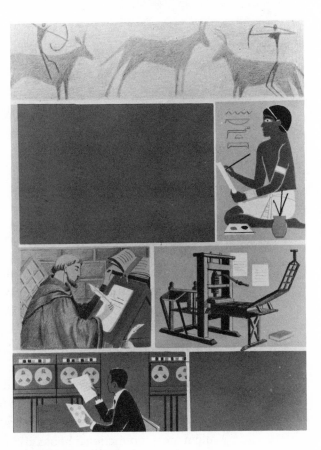

From cave art to computer language, the
history of writing spans a series of milestones that mark the growth of this highly
skilled form of human communication.
From The Story of Writing *by William and
Rhoda Cahn, illustrated by Anne Lewis. Copyright* © *1963 by William and Rhoda Cahn,
illustrations* © *1963 by Harvey House, Inc.
Reproduced by permission.*

- Does the book open up new fields of inquiry?
- Does the book take language out of the realm of the obvious by developing a fresh awareness of the power and importance of language?

REFERENCE BOOKS

Designed to answer a wide variety of questions about
many subjects frequently asked by children in the elementary and second-
ary schools, reference books present factual information in an ordered,
accurate, and concise way. Many of the references are alphabetically
arranged and graphically prepared to make investigation handy and useful. Consisting chiefly of dictionaries and encyclopedias, the criteria applicable are essentially the same as the criteria for informational books in
general because many of them deal with each of the specific subjects
covered by the major subject groupings. A few more specific criteria,
however, may be useful:

- Are specific facts provided for each of the subjects considered? Is there
  also generalized information?
- Are the facts presented in an interesting style and in large, readable print?

429

- Is the style free of condescension?
- Does the content stimulate interest for further study?
- Can the information be easily located?
- Are there a useful table of contents and index?
- Are the illustrations and diagrams made clear and illuminating?
- Does the reference keep in mind the reading level of the audience for which it is intended?

Books of information constitute an enormous division of nonfictional material covering a wide range of subjects for many levels of maturity. Not always designed to meet literary standards of distinction, books of information aim to provide children with knowledge they may be seeking as they discover and learn more about the world in which they live and the worlds that lie just beyond their reach. Well-written and well-illustrated informational books do more than inform children who seek specific facts and figures; they stimulate interest, lead to other areas of inquiry, provide fresh material, and add extensions of information that contribute to children's reading growth and background.

Along with providing specific information within school curriculum areas, nonfictional books also supply with clarity the directions one must follow in order to construct or build or create something that interests him.

Informational books also acquaint children with people, places, and customs, both in their immediate environment and in widely separated communities. They provide for children vivid glimpses of life and how it is lived under varied conditions and cultural influences. Thus children's books in the areas of social studies and social living sharpen children's awareness of man's need to adjust, to produce, to rely on each other, to survive in a universalizing way.

Facts and figures change, and scientific concepts reflect trends and developments, but boys and girls the world over remain essentially the same with unchanging needs for food, clothing, shelter, art forms, holidays, hobbies, fun, games, and heroes. Informational books, varied as the needs and interests of children, represent the major sources for fulfilling their unchanging needs and augmenting their firsthand experiences.

The enormity of this division of children's books has prohibited detailed analyses of books in each of the subject areas at various levels of growth; nor has it allowed for an exhaustive bibliography in specific curriculum groupings. The following list at least will serve as a guide to book selections, and through its annotations, it will indicate certain qualities that are fundamental to informational literature for children.

References

ARBUTHNOT, MAY HILL, "Reading for Information," in *Children and Books*, 3rd ed. Chicago: Scott, Foresman & Company, 1964.

HOLLOWELL, LILLIAN, "Biography," in *A Book of Children's Literature*, 3rd ed. New York: Holt, Rinehart & Winston, Inc., 1966.

HUCK, CHARLOTTE S., and DORIS A. YOUNG, "Children Seek Information About the Physical World," "Children Seek Information About People and Places," in *Children's Literature in the Elementary School*. New York: Holt, Rinehart & Winston, Inc., 1961.

JOHNSON, EDNA, et al., "Earth, Sky, and Sea," "Biography," "Travel and History," in *Anthology of Children's Literature*. Boston: Houghton Mifflin Company, 1959.

SMITH, LILLIAN H., "Books of Knowledge," in *The Unreluctant Years*. Chicago: American Library Association, 1953.

Information in Children's Literature

SCIENCE AND MATHEMATICS

Science

THE GIANT GOLDEN BOOK OF BIRDS
*Written by Robert P. Allen.
Illustrated by Arthur Singer.
Golden Press, Inc., 1963.*

Written especially for younger children, the text of the book is kept to a minimum, and the illustrations are perhaps the most outstanding since Audubon. The information is slight, but it can be enjoyed by old and young alike.

WILDLIFE IN AMERICA'S HISTORY
Written by Will Barker. Illustrated by Howard Jerome Smith. David McKay Co., Inc., 1966.

An informative book that discusses such animals as the buffalo, elk, deer, and eagle and their influence on American history. These illustrations of America's wildlife are enlightening to children of all ages, but especially to those in the intermediate grades.

THE WIND
Written and illustrated by Jeanne Bendick. Rand McNally & Co., 1965.

An understandable and accurate explanation of the wind and of weather in general. Tells about the effect of wind and weather on nature and mankind. Many helpful diagrams and maps. Suitable for younger children.

BOOK OF REPTILES AND
AMPHIBIANS
Written and illustrated by Michael H. Bevans. Doubleday & Company, Inc., 1956.

An excellent book for very young nature lovers and hobbyists, this illustrated work describes the characteristics, habits, and habitats of over one hundred species of snakes, lizards, turtles, frogs, toads, and salamanders in the United States.

LOOKOUT FOR THE FOREST
Written by Glenn O. Blough. Illustrated by Jeanne Bendick. McGraw-Hill Book Company, 1955.

This book of simple science tells how foresters thin, reset, cultivate, and protect the trees and wildlife of our land. It shows how everyday citizens can aid in protecting our forests. Giving even the youngest an appreciation of great forests and an understanding of the importance of taking care of them, the book blends beautiful three-color pictures with singing prose.

BIOGRAPHY OF AN ATOM
Written by J. Bronowski and M. E. Selsam Illustrated by Pursell Weimer. Harper & Row, Publishers, 1965.

How and why are substances classified? What is the nature of the atom? Both questions are answered with an up-to-date and exciting approach. Detailed diagrams help to clarify the text for younger children.

RAIN FOREST
Written by Bill Brown. Coward McCann, Inc., 1962.

The story of the greatest forest on earth, the vast Pacific Coast Rain Forest, this book tells how nature created the forest and how man nearly destroyed it through abuse, and how man has learned to maintain, preserve, and use it. Geared for upper grade use. Good, clear material, fine photographs. Glossary and index.

SMALL PETS FROM WOODS AND
FIELDS
Written and illustrated by Margaret Waring Buck. Abingdon Press, 1960.

Information is given on locating small, wild creatures with directions for raising them in comfortable captivity. A wealth of suggestions is presented for young children's nature projects. Species are identified and drawn in clear, ink lines with an excellent nature bibliography.

UNDERGROUND RICHES
Written by Walter Buehr. William Morrow & Co., Inc., 1958.

This book gives the more mature reader a concise account of the minerals of the world. Included are descriptions of mining methods from the earliest to the scientific procedures used today.

DASH AND DART
Written by Mary and Conrad Buff. Illustrated by Conrad Buff. The Viking Press, Inc., 1942.

The story of two baby deer in the Southwest, illustrated in full color and black and white, is written with a beautiful simplicity and deep feeling for wildlife and the out-of-doors. This can be an especially meaningful book in the primary grades offering vicarious experiences for the city child who has little personal contact with nature.

SNOW SURVEYORS
Written by C. B. Colby. Coward-McCann, Inc., 1959.

Describes graphically the life and work of those men of the Soil Conservation Service whose job it is to measure the depth of the mountain snow cover each winter in order to predict flood or drought for the next spring and summer. This book helps

one realize the importance of snow surveying and how it can defend us against
flood and drought. Intermediate and upper
grades.

PROJECT APOLLO: MISSION TO
THE MOON
Written by Charles Coombs.
William Morrow & Co., Inc., 1965.

What course of action will the United
States follow when the mission to the
moon is a confirmed accomplishment
rather than a dream? The author, through
the use of accurate, technical information
and good illustrations and photographs,
offers some suggestions. Suitable for upper
grades.

ANIMALS EVERYWHERE
*Written and illustrated by Ingri and
Edgar Parin d'Aulaire. Doubleday
& Company, Inc., 1954.*

In this gay picture book, the authors tell of
animal life from the tropics to the Far
North. Four-color illustrations showing
the animals of the cold, hot, and temperate
zones in their native surroundings, complement the text to make this book an excellent source for primary-grade children on
animal life and the different regions of
climate of the earth.

AMERICANS IN SPACE
*Written by John Dille. Harper &
Row, Publishers, 1965.*

With enthusiasm the author relates the
story of American achievements in the
space program. Numerous details, good
photographs, and selective words are assets
to the book. Upper grades.

ABOUT FORESTERS
*Written by Norma Dobrin.
Illustrated by Arnold Dobrin.
Melmont Publishers, Inc., 1962.*

Emphasizes the role of forests in our
country's economy and stresses the importance of foresters. The many and varied
duties of the forester having to do with the
preservation of trees, protection of wildlife, the conservation of water and soil,

and even the pursuit of research projects
are taken up each in its turn. Mrs. Dobrin
writes clearly and precisely. Very informative yet distinctly readable text gives a
child respect for forests and foresters.

ATOM POWER
*Written by Joseph M. Dukert.
Illustrated by John T. Gorsuch.
Coward-McCann, Inc., 1962.*

In the clearly written, well-illustrated text,
the author tells the story of atom power.
He explains how atomic energy is produced, how it is presently being used, and
how it might be used in the future. More
mature readers.

THE SNOW BOOK
*Written by Eva Knox Evans.
Illustrated by Aldren A. Watson.
Little, Brown & Co., 1965.*

A simple, clearly written, and rather dull
book about snow and its effects. For younger children.

THE STORY OF DAMS
*Written by Peter Farb. Illustrated
by George Kanelous. Harvey
House, Inc., Publishers, 1961.*

An exciting story of what is being done to
harness the world's rivers for the benefit
of mankind. Through a knowledge and
understanding of the engineering facts
of water control, youth will be prepared
to carry out its future responsibility of
assuring that there will be enough, but
not too much water at the right time and at
the right place. Reviewed for scientific
accuracy by the U.S. Army Corps of
Engineers. Upper grades.

THE LAND WE LIVE ON
*Written by Carroll and Mildred
Fenton. Photographs. Doubleday &
Company, Inc., 1944.*

Photographs and clear simple text describe thirty-four land formations and the
kinds of land in different parts of the country, how it is changed by such agents as
water, fire, dust storms, and men, and how
it can be used and conserved. This photo-

graphic picture book grew out of the author's radio program "Science Every-where." A physical geography book for older children.

WHEN WINTER COMES
Written by Charles P. Fox. Reilly
& Lee Co., 1962.

This is a fascinating story of how and where animals live when snow covers the earth. The style is simple, clear and concise. The photographs have been well co-ordinated with the textual information and help bring the story to life. Intermediate grades.

THE TRUE BOOK OF CONSERVATION
Written by Richard Gates.
Children's Press, Inc., 1959.

The author makes clear the responsibility everyone has for protecting our great natural resources, gives an elementary idea of balance in nature, and stresses the im-portance of conservation of plants, animals, and soil. The author's ideas are not beyond the understanding of children in the pri-mary grades. Many illustrations in full color make this book attractive, but those in black and white are superior. Recommended if easier material on con-servation is needed.

WAIT AND SEE
Written by Constantine Georgiou.
Illustrated by Janet and Alex
D'Amato. Harvey House, Inc.,
Publishers, 1962.

A meaningful science experience that deals with the incubation of young chicks in an exciting as well as factual manner. It may serve to stimulate children to ex-plore the subject further by setting up a similar experiment. All ages.

WHITEY AND WHISKERS AND
FOOD
Written by Constantine Georgiou.
Illustrated by Taylor Oughton.
Harvey House, Inc., Publishers,
1965.

Two white mice, Whitey and Whiskers, are used in an experiment to find out about

food. Whitey is fed food indicated on a "good food chart"; Whiskers is fed "goodies." Stressing the nutritive values of various types of food, the book under-scores the scientific method and the im-portance of a proper diet. Fourth-graders and younger children can benefit from this helpful science book.

HOUSES FROM THE SEA
Written by Alice E. Goudey.
Illustrated by Adrienne Adams.
Charles Scribner's Sons, 1959.

A beautifully illustrated and scientifically accurate book on seashells and the delight two children find in spending a day at the beach collecting them. The rhythmic prose makes this a good book for reading aloud to all children, especially those in the lower grades.

WILDLIFE IN DANGER
Written by Ivah Green. Coward-
McCann, Inc., 1960.

Brief accounts of twenty-nine birds and animals that are either extinct or threat-ened with extinction stress the importance of wildlife conservation. Each account is illustrated by an excellent photograph. Of general interest as well as useful in schools.

THE BIG BOOK OF WILD
ANIMALS
Compiled and edited by Margaret
Green. Pictures by Janusz
Grabianski. Franklin Watts, Inc.,
1964.

Here are many stories of wild animals as they really are—not as beasts who speak in the language of men. These are the animals as they have been observed by woodsmen, explorers, and zoo keepers, to name a few. Exciting illustrations bring beauty, terror, and moments of playfulness to the beholder. All ages.

FROGS AND POLLIWOGS
Written by Dorothy Childs Hogner.
Illustrated by Nils Hogner. Thomas
Y. Crowell Company, 1956.

Here is a delightful introduction to many species, from the common Bullfrog, or Jumbo, which lives east of the Rockies, to the large Goliath of West Africa whose body may be a foot long. The concluding chapter discusses ways to study these creatures at home in an aquarium or vivarium and gives directions for making the latter. Illustrations are excellent.

WILD WAYS
Written and illustrated by Ross E. Hutchins. Rand McNally & Co., 1961.

Illustrated by fifty photographs that show the strange ways of the animal world, this book deals with varied creatures and delights the reader with a storehouse of knowledge and often startling facts about them. Upper grades.

HORSES OF LONG AGO
Written and illustrated by Dahlov Ipcar. Doubleday & Company, Inc., 1965.

The author begins his history by relating the beginnings of the very first twelve-inch eohippus of fifty-five million years ago and explores all aspects of horsedom right down to the draft horse of the present day.

ANIMAL HIDE AND SEEK
Written and illustrated by Dahlov Ipcar. William R. Scott, Inc., 1947.

This gracefully prepared book uses colored pictures with brief texts to show how small forest animals achieve protective coloration. It is charming and stimulating for the young set. The artist's drawings are realistic, and her simple prose tells you what to look for among the arabesques of leaves and branches, a device useful in developing a prime requisite for enjoyment of life— the seeing eye.

THE RIVER'S JOURNEY
Written and illustrated by Anne Marie Jauss. J.B. Lippincott Co., 1957.

Descriptions of life on river banks and man's use of the river help to unfold the exciting story of a river's journey from its source to the sea. Children from nine to twelve will delight in this story told in attractive text and pictures.

THE SEASONS
Written by Derek Jervis. Illustrated by Joan Beals. The John Day Company, Inc., 1962.

This is the story of the earth's movement around the sun. It clearly explains seasonal differences. Experiments are included that make the story fun and interesting to young readers. Colorful illustrations further strengthen the book.

ALL ABOUT THE PLANET EARTH
Written by Patricia Lauber. Illustrated by Lee J. Ames. Random House, Inc., 1962.

The author whisks the reader away to explore space, the ocean, and the earth. A superbly illustrated account that answers many questions a young child may have.

THE STORY OF SHELLS
Written by Curtis Martin. Illustrated by Christopher Williams. Harvey House, Inc., Publishers, 1966.

Intermediate-grade children will enjoy reading this informative guidebook with sections on the five main classifications of sea shells. A do-it-yourself guide for making articles from shells and pearls lends wonder and delight to this colorfully illustrated book.

ENGINES
Written by Jerome S. Meyer. Illustrated by John Teppich. World Publishing Co., 1962.

This science concept book explains in clear language the history of engines as well as the principles of each. The lucid introductory account is illustrated in black and white.

THE FABULOUS ISOTOPES
Written by Robin McKown. Illustrated by Isadore Steinberg. Holiday House, 1962.

What are isotopes and what do they do? This book shows and tells in a direct manner the fascinating answers to some of these questions asked by children in all grades.

WORLD PROVIDER: THE STORY OF
GRASS
*Written by Sarah Riedman.
Abelard-Schuman Limited, 1962.*

Drawings and photographs help to unfold for the older reader the thousands of species of the grass family, its cultivation and varied uses.

A PICTURE STORY OF FORCE AND
MOTION
*Written by Hy Ruchlis. Illustrated
by Alice Hirsh. Harper & Row,
Publishers, 1958.*

An enthralling explanation of the laws of force and motion. Well substantiated by diagrams and photographs.

THE STORY OF ROCKS AND
MINERALS
*Written by David M. Seaman.
Illustrated by L. Oviatt Welcome.
Harvey House, Inc., Publishers,
1966.*

This beautifully illustrated earth science book tells how rocks and minerals are made, and about uranium prospecting, clues for detecting minerals, the lost Inca emerald mines, and minerals from outer space.

HERE COMES THE NIGHT
*Written by Miriam Schlein.
Illustrated by Harvey Weiss. Albert
Whitman & Co., 1957.*

In rhythmic prose style the author tells how night visits the farm, the sea, and the city. The text is illustrated with imaginative pictures that supplement the text perfectly.

EVERYDAY WEATHER AND HOW
IT WORKS
*Written by Herman Schneider.
Illustrated by Jeanne Bendick.*

*McGraw-Hill Book Company,
1961.*

This informative book explains many concepts about the weather with the use of simple diagrams and experiments.

YOU AMONG THE STARS
*Written by Herman and Nina
Schneider. Illustrated by Symeon
Shimin . Scott, Foresman &
Company, 1951.*

This book lucidly introduces a child to some difficult concepts concerning the universe. Some of the ideas are hard to grasp, but the colorful illustrations are helpful.

GREAT HERITAGE
*Written by Katherine Shippen.
Illustrated by C. B. Falls. The
Viking Press, Inc., 1947.*

A historical discussion of fourteen of the principle resources of America from the time it was first settled to the present. Among the subjects are wheat, fur, corn, flour, coal, gold, timber, and how man's use and abuse of them have affected the nation. The folklore and personalities connected with these resources have a part in the book. Illustrations admirably depict the resources of this enormous land. The book is brilliant in execution. All ages.

THE STORY OF ROCKS
*Written by Dorothy Shuttlesworth.
Doubleday & Company, Inc., 1956.*

The color illustrations in this book are beautiful and useful for rock identification and classification and for assembling rock collections. There is also a state-by-state listing of rocks and minerals included to aid the beginning rock collector. Intermediate grades.

THE STORY OF CATS
*Written by Dorothy Shuttlesworth.
Illustrated by G. Don Ray.
Doubleday & Company, Inc.,
1962.*

This book, beautifully illustrated in tints and shades of browns, grays, and yellows, tells the story of feline evolution from prehistory to today. It tells how to differentiate between breeds and describes some of the superstitions and legends about cats. All ages.

GUARDING THE TREASURED LANDS:
THE STORY OF THE NATIONAL
PARK SERVICE
*Written by Ann and Myron
Sutton. (Foreword by Stewart L.
Udall). J. B. Lippincott, Co., 1965.*
A brief but effective recruitment book designed to interest boys and girls in careers with the National Park Service. Thrilling tales of rescue and humorous anecdotes combine with career information. Upper grades.

TO SAVE THE SOIL
*Written by Naomi Talley.
Photographs courtesy of Soil
Conservation Service, Department
of Agriculture. The Dial Press, Inc.,
1965.*
The nature and causes of soil erosion are outlined and traced in a history of soil conservation in this country. The book includes a description of the U.S. Conservation Service and examples of specific conservation projects throughout the United States. Good photographs supplement the informative text. All ages.

THE LAND RENEWED
*Written by William Van Dersal
and Ed Graham. Photographs.
Oxford University Press, Inc., 1946.*
A clear, vivid story of how the rich soil of America has been damaged by erosion and the methods by which it can be renewed for ourselves and for future generations. The striking photographs carry further the points made by the text. Mature readers.

WATER FOR AMERICA
*Written by William R. Van Dersal
and Ed H. Graham. Photographs.*

*Henry Z. Walck, Inc., Publishers,
1956.*
This comprehensive treatment of water conservation describes the many ways in which water affects life and tells all about water in its various forms, sources, and uses. The practice of confining each topic to exactly one page with a related photograph facing it makes an attractive book, but does not always allow for the simplicity or difficulty of a subject. Complex subjects have been subdivided for easy understanding. The book will be a help in the study of either water or conservation. Ages twelve and up.

Mathematics

REALM OF NUMBERS
*Written by Isaac Asimov. Diagrams
by Robert Belmore. Houghton
Mifflin Company, 1959.*

An explanation of mathematical principles and procedures starting with simple arithmetic and the abacus and continuing to more advanced mathematics—square root, logarithms, rational and irrational numbers. Short cuts, tricks, and puzzles provide entertainment for those with some math background. For intermediate and upper grades.

THE FIVE ROLLATINIS
*Written and illustrated by Jan B.
Balet. J. B. Lippincott Co., 1959.*

Brilliantly illustrated in full color and written with humor and sympathy, this is a description of the magic and activity of a small traveling circus. It offers meaningful experience to young children in the development of number concepts as well as the concept of sets that is an integral part of the new math now being taught in elementary school. For the lower grades.

ALL KINDS OF TIME
*Written and illustrated by Harry
Behn. Harcourt, Brace & World,
Inc., 1950.*

In this poetically and imaginatively written book, the author describes a child's feelings about time, the mystery of seconds, minutes, hours, days, and seasons. Delicately colored illustrations join with text to make this an excellent introduction to the meaning of time in terms that the young child can understand and appreciate. For the lower grades.

A CAT CAN'T COUNT

Written by Blossom Budney.
Illustrated by William Wondriska.
Lothrop, Lee & Shepard Co., Inc.,
1962.

Using the new concept of counting and measuring, gay pictures and verse invite the young child to count and see how many objects he can find. For the lower grades.

THINGS THAT MEASURE

Written by Philip Carona.
Illustrated by John Kaufmann.
Prentice-Hall, Inc., 1962.

An introduction to the various new methods of measurement developed for space age needs. Indexed.

DANCING IN THE MOON

Written and illustrated by Fritz
Eichenberg. Harcourt, Brace &
World, Inc., 1955.

This book introduces young children to the numbers from one to twenty by means of nonsensical counting rhymes. The humor of the text is reflected in the delightful and very amusing illustrations that accompany each rhyme. The book has real value in teaching number concepts to children in that it presents the abstract number symbol in the text with a concrete example of what the symbol stands for in the illustrations. For the lower grades.

THE WING ON A FLEA

Written and illustrated by Ed
Emberley. Little, Brown & Co.,
1961.

Three basic geometric shapes (square, triangle, circle) are examined as they appear in familiar, everyday things. Simply written and cleverly illustrated, this is an excellent introduction for young children to the systematic study of shape and form, namely geometry. It can also be used to encourage them to discover things besides those listed in the book that contain the three shapes discussed. This book can also be used in the area of art. For the lower grades.

JEANNE-MARIE COUNTS HER SHEEP

Written and illustrated by Françoise.
Charles Scribner's Sons, 1951.

In this gay, childlike picture book, a little French girl counts the seven little lambs that she hopes her pet sheep will have and plans what she will do with the money the wool brings. This book presents the young child with a story that delights him and at the same time teaches him to count to seven in a meaningful way. For the lower grades.

THE WONDERFUL WORLD OF MATHEMATICS

Written by Lancelot Hogben.
Doubleday & Company, Inc., 1955.

A book containing many colored illustrations that show the development of mathematics as a science from ancient times to the present. For intermediate and upper grades.

NEW WAYS IN MATH

Written by Arthur Jonas. Illustrated
by Aliki. Prentice-Hall, Inc., 1962.

The history of mathematics from the days of bartering up to the present binary numbers, flip flop switches, and computer programming. Indexed.

I MADE A LINE

Written and illustrated by Leonard
Kessler. Grosset & Dunlap, Inc.,
1962.

This is the simply written and imaginatively illustrated story of a young boy who loves to draw. In doing so he creates a whole world just with his use of a pencil. This book opens up a wide area of possibilities for creative art experiences for children in the primary grades.

INCH BY INCH
Written and illustrated by Leo Lionni. Ivan Obolensky, Inc., 1960.

The adventures of an inchworm told in simple text and colorful illustrations provide an excellent introduction to the concept of measurement. For the lower grades.

HOW BIG IS A FOOT?
Written and illustrated by Rolf Myller. Atheneum Publishers, 1962.

The answer to the question is a humorous one and the story sheer nonsense, but the basis is the important concept of the need for standard measures. Written and illustrated with charm and humor, this book offers a meaningful introduction to a unit in linear measurement for young children. For the lower grades.

THE STORY OF MATHEMATICS
Written by Hy Ruchlis and Jack Engelhardt. Harvey House, Inc., Publishers, 1965.

An absorbing, extremely well-illustrated approach to the study of mathematics. For intermediate and upper grades.

HOW BIG IS BIG: FROM STARS TO ATOMS
Written by Nina and Herman Schneider. Scott, Foresman & Company, 1950.

Concepts of relative size are presented in easy step-by-step comparisons. Pictures illustrate the changes in size. Lower and intermediate grades.

SOCIAL STUDIES

The World: Past and Present

THE GREEKS: A GREAT ADVENTURE
Written by Isaac Asimov. Houghton Mifflin Company, 1965.

The story of the heritage of Greece is superbly presented in text and pictures. Upper grades.

EXPLOITS IN AFRICA
Written by John Bayliss. N.Y. Graphic Society, 1964.

Thirteen exciting and well-told stories of true adventure in Africa, ranging from a visit with Dr. Schweitzer to an air race in Johannesburg. Upper grades.

PARIS IN THE RAIN WITH JEAN AND JACQUELINE
Written by Thea Bergere. Illustrated by Richard Bergere. McGraw-Hill Book Company, 1963.

Rainy days are always special days for boys and girls all over the world. In this book the reader has fun walking around Paris in the rain in spring, summer, fall, and winter in the company of Jean and Jacqueline, two charming French children. The text is poetically written and full of beautiful descriptions of life in Paris, including simple French words that young children will find easy to learn. The superb illustrations, in shades of blue with accents of red, capture the feeling of Paris in the rain as seen through the eyes of the two children.

CORTEZ AND THE ATZEC CONQUEST
Written by Irwin R. Blacker. Consultant: Dr. Gordon F. Ekholm. Harper & Row, Publishers, 1965.

The text is an expert summary of the fascinating story of Cortez supported by a rich array of maps, artifacts, and drawings. Intermediate and upper grades.

PEOPLE
Written by Irvin Block. Franklin Watts, Inc., 1956.

This introduction to anthropology describes the ways of living of six different groups of people and fosters understanding and respect for differences in beliefs and behavior. Intermediate and upper grades.

HISTORY AND HISTORIANS
*Written by Fon W. Boardman, Jr.
Henry Z. Walck, Inc., Publishers,
1965.*

An absorbing survey of historians and their methods over nearly 2,500 years. For the upper grades.

ASPECTS OF LIVING: THE STORY
OF SCHOOLS FROM ANCIENT TIMES
TILL NOW
*Written by Peggy Boehm. Sterling
Publishing Co., Inc., 1958.*

A brief picture story of the beginnings and development of schools throughout the world from the first open-air schools of ancient Greece to the modern American school. Intermediate grades.

THE FIRST BOOK OF PAKISTAN
*Written by Jean Bothwell.
Photographs. Franklin Watts, Inc.,
1962.*

A view of Pakistan, its history, problems, ways of living, and future. Intermediate grades.

THE SPANISH CONQUISTADORES IN
NORTH AMERICA
*Written by Walter Buehr. G. P.
Putnam's Sons, 1962.*

The story of the great Spanish explorers and the part they played in the history of North America. Intermediate grades.

MAIN STREETS OF SOUTHEAST ASIA
*Written by Hal Buell. Photographs.
Dodd, Mead & Co., 1962.*

A picture tour of Southeast Asia, which introduces the land and people of today. Intermediate and upper grades.

THE PICTURE STORY OF JAPAN
*Written by Rachel Carr. Illustrated
by Kazue Mizumura. David
McKay Co., Inc., 1962.*

A brief but comprehensive introduction to Japan—past and present. Intermediate grades.

SLAVIC PEOPLES
*Written by Thomas Caldecot
Chubb. Illustrated by W. T.
Mars. World Publishing Co., 1962.*

A clear introduction to the history and culture of the Slavic nations of middle Europe. A "Major Cultures of the World" book. Upper grades.

MAPPING THE WORLD
*Written by C. B. Colby.
Photographs. Coward-McCann, Inc.,
1959.*

The project of the U.S. Army Corps of Engineers to map the world accurately is explained in text and photographs. Surveying and cartography are described. Intermediate grades.

CRETE: ISLAND OF MYSTERY
*Written by Leonard Cotrell.
Illustrated by W. T. Mars.
Prentice-Hall, Inc., 1965.*

A renowned archeologist and author shows how the culture of Crete combines myths and history. An outstanding book for all ages.

BAGHDAD AND BEYOND
*Written by Mora Dickson. Rand
McNally & Co., 1962.*

A picture of Baghdad's daily life with descriptions of trips to various sights outside the city. Upper grades.

UNITED NATIONS
*Written by Myron Ehrenberg.
Photographs. Doubleday &
Company, Inc., 1965.*

Behind the scenes at the UN. Intermediate and upper grades.

THE COMMON MARKET
*Written by Harry B. Ellis.
Photographs. World Publishing Co.,
1965.*

An authoritative discussion of the Common Market and its role in the world's economy. Upper grades.

SOVIET UNION
Written by Frank Folsom. Thomas Nelson & Sons, 1965.

A firsthand report on the careers, attitudes, and activities of Soviet teenagers, and a general view of the U.S.S.R. based on the author's extensive tour of Russia. Upper grades.

WHERE IN THE WORLD DO YOU LIVE?
Written by Al Hine and John Alcorn. Illustrated in color by John Alcorn. Harcourt, Brace & World, Inc., 1962.

This approach to geography for lower grades shows them their relationship to the physical world.

NOTHING TO WEAR BUT CLOTHES
Written by Frank Jupo. E. P. Dutton & Co., Inc., 1953.

This simple story of clothes, from skins worn by primitive people to space suits of our modern day, is presented in interesting text and appropriate drawings. Good general information to arouse interest in the subject. Lower to intermediate grades.

THE FIRST BOOK OF COMMUNIST CHINA
Written by William Kinmond. Photographs. Franklin Watts, Inc., 1962.

Life in China today with background material by a Canadian journalist who went there. Upper grades.

AFRICA: AWAKENING GIANT
Written by Sidney Lens. Photographs. G. P. Putnam's Sons, 1962.

A presentation of the men and events that led up to the creation of independent nations in Africa.

SOCIOLOGY
Written by Dale McLemore and M. Vere DeVault. Illustrated by Ralph White. Steck-Vaughn Co., 1962.

A simple explanation of sociology: Primary groups, status, role, folkways, mores, and laws. For intermediate grades.

THE EPIC OF THE MACCABEES
Written by Valerie Mindlin and Gaalyahu Cornfeld. The Macmillan Company, 1962.

Adopted from the Apocrypha of the Old Testament, this book re-creates a historical epic battle. For intermediate and upper grades.

THE PAGEANT OF SOUTH AMERICAN HISTORY, REV. ED.
Written by Anne Merriman Peck. David McKay Co., Inc., 1962.

First published in 1941, this is the history of South America from the primitive Indian cultures up to the past twenty years. For the upper grades.

A MAP IS A PICTURE
Written by Barbara Rinkoff. Illustrated by Robert Galster. Thomas Y. Crowell Company, 1965.

An extraordinarily interesting book in which the reader is led through a graded series of maps beginning with a pirate's sketch for locating buried treasure and progressing through maps of the world, countries, cities, neighborhoods, even maps of the sea and air. Directions, legends, and scales of miles are carefully discussed. Commendably clear illustrations. Primary grades.

THE FIRST BOOK OF ANCIENT BIBLE LANDS
Written by Charles Alexander Robinson, Jr. Photographs. Franklin Watts, Inc., 1962.

A history of Palestine and surrounding lands and the religions that grew there. Suitable for intermediate grades.

FIRST BOOK OF ANCIENT
MESOPOTAMIA AND PERSIA
*Written by Charles Alexander
Robinson, Jr. Photographs. Franklin
Watts, Inc., 1962.*

A history and description of the civilizations of the ancient Near East with emphasis on the culture and ideas of these
ancient peoples. For intermediate and
upper grades.

THE KEY TO MOSCOW
*Written by Harrison E. Salisbury.
J. B. Lippincott Co., 1963.*

A history of the capital of the U.S.S.R.
and a vivid portrait of the city as it is
today by the Pulitzer Prize winning former
Moscow correspondent of *The New York
Times.* Intermediate grades.

LET'S FIND OUT ABOUT THE
UNITED NATIONS
*Written by Martha and Charles
Shapp. Illustrated by Angela Conner.
Franklin Watts, Inc., 1962.*

The meaning of the United Nations is
captured in the clear and simple termi-
nology of the text and the expressiveness
of the pictures. It is very important that
children know the place of the United
Nations in today's struggle for peace, and
this book provides a meaningful learning
experience in this area. For the primary-
grade child.

FIRST BOOK OF BRAZIL
*Written by Sally Sheppard.
Photographs. Franklin Watts, Inc.,
1962.*

Brazil as it is today, with enough history
and geography to establish its background.
For the upper grades.

THE POOL OF KNOWLEDGE: HOW
THE UNITED NATIONS SHARE
THEIR SKILLS, REV. ED.
*Written by Katherine B. Shippen.
Photographs. Harper & Row,
Publishers, 1965.*

Deals with the programs of the United
Nations Technical Assistance Board and

Special Fund and includes some of the
recent projects undertaken by the UN in
such fields as health, agriculture, and
education. It shows how the Technical
Assistance Program is organized, how it
operates, and what it has accomplished
in helping the developing countries in the
world. Upper grades.

PLAYTIME IN AFRICA
*Written by Efua Sutherland.
Photographs. Atheneum Publishers,
1962.*

A book about the happy playtime activities of African children. Intermediate
grades.

THE PEOPLES OF AFRICA
*Written by Colin Turnbull.
Illustrated by Richard M. Powers.
World Publishing Co., 1962.*

A fascinating survey of the basic tribal
cultures of Africa—hunters, pastoralists,
and cultivators. A "Major Cultures of
the World" book.

America: The Land and Its People

OUR FEDERAL GOVERNMENT AND
HOW IT WORKS
*Written by Patricia C. Acheson.
Dodd, Mead & Co., 1958.*

This introduction to the United States
Government outlines its complex framework and the functions of major divisions
with great clarity. Upper grades.

IN NAVAHO LAND
*Written and illustrated with
photographs by Laura Adams Armer.
David McKay Co., Inc., 1962.*

These personal experiences of life on an
Arizona Indian reservation reveal the
customs and the art of the Navaho. Upper
grades.

THE STORY OF YANKEE WHALING
*Written by the editors of American
Heritage. Illustrated with drawings,
period prints, paintings, and
photographs. Golden Press, Inc.,
1959.*

This is a rich source of information about the American whaling industry. Rare illustrations make this a beautiful book. Intermediate and upper grades.

STEAMBOATS ON THE MISSISSIPPI
Written by Ralph K. Andrist.
Duell, Sloan & Pearce, 1962.

A book about the Missouri-Mississippi river system, which was graced by a fleet of steamboats for nearly seventy-five years. Intermediate to upper grades.

THIS IS THE DESERT
Written by Phil Ault. Illustrated by
Leonard Everett Fisher. Dodd,
Mead & Co., 1959.

The dramatic story of the American desert is skillfully handled as the author tells of exciting events, resources of the land, and potential utilization. Intermediate and upper grades.

AMERICANS BEFORE COLUMBUS
Written by Elizabeth Baity.
Photographs. The Viking Press,
Inc., 1951.

Thirty-two pages of photographs precede the text. The author gives a clear account of the settlement of the American continents by wandering hunters from Asia and the development of cultures such as those of the Mayan and the Aztec. New York Herald Tribune Spring Festival Award, 1951. Intermediate and upper grades.

AMERICA'S BURIED PAST
Written by Dr. Gordon C.
Baldwin. Photographs. G. P. Putnam's
Sons, 1965.

The story of the American Indians who populated North America 25,000 years before the arrival of Columbus. Intermediate and upper grades.

THE SIOUX INDIANS
Written by Sonia Bleeker. Illustrated
by Kisa Sasaki. William Morrow
& Co., Inc., 1965.

A study of this powerful tribe whose life on the Great Plains centered around the hunting of buffalo. Intermediate grades.

LET'S GO TO THE FIRST
INDEPENDENCE DAY
Written by Mary Jo Borreson.
Illustrated by Gustav Schrotter.
G. P. Putnam's Sons, 1962.

A trip back in time to the signing of the Declaration of Independence. Intermediate grades.

LET'S GO TO MOUNT VERNON
Written by Mary Jo Borreson.
Illustrated by Moneta Barnett.
G. P. Putnam's Sons, 1962.

A trip to Mount Vernon, giving a picture of the estate as it was when George Washington lived there and as it is today. Intermediate grades.

ETHAN ALLEN AND THE GREEN
MOUNTAIN BOYS
Written by Slater Brown. Illustrated
by William Moyers. Random
House, Inc., 1956.

The story of Vermont's hero, Ethan Allen, and his role in the War of Independence. Intermediate grades.

THIS HALLOWED GROUND
Written by Bruce Catton.
Doubleday & Company, Inc., 1965.

An oversized and especially abridged edition of Mr. Catton's famous book; more than one hundred illustrations, including historic lithographs, detailed maps. Intermediate and upper grades.

MEET THE PRESIDENTS, REV. ED.
Written by Frances Cavanah.
Macrae Smith Company, 1965.

Through anecdotes, vignettes, and stories, this book presents our Presidents—from Washington to LBJ. Tells how they shaped their country's destiny. Valuable "President at a Glance" section. Intermediate grades.

THE BOOK OF THE WEST
*Written by Charles Chilton.
Illustrated by Eric Tansley.
Bobbs-Merrill Company, Inc., 1965.*

An authentic, highly readable account of the history and development of the American West. Intermediate and upper grades.

THE DESERT PEOPLE
*Written by Ann Nolan Clark. The
Viking Press, Inc., 1965.*

Tells in singing prose of an Indian boy's daily life, his home, his brothers, customs, and animals. Lower and intermediate grades.

HIGH COUNTRY
*Written by Libra Jan Cleveland.
Illustrated by Tom Dunnington.
Childrens Press, Inc., 1962.*

Tells the story of the Rocky Mountain and Plateau states, their history, people, arts, wildlife, and national parks. Intermediate and upper grades.

PACIFIC SHORES
*Written by Libra Jan Cleveland.
Illustrated by Tom Dunnington.
Childrens Press, Inc., 1962.*

The story of the Pacific states including Alaska and Hawaii, their history, people, customs, and art. Intermediate and upper grades.

HOW MONEY IS MADE
*Written by David C. Cooke.
Dodd, Mead & Co., 1962.*

Fascinating information about who makes our money, how it is done, and how to identify counterfeit currency. Illustrated photographs. Intermediate grades.

PRESIDENT KENNEDY SELECTS SIX
BRAVE PRESIDENTS
*Written by Bill Davidson.
Photographs. Harper & Row,
Publishers, 1962.*

Based on the author's interviews with President Kennedy about the six American Presidents whose courage meant the most to him. Upper grades.

COLONIAL LIFE IN AMERICA
*Written by Margaret C. Farquhar.
Holt, Rinehart & Winston, Inc.,
1962.*

A fascinating account of everyday life in America's thirteen original colonies. Lower grades.

THE SUPREME COURT IN
AMERICAN HISTORY: TEN GREAT
DECISIONS
*Written by Marjorie G. Fribourg.
Macrae Smith Company, 1965.*

The people, the times, and the issues of ten major cases with far-reaching implications. Bibliography, list of judges, index. Upper grades.

SAN FRANCISCO
*Written by Jean Fritz. Illustrated by
Emil Weiss. Rand McNally & Co.,
1962.*

Part of the "Cities of the World" series, this book takes a tour through the past and present of San Francisco. Intermediate grades.

MOUNTAINS
*Written by Delia Goetz. Illustrated
by Louis Darling. William Morrow
& Co., Inc., 1962.*

A picture of the life of mountain folk with information on the formation and location of mountains. Intermediate grades.

YOU AND DEMOCRACY
*Written by Dorothy L. Gordon.
E. P. Dutton & Co., Inc., 1951.*

Simple text and many pictures make up this small concise book on what democracy is and what privileges the people enjoy. Intermediate and upper grades.

HOW THE PILGRIMS CAME TO
PLYMOUTH
*Written by Olga Hall-Quest.
Illustrated by James MacDonald.
E. P. Dutton & Co., Inc., 1953.*

The many difficulties encountered by the Pilgrims in leaving England, during their stay in Holland, in crossing the Atlantic, and in settling at Plymouth are simply stated. One map shows the route followed, and full-page drawings preface each of the book's nine chapters. Intermediate and upper grades.

FRONTIER LEADERS AND PIONEERS
Written by Dorothy Heiderstadt.
Illustrated by Clifford N. Geary.
David McKay Co., Inc., 1962.

A collection of twenty brief biographical stories about American pioneers and leaders, including Daniel Boone, Jim Bowie, and John Muir. Intermediate grades.

FRUITCAKE AND ARSENIC
Written by Josephine Hemphill.
Illustrated by Marvin Friedman,
Little, Brown & Co., 1965.

How the U.S. Food and Drug Administration protects us. Upper grades.

WHAT THE PRESIDENT DOES ALL DAY
Written by Roy Hoopes.
Photographs. The John Day
Company, Inc., 1962.

What the President does in a routine office day, presented through photographs and text. Lower grades.

WHAT DOES A SECRET SERVICE AGENT DO?
Written by Wayne Hyde. Illustrated
with photographs. Dodd, Mead &
Co., 1962.

The informational story of the Secret Service, how the agents are trained, and what they do. Intermediate grades.

THE REAL BOOK ABOUT OUR ARMED FORCES
Written by Clayton Knight. Garden
City Books, 1959.

A summary of the historical achievements and modern equipment and training methods of the five branches of U.S. fighting forces. Intermediate and upper grades.

THE CHANGING SOUTH
Written by Myrick and Barbara
Land. Photographs. Maps by Marian
Manfredi. Coward-McCann, Inc.,
1958.

An up-to-date book about the southern United States, describing its resources, industries, atomic energy research, and experiments in space flight. Intermediate and upper grades.

MEN AT WORK IN THE GREAT LAKE STATES
Written by Henry B. Lent.
Photographs. G. P. Putnam's Sons,
1958.

An interesting selection of facts about the major products and industries of one of America's most productive regions. Indexed for reference. Intermediate grades.

ALASKA
Written by Dorothy Les Tina.
Illustrated by Aliki. Holt,
Rinehart & Winston, Inc., 1962.

Stresses the geography, natural products, animal life, and native Indians and Eskimos of the forty-ninth state. Lower grades.

GOLD RUSH ADVENTURES
Written by Edith McCall.
Childrens Press, Inc., 1962.

Stories of the mad Gold Rush in California and of the people who stayed and found their fortunes in wheat, fruit, and the building of a new state. Intermediate grades.

GROWING UP IN PUERTO RICO
Written by Dorothy Loa McFadden.
Photographs. Silver Burdett
Company, 1958.

Through stories about today's children in Puerto Rico, the reader learns about everyday life, work problems, and progress in this part of the United States. Glossary of Spanish words. For intermediate grades.

ROOSEVELT'S AMERICA
Written by Robin McKown.

*Photographs. Grosset & Dunlap,
Inc., 1962.*

A re-creation of the life and times of FDR,
America's only four-term president. Intermediate and upper grades.

THE PONY EXPRESS
*Written by Carl Memling.
Illustrated by William Moyers.
Parent's Magazine, 1962.*

The story of the mailmen of 1860–61,
who plunged through 2,000 miles of
wilderness on horseback. Lower and intermediate grades.

DIARY OF DEMOCRACY: THE
STORY OF POLITICAL PARTIES IN
AMERICA
*Written by Harry Edward Neal.
Photographs. Julian Messner, Inc.,
1962.*

Traces the changes in the governing process of the United States as reflected in the
political parties. Upper grades.

THE WHITE HOUSE
*Written by Mary Kay Phelan.
Illustrated by Ed Emberley. Holt,
Rinehart & Winston, Inc., 1962.*

How the executive mansion was built and
has changed over the years as seen through
the eyes of the Presidents' young relatives.
Lower grades.

ALL ABOUT OUR FIFTY STATES
*Written by Margaret Ronan.
Illustrated by Frank Ronan and
William Meyerjecks. Random
House, Inc., 1962.*

Information about each state in the union.
Intermediate and upper grades.

ALOHA FROM BOBBY
*Written and illustrated by Arnold
Spilka. Henry Z. Walck, Inc.,
Publishers 1962.*

Bobby and his pet goose search the island
of Hawaii for a suitable subject of a painting to be presented to Uncle Herman as a
souvenir of his trip there. Bobby's travels

present the reader with a panoramic view
of life in Hawaii. For the lower grades.

JOHN F. KENNEDY AND PT 109
*Written by Richard Tregaskis.
Photographs. Random House, Inc.,
1962.*

An account of Lt. John F. Kennedy's
World War II experiences as skipper of a
motor torpedo boat. Intermediate and
upper grades.

COLONIAL CRAFTSMEN AND THE
BEGINNINGS OF AMERICAN INDUSTRY
*Written by Edwin Tunis. World
Publishing Co., 1965.*

A meticulously researched, fascinating
study of the crafts and craftsmen of
America from earliest pioneer days to the
mid-1800's. Provides an excellent insight
into how our ancestors designed and made
silver, furniture, and glassware. Intermediate and upper grades.

WE ELECT A PRESIDENT
*Written by David E. Weingast.
Photographs. Julian Messner, Inc.,
1962.*

The story of how the American people
elect a man to the Presidency. Upper
grades.

A NATION FIGHTS BACK: THE
DEPRESSION AND ITS AFTERMATH
*Written by Irving Werstein.
Photographs. Julian Messner, Inc.,
1962.*

The years between the 1929 stock market
crash and the New Deal. Upper grades.

HILLS AND HARBORS
*Written by Dorothy Wood.
Illustrated by Vernon McKissack.
Childrens Press, Inc., 1962.*

Presents the great cities, world seaports,
mountains, ocean beaches, rivers, lakes,
and valleys of the Middle Atlantic states.

NEW ENGLAND COUNTRY
Written by Dorothy Wood.
Illustrated by Tom Dunnington.
Childrens Press, Inc., 1962.

Life in the Northeastern states from the Norsemen, through the Indian and Pilgrims, to the present day. Intermediate grades.

GULF LAND AND CENTRAL SOUTH
Written by Frances E. Wood.
Illustrated by Katherine Grace.
Childrens Press, Inc., 1962.

The story of the region that combines the Deep South and the West, its settlers, and its empires of cattle, cotton, and oil. Intermediate grades.

ASPECTS OF LIVING

Farms and their produce

THE PICTURE BOOK OF GRAINS
Written by Anita Brooks. Illustrated with photographs. The John Day Company, Inc., 1965.

The world-wide story of wheat, rye, barley, rice, maize, and millet from seed through processing. For intermediate grades.

APPLE ORCHARD
Written by Irmengarde Eberle.
Illustrated by Ezra Jack Keats.
Henry Z. Walck, Inc., Publishers, 1962.

The story of one orchard: fertilizing, harvesting and marketing, and tree care. For intermediate readers.

OF CABBAGES AND CATTLE
Written by Dirk Gringhuis. The Dial Press, Inc., 1965.

Introduction to the many different kinds of farms in America today. For intermediate readers.

TEN BIG FARMS
Written by Dahlov Z. Ipcar.
Alfred A. Knopf, Inc., 1958.

A family visits ten specialized farms before deciding to buy a little farm that has "everything." Information about many aspects of farm life in simple text and striking illustrations. For lower to intermediate grades.

ABOUT TRUCK FARMING.
Written by Irma Bolan Johnson.
Illustrated by Nixon Galloway.
Melmont Publishers, Inc., 1962.

A picture of truck farming from the time the seed bed is prepared until the produce is marketed. For the intermediate grades.

THE LITTLE FARM
Written and illustrated by Lois Lenski.
Henry Z. Walck, Inc., Publishers, 1942.

Life on a farm is beautifully and clearly presented in both text and illustrations as Miss Lenski's story of Farmer Small unfolds.

LAKES, HILLS AND PRAIRIES
Written by Frances E. Wood.
Illustrated by Tom Dunnington.
Childrens Press, Inc., 1962.

The beauty of the Midwestern states and their life: farming, dairying, manufacturing, and transportation. For intermediate and upper grades.

The city and its life

A WORLD FULL OF HOMES
Written by William A. Burns.
Illustrated by Paula Hutchison.
McGraw-Hill Book Company, 1953.

An interesting history of homes in many parts of the world from earliest to modern times. Good material to use as a basis for understanding why people live in different ways. For intermediate grades.

SKYSCRAPER ISLAND: HOW SHIPS
BUILT NEW YORK
*Written by Sturges F. Cary.
Illustrated by Walter Galli.
Coward-McCann, Inc., 1957.*

The influence of ships and a harbor on the growth and economic life of New York City. For intermediate grades.

A WALK IN THE CITY
*Written and illustrated by Rosemary
and Richard Dawson. The Viking
Press, Inc., 1950.*

What a small boy sees, hears, and does when he goes walking with his mother is told in charming verse and gay pictures. This is the kind of book that can be used to promote an awareness of the sights and sounds of one's own neighborhood.

THIS IS A DEPARTMENT STORE
*Written by Nicholas P. and Louis
G. Georgiady. Follet Publishing
Company, 1965.*

Tells how a department store serves the community with its many wares. For intermediate grades.

LET'S FIND OUT ABOUT FIREMEN
*Written by Martha and Charles
Shapp. Illustrated by Peter
Costanza. Franklin Watts, Inc.,
1962.*

Firemen are the subject of a book that helps the youngest reader with reading and vocabulary building. For the lower grades.

LET'S FIND OUT ABOUT
POLICEMEN
*Written by Martha and Charles
Shapp. Illustrated by Peter
Costanza. Franklin Watt, Inc.,
1962.*

Introduces beginning readers to policemen and how they give protection and make our streets safe for our citizens. For the lower grades.

I KNOW A CITY: THE STORY OF
NEW YORK'S GROWTH
*Written by Katherine B. Shippen.
The Viking Press, Inc., 1954.*

The book shows how the facilities of a modern city—any city—grow out of the needs of the people. For intermediate grades.

SAD DAY, GLAD DAY
*Written by Vivian L. Thompson.
Illustrated by Lilian Obligado.
Holiday House, 1962.*

When her family moves from the city to the country, Kathy finds it very difficult to make the adjustment. Movingly written and sensitively illustrated, this is the story of how Kathy learns to live in the country and like it. Besides dealing with a problem that many children often have to face, this book offers an excellent opportunity for children to see the difference between life in the city and life in the country. For the lower grades.

LET'S GO TO A CITY HALL
*Written by Louis Wolfe.
Illustrated by Jerry Robinson. G. P.
Putnam's Sons, 1959.*

An introduction to the functions of city government with explanations of the work of a city council and the various departments. For intermediate grades.

THE SKYSCRAPER
*Written by Yen Liang. J. B.
Lippincott Co., 1958.*

Handsome, detailed pictures show the happenings, workers, and tools that change a crowded old city neighborhood into a proud new apartment area. For lower grades.

Transportation: old and new

ROADS
*Written by Fon W. Boardman, Jr.
Illustrated by Paul Sagoorian.*

Photographs. *Henry Z. Walck, Inc., Publishers, 1958.*

This distinguished book presents comprehensive information about roads of the past and present—their construction, use, and role in history. For intermediate grades.

THE STORY OF SHIPS
Written by Frank O. Braynard. Illustrated by Fouille. Grosset & Dunlap, Inc., 1962.

The history of vessels, primarily seagoing, from floating logs to atomic ships. For intermediate and upper grades.

BEHIND THE SCENES AT AN AIRPORT
Written by David C. Cooke. Photographs. Dodd, Mead & Co., 1958.

Aspects of airline business are presented through a brief factual text and excellent photographs. For intermediate grades.

TRAINS AT WORK
Written by Mary Elting. Illustrated by David Lyle Millard. Harvey House, Inc., Publishers, 1962.

The story of railroading, the tank cars, hoppers, gondolas, and diesels, and the men who run them. For intermediate grades.

TRUCKS AT WORK
Written by Mary Elting. Illustrated by Ursula Koering. Harvey House, Inc., Publishers, 1962.

The story of all trucks and a description of the languages and rules of truck drivers. For intermediate grades.

SHIPS AT WORK
Written by Mary Elting. Illustrated by Manning DeV. Lee. Harvey House, Inc., Publishers, 1962.

A description of the lives of seamen and their ships, along with the story of the development of ships from canoes to ocean liners. For intermediate grades.

BOATS ON THE RIVER
Written by Marjorie Flack. Illustrated by Jay Hyde Barnum. The Viking Press, Inc., 1947.

The pleasing rhythmical text and large full-page pictures are full of color and movement that give the reader a first-hand experience of watching life on the river from dawn to dusk. For the lower grades.

THE EARLY DAYS OF AUTOMOBILES
Written by Elizabeth Janeway. Illustrated by Hertha Depper. Photographs. Random House, Inc., 1956.

A lively, informative account of the history of the automobile in America. For intermediate grades.

THE ROMANCE OF AMERICAN TRANSPORTATION, REV. ED.
Written by Franklin M. Reck. Thomas Y. Crowell Company, 1962.

A rewritten and modernized edition of the classic history of American transportation from 1789 to the present day. For intermediate and upper grades.

THE FIRST BOOK OF THE CHINA CLIPPERS
Written by Louise Dickinson Rich. Illustrated by Henry S. Gillette. Franklin Watts, Inc., 1962.

The years of the China trade, the clippers, and the men who sailed them. For upper grades.

CARAVAN IN PERIL
Written by Karl Rolf Seufert. Pantheon Books, Inc., 1962.

The true story of the six men who were the first to plot trade routes into deep Africa and map the entire Sahara Desert. For upper grades.

LET'S FIND OUT ABOUT WHEELS
Written by Martha and Charles Shapp. Illustrated by Peter

*Costanza. Franklin Watts, Inc.,
1962.*

Wheels that move things and wheels that make work easier are described. For the lower grades.

ABC OF BUSES

*Written by Dorothy Shuttlesworth.
Illustrated by Leonard Shortall.
Doubleday & Company, Inc., 1965.*

Gay verses and big, bright, color pictures carry the story of buses through the alphabet.

ABOUT CARGO SHIPS

*Written by Melvin John Uhl.
Illustrated by Madalene Otteson.
Melmont Publishers, Inc., 1962.*

Tells about the various kinds of freighters and tankers, their likenesses and their differences. For intermediate grades.

WONDERS OF FLIGHT

*Written by Robert Wells. Dodd,
Mead & Co., 1962.*

How birds and men fly and the problems man encounters in keeping a heavier-than-air machine aloft. Includes mention of other kinds of flight and the latest wingless airplanes. For intermediate grades.

YOUR FREIGHT TRAINS

*Written and illustrated by George
Zaffo. Garden City Books, 1958.*

A colorful, comprehensive book that presents accurate and detailed pictures and text about freight trains and freight yard operations. For lower grades.

I LIKE TRAINS, REV. ED.

*Written by Catherine Woolley.
Pictures by George Fonseca. Harper
& Row, Publishers, 1965.*

A perennially popular book, now revised and newly illustrated to provide up-to-date facts about all kinds of trains. For lower grades.

Social graces

MANNERS MADE EASY

*Written by Mary Beery. McGraw-
Hill Book Company, 1967.*

For teen-agers, this is the book to read. It offers practical information on how to conduct oneself when out on a date, and it will help one over hurdles such as menus in foreign restaurants.

WHITE GLOVES AND PARTY MANNERS

*Written by Marjabelle Young and
Ann Buchwald. Robert B. Luce,
Inc., 1967.*

This book should prove helpful to girls just starting out in the social whirl. Directed at both young girls and their older sisters, it gives pointers on the proper way of using the telephone, keeping well groomed, and many of the other things a young girl beginning to grow up needs to know.

THE ART OF DATING

*Written by Evelyn Mills Duvall.
Association Press, 1967.*

The author, aware of the problems and questions teen-agers have about dating, gives answers with suggestions rather than rules. This approach should appeal to young people.

PARTY PLANS FOR TEENS

*Written by Kate Harris. Follett
Publishing Company, 1967.*

Today's social-minded teenager will never be bored with the suggestions offered in this book. Events are planned for every month of the year beginning with New Year's Eve and including one called "Lawn Dance in the Basement."

THE COMPLETE CHILD

*Compiled by Lois Wyse and Joan
Javits. Illustrated by Ouida. World
Publishing Co., 1967.*

The authors use comparisons to help both boys and girls acquire the social graces of manners, etiquette, and poise. The quaint pastel-colored illustrations add an extra touch.

HOW TO BE A SUCCESSFUL TEEN-AGER
Written by William C. Menninger and others. Sterling Publishing Co., Inc., 1967.

Compiled to help teen-agers understand themselves and get along with others, this collection of articles discusses sex, friendship, parents, and other problems faced by young people.

ETIQUETTE, JR
Written by Mary Elizabeth Clark and Margery Closey Quigley. Doubleday & Company, Inc., 1967.

Aimed at the ten-to-fourteen age group, the text offers advice on conduct, clothes, and conversation. A chapter on the first job is also included.

THE CALLING ALL GIRLS PARTY BOOK
Written by Rubie Saunders. Parents' Magazine, 1967.

Written to meet the needs of the eight-to-twelves, this book provides recipes for food, fun, and games that appeal to this age group.

A NEW YOU: THE ART OF GOOD GROOMING
Written by Emily Wilkens. G. P. Putnam's Sons, 1967.

What every girl should know in order to make the most of what she has is spelled out in terms of diet, grooming, dressing, make-up, and manners.

BIOGRAPHIES

Figures in the fine arts

STORY LIVES OF GREAT COMPOSERS
Written by Katherine Bakeless. Photographs. J. B. Lippincott Co., 1962.

A collection of interesting although somewhat cursory sketches of the lives of thirteen composers. Full-page photographs of each of the musicians add interest to the book, which also contains a list of recordings representing some of the work of each composer. Intermediate and upper grades.

PABLO CASALS: CELLIST FOR FREEDOM
Written by Aylesa Forsee. Photographs. Thomas Y. Crowell Company, 1965.

A portrait of a great composer, musician, conductor, teacher, and man. Casal's life is traced from his years as a brilliant child musician and protégé of Spain's Queen Regent. He survived years of war and revolution in his homeland and finally achieved a triumphant culmination to his career as an artist. A sensitive and moving story with beautifully descriptive pictures. For upper-grade children.

BOYHOODS OF GREAT COMPOSERS, BOOK II
Written by Catherine Gough. Illustrated by Edward Ardizzone. Henry Z. Walck, Inc., Publishers, 1965.

The childhoods of six composers—Handel, Mozart, Schubert, Mendelssohn, Grieg, and Elgar—are described in a lively and interesting manner. The author discusses the beginnings of their musical lives, emphasizing the humorous as well as important aspects of their development. Intermediate grades.

THE LION OF POLAND
Written by Ruth and Paul Hume. Illustrated by Lili Rethi. Hawthorne Books, Inc., 1963.

An exciting and inspiring story of a great pianist, Ignace Jan Paderewski. Paderewski showed early promise as a composer but was told that he would never become a pianist. He achieved his goals of becoming a great concert pianist and of helping his beloved Poland become a free nation after World War I, when he became its premier. Intermediate and upper grades.

AMERICAN COMPOSERS OF OUR TIME
Written by Joseph Machlis. Thomas Y. Crowell Company, 1963.

A substantial survey of the lives and work of sixteen notable contemporary composers, introduced by a summarizing essay on the development and current significance of American music. Each chapter deals with a composer biographically and musically and ends with a brief analysis of one of his representative works. Actual listening is stressed. Upper grades.

LUCREZIA BORI OF THE METROPOLITAN OPERA
Written by John Francis Marion. Photographs. P. J. Kenedy & Sons, 1963.

An interesting and vivid account of the life of a young girl and her rise in the music world to become a great opera singer. Intermediate and upper grades.

FAMOUS BALLET DANCERS
Written by Jane T. McConnell. Photographs. Thomas Y. Crowell Company, 1955.

Here are the stories behind fifteen of the most famous names in the history of ballet. The biographies are moving and informative, and the world of ballet is excitingly re-created. For upper grades.

MOZART
Written by Reba Paeff Mirsky. Illustrated by W. T. Mars. Follett Publishing Company, 1960.

Charming letters from Mozart to his family lend authenticity to this affectionate biography. The composer's short life was a brilliant one, and his contributions to music were enormous. The book traces the life of this child prodigy through the hardships and poverty he later suffered. The descriptions of his meetings with other musicians, especially young Beethoven,

add to the excitement of the book. For intermediate and upper grades.

HAYDN
Written by Reba Paeff Mirsky Illustrated by W. T. Mars. Follett Publishing Company, 1963.

A warm and revealing portrait of "Papa Haydn" from his early display of genius at the age of five to the height of his fame. His relations with the nobility and the affection with which he was viewed by the public make exciting reading for children in the intermediate and upper grades.

BEETHOVEN
Written by Reba Paeff Mirsky. Illustrated by W. T. Mars. Follett Publishing Company, 1965.

An understanding, compassionate, and informative book about one of the great musical geniuses of all time. The author, a music scholar and devotee of Beethoven, traces the composer's life and music from early childhood influences to the height of his fame following his deafness. The composer, whose genius made him a master, is seen as a human being with all of man's frailties. Intermediate and upper grades.

LEONARDO DA VINCI
Written by Elizabeth Ripley. Oxford University Press, Inc., 1952.

This book is almost an autobiography. It is filled with notes and sketches from da Vinci's numerous notebooks that convey this man's genius in a wide variety of areas. Upper grades.

VINCENT VAN GOGH
Written by Elizabeth Ripley. Oxford University Press, Inc., 1954.

A warm portrayal of Van Gogh's childhood and development into an artist. Text alternates with photographs of Van Gogh's works. This helps in understanding the man and the artist. Upper grades.

RAPHAEL
Written by Elizabeth Ripley. J. B. Lippincott Co., 1961.

An excellent biography of the man and artist, it portrays his relationships with Michelangelo, da Vinci, the Rennaissance Popes, and other great men of his period. Photographs of the artist's works make this a memorable book. For the upper grades.

TITIAN
Written by Elizabeth Ripley. J. B. Lippincott Co., 1962.

A fine portrayal of Titian's life and works. The adventures of this great master of Renaissance art are vividly presented and illuminated by many photographs of his work. For children in the upper grades.

WOLFGANG AMADEUS MOZART
Written by Victor Seroff. The Macmillan Company, Inc., 1965.

In this fascinating account of the tragic life of the composer, the author has focused on the factors that were of the greatest influence. Seroff's insights into society and into the lives of people who affected the composer make this book an exceptionally interesting one for older children.

THE GREAT ADVENTURE OF MICHELANGELO
Written by Irving Stone. Doubleday & Company, Inc., 1965.

In this abridged version of *The Agony and the Ecstasy*, Stone traces Michelangelo's life from his early artistic manifestations. Michelangelo battles with kings and Popes to do justice to the genius he knows he possesses. His love of marble, his great art, and his strong personality are faithfully and beautifully portrayed in the text and accompanying illustrations. For intermediate grades.

HEAR THE DISTANT APPLAUSE: SIX GREAT LADIES OF THE AMERICAN THEATRE
Written by Marguerite Vance. E. P. Dutton & Co., Inc., 1963.

Biographies of famous actresses such as Charlotte Saunders Cushman, Minnie Maddern Fiske, and Maude Adams. The stories are warmly human, showing the hopes, tribulations, hard work, and successes of each woman as she tried to become an actress. The book also contains a great deal of information concerning important people in the theatre and the plays they produced. Upper grades.

FAMOUS AMERICAN ACTORS AND ACTRESSES
Written by Frederick Wagner and Barbara Brady. Illustrated by Gerald McCann. Dodd, Mead & Co., 1961.

The authors have created a panorama of the history of the American theater through the biographies of some of its most notable personalities such as the Drews, the Barrymores, and George M. Cohan. The accurate and realistic portraits make enjoyable reading for children in the upper grades.

Historical figures

ALLAN PINKERTON: YOUNG DETECTIVE
Written by Kathryn Borland and Helen Speicher. Bobbs-Merrill Company, Inc., 1965.

Born in Scotland in 1819, young Allan grew up to become one of the most famous detectives in the United States. Here is an exciting account of the boy's developing interest in the work of a detective and how he managed to become one. Upper grades.

MARTIN LUTHER KING: THE PEACEFUL WARRIOR
Written by Ed Clayton. Illustrated by David Hodges. Prentice-Hall, Inc., 1964.

Martin Luther King, who learned about prejudice the hard way when he was a boy, had become one of the leading fighters for Negro rights in America. His approach was a peaceful but forceful one. This clearly and objectively written book tells about this dedicated man's efforts to bring about peaceful racial integration in the United States. For children in the intermediate grades.

CRUSADERS FOR FREEDOM
Written by Henry Steele Commager.
Illustrated by Mimi Korach.
Doubleday & Company, Inc., 1962.

The rights and freedoms of mankind have often been won only through the vigorous and courageous efforts of determined men and women. This book tells their stories in a dramatic way. The author has grouped the biographies by categories. For upper-grade children.

P. T. BARNUM: ENTERTAINING
THE WORLD
Written by Fred J. Cook.
Britannica Press, 1962.

P. T. Barnum was one of the earliest and best-known American showmen. He knew what kept the public entertained, and he provided it for them. Here is the story of the magical master of the circus and the founding of the world-famous Barnum and Bailey Circus. For intermediate and upper grades.

CLARENCE DARROW: DEFENDER OF
THE PEOPLE
Written by Doris Faber. Illustrated by
Paul Frame. Prentice-Hall, Inc.,
1965.

A well-written book about Clarence Darrow. The focus is placed upon his years as a lawyer and upon some of his more famous and controversial cases. An enjoyable, short biography for pre-adolescents.

FATHERS OF INDUSTRIES
Written by Leonard M. Fanning.
Illustrated by Albert Orbaan. J. B.
Lippincott Co., 1962.

Concentrating on modern industry as the backbone of the economy of all the developed countries in the world, this book contains twenty-four brief biographies of the inventive geniuses whose discoveries led to this development. The stories are

well told with emphasis on inventions and their effects on industries. Upper grades.

CLARENCE DARROW
Written by Miriam Gurko. Thomas
Y. Crowell Company, 1965.

Clarence Darrow's turbulent career as a defender of the rights of man is sympathetically related in this biography. Concentrating on his more famous cases, including his defense of Debs, Haywood, Leopold and Loeb, and Scopes, the author emphasizes the principles behind each and explains the background of the issues. A well-presented life story. Upper grades.

AMERICA'S ETHAN ALLEN
Written by Stewart Holbrook.
Illustrated by Lynd Ward. Houghton
Mifflin Company, 1949.

Presented as an idealized figure who fought for God and country, this neatly turned biography possesses the charm and appeal suitable for the intermediate-grade child. Filled with events, people, and handsome illustrations, this book captures the drama of the times and its key characters.

RALPH J. BUNCHE: FIGHTER FOR
PEACE
Written by Joseph A. Kugelmass.
Julian Messner, Inc., 1952.

From a background filled with poverty and discrimination, the young Negro, Ralph Bunche, struggled for an education, and with determination managed to become a distinguished anthropologist, an expert on colonization, and a Nobel Peace Prize winner. This biography covers the period from childhood on. The author shows a strong enthusiasm for his subject. Upper grades.

CHAMPION OF WORLD PEACE
Written by I. E. Levine. Julian
Messner, Inc., 1962.

Dag Hammerskjold's life is traced from his boyhood in Sweden to the years he spent as Secretary General of the United Nations—the office he held until his death in 1961. The book focuses on the work of

Hammerskjold as he carved out the role of the United Nations for the world.

THE FIGHTING DOUGLAS
MACARTHUR
Written by Clarke Newlon.
Photographs. Dodd, Mead & Co.,
1965.

A stirring and inspiring biography of America's most decorated soldier. This narrative, illustrated with photographs and maps, is a good book for teen-agers.

JOHN H. GLENN: ASTRONAUT
Written by Lt. Col. Philip Pierce,
USMC, and Karl Schuon. Franklin
Watts Inc., 1962.

John Glenn, the first American to orbit the earth, has had a glorious and exciting military career. Here is his story, told with conviction by men who know him. Upper grades.

ADMIRAL RICHARD E. BYRD:
CONQUERING ANTARCTICA
Written by Paul Rink. Britannica
Press, 1962.

This exciting story of Rear Admiral of the U.S. Navy, Richard Byrd, who led the U.S. explorations of the Antarctic polar regions, relates his adventures on those expeditions. Intermediate and upper grades.

FRANKLIN DELANO ROOSEVELT
Written by Henry Thomas. G. P.
Putnam's Sons, 1962.

Here is the story of one of America's most dynamic Presidents. His childhood at Hyde Park, his marriage to his cousin Eleanor, his politics, and his sudden attack of polio are all recounted to help the reader understand this great personality who rose to fame and power despite his great physical handicap. Suitable for intermediate-grade children.

JOHN MARSHALL
Written by Caroline Tucker.
Farrar, Straus & Geroux, Inc.,
1962.

John Marshall was one of the greatest and most influential Chief Justices that the United States Supreme Court has ever had. He is responsible for many of today's legal precedents. This is the absorbing story of his life and some of the momentous events in it. For upper-grade children.

SCOTLAND'S QUEEN
Written by Marguerite Vance. E. P.
Dutton & Co., Inc., 1962.

Mary Stuart lived in a time of religious conflict. This, together with her personal intrigues, caused her to live a short and unhappy life. She is portrayed as wise and impulsive, charming and conniving. The many unfortunate events in her life brought her general unpopularity and a nineteen-year imprisonment that ended with her execution. Suitable for mature readers.

Literary figures

LEWIS CARROLL
Written by Roger Lancelyn Green.
Henry Z. Walck, Inc., Publishers,
1963.

Here is a fascinating biography of the beloved English author of *Alice in Wonderland.* The story of the college professor and his journey into children's literature is beautifully told by a writer who knows and admires Carroll's work. Intermediate grades.

EMILY DICKINSON: HER LETTER TO
THE WORLD
Written by Polly Longsworth.
Thomas Y. Crowell Company,
1965.

A sensitive and accurate account of the life of a shy and gentle poetess. Emily Dickinson's life is traced from her lively childhood to her increasingly quiet adult years. This book is enhanced by selections of Emily Dickinson's poetry. Suitable for older children.

MARK TWAIN: WRITING ABOUT
THE FRONTIER
*Written by Jean Rikhoff. Britannica
Press, 1963.*

Here is a thrilling account of the life of
Mark Twain, who led, not one life, but
many. The author covers aspects of
Twain's several exciting lives and their
influence on his writing. Upper-grade
children.

ERNEST HEMINGWAY: REMAKING
MODERN FICTION
*Written by Paul Rink. Britannica
Press, 1963.*

Ernest Hemingway is portrayed as one of
the most influential writers of the twentieth
century, and Mr. Rink vividly describes
the adventures of this man whose style
of writing ushered in a new school of
modern fiction. Suitable for mature
readers.

FAMOUS AMERICAN NEGRO POETS
*Written by Charlemae Rollins.
Photographs. Dodd, Mead & Co.,
1965.*

In this introduction to twelve Negro
poets whose works have a special appeal to
children and adolescents, the author
describes their lives and works. She
appraises their writings against the background of their lives and aspirations and
includes selections from their poetry.

THE YOUNG SHELLEY
*Written by Philip Rush. Illustrated
by Anne Linton. Roy Publishers,
Inc., 1963.*

Here is a sensitive and captivating portrait
of England's famous lyric poet, Shelley,
whose actions as a youth earned him the
name "mad Shelley." Appropriate for
the upper grades.

Scientists

A WEED IS A FLOWER: THE LIFE
OF GEORGE WASHINGTON CARVER
*Written by Aliki. Prentice-Hall,
Inc., 1965.*

This enthusiastic and affectionate story of
George Washington Carver tells about his
childhood, his desire to go to school, and
his position as a teacher at Tuskegee
Institute. It describes how he taught the
farmers in the area about crop rotation,
and, since there was no market for sweet
potatoes or peanuts, how he discovered
hundreds of uses for them. For younger
children.

THE FRONTIER DOCTORS
*Written by Wyatt Blassingame and
Richard Glendinning. Franklin
Watts, Inc., 1963.*

Inspiring and exciting biographical
sketches of the unheralded men who
brought the art and science of medicine to
the frontier. They had nothing to rely on
but their own observations, experience,
and intelligence. An exciting and often
overlooked segment of American history.
Good reading for children in the upper
grades.

ELIAS HOWE
*Written by Jean Corcoran.
Bobbs-Merrill Company, Inc., 1965.*

The absorbing story of Elias Howe, whose
lameness and lack of education did not
prevent him from becoming the inventor
of the sewing machine, which helped to
further the industrial revolution. For
younger children.

THE DISCOVERER OF OXYGEN
*Written by William D. Crane.
Julian Messner, Inc., 1963.*

Here is an interestingly written account of
Joseph Priestley's contributions to science.
His early scientific experiments in the
field of electricity and his later work
leading to the discovery of oxygen are
accurately portrayed. For upper graders.

THE GREAT ARCHAEOLOGISTS
*Written by Charles Michael
Daugherty. Illustrated by Leonard
E. Fisher. Thomas Y. Crowell
Company, 1962.*

The author gives capsule biographies of more than twenty men who helped make archaeology a science rather than merely the collecting of relics. Humorous anecdotes and interesting detail make this an enjoyable excursion into both history and science for children in the upper grades.

GREAT MEN OF SCIENCE
Written by Arnold Dolin.
Illustrated by Rafaello Busoni.
Hart Publishing Co., Inc., 1960.

Here is an exciting series of biographies of some of the men who made discoveries that greatly affected the course of the world. Among those discussed are Alexander Graham Bell and the telephone, and the development of atomic energy. For the intermediate grades.

GREAT MEN OF MEDICINE
Written by Ruth Fox Hume.
Illustrated by Robert Frankenberg.
Random House, Inc., 1961.

Ruth Hume describes the foundations of modern medical science through the stirring and informative biographies of ten of the great men of medicine. She concentrates on their medical careers and achievements. For children in the intermediate grades.

JUNGLE DOCTORS
Written by Mike McGrady.
Photographs. J.B. Lippincott Co., 1962.

This absorbing book contains short and vivid biographies of heroic men and women who dedicated their lives to helping unfortunate people in other lands. Illustrated with moving photographs, this book is suitable for intermediate and upper graders.

NIELS BOHR: THE MAN WHO MAPPED THE ATOM
Written by Robert E. Silverberg.
Macrae Smith Company, 1965.

A biography of the giant figure of modern physics who won both a Nobel Prize and the first Atoms for Peace Award. An exciting book, which is both interesting and informative. For intermediate and upper grades.

POLIO PIONEERS
Written by Dorothy Sterling.
Doubleday & Company, Inc., 1955.

In this book, replete with photographs, the author has given a vivid and exciting picture of the doctors, scientists, and technicians who contributed in the fight against polio. For the intermediate grades.

Sports figures

FAMOUS NEGRO ATHLETES
Written by Arna Bontemps. Dodd, Mead & Co., 1964.

This collection of biographical sketches is about each athlete's struggle to succeed. The book includes sketches of Joe Louis, Sugar Ray Robinson, Jackie Robinson, Leroy Paige, Willie Mays, Jessie Owens, Wilton Chamberlain, James Brown, and Althea Gibson. Each athlete struggled not only to be an outstanding sportsman, but also to overcome the race barrier. Appropriately written for the upper grades.

WILLIE MAYS: COAST TO COAST GIANT
Written by Charles Einstein. G. P. Putnam's Sons, 1963.

This biography of the New York Giants' "Number 24" is a recent account of a star baseball player. His batting and catching techniques are given due attention as are his personal contacts and relationships with other teammates and teams. Written in lively style, the book concludes with his records in chart form followed by an index. Suitable for intermediate and upper grades.

LOU GEHRIG: A QUIET HERO
Written by Frank Graham. G. P. Putnam's Sons, 1942.

This is an illustrated biography of a great baseball player. Because Lou Gehrig was an unusual person, the book emphasizes not only his baseball career, but also his courageous personal life. A child need not be sports-minded to read and enjoy this touching book. Intermediate and upper grades.

THE JOHNNY UNITAS STORY
Written by Lee Greene. G. P.
Putnam's Sons, 1962.

A fascinating account of the life and career of a professional football player. Mr. Greene has re-created all the excitement of the game. The reading level here is suitable for the intermediate grades.

THE AL KALINE STORY
Written by Al Hirschberg. Julian
Messner, Inc., 1964.

One of the youngest professional baseball players, Al Kaline of the Detroit Tigers is highly respected for his throwing ability, running speed, and batting average. His father encouraged him to play ball at an early age; the day after high school graduation, he signed a contract with the Detroit Tigers. After playing on that team for eleven years he comments, "I don't think I've ever achieved my potential." The book concludes with a chart of his records and an index. Suitable for intermediate-grade children.

BASEBALL'S GREATEST PLAYERS
Written by Tom Meany. Grosset
and Dunlap, Inc., 1953.

This fascinating book relates the personal lives and outstanding achievements of twenty-five of the greatest baseball players of the century. Writing in provocative style, with humorous analogy, Mr. Meany captures the disappointments and hardships as well as the glory. The book is illustrated photographically and has charts. It can be as easily enjoyed by an adult as it can by a child.

BABE DIDRIKSON ZAHARIAS:
STRIVING TO BE CHAMPION
Written by Helen Markley Miller.
Britannica Press, 1963.

An inspiring and compassionate account of the life of a champion woman golfer and her battle with cancer. Upper grades.

BREAKTHROUGH TO THE BIG
LEAGUE: THE STORY OF JACKIE
ROBINSON
Written by Jackie Robinson and
Alfred Ducket. Harper & Row,
Publishers, 1965.

This autobiography of Jackie Robinson is enlightening. Beginning with his poverty-stricken childhood, he tells of early racial problems and the success in sports that enabled him to go to college. To his own amazement, he soon finds himself to be the first Negro player in major league baseball. The very direct sharing of personal experiences make this book excellent for the upper grades.

BOB FELLER: HALL OF FAME
STRIKEOUT STAR
Written by Gene Schoor. Doubleday
& Company, Inc., 1962.

This book relates the story of Bob Feller, the St. Louis Cardinals' star pitcher. Bob's natural throwing arm plus a study of opposing batters' habits leads to his Hall of Fame status. It is enthusiastically written for the junior high school level.

THE STAN MUSIAL STORY
Written by Gene Schoor. Julian
Messner, Inc., 1963.

Appropriate for the middle grades, this photographically illustrated biography traces Stan Musial's athletic career from high school through many happy years with the St. Louis Cardinals. Superb batting and an unusual pitching arm help this Pennsylvania boy to fame and success. The book concludes with an index.

MICKEY MANTLE OF THE YANKEES
Written by Gene Schoor. G. P.
Putnam's Sons, 1958.

This unillustrated biography traces Mickey Mantle's life from infancy through the highlights of his baseball career. It stresses the influence his parents had on his early interest in baseball as well as his phenomenal batting performance as a professional player. His shyness and modesty, which are well illustrated in this book, keep him from being too sure of himself and add to the human aspect of the story. Aimed at more mature readers.

JACKIE ROBINSON: BASEBALL HERO
Written by Gene Schoor. G. P. Putnam's Sons, 1958.

This book deals not only with the fantastic story of Jackie Robinson's fielding and batting for the Brooklyn Dodgers, but also with the dramatic events of his being the first Negro player in organized major league baseball. The book illustrates how people such as his older brother, his mother, Branch Rickey, Joe Louis, and his wife Rachel influenced his career and life, although Jackie attributes the major events to God's help. The abnormal hardships Jackie had getting into baseball and staying there make this story a unique and touching one for readers of the middle grades and up.

Famous women

GREAT AMERICAN HEROINES
Written by Arnold Dolin. Illustrated by Rafaello Busoni. Hart Publishing Co., Inc., 1963.

These true stories about the women who have played an important part in the making of American history are both interesting and inspiring. Their courage and intelligence, which are shown through their adventures, make them women to be admired. For children in the intermediate and upper grades.

LILLIAN WALD: ANGEL OF HENRY STREET
Written by Beryl W. Epstein. Julian Messner, Inc., 1948.

Lillian Wald's career as a nurse, social worker, and founder of the Henry Street Settlement House is interestingly described. For the upper grades.

WOMEN WHO MADE AMERICA GREAT
Written by Harry Gersh. Illustrated by Mel Silverman. J. B. Lippincott Co., 1963.

The life stories of ten rebellious, adventurous women whose careers and interests carried them into fields then closed to women are accurately portrayed. They make exciting and inspiring reading for intermediate and upper graders.

RELUCTANT FIRST LADY
Written by Lorena S. Hickok. Dodd, Mead & Co., 1963.

In this revealing portrait of Eleanor Roosevelt, the author has focused on Mrs. Roosevelt's transition from a private citizen to First Lady of the land. The account demonstrates the sacrifices demanded of the wife of the President of the United States. Upper grades.

BRIDE OF GLORY
Written by Margaret Leighton. Farrar, Straus, & Giroux, 1962.

The adventurous life of Libbie Bacon Custer, wife of the colorful, dashing, fearless General. For upper graders.

ASTRONAUT'S NURSE: THE STORY OF DEE O'HARA
Written by Virginia McDonnell. Thomas Nelson & Sons, 1965.

The story of Dee O'Hara, the Air Force Nurse who was responsible for the health of the original astronauts at Cape Kennedy. Her engrossing story continues at the Manned Spacecraft Center in Houston where the new astronauts are training. For upper graders.

TONGUE OF FLAME: THE LIFE OF LYDIA MARIA CHILD
Written by Milton Meltzer. Thomas Y. Crowell Company, 1965.

In this absorbing biography we follow the exciting life of a staunch abolitionist, author, and founder of the first American magazine for children. Upper grades.

FIRST WOMAN AMBULANCE
SURGEON
*Written by Iris Noble. Julian
Messner, Inc., 1963.*

In this biography of Emily Barringer, the author vividly describes the conditions existing in the field of medicine at the turn of the century. The story concentrates on Emily's experiences, which led to her becoming the first woman allowed to intern in a hospital. For children in the upper grades.

AMELIA EARHART: PIONEER IN THE
SKY
*Written by John Parlin. Garrard
Press, 1963.*

This biography is a dramatic account of the life of a fearless woman who was one of our country's first woman pilots. Amelia Earhart's adventures are faithfully described. For intermediate grades.

AFRICAN TRAVELER
*Written by Ronald Syme. Illustrated
by Jacqueline Tomes. William
Morrow & Co., Inc., 1963.*

This lively biography is concerned with the adventures of Mary Kingsley. A Victorian woman, she became, in the 1890's, the first person to explore much of West Africa. For children in the intermediate and upper grades.

FINE ARTS

DANCERS OF THE BALLET
*Written by Margaret F. Atkinson
and May Hillman. Alfred A.
Knopf, Inc., 1955.*

This book contains brief biographies of a cross section of leading ballerinas and *premiers danseurs* of the United States, England, and France. The text is poetic and gives details of each dancer's life in vivid terms. It shows the hard work necessary to learn to dance, but it also reveals the satisfaction derived from such a life. There are lovely photographs showing the dancers in major roles. Intermediate grades.

LOOKING AT ART
*Written by Alice Elizabeth Chase.
Reproductions in color and black-and-
white. Thomas Y. Crowell Company,
1966.*

An unusually attractive book consisting of brief text and about one hundred illustrations in full color and black-and-white.

ALL ABOUT THE SYMPHONY
ORCHESTRA AND WHAT IT PLAYS
*Written by Dorothy Berliner
Commins. Drawings by Warren
Chappell. Random House, Inc.,
1961.*

This book contains a comprehensive explanation of the various parts of an orchestra on a fairly abstract level. It is illustrated with diagrams and excellent photographs and includes detailed explanations of the instruments, the conductor, his history, and how he uses his baton. There are also brief biographies of some of the great composers. Intermediate and upper grades.

PITIDOE THE COLOR MAKER
*Written and illustrated by Glen Dine.
The Macmillan Company, 1959.*

This charming, fanciful, and colorfully illustrated story is about what happens in the land of Soo when the young apprentice to the color-making wizards is left in charge of the color dust. It aids in enhancing the young child's awareness of all the colors of the rainbow.

DISCOVERING DESIGN
*Written by Marion Downer.
Photographs. Lothrop, Lee &
Shepard Co., Inc., 1947.*

An excellent book that describes in simple but imaginative and poetic language the principles underlying art—line, rhythm, balance, and so forth. With beautiful photographs and drawings of things from everyday life, the author shows the relationship between scenes in nature and painting itself. The book, a work of art itself, is a fine way to introduce art to children. Intermediate and upper grades.

THE AMERICAN MOVIE
Written by William K. Everson.
Photographs. Atheneum Publishers,
1963.

This beautifully designed book traces the development of the American moving picture. Without becoming unduly technical, it explains how the devices of an early director like D. W. Griffith developed a "grammar" and changed a mere mechanical novelty into an art form. The excellently chosen stills and the text effectively evaluate film acting and actors and illustrate the changes in American cinematic taste during the last sixty years. More mature readers.

PET OF THE MET
Written and illustrated by Lydia
and Don Freeman. The Viking Press,
Inc., 1953.

The story of Mozart's "Magic Flute" is re-enacted by a family of music-loving white mice who live in the attic of the old Metropolitan Opera House and a music-hating cat, appropriately named Mephisto, who lives in the Met's basement. The adventure and excitement of the story are reflected in the superb full-color illustrations. This book might very well serve in the primary grades as an introduction to opera and the playing of excerpts from the "Magic Flute."

ART AND ARCHAEOLOGY
Written by Shirley Glubok.
Designed by Gerard Nook.
Harper & Row, Publishers, 1966.

Blending archaeological facts with information about art, this outstanding book reveals the work of archaeologists who find and restore art treasures in an attempt to preserve the masterpieces of all times. All ages.

THE ROYAL BOOK OF BALLET
Written by Shirley Goulden.
Illustrated by Maraja. Follett
Publishing Company, 1965.

The beautiful stories of six famous ballets—*Swan Lake*, *The Sleeping Beauty*, *Giselle*, *The Nutcracker Suite*, *Petrushka*, and *Coppelia* are recounted here and illustrated with detailed and charming pictures that capture the grace of the dance. All ages.

STORY OF PAINTING FOR YOUNG
PEOPLE: FROM CAVE PAINTINGS
TO MODERN TIMES
Written by Horst W. and Dora Jane
Janson. Illustrated with reproductions.
Harry N. Abrams, Inc., 1962.

This is a large, comprehensive book, clearly written, with advanced concepts for the intermediate-grade reader. It gives the story of how painting began and how it developed through the ages. The authors show how art is related to man's history and to cultures of particular times and peoples. They also describe the various artistic techniques used in each period. The reproductions are fairly good.

STAGESTRUCK: YOUR CAREER IN
THEATRE
Written by Burt Hirschfeld. Julian
Messner, Inc., 1963.

Theater, warns the author, is "a game in which most of the players are losers." Too many dreams of names in lights and resounding applause are shattered because they never go beyond the flimsy fabric of dreams. This book presents a pragmatic view of a tough career field, putting the stage in historical and cultural context. It points to acting as just one phase of the stage, and gives full treatment to the more anonymous off-stage opportunities—designing, directing, stage managing, composing. Upper grades.

DRAWINGS TO LIVE WITH
Written by Bryan Holme. Illustrated
with reproductions. The Viking Press,
Inc., 1966.

A wonderful introduction to drawing and its varied aspects as well as the artists who utilized this medium in producing their masterpieces. Over 140 reproductions illuminate the concise text of a highly informative book on art. All ages.

THE TWELVE DAYS OF CHRISTMAS
Illustrated by Ilonka Karasz.
Harper & Row, Publishers, 1949.

Miss Karasz has illustrated this well-known Christmas carol with colorful and delicately drawn pictures that have a tapestry-like quality to them. Each verse has its own illustrations. Children can also have fun searching the pictures to count the different characters. All ages.

THE WORM, THE BIRD, AND YOU:
A LONG AND SHORT LOOK AT THE
WORLD ABOUT YOU
*Written and illustrated by Leonard
Kessler. Dodd, Mead & Co., 1962.*

Mr. Kessler has written and illustrated a captivating picture book that points up the essentials of perspective in simple and clearly understandable terms. Younger children.

AIR IS EVERYWHERE
*Written and illustrated by Leonard
Kessler. Dodd, Mead & Co., 1959.*

This is a captivating book about the universality of art. It encourages children to savor the things around them and then paint and draw them as they see and feel them. The author offers many practical suggestions and helps children to discover the fun of mixing paints and the variety of techniques available. He has a good understanding of children's vocabulary and integrates his illustrations with his text well. Intermediate grades.

FLUTES, WHISTLES, AND REEDS
*Written and illustrated by Larry
Kettlekamp. William Morrow &
Co., Inc., 1962.*

The author clearly explains how each type of wind instrument is made, how it makes its sounds, and what its history is. He relates his explanation to objects in the child's experiences and gives helpful diagrams. For energetic youngsters, he has provided ways of making their own instruments out of readily available materials. Primary and intermediate grades.

OL' DAN TUCKER
*Retold by John Langstaff. Illustrated
by Joe Krush. Harcourt, Brace &
World, Inc., 1963.*

Ol' Dan Tucker, a legendary character who grew out of American pioneer life, is immortalized in a book full of the humor and boisterous exaggerations that are a vital part of an American tradition. From the many existing versions of this 120-year-old banjo dance tune, Mr. Langstaff has chosen the verses he likes best and, with the interpretive assistance of Mr. Krush, has made this into a picture book as gay and lively as the song itself. All ages.

WHEN I GROW UP
*Written and illustrated by Lois Lenski.
Music by Clyde Robert Bulla.
Henry Z. Walck, Inc., Publishers,
1960.*

Charmingly written and illustrated, this book contains songs for both boys and girls to read and sing. There are a number of occupations suggested for children when they grow up: sailor, cowboy, farmer, teacher, mother. The text is simple and short in catchy poetic form. There are musical scores provided for each set of words. Younger children.

THE LOVE FOR THREE ORANGES
*Retold by John Moreton. Illustrated
by Murray Tinkelman. G. P.
Putnam's Sons, 1966.*

Prokofiev's complex and humorous opera is given an abrupt handling in this re-working of the story for children. The drawings that supplement the text are attractive representations of the dramatic aspect of the opera, but one wonders if one picture is worth a thousand words. Older children.

THE FIRST BOOK OF MUSIC
Written by Gertrude Norman.
Illustrated by Richard Gettenbach.
Franklin Watts, Inc., 1954.

The principles of rhythm, melody, and harmony are presented in this book in a simple manner. A history of instruments and types of music is also included. The illustrations are fair. An appendix gives brief biographical sketches of famous musicians and composers and a list of music appreciation records for children in elementary school.

THE STORY OF LOHENGRIN: THE KNIGHT OF THE SWAN
Retold by Doris Orgel. Illustrated by Herbert Danska. G. P. Putnam's Sons, 1965.

A smooth, concise narrative and stylized angular drawings evoke the strange appeal of this medieval story. It is pleasing to the eye and will provide exciting reading for the child who has a lively sense of pageantry.

SHAPES
Written by Miriam Schlein.
Illustrated by Sam Burman.
William R. Scott, Inc., 1952.

With a deceptively delicate touch, the author helps children from the ages of four to seven to start noticing what different shapes are like. This is an excellent book that will begin to train children in recognition of shapes and make them aware of form and design. Younger children.

IT LOOKED LIKE SPILT MILK
Written and illustrated by Charles G. Shaw. Harper & Row, Publishers, 1947.

What is it that looks like spilt milk and many other things but is not? The reader is taken from one shape to another until he finds that it is a white cloud in the sky that looks like all these things. The use of white forms against a dark blue background provides a vivid introduction to shape and form for the young child.

SELECTED STORIES FROM THE BALLET
Written by Ursula Roseveau. Pitman Publishing Corp., 1954.

This book contains stories from sixteen ballets, published "by popular demand" of children and adults who heard them over the BBC. A description of the action of each ballet is given and illustrated by photographs. This book is an excellent supplement to actually viewing the ballets and to other books that deal more with the dance aspect of ballet. All ages.

THE MEANING OF MUSIC
Written by Jean Seligmann and Juliet Danziger. Illustrated. World Publishing Co., 1966.

In lively conversational prose, the authors unfold the exciting story of music, the men who moved it, and the elements of the art. Stories and technical explanations are presented with an infectious respect and love for this powerful art form. It is a difficult job beautifully executed. All ages.

THE STORY OF PRINTING
Written by Irving B. Simon.
Drawings and photographs by Charles E. Pont. Harvey House, Inc., Publishers, 1965.

This book gives a fascinating view of the development of printing from Gutenberg's workshop to today's billion-dollar printing industry. The author also includes information on careers in printing, the effects of automation, and the future of graphic arts. There is both technical detail and human interest information about the inventors' lives. The illustrations help one to understand the text. Intermediate grades.

THE MAGIC FLUTE
Retold by Stephen Spender.
Illustrated by Beni Montresor. G. P. Putnam's Sons, 1966.

The difficult job of translating this complex operatic plot into an enjoyable story for children of all ages is admirably attempted but dryly executed by Mr. Spender. Mr.

Montresor's illustrations carry the splendor of his actual sets for the City Center's production of Mozart's opera onto the pages of the book.

KIMO MAKES MUSIC
Written by Vivian L. Thompson.
Illustrated by Frances Walter.
Golden Gate Junior Books, 1962.

This is the story of a young Hawaiian boy whose love of music leads him to musical discoveries both with familiar musical instruments as well as objects of nature (sea shell, bamboo, and so forth). Like its young hero, the story is full of music and rhythm both in its poetic text and lovely two-color illustrations. Elementary school.

HOBBIES AND GAMES

DOLLS TO MAKE FOR FUN AND PROFIT
Written by Edith Ackley.
Illustrated by Telka Ackley. J. B.
Lippincott, Co., 1951.

Good directions for making and dressing cloth dolls, baby dolls, boy and girl dolls, and novelty dolls. Patterns are full size for tracing or copying. For intermediate grades.

HEADS UP—HEELS DOWN
Written and illustrated by Clarence
W. Anderson. The Macmillan
Company, 1954.

A handbook of horsemanship and riding that tells about the selection, care, and handling of horses. Excellent sketches by the author-artist. Intermediate grades.

EXPERIMENTS WITH A MICROSCOPE
Written by Nelson F. Beeler.
Illustrated by Anne Marie Jauss.
Thomas Y. Crowell Company, 1957.

Making discoveries through the use of the microscope in examining common and uncommon things. Introduction to real science that will appeal to intermediate-grade children. Unusual information.

HOT ROD ANGELS
Written by Robert S. Bowen.
Chilton Books, 1960.

This is the fast-moving story of high school seniors who want to turn a deserted airstrip into a hot-rod field and how they go about achieving their goal. It is an easy-to-read book for slower readers. Upper grades.

HOW TO MAKE A HOME NATURE MUSEUM
Written by Vinson Brown. Illustrated
by Don G. Kelley. Little, Brown &
Co., 1954.

An information book for older boys and girls who like to collect and keep. Collecting, classifying, mounting, labelling specimens, making models, diagrams, and charts are a few of the activities discussed. In addition, there are many suggestions for individual projects that club leaders, campers, and teachers will find helpful.

TRACK TECHNIQUES ILLUSTRATED
Written by Don Canham. Illustrated
by Tyler Micoleau. The Ronald
Press Company, 1952.

This illustrated handbook of track techniques begins with a discussion of equipment, short-distance running, the importance of training, and long-distance running. Hurdling and relay running are also included. This clear, concisely written book is concluded with a glossary.

PETS: A COMPLETE HANDBOOK ON THE CARE, UNDERSTANDING AND APPRECIATION OF ALL KINDS OF ANIMAL PETS
Written by Frances W. Chrystie.
Illustrated by Gillet G. Griffen.
Little, Brown & Co., 1953.

An unusually fine book describing the attention appropriate to certain pets ranging from the usual to the rare. Sensitively beautiful text is supported by loving sketches of pets. Includes a chapter on first aid and common diseases. All ages.

SCIENCE IN YOUR OWN BACK
YARD
*Written by Elizabeth K. Cooper.
Harcourt, Brace & World, Inc.,
1958.*

A basic introduction to various fields of
nature study with special emphasis on
things that can be observed in the area
around the average home. A number of
easy experiments are included. All ages.

101 HAND PUPPETS
*Written and illustrated by Richard
Cummings. David McKay Co.,
Inc., 1966.*

An unusual book of detailed instructions
for designing hand puppets. Also included
are scripts for three plays and some simple
designs for stages and props. Intermediate
and upper grades.

KITES: HOW TO MAKE THEM AND
FLY THEM
*Written and illustrated by Marion
Downer. Lothrop, Lee & Shepard
Co., Inc., 1959.*

This handbook of kites gives very clear
directions and simple illustrative sketches
on how to make various kinds of kites.
Tools, materials, and methods of construction are discussed first, followed by
an overview of kite contests. The latter
part of the book is illustrated with stimulating photographs of kite-flying events.
Primary and middle grades.

THE FIRST BOOK OF SECRET CODES
AND CIPHERS
*Written by Sam and Beryl Epstein.
Illustrated by Laslo Roth. Franklin
Watts, Inc., 1956.*

Deals with invisible inks, secret codes,
ciphers, and contains a section on deci-
phering secret messages. Intermediate
grades.

HOW TO PITCH
*Written by Bob Feller. The
Ronald Press Company, 1948.*

This short illustrated explanation of how to
pitch is by an expert. Feller vividly describes how to throw various kinds of
pitches from the fast ball to the curve ball.
This is an appropriate book for the junior
high level and up.

THE SECRET OF COOKIES, CANDIES
AND CAKES
*Written by Helen Jill Fletcher.
Illustrated by Margaret Zimmerman.
Harvey House, Inc., Publishers,
1965.*

Simple, easy-to-make recipes for cookies,
candies and cakes for the youngest cook.
How to decorate cakes, make lollipops
and other sweets for parties. Cleanliness
and safety rules. Intermediate grades.

BIRDS WILL COME TO YOU
*Written by Charles Philip Fox.
Reilly & Lee Co., 1963.*

Here is an excellent manual on attracting
birds in winter and in summer. Clarity
and simplicity distinguish this useful book
complete with fine photographs, diagrams,
and simple instructions for making bird
feeders and bird houses. The manual also
provides suitable advice for bird feeding.

FUN WITH YOUR CAMERA
*Written by Mae and Irma Freeman.
Random House, Inc., 1955.*

Advice in text and photographs will help
a beginner get good results from his
camera. Suggestions on use of light, focus,
and other pointers a beginner needs.
Younger shutterbugs.

MATHEMATICAL FUN, GAMES AND
PUZZLES
*Written by Jack Frohlichstein.
Dover Publications, Inc., 1962.*

Some four hundred puzzles, games, and
fun projects or novelties identified as easy,
average, or difficult. All ages.

MODEL PLANES FOR BEGINNERS
*Written and illustrated by H. H.
Gilmore. Harper & Row,
Publishers, 1957.*

Simple diagrammed instructions of how to
make ten well-known American planes.
Intermediate and upper grades.

MODEL ROCKETS FOR BEGINNERS
Written and illustrated by H. H. Gilmore. Harper & Row, Publishers, 1961.

How to build models of ten modern missiles and space rockets with helpful pictures and diagrams. Intermediate grades.

COLLECT, PRINT, AND PAINT FROM NATURE
Written by John Hawkinson. Albert Whitman & Co., 1963.

Experiments in printing and painting leaves, blossoms, ferns, pine needles, and other natural specimens are suggested. Illustrations are in rich, clear watercolors and accompany pages of detailed diagrammed instructions. Primary and intermediate grades.

STRINGS ON YOUR FINGERS: HOW TO MAKE STRING FIGURES
Written by Harry and Elizabeth Helfman. William Morrow & Co., Inc., 1965.

How to do a number of clever things with your two hands and a loop of string. The instructions are very clear and the illustrations back them up at every point. Elementary school.

MR. WIZARD'S EXPERIMENTS FOR YOUNG SCIENTISTS
Written by Don Herbert. Doubleday & Company, Inc., 1959.

Directions and diagrams for thirteen science experiments that can easily be done with equipment found in the home. Each experiment is explained so that the more mature reader can understand the methods used by adult scientists in research.

HOW TO MAKE ORIGAMI
Written and illustrated by Isao Honda. Ivan Obelensky, Inc., 1959.

An excellent introduction to the Oriental art of folding paper, a hobby that offers almost limitless possibilities. Stunningly designed and colorfully illustrated. Intermediate grades.

MY HOBBY IS COLLECTING STAMPS
Written by Ernest A. Kehr. Childrens Press, Inc., 1958.

Information on how to start a collection and how to secure stamps from auctions, catalogs, and other sources. A good introduction to the hobby for the whole family.

SPORTS AND GAMES
Written by Harold Keith. Thomas Y. Crowell Company, 1960.

This introductory book deals with fifteen sports, briefly tracing the history of each and then describing how to play it. General rules are included. Diagrams of various playing fields and positions illustrate the book. Middle and upper grades.

FUN WITH PAPER DOLLS
Written by Tina Lee. Illustrated by Manning Lee. Doubleday & Company, Inc., 1957.

Complete instructions on how to make dolls, plan wardrobes, and design doll houses. For the elementary school grades.

FUN FOR YOUNG COLLECTORS
Written by Joseph Leeming. Illustrated by Jessie Robinson. J. B. Lippincott Co., 1953.

Suggestions are given for starting and maintaining collections of many different kinds and for effectively displaying them. All ages.

HERE IS YOUR HOBBY: ART
Written by Andrew Lessin. G. P. Putnam's Sons, 1965.

The necessary instructions for setting a style and creating an individual piece of work, whether it be a drawing, an oil painting, a collage, a mobile, or a poster. Also some history of art. All ages.

THE STORY OF THE WORLD SERIES
Written by Fredrick G. Lieb. G. P. Putnam's Sons, 1965.

This book is a series of succinct capsules of the World Series from 1949 through 1964. It covers major plays of the games, turns of the tide, players' and managers' feelings, as well as box office sales. It is enthusiastically written for the upper grades.

MAKE IT AND RIDE IT
Written by C. J. Maginley.
Illustrated by Elizabeth D. McKee.
Harcourt, Brace & World, Inc.,
1949.
Directions and clear diagrams are given for making soapbox racers and other kinds of four-wheeled vehicles with hand tools, using scrap materials whenever possible. Upper grades.

MAKE YOUR OWN MUSICAL
INSTRUMENTS
Written and illustrated by Muriel and Robert E. Wood. Sterling Publishing Co., Inc., 1957.
Easy-to-follow illustrations and directions for making musical instruments from inexpensive materials. Intermediate grades.

DRAGGING AND DRIVING
Written by Tom MacPherson.
Illustrated by Denny McMains.
G. P. Putnam's Sons, 1965.
A handbook of mechanical information and driving safety for the teen-ager, whether he races a hot-rod at 150 miles per hour or merely borrows the family car. All ages.

FUN WITH TOOLS
Written by William and Robert Cymar. Photographs. Random House, Inc., 1957.
A good book for enthusiastic woodworkers. Detailed instructions on how to make such articles as lamps, puzzles, game tables. Upper grades.

THINGS A BOY CAN DO WITH
ELECTRICITY
Written by Alfred Morgan.
Charles Scribner's Sons, 1956.
Detailed information for interested youngsters with many suggestions for experiments. More mature readers.

A COOKBOOK FOR GIRLS AND BOYS
Written by Irma S. Rombauer.
Bobbs-Merrill Company, Inc., 1952.
This is more than a book of recipes. It gives interesting information about foods and their preparations, a picture table of utensils used in cooking, and many helpful hints that make cooking easier for the beginner. All ages.

SCIENCE FUN WITH MILK CARTONS
Written by Herman and Nina Schneider. Illustrated by Jeanne Bendick. McGraw-Hill Book Company, 1953.
Bridges, ships, trains, elevators, and turbines can be built with milk cartons. Clear directions. Older children.

101 GIFTS AND NOVELTIES
CHILDREN CAN MAKE
Written by Becky Shapiro. Sterling Publishing Co., Inc., 1958.
An infinite variety of household items are employed in the making of simple gifts and novelties. A fine book to have around the house for children of all ages.

PAPER, INK AND ROLLER:
PRINT-MAKING FOR BEGINNERS
Written by Harvey Weiss.
William R. Scott, Inc., 1958.
Easily understood, well-illustrated instructions for print-making for the beginner. Methods described are for use with leaves, bottlecaps, potatoes, corks, linoleum, cardboard. Upper grades.

CLAY, WOOD AND WIRE: A
HOW-TO-DO-IT BOOK OF
SCULPTURE
Written by Harvey Weiss. William R. Scott, Inc., 1956.
Step-by-step instructions of the use of clay, plasticene, pipe cleaners, wood,

papier-mâché. The reader is urged to use his creativity and imagination. All ages.

GENERAL HOLIDAY COLLECTIONS

THE FIRST BOOK OF HOLIDAYS
Written by Bernice Burnett. Illustrated
by Marjorie Glaubach. Franklin
Watts, Inc., 1955.

Gay illustrations complement this simple, well-written text telling of the origins and ways of celebrating many holidays including April Fool's Day, Christmas, Easter, and others.

HOLIDAY STORYBOOK
Compiled by the Child Study
Association of America. Illustrated
by Phoebe Erickson. Thomas Y.
Crowell Company, 1952.

Simple, well-written verses and stories about various holidays with very good black-and-white illustrations quite suitable for even preschool children.

HOLIDAY PROGRAMS FOR BOYS
AND GIRLS
Written by Aileen Fisher. Plays,
Inc., 1959.

A treasury of classroom and assembly material—plays, poems, skits, group readings, and recitations—for presenting balanced and effective holiday programs. An excellent collection for teachers. For all ages.

THE BOOK OF PATRIOTIC HOLIDAYS
Written by Marguerite Ickis.
Illustrated by Miriam Fabbri. Dodd,
Mead & Co., 1962.

This book tells of the origins and reasons for celebrating our many patriotic holidays, including the Fourth of July, the birthdays of some of our important Presidents, and others. It provides children with a good basic understanding of these holidays. More mature readers.

WHY IT'S A HOLIDAY
Written by Ann McGovern.
Illustrated by Arnold Kohn.
Random House, Inc., 1960.

A holiday book with numerous good illustrations that trace the origins of many holidays. Older children.

THE TRUE BOOK OF HOLIDAYS
AND SPECIAL DAYS
Written by John W. Purcell.
Illustrated by Arnold Kohn.
Children's Press, Inc., 1955.

A simply written book about many holidays for very young children. Preschool children especially will love the attractive illustrations and the lovely lilting prose.

THE DAYS WE CELEBRATE
Written by Robert H.
Schauffler. Dodd, Mead
& Co., 1956.

This collection tells how we celebrate our important patriotic holidays. Includes poems, plays, stories, and essays about each holiday. Also, some good material for assembly program use. Suitable for elementary school.

RED LETTER DAYS
Written by E. H. Sechrist.
Illustrated by Guy Fry. Macrae
Smith Company, 1940.

A complete, interesting, readable account of the traditional customs associated with holidays and special days. Aimed at the upper grades.

STORIES AND INFORMATION FOR SPECIFIC HOLIDAYS

Christmas

BROWNIES—IT'S CHRISTMAS
Written by Gladys L. Adshead.
Illustrated by Velma Ilsley.
Oxford University Press, Inc., 1956.

This easy-to-read, gay story for beginning readers tells how an old couple fell asleep before they finished trimming their Christmas tree and how the Brownies helped them. And then there was a surprise for the Brownies!

CHRISTMAS IS A TIME OF GIVING
Written and illustrated by Joan Walsh Anglund. Harcourt, Brace & World, Inc., 1962.

This charming book conveys the delights of gifts and a tree, making cookies, and the memories enjoyed as families gather. Christmas is described as a "time of giving." All ages.

FRIENDLY BEASTS
Written by Laura Nelson Baker. Illustrated by Nicolas Sidjakov. Parnassus Press, 1958.

An adaptation of a fourteenth-century English carol about the Nativity. The illustrations are very rich in color and have a stained glass quality. The story tells what the animals offered the Christ Child. Children of all ages.

JOY AND THE CHRISTMAS ANGEL
Written and illustrated by Pamela Bianco. Oxford University Press, Inc., 1949.

A story of a small brother and sister who do not want to part with their Christmas tree. When it becomes inevitable, they give a party for the wax angel from the top of their tree. The next morning they find that the angel has left them the gifts they wanted most. The book handles this delicate theme beautifully in words and graceful drawings. Intermediate grades.

CHRISTMAS TREES AND HOW THEY GROW
Written by Glenn O. Blough. Illustrated by Jeanne Bendick. McGraw-Hill Book Company, 1962.

The author presents the natural history of Christmas trees and their companions who end up as books, houses, and telephone poles. He slips in some hints about conservation, tells how to keep the festive tree green longer, and how to use it as a source of supplies for hungry winter birds. A wonderful combination of pleasant conversation and sound scientific fact makes learning a pleasurable experience. Very fine for younger children.

ON CHRISTMAS EVE
Written by Margaret Wise Brown. Illustrated by Beni Montresor. William R. Scott, Inc., 1961.

With poetic vividness and an incomparable memory for the feelings of children, the author catches the impatience of the night before Christmas. Unusual pictures capture the color, the stillness, and the radiance of Christmas Eve. Suitable for very young children.

CHRISTMAS TREE HESSIAN
Written by Cona Cheney. Illustrated by Edith Ballinger Price. Holt, Rinehart & Winston, Inc., 1957.

Tells the story of Abe Smith, a brave patriot boy who tries to take the place of his absent father and Konrad, a young Hessian soldier of the American Revolutionary period. It is a good tale, ending with what may have been the first Christmas tree in America. Older readers will find valuable information and suspense.

THE NOBLE DOLL
Written by Elizabeth Coatsworth. Illustrated by Leo Politi. The Viking Press, Inc., 1962.

The loving heart of a little girl who trusts St. Francis brings unexpected help to a poor lady. The setting is a Mexican Christmas. The charm of Mexico, the the kindness of the people, and the gaiety of Christmas fill this picture book. This story is perfectly interpreted by Mr. Politi's characteristically warm, happy, and evocative Mexican illustrations. Younger children.

A CHRISTMAS CAROL
Written by Charles Dickens. Illustrated by Ronald Searle. World Publishing Co., 1962.

A newly illustrated edition of this marvelous Christmas story. Charles Dickens' Preface, dated December 1843, is included: "I have endeavoured in this Ghostly little book to raise the Ghost of an idea, which shall not put my readers out of humor with themselves, with each other, with the season, or with me. May it haunt their houses pleasantly, and no one wish to lay it." The book is a delight to read and to behold, for Searle really catches the rich comic flavor of the old masque admirably and without sacrificing the nightmarish quality, which is part of its charm. The illustrations are a tribute to Dickens and the Victorian era. All ages.

ONE THOUSAND CHRISTMAS
BEARDS
Written and illustrated by Roger
Antoine Duvoisin. Alfred A. Knopf,
Inc., 1956.

This nonsense picture storybook tells how the true Santa Claus, indignant because there are so many fake ones around, deprives them of their beards. He is set right by Mrs. Claus as to the world's need for the imposters. This story can be enjoyed by preschool and primary grades.

THREE KINGS OF SABA
Written by Alf Evans. Illustrated by
Helen Sewell. J. B. Lippincott Co.,
1955.

This charming retelling of the story of the three wise men who came to Bethlehem at the time of the birth of Christ is excellent for reading aloud to the primary grades or for children in the intermediate grades who can read it themselves.

CHRISTMAS FLOWER
Written by Joseph Henry Jackson.
Illustrated by Tom Lea. Harcourt,
Brace & World, Inc., 1951.

The Mexican legend of the miracle brought about by a small Indian's gift of poinsettia leaves to the Christmas manger in the village church. This short story is written with sensitive restraint, warm feeling, and validity. The author catches

the wonder of the myth with a magical touch of his own. The illustrations are quite unusual. Preschool and up.

CHRISTMAS STORIES 'ROUND THE
WORLD
Edited by Lois Elizabeth Smith
Johnson. Illustrated by Beth Krush.
Rand McNally & Co., 1961.

This is a useful book for home, school, and library use. It contains fourteen short stories about Christmas in many lands including Austria, Canada, Iceland, Japan, Mexico, Ireland, and the United States. Each story is prefaced with a few paragraphs about the observance of Christmas in that country. The black-and-white illustrations are very well done and add to the enjoyment of the book. All ages.

TELL ME ABOUT CHRISTMAS
Written by Mary Alice Jones.
Illustrated by Marjorie Cooper.
Rand McNally & Co., 1959.

In a simple, natural way the author gives the answers of one mother to the probing questions of her children. She supplies and applies the story of Jesus to everyday living and shows that Christmas is the expression of God's love for man. Intermediate grades

THE YEAR WITHOUT A SANTA
CLAUS
Written by Phyllis McGinley.
Illustrated by Kurt Werth. J. B.
Lippincott Co., 1957.

Against a background of vibrating colored illustrations, the author in witty, humorous verse tells of the year a tired old Santa decides not make his annual journey and the effect his decision has upon the boys and girls who expect him. Poetic and original, this beautifully drawn book is ageless in its appeal and delight.

WITH BELLS ON
Written and illustrated by Katherine
Milhous. Charles Scribner's Sons,
1955.

Old Pennsylvania customs form the

background for this story of two children who make a Christmas manger scene to greet their older brother when he returns from his trip to Philadelphia. It is a charming story full of interesting old customs and the true spirit of Christmas. All ages.

THE FIRST CHRISTMAS TREE
Written by Hertha Pauli. Illustrated by Kurt Werth. Ives Washburn, Inc., 1962.

This is a wonderful version of a little-known but beautiful story of one of the many child-legends surrounding Christmas. It is one that can be dramatized easily to grace any Christmas program. Intermediate grades.

JOY TO THE WORLD: CHRISTMAS LEGENDS
Retold by Ruth Sawyer. Illustrated by Trina Schart Myman. Little, Brown & Co., 1966.

A radiant collection of Christmas stories by a storyteller whose gifts are beautifully expressed in retellings of Christmas legends from a variety of sources. Handsome illustrations resembling medieval illuminations decorate the book with a touch of reverence. To be read to children in the elementary grades and by children in the upper grades.

TOP O' CHRISTMAS MORNING
Written by Alta Halverson Seymour. Illustrated by Mary Stevenson. Follett Publishing Company, 1955.

In this story of Ireland, a lonely young Irish girl meets a lively family who introduce her to horses and a typical Irish Christmas. The book offers interesting information to intermediate-grade children seeking to learn about Christmas in the Emerald Isle.

CANDLE LOVE FEAST
Written by Julia Montgomery Street. Illustrated by Anna Marie Magagna. Coward-McCann, Inc., 1960.

This is a very simple, sincere, and charming picture story of the Moravian Christmas celebration in which families gather in church for a love feast of carols, delicious brown buns, steaming coffee, and lighted candles. Younger children.

Columbus Day

SON OF COLUMBUS
Written by Hans Baumann. Illustrated by William Stobbs. Oxford University Press, Inc., 1957.

An exciting and well-written story about the events of Columbus' fourth voyage in the West Indies, as seen by Fernando, the Admiral's younger son. Suitable for intermediate-grade children.

THE COLUMBUS STORY
Written by Alice Dalgliesh. Illustrated by Leo Politi. Charles Scribners Sons, 1955.

The story and pictures in this book—planned for reading aloud—follow highlights of Columbus' life from his boyhood in Genoa, through study and work, voyage and discovery, to the triumphant start of his second voyage. It is well-written, simple, and vivid. The pictures radiate Italian and Spanish charm. Younger children.

COLUMBUS
Written and illustrated by Ingri and Edgar d'Aulaire. Doubleday & Company, Inc., 1955.

This book presents the life of Christopher Columbus from his boyhood, through his four voyages, to his old age in Spain. For younger children.

CHRISTOPHER COLUMBUS, DISCOVERER
Written by Alberta Powell Graham. Illustrated by Janice Holland. Abingdon Press, 1950.

A fictionalized biography of Columbus. It is easy to read and brings out the personality of the great discoverer with informative details of the man, time, place, and social order. Intermediate grades.

SONS OF THE ADMIRAL
Written by Seth and Shumway Harmon and Harry Irving. Illustrated by Paul Quinn. L. C. Page & Company, Inc., 1940.

The story of Christopher Columbus as told from the viewpoint of his young sons Diego and Fernando. The friendship of the boys, so different from each other, is stressed as much as their firm belief in their father. Older readers.

CHRISTOPHER COLUMBUS AND HIS BROTHERS
Written and Illustrated by Amy Hogeboom. Lothrop, Lee & Shepard Co., Inc., 1951.

This biography in story form emphasizes the great bonds of love and cooperation that existed between Columbus and his brothers, Diego and Bartholomew. Christopher's son Ferdinand also enters into the story. Suitable for the intermediate grades.

VOYAGES OF COLUMBUS
Written by W. Irving. Illustrated by Henry Pitz. The Macmillan Company, 1931.

This abridgment of Irving's life of Columbus offers new material on the character of Columbus and gives many incidents not usually included in textbooks. Excellent supplementary reading. Upper grade children.

I DISCOVER COLUMBUS
Written and illustrated by Robert Lawson. Little, Brown & Co., 1941.

This purports to be the true story of Christopher Columbus, the discovery of America. The narrator is Aurelio, a parrot who was blown from his native Caribbean to Spain by a hurricane. In Spain he meets Columbus and inspires him to take the trip of discovery for the simple reason that he misses his native

foods and can not think of any other way to get back to them. Beautiful reading for intermediate-grade children.

VOYAGES OF CHRISTOPHER COLUMBUS
Written and illustrated by Armstrong Sperry. Random House, Inc., 1950.

This is a fictionalized biography of Christopher Columbus. It brings to life a great event from our nation's past. The intermediate-grade children who read this book will never forget Columbus—the man, his work, his place in history.

Easter

EASTER TREAT
Written and illustrated by Roger Duvoisin. Alfred A. Knopf, Inc., 1954.

A picture story book about the time Santa Claus decided to take a trip to the city at Easter. Truly delightful, especially for young children. Preschool.

EASTER BUNNY THAT OVERSLEPT
Written by Priscilla and Otto Friedrich. Illustrated by Adrienne Adams. Lothrop, Lee & Shepard Co., Inc., 1957.

A picture storybook about the Easter bunny who overslept and tried to deliver Easter eggs on Mother's Day. Nobody wants them, so he redecorates them and tries to give them out on the Fourth of July. That too is unsuccessful. But when a big wind takes him up to Santa Claus' house, his good luck begins. The Easter bunny tries to persuade people that Easter eggs can be fun any time of the year. The illustrations are charmingly detailed pictures in pastel colors that make the bunny appealing and his adventures worth following. Younger children.

EASTER BOOK OF LEGENDS AND STORIES
Written by Alice I. Hazeltone and Elva S. Smith. Illustrated by Pamela

Bianco. Lothrop, Lee & Shepard, Inc., 1947.

Here is a lovely book that includes a rich collection of poems, stories, and legends. The illustratrations are wonderful. All ages.

THE EGG TREE
Written and illustrated by Katherine Milhous. Charles Scribner's Sons, 1950.

The fascinating and colorful traditions and folk art of the Pennsylvania Dutch are superbly described in both words and pictures. This is an excellent source for primary-grade children on life among the Pennsylvania Dutch, particularly as they celebrate the holiday of Easter.

PICCOLINA AND THE EASTER BELLS
Written by Pauline Priolo. Illustrated by Rita Fava. Little, Brown & Co., 1962.

This sunlit story is based on a Sicilian custom—as the Easter Bells ring out, children are lifted high in the air by their tallest relatives, with the admonition, "Grow, child, grow!" Piccolina is so tiny that she longs for the day on which her father will lift her and she will begin to grow. When the day comes her father's arrival is delayed, but Piccolina is lifted high by the miller! There is a glossary of Sicilian terms. The colored drawings fill the pages with Italian people and the Italian countryside. Intermediate grades.

IT'S TIME FOR EASTER
Written by E. H. Sechrist and J. Woolsey. Illustrated by Elsie J. McConkell. Macrae Smith Company, 1961.

Beginning with a brief form of the Biblical narrative from the Synoptic Gospels, the authors trace the origins of curious symbols and Easter folklore through the folkways of many lands, ancient and modern. Also included are many Easter songs good for upper grades.

EASTER: ITS STORY AND MEANING
Written by A. W. Watts. Abelard-Shuman, Ltd., 1950.

A history of Easter festivals reaching back to pagan times, showing the origins of the observances of Holy Week and the symbolism of Easter. An unusually informative source for older children.

Halloween

TWO TOO MANY
Written and illustrated by Nora S. Unwin. David McKay Co., Inc., 1963.

Two black kittens named Two and Too Many find themselves in the dark forest searching for a warm place and a saucer of milk. Frightened by the awesome witch, they hide themselves in her broom, and when the witch mounts it, they are carried away in the Grand Race over the moon. The kittens are as vivid in the texts as they are in the illustrations, which are black, white, and October yellow. Suited for primary-grade children.

HEIGH-HO FOR HALLOWEEN
Written by E. H. Sechrist. Illustrated by Guy Fry. Macrae Smith Company, 1948.

After an explanation of the origin of Halloween, the book consists of stories, poems, plays, games, parties, and suggestions for making cards. A very practical book for younger children.

A LITTLE BOOK OF HALLOWEEN
Written by E. H. Sechrist. Illustrated by Guy Fry. J. B. Lippincott Co., 1934.

Simple directions for more than fifty games suitable for Halloween, and also several ghost stories. A book planned for little children in order to help them in arranging and conducting their own parties.

THE FIRST BOOK OF FESTIVALS
AROUND THE WORLD
Written by Alma Kohoe Reck.

Illustrated by Helen Borten.
Franklin Watts, Inc., 1957.

A short story telling about Halloween in the United States. Also, may other stories of holidays and the festivities that surround them.

Hanukkah

THE JEWISH NEW YEAR
Written by Molly Cone. Illustrated by Jerome Snyder. Thomas Y. Crowell Company, 1966.

Rich in history and rooted in tradition, this distinguished book explains the ten High Holy Days connected with the harvest season, when the Jewish New Year begins. From Rosh Hashanah to Yom Kippur, the solemnity of these special days is deeply expressed in the lyrical prose illumined by distinctive pictures. Also by the same author and illustrated by Ellen Raskin, *The Jewish Sabbath*, suitable for younger children.

HANUKKAH
Written by Norma Simon. Illustrated by Symeon Shimin. Thomas Y. Crowell Company, 1966.

This reverently written book describes the Festival of Lights that commemorates deliverance of the Jews who won their freedom to worship according to the dictates of their own conscience. By skillfully retracing the ancient Hanukkah story, the author also explains the religious observances and certain other colorful ones that have become part of that glorious festival. Highlighted by simple, beautifully shaded, three-color illustrations, the book speaks its message to younger children in particular.

Lincoln's Birthday

ABE LINCOLN GETS HIS CHANCE
Written by Frances Cavanah. Illustrated by Paula Hutchison. Rand McNally & Co., 1959.

Miss Cavannah tells with simplicity and warmth a smoothly flowing story that makes her hero and the people among whom he grew up seem very real. She focuses on Lincoln's childhood, his desire for education, and his close relationship with his stepmother. Older children.

ABRAHAM LINCOLN: AN INITIAL BIOGRAPHY
Written and illustrated by Genevieve Foster. Charles Scribner's Sons, 1950.

An introductory biography of Abraham Lincoln telling of the childhood and manhood of the great President. Contains an interesting text and lively pictures in two colors that add to its appeal for eight to twelve year-olds.

THE REAL BOOK ABOUT ABRAHAM LINCOLN
Written by Michael Gorham. Illustrated by Elinore Blaisdell. Garden City Books, 1951.

Anecdotes and real incidents from Lincoln's full life. It is an affectionate collection of almost legendary stories about the great President. All ages.

NANCY HANKS OF WILDERNESS ROAD: A STORY OF ABRAHAM LINCOLN'S MOTHER
Written by Meridel Le Seur. Illustrated by Betty Alden. Alfred A. Knopf, Inc., 1949.

A biography of Lincoln's mother told in the form of a folk legend. It is made up of an incident remembered by the narrator's grandmother and Dennis Hanks, Nancy's cousin. The richness of the relationship—too soon ended—between Nancy Hanks Lincoln and her small son is well drawn, as is the realistic, vigorous portrait of his father. Lyric style prevails and turns the brief biography into a poetic elegy. It is in large print with bright colors. Primary and intermediate grades.

AMERICA'S ABRAHAM LINCOLN
Written by May Y. McNeet. Illustrated by Lynd Ward. Houghton Mifflin Company, 1957.

A short biography of Lincoln that reads

a little like a prose poem. Lynd Ward's strong illustrations in muted tones and glowing colors are very good for the intermediate grades.

INDY AND MR. LINCOLN
Written by Natalia Belting.
Illustrated by Leonard Everett Fisher. Holt, Rinehart & Winston, Inc., 1960.

The story is built around fact and combines the appeal of animals and the charm of historical reality. Indiana (Indy for short) was a pet pig who lived in New Salem, Indiana, when Abraham Lincoln lived there. Everyone knew Indy and was amused by her and by her adventures, particularly one in which Mr. Lincoln became involved. It is a humorous story that has rhythmic style and genuine folk tale flavor. Younger children will find it most appealing.

WHEN LINCOLN WENT TO GETTYSBURG
Written by Adele Nathan Gutman.
Illustrated by Emil Weiss. Aladdin Books, 1955.

A fictionalized account of Lincoln's trip to Gettysburg and of the activities in the little town at the time the battlefield was dedicated in 1863. Very useful for work in history at the intermediate-grade level.

HENRY'S LINCOLN
Written by Louise A. Neyhart.
Illustrated by Charles Banks Wilson. Holiday House, 1945.

A story of the great Lincoln-Douglas debate of August 27, 1858, as seen through the eyes of a young farm boy. The children of today may here share warmly in that historic event, see people and places, and hear the brilliant speeches. It is a vivid, intimate, personal story, well told and printed in an attractive book. The lively illustrations match the text beautifully. Primary grades.

A MAN NAMED LINCOLN
Written by Gertrude Norman.

Illustrated by Joseph Cellini. G. P. Putnam's Sons, 1960.

This book gives a concise, overall, and, within the limits of space and vocabulary, a sound foundation on which later reading and understanding can be based. Primary grades.

ABE LINCOLN: LOG CABIN TO WHITE HOUSE
Written by Sterling North. Illustrated by Lee Ames. Random House, Inc., 1956.

This vivid and accurate biography tells the story of Lincoln's boyhood and young manhood on the Midwestern frontier. It is one of the best books about Lincoln for the young reader.

Thanksgiving

FIRST THANKSGIVING DAY
Written by Lena Barksdale.
Illustrated by Lois Lenski. Alfred A. Knopf, Inc., 1942.

Before they were married, and many years before this story begins, little Hannah's grandparents had been present at the very first Thanksgiving feast. The year that Hannah comes down from Maine to stay with her grandmother, she is one of the many children to hear from Grandmother's lips the tale of that first day the Pilgrims and their Indian friends gave thanks for the feast. This charming little story conveys the spirit of early America. Children can easily identify with the book and understand the text. The pictures are wonderful. All ages.

THE THANKSGIVING STORY
Written by Alice Dalgliesh.
Illustrated by Helen Sewell. Charles Scribner's Sons, 1954.

Dealing with the journey of the *Mayflower* and the founding of Plymouth, the story centers upon one family. This familiar story is told simply enough for the beginning reader, without loss of significane or dignity. Sewell's pictures are done in the manner of American primitives, bringing the scenes and characters to life and adding a note of childlike gaiety. From the somber tones of the first part of the book, the pictures build up to a climax of glowing autumn colors. A conjectural plan of the *Mayflower* and a map of the Plymouth Rock area by Rafael Palacios are interesting and informative.

PILGRIM THANKSGIVING
Written by Wilma Pitchford Hays.
Illustrated by Leonard Weisgard.
Coward-McCann, Inc., 1955.

A little Pilgrim girl, Damaris, her brother Giles, and her little dog experience their first Thanksgiving when the Indians come from the forest to join the feast. Suitable for very young children.

IT'S TIME FOR THANKSGIVING
Written by Elizabeth Hough and
Woolsey Sechrist. Illustrated by Guy
Fay. Macrae Smith Company, 1957.

A potpourri of Thanksgiving treats for everyone. This special collection is a holiday delight. It contains stories, poems, games, and recipes. The gay illustrations will delight young children and adults.

THANKSGIVING: OUR AMERICAN HOLIDAY
Edited by Robert Haven Schauffler.
Dodd, Mead & Co., 1954.

This book gives the origin, celebration, and significance of Thanksgiving in prose and verse. It is one of a series of anthologies for the use of students and teachers, consisting of verse, plays, stories, addresses, special articles, orations, and so forth. Very good as a reference or for reading to a class. All ages.

Valentine's Day

VALENTINE PARTY
Written and illustrated by Pamela
Bianco. J.B. Lippincott Co., 1955.

Cathy, aged five, is unhappy because she has only one valentine and has not been invited to a party. This story describes what

happens when she tries to go to the party uninvited. There are delicate illustrations, filled with wonder, and exquisite, colorful pictures. It is well suited to the holiday and the giving of cards. Beautifully designed for the primary grades.

THE VALENTINE CAT
Written by Clyde Robert Bulla.
Illustrated by Leonard Weisgard.
Thomas Y. Crowell Company,
1959.

Abandoned in wood as a tiny thing, then kidnapped by a chimney sweep to be used uncomfortably and ignominiously as a "magic broom" to clean out narrow parts of sooty chimneys, the Valentine cat was twice rescued—by an artist and by a princess. Both of them feel they own the cat, and their claims are reconciled on Valentine's Day. A happy, satisfying story with handsome pictures full of design and color that aid in making this a wonderfully imaginative Valentine story for younger children.

Washington's Birthday

GEORGE WASHINGTON: FIRST PRESIDENT
Written by Elsie Ball. Illustrated by
Manning de V. Lee. Abingdon Press,
1954.

A brief biography of Washington, beginning with his eleventh year and ending with his death. Good elementary-school factual content.

GEORGE WASHINGTON
Written and illustrated by Ingri and
Edgar Parin D'Aulaire. Doubleday &
Company, Inc., 1936.

This is a large, easy-to-read, picture book about the father of our country. Broad, striking color pages portray George Washington, and historical details enhance the value of the biography.

GEORGE WASHINGTON: AN INITIAL BIOGRAPHY
Written and illustrated by

Genevieve Foster. Charles Scribner's Sons, 1949.

A brief yet dignified biography; easy reading yet informative. The material is simplified without writing down, and the illustrations are beautiful. Suitable for intermediate grades.

GEORGE WASHINGTON: FRONTIER COLONEL
Written by Sterling North. Illustrated by Lee Ames. Random House, Inc., 1957.

A biographical study of George Washington's formative years especially the period when he served as a frontier fighter in the French and Indian War. Quotes from some of Washington's own writings give the reader a sense of nearness as well as a sense of time and place. Best suited for upper-grade children.

WASHINGTON: THE NATION'S FIRST HERO
Written by Jeanette Eaton. Illustrated by H. Pitz. William Morrow & Co., Inc., 1951.

This simply written book tells of Washington's part in the French and Indian War and the Revolution. A few final pages summarize the rest of his life. A handsome first book about the President.

WASHINGTON: THE LIFE OF A PATRIOT
Written by André Maurois. Illustrated by H. Pitz. Didier Pubs, 1947.

A brief biography that highlights Washington's frontier training, military service, and life as the master of Mount Vernon. The illustrations have great strength and appeal. For older children.

LANGUAGE SKILLS

THE STORY OF WRITING: COMMUNICATION FROM CAVE ART TO COMPUTER

Written by William and Rhoda Cahn. Illustrated by Anne Lewis. Harvey House, Inc., Publishers, 1963.

An exciting survey, for older children interested in the history of communications, of picture writing, of monks copying and recopying the Bible, and of electronic brains. Useful for its bibliography, glossary, maps, and pronouncing index. Upper grades.

A FRENCH ABC
Written and illustrated by Francine Le Grand Dauphin. Coward-McCann, Inc., 1947.

For each of the twenty-six letters of the alphabet, there is a full page drawing in lovely color showing little French children engaged in characteristic games and occupations. The simple descriptive text for each picture is given both in French and English providing an opportunity for the older primary-grade child to compare words in English and French to find the similarities and differences in the two languages. This could serve as the basis of a lesson, in very simple terms, on the origin of certain words with which children are familiar. This book can also be used in the area of social studies. For the lower grades.

A FOR THE ARK
Written and illustrated by Roger Duvoisin. Lothrop, Lee & Shepard Co., Inc., 1952.

By tying the alphabet in with the story of Noah and his Ark, Mr. Duvoisin has very cleverly written and illustrated a book that can serve a number of purposes in the area of language arts. As the story of Noah unfolds, young children are introduced to the letters of the alphabet, the order in which the letters appear, and a listing of words beginning with each letter—the names of animals that entered the Ark. For the lower grades.

APE IN A CAPE
Written and illustrated by Fritz Eichenberg. Harcourt, Brace & World, Inc., 1952.

Simple nonsense rhymes provide the young child with an introduction to the letters of the alphabet. Each letter has its own rhyme about an odd animal accompanied by a humorous and well-drawn picture of the animal described. For the lower grades.

SEE AND SAY: A PICTURE BOOK IN FOUR LANGUAGES
Written and Illustrated by Antonio Frasconi. Harcourt, Brace & World, Inc., 1955.

In this picture book, striking three- and four-color woodcuts accompany words in English (printed in black), Italian (blue), French (red), and Spanish (green). Words are chosen on the basis of their importance to children and pronunciations are given in each case. This, too, can form the basis of a lesson on word origins and derivations. For the lower grades.

SEE AGAIN, SAY AGAIN
Written and illustrated by Antonio Frasconi. Harcourt, Brace & World, Inc., 1964.

A delightful multilingual book introduces familiar things in Italian, French, Spanish, and English, with color woodcuts clarifying each phonetically printed word. For the lower grades.

I READ SIGNS
Written and illustrated by Tom Funk. Holiday House, 1962.

As they walk downtown, Peter and his dog find a multitude of signs, always so fascinating to young children. Simple text and colored pictures on every page encourage the beginning reader to join with Peter and his dog as they try to discover the meanings of the signs by

reading them. Makes an excellent supplement to a basic reader. For the lower grades.

PLAYS AND CREATIVE WAYS WITH CHILDREN
Written and edited by Gertrude Lerner Kerman. Illustrated by Margaret Zimmerman. Harvey House, Inc., Publishers, 1961.

An unusually fine collection of non-royalty plays with expansible casts, staging suggestions, creative dramatic techniques for children, and valuable step-by-step instructions. For upper grades.

SHAKESPEARE FOR YOUNG PLAYERS
Adapted by Gertrude Lerner Kerman. Illustrated by Anne Lewis. Harvey House, Inc., Publishers, 1964.

An exciting book of six Shakespearean plays with original lines from *Romeo and Juliet, Twelfth Night, The Taming of the Shrew, A Midsummer Night's Dream, The Tempest,* and *As You Like It.* Included is an introduction providing information about Shakespeare's times and the Elizabethan period in England. Detailed staging directions increase the value of this beautiful book. For upper grades.

THE B BOOK
Written by Phyllis McGinley. Illustrated by Robert Jones. Crowell Collier, 1962.

When a small brown bee, tired of being just a bee, flies off to find something more beautiful he can become, he discovers that the best things begin with the letter B. The humor of the text and attractiveness of the illustrations make this a meaningful introduction to the letter B and words beginning with this letter. This book can become a stimulus for young children to explore language by writing and illustrating stories about the other twenty-five letters of the alphabet with a list of words for each letter. For the lower grades.

ALL THE SOUNDS WE HEAR
Written by Lee Nelson. Illustrated
by Audrey Zinser Ashley.
Steck-Vaughn Co., 1960.

This book serves to promote in young children an awareness of all the sounds they hear around them. The simple text is written in such a way as to provide a verbal description of each sound discussed. The accompanying illustrations more than adequately supplement the text by providing appropriate pictorial representations for each sound. Both text and illustrations make this a book with great appeal to the senses. For the lower grades.

THE LITTLE GREEK ALPHABET
BOOK
Written by Ennis Rees. Illustrated
by George Salter. Prentice-Hall,
Inc., 1968.

In an informative book about the Greek alphabet, light verse and large handsomely drawn letters are provided to give sound and meaning as well as image and form to the ancient alphabet. Based on scholarly research, the information in the clever verses is matched with elegant calligraphy in the production of an informative and entertaining alphabet book.

ANIMALS IN THE ZOO
Written and illustrated by Feodor
Rojankovsky. Alfred A. Knopf, Inc.,
1962.

Here is a book that offers a delightful introduction to the alphabet. Each letter stands for an animal and striking illustrations that make them come alive. Young

children could have fun in discovering for themselves a new group of animals for each letter of the alphabet. For the lower grades.

THE STORY OF PRINTING
Written by Irving B. Simon.
Drawings and photographs by Charles
E. Pont. Harvey House, Inc.,
Publishers, 1965.

Lucid text reinforced by substantial photographs and clear drawings make this a fascinating book about the development of printing from Gutenberg's workshop to today's billion-dollar plants. Here are described the major printing processes and machines from hand-set type to typesetting machines operated by electronic tapes. Also included is information on careers in the industry, on automation, and a glimpse into the future of the graphic arts. For upper grades.

A FRIEND IS "AMIE"
Written and illustrated by Charlotte
Steiner. Alfred A. Knopf, Inc.,
1956.

Two charming little girls, one American and one French, overcome a language barrier. As they play, each learns a few words of the other's a language. Colorful illustrations gaily complement the rhyming text by presenting pictorial representations of the items discussed. This is another book in which the concept of language structure and usage can be meaningfully explored. This book can also be used in the area of social studies. For the lower grades.

SUBJECT AND
TITLE INDEX

AUTHOR AND ILLUSTRATOR INDEX